AN EXPLORER'S GUIDE

North Carolina

AN EXPLORER'S GUIDE

North Carolina

Jim Hargan
with photographs by the author

FIRST EDITION

The Countryman Press ✷ Woodstock, Vermont

Explorer's Guide North Carolina
ISBN 978-0-88150-845-1

Interior photographs by the author unless otherwise specified
Maps by Erin Greb Cartography, © The Countryman Press
Book design by Bodenweber Design
Composition by PerfecType, Nashville, TN

Published by The Countryman Press, P.O. Box 748, Woodstock, VT 05091

Distributed by W. W. Norton & Company, Inc., 500 Fifth Avenue, New York, NY 10110

Printed in the United States of America

10 9 8 7 6 5 4 3 2 1

Dedicated to the State of North Carolina, and its wonderful people.

EXPLORE WITH US!

Come join us on a trip through one of the most varied states in the nation. We'll visit miles of beaches and mile-high peaks, quaint country villages and large vibrant cities, vast tracts of public lands and lovely little gardens, and sites from every period of American history, from Sir Walter Raleigh's day right down to the present. We'll pedal down bicycle paths, hike the Appalachian Trail, kayak Olympic whitewater, and drive along hundreds of miles of scenic highway. And along the way we'll stay in only the quaintest and friendliest hotels and B&Bs, and eat only good local food, prepared from scratch.

This *Explorer's Guide* does a few things differently from most guidebooks you may have seen. For one thing, it doesn't stop at the state line; if there's something really great just over the line, we'll tell you all about it. This especially includes full coverage of the Great Smoky Mountains National Park, including hotels and restaurants in Gatlinburg and Townsend, Tennessee. Second, we'll tell you what an area will look like, and include a scenic drive and a walk or two, for those who enjoy beautiful scenery. And we'll describe the large tracts of public lands—national forests, national wildlife refuges, wild seashores, state game lands—in which you can wander freely, and explore nature on your own terms. We'll also cover the beaches (right down to parking), the rivers, and the great man-made recreation lakes. Then come all the best sites, the museums and galleries, the restaurants and hotels, but now in a context of the natural beauty of their region. It's a different approach—an approach for explorers.

PRICES

Prices were checked in mid- to late 2010. These will, of course, slip as this book ages—mainly upward—but the relative brackets should remain comparable. These brackets have been chosen so that the lowest and highest brackets are very rare, but not unheard-of.

DINING PRICES Typical price for one full meal, with tea in a simple family restaurant or wine in an upscale restaurant:

$: Up to $7

$$: $8–15

$$$: $16–29

$$$$: $30–59

$$$$$: $60–119

$$$$$$: $120-plus

HOTELS AND B&B PRICES These brackets are for double occupancy for one night, excluding tax. Some establishments may require reservations for more than one night; these have been pro-rated for comparison purposes.

$: Up to $69

$$: $70–119

$$$: $120–169

$$$$: $170–349

$$$$$: $350–999

$$$$$$: $1,000-plus

ATTRACTION PRICES These range from museums to driving a race car on a dirt track; prices are for one adult for one day unless noted in the text.

$: $1–4

$$: $5–9

$$$: $10–24

$$$$: $25–99

$$$$$: $100–999

$$$$$$: $1,000-plus

RESTAURANTS

Please note the distinction between *Dining Out* and *Eating Out*. *Dining Out* places are more formal, more gourmet-oriented, and more expensive; *Eating Out* places are more casual and cheaper.

KEY TO SYMBOLS

This particular edition of the *Explorer's Guide* series uses only two symbols, both applying to hotels and B&Bs, and to some restaurants as well.

- The crayon designates kid-friendly establishments. If this is missing, assume that your prospective hotel will *not* allow children under 12. If young children are allowed, but restrictions or fees apply, this will be noted in the text.
- The paw print designates pet-friendly establishments. Again, if this is missing, assume that pets are prohibited. With pets in hotels, restrictions and fees are the norm, and you should always contact the landlord in advance.

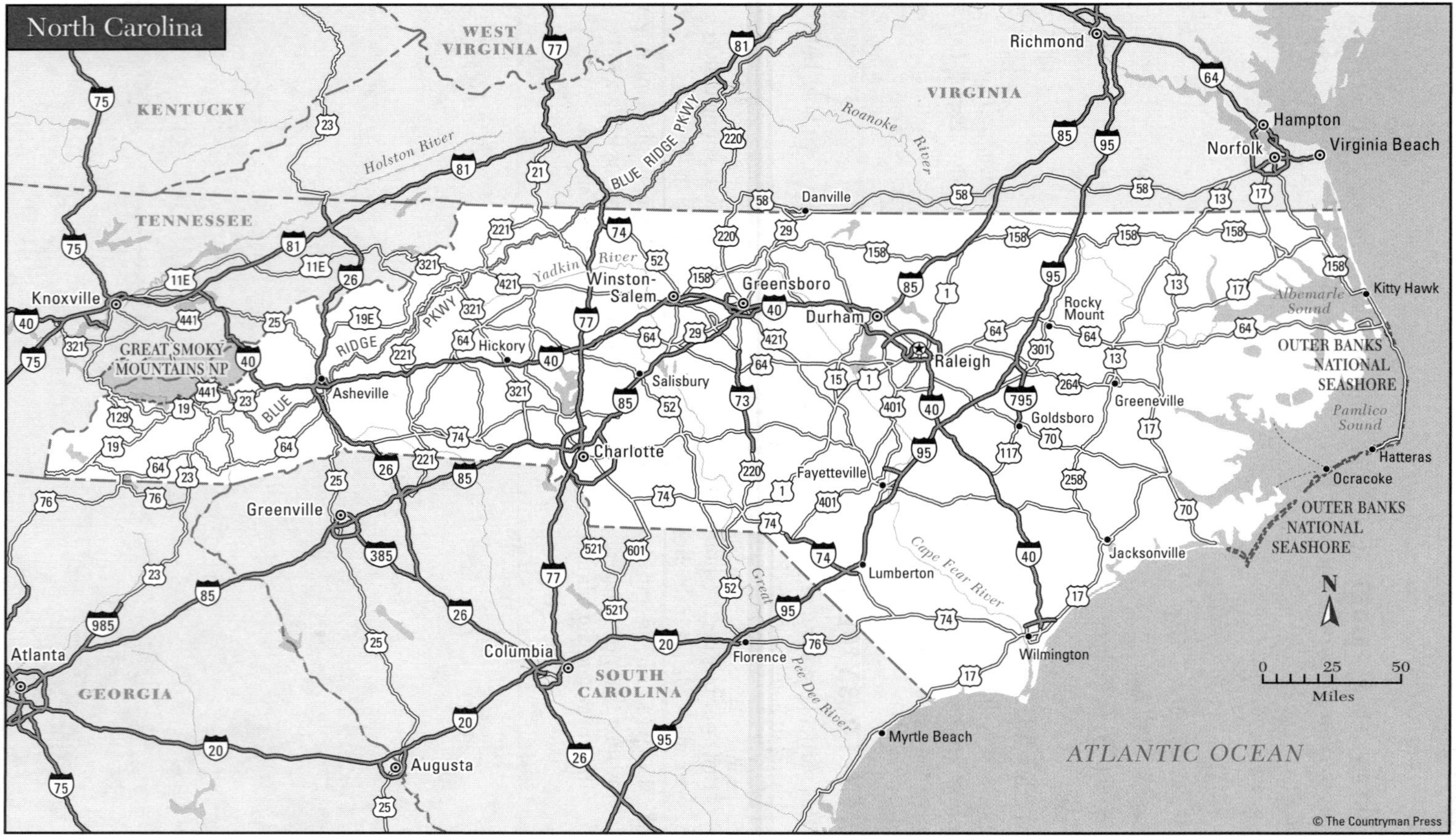
North Carolina
KENTUCKY
WEST VIRGINIA
VIRGINIA
TENNESSEE
SOUTH CAROLINA
GEORGIA
Richmond
Hampton
Norfolk
Virginia Beach
Danville
Kitty Hawk
Albemarle Sound
Pamlico Sound
OUTER BANKS NATIONAL SEASHORE
Hatteras
Ocracoke
OUTER BANKS NATIONAL SEASHORE
Knoxville
GREAT SMOKY MOUNTAINS NP
Asheville
Hickory
Winston-Salem
Greensboro
Durham
Raleigh
Rocky Mount
Greeneville
Goldsboro
Salisbury
Charlotte
Fayetteville
Lumberton
Jacksonville
Wilmington
Greenville
Columbia
Florence
Myrtle Beach
Augusta
Atlanta
Holston River
Roanoke River
Yadkin River
Cape Fear River
Great Pee Dee River
BLUE RIDGE PKWY
ATLANTIC OCEAN
N
0 25 50
Miles
© The Countryman Press

CONTENTS

INTRODUCTION

Let's start with the numbers: North Carolina is 500 miles long, 240 miles wide at its eastern end, and 16 miles wide at its western end. In other words, North Carolina is a big pie slice. The rim of the pie slice, suitably rounded, sticks out into the Atlantic as a crescent of beaches called the Outer Banks. There's actually about 300 miles of beach (like all pie edges, this one is crinkly), ranging from big resorts to utter wilderness, and it's all spectacular. At the other end of the state, the slice's point includes the tallest mountains in the East, the Blue Ridge and Smoky Mountains, with America's two most popular national parks. Call it the lumpy end of the pie. Before North Carolina narrows to a point, it manages to fit in about 250 miles of lumps. Between the beaches and the mountains are the cities, some of the greatest of the old New South, forming a continuous urban arc nearly 200 miles long. Within these urban areas, money from tobacco, textiles, and furniture has produced a flood of museums, theaters, parks, historic restorations, professional sports teams, skyscrapers, zoos, and more than a smattering of eccentricity.

And if this makes North Carolina sound something just shy of complete chaos—well, that's part of its charm. It's exciting, and you can never run out of things to see or do.

North Carolina dates back to the late 17th century—not counting Sir Walter Raleigh's failed attempt to settle Roanoke Island in the late 16th century. Between Sir Walter and 1700 it was just "Carolina," ruled from faraway Charles Towne (modern Charleston, South Carolina). European settlement consisted of a scatter of people in the far northeastern corner, who rather liked the fact that the constantly shifting shoals of the Outer Banks blocked the military ships that might bring lawmen and tax collectors. Sometime around 1700 the English started appointing a separate governor for this unruly district, the better to keep it under control. It didn't always work. In 1718 North Carolina's Governor Eden evidently made a deal with Blackbeard, the most notorious pirate of the day, to declare his booty "abandoned goods" in exchange for a 20 percent cut. Blackbeard even rented a house in Bath, where Governor Eden lived. Fifty years later the royal governors were still as blatantly corrupt; Governor Tryon raised taxes on his colony to get the money to build himself the biggest mansion in the South, Tryon Palace, now a stunning historic site in New Bern. This actually touched off an armed rebellion, the Regulation War, five years before the Revolution.

By that time North Carolina was becoming well settled. In the flat, sandy plains along the coast, planters with giant plantations, each with hundreds of slaves, placed a choke hold on local growth and politics. The Piedmont, however, was being rapidly settled by small farmers, with few or no slaves. Many (perhaps most) of these yeomen came, not from the eastern parts of the state, but from Pennsylvania and Virginia via the Great Wagon Road that connected what is now Roanoke, Virginia, with the area then known as Wachovia, modern Winston-Salem. The first of these were Moravians, religious refugees, whose main settlement is preserved as Old Salem. And at the far western end of the Piedmont, North Carolinians like Daniel Boone (whose family had migrated from Pennsylvania down the Great Wagon Road when he was a kid) were pushing deep into the Blue Ridge Mountains.

Still, when the British overlords looked at North Carolina, they saw little more than a coastal crust of privilege on top of an enormous, unknown backcountry. This would be their downfall during the Revolution. An attempt to use Loyalist settlers to battle the Patriot armies failed spectacularly at the Battle of Kings Mountain, leaving the state in the hands of the Patriots. When Lord Cornwallis tried to recapture it a year later, his troops were so devastated that he was forced to retreat—to Yorktown, Virginia, where his army was surrounded and forced to surrender, ending the war. In this campaign the decisive battle was fought at Guilford Courthouse, near modern Greensboro (named after the victorious general, Nathanael Greene).

REVOLUTIONARY WAR REENACTORS AT MOORES CREEK BATTLEFIELD

It was in the aftermath of the Revolution that the deep mountains of the Blue Ridge and Smokies were settled by Europeans. The native Cherokees had sided with the British against the land-hungry Patriots, and losing control of the Blue Ridge was the price of their defeat. The most conservative, anti-European Cherokees retreated deep into the Great Smoky Mountains, while the accommodationist factions formed the independent Cherokee Nation, over the state line in Tennessee and Georgia. Then the ultimate disaster struck: Gold was discovered in the Georgia Cherokee lands. The Georgia government in particular, strongly aided by Tennessee, lobbied hard for the illegal expulsion of the Cherokees, and won. When the U.S. Supreme Court forbade it, President Andrew Jackson simply ignored the ruling and sent in the troops. The result was the horrific Trail of Tears, in which Cherokees were rounded up into concentration camps and then deported in large groups so ill equipped that death from disease and malnourishment dogged them all the way to Oklahoma. This expulsion did not, however, include the North Carolina Cherokees, known as the Qualla, who had refused to join the Cherokee Nation and were therefore exempt. In this they were protected by the mountains' most powerful politician, William Holland Thomas, so openly pro-Cherokee that he was widely acknowledged as their Principal Chief. (Bear in mind that the Cherokees had no money and no vote; Thomas did this out of conviction, with the evident approval of the white mountain folk who elected him year after year.) Thomas used all his influence and money to establish the Qualla on their own land forever—an area correctly known as the Qualla Boundary or the Eastern Band (and incorrectly called the Cherokee Reservation), centered on the town of Cherokee at the southern entrance of the Great Smoky Mountains National Park.

Back on the coast, the owners of giant plantations controlled the state government by gerrymandering, and by manipulating the votes of the poor white farmers who were wholly dependent upon them. Some slave owners (particularly the smaller ones) tried to treat their human property humanely; it was not unusual for some plantations' slaves, like those of Poplar Grove near Wilmington, to have access to education, and even be allowed to work side jobs for money. But these owners did not control the legislature. The largest and oldest plantations, with played-out soils, were making their money as human breeding farms, in an economy where a prize worker could cost as much as a racehorse. They could not afford any slackening of the institutions of slavery, and made manumission virtually impossible.

While the coastal plains may have been falling asleep under its stultifying slave economy (North Carolina was known as "the Rip Van Winkle State"), the Piedmont was roaring ahead. Antebellum industry relied on waterpower, not steam, and a sophisticated factory based on waterwheels could do anything a steam engine could, for free; examples still abound, particularly around Burlington. When the Piedmont finally managed to send a native son, John Morehead, to the governor's mansion, that energy burst upon the state, with improved education, turnpikes, river navigation—and that newfangled monstrosity, the railroad. In the early 1840s Morehead pushed into existence what was then the longest railroad line in the world, the North Carolina Railroad, still in existence under its original name and original owner (the state of North Carolina). Along its line sprang a great curve of industrial cities: Durham, Burlington, Greensboro, Winston-Salem, High Point, Hickory, Charlotte. In the 20th century these Piedmont rail towns would grow together into one giant urban crescent—the fourth largest manufacturing region in America—with more than six million inhabitants, nine major universities, and three international airports.

At the start of the Civil War, North Carolina was the last state to join the Confederacy, and the most reluctant. The planters who still controlled the state legislature rammed secession through in May 1861. This was so unpopular that voters turned the secessionist planters out at the next election, and elected as governor Asheville's Zebulon Vance, whose log cabin home is a state historic site north of town. Vance, who became one of the state's most beloved political figures, protected his people from the worst excesses of the Confederacy, prohibiting forced conscription, keeping the courts open, and (alone in the U.S., North or South) retaining the use of *habeas corpus.* He had a lot on his hands, as North Carolina's

INSIDE A LOG FARMHOUSE AT THE MOUNTAIN FARM MUSEUM IN THE GREAT SMOKY MOUNTAINS NATIONAL PARK

major role in the war was to supply the Confederacy with cannon fodder, sending more soldiers into Confederate armies than any other state. He had his own civil war on his hands as well; as with Tennessee and Virginia, the people who lived deep in the North Carolina mountains were Unionists, and preventing atrocities against them (such as the slaughter at Shelton Laurels north of Asheville) proved difficult. Late in the war Sherman completed his March Through Georgia by turning up the coast and heading into North Carolina. Here he was confronted by a much smaller southern force at Bentonville, which he trounced soundly. The North Carolina forces formally surrendered at Bennett Place, outside Durham, 17 days after Lee's surrender at Appomattox.

In the years following the war, North Carolina slowly climbed out of chaos and depression, with an economy increasingly fueled by factory growth along the Piedmont Crescent, and tobacco farms along the coastal plains. Textile mills migrated from New England, and furniture mills set up at railheads to take advantage of cheap Blue Ridge oak, maple, and hickory; indeed, the city of High Point remains a design center of the furniture industry. Tobacco, however, was and is the signature industry. The played-out soils left behind by the planters turned out to be ideal for growing a fine cigarette tobacco known as Bright Leaf, whose light color and mild taste come from starved, dry soils. The American cigarette industry started in Durham, where the farmstead it originated upon is a state historic site, and the massive brick factories it once required now house malls, restaurants, offices, and condos. However, the industry remains, and operates at full throttle, at Winston-Salem, where the R. J. Reynolds Tobacco Company was founded and continues to operate. There, tobacco-related tourism is not just factory tours; it's the mansions, gardens, and art museums left behind by the tobacco magnates.

THE LUCKY STRIKE CIGARETTE LOGO DECORATES THE OLD AMERICAN TOBACCO COMPANY PLANT IN DURHAM.

The Blue Ridge Mountains did not participate in this boom. Too isolated to attract industry, the most remote mountain communities slid into the deep, permanent depression that would later lead to the neologism *Appalachia* as a synonym for poverty and backwardness. By the late 19th century the era's destructive farming and logging techniques, applied to steep mountain slopes, had left the area devastated, with muddy streams and treeless slopes in all but the deepest mountains. In the middle of this, however, the mountain town of Asheville had a thriving summer tourism industry that attracted the wealthiest members of the northeastern elite. Chief among them was Cornelius Vanderbilt, who built the Biltmore Estate, still the largest private home in America, on the edge of town, and purchased every single inch of raw, damaged land that he could see from the wide view in his garden. (It came to 125,000 acres.) He then hired America's foremost forester, Gifford Pinchot, to restore it. After three years Pinchot moved on to found the U.S. national forest system as first director of the National Forest Service. At first an agency to manage government-owned forests in the West, Pinchot's operation reentered his old stomping grounds in 1911, when the Weeks Act, which aimed to protect navigable rivers from siltation, lead directly to the creation of the Nantahala and Pisgah National Forests.

These two tracts of public land, much expanded since, now protect vast swaths of mountain ranges and make them open to public recreation. In 1914 Vanderbilt's widow sold much of the forest Pinchot had helped restore to the Pisgah National Forest, and in 1940 the Department of the Interior protected a further half million acres as the Great Smoky Mountains National Park. In later decades, at the far end of the state, 150 miles of wild beach in the Outer Banks would be added to the system of public lands, as well as hundreds of thousands of acres of coastal wetland. These enormous tracts have become the foundation of the travel experience in the state's two opposite tourism regions. Hiking, backpacking, camping, hunting, fly fishing, surf fishing, kayaking (either in mountain whitewater or the calm waters of a coastal marsh), and just plain old glorious sightseeing in beautiful lands that never seem to end—these are here in plenty because of the great public lands.

In the Piedmont, public lands take a different form. Already thickly settled and heavily industrialized when Pinchot was starting his reforms, it missed out on the great forests. What it got was lakes, huge lakes, constructed to provide electrical power to the region's mills. The biggest player was tobacco scion James Buchanan Duke, whose Duke Power Company (now Duke Energy) dammed pretty much all of the Piedmont's two major rivers, the Catawba and Yadkin/Pee Dee. Seventeen such lakes (with more in the mountains and Piedmont), built by Duke and his competitors, make for fine outdoor recreation, and are described in detail in this book.

WHAT'S WHERE IN NORTH CAROLINA

AIRPORTS AND AIRLINES North Carolina has four major airports. Raleigh-Durham (RDU) and Charlotte (CLT) have regular international flights as well as flights to virtually every domestic destination. Piedmont Triad Airport (GSO), located between Greensboro and Winston-Salem, and Wilmington (ILM) on the south coast, each offers a large number of nonstop flights to eastern cities. Of note is Asheville's airport (AVL), a small regional airport with good connections because of its central location in the heart of the Blue Ridge Mountains. For the Outer Banks, Norfolk, Virginia (ORF), has the closest airport, with nonstop flights to many eastern cities.

AMTRAK (amtrak.com). North Carolina has two sets of passenger trains: two Amtrak-owned routes, and two additional routes sponsored by the state on the railroad it's owned since the 1840s, the North Carolina Railroad.

The Crescent shuttles between New York and New Orleans, one train a day each way (two physical trains). In North Carolina it stops at Greensboro, High Point, Charlotte, and two smaller towns.

The Silver Service/Palmetto groups three parallel routes together, all running between New York and Florida: the Silver Meteor, the Silver Star, and the Palmetto (which terminates in Savannah, Georgia). They share the same route as they enter North Carolina (with three stops, including Rocky Mount). Then they branch, with the Silver Star heading inland to Raleigh and Southern Pines (among other places), and the Silver Meteor and Palmetto following the coast to Fayetteville and points south. (The Silvers branch again in Florida, with the Star heading to Tampa and the Meteor going straight to Miami.) Each of these is two physical trains a day, one in each direction.

The Carolinian, starting in New York, follows the route of the Silver Star as far as Raleigh, then branches west to Durham, Burlington, Greensboro, and High Point (as well as other places) before terminating in Charlotte.

The Piedmont shuttles between Raleigh and Charlotte and then back again, stopping at the same stations as the Carolinian. This route consists of two physical trains that depart Raleigh five hours apart, so that it creates two stops a day (each way) at these stations.

So if you've lost track, here's the score: Little Rocky Mount is the winner with six trains a day in each direction; Raleigh, Greensboro, High Point, and Charlotte each has four; Burlington and Durham each has three; Fayetteville has two; and Southern Pines has one. While this wouldn't impress a European, it's the best of any state in the South.

ARTISTS AND ART GALLERIES Major cities have major art galleries, reflecting their concentrations of corporate headquarters both past and present. The state's great traditional galleries tend to group in the tobacco and textile cities of Winston-Salem and Greensboro, as well as the state capital of Raleigh and the main state university at Chapel Hill (as the state is the biggest corporate donor of them all). Charlotte, the scene of rapid growth of Fortune 1000 companies, is also seeing rapid growth of art galleries.

The liveliest art scenes, however, are far away from these centers of corporate patronage. Asheville has one of the largest and most varied artists' communities in the South, big enough to take over and transform multiblock urban districts. It centers on fine crafts, and this specialty spreads far into the surrounding countryside, with surprising finds in tiny shops by courthouse squares. The other major district is at Seagrove, an isolated rural area in the eastern Piedmont, which happens to have some of the finest pottery clay on the continent. A folk craft of hand pottery making has flourished here continuously since colonial times, and flourishes still; you can go to several Seagrove potters and specify your wedding china. All this activity has attracted a core of 60 or so fine craft potters and other artists. Finally, the wild scenery of the Outer Banks has attracted a number of excellent landscape artists, whose work can be found in coffeehouses, small galleries, and gift shops along the coast.

BARBEQUE North Carolina is noted for its barbeque, with two distinct regional styles. In the Eastern Style, a whole hog is cooked over greenwood and basted with a vinegar-pepper sauce—a more traditionally southern approach, except for the fact that the meat is served chopped, frequently with the cracklings (crunchy skin) and gristle intentionally mixed in. In the Lexington (or Piedmont) Style, only the shoulder is cooked, and over charcoal rather than wood (so the smoke flavor comes from burning drippings); it is basted with a ketchup/vinegar/hot pepper sauce, and this baste is used to make the mayo-free coleslaw. Both styles require slow cooking—at least eight hours. You'll find more details, along with restaurants, in the listings.

BUGS (SUMMER) First the good news. The Smokies and the Blue Ridge are largely free of swarming blackflies, midges, and mosquitoes—the kind that in some other states, form clouds around your face and fill your nose when you try to breathe. Down on the coast, however, summers are choked with mosquitoes and biting flies, unless you are on the beach with a sea breeze. The Piedmont is pretty much like any other place in the summer. All three regions have chiggers in the forests, microscopic larvae that burrow into your skin anytime you sit down, and ticks. If you venture in the woods at the height of summer, it's best to wear long sleeves and trousers, and spray insect repellent on your ankles, wrists, belt, and neck.

BED & BREAKFASTS A rare sight 30 years ago, bed & breakfasts are now found in every part of the state. They are generally price-competitive with local motels, and a whole lot nicer. Small and friendly, a B&B is a good way to relax and meet the locals. A typical B&B will have a wide porch with rocking chairs and a view over a garden, a great room with comfortable sofas and chairs grouped around a wood fire, a friendly group of guests who swap experiences over a luxurious breakfast or an evening glass of wine, and a gregarious host who never seems to tire of meeting new people and giving a helping hand to visitors.

By the way, you might want to check the Internet for a B&B's web page before calling for a reservation. Nearly all of them have one, and show photos of the individual rooms.

BICYCLING North Carolina offers a number of wonderful opportunities for bicyclists, and this book tries to highlight the best with their own listings. Apart from these greenways, ask at one of the listed bike rental shops about back roads, with wonderful scenery and light traffic. The premier road biking experience is the Blue Ridge Parkway, where the scenery is nonstop and wide shoulders, gentle curves, and frequent pullovers reduce traffic problems. The huge tracts of national forest land found throughout the state offer many miles of trail biking, mainly down old logging roads. For those who don't travel with their bicycles, this book lists bicycle rentals in most areas.

CAMPING Campgrounds are found in abundance throughout the state. The national parks and forests contain scores of public campgrounds, generally cheap and scenic but frequently without hookups. (The popular campgrounds within the Great Smoky Mountains National Park don't even have showers.) While many of the public campgrounds stay booked up all summer, you can always find a good site in a remote, beautiful little national forest campground down a gravel road; ask a ranger at the nearest district station. Private campgrounds are the best bet for RVers who want electricity and running water.

CANOEING AND KAYAKING This state has abundant whitewater and stillwater, with suitable streams in nearly every chapter. Famous whitewater streams include the Ocoee, site of the 1996 Summer Olympics; the Nantahala, well known as a training ground for Olympic medalists; and the Chattooga, made famous in the novel *Deliverance*. Other rivers, such as the New River, the French Broad River, the Cape Fear River, and the Neuse River, offer excellent areas for long, scenic canoe trips, perfect for overnight camping. Places to hire canoes and kayaks, join a whitewater rafting party, or have your boat shuttled to a drop-off point are noted throughout this book.

CHEROKEES Before the arrival of the European settlers, the Cherokee tribes inhabited all of the fertile mountain valleys south and west of the Great Smoky Mountains. The Cherokees lived in villages ranging from half a dozen to several score houses, made of logs, and surrounded by cultivated fields. These were organized along clan lines, similar to the Scottish Highlands but without the constant warfare; the Cherokee villages shared a traditional legal code, enforced through consensus and the leadership of chiefs. Until the wars of the late 18th century, the Cherokees had three major settlement areas: an area of villages in the South Carolina upstate, a second area in the deep mountains to the immediate south of the Smokies, and a third area (called the Overhill area) at the foot of the mountains in Tennessee. The more northern mountains, around present-day Burnsville and Boone, were kept as a hunting ground.

In the late 18th century, the Cherokees tried to defeat the European invaders in battle, with disastrous consequences. After that tribal consensus swung toward working within the invaders' legal system. Led by wealthy, Europeanized chiefs, the tribe formed itself into a quasi-autonomous legal entity known as the Cherokee Nation, located in northern Georgia, southeastern Tennessee, and the westernmost corner of the North Carolina mountains. In 1838 President Andrew Jackson's administration expelled the Cherokee Nation to Oklahoma, forcing the Cherokees into a deadly winter march known as the Trail of Tears.

About 600 Cherokees remained in the deep coves of the Smokies, and their descendants still live, work, and thrive in these mountains. The Eastern Band of the Cherokee Nation, some 10,000 strong, inhabits a sizable reservation, properly called the Qualla Boundary, located on the North Carolina side of the Great Smoky Mountains National Park.

CHILDREN, ESPECIALLY FOR This region is jammed with child-appropriate, family-friendly stuff. The text makes a serious effort to mention anything that will challenge a child's patience, endurance, or safety, making it easy to judge what's right for your kids. Please note that most B&Bs do not accept children under 12; the text notes those that do with a family-friendly (🖍) icon.

THE CIVILIAN CONSERVATION CORPS (CCC) When President Franklin D. Roosevelt founded the Civilian Conservation Corps in 1933, he meant it to attack two of the Great Depression's problems at once. The first, and most visible, was a veritable army of unemployed, and unemployable, older teenage men. The second, hidden from city folk's view but just as serious, was tens of millions of acres of land destroyed by exploitative forestry—abandoned and covered with tinder-dry waste. He formed the veritable army into an actual one, run by the U.S. Army (and spied upon by suspicious Nazis), that fanned out through America's ruined forests to restore them.

Today we are reaping the harvest that Roosevelt and his CCC army sowed. The CCC restoration efforts have provided us with the luxuriously deep forests that now blanket the mountains of the Virginias. The CCC also provided us with some of our finest architecture. Combining standard plans, local materials, handcraftsmanship, and lots of imagination, these classic structures—ranging from camp offices and workers' cabins to picnic shelters and hiking paths—present a coherent style of notable simplicity and beauty. This book will highlight surviving CCC recreation areas wherever it finds them, and you can be assured of finding both beauty and thoughtful quality at these spots.

COTTAGE RENTALS Cottage rentals have long been a tradition in the mountains and along the coast, and have become increasingly popular in recent years. In some parts of the Blue Ridge, small compounds of log cabins, recently built in traditional styles and luxuriously furnished, have been springing up faster than chain motels. In both regions, second homes are widely available for rentals. A rental cabin can be a pleasant retreat for a couple, with its ample space, separate living room, and porch; for a family with kids, it can also be a major money saver, allowing breakfasts and dinners at home with picnic lunches on the road.

EMERGENCIES There is nothing more frightening that having a serious medical emergency and not knowing where to go for help. For this reason, each chapter introduction includes the location of the nearest emergency room.

FALL FOLIAGE The Smokies and the Blue Ridge have one of America's outstanding autumn color displays—the result of a large variety of species, spread over a large range of elevations and habitats. Look for color to begin in early October and reach its peak in the middle of the month. From then, colors will last until the first strong wind, generally in the third or fourth week of October. In most years, color is nearly gone by early November, and lasts a week or two longer in the Piedmont and along the coast. If you are coming for the color, you can check out the views on webcams on these sites:

- nature.nps.gov/air/WebCams lists two webcams within the Great Smoky Mountains National Park and showing elevations between 5,000 and 1,000 feet.
- webcam.srs.fs.fed.us, a National Forest Service webcam pointed at the Shining Rock Wilderness, shows elevations from 6,000 to 3,000 feet.

HIKING Sooner or later, nearly everyone gets out of their car and walks through the woods. There are thousands of miles of walking trails to choose from, with good choices in nearly every chapter of this book. The *Exploring the Area* section contains a suggestion or two, very rewarding and not particularly difficult. Other sections will mention still more trails, each with a brief indication of the type of scenery, as well as its difficulty and length.

HUNTING The state's main hunting season runs from September through January. Remember that hunting is allowed in all national forest lands, including the wilderness areas, as well as all state game lands and most national wildlife refuges; you should always wear hunter orange anytime you enter these areas during the season. If you wish to avoid hunting areas altogether, you should stay in the national parks and state parks (which, fortunately, offer plenty of outdoor opportunity). Hunting is also prohibited on Sunday in the state of North Carolina, making that a good day to enjoy God's creation (but wear hunter orange anyway, just in case).

HIGHWAYS AND ROADS This book uses these conventions for naming highways: interstates are "I-81," U.S. primary highways are "US 25" or "US Bus 19" (*Bus* for "Business," *Alt* for "Alternate," *Byp* for "Bypass").

ECCENTRIC HIGHWAYS OF NORTH CAROLINA

The state of North Carolina designates certain roads as highways, giving them numbers on special diamond signs, which are supposed to hurry through-traffic on its way to its destination. Some of these designations seem less than completely thought out, and a few of them are downright eccentric—so much so that road buffs will want to search these out for themselves.

NC 210: You'd expect a highway to make a beeline for its destination—or at least go *somewhere*. NC 210 doesn't. Instead it traces out two-thirds of an oval, starting at Smithfield in the Coastal Plains (see "The Coastal Plains"), and ending south of Jacksonville on the South Coast (see "Albemarle Sound"). In doing so it traces out a 191-mile route that end up only 81 miles from its starting point, along the way heading in every direction of the compass rose. It's an attractive rural drive, whose high points include the military tourism of Fayetteville, the natural Bladen Lakes, and the beaches of remote Topsail Island.

NC 90: In the 1920s this was one of the state's most important east–west highways, but in the intervening decades bits and chunks of it were whittled off to become main U.S. highways. Now the only part left is its extreme western terminus, as it enters the mountains, loses its pavement, and disappears, its end unmarked, in a welter of Forest Service roads. Its final miles at the foot of the Blue Ridge below Boone make for an attractive and interesting drive.

NC 197: Another one of North Carolina's unpaved "highways," this particularly scenic drive north of Asheville crosses a high shoulder of Mount Mitchell, the tallest mountain in the East, visiting some lovely little communities on both sides of this gap before ending up at the pleasant county seat of Burnsville.

State highways are designated as "NC 80" or "TN 70." Although these are supposed to be main through-highways, some are no better than local roads with fancy signs, and three of them are gravel-surfaced (NC 281, NC 197, and NC 90). Local roads have names in Tennessee, Georgia, and South Carolina, but four-digit numbers in North Carolina. National Park Service roads always have names. National Forest Service have numbers such as "FS 712"; please note that many Forest Service roads are not passable for passenger autos.

This book occasionally recommends touring on gravel-surfaced roads. These are roads that have been improved by pounding in a mixture of gravel and rock dust, the rock dust acting as a sort of temporary cement. Gravel roads form potholes and washboard-like ridges if not graded once or twice a year, a condition most apt to occur on Forest Service roads. The text will highlight known problems. In

general, if a road starts looking too rough for you, don't hesitate to turn around and go back.

HIGHWAYS AND ROADS (STATE) Unlike other states, North Carolina has no local roads outside cities. All of its rural roads are state roads, from the largest freeway down to the roughest dirt rut. The state's Department of Transportation (known as NCDOT, or NickDot) distinguishes "state highways" from "state roads." State highways are considered major thoroughfares, with regular state highway signs and two- or three-digit numbers, such as "NC 90" or "NC 197." State roads have four-digit numbers, sometimes marked on stop signs with those little home address stick-on numbers, but more often found on the standard green street signs now used everywhere in America. In this book, state roads are denoted as, for example, "SSR 1300" or "SSR 1407," the *SSR* standing for "state secondary road." However, don't expect locals to direct you to an SSR number; no one in North Carolina pays attention to them.

INFORMATION As much as we like to be encyclopedic in our coverage, we admit that there is nothing like fresh, local information. Each chapter of this book lists the relevant chambers of commerce, along with their toll-free numbers and web page. We also describe the local tourist information center, so you can drop by and talk to someone friendly and in the know.

THE INTRACOASTAL WATERWAY Authorized by Congress in 1919 and completed in 1940, the Atlantic Intracoastal Waterway (run by the U.S. Army Corp of Engineers) provides a safe inland passage between Norfolk, Virginia, and Jacksonville, Florida, with a target depth of 12 feet (sometimes missed due to consistent underfunding). It consists of a connected series of inland canals, dredged tidal inlets and lagoons, and open water. North Carolina possesses 308 miles of the Intracoastal Waterway, and this is described in some detail in the chapters through which it passes, with emphasis on the scenery and the location of services.

LAKES There are a few natural lakes in the state—the Bladen Lakes in the coastal plains, and the Croatan National Forest lakes in the southern tidewater area—but most of the lakes are man-made, nearly always for hydropower and flood control. Of particular note is the chain of 17 large hydropower lakes in the Piedmont, ranging in character from narrow, wild gorges to wide, home-lined waters. These are wonderful recreational opportunities; this book describes them in detail, and includes places where you can rent a boat.

LOG CABINS While most of us associate log cabins with the first generations of settlers, log construction continued in the mountains into the early 20th century. This was not a matter of isolation or tradition so much as saving money; logs were free, while milled studs required scarce dollars. The Great Smoky Mountains National Park displays a superbly crafted log cabin built by its owner in 1902. The log cabin tradition in the Piedmont died out during the 19th century, but you will find many surviving examples in the historic sites listed in this book.

In North Carolina, all vernacular log cabins were built with planked logs—that is, logs that had their vertical sides hewn flat. Planking reduced rot by allowing rainwater to run straight down, rather than beading up on the underside of a round log. While barns frequently used round logs, a round log cabin is invariably modern.

This book will sometimes describe a log cabin in terms of its cribs. A crib is the rectangle made when the logs are fitted together; doors and windows are then cut out of the cribs. The simplest cabins had one crib, covered with a roof. Larger cabins had two cribs, and the cribs could be placed together to form a two-room cabin, separated by a chimney (a rare form in the South), or (most commonly) separated by a roofed central breezeway, or dog-trot.

Log cabins were an important part of mountain life—but today, all the log cabins you will see will be carefully restored museum pieces, or else abandoned hulks. Not so with log barns; keep an eye peeled for log barns still in use along any back road, and particularly in the mountains.

LONG-DISTANCE FOOTPATHS (Appalachian Trail Conservancy: appalachiantrail.org; Friends of the Mountains-To-Sea Trail: ncmst.org; detailed maps of the Mountains-to-Sea Trail: artshikingmaps.info). North Carolina has two prominent long-distance paths and several shorter, less famous ones. The Appalachian Trail, the granddaddy of them all, runs for almost 2,200 miles between northern Georgia and central Maine, following the spine of the eastern mountains. It spends 288 miles in North Carolina (including 200 miles following its border with Tennessee). The Mountains-to-Sea Trail, sponsored by the state of North Carolina, runs for 1,000 miles, from 6,643-foot Clingman's Dome in the Great Smoky Mountains National Park (where it meets the Appalachian Trail) to Cape Hatteras. It's about 50 percent off-road footpath, connected by back road segments while the trail is being extended.

LOST Even with the best maps you are likely to get lost once you stray from a main highway. On these twisting roads, even the sharpest explorers will lose their sense of direction. GPS units are popular, but be advised that they are no better than their computer maps—and these can be pretty lousy, especially within the mountains and the national forests. Your best defense is a compass—one of those round ones you stick on your dashboard. Pay attention to it along several twists, and take an average. This will at least tell you if you are going generally toward your destination or away from it. And relax. How bad can it be? Getting lost is an adventure, not a disaster.

MUSIC, MOUNTAIN Mountain music isn't bluegrass, and it definitely isn't country. Mountain music is the music people knew before radios came along, the music they used to play deep in the coves and hollows. Mountain music was already a fast-disappearing anachronism when Mars Hill native Bascom Lamar Lunsford started his vast collection of mountain folk music in the closing years of the 19th century. Today the music collected by Lunsford and others represents a carefully preserved folk tradition, still popular and readily available throughout this region. This book cites mountain music venues wherever it can.

PETS Only a few B&Bs allow pets, and these are highlighted in the text. You will have better luck with a cottage rental, which fortunately are very common, but verify in advance that your pet will be welcome. Of the places that allow pets, many charge an extra fee or restrict pets to special units. The Great Smoky Mountains National Park is notoriously pet-hostile, prohibiting pets on all hiking trails with no exceptions, and requiring dogs to be kept on leashes at all times anywhere else.

PUBLIC LANDS: THE NATIONAL PARK SERVICE (nps.gov). The National Park Service, a bureau of the U.S. Department of the Interior, maintains a number of tracts in this state, of which the largest are the Great Smoky Mountains National Park, Blue Ridge Parkway, Hatteras National Seashore, and Cape Lookout National Seashore. Each has its own management style. The Great Smoky Mountains National Park—the only designated "national park" of the four and the most visited such park in America—has always been maintained as a wilderness park with the emphasis on hiking, camping, picnicking, and fishing. The Blue Ridge Parkway (the most visited property managed by the National Park Service in America) is more purely recreational, with hotels and restaurants along its length. The national seashores are also recreation-oriented, and even have limited hunting seasons (unusual in the national park system). They are all preserves, each safeguarding a precious resource for the future. All prohibit gathering plants, rockhounding, and picking wildflowers.

PUBLIC LANDS: THE NATIONAL FOREST SERVICE (cs.unca.edu /nfsnc). People frequently confuse the National Forest Service with the

National Park Service, yet the two agencies couldn't be more different. While the National Park Service preserves our finest natural and historic lands, the National Forest Service—part of the Department of Agriculture—manages forestlands for sustainable exploitation. The National Forest Service logs many of its tracts, getting much of its operating revenues from timber sales. It allows hunting on virtually all of its lands, including congressionally declared wildernesses. The actual type of use given to any tract of national forest land—logging, recreation, preservation—is set by a plan that is revised every eight years.

North Carolina has four national forests: the Nantahala National Forest in the southern half of the mountains, the Pisgah National Forest in the northern half of the mountains, the Uwharrie National Forest in the Piedmont, and the Croatan National Forest on the coast north of Wilmington. All are managed from a headquarters building in Asheville.

PADDLE TRAILS (STATE DECLARED) (ncsu.edu/paddletrails). In 2001 the state of North Carolina declared a number of canoe and kayak streams in the coastal plains and estuaries as "NC Coastal Paddle Trails." These range from the Cape Fear River, improved (but no longer used) for commercial traffic, to obscure creeks lost deep in swamplands. The program has published a fairly thorough guide on its website—which, however, was marked "Last update: 6/12/2001" at press time. It's a good place to find ideas for exploration, particularly obscure creeks, but don't assume that being included in the guide means that anyone is removing deadfalls.

SKIING Many people think that North Carolina's mountains are too far south for skiing. They're right; snow seldom sticks around more than a week or so at even the highest elevations, and cold rain is a lot more common than fleecy blizzards. However, a number of ski slopes stay in business using manufactured snow. Mostly the result of a speculative boom in the 1960s (during a series of cold winters), some of these slopes are old and unpleasant, while others keep themselves up. None is particularly fancy. Winter skiing isn't really an environmentally friendly sport, as it carves great scars on hillsides and breaks the winter silence with the sideshow roar of diesel generators and massive snowblowers. However, this book lists several of the better slopes, for those so inclined.

SIX-THOUSAND-FOOT PEAKS (tehcc.org/Beyond6000.htm). Most of the East's mountains stay below 4,000 feet. Of those that rise higher, a handful reach the mile-high mark, and only 41 top 6,000 feet. Of these 41 6'ers, 40 are within North Carolina or on her border with Tennessee, including the 1st through 16th tallest peaks. (The 17th tallest peak in the east, Mount Washington, is located in New Hampshire.) Bagging 6'ers is beginning to catch on as a hobby, akin to bagging Scottish Munros or Coloradan 14'ers, only easier. If you are looking for a reason to choose one mountain walk over another, bagging 6'ers will lead you to a lot of really great places, and the Tennessee Eastman Hiking and Canoeing Club will give (well, sell) you a neat patch.

WALKING Frequently the best way to enjoy an area is to get out and walk around. Most chapters of this *Explorer's Guide* offer a few good walks, mainly short and easy, that highlight major features of the locale. This list-

ing is by no means encyclopedic; rather, it's more by the way of a sampler, oriented toward the rushed traveler who doesn't have time to spend on a long, hard hike. There are numerous specialized hiking guides for the enthusiast, starting with Backcountry Press's *Fifty Hikes in the Mountains of North Carolina*, which includes a number of fine Piedmont hikes as well.

WATERFALLS Erosion—50 million years' worth—has not yet smoothed away all the rock ledges in the mountains and Piedmont. Waterfalls abound throughout this region, ranging from half a dozen feet high to over 400. The tallest waterfalls, deep in the mountains, often require difficult hikes down gorges, but some can be reached down an easy path, and a few can be viewed from the roadside. The text highlights the best of the waterfalls.

WINE (Winegrowers Association: ncwinegrowers.com; official state site: visitncwine.com). The North Carolina winemaking industry was almost invisible a few decades ago; now there are nearly 100 wineries that offer tastings, far more than is possible to list in this book. Wineries can be found anywhere in the state, from the Outer Banks to the westernmost mountains. Coastal wines frequently feature the native Scuppernong grape, a type of muscadine first described by Sir Walter Raleigh's explorers in the 1580s, while Piedmont and mountain wineries favor European varietals. Within this scatter are three official appellations (federally declared American Viticultural Areas, or AVAs): Haw River, centered on Burlington; Yadkin Valley in the high Piedmont between Winston-Salem and the Blue Ridge; and Swan Creek, in the Brushy Mountains (a Blue Ridge outlier in the Piedmont).

WILDLIFE Bears, of course. People are sometimes surprised to learn that bears are common enough to be hunted in parts of our national forests (and a bear hunt is a massive enterprise, resembling a military search-and-destroy mission). Bears are common enough that you might walk up onto one by accident in the mountain back-country, and even in some remote wildlife refuges in the tidewater; treat it as very, very dangerous, and get away without showing panic or fear. The infamous begging bears of the Great Smoky Mountains National Park are less of a pest now than in the past, but are still to be avoided as dangerous.

Wildlife is common throughout the state, but timid. The author has seen, in his small rural property in the Blue Ridge mountains, foxes, many deer, groundhogs, innumerable rabbits, skunks, squirrels, turkeys, a bobcat, and two bears—a pretty typical cross section. Deer are particularly common, especially in the national parks. Rangers offer regular wildlife walks in all the national parks and forests, as well as all the state parks, with schedules available at park offices and websites.

1

The Coastal Region

INTRODUCTION

North Carolina's coast could have been made specifically for outdoor recreation. A thin crust of beach, 300 miles long, presents uniformly high quality sand and water, and every level of development from outright wilderness to plush resorts, with two national seashores protecting about half of this long strand. Behind are massive bays and sounds, with broad expanses of water, and, behind that, large wild marshlands, government-owned refuges managed for hunting, fishing, boating, and wildlife observation. "Outdoorsmen's Paradise" is a cliché everywhere but here.

It is less well known that the coastal region is rich with historic sites. This was where English settlement first began, and historic sites preserve and present all aspects of this rich heritage, from Sir Walter Raleigh's Lost Colony (in 1584, the year Shakespeare turned 20) to the maritime legacy of the Outer Banks. This includes the colonial towns of Edenton and Bath (where Blackbeard lived in 1718), the antebellum city of Wilmington, an entire series of plantation houses, the lighthouses of the Outer Banks and southern beaches, the tobacco farms of the inland sandy plains, and the outstanding military tourism of Fayetteville.

FERRIES The North Carolina State Ferry System (800-273-3779; ncdot.org/transit/ferry). In the mid-1940s the state of North Carolina began to extend its highway system across its large bodies of water, first by subsidizing and purchasing existing private ferries to the Outer Banks, then by replacing and expanding this system with its own fleet. It now runs seven routes, four of them free, linking the remotest parts of the coast. Ranging from 20 minutes to 2½ hours in length, these are a fun addition to any sightseeing trip. In good weather seagulls will flock to your ferry looking for handouts, and someone will invariably be feeding them bits of bread.

Here's a list of all seven, from north to south.

Route 1: Currituck to Knotts Island (252-232-2683). Open daily 6–5:30, running six times a day. Free. This 45-minute ferry links Currituck County's seat with Knotts Island, a remote part of the same county. Actually, Knotts Island has a bridge to the mainland, but it leads into Virginia, which is evidently a problem for North Carolina school buses—hence this ferry. Knotts Island has some notable outdoor recreation opportunities in its MacKay Island National Wildlife Refuge.

Route 2: Hatteras to Ocracoke (800-368-8949; 252-986-2353). Open daily 5 AM–midnight, usually running every half hour. Free. The most popular ferry in the state links beautiful Ocracoke Island with the rest of the Outer Banks. It's a 2½-hour drive from Kitty Hawk on a good day, plus another half hour from the Ocracoke ferry terminal to Ocracoke village. The ferry ride itself is 40 minutes, but on a peak day you might have to wait quite a long time before getting onto the boat. The above phone numbers are for the Hatteras Village terminal; for Ocracoke, call 800-345-1665 or 252-928-3841.

Route 3: Swan Quarter to Ocracoke (800-773-1094; 252-926-1111). Open daily at 6:30 AM, running two to four times a day. $$$. This ferry runs eastward from marshy Hyde County's tiny and remote county seat, Swan Quarter, to the Outer Banks village of Ocracoke—also in Hyde County, as it turns out. Expect it to take 2½ hours, much faster than driving down the Banks from Kitty Hawk. The above phone numbers are for the Swan Quarter terminal; for Ocracoke, call 800-345-1665 or 252-928-3841.

Route 4: Cedar Island to Ocracoke (800-856-0343; 252-225-3551). Open daily, starting at 7 AM, running four to six times a day. $$$. This ferry connects the Outer Banks island of Ocracoke with the lands to the south, a 2½-hour journey that ends at the remote community of Cedar Island deep in the coastal marshes that surround the New Bern–Morehead City–Beaufort region. From Cedar Island it's another 40 miles to Beaufort, the nearest town of any size. The above phone numbers are for the Cedar Island terminal; for Ocracoke, call 800-345-1665 or 252-928-3841.

Route 5: Bayview to Aurora (252-964-4521). Open daily, 5:30 AM–11 PM, running about once every 90 minutes. Free. North of New Bern, the wide tidal waters of the Neuse and Pamlico Rivers form a peninsula large enough to contain one entire county and parts of two others—a large and prosperous area that relies on ferries to reach the wide world to its north and east. This 30-minute ferry provides the northern link.

Route 6: Cherry Branch to Minnesott (near New Bern) (800-339-9156; 252-447-1055). Open daily, 5:15 AM–midnight, typically running every 45 minutes. Free. This 20-minute ferry ride provides the eastern link for the peninsula isolated by the Pamlico-Neuse Rivers. It links the large marine base at Havelock with Pamlico County, and is very heavily used.

Route 7: Southport to Fort Fisher (near Wilmington) (800-368-8969; 910-457-6942). Open daily, 5:30 AM–7 PM, typically running every 45 minutes. $$. This ferry allows you to travel between the beaches in the Wilmington urban area and those farther to the south without having to drive through Wilmington. Because the ferry takes about half an hour, it doesn't really save time, but it's fun and scenic.

CABLE FERRIES Before the road-building projects of the 1930s, cable ferries were the way most people got their wagons and cars across rivers. The ferry, which has a small diesel engine on board, is guided by a cable running across the river; when the ferry isn't running, the cable sits on the bottom out of the way of boat traffic. The state of North Carolina still operates three cable ferries, all on wide and remote rivers near the coast, and all free. They are interesting in their own right, and all are in scenic locales worth driving a bit out of the way.

Parkers Ferry. Open daily, daylight hours. Free. Located at the far northeastern corner of Tobacco Country, Parker's Ferry allows a backwoods shortcut for locals traveling between Winton, North Carolina, and Franklin, Virginia—a route otherwise blocked by the marshlands of the Chowan and Meherrin Rivers. It's been in operation since the 1850s, and has been owned by one government or another since 1886. To find it, go about a mile west of Winton on US 158, then turn right onto SSR 1175 (Parkers Ferry Rd.).

SANS SOUCI CABLE FERRY, ON THE CASHIE RIVER

Sans Souci Ferry. Open daily, daylight hours. Free. North of Plymouth in the middle of the Tidewater Region, this remote ferry crosses the Cashie River on dirt-surfaced SSR 1500 (San Souci Rd.). Its purpose is to link a peninsula of farmland that projects into the massive marshes of the Roanoke River to the farmlands north of the river. It's been in business since the 19th century, coming under state ownership in 1934. It only gets about 30 cars a day, but is important enough to local farmers to be worth the cost. It is remarkably scenic, with a 0.25-mile stretch of road hard by the river to give wide views.

Elwell Ferry. Open daily, 6 AM–6 PM (or dawn to dusk when days are short). Free. Founded in 1905, Elwell Ferry crosses the Cape Fear River on SSR 1730 (Elwell Ferry Rd.), a back road in the Bladen Lakes area of Tobacco Country, about 35 miles northwest from Wilmington. Owned and operated by the North Carolina Division of Highways, it gets 60 to 80 cars a day despite being only 8 miles from a bridge.

THE OUTER BANKS

With 125 miles of high-quality sand beach, the Outer Banks is one of North America's premiere oceanside resort areas. The beaches get much of their interest from their mixture of wild and developed character, with a large developed area on the northern half and small enclaves of development buried like raisins in the wild beaches of the Hatteras National Seashore, the southernmost 78 miles. Even better, all of the wild beach can be easily reached from the family car, with no need for expensive ferries or special vehicles. NC 12 parallels the beach behind its dune line nearly the entire way, with parking lots and dune crossings every 1 to 4 miles.

The Banks stand a dozen miles off the North Carolina coast and remain isolated by this great distance. In the old days this isolation was profound, requiring a long boat trip and becoming completely cut off in bad weather. Despite this it carried a substantial population of fisherfolk, with its frequent lifesaving stations and four lighthouses furnishing stable paying jobs after 1874; some towns, such as Corolla, Ocracoke, and Portsmouth, had populations over 500. The Bankers (as these residents were called) developed a distinctive culture, dialect, and architecture. Of this, only the architecture survives, not only in the many historic buildings scattered about the islands, but also in kindly imitation by modern structures, for traditional Banker architecture turns out to be very practical as well as attractive.

The Banker traditions ended after the automobile came. The first bridge, US 158 to Kitty Hawk, was erected in the early 1930s, and the beach-side NC 12 came soon after. The U.S. Congress moved to protect the empty beaches in 1937, and this was completed in 1953 with the opening of Hatteras National Seashore, containing all the beaches and much of the back-island from Nags Head south to Ocracoke. However, they left six back-island Banker communities in private hands, and these—Rodanthe-Waves-Salvo, Avon, Buxton, Frisco, Hatteras, and Ocracoke—are now islands of development surrounded by great seas of wilderness. North of the national seashore, the Banks have developed thickly and completely for 36 miles. This is not, however, the splashy condo-tower development of Miami or Hilton Head. It is, rather, a very low-rise, small-scale, and family-friendly development, with many mom-and-pop stores and cafés.

Except at Cape Hatteras the Banks are very narrow, typically from 500 to 5,000 feet wide. There will be a wide sand beach (usually 100 feet in the developed areas and much wider in the wild areas), followed by a dune line, very wide in the wild areas but narrow or missing in the developed areas. Behind this there may be a

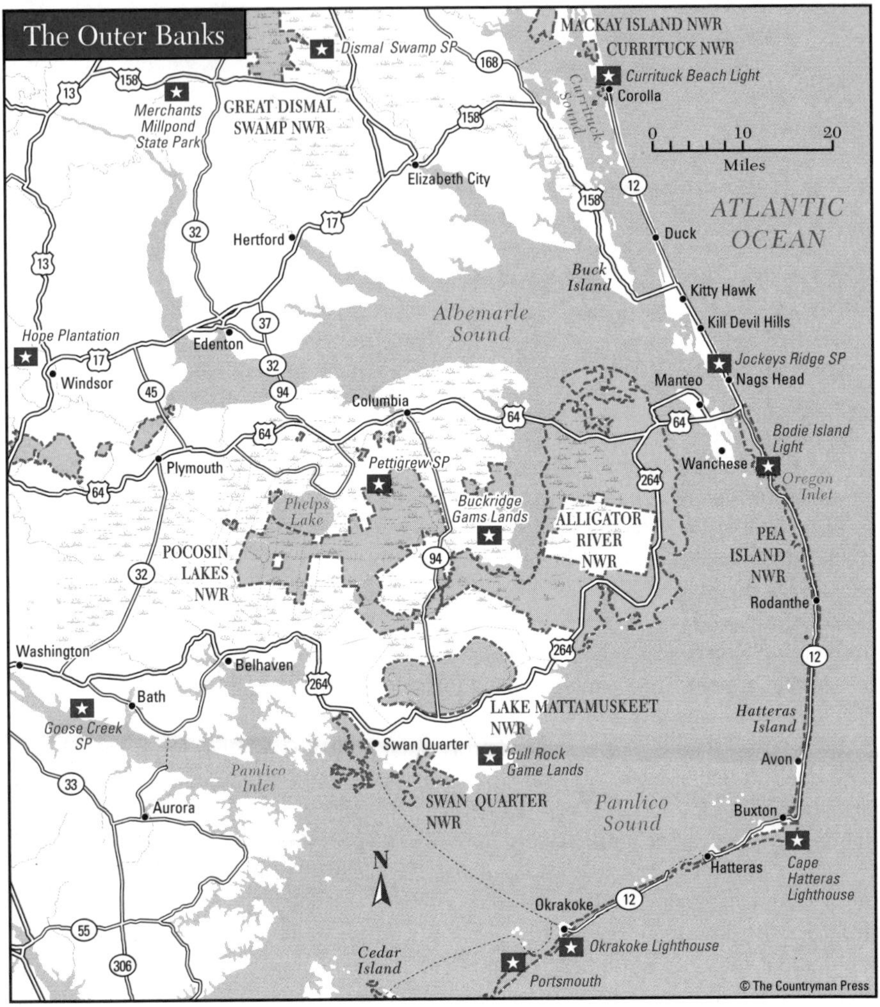

"maritime forest," an old stand of twisted oaks and woody scrub, rich in wildlife. On the far back side, along the sound, is marsh, mainly dense reeds cut by many tiny inlets that flood at high tide, a nursery for sea life. About 70 miles of this natural order survives, 10 or so miles north of Corolla and 60 or so miles within the national seashore. In this chapter you will find the beach-to-sound wild lands described under *Public Lands*; the individual beaches, both wild and developed, get examined, in detail, in their own section.

The tourist season is very sharply defined, from May to September. Most of the national seashore and some of the private enterprises close during September, and the entire national seashore closes and winterizes in November, including all the campgrounds. By New Year's, most of the shops and cafés have closed as well, and the Banks are nearly empty in January and February. September and October are hurricane season; do *not* make uncancellable reservations for these months. You will not be marooned on the island during a hurricane; rather, you will be evacuated (whether or not you want to be) and kept off the islands until the danger is passed. Apart from hurricanes, September is a nice time to visit, as it is still warm enough to swim and the waves may be larger than normal.

GUIDANCE **OuterBanks.org (Dare County)** (877-629-4386; 252-473-2138; outerbanks.org; information@outerbanks.org), 1 Visitors Center Circle, Manteo 27954. All of the Outer Banks except for the northernmost 23 miles and Ocracoke Island to the south is within giant Dare County, whose seat of government is in Manteo on Roanoke Island. The Outer Banks Visitors Bureau is a county agency, and sponsors this website and four visitors centers. The main center in Manteo is at the foot of the US Byp 64 bridge to the mainland, and its contact information is given above. They also have a large visitors center at milepost 1 in Kitty Hawk, an information desk just inside Hatteras National Seashore, and a satellite office in Hatteras, in the historic **Weather Bureau Building**.

VisitCurrituck.com (877-287-7488; 252-453-9612; visitcurrituck.com; info@visitcurrituck.com), 500 Hunt Club Dr., Corolla 27927. Open daily 9–5. The northernmost 23 miles of the Outer Banks are in Currituck County, including Duck and Corolla, and for this you need to consult the website and visitors center maintained by the Currituck County government (Dare County's outerbanks.org silently neglects this worthy section). Their visitors center is on NC 12, 13.6 miles north of its intersection with US 158. If you are traveling south from Newport News they maintain a second visitors center on NC 168 at the state line.

Carolina Environmental Diversity Explorations (learnnc.org/lp/editions/cede_nobx/cover). This website, posted by the University of North Carolina School of Education, features online "field trips" by experts in ecology, well written and worth your time. The Outer Banks field trip, written by the late marine scientist Dirk Frankenburg and geologist Blair Tormey, is spritely and fascinating.

GETTING THERE *By car:* There are two points at which bridges link the Outer Banks with the mainland: US 158 at Kitty Hawk, and US 64 at Manteo and Nags Head (which actually has two bridges, an old one and a new one). From points north you'll want to

A FISHING BOAT ON A SMALL CREEK, OCRACOKE ISLAND, HATTERAS NATIONAL SEASHORE

approach the Outer Banks via Norfolk, Virginia, taking VA/NC 168 (an expressway in Virginia) to US 158 and thence to Kitty Hawk. From all other directions you will find it faster and easier to take US 64, which has been upgraded to expressway along nearly all of its route.

You can also get to the Banks via toll ferry to Ocracoke, either from Cedar Key or Swan Quarter. This is faster and cheaper if you are coming from Beaufort (Cedar Key), or want to go directly from the mainland (Swan Quarter) to Ocracoke, avoiding a 150-mile drive and saving about 1½ hours. Otherwise, consider it a worthwhile touring excursion, perhaps added to the end of a trip.

Once you're on the Outer Banks it's hard to get lost. NC 12 travels its entire length from Corolla to the village of Ocracoke. Between Kitty Hawk and Nags Head, US 158 parallels it on the sound side, faster but less entertaining.

By air: **Norfolk International Airport** (757-857-335; norfolkairport.com), 2200 Norview Ave., Norfolk, VA 23518. Norfolk's airport is the closest to the Outer Banks, at 93 miles from Kitty Hawk. It is a major airport, served by six airlines with nonstop service from 25 cities.

By train or bus: The Outer Banks has no train or bus service.

MEDICAL EMERGENCIES The Outer Banks Hospital (877-359-9179; 252-449-4500; theouterbankshospital.com), 4800 S. Croatan Hwy. (US 158), Nags Head 27959. This, the only hospital in the Outer Banks, is full service and fully accredited despite its tiny size (only 21 beds). During the summer it also runs a minor care unit; just walk up to the emergency desk and ask. It is a not-for-profit, part of the Greenville (NC) based University Health Systems.

✷ Exploring the Area

EXPLORING BY CAR NC 12, Part I: Corolla to Nags Head. *Length: 37.2 miles*. NC 12 follows the Outer Banks beach from Corolla Lighthouse on the north to Ocracoke Harbor on the south—at 113.7 miles, the ultimate beach drive. The first three dozen or so miles traverses the heavily developed areas to the north of Hatteras National Seashore, and are the subject of this drive.

Up to 1984 this section was much shorter. The state highway stopped at the US 158 bridge at Kitty Hawk; to reach Corolla, you had to take a bad county road half the way, then drive on the beach for the rest. Your reward was a stunning exploration of lonely beach wilderness, ending at the most isolated and traditional village in the Banks. No longer. With the extension of the state highway, Corolla has become a fashionable little resort village with a core of restored Banker buildings, and the rest of the Northern Reach has become nonstop vacation homes, a 22-mile string of McMansions.

This drive starts at the beach access north of Corolla Village, the northern terminus of NC 12. Here a sand track continues over the dunes to a beach drive that leads, ultimately, to the Virginia state line—where Virginia authorities have erected a giant fence to keep out beach-driving Tarheels. Along this northernmost stretch (called Carova or, more simply, the Four-Wheel-Drive Area by the locals) are somewhere around 100 houses, set back in the woods, ranging from modest cabins to elaborate mansions. These houses can be reached only by driving along the beach and have no services at all, yet all are in use and a few more are built every

SAND DUNES ON OREGON INLET, HATTERAS NATIONAL SEASHORE

year. Also along this stretch is the Outer Banks' largest herd of **wild horses**, wandering everywhere and easily spotted should you be able to make the drive.

Corolla Village, to your left as you drive south from the beach ramp, is attractive, with numerous historic buildings. Its tall brick **lighthouse** is its main attraction, along with the adjacent **Whalehead Club**, a restored hunt club from the 1920s, and the **Wild Horse Museum** in the old school. There's public beach access at the end of the village—your last until Kitty Hawk. The next 17 miles, in which the highway follows the sound rather than the beach, are the most recently developed, and so display the most grandiose construction. Then, on your right, you pass the Coast Guard Research Station, closed to the public but with a large exhibit board by the roadside. Past that you enter **Duck**, once a sound-side Banker harbor, now a collection of shops. NC 12 continues sound-side for another 5.6 miles, reaching Kitty Hawk and swerving toward the beach a block short of US 158 (watch for the sign).

The next 14.8 miles closely follow the beach through the completely built-up towns of **Kitty Hawk**, **Kill Devil Hills**, and **Nags Head**, with plentiful beach access and parking. For the first 3 miles of this stretch the beach will be hard upon the highway; this common sight, misleadingly called beach erosion, is simply the result of natural forces sweeping sand southward, stripping some beaches and enlarging others. Past that you will drive through a continuous strip, not without interest, of motels, restaurants, shops, and piers. At 6.2 miles along this section you'll pass, on your left, the former main entrance (when this was the main highway) to **Wright Brothers National Memorial**, with its impressive marble tower atop the sand dune (now grassed) where the world's first heavier-than-air flight took place. At 7.9 miles a left onto Ocean Acres Drive leads 1.2 miles (watch the jog left at US 158) to **Nags Head Woods Ecological Preserve**, the finest back-island natural site in the Outer Banks. At 10.3 miles E. Hollowell Street leads left three blocks to **Jockeys Ridge State Park**, containing the tallest sand dunes in the eastern United States, and popular with hang gliders and kite flyers. At 11.1 miles, as you approach East Soundside Drive on your right, the unpainted houses on your left are the **original core of Kitty Hawk**, with some as old as the 1830s. This drive ends 5 miles later, at Gulfstream Drive, which heads left two blocks to the northern gate of **Hatteras National Seashore**.

NC 12, Part II: Hatteras National Seashore. *Length: 78.0 miles*. Opened to the public in 1953, Hatteras National Seashore protects 77.3 miles of beach on three islands—and this stretch of NC 12 gives access to virtually all of it, running just behind the dune line nearly the entire way.

Start where Part I (above) left off, in Nags Head, at NC 12's intersection with US 64/264, near the bridge to Manteo—milepost 0 for this drive. A large sign announces your entrance to the **Hatteras National Seashore**, part of the U.S. National Park System; 500 feet later, on your right, is a small **information office**. For the next 4.6 miles you'll slip easily through back-of-the-island wild lands, mainly marsh with some maritime forest. You will, however, be paralleling the last, highly developed strip of Nags Head Beach, on your left, unseen and with no connections until its beach road, named Old Oregon Inlet Road, enters the park and connects with NC 12 at milepost 4.7. Here your road curves east to the dune line.

This dune line (and its siblings farther south) will be your companion during much of the drive to Ocracoke village; you will lose it only in the settled enclaves within the national seashore. It ranges up to 30 feet tall, and is typically from 50 to 200 yards wide. Unlike many dune lines in North Carolina, you are legally allowed to park your car on the verge and walk over the dunes anyplace you want. This is, however, a bad idea. The roadside verge can have sand deep enough to sink a four-wheel-drive vehicle, and tow trucks can be mighty scarce. The dunes themselves are covered with sandspurs and briars, and are infested with poisonous snakes. It's best to use the access points, which can include auto access as well as pedestrian, as driving on the beach is legal, although highly restricted.

At milepost 5.8 you reach your first major site, at a rare full intersection. On your left is the park's first major beach access, **Coquina Beach** (lifeguards and showers in summer), notable for its 19th-century shipwreck hidden between the drifting dunes. On your right is the access road to **Bodie Island Lighthouse**, the most dramatic of the four Banks lighthouses, with a museum and visitors center. The lighthouse is adjacent to a large marsh-lake, which gives a wonderful view from the main road at milepost 6.6, particularly impressive at sunrise and sunset. **Bodie Island Campground** is on your left at milepost 8.0 (open Easter–Columbus Day), and the concessionaire-run **Oregon Inlet Marina** is on your right at milepost 8.1. **Ramp 4**, offering pedestrian and four-wheel-drive access to the beach, is on the right at milepost 8.2; the beach here is growing toward Oregon Inlet, and its farthest tip is popular with surf fishermen.

Immediately in front of you is the **Herbert C. Bonner Bridge**, curving gracefully high over the beach and Oregon Inlet for 2.7 miles. It is slated for replacement, probably by a parallel structure immediately to its west, although details have not been decided at press time. At the far end (milepost 10.8) is a boat ramp and access to a **fishing boardwalk** hung from the bridge. Just beyond is the restored **Old Oregon Inlet Life-Saving Station**, and the duniest beach in the banks, the dunes having swallowed most of the station's outbuildings. You are now on Hatteras Island, and will stay on it until you reach the ferry to Ocracoke. You are also in **Pea Island National Wildlife Refuge** for the next 11.9 miles, unusual for such refuges in that it prohibits hunting. Within it, natural marshlands have been converted into ponds for migrating waterfowl, and these stretch on your right for 3.5 miles, starting at mileposts 13.4; their dikes are popular with hikers and birdwatchers. The 11-mile Pea Island beach has only four pedestrian access points, and vehicles are prohibited on it, making it a good place for a wild beach walk or a lonely swim.

At milepost 22.7 you reach **Rodanthe**, followed immediately and with no clear border by Waves and Salvo—the first of five private enclaves within the park. **Chicamacomico Life-Saving Station**, probably the finest restored station in the nation, is immediately on your left. Your next 4.9 miles will be lined by development, modest and mostly light, but continuous. It has a fine beach and a pier, and all sorts of places to eat, sleep, and shop. There's a spot, about 0.8 mile north of the pier, where the shifting beach line has led to the sea swallowing an impressive number of houses, a site worth seeing.

Your road reenters the park's lands at milepost 27.6, and your next 11.5 miles are a remarkable drive through wild back-dune lands. Beach driving resumes here, and there are four access ramps shared by pedestrians and vehicles. The former **Salvo Campground**, on your right at milepost 28.2, is now a very large and underused picnic area with a shower, worthwhile for its sound-side walks and kayak launching places. At milepost 36.6 on your right is the restored **Little Kinnakeet Life-Saving Station**, with only its exterior open to the public at press time. Then, at milepost 39.1 you enter the second and smallest of the five enclaves, **Avon**, much like Rodanthe; it, too, has a pier, and its old harbor (right at milepost 40.5) retains its Banker charm. At 42.6 miles you are back in the parklands. For the next 3.8 miles you'll be on another back-dune drive, this time down the narrowest part of Hatteras Island, a slender neck that washed out completely in 2003, and was repaired by dredge-and-fill. There's a combined pedestrian and vehicle beach access at the northern end of this stretch, and a pedestrian-only access point at the southern end (which has a unique sound-side beach as well, due to the 2003 sand fill).

At milepost 46.4 Hatteras Island makes a right-angled bend to the west and its character changes radically, becoming a series of relic parallel ridges as much as 4 miles wide. Here the Outer Banks makes its grand curve west at Cape Hatteras—but your road swerves several miles shy of this famous point, to wander down the back of the island. You are now in the largest private enclave, 8.2 miles long, containing the settlements of **Buxton** and **Frisco**. This is the most thinly developed of all the enclaves, yet because of its size contains the most services, including a full-sized K–12 school. This enclave is long but skinny; most of the Cape Hatteras section is either state or federal conservation lands.

At 46.9 miles a left turn takes you 1.1 miles to the most famous of the Outer Banks landmarks, the **Cape Hatteras Lighthouse**. Now 1,500 feet inland after having been moved from its precarious seaside perch in 1999, it is the center of a museum compound, and gives wide views to those who climb its 208 steps. Opposite the lighthouse entrance is a nature trail exploring the remarkable (and, in summer, buggy) maritime forest known as **Buxton Woods**. Continuing on this side road takes you past the historic and attractive **Hatteras Coast Guard Station** at 1.7

miles, still active and therefore not open to tours, past the Cape Point Campground (open Memorial Day–Labor Day) at 2.5 miles, to end at pedestrian and vehicle access to **Cape Hatteras** itself.

Back at the main road, at milepost 50.6 a left turn onto sand-surfaced Water Association Road lets you drive into the lightly regulated Buxton Woods State Game Lands, a good access point for independent exploration of this unique area. Then at 53.5 miles a paved side road on the left goes past **Billy Mitchell Airport**, where General Billy Mitchell, in 1923, demonstrated how easily bombers could sink battleships, a crucial step in the founding of U.S. airpower. At its end in 1.0 mile is the **Frisco Campground** (open Easter–Veterans Day). At 54.6 miles you reenter parkland for another 1.5 miles, with a major beach access point; this, too, washed away completely in 2003 and had to be pumped back.

At milepost 56.2 you enter the fourth enclave as the road swerves far back away from the beach to the old Banker village of **Hatteras**, now gentrifying, but its pleasant old harbor hidden away down Kohler Road. The road ends at milepost 59.0, but the highway doesn't; NC 12 continues to Ocracoke Island in the form of a **free 5-mile ferry**.

Once on **Ocracoke Island** you have a 12.6-mile journey along the back of the sand dunes; there are five pedestrian and four vehicular access points widely spread along this long section. Keep an eye on the sound side as well, as local fishermen sometimes moor in the little creeks. At 9.6 miles you'll reach the fourth of the park's campgrounds, **Ocracoke Campground** (open Feb.–late Oct., and the only campground accepting reservations). At the end of this you enter the village of Ocracoke, quaint and lively, with its fine harbor. Hidden away in an old Banker neighborhood on your left, 13.3 miles from the ferry, is the pretty little **Ocracoke Lighthouse** set behind picket fences, and the **Springers Point Nature Preserve**, the spot where Blackbeard met his fate. NC 12 ends at the far end of town, at a terminal where multihour toll ferries take you to Swan Quarter and Cedar Point.

✱ Towns and Islands

Carova (the Four-Wheel-Drive Area). The Outer Banks start as a long sand ridge (named Sand Ridge) extending south from Virginia Beach, Virginia. Originally (in the 19th century) it was 28 miles long, but two previously navigable inlets have since sanded shut and disappeared, adding another 40 miles to this peninsula. The part of this ridge that enters North Carolina was subdivided in 1967, but the state of Virginia quickly moved to cut off road access to the new development—and so it remains to this day, a strong fence that marks the state line with signs that forbid vehicles from crossing into Virginia. Yet the development of **Carova** did not die. One by one, people bought lots and built houses, reaching their lands by driving on the beach from North Carolina. Today there are somewhere over 100 houses scattered about, many of them substantial mansions. There are no services of any sort in Carova other than electricity and phone lines to the private homes, and you must have a four-wheel-drive vehicle to reach it. Not surprisingly, it is frequently called the Four-Wheel-Drive Area or the 4x4 Area. The only surviving wild horse population in this chapter lives and thrives in this area, managed and protected by the **Wild Horse Fund** of Corolla.

Corolla and Duck (corollaguide.com). The village of **Corolla** (pronounced *cuh-RAH-luh*) sits at the northernmost end of the paved road, 36 miles from Kitty

A SPORTFISHING BOAT ON PAMLICO SOUND, OFF OCRACOKE ISLAND

Hawk via NC 12, and as far as you can go without a four-wheel drive. Indeed, until the 1980s you couldn't even get this far; Corolla had no road access, making it the last of the Banker settlements. With the coming of NC 12, however, the landscape changed radically, and all 36 miles of this former wilderness have been completely built up in the last quarter century. Corolla now consists of a tiny old Banker village center surrounded by endless tracts of giant modern vacation homes. The center of the village has been largely restored, and preserves the look of a Banker settlement more than any village in the Outer Banks (apart from the uninhabited historic site of Portsmouth). Here in the old village you'll find the **Currituck Lighthouse**, its warm red brick making it the most attractive of the four Outer Banks Lights, the **Corolla Wild Horse Museum**, and the **Historic Whalehead Club**, once a 1920s luxury resort and now a historic museum. Two long **boardwalks** allow you to enjoy the luxuriant sound-side marshes with their rich bird life and wide views. Or you can just wander about; imagine the pavement gone, and see what it would be like to live, isolated, in a Banker settlement around 1935.

Duck, 6 miles north of US 158, marked the end of the paved road in the 1970s. This sound-side settlement has a small harbor and a number of shops and cafes.

Kitty Hawk, Kill Devil Hills, and Nags Head. In the 1930s the state bridged the back marshes of Currituck to bring US 158 onto the Outer Banks; in the 1960s, they matched this with a second bridge, US 64, 15 miles to the south. Between these two bridges an urban area of about 12,000 permanent inhabitants has grown up, made up of three incorporated towns: **Kitty Hawk** to the north, **Kill Devil Hills** in the center, and **Nags Head** to the south. Two-lane NC 12 closely parallels the beach, and the thickest and oldest development fronts it. US 158 moves along the back side of the island in all its four-lane glory, lined by all the newer development. This was, of course, the site of the first powered heavier-than-air flight in the world, commemorated by the **Wright Brothers National Memorial** at the center of Kill Devil Hills (not Kitty Hawk, as often erroneously stated). The town of Nags Head offers two outstanding nature sites, **Jockeys Ridge State Park** with the largest sand dunes in the state, and The Nature Conservancy's **Nags Head Woods** site, with many miles of trail and boardwalk looping through a 1,400-acre maritime forest. The three towns together have 20 miles of excellent beaches, with good access.

Roanoke Island: Manteo and Wanchese. The site of the first English colony in North America, the unsuccessful "Lost Colony," Roanoke Island sits immediately behind the Outer Banks, just off Nags Head; it is reached from the mainland by US 64. It is substantial in size, about 8 miles long and 2 miles wide, and has a permanent population of around 7,000. Its only incorporated place is **Manteo** at its northern end, a county seat with an exceptionally handsome commercial center along an extensive waterfront fronting Shallowbag Bay. The center is not, however, on the main highway; to find it, take US Bus 64 north from US 64 for 1.4 miles to a right turn onto Budleigh Street, then go three block to the waterfront. Here you'll find **Roanoke Island Festival Park**, a state historic site celebrating the first colony with a reproduction of its ship, its village, and an Algonquin village; also in the town center is a branch of the **North Carolina Maritime Museum** featuring boatmaking displays, and a restored **channel lighthouse**. Nearby on Roanoke Island is the national park dedicated to the first colony, **Fort Raleigh National Historic Site**, which includes a reconstructed fortress and an Elizabethan Garden noted for its tulip display. Also nearby is the **North Carolina Aquarium at Roanoke Island**, one of the state's three aquariums. At the south end of Roanoke Island, the unincorporated settlement of **Wanchese** retains its fishing fleet, virtually alone among Banker communities.

Bodie Island. Originally settled by the Body family (whose name furnished the correct pronunciation), modern Bodie Island has no settlement apart from the southern fringe of Nags Head, a neighborhood sometimes known as Whalebone. Here you will find the entrance to the Hatteras National Seashore, on US 64 just east of the bridge, and from that entrance NC 12 runs southward into the park to start its lonely 78-mile journey to Ocracoke. At its northern end, Bodie Island is connected to the Sand Ridge peninsula, its former inlet (north of the US 64 bridge) having filled with sand long ago. At its southern end are the **Bodie Island Lighthouse**, **Oregon Inlet Marina**, and the 3-mile-long Herbert C. Bonner Bridge, flying high over Oregon Inlet (which used to be a lot wider than it is now), and onto Hatteras Island.

Northern Hatteras Island: Rodanthe (with Waves and Salvo) and Avon. Hatteras Island, very long and very skinny, stretches for 40 miles south to Cape Hatteras, then makes a sudden bend westward to go on for another 14 miles. All of it is national park land except for four urbanized enclaves; NC 12 traverses its entire length. The first dozen miles are wilderness beach, mainly taken up by **Pea Island National Wildlife Refuge**, with **Old Oregon Inlet Lifeboat Station** an important historic site at its northern end. Then comes **Rodanthe** (pronounced *ro-DAN-the*), followed by Waves and Salvo—a dispersed unincorporated settlement once known as Chicamacomico. You'll find all three of these (they run together with no firm boundaries) to be scattered, and rather modest, with services sprinkled along their 4.9-mile length of highway. It's the site of the best-selling novel and movie *Night in Rodanthe*, which was filmed here.

Avon sits to the south of Rodanthe-Waves-Salvo, separated by 11.5 miles of wild beach. This enclave is 3.5 miles long, and, like Rodanthe, has dispersed settlements and scattered services that tend to close in the winter. Unlike Rodanthe, Avon has a Banker-era wharf hidden in its back streets, and worth the trouble to find.

South of Avon is 3.8 miles of wild beach, the narrowest in the Outer Banks. Indeed, in 2003 this thin neck washed out completely during Hurricane Isabel, forming Isabel Inlet and turning the Cape Hatteras portion into its own island, dubbed Little Hatteras Island. This was a natural but inconvenient turn of events, and the U.S. Army Corp of Engineers quickly reversed it, using sand from the Hatteras–Ocracoke ferry channel to fill the new inlet.

Southern Hatteras Island (Cape Hatteras): Buxton, Frisco, and Hatteras. At the southern end of Hatteras Island is this west-facing bulbous section, 14 miles long. It's made up of parallel beach ridges, which form an unusual maritime forest known as the **Buxton Woods**, half within the national seashore and half protected as a state conservation land. Its most famous site is **Cape Hatteras**, a sandy promontory that is still rapidly extending itself southward into the ocean; 2.5 miles to its north, the iconic **Cape Hatteras Lighthouse** still protects mariners from these dangerous shoals. While parklands (state and federal) protect most of this section, the lagoon-side portion is privately owned, and this is where NC 12 goes. This 8.2-mile private enclave bears the community name **Buxton** on its east and **Frisco** on its west, but neither has any real center; instead you get the sort of dispersed and modest development you saw in Avon and Rodanthe. This ends in a 1.5 miles stretch of national seashore (with a developed beach day area).

Beyond that is Hatteras, often called Hatteras Village to distinguish it from the cape and the island. The village sits on its own little back-island (now connected to the main island with marshes), and so NC 12 loops rather out of its way to reach it before returning to the main island for the ferry terminus. A new yacht basin and commercial development marks the farthest point. The highway ends at the Hatteras Ferry Terminal, whose free ferries qualify as attractions in themselves; there's a marina here as well. Beyond is four-wheel-drive access to 3.5 more miles of wild national seashore, to the end of the island—0.8 mile more beach than when the park was established in 1953.

Ocracoke. With NC 12's extension to Corolla in 1986, **Ocracoke** became the only town in North Carolina not accessible by road. Far from declining, it has become the liveliest village in the Outer Banks, a quaintly attractive summer party spot. The village (founded in 1750) centers on a natural oval harbor called Silver Lake, 2,000 feet long and nearly 1,000 feet wide, ringed by roads that offer fine views. On its southwestern side is **Ocracoke Lighthouse**, the oldest in the Banks and very photogenic behind its picket fence, and **Springers Point**, the land opposite which Blackbeard the pirate was killed in 1723, now a nature preserve explored by a short trail. On its farthest (northern) end is the dock for the two pay ferries that ply the long journey between it and the mainland, Swan Quarter (a three-hour trip to the mainland), and Cedar Island (linking it to the Beaufort and New Bern tourist areas). Here also is the private pay ferry to **Portsmouth**, the deserted Banker town now restored by the National Park Service. From the village, paved

NC 12 runs 14 miles eastward, through the wild lands of the national seashore, to the free ferry from Hatteras. The island's services (many of which close in the winter, when the population shrinks to 700) tend to group between Silver Lake and the national seashore's border.

✷ Green Spaces

PUBLIC LANDS *Note:* By local convention, distances are described, not by counting traffic lights or turns, but by citing "mileposts" or "mile markers" (sometimes real, and sometimes mythical). These mileposts are counted north-to-south as follows:

1. The US 158 bridge's Kitty Hawk terminus is taken as milepost 0, and mileages are counted south from there along US 158 to its end at NC 12, where the Hatteras National Seashore begins.
2. Within the national seashore, the NC 12 entrance is taken as milepost 0, and mileages are counted all the way to the end of the pavement at the Hatteras–Ocracoke ferry.
3. On Ocracoke Island, the Hatteras ferry becomes milepost 0, and mileages follow NC 12 to its end at Ocracoke Village.

Tradition holds that mileposts are not cited north of Kitty Hawk, or on Manteo.

Hatteras National Seashore (252-473-2111; nps.gov/caha), 1401 National Park Dr., Manteo 27954. Admission is free. In 1937, shortly after the first bridge opened to the Outer Banks, the U.S. Congress moved to protect these great lonely expanses from development. In 1953, with all the beach and most of the back-island purchased between Nags Head and Ocracoke, Hatteras National Seashore opened to the public, the first national park dedicated solely to a beach. It remains an impressive achievement, protecting 78 miles of beach, along with 60 miles of back-island.

It is also wholly accessible by the auto-bound. NC 12 runs through the entire length of the park, and those parts of the beach not within an easy stroll of a parking area can be reached (restrictions permitting) by a four-wheel-drive vehicle with high clearance and low air in its tires. For, unusual with conservation areas, this national park allows driving on the beach. Indeed, this privilege is heavily restricted in summer, when humans' crowding cycle and nature's breeding cycle overlap; during this period, night driving is prohibited. However, even then you'll find 30 or so miles of tire-friendly beach, in scattered sections. Restrictions relax after Labor Day, and nearly (but not quite) disappear after Veterans Day, when night driving becomes allowed. This happily corresponds to the height of the surf-fishing season. The National Park Service publishes a Google Earth map overlay of the current restrictions, and updates it at least once a week; go the website for the latest version.

Beach walking can be restricted as well as beach driving; when a bird breeding location is identified, temporary signs will go up prohibiting everyone, not just vehicles. This is a problem for long-distance beach hikers, particularly on the Mountains-to-Sea Trail, as there are no alternatives, no handy walk-arounds.

Even more oddly for a national park, hunting is allowed (outside Pea Island National Wildlife Refuge). This includes waterfowl hunting along the sound side, and general hunting in the Buxton Woods State Game Lands. Special regulations apply only on Bodie Island (which requires a permit from the Park Service) and Buxton Woods. Otherwise, ordinary state regulations apply, which include a prohibition on Sunday hunting. If you venture into the back-island marshes or the game lands between November and March, wear hunter orange.

The park winterizes after Veterans Day, and stays that way until Easter holiday. This means that all four campgrounds close (and three of them close long before), all the restrooms close and their showers and spigots go dry, and all the park museums, information desks, and lighthouses close. Most privately owned facilities close as well, although many stay open until New Year's.

The park's headquarters are outside its boundaries, at Manteo's Fort Raleigh National Historic Site, where the same staff run Fort Raleigh, Wright Brothers National Memorial, and the seashore.

The public lands of Carova (fws.gov/currituck). The 11 miles of roadless beach lands that stretch between Corolla and the Virginia line are best known for their wild horses and their continuing development into remote, serviceless mansions. There are, however, significant tracts of protected public lands, owned by the state, the feds, and private land trusts. The most significant of these is the Currituck National Wildlife Refuge, at 4,500 acres and still acquiring land. Here's where to find the conservation lands, as you drive or walk north on the beach from the end of NC 12.

The first 1.6 miles are entirely conservation lands, from the tide line to the sound shore. The first half of this is part of the state's coastal estuarine reserve program, while the second half is part of the wildlife refuge.

At 3.6 miles you will be opposite the center of the old Swan Beach subdivision, an area of heavy development despite the fact that its roads have been wiped out by storm overblow. Its back-island areas of overwashed sand, marine forest, and marsh are part of the wildlife refuge.

From 4.2 to 6.5 miles the entire island, from beach to back, is within the wildlife refuge.

North of here to the Virginia line stretches the old Carova Beach development, whose gridiron of streets, still discernible in most places, extends up to six blocks back. From 9.8 miles to the state line, the back-island forests and marshes west of the gridiron's end are within the wildlife refuge.

At 10.9 miles you reach the state line; further driving is blocked by a sturdy fence and prohibited by state and federal law. You can, however, walk, for the next 10 miles of beach and island are wholly within Virginia's False Cape State Park and Back Bay National Wildlife Refuge, both strictly pedestrian only.

Pea Island National Wildlife Refuge, Hatteras Island (fws.gov/peaisland). Established in 1938, Pea Island occupies the uppermost 13 miles of Hatteras Island, with 5,800 land acres and another 20,000 water acres on the sound side. Its main feature, apart from its long, wild beach, is its 3.5 miles of man-made ponds, three huge diked and flooded marshes maintained for the use of migrating waterfowl. The 2.5 miles of dikes along the northernmost pond are open to walkers, with some of the finest bird-watching in the state; the other two ponds are closed to the public. Birders will find observation platforms, birding blinds, and a tower along the dike system. There are weekly bird walks all year, making this one of the few places in the Banks to actively support winter recreationists.

The refuge is within the Hatteras National Seashore, but run by the U.S. Fish and Wildlife Service, rather than the National Park Service, so that its regulations are more wildlife-centered and less recreation-friendly. This long stretch of beach has only four access points, making it hard to reach but a good place for a long, lonely stroll. These points are pedestrian only; vehicles are not allowed. Hunting is prohibited as well; this is a refuge in the truest sense. Fishing is allowed in the sound waters and the surf, but not in the ponds. The refuge maintains a visitors center at milepost 14.9, with an information desk, gift shop, and wildlife-viewing platform.

As you drive along NC 12 through the refuge you will notice a great abundance of construction equipment and earthmovers along the way. Natural forces have been trying to push the beach westward, destroying the highway and endangering the dike system. The refuge has been trying to prevent this for years, and it has now become a continuous struggle.

Buxton Woods, Cape Hatteras. The Buxton Woods are an exceptionally large and well-preserved maritime forest covering about 6 square miles of relic dunes behind Cape Hatteras. Nearly all of it is in public ownership, split among Hatteras National Seashore, the North Carolina Coastal Preserve, and the Buxton Woods State Game Lands. For a short introduction to this area, visit the nature trail opposite the **Cape Hatteras Lighthouse**. For a longer exploration (outside the hunting season or on Sunday) turn to the state game land, which allows hikers and birders to wander freely on its network of old sand tracks. Access is directly off NC 12 in Buxton, either at Old Doctor's Road at milepost 34.4, or at Water Association Road at milepost 35.6. Be sure to use bug spray in summer.

THE OLD HARBOR AT AVON, HATTERAS NATIONAL SEASHORE

PARKS AND GARDENS The Boardwalks of Corolla. The two best places to explore the quiet, bird-rich marshlands of the back-island are both in Corolla, boardwalks erected by the North Carolina Coastal Preserve. The first is 1,065 feet long, and sits opposite the **Currituck Island Lighthouse** and adjacent to the **Whalehead Club**, off Corolla Village Road. It moves quickly through maritime forest to pass through the usually impenetrable reeds of the marshes for 1,000 feet, then goes over open water for its last 200 feet with wide views over the sound and back to the historic lighthouse and club. The second has its own paved trailhead on NC 12, 21.6 miles from US 158 (on a very sharp curve just north of the village). At 1,850 feet it is the longer of the two, and wanders prettily through the back-island forests before finally breaking out into reeds at a quiet tidal inlet, superb for bird-watching. About 500 feet from the trailhead a footpath forks away to the right, exploring the forests for another 0.7 mile until it, too, reaches the sound.

Pine Island Audubon Sanctuary and Center (252-489-5303; nc.audubon.org/centers-chapters/pine-island-audubon-sanctuary-and-center; mbuckler@audubon.org). Open in daylight hours, all year. This sprawling 2,600-acre tract, the largest remaining wild land between Kitty Hawk and Corolla, opened in early 2010. It features a 2.5-mile trail following an old sand track that parallels the sound, leading to two sound-side observation towers. There are also regularly scheduled bird walks throughout the summer. To find it, take NC 12 north from US 158 for 12.3 miles to a left onto Audubon Drive, then go one block to a left onto Racquet Club Drive; the trail starts behind the club.

Run Hill State Natural Area, Kill Devil Hills. There were originally nine giant dunes on the northern Outer Banks, a great field of shifting sand stretching from Kitty Hawk to Nags Head. All but two are now gone—harvested for fill, bulldozed out of the way for houses, or covered with lawn grasses to make them into normal, usable hills. The state of North Carolina preserves the remaining two, Run Hill and Jockeys Ridge, allowing them to drift where the wind takes them. Of these, Run Hill is the smaller. It gains its interest, however, from being very little visited (unlike its big brother 3 miles to the south), and from the way it creeps into adjacent Nags Head Woods, enveloping the old trees one by one. This is not bad; it's normal dune behavior, and this area is managed to allow it to continue. To find it go to Airstrip Road at milepost 9.0 and go west (away from the beach) to its end (in 0.8 mile), then turn right onto 10th Street; the natural area is one block ahead.

Nags Head Woods Ecological Preserve, Kill Devil Hills (252-441-2525; nature.org/wherewework/northamerica/states/northcarolina/preserves/art5618.html), 701 W. Ocean Acres Dr., Kill Devil Hills 27948. Open daily, dawn to dusk. Admission is free. Owned and operated by The Nature Conservancy, this park-like tract preserves 1,400 acres of pristine maritime forest in the urbanized heart of Nags Head—a 2.5-mile length of the wild back-island, sandwiched between the large active dune fields of Jockeys Ridge to the south and Run Hill to the north. It's located at milepost 9.6, then west (away from the beach) on Ocean Acres Drive for 0.9 mile to the visitors kiosk—a handsome information stand by a natural back-dune pond, with boardwalk views. From here, 3.4 miles of trails explore the forest-covered dunes, the lush ponds and marsh-forests between them, and the sound-side grasslands. A separate trail can be found at milepost 10.9, then west on Barnes Street to its end at a town park; it runs 0.8 mile (one way) directly across this relic dunescape to Roanoke Sound.

Jockeys Ridge State Park, Kitty Hawk (252-441-7132; Friends of Jockeys Ridge: jockeysridgestatepark.com; official: ncparks.gov/Visit/parks/jori/main.php; jockeys.ridge@ncmail.net), P.O. Box 592, Nags Head 27959. Opens daily at 8; closes at 9, June–Aug.; at 8, Mar.–May and Sept.–Oct.; at 6, Nov.–Feb. Admission is free. This state park protects what is said to be the tallest sand dune in the eastern United States, Jockeys Ridge, with the park entrance at milepost 12.0. That actual elevation, however, is vague; the state park claims 80 to 100 feet, depending on the wind, while the USGS topographic map marks it as topping out at 138 feet. Whatever its peak height, its eastern edge is certainly impressive, hard up against US 158 for half a mile south of the park entrance and instantly rising 80 feet straight up. And yes, you can park in the little shopping center (you'll find **Kitty Hawk Kites** there) and walk up it. But it's even better to go to the visitors center in the middle of the park. Here you'll find an interpretive center, picnic tables, and a boardwalk to a good view. Beyond the boardwalk is pure sand, with hardly any vegetation. It's always blowing about, so there's no trail; the 1.5-mile-long (round-trip) nature trail, named Tracks in the Sand, uses posts to guide you to Roanoke Sound and back. Rather than the nature trail, however, you might want to head out eastward and uphill. Here, at the tallest parts of the ridge, you will find popular hang-gliding sites (permit required), great kite flying, and wide views. There's also a sand-boarding area on the farthest, sharpest face (permit required).

On the southwest corner of the park is a separate entrance point; to find it, go 0.8 mile south of the park entrance (milepost 12.8) to a right turn onto Soundside Road, then go 0.5 mile to the park entrance on your right. Here you will find a kayak and windsurfing launching spot, and a 1-mile loop trail along the sound, into a small maritime forest, and around the back face of the dune. Here also the dune forms a small sandy beach on Roanoke Sound, surprisingly popular with sea bathers.

Springers Point Nature Preserve, Ocracoke (coastallandtrust.org/pages/springers_point.html). This 120-acre nature preserve, owned and run by the North Carolina Coastal Land Trust, overlooks Teach's Hole, where, in 1718, Blackbeard met his fate at the hands of the Virginia navy. It seems (although this is controversial) that Blackbeard had bought off North Carolina governor Charles Eden, and was maintaining a household in Bath (under his *nom de guerre* of Edward Teach) while anchoring his pirate ship off Ocracoke's Springers Point. Governor Eden would officially declare Blackbeard's loot as "salvage" and take 20 percent of the cut. The Virginia governor became fed up with these shenanigans and sent a small fleet to deal with it; although Blackbeard put up quite a fight, the Virginians returned with his decapitated head tied upon a bowsprit. Today walking trails lead the short distance to the natural sand beach overlooking Teach's Hole, passing through maritime forests unchanged since Blackbeard's time.

ESTUARIES Behind the Outer Banks lies a single huge estuary, 150 miles long and anywhere from 3 to 30 miles wide. Its northern end terminates in Virginia marshland just south of Newport News. Its southern end also terminates in marsh, just north of Beaufort. It has three distinct names: Currituck Sound from its northern end to Kitty Hawk, Albemarle Sound between Kitty Hawk and Manteo, and Pamlico Sound (by far the biggest of the three) from Manteo to Cedar Island, ferry terminal and the start of the southern marshes. In any other area, these sounds, with their superb fishing and vast open stretches of water, would be *the* tourist draw. In the Outer Banks, however, they are completely overwhelmed. There are, of course, marinas that cater to sound-side fishermen and recreationists. They are scattered all over, with the largest at Manteo and the village of Hatteras.

BEACHES (nps.gov/caha). The purpose of this section is simply to help you choose the beach you want to visit on a day trip, driving in from wherever you are

VIEW ACROSS THE OLD TOWN HARBOR ON PAMLICO SOUND

staying. It aims to distinguish between a large number of excellent beaches, not to pick out one or two best, but to give you the information you need to make a decision. How's the parking? Is it a long walk in? Do I have to trudge through sand, or is there a boardwalk? Is it wild or developed, crowded or empty? Are there restrooms and a shower?

Within the national seashore, pedestrians need not use the access points; it's perfectly legal to park by the roadside and walk across the dunes anywhere you want. It's a bad idea, however. Verges can conceal soft, deep sand that can swallow your car up to its axles, and the dunes (which can be 1,000 feet wide) are covered in sandspurs and briars, and home to poisonous snakes.

Lifeguards are only on duty between Memorial Day and Labor Day; outside those months, you are on your own. Between Corolla and Nags Head there are roving lifeguards who use ORVs, and stationary lifeguards near the biggest parking areas. There are lifeguards within the Hatteras National Seashore as well, generally limited to the large parking areas; check their website for details.

Carova Beach (the 4x4 Area). The 11 miles of beach that stretch northward from Corolla have never had road access, and never will. You can explore it, however, by driving a high-clearance four-wheel-drive vehicle off the far northern end of NC 12, then northward along the beach. During the 1960s speculators attempted to develop this long stretch of wild beach, and, while their street networks never really existed and are now covered by drifting sand, more than 100 houses now exist along them, ranging from modest cottages to huge mansions, with more being built every year. These tend to be grouped in two areas, corresponding to the two biggest developments: Swan Beach, centered about 3.5 miles up from Corolla, and Carova Beach, starting at 6.5 miles and continuing to the state line. Scattered between and behind these are great tracts of public lands, owned by both the state and federal governments. This beach is most famous, however, for its large population of wild horses. Descendants of 16th-century Spanish shipwreck survivors, this herd wanders freely among the houses and along the beach, and you are likely to see some when you visit.

Beaches from Corolla to Kitty Hawk. The beaches north of Kitty Hawk, excellent in quality, are nevertheless lightly visited. Largely roadless until the 1970s, this 22-mile stretch developed very quickly after NC 12 opened in the mid-1980s. Unlike the beaches to its south, however, the stretch is almost wholly dominated by expensive second homes, which fill the space between sound-side NC 12 and the beach. With no beach-side highway, there are no oceanfront resorts, restaurants, or town centers; just house after house.

Not surprisingly, these beaches are run for homeowners and their renters. There is no general public access for the first 13 miles of beaches at all; Dare County limits all seven of its access points to residents and renters only, and enforces this by prohibiting parking. (And if you are renting, make sure that you don't have to walk a mile or so to the nearest access point.) Farther north, Currituck County furnishes full beach access (pedestrians and vehicles) with restrooms, showers, and summer lifeguards 13.5 miles from US 158, with the county's welcome center diagonally across the highway. Then, starting at 17.1 miles, there are five more public access points with parking hidden away within the old subdivision of Whalehead Beach. They are all on Whalehead Drive, at its intersections with Shad, Sturgeon, Perch, Bonita, and Sailfish Streets, plus vehicular access at Albacore Street; to reach Whalehead Drive turn right off NC 12 onto either Albacore Street at 17.1 miles, Bonita Street at 18.4 miles, or Shad Street at 20.2 miles.

Beaches from Kitty Hawk to Nags Head. The people's beach starts opposite the US 158 bridge to the mainland. From here all the way to Ocracoke you will have no trouble finding a place to park and cross the dunes.

This first stretch, 19.4 miles in length, is within the municipalities of (north to south) Kitty Hawk, Kill Devil Hills, and Nags Head. It is the exemplar of Outer Banks beaches—white and fluffy, and lined by a continuous procession of hotels, cafés, pubs, shops, and stilt homes. There are five fishing piers, at mileposts 0 (part of the Hilton Garden Inn resort), 6, 11.5, 15 (**Jennette's Pier**), and 18.5. A road closely parallels the beach for its entire length, with access points and parking typically every two or three blocks. There are several big access parks with massive parking, but you can use the plentiful neighborhood access points as well, as legal street parking is usually nearby.

For most of the first 16 miles of this stretch you'll find about 100 feet of sand and a 50-foot dune line that you cross either by a vehicle access track or a boardwalk. The quality of the beach is so even that you will want to pick your access point by how you feel about the adjacent development, and how easily you can park. After milepost 16 (apart from the beaches around the pier at 18.5) erosion has narrowed the beach, so much so that some houses sit upon the beach itself, the land having washed out from under them. If you want a really wide beach, those of the national seashore, where natural forces hold sway, are wider than those of any of the developed areas.

Jennette's Pier, Nags Head (ncaquariums.com/aquarium-piers/jennettes-pier). Located on NC 12 just as it approaches the beach from the Roanoke Island Bridge, Jennette's Pier, constructed in 1939, was the oldest in North Carolina until it was destroyed by a hurricane in 2004. It has now been completely rebuilt, stormproofed, and green-certified by the North Carolina State Aquarium, part of a proj-

DRIVING ON THE BEACH

(nps.gov/caha). Driving on the beach is a long-standing tradition in the Outer Banks. You cannot, however, toodle down the strand in your family station wagon and expect anything other than an expensive tow. First of all you need a four-wheel-drive vehicle with high clearance, designed for off-road use. Do not use an AWD (all-wheel drive); they perform no better on sand than an ordinary car. Then you need to lower the pressure in your tires to 18 psi, and check a tide chart to make sure that the tide is low and ebbing. Now pack a shovel for digging yourself out and a cell phone for calling a tow truck, and you are ready!

On the beach you'll either drive on the hard-packed sand between high and low tides (you did check the tide chart, right?), or in the soft sand along the dune line; the center of the beach is for pedestrians and parking. ORVs are not allowed, and you cannot drive on the dunes. Pedestrians always have the right-of-way. The Hatteras National Seashore has many restrictions on beach driving, and these vary from day to day; download the latest rules from their website (you will need to install Google Earth) before setting out.

So, where to go? The Carova Beach area is a hoot, with its wild horses, stunning beaches, superb wildlife observation, and strange, scattered community. A serious four-wheeler will find ample rentals there as well, for a weeklong four-wheel holiday. Between Corolla and Nags Head you'll find the beaches narrow and best left to the pedestrians who throng them. In the national seashore much of the four-wheeling deals with getting surf fishermen to the inlet beaches where the fish really run, a drive of 2 to 3 miles from a ramp. Cape Hatteras is noteworthy, but Oregon Inlet gives a dramatic sunset view through the high arches of Bonner Bridge, while Hatteras Inlet (from Hatteras Island beyond the Ocracoke ferry) leads you past the ruins of World War II's Fort Clark. Finally, on Ocracoke Island, beach driving (if restrictions allow) can let you find a perfect spot in a 10-mile stretch of wild beach, along which mere pedestrians must fight it out for fewer than 100 parking spaces spread up to 5 miles apart.

ect to connect all three state aquariums with beach access. Its handsome on-pier visitors center has exhibits and research offices as well as the traditional tackle shop, and there is parking and a bathhouse for beachgoers.

Bodie Island beaches. The beaches of the national seashore are characteristically wider than those of the developed areas, and separated from NC 12 by a very wide dune line. They preserve their wild scenery by placing access points 2 or 3 miles apart; you can rejoice in crowded humanity near the access point, or gain solitude with a short walk. This first section of park is no exception. The 5.4 miles of Bodie Island sand has three access points, all allowing vehicles as well as pedestrians. The first is at the southernmost end of Nags Head, at the national seashore border. The second is Coquina Beach at milepost 5.8 (from the park entrance at the intersection of NC 12 and US 158), with showers, lifeguards (in season), and a very large parking lot. Although you are only a mile south of Nags Head, the beach here is 250 feet wide with 200 feet of dunes to cross on a boardwalk before you get there. Across the street is the entrance to Bodie Island Lighthouse. The third access point is at the southern end of the island, milepost 8.2, a vehicle track that pedestrians may use. From this point the beach curves gently around the base of the island and widens dramatically as it enters Oregon Inlet, becoming as much as 0.3 mile wide as it reaches the Bonner Bridge, a distance of about 2 miles from the access point.

Beaches of Northern Hatteras Island. This stretch follows 35 miles of very skinny barrier island, anywhere from 500 to 5,000 feet wide, with two town areas (Rodanthe-Waves-Salvo and Avon) breaking the parklands into three sections. In general, your choice of beaches mirrors what we've seen farther north: developed areas with plentiful facilities but comparatively narrow beaches and dunes, and undeveloped areas with limited facilities but a very wide beach and dune line. The first section is the 12 miles of beach managed by the U.S. Fish and Wildlife Service as part of the Pea Island National Wildlife Refuge. Because it's managed for wildlife rather than recreation, it has no vehicle access and only a few crossover points for pedestrians; this makes it particularly appealing for those looking for a wild and remote beach experience. The first access point is an informal dune walkover at the Old Oregon Inlet Life-Saving Station at the top of the island (milepost 11.2); this is an unusually large and aggressive dune complex, having swallowed the outbuildings of the old station, and makes for interesting beachcombing. Next up are two boardwalk crossovers with tiny parking lots that fill up fast, at mileposts 13.1 and 14.5. The major Pea Island access point, with showers and restrooms, comes at milepost 17.2, with additional parking at 17.5.

The Rodanthe-Waves-Salvo developed area, entered at milepost 22.6 and exited at milepost 27.6, is best visited from the ample parking lot at Rodanthe Pier, milepost 24.2. For wider beaches, make your way south from the pier. Then comes another 11.5 miles of wild beach, with four access points. The first, at milepost 28.0, has a 0.25-mile dune crossing on soft sand, so is better suited for vehicles than pedestrians. Then comes one at 32.3 with a boardwalk as well as a vehicle ramp; one at 34.5 with no boardwalk but a vehicle ramp 100 yards long; and one at 38.7 with a boardwalk and a vehicle ramp. After this you are in the Avon area, and your best bet is once again the pier, at milepost 40.9. The final 3.8 miles of this stretch are wild beach, but with a narrower dune line and wide sands. There's a boardwalk and vehicle ramp at milepost 42.7, then again at milepost 44.3—a major access point on the sound side with ample parking, restrooms, showers, and short (200 feet) sandy paths over the dunes to the oceans. There is also a unique sandy beach on the calm sound-side waters, formed when this neck of the island was replaced by sand dredging after it blew out in 2003.

Cape Hatteras beaches. The thick, western-pointed end of Hatteras Island, often called Cape Hatteras from its most prominent feature, is nearly all in public ownership with spectacular wild beaches. You wouldn't guess this, however, from NC 12, which hugs the sound side the entire way, and enters parklands for only 1.5 miles in the 12.6 miles it spends meandering to the Ocracoke ferry terminal. The beaches—18 miles of them—are mainly far to the south of NC 12 and, with one exception, must be reached by side roads or four-wheel-drive ramps. All of the beaches are very wide, as much as 1,000 feet at Cape Hatteras itself.

The first 0.9 mile of beach is closely bordered by Buxton private development, ending in a large, but locked-down, Coast Guard base. The wild public beaches cannot be reached from here; instead, turn left onto Lighthouse Road, milepost 46.9. The first public access, in 0.8 mile, is the old lighthouse location, pedestrian only, with ample parking and sand trails 200 to 400 feet long. The lighthouse's old location is marked only by the riprap and jetties that protected it for so long, and the runway-style road built to move it is easy to spot. The Cape Hatteras Lighthouse, at 1.0 mile, has no beach access. At the end of the road, however, three access points get you closest to Cape Hatteras. For the first, enter the Cape Point Campground (at 2.3 miles) and continue all the way through it to a large parking lot at its far end in 0.9 mile. This is pedestrian only; a 0.4-mile sand walk brings you to the beach, 1.4 miles west of the growing tip of Cape Hatteras. Then, at 2.4 miles, Salt Pond Road on your right gives four-wheel-drive access to a couple of miles of back-dune sand tracks, with three ramps exiting on the beach. Finally, at the end of the paved road (at 2.6 miles), is a paved parking lot on the beach—although it might be more accurate to say that the beach is on it, as drifting dunes have been trying to cover it for years and the Park Service has to keep bulldozing it clean. There's a vehicle ramp here as well. From here it's 1.4 miles to the tip of the cape. At about the 0.5-mile mark you will be even with the large, brackish Salt Pond on the far side of the dunes on your right, giving you the unusual opportunity to watch for marsh birds while lying on the beach.

Your next beach access is a left onto Park Road at milepost 53.5, then a mile to its end. There is a vehicle ramp here with very limited parking and a 0.3-mile walk along the sand track to the beach. In front of you is the Frisco Campground, with two very long boardwalks (0.2 mile with some soft sand) to the beach. Then comes a short stretch of developed beach with parking at a pier at milepost 54.4, followed by a major national park access point (pedestrian only, restrooms and showers) at milepost 54.7, with a short boardwalk. There's a second parking lot at milepost 55.5, with a very short boardwalk to the ocean, and a small sound-side beach as well.

The village of Hatteras has 1.9 miles of beach, all of it wide and with a fine dune line but bordered by development, with no public access points. The road takes an extra mile to loop around this, but rejoins park beaches just past the Ocracoke ferry terminal at milepost 59.0. The last pedestrian access point is just beyond, at the Graveyard of the Atlantic Museum, with a 350-foot boardwalk. Immediately after this starts a long four-wheel-drive track paralleling the beach, reaching the scant remains of World War II–era Fort Clark at 1.7 miles and the end of the island at 3.2 miles.

Ocracoke beaches. Ocracoke Island's 17.1 miles of beaches are, without exception, wide, wild, and deep with fluffy sand and drifting dunes. The first 12.6 miles (counting from the Hatteras Ferry terminal) are paralleled by NC 12—surprisingly, with the worst beach access in the national seashore. There's a vehicle access ramp at 0.5 mile (1,000 feet from the beach), and a small parking lot for pedestrians at 0.6 mile with a 400-foot sand path. From there, however, it's almost 5 miles to your next access point, pedestrian only with a tiny parking lot adjacent to the beach, at 5.3 miles. Then there's a second, somewhat larger lot at 6.1 miles (still pedestrian only) with a short boardwalk, followed by a vehicle ramp at 8.3 miles. Ocracoke Campground, at 9.4 miles, has two small parking lots, one on each side of the road, plus a vehicle ramp, but pedestrian access comes by walking 400 feet through the churned, rutted sands of the ramp. All in all, there are fewer than 100 parking spaces for the first 10 miles of this beach! The major parking lot, just outside the village of Ocracoke at 11.6 miles, doubles that total, and adds restrooms and showers. It's pedestrian only, and has a 350-foot boardwalk. Vehicle access comes at 12.0 miles (at the airport), then again at 12.5 miles, where a sand track wanders well behind the dune line to finally reach the beach after 1.7 miles, and the end of the island at 3.6 miles. (Do not assume that you can bypass this back-dune road by driving on the beach, as bird or turtle breeding zones can block it at anytime from April to November.)

✷ To See

LIGHTHOUSES AND LIFESAVING STATIONS No stretch of the American Atlantic endangered mariners like the North Carolina coast. Its constantly shifting shoals, extending far out to sea, destroyed so many ships and killed so many men that it became known as the Graveyard of the Atlantic. As early as 1795 the newly formed American Republic took steps to protect sailors and ships, building lighthouses at **Cape Hatteras**, **Ocracoke**, and **Bald Head Island**. Other lighthouses followed, and these were accompanied by life-saving stations, staffed and equipped to rescue shipwrecked sailors.

The role of a lighthouse is simple: to supply a readily identifiable point from which navigators can calculate their position. In the daylight, they are not only very tall (from 8 to 20 stories high), but each also has a distinctive look: Stripes, spirals, plain brick, and pure white are the designs you'll find here. At night they each shine a light, visible far out to sea, each with its own readily identifiable pattern. The invention of the Fresnel (pronounced *frey-NELL*) lens in 1823 allowed a comparative dim light to be magnified greatly; by rotating a set of lenses around a light source, the characteristic timed blink was created. None of these functions required the lighthouse to be particularly near the water, and all of the Outer Banks' lights were set well back from the beach in a protected position. All the lighthouses in this chapter are still in active use as navigation aids, and all are open to the public.

Founded in 1848, the U.S. Life-Saving Service maintained a series of rescue stations along the coast until it merged with the Revenue Cutter Service to form the U.S. Coast Guard in 1915. In the Outer Banks these stations had to be close together—much closer, in fact, than the villages—and nearly two dozen were cre-

SANDPIPER IN THE SURF AT RODANTHE, HATTERAS NATIONAL SEASHORE

ated at one time or another. A station would be manned full-time from April through November, and would have equipment to mount a beach-based rescue operation. In addition to small, surf-launchable boats, this included a Lyle Gun, a cannon used to shoot a line over the wrecked vessel, which its mariners would use to haul in a heavier line for transport to shore. To this would be attached the breeches buoy, a trousers-harness sewn into a life ring; mariners could sit in it and be hauled back along the line. This rescue method is demonstrated weekly during the summer at **Chicamacomico Life-Saving Station**.

Many of the old lifesaving stations survive, restored, and five house businesses that will welcome your visit. Two of the Outer Banks' lifesaving stations are now restaurants: Caffeys Inlet Life-Saving Station is the restaurant for the resort hotel the **Sanderling at Duck** (1471 Duck Rd.), and the Kitty Hawk Life-Saving Station is now the **Black Pelican Restaurant** (3848 Virginia Dare Trail). The real estate firm Twiddy & Company, indefatigable restorers of the northern Outer Banks, has saved two lifesaving stations, and uses both as sales offices: the Kill Devil Hills Station, which they moved 20 miles to Corolla, and the large and remarkable Wash Woods Coast Guard Station (built in 1917) in the Carova area, accessible only by four-wheel drive. Finally, Durants Life-Saving Station, of Hatteras Village, has been restored as the clubhouse of the Durants Station condominiums, east of the village on NC 12.

Currituck Beach Lighthouse (252-453-8152; currituckbeachlight.com; info@currituckbeachlight.com), 1101 Corolla Village Rd., Corolla 27927. Open daily 9–5, Easter–Thanksgiving. Admission to the site is free. The last of the Outer Banks lighthouses, this 1875 lighthouse is a cylinder of plain red brick 162 feet tall, in the center of historic Corolla village. Left unpainted to make it easy to distinguish from other nearby lighthouses, Currituck glows golden in late-afternoon sun. It sits on a large plot of village land, behind its keeper's cottage, a nicely restored Victorian farmhouse, not the slightest bit out of place, as if every small town home should have a 16-story tower behind it. You may climb the 214 steps to the balcony outside the light itself for some fabulous views (fee). Adjacent to it is a lovely boardwalk out to the sound-side marshes, with excellent bird-watching; the **Whalehead Club** and **Wild Horse Museum** are each within easy walking distance. The lighthouse and keeper's cottage are owned and operated by Outer Banks Conservationists, a nonprofit organization, which funded the restoration.

Bodie Island Lighthouse. Open daily May–Sept.; the site is always open. Admission to the museum and grounds is free. There may be a charge to climb the tower, unknown at press time. Bodie Island is the most dramatic of the four lights of the Outer Banks (now that Cape Hatteras Lighthouse has been moved away from the beach), a 156-foot-tall white-and-black-striped tower, reflecting in the marshes that separate it from NC 12 and the beach. You'll find it at the southern end of Bodie Island; its entrance road is at milepost 5.8, and excellent roadside views at 6.5 miles. Under restoration at press time, it should be open again by the time you read this. You may climb to the top, and the lightkeeper's cottage contains a fine little museum.

Oregon Inlet Life-Saving Station. Sitting at the southern end of the Bonner Bridge over Oregon Inlet (milepost 11.2), this was for many years the most evocative, as well as mysterious, ruin in the national seashore. Still under expansion and improvement as late as 1979, this 1878 station was utterly abandoned in 1988, as

BODIE ISLAND LIGHTHOUSE

drifting sand dunes began to envelop it. Within a decade, dunes had covered the road, swallowed outbuildings, and broken through windows to enter the original historic structure.

Then in 2008, the North Carolina Aquarium at Roanoke Island acquired title. They have removed both the sand and the modern outbuildings, and completely restored the historic structure. At press time it sits near the highway, handsome and loved—and still abandoned, as the aquarium has not come up with a final purpose for it. They are waiting for NCDOT to finalize plans for the rebuilding of Bonner Bridge, which might require them to move the station.

Chicamacomico Life-Saving Station (252-987-1552; chicamacomico.net), 23645 NC 12, P.O. Box 5, Rodanthe 27968. Open weekdays 10–5, Apr.–Nov. Beach Apparatus Drill held Thu. at 2, June–Aug. $$. Located at the northern edge of Rodanthe at milepost 39.5, Chicamacomico (pronounced *chick-a-ma-COMIC-oh*) is America's largest, most complete, most thoroughly restored, and most accurately presented lifesaving station, and one of only a handful to retain all of its original buildings. Most important, it is the only lifesaving station in America to regularly perform the full Beach Apparatus Drill, an impressive training exercise from the 1870s, done with authentic replica equipment. Owned, restored, and operated by the nonprofit Chicamacomico Historical Association, it boasts a crew of uniformed surfmen that would do the old service proud.

The site centers on its two historic stations, an 1874 station in the exuberant architecture that characterized the earliest years of the service, and its 1911 replacement, a large and handsome structure in the Banker style. Five outbuildings round out the site, including the beach-side Drill Pole, whose function becomes clear when you witness a Beach Apparatus Drill.

Cape Hatteras Lighthouse. Open daily May–Sept.; the site is always open. Admission to the site and museum is free; $$ for climbing the lighthouse. The prince of Outer Banks lights, 200-foot-tall Cape Hatteras is the tallest lighthouse in America and the 23rd tallest in the world. It was once the most dramatic of the Banks lighthouses as it loomed above the beach, protected from the fury of the ocean by a thin shell of seawall and riprap. Constructed in 1874 to replace a 1795 tower, it was originally 1,500 feet away from the shore—but near a spot unusually exposed to the erosional forces of lateral currents, waves hitting the sand at an angle. Within 20 years 1,200 of those feet had disappeared, and by 1935 the last 300 feet were gone; the Coast Guard abandoned it, expecting it to topple into the ocean during the next big storm. It was tougher than that, however, and by 1950 it was back in service, having regained (through natural forces) more than 500 feet of its missing beach. This, as with all beach lines, was not to last: By the 1980s its protective beach had once again disappeared and storm waves crashed against its foundation. In 1999 the National Park Service moved it to its current location, a slow-motion affair that took 23 days and looked rather like a brick space shuttle being moved to its pad. You can still see (and park on) the runway-like road built for this purpose. The current site is about 1,500 feet inland, the same distance as the original site, and hopefully will stay that way.

Cape Hatteras Lighthouse today is set in a large grassy meadow carved out of a stand of maritime forest, 20 stories of white-and-black spiral stripes. With nothing more than the salt-stunted trees to give it perspective, however, it can be a bit of a disappointment visually, particularly if you come primed by photos of it in its old location (still, alas, common in those travel media that prize sensation over accuracy). On the bright side, you can now climb it ($$), 268 steps on an ancient wrought-iron stairway. Compared with the old site, the new location has been much improved by the creation of an excellent museum on lighthouses and the Banker life, housed within the two original keepers' cottages, which have been moved along with the lighthouse.

Hatteras Village Weather Station (877-629-4386; 252-986-2203), 57190 Kohler Rd., Hatteras 27943. Open daily 9–5, Mar.–Dec. Admission is free. The dangers of the North Carolina coast were such that the federal government established early weather stations at Hatteras. These varied in location until the Weather Service purpose-built a station in 1901 at the center of Hatteras Village, on what is now Kohler Road just off NC 12. The unique structure consists of a full-sized house for the weather observer and his family downstairs, with an observation unit as its second floor. It was decommissioned in 1946, and now, fully restored, holds the Outer Banks Visitors Center; unfortunately, there are no exhibits about the old station inside.

Ocracoke Lighthouse. The site is open daily during daylight hours. Admission to the site is free. The oldest, shortest, and quaintest of the Banks lighthouses stands off a back street in Ocracoke village. Built in 1823, it's a squat, whitewashed tower only 75 feet tall, so much wider at its base than its top as to make it almost a cone. Picket fences and a location in an old Banker neighborhood make it unusually homey. You are free to admire it from the outside, but, unlike the other three lights, it cannot be climbed, and its lightkeeper's cottage is a private residence and closed to the public.

CULTURAL SITES **North Carolina Aquarium on Roanoke Island** (866-332-3475; 252-473-3494; ncaquariums.com/roanoke-island), 374 Airport Rd., Manteo 27954. Open daily 9–5. $$. Founded in 1976, North Carolina's state aquarium program features three separate, full-sized aquariums, one in each section of the coast. Each has its own specialty: the species indigenous to its local waters, from the rivers that drain from the state's interior, to the estuaries, along the beaches, and out into the oceans.

The Aquarium on Roanoke Island features the fauna of the Roanoke River, the Albemarle Sound, and the Outer Banks. Its centerpiece is a 280,000-gallon tank featuring sharks, while other exhibits include river otters and alligators. There's a daily dive show at 10:30, and feedings at 3. Sharks are fed separately, behind the scenes, but this can be watched as part of a special behind-the-scenes tour (fee), one of several offered (including some off-site). The aquarium owns and operates **Jennette's Pier** in Nags Head as its beachfront satellite, and the **Old Oregon Inlet Life-Saving Station**. It's located on the northern end of Manteo; to find it, take US Bus 64 3.5 miles north from its intersection with US Byp 64, then turn left onto Airport Road and take it to its end in 1.3 miles.

HISTORIC SITES **Historic Corolla Village** (twiddy.com/history/historic-corolla-village.aspx). Corolla, the last of the old Banker villages to be modernized, is the only one (other than the abandoned museum-piece Portsmouth) to avoid being smashed by development. One of the area's more prominent developers, a family-owned Realty named Twiddy & Company, had a big hand in its saving, restoring buildings and promoting the historic core.

Originally named Jones Hill, Corolla was founded in the 1870s, a grouping of Bankers around a lifesaving station (now gone) and lighthouse. Despite being accessible only by boat, the village thrived; by the 1890s it had a population of around 200. It continued to grow during the 1920s as an exotic destination for wealthy sportsmen, and weathered the Depression nicely (being not much dependent on the great outside world). When World War II approached the Coast Guard turned the nearby Wash Woods Station (in the Carova area, now restored and a Twiddy office) into a major anti-submarine post, and the village grew to 1,000 residents. That, however, was its high point; with no road access and no electricity, its population drifted away after the war, reaching its low point of 15 souls in the early 1970s. Its current prosperity (and near eclipse) comes from the extension of NC 12 northward from Kitty Hawk in 1984.

The old village center sits just to the west of NC 12, four blocks of modestly attractive Banker buildings. You'll get little hint of its existence, however, from the highway. The old village centers on Corolla Village Road, paralleling NC 12 about 200 yards to its west, starting at the lighthouse; wealthy hunters built the Whalehead Club immediately adjacent to the old village's southern border. The Currituck Beach Lighthouse anchors the old village's southwestern corner, looking at home with its Victorian farmhouse cottage and its wood fence. Opposite it, a 1,065-foot boardwalk extends through the back-island marshes to a bird-viewing platform on the sound. North from the lighthouse is the Wild Horse Museum, run by a foundation dedicated to protecting the largest wild horse herd in the Outer Banks, and housed in the village's one-room schoolhouse (in use until the 1950s). Now you enter the village's old center, an off-the-beaten-track collection of odd little shops. In the middle of it is the Island Garden, a demonstration of how Banker garden-agriculture worked. At the northern end, the 1885 Corolla Chapel holds regular interdenominational services year-round. On NC 12, the restored (and moved) Kill Devil Hills Life-Saving Station has close associations with the Wright Brothers and their First Flight; it now houses the Twiddy sales offices.

The Whalehead Club (252-453-9040; whaleheadclub.org), 1100 Club Rd., Corolla 27927. Open daily 9–5. House tours $$. Admission to the site is free. In 1922 a wealthy industrialist purchased about 4 miles of Outer Banks just south of the village of Corolla, and built for himself and his wife a hunting lodge, suitable for entertaining friends during the waterfowl migrations. Today this amazing "cottage," restored by Currituck County, is the centerpiece of 39-acre Currituck Heritage Park. It's 21,000 square feet, luxuriously appointed, built in an oddly charming combination of Banker and Art Nouveau styles and painted a startling yellow. Also on-site is a small harbor, now a yacht basin and kayak launch, and an environmental education center, plus picnicking and walking paths. The Currituck Beach Lighthouse and one of the two Corolla Marsh Boardwalks are both immediately adjacent.

Wright Brothers National Memorial, Kill Devil Hills (252-441-7430; nps.gov/wrbr). Open June–Aug., 9–6; Sept.–May, 9–5. $. While Orville and Wilbur Wright were developing their airplane in Dayton, Ohio, they were dogged by industrial spies, intent on stealing their ideas before they could patent them. So in late 1903, they fled Ohio to test their plane in the Outer Banks, where winds were favorable and prying eyes were absent. They first tested their wing design by making gliding flights off the 90-foot-high sand dune known as Kill Devil Hill; then, on December

17, 1903, they tested their powered aircraft for the first time, on the flat sands to the north of the dune. This 400-acre park at milepost 7.9, operated by the National Park Service, preserves the site of that first successful sustained powered flight. Its centerpiece is a massive marble tower on top of Kill Devil Hill, a remarkable art deco structure six stories tall, built in 1932; views from its base are stunning. A visitors center has exhibits on the Wright Brothers, including a full-scale, working replica of their first airplane. Adjacent to it, the Centennial Pavilion houses additional exhibits, on the Outer Banks in 1903 and the evolution of manned flight (up to, and including, NASA exhibits). Just outside is a re-creation of the first flight's locale—the crude wooden buildings the Wrights threw up, bronze statues of their plane, themselves, and the witnesses in their original locations, and a flight line with monuments where the plane left the ground and landed. The park has its own airstrip, for those who wish to land their private aircraft at the site of the first flight.

Nags Head's Historic Core. Almost unmentioned in the tourist literature and unnoticed by the hordes of visitors that pour through every year, a group of original cottages survive in the urban heart of the Outer Banks, "the unpainted aristocracy of Nags Head"; you'll find them facing the ocean around the intersection of NC 12 and E. Soundside Dr. (milepost 12.8). The oldest of these date to the 1830s, and were built as vacation cottages from the beginning—hence they're large and impressive enough to survive both storms and developers. These earliest cottages define the Banker style, with their unpainted shingle sides. Their stilts were an original innovation as well, a very effective protection against storms and now much copied.

Fort Raleigh National Historic Site and Elizabethan Gardens, Roanoke Island (252-473-5772; nps.gov/fora; elizabethangardens.org; thelostcolony.org), 1401 National Park Dr., Manteo 27954. The fort is open daily 9–5. The gardens are open at about the same time (shorter in winter, longer in summer). *The Lost Colony* performs June–mid-Aug., Mon.–Sat. at 8. Admission to the fort is free; gardens $$; theater $$$–$$$$. This 350-acre national park occupies the spot of the first two English attempts to colonize North America, sponsored by Sir Walter Raleigh in 1584 and 1587. The first settlement, consisting of 114 men, was meant as a temporary exploration party, wintering over to look for gold and pearls. They did no planting and fishing, and managed to make enemies of some (but not all) of the local tribes, so that by spring they found themselves on short rations and were rescued by Sir Francis Drake. Raleigh meant his second attempt to be a permanent colony, and sent over married couples ready to farm. Now known as "the Lost Colony," this group of 117 men and women inherited the Indian conflicts stirred up by their predecessors, but did not want to give up; instead, they sent their leader, John White, back to England to get additional supplies. Back in England, however, he couldn't find a ship; Spain's Armada attacked within the year, and open-seas warfare (mainly privateering) occupied all English shipping for the following two years. Finally, in 1590, White found a merchant ship willing to go out of its way to face the dangers of the Carolina shoals. When he finally arrived at Roanoke he found that that the camp had been systematically dismantled and the word CROATOAN (the name of Hatteras Island at the time), carved on a tree. No trace of colonists has ever been found, and their fate is unknown, although some 20 years later Chief Powhatan told John Smith that he had murdered the colonists as part of his genocide of the Chesepian tribe, with whom they were living. The National Park Service commemorates this settlement with a reconstruction, based on archaeological evidence, of its fort, together with an interpretive center.

On the same site is the 10-acre Elizabethan Gardens, created by the Garden Club of North Carolina as a memorial to the Lost Colony. It is noted for its variety, its spectacular tulip display, and its statues, garden architecture, and Tudor-style buildings.

Also on the site (and pre-dating the national park by 15 years) is Waterside Theater, a spectacular amphitheater overlooking Roanoke Sound. It is the site of *The Lost Colony* outdoor drama, written by Pulitzer Prize winner Paul Green in 1937, and accompanied by a symphonic orchestra.

Roanoke Island Festival Park (252-475-1500; roanokeisland.com; FestivalParkInformation@ncdcr.gov), 1 Festival Park, Manteo 27954.Open daily 9–5, Mar.–Dec. $$ (good for two consecutive days). Admission to the site, including the art gallery, history center, and paths, is free. This state historic site sits adjacent to downtown Manteo on its own little island. It was founded in 1984 as the permanent mooring of the *Elizabeth II*, a full-sized accurate replica of the three-masted barks that brought the doomed Roanoke Colony to this location in 1687. It remains the park's centerpiece, fully rigged, seaworthy (they take it out for a sail every once in a while), and manned by sailors in period dress who cheerfully answer questions and welcome visiting children to help them with their tasks. To this have been added ambitious re-creations of the Roanoke Colony and of an Algonquin settlement. The colony, called the Settlement Site, features costumed docents performing typical daily tasks, including farming, blacksmithing, carpentry, shoemaking, and the games of 300 years ago. Nearby is the Algonquin settlement, called American Indian Town, patterned after coastal settlements of the 16th century,100 years or so before the Lost Colony. Here you'll find authentically re-created longhouses, agricultural areas, and a ceremonial area, and visitors can try their hand at the daily tasks of building and living in such a settlement.

Also on the site is the Roanoke Adventure Museum, a hands-on history museum dedicated to Outer Banks history, notable both for its child-friendliness and for its embracing of Native and African-American themes. Its film, *The Legend of Two-Path*, examines the attitudes of, and choices made by, the coastal Algonquins during their initial contact with Europeans. A free Art Gallery (separate opening hours) features works by regional artists. The Outer Banks History Research Center is an archive and library (free, with separate opening hours) for those who wish to delve more deeply into Banker history. A large festival area, an amphitheater bowl with grass seating, is behind the museum, and features regular events during the summer season. The Festival Park also runs the harbor lighthouse and the Maritime Museum, both in downtown Manteo.

Downtown Manteo, Roanoke Island. Manteo's small and wonderfully strollable downtown is made up of a jumbled mixture of old and new buildings, filled with shops and cafés. Founded in 1873 as the seat of newly created Dare County, it spent its first century cut off from the mainland, and is centered on its harbor rather than on a traditional "Main Street." Not surprisingly, its main feature is its waterside boardwalk, lined with sailboats and small yachts, created in 1984 to celebrate the 400th anniversary of European settlement in North America, and the

300th anniversary of the first attempted English settlement (only a mile or two away). From it you can get a good view of the *Elizabeth II*, a faithful reproduction of one of the early colonists' ships, now part of adjacent Roanoke Festival Park. One of the harborside docks holds the strange and lovely Roanoke Marsh Light, a faithful reproduction of a channel light that stood on stilts in the open waters of Croatan Sound from 1858 to 1955. It's a charming square cottage with a bright red roof, topped with a light that could have come from one of the great coastal towers, and is used for education programs. Just beyond the southern end of the boardwalk is the Maritime Museum (free), also known as Creef/Davis Boathouse. Built in 1982 in the form of a traditional Banker boatbuilder's shop, it housed the construction of the *Elizabeth II* and now holds exhibits on Banker boats and boatbuilding, along with boatbuilding projects.

Island Farm, Roanoke Island (252-473-6500; theislandfarm.com), P.O. Box 970, Manteo 27954. Open weekdays 10–4, Jun.–Nov. $$. This living history museum recreates the antebellum farmstead that existed at this site from 1757, as it was in 1847, when its surviving farmhouse was built; you'll find it just north of Manteo off US Bus 64, 2.5 miles from its intersection with US Byp 64. This was the farm of a prosperous small freeholder, as witnessed by the fact that it included five enslaved people—not quite a plantation, yet far removed from a Banker's subsistence plot. The house is original, and furnished with period antiques; 12 outbuildings have been added. There are farm animals, and hands-on demonstrations and activities.

The Graveyard of the Atlantic Museum, Cape Hatteras (252-986-2995; graveyardoftheatlantic.com), P.O. Box 284, Hatteras 27943. Open Mon.–Sat. 10–4. Admission is free. The newest member of the state of North Carolina's Maritime Museum system occupies a large new building reminiscent of a wrecked ship, immediately upon the beach near Cape Hatteras, at the end of NC 12 (milepost 59). It is dedicated to its namesake, the vast area of ocean immediately off the coast, notorious for its hundreds of shipwrecks. Large areas of shallow sand, called shoals, extend for many miles off the coast of North Carolina, with Cape Hatteras the most visible landmark at the center of the most dangerous area. These shoals are in fact former Outer Banks, deposited at various points during the last ice age when sea levels were up to 500 feet lower and the Outer Banks coast up to 30 miles offshore. Each successive rise in sea level led to the old barrier islands drowning and a new set being formed to the west, and those drowned islands are now shoals, moving with the currents and exposed by tides and storms. The museum shows remains of the many shipwrecks, the treasures they contained, and the efforts to prevent them and save their sailors.

Portsmouth (252-928-4361; supporting organization: friendsofportsmouthisland.org; Austin Boat Tours, the ferry and guide service: portsmouthnc.com), P.O. Box 375, Ocracoke 27960. Open during daylight hours. Admission is free, but access is only by boat. This Banker ghost town sits opposite Ocracoke Island, at the tip of Cape Lookout National Seashore (see "New Bern and Beaufort"), is accessible by boat only. In antebellum times it was one of the state's most important ports, where goods were transferred from oceangoing vessels to smaller boats to be moved up rivers to plantations far inland, and in 1860 it reached its maximum population of 865. Shifting shoals and mainland railroads drove this trade elsewhere, but Portsmouth struggled on for another century as a commercial fishing center. This, too, died out in the 1950s, and the last two elderly residents moved out in 1971.

In 1976 the National Park Service took over the site and began a program of stabilizing, then restoring, the historic buildings. There are now 21 surviving structures, five of which are fully restored and open to the public as museums (others are privately occupied). These include a visitors center, the old general store and post office, the Methodist Church (the site of a homecoming in even-numbered years), the one-room schoolhouse, and the Portsmouth Life-Saving Station, whose 1937 closure was the beginning of the end for the town. The site itself is visually striking, with old Banker buildings set far apart, framed by small drifting dunes. A 1.5-mile path leads across tidal flats to a wide beach.

Getting there: There are two docks, one at town center, and another at the sound end of the beach. For a ferry, contact Austin Boat Tours of Ocracoke, the official park concessionaire, whose website is the best source of information on the island. (The National Park Service's website hardly mentions Portsmouth.) The contact information above is for Austin Boat Tours, whose tours leave the Ocracoke Community Docks twice a day in season. In summer prepare yourself for mosquitoes, and bring your own drinking water.

✷ To Do

BEACH GEAR rentals include such things as umbrellas and folding chairs. The merchants listed here, however, go a bit farther and rent active outdoor equipment as well. This can include bicycles (particularly fat-tire beach cruisers), surfboards, and kayaks. Specialized surfboard shops that offer rentals are also in this category.

Duck Village Outfitters (252-261-7222; duckvillageoutfitters.net; contactus@mydvo.com), 1207 Duck Rd., Duck 27949.This company rents bicycles, primarily beach cruisers, but also mountain bikes and children's bikes with trainer wheels. They rent surfboards and kayaks, and sponsor kayak tours. They have a second location in Salvo.

Just for the Beach Rentals (252-441-9480; justforthebeach.com), 1006 S. Virginia Dare Trail, Kill Devil Hills 27948. This shop rents bicycles, kayaks, and surfboards, as well as more ordinary beach gear (including stuff that you might need for your rental cottage). They have a shop in Corolla as well.

Ocean Atlantic Beach Rentals (800-635-9559; 252-441-7823; oceanatlanticrentals.com; info@oceanatlanticrentals.com), 2001 S. Croatan Hwy., Kill Devil Hills 27948. This beach rental offers a full selection of adult and kids' bicycles, kayaks, and surfboards, as well as a very complete selection of beach gear and cottage gear. They also have stores in Corolla, Duck, and Avon.

Hatteras Island Boardsports, Avon (866-442-9283; 252-995-6160; hiboardsports.com). This surfboard shop on NC 12 in Avon rents a variety of boards, as well as wet suits and kayaks.

CANOES AND KAYAKS **Coastal Explorations, Corolla** (252-453-9872; coastalexplorations.com; hadley@coastalexplorations.com). This company rents kayaks, and offers kayak and motorized boat tours of the back-island marshes.

Kitty Hawk Kayaks (866-702-5061; 252-261-0145; khkss.com; info@khkss.com), 6150 N. Croatan Hwy., Kitty Hawk 27949. This company rents kayaks, stand-up paddleboards, and surfboards; they have an outlet in Corolla, as well as their main shop on US 158.

DEEP-SEA FISHING BOAT AT OREGON INLET MARINA, HATTERAS NATIONAL SEASHORE

Coastal Kayak Touring Company (252-261-6262; joe@coastalkayak.org). This company offers a variety of guided kayak tours in the back-island area between Corolla and Pea Island.

Grog's Watersports (252-441-8875; grogswatersports.com; info@grogswater sports.com), 7649 S. Virginia Dare Trail, P.O. Box 3275, Nags Head 27959. This company offers kayak rentals and tours, as well as skiff and pontoon boat rentals, parasailing, and dolphin-sighting tours. They are located on the sound, just as US 64 enters Nags Head.

Hatteras Watersports, Salvo (252-987-2306; hatteraswatersports.com; info @hatteraswatersports.com), 27130 NC 12, Salvo 27972. Located at milepost 42.5, this Rodanthe-area company has kayak rentals and tours, and rents Hobie Wave sailboats. Their sound-front location, with a wide lawn, has a picnic area, restrooms, and showers.

KITES **Kitty Hawk Kites** (800-441-4778; 252-449-2210; kittyhawk.com; nagshead @kittyhawk.com), 3933 S. Croatan Hwy., Nags Head 27959. Claiming to be the largest kite company in the world, Kitty Hawk Kites started by helping people hang glide and fly kites from the top of the 100-foot sand dunes in Jockeys Ridge State Park immediately in front of their main store. They have now grown to a dozen outlets, spread from Corolla to Ocracoke, and offer kayaking, parasailing, and kiteboarding as well.

REAL Kiteboarding, Waves (866-732-5548; 252-987-6000; realkiteboarding .com; info@realwatersports.com), 25706 NC 12, P.O. Box 476, Waves 27982. Located in the Rodanthe area, this large and modern facility claims to be the largest kiteboard school and retailer in the world. They rent surfboards and stand-up paddleboards as well as kiteboards.

SAILING AND MOTORBOAT RENTALS **Nor'banks Sailing, Duck** (252-261-2900; norbanks.com), 1308 Duck Rd., Duck 27949. In business since 1979, this company rents five types of small sailboats and offers instructions. They also rent kayaks, stand-up paddleboards, and power fishing boats, and offer parasail rides.

OFF-ROAD TOURS **Back Country Outfitters and Guides, Corolla** (252-453-0877; outerbankstours.com; info@outerbankstours.com), 107-C Corolla Light Town Center, Corolla 27927. This eco-tour company offers wild horse tours in the Carova Beach area, using family-sized four-wheel-drive vehicles, taking 2-plus hours. They also offer Segway tours of Corolla's historic center, and a special tour that uses four-wheel drive to reach a horse reserve, then explores it with off-road Segways. A third tour option, taking 3-plus hours, combines four-wheel exploration with a kayak tour of the remote back-island.

Barrier Island Eco-Tours, Corolla (252-722-4014; barrierislandecotours.com; barrierislandecotours1@yahoo.com), 795 Sunset Blvd. (in Timbuck II, a shopping plaza), Corolla 27927. This company's 2½-hour four-wheel-drive tour of Carova Beach is done from a converted vehicle that looks like a Monster School Bus. They also offer several airboat tours of the marsh areas, venturing into Virginia's conservation areas.

Beach Jeeps of Corolla (252-453-6141; beachjeepsofcorolla.com), 1159 H Austin St., Corolla 27927. This company rents rag-top jeeps for self-driven tours of Carova Beach's wild horse area; following county ordinance, a guide accompanies you, and the company will guarantee that you see horses.

Bob's Off-Road Wild Horse Adventure Tour, Corolla (252-453-0939; corolla wildhorsetours.com), 1066 Ocean Trail (Inn at Corolla Light), Corolla 27927. This company runs four-wheel tours of Carova Beach using open-air, canvas-covered touring trucks, built for the purpose. They seat 17, and run as often as once an hour during the season.

Corolla Outback Adventures (252-453-4484; corollaoutback.com; cobainfo@mac.com). A guide leads a convoy of guest-driven vintage Toyota four-wheel-drive vehicles through the Carova Beach area. Passenger tours are also available, from customized open-air vehicles. The owner was raised in Carova, by parents who were offering tours in the off-road area as far back as the 1960s.

Wild Horse Adventure Tours (800-460-4136; 252-489-2020; wildhorsetour.com), 610 Currituck Club Dr., Corolla 27927. These Carova Beach wild horse tours give you the choice of a closed Suburban or an open-top jeep, driven by a guide; they also will rent you a self-driven jeep, with a guide present (as required by county ordinance).

Corolla Wild Horse Fund (252-453-8002; corollawildhorses.com; info@corolla wildhorses.com), 1126 Old Schoolhouse Lane, Corolla 27927. This not-for-profit manages and protects the wild horse herd of Carova Beach, and runs a museum in the Old Schoolhouse in Corolla's historic center. For a charitable contribution of $250 to $500, a staff member will personally conduct your family on a four-wheel-drive tour of the wild horses.

✷ Lodgings

HOTELS AND RESORTS **Blackbeard's Lodge, Ocracoke** (800-892-5314; 252-928-3421; blackbeardslodge.com; info@blackbeardslodge.com), 111 Back Rd., P.O. Box 298, Ocracoke 27960. $–$$$$. Blackbeard's Lodge is located on a back street in the center of the village of Ocracoke. Built in 1936 as the Wahab Village Hotel, it has a strangely meandering exterior, a kind of Dr. Seuss version of Banker architecture, with an interior that features high ceilings and authentic cedar paneling. Each of the 38 guest rooms, suites, and apartments has its own character, with a family rather than a luxury emphasis; rooms without kitchens will have a small fridge. There are king, queen, and double beds, and 10 rooms are pet-friendly. The attractive common areas include a pool table, and WiFi is available in the commons. Breakfast is not included.

BED & BREAKFASTS The Cypress House Bed and Breakfast, Kill Devil Hills (800-554-2764; 252-441-6127; cypresshouseinn.com; cypresshouseinn@charter.net), 500 N. Virginia Dare Trail, Kill Devil Hills 27948. $$–$$$$. This handsome Banker house, on NC 12 across from the beach, was built in 1947 as a hunting lodge; its current name reflects the fact that walls and ceilings are paneled in cypress. Its six rooms all have sitting areas and large windows, with queen beds. WiFi is available, as are free beach gear and bicycles. The tariff includes a full breakfast, served at 8:30 (although other arrangements can be made), along with afternoon tea with homemade cookies.

The Cameron House Inn B & B, Manteo, Roanoke Island (800-279-8178; cameronhouseinn.com; Innkeeper@CameronHouseInn.com), 300 Budleigh St., Manteo 27954. $$$–$$$$. This handsome 1919 bungalow sits in Manteo's historic district, at the edge of its attractive and shop-filled downtown. Its six rooms are decorated in the Arts and Crafts style from which such bungalows emerged. All are spacious, with sitting areas and desks, and all have WiFi; there's a choice of king, queen, and double beds. One room is outside the main house, and this is the pet-friendly room. The tariff includes a homemade continental breakfast and a hospitality fridge stocked with soft drinks and goodies. Bicycles are also provided free. If you wish them to accommodate children or pets you *must* make prior arrangements.

The White Doe Inn Bed and Breakfast, Manteo, Roanoke Island (800-473-6091; 252-473-9851; whitedoeinn.com; whitedoe@whitedoeinn.com), 319 Sir Walter Raleigh St., Manteo 27954. $$$$. This stunning Queen Anne mansion, built in 1910 and listed in the National Register, features a wide wraparound veranda with Doric columns and a corner turret, and lots of old wood on the inside. Its eight rooms are all large, with sitting areas, tastefully decorated in period, with a choice of king or queen beds. All rooms have gas fireplace, and either a whirlpool tub or an extra-large club-footed tub is available, as is WiFi. A four-course full breakfast, served daily 8:30–9:30, is included in the tariff, as is afternoon coffee (including cappuccino and espresso) with freshly baked goodies. Bicycles and beach equipment are available free.

The Island House of Wanchese Bed and Breakfast, Roanoke Island (866-473-5619; islandhouse-bb.com; islandhousebb@earthlink.net), 104 Old Wharf Rd., Wanchese 27981. $$–$$$. This large Banker house with a wraparound screened porch, about 100 years old, is made of wood cut on the site; it sits off a back road in the dispersed fishing of Wanchese, 3 miles south of US Byp 64. It has three cheerful, comfortable rooms with seating areas, plus a suite where pets and children as young as 8 are allowed with prior arrangement. Broadband is available, and a full southern buffet breakfast is included in the tariff, along with guest pantry with ice machine, microwave, and fridge.

The Thurston House Inn Bed and Breakfast, Ocracoke (252-928-6037; thurstonhouseinn.com; stay@thurstonhouseinn.com), 671 NC 12, P.O. Box 1115, Ocracoke Island 27960. $$–$$$. Located in a 1920s home near the center of the village, this B&B is owned and run by the descendants of its builder, an early Outer Banks captain and guide. The 10 large rooms, with seating areas, comprise 4 in the original home and 6 in an annex. King, queen, and two twin beds are available (the twins convert to a king, so call ahead), and WiFi is available. The full southern-style breakfast, served 8:30–9:30 and included in the tariff, includes fig cake made from figs grown on the property.

✷ Where to Eat

DINING OUT **The Pearl Restaurant, Kill Devil Hills** (252-480-3463; thepearlobx.com; thepearlobx@embarqmail.com), 1731 N. Virginia Dare Trail, Kill Devil Hills 27948. Open for dinner Tue.–Sun., and for lunch Fri.–Sun. $$$–$$$$. The Outer Banks' only oceanfront restaurant offers white-tablecloth dining, both in its elegant, brightly lit dining room and on a terrace bordering the dunes. The cuisine is strongly French, built around ingredients from local farms and waters by its owner-chef, the son of the chef who owned and operated Chanticleer on Nantucket Island. You'll find it tucked away in the Sea Ranch Hotel, on NC 12 near milepost 7.

THE HARBOR AT OCRACOKE VILLAGE

EATING OUT Tale of the Whale, Nags Head (252-441-7332; taleofthe whalenagshead.com; info@taleofthe whalenagshead.com), 7575 S. Virginia Dare Trail, Nags Head 27959. Open for dinner daily. $$$–$$$$. Founded in 1980 and still owned by the founder's family, this casual seafood restaurant sits overlooking the sound beside US 64 as it enters Nags Head, with a waterside boardwalk and pier. Its interior is attractive, with lots of wood accents and wide views through large windows. Their menu features local catches among a wide choice of items, and portions are large unless you order from the (less expensive) "Lighter Fare" menu.

Adrianna's Waterfront Restaurant, Manteo, Roanoke Island (252-473-4800; adriannasrestaurant.com; reser vations@adriannasrestaurant.com), 207 Queen Elizabeth Ave., Suite 5, Manteo 28754. Open for lunch and dinner Mon.–Sat. $$$–$$$$. Expect intelligent and imaginative menus at this small waterfront restaurant on Manteo's harbor boardwalk. Indeed, the first thing the new owners did in 2008 was to rip out the bank of deep-fat fryers. All food is made from scratch using fresh ingredients; lunch visitors will be greeted by creative specials at reasonable prices. Call ahead, as this open, attractive space, with its large windows onto the waterfront, is popular for private events.

Full Moon Café and Grille, Manteo, Roanoke Island (252-473-6666; thefullmooncafe.com; info@thefull mooncafe.com), 208 Queen Elizabeth St., Manteo 27954. Open daily (in-season) for lunch and dinner. Lunch: $$–$$$; dinner: $$$–$$$$. This downtown Manteo restaurant has sidewalk terrace dining a short block from the waterfront. Their original recipes have an international slant, and are prepared fresh, using local ingredients when available, including local seafood. The wine list has many inexpensive choices, some below $20, and regional craft brews are available on tap, including Full Moon Lager, special to this restaurant.

The Back Porch Restaurant, Ocracoke (252-928-6401), 110 Back Rd., Ocracoke 27960. Open daily for dinner. $$–$$$$. Located on a back street in the middle of the village of Ocracoke, this restaurant occupies a pretty little board-and-batten building with a large, screened terrace cooled by the trees of a relic maritime forest—the "back porch" of its name. The food, made fresh from scratch, blends French, Vietnamese, and Banker elements, and features locally caught seafood.

Howard's Pub, Ocracoke (252-928-4441; howardspub.com; info@ howardspub.com), 1175 Irvin Garrish Hwy., Ocracoke 27960. Open daily for lunch and dinner, closing at midnight, Mar.–Nov. $$–$$$. This Outer Banks landmark sits just outside the village of Ocracoke on NC 12. It's beachy and pubby, an open, friendly place that welcomes kids in their indoor dining room and large screened and covered terrace. Pub meals feature fresh local seafood including a raw bar; even the burgers and fries are made to order from fresh ingredients. Their selection of two dozen tap beers includes many regional craft brews. On some nights they offer entertainment later in the evening.

✷ Entertainment

POPULAR OBXNightOut.com. During the summer season, live late-night entertainment is scattered all along the Banks. This website is dedicated specifically to the live entertainment venues and the bands playing at them during the weekend of your visit.

✷ Selective Shopping

Shopping in the Outer Banks is highly dispersed. Duck has the largest concentration of boutique and craft shops, and Corolla's old village center is emerging as a good place to find fine crafts by beach artists.

✷ Special Events

As with entertainment and shopping, festivals in the Outer Banks tend to be common, but small and spread out. There is something fun going on virtually every weekend during the season, somewhere along the 125 miles of beach. None of it, however, is the sort of monster event that attracts crowds numbering in the many tens of thousands; they are all smaller-scale, more family-friendly. Look especially for kite and hang-gliding events on the dunes of **Jockeys Ridge**, and sandcastle events in all sorts of places. During National Speak Like a Pirate Day, September 19, pirates invade Banks restaurants looking to shanghai crew members. The popular Beach Music Festival, in Manteo during May, didn't come off during the year this book went to press, but it might be revived by the time you visit.

THE TIDEWATER REGION: ALBEMARLE SOUND

Behind the Outer Banks, three massive tidal inlets define the Tidewater Region of North Carolina. Here land and water meet and mix, with salinity as much as solidity distinguishing "land" from "sea." Three massive bays define the region: Albemarle Sound to the north, Pamlico Inlet in the center, and New River Inlet to the south. These are major barriers to anyone on a north–south drive, and make it necessary to divide the Tidewater into two chapters.

This chapter deals with Albemarle Sound, and the peninsula formed by Albemarle Sound and Pamlico Inlet, an area rich with colonial history (including Blackbeard, who lived here) and vast tracts of public land. The next chapter will deal with the peninsula formed by Pamlico Inlet and New River Inlet, the New Bern area, and the Cape Lookout Coast.

GUIDANCE **Edenton** (800-775-0111; 252-482-3400; visitedenton.com), 116 E. King St., Edenton 27932. The website and visitors center cover the area around the colonial-era town of Edenton, on the northwestern edge of Albemarle Sound's northern shore.

Hertford (252-426-5657; visitperquimans.com; chamber@perquimans.com), 118 W. Market St., Hertford 27944. The Perquimans County Chamber of Commerce covers the area around the small town of Hertford, on Albemarle Sound's north shore (between Edenton and Elizabeth City).

Elizabeth City (252-335-5330; 252-335-5330; discoverelizabethcity.com), 400 S. Water St., Suite 101, Elizabeth City 27909. The Elizabeth City Area Convention and Visitors Bureau covers the area around this small city on the northeast edge of Albemarle Sound.

Plymouth and Washington County (252-793-3248; Washington County: gowildnc.org; visitplymouthnc.com; chamber@washconc.org), 701 Washington St., Plymouth 27962. Located at the head of Albemarle Sound, the town of Plymouth is the largest settlement in Washington County, on the sound's southwestern shore. There's a countywide website run by the Tourism Development Authority (TDA), and a website specifically for Plymouth tourism, run by the town government. The

TDA site is unusual in having a series of in-depth articles on the area's natural history, written by an expert. The address and phone number are for the visitors center, run by the TDA.

Columbia and Tyrrell County (252-796-1996; visittyrrellcounty.com; visitrtc@embarqmail.com), P.O. Box 170, Columbia 27925. Tyrrell County covers the southeastern shore of Albemarle Sound, with the small town of Columbia its seat and only urban center. The county's chamber of commerce provides its official tourism website and maintains a visitors center in Columbia, where US 64 crosses the Scuppernong River.

Town of Washington and Beaufort County (800-546-0162; 252-958-9415; visitwashingtonnc.com), 138 S. Market St., P.O. Box 1765, Washington 27889. The Washington Tourism Development Authority covers the small city of Washington and the western end of Pamlico Sound.

Hyde County (888-493-3826; 252-926-9171; hydecounty.org; hydecountychamber.org; info@hydecountychamber.org), 20646 US 264, Swan Quarter 27885. Remote and lightly populated, Hyde County sits at the mouth of Pamlico Inlet. While it includes Ocracoke Island, a popular part of the Outer Banks, this chapter concerns itself only with Hyde County's mainland portion. The contact information is for the Hyde County Chamber of Commerce.

GETTING THERE *By car:* From points north, take US 17 from Norfolk, Virginia, an expressway that goes near Elizabeth City and past Hertford and Edenton to US 64. From other directions, your best bet is US 64, now an expressway nearly its entire length from the Raleigh area to Plymouth and Columbia. US 264, not quite as good a road as US 64 but still an easy drive, parallels it to the south, reaching Washington and Hyde County. When traveling north–south within this area you'll be using good state highways; these are not, however, consistently numbered, and a map is recommended.

By air: The Norfolk, Virginia, International Airport (ORF) is about 100 miles north of the center of this chapter's area via expressways; Raleigh-Durham (RDU) is 140 miles west via expressway; and Wilmington (ILM) is 160 miles south via two-lane highways.

By bus or train: **Greyhound** (greyhound.com) runs a daily bus in each direction between Raleigh and Norfolk, Virginia, that stops at Washington, Edenton, and Elizabeth City. There is no rail service to this area.

MEDICAL EMERGENCIES **Chowan Hospital, Edenton** (252-482-0629; uhseast.com), 211 Virginia Rd., Edenton 27932. This 95-bed hospital, just north of town on NC 32, is run by University Health Systems of Eastern Carolina, a not-for-profit affiliated with East Carolina University's College of Medicine.

Albemarle Health, Elizabeth City (252-335-0531; albemarlehealth.org), 1144 N. Road St., Elizabeth City 27909. The largest hospital in this chapter's area, Albemarle Health is another University Health Systems affiliate, and is located at the center of Elizabeth City.

Beaufort County Hospital, Washington (252-975-3498; beaufortregionalhealthsystem.org), 628 E. 12th St., Washington 27889. This 95-bed hospital near the center of Washington is run by Beaufort Regional Health Systems, an independent not-for-profit.

✷ Exploring the Area

EXPLORING BY CAR The Albemarle Peninsula. Defined by Albemarle Sound on its north and Pamlico Inlet on its south, the 2.4-million-square-mile Albemarle Peninsula is the emptiest and wildest region in the state of North Carolina. This 173-mile loop will take you to the best of the sights without (it is hoped) trying your patience with too many miles of scenic emptiness.

Start at Washington's waterfront, at the peninsula's southwest corner. *Take NC 32 east from US 17.* This leads you into Washington's attractive two-block downtown, well kept and traditional; its recently renovated waterfront, with sound-side parks and yacht moorings, is a block to your right. The **North Carolina Estuarium** is at the eastern end of the waterfront, using art and science to present the state's estuaries. *Continue on NC 32* as it turns north (at 5.3 miles), crosses US 264 (at 8.3 miles), and travels across the peninsula for 28 miles. This section follows a low ridge with mixed forests and farms, and a string of houses favoring the high ground.

A FISHERMAN LAUNCHES ON THE PUNGO RIVER AT SUNRISE

Cross US 64 at 36.6 miles, and reach the Plymouth waterfront at 37.2 miles. Two blocks to your left sits the **Roanoke River Lighthouse**, a cottage on stilts with a light atop that once served as a channel beacon, reconstructed in a riverside park and coupled with the **Roanoke River Maritime Museum** across the street. *Turn right onto Water Street,* going through the town's little waterfront downtown and along the river to its **Port o' Plymouth Museum**, housed in a fine brick train depot by the river, with a replica of a Confederate ironclad rammer (almost a submarine) moored beside it. *Turn left onto Main Street and follow it to its end at US 64, then turn left onto US 64 and follow it for 2.2 miles, then continue straight on NC 32 (Old US 64) for 4.6 miles, to a right turn onto Newland Road (SSR 1126).* This attractive paved road wanders through the backcountry, mainly open farmland, and its narrow shoulders and lack of fences bring you close into the scenery. After 8.2 miles of nearly complete emptiness, a little jog marks the beginning of an imperceptible ridge in the flat marshlands; the road becomes lined with vernacular houses from every period, as it curves crazily in a search for high ground.

After 11.7 miles on Newland Road, turn right onto Weston Road (SSR 1164), then go 2.4 miles to a left onto Lake Shore Road, which you take it to its end at a T-intersection in 3.0 miles. On your right is natural Phelps Lake and **Pettigrew State Park**; a hike-bike trail follows the lake to your right, and a walking path heads off along the shoreline to your left. The park's main entrance is at 2.1 miles on your right. Then at 2.6 miles on your right is **Somerset Place**, a restored plantation house that, before the Civil War, commanded a 100,000-acre commercial operation; now a state historic site, is run as a representative 19th-century farm with a dozen outbuildings.

Turn left onto Magnolia Road (SSR 1118); this modest paved back road passes through miles of farmland cleared by slaves in the 18th century. *Turn left after 4.4 miles onto Magnolia Cross, then go 0.2 mile to a left turn onto Spruill Bridge Road (SSR 1142).* This will take you to the village of Creswell in 2.1 miles, and back to US 64 in 3.0 miles.

We are now done with back roads. *Take the US 64 expressway east for 8.5 miles, to Columbia.* The seat and only town of the state's least populated county has a lovely waterfront on the Scuppernong River, with a boardwalk and nature trail behind the visitors center. *Turn right onto NC 94*; you are now heading south to re-cross the peninsula. Civilization will quickly drop away and leave you surrounded by farmland, unfenced and devoid of population. At 12.8 miles a rare side road on your left leads some miles to the **Buckridge Game Lands**, where a very remote boat ramp gives access to the vast wilderness estuary known as Alligator River. Then, at your first real curve (13.6 miles), your scenery changes to the marsh hardwoods of the **Pocosin Lakes National Wildlife Refuge**. At 24.3 miles you cross the **Intracoastal Waterway** on a high bridge with sweeping views. Finally, at 28.9 miles, you reach **Lake Mattamuskeet**, then go right across the center of this massive natural lake on a 5.2-mile-long causeway. At 33.4 miles dirt-surfaced Headquarters Road goes off to the left for 2.2 miles to historic and picturesque **Mattamuskeet Lodge**, with its strange tower overlooking the lake; here the **Mattamuskeet National Wildlife Refuge** provides boardwalks and bird walks. *After 35.0 miles you reach US 264; turn left.*

Turn right onto US 264, surprisingly narrow and curvy after NC 94, and go 33.5 miles to Belhaven. At the 7.0-mile mark, Swan Quarter is 1.5 miles to your left via Main Street (SSR 1129); this tiny village is the seat of Hyde County and site of the **auto ferry to Ocracoke Island** in the Outer Banks. At 10.7 miles a dirt-surfaced side road leads 2.0 miles through **Swanquarter National Wildlife Refuge** to the 1,000-foot-long Bell Island Pier, with stunning views over Rose Bay. At 21.0 miles you re-cross the Intracoastal Waterway, and then cross the wide Pungo River at 25.6 miles. While the main highway misses Belhaven, a short jog to your left will bring you into this attractive fishing village with a nice local museum and good restaurant.

At Belhaven go straight onto NC 99, crossing two wide inlets with good water views in the first 4.4 miles. At 16.9 miles you reach the village of **Bath**, noted both for its colonial era buildings (several open to the public as part of a state historic site) and as the town where Blackbeard the pirate kept a home during 1718, the last year of his life. You regain NC 32 in another 8.7 miles; Washington is 6.3 miles farther ahead.

EXPLORING BY BICYCLE **The Dismal Swamp Canal Trail**. This 4.5 mile paved path, 10 feet wide, follows the historic 1805 Dismal Swamp Canal, famously promoted by George Washington and now part of the **Intracoastal Waterway**. It starts just north of the village of South Mills, with a paved trailhead at the intersection of the new US 17 expressway with the old US Bus 17. Its first 2.9 miles follow the old US 17 roadbed on the eastern side of the canal, occasionally coming quite close to the new highway. Then, at the **Dismal Swamp State Park** headquarters, it crosses the canal on a unique drawbridge (boats have the right-of-way) to follow the wild western side of the canal, through dense forests within the state park. The pavement ends well shy of the state line, but bicycling continues on the sandy canal dikes that extend deep into the park. You can also extend its southern end into the center of South Mills and its handsome old drawbridge, as dual paved shoulders along former US 17 (each 5 feet wide) have been declared bicycle paths.

EXPLORING BY BOAT **The Intracoastal Waterway in the Northern Tidewaters**. Created by Congress in 1919, the Atlantic Intracoastal Waterway runs for 741 miles from its northern terminus at Portsmouth, Virginia (part of the Norfolk urban area) to the mouth of the St. Johns River near Jacksonville, Florida, staying a short distance inside the coastline the entire way. The Florida Intracoastal Waterway, never completed, continues down to Miami and Key West, and through Lake Okeechobee to the Gulf of Mexico; the Gulf Intracoastal Waterway, also never completed, picks up from there to go along the coast to Texas, with a big chunk missing between Tallahassee and Clearwater. It is possible to extend this inland shipping route northward from Portsmouth as well, going as far as Rhode Island before hitting open ocean. In all, it was supposed to tie together to form a 3,000-mile-long sheltered channel from Boston to Brownsville—the Atlantic Intracoastal being the first link, the granddaddy of them all. While the western Gulf segment still gets heavy commercial use, the Atlantic Intracoastal had its last heyday during World War II when shipping used it to avoid U-boats. It is supposed to have a project depth of 12 feet, but lack of commercial shipping has given dredging a low priority, and the inevitable shoaling has further damaged its commercial shipping.

The main channel of the Intracoastal Waterway spends 154 miles in the northern Tidewaters. There's a secondary channel as well, the purely recreational Dismal Swamp Canal, much narrower, with locks, and a project depth of 6 feet. It's spectacularly beautiful, passing through prime recreation lands of the **Great Dismal Swamp National Wildlife Refuge** and **Dismal Swamp State Park**, then twisting along the wild Pasquotank River. It has the final advantage of ending at Elizabeth City, noted for its friendliness to recreational boaters.

The main channel also follows a historic canal, the Albemarle & Chesapeake, which runs overland well to the east of the Dismal Swamp. This is the choice of commercial traffic, as well as those pleasure craft that can't hang with a 6-foot-deep channel. By the time this branch crosses the state line it has already entered the coastal waters of Currituck Sound, just behind the Outer Banks. Before it reaches the first Banker marina, however, it jogs west up a shallow creek, cuts through a peninsula, then runs down another minor creek to rejoin the Dismal Swamp branch well out into Albemarle Sound.

For the next 82 miles the waterway carefully avoids the wide, stormy waters behind the Outer Banks to cut a more sheltered course through the empty marshlands to its west. After crossing Albemarle Sound (a distance of 15 miles) it enters the long bay known as Alligator River, surrounded by the lands of the **Alligator River National Wildlife Refuge**, **Pocosin Lakes National Wildlife Refuge**, **Alligator River Game Lands**, and **Buckridge Game Lands**, a 25-mile segment. The emptiness continues as the waterway cuts straight overland for another 22 miles, to finally empty into the wide inlet formed by the mouth of the Pungo River where Belhaven, in 8 miles, has marina services. After 18 miles in the Pungo Inlet, the waterway crosses the Pamlico Inlet (a mere 5 miles wide here), and enters the next chapter.

✷ Towns

Edenton. The westernmost of the three north shore towns, Edenton sits on the northwest corner of Albemarle Sound at the mouth of the Chowan River. Named after the early colonial governor who pardoned Blackbeard and declared his piratical booty to be "naval salvage" in exchange for a 20 percent "fee," Edenton is noted for the stunning harbor views from its historic center. Edenton acquired its colonial core while it served as the colony's capital from 1722 to 1743; by that time it had become an established port, and continued to thrive. Today its a handsome town of 5,000 that barely manages to spill out of its original street plan, a grid of two long blocks paralleling its sound-side port and extending 11 blocks inland. Years ago US 17 ran right up the middle of that grid, causing much congestion—but now a modern expressway siphons off through-traffic, and the quiet bustle of a small town reigns supreme. Its centerpiece is its harborside park with a fine yacht basin; behind this another park extends inland to incorporate the 1767 Chowan County Courthouse, elegantly Georgian and still in use. It has a traditional downtown on the opposite (eastward and inland) street, Broad Street, with three pleasantly strollable blocks and plentiful parking in the rear, to the east.

HERTFORD TOWN CENTER

Hertford. The middle and smallest of the Albemarle's three north shore towns, Hertford sits on a tiny peninsula at the head of 12-mile-long Perquimans River Inlet. Its one-block downtown is made up of old-fashioned red-brick buildings that face its charming little courthouse. From there, US Bus 17 curves into the cypress-lined mouth of the Perquimans, crossing it on a classic bridge from the 1930s with acorn lamps, a steel truss center, and wide views from its sidewalk.

Elizabeth City. The largest and easternmost of the three shore towns, Elizabeth City boasts a population of 21,000, and has the character of a small city. Located at the head of the Pasquotank River's tidal inlet, it is best noted for the friendliness of its port facilities, catering to pleasure craft of all type; it certainly does no harm that the Dismal Swamp Branch of the **Intracoastal Waterway** runs inside its harbor area. Its large, traditional downtown is four blocks long and extends three blocks back from the harbor area; the **Museum of the Albemarle** sits opposite a harborside park at the south end, and two discontinuous boardwalks give views over the water.

Washington. The only sizable town on the Albemarle Peninsula, Washington boasts a population of 13,000; it sits on the peninsula's far southwest corner, with an extensive frontage at the tidal Pamlico Inlet's head. Its fine old downtown stretches for two blocks along NC 32, one block in front of its waterfront. Its old harbor has become a four-block park with a sound-side walk, ending at the **North Carolina Estuarium**.

✷ Green Spaces

PUBLIC LANDS The Great Dismal Swamp (national wildlife refuge: fws.gov/northeast/greatdismalswamp; state park: ncparks.gov/Visit/parks/disw). George Washington called this marsh "a glorious paradise"—but given its name, others seem to have disagreed. Located astraddle the Virginia state line just west of US 17, the Great Dismal Swamp is the northernmost of a string of forested wetlands that sit some distance behind the Atlantic coast, ranging from here southward to Georgia's Okeefenokee Swamp, terminating in northern Florida's Big Bend region; they represent the continent's former coastline, a series of offshore lagoons that have been filled by deposition and built up by peat. At a mere 200 square miles, the Great Dismal Swamp is far from the largest of these, but nevertheless provides plenty of elbow room for the serious nature lover. Access to its center is via the banks of old canals, straight and easy walking.

Nearly of the Great Dismal Swamp is government-owned and freely open to the public. The Great Dismal Swamp National Wildlife Refuge controls 175 square miles, including all of the Virginia swamp. While it provides no developed facilities in North Carolina, it has several just over the line in Virginia. The largest and best of these is at its headquarters, on the west side of the swamp. Here you'll find a boardwalk exploring the forest around the headquarters building, and the 4.5-mile (one-way) walk to Lake Drummond, a large natural lake, with views from a pier. There's also a motorable road to the lake, ending in a boat ramp, but you must get a permit from the headquarters building to drive it.

On the southeastern corner of the swamp, within North Carolina, is the 22-square-mile Dismal Swamp State Park, with its entrance within the state's Welcome Area on US 17, 3.2 miles south of the state line. Here a branch of the Intracoastal Waterway follows an 1805 canal (promoted by George Washington) along the eastern side of the swamp; the park headquarters is immediately over the canal via a unique hydraulic bridge. (Boaters have the right-of-way.) Here also the Dismal Swamp Canal Trail, a 4.5-mile paved hike-bike trail, passes through the park on the canal bank. Behind this is a 2,000-foot boardwalk, as well as a network of canal dike trails, most of them open to off-road bicycles.

MacKay Island National Wildlife Refuge (252-429-3100; fws.gov/mackay island), 316 Marsh Causeway, P.O. Box 39, Knotts Island 27950. The refuge is open Mar. 15–Oct. 15 to hiking, trail biking, birding, fishing, boating, and crabbing. There are limited closures (including the impoundments) Oct. 16–Mar. 14 to protect migrating waterfowl. Deer hunting is allowed with a special refuge permit, but waterfowl hunting is prohibited. Located in the far northeastern corner of this chapter's area, MacKay Island is, in fact, a peninsula into Currituck Sound, linked to the mainland by a narrow strip of marsh extending northward into Virginia and traversed by a state road (VA/NC 615). It can be visited without driving three sides around a square by taking the free state-run auto ferry from Currituck on NC 168 (see in the introduction to part 1). The 8,200-acre federal refuge takes up the entire western three-quarters of the "island"; the eastern quarter is a high sand ridge, settled and farmed, known as Knotts Island. The refuge has two areas for public recreation. The first comes 2.7 miles north of the ferry terminal, at a left turn onto MacKay Island Road, a very scenic drive along a good gravel road that goes 1.6 miles into the refuge, following a wide, canoeable canal for most of its length. It ends at a series of wildfowl impoundments, with a disabled accessible fishing and observation boardwalk at the parking area, and 5.9 miles of hike-bike trails on the dikes that lead to wide views over the sound. The second area comes 4.6 miles from the ferry, as the main paved road turns west to head across the marshes and into Virginia. The next 3.7 miles of highway pass through the heart of the refuge, with fine wild scenery and many opportunities for wildlife observation, particularly along its parallel canal. At 5.0 miles from the ferry, the 0.3-mile Great Marsh Trail circles a small pond on your left, whose many trees only partially conceal its wildlife. After that the scenery becomes very open, over wide reed lands. At 6.5 miles you break into open water, marked by a wooden observation tower. At the end of the refuge, as the road climbs to high ground, a paved road to your left leads 0.9 mile to the refuge headquarters, with visitors information and views over the sound.

Pocosin Lakes National Wildlife Refuge (252-796-3004; fws.gov/pocosinlakes; pocosinlakes@fws.gov), 205 S. Ludington Dr., P.O. Box 329, Columbia 27925. Open all year; Pungo Lake and New Lake fishing is open Mar.–Nov. Hunting is allowed as per North Carolina law; during hunting season, confine wildlife observation, hiking, and canoeing to Sundays and wear hunter orange. With more than 110,000 acres, Pocosin Lakes sprawls across the center of the Albemarle Peninsula. It is dominated by vast tracts of *pocosin*, a swamp ecology made up of impenetrably dense evergreen shrubs; it is best known, however, for its substantial holdings around natural Lake Phelps and Pungo Lake, and along the Scuppernong and Alligator Rivers. This refuge is quite new (founded in 1990) and most (if not all) of its tracts have been exploited at one time or another, so that much of the refuge's energies are concentrated on habitat restoration. On the bright side, this history has left a large network of canal dikes for exploring, many of them open to driving by licensed vehicles, and all of them open for walking. Four areas of the refuge offer public recreation.

- The refuge's headquarters on the Scuppernong River in Columbia has a fine 0.7-mile boardwalk along this tidal waterfront and back into ancient cypress forests, as well as exhibits on wildlife.

- Four miles of Lake Phelps shoreline can be reached via paved Shore Road, which branches right from Newland Road 6.9 miles east from Roper; two motorable and three hiking trails along old farm dikes head southward into the heart of the pocosin, and a third motorable trail wanders eastward through the largest and densest tract to eventually meet NC 94.
- A large detached tract gives access to Alligator River's west shore, including the large wild bay known as the Frying Pan; go 7.0 miles south of Columbia on NC 94 to a right turn onto Frying Pan Road, which leads to the Frying Pan and refuge dike paths in another 6.0 miles.
- Pungo Lake (wholly within the refuge) has small boat access and an observation tower on its southern edge, reached via a dirt-surfaced refuge track designated the Charles Kuralt Trail (which might not be suitable for ordinary cars when you visit, so use caution); you can reach it by taking NC 45 for 17.1 miles south from Plymouth, to a left turn onto the Charles Kuralt Trail, which leads 4.9 miles to the lake.

Alligator River National Wildlife Refuge (252-473-1131; fws.gov/alligatorriver; alligatorriver@fws.gov), 708 N. US 64, Manteo 27954. Open all year with few, if any, seasonal use restrictions. Hunting is allowed as per state law. During hunting season, enjoy wildlife observation on Sundays only and wear hunter orange. This enormous refuge, with 154,000 acres, occupies a subpeninsula formed by Alligator River (a large bay) and Albemarle Sound, on the eastern side of the Albemarle Peninsula. Access is via US 64 through its northern portion, and US 264 along its eastern edge. The nearest town is Manteo, in the Outer Banks, where its headquarters is located. It's noted for its program of reestablishing nearly extinct red wolves, a program it shares with Pocosin Lakes to its west; however, these wolves are very skittish and are almost never seen by visitors. Bears, on the other hand, are common, and you have a good chance of seeing one if you drive slowly down Milltail Road (off US 64, 6.3 miles west of the Manteo bridge).

A COMMERCIAL FISHING SUPPLIER IN BELHAVEN

The main recreation area focuses on a large commercial farm recently purchased by the refuge and kept open to supply open, seed-rich habitat; known as the Farmlands, it forms a 10-mile crescent immediately south of US 64 and curving around toward US 264. Here you'll find the refuge's two short nature trails, each carefully developed to lead through varied ecosystems with good wildlife observation. The 0.5-mile paved Creef Cut Wildlife Trail, at Milltail Rd. and US 64, features a disabled-accessible fishing platform, a 250-foot boardwalk, and an observation platform in a migratory bird impoundment. The 0.5-mile Sandy Ridge Wildlife Trail explores a cypress swamp with 2,300 feet of boardwalk; to find it, take US 64 west for 9.7 miles from the Manteo bridge, then go left onto the good dirt-surfaced Buffalo City Road, which ends at the trailhead in 2.2 miles. This trailhead is also an important canoe and kayak access point; four small blackwater streams wander away from here, with a total of 15 miles of maintained water trails. The Farmlands contain many dike-top foot trails, and a wildlife vehicle trail has been designated along several of its sand roads. To its south, more dike roads lead deep into the forest.

If you look at the refuge on the map, you will note that a large rectangle has been sliced out of its southern half. This is a naval bombing range, and when it isn't being strafed (which is most of the time), it's open as a state game land. If this range were ever incorporated into the refuge, the refuge would be nearly 200,000 acres!

Lake Mattamuskeet National Wildlife Refuge (252-926-4021; fws.gov/mattamuskeet; mattamuskeet@fws.gov), 38 Mattamuskeet Rd., Swan Quarter 27885. Open all year; most impoundment levies are closed Nov.–Feb. Hunting requires a refuge permit, issued via a lottery. Established in 1934, this 50,000-acre refuge encircles the 40,000-acre Lake Mattamuskeet, a natural oval 14 miles long and 5 miles wide; its lakeside headquarters is about 10 miles east of Swan Quarter via US 264, then north 0.7 mile on Headquarters Road. This very shallow lake is encircled by paved state roads, and bisected by NC 94, which crosses it on a causeway for good fishing access and great views. A network of canal dikes around the headquarters gives year-round access to the lake, canal fishing, and bird-watching; this is a major migration destination, and over 100,000 tundra swans, snow geese, and Canadian geese overwinter here. Two more impoundments, one on each end of the lake, are closed during the migration season (Nov.–Feb.), but are open to dike walking the rest of the year.

Its most remarkable site, however, is Mattamuskeet Lodge, now owned by the state and under restoration at press time. Built in 1914 as a pumping station (the world's largest, meant to drain the lake into farmland) and later converted into a hunting lodge, this grand old structure straddles the large outflow canal, its elegant lines and peculiar tower reflected in the still waters. When finished it will hold a conference center and lodge with 16 rooms, a restaurant, and a small museum.

MORE PUBLIC LANDS OF THE ALBEMARLE PENINSULA (game land maps: ncwildlife.org/Hunting/H_GL_Maps_Coast.htm). The following four public tracts, together totaling 83,500 acres, all provide worthwhile opportunities for hiking, wildlife observation, and bird-watching.

Alligator River State Game Lands. Located on the west shore of Alligator River, to the south of US 64, this tract provides numerous old canal banks that penetrate deep into the hardwood marshes. Of particular note is a 600-acre set of waterfowl impoundments with easy dike-top walking, 8.7 miles east of Columbia, then right on a dirt road.

Buckridge State Game Lands. This large area on the west shore of Alligator River, 13.6 miles south of Columbia via NC 94, features a long and fascinating drive (be sure to download the game land map) to a very remote boat launch on the Alligator River, as well as many good opportunities to explore the forests on foot.

Swanquarter National Wildlife Refuge. Founded in 1932, this large refuge surrounds the village of Swan Quarter (note the different spelling). It's mainly water and makes for fine boating, with several ramps in the area. Its Bell Island Dock is a remote 1,000-foot-long fishing pier in Rose Bay, with good fishing and great views, located off US 264 1.6 miles west of NC 45, then right on a dirt road to its end in 2.0 miles.

Gull Rock State Game Lands. Outfall Canal Road, impressively remote and empty even by Albemarle Peninsula standards, leads 6.7 miles south from US 264 (2.3 miles west of NC 94), passing through these game lands to end at a boat ramp on Pamlico Sound. At 5.6 miles a side track bridges the wide canal to explore deep into the game lands.

PARKS AND GARDENS **Merchants Millpond State Park** (252-357-1191; ncparks.gov/Visit/parks/memi/main.php; merchants.millpond@ncmail.net), 176 Millpond Rd., Gatesville 27938. Admission is free. Located at the far northwestern edge of this chapter's area (22 miles west of US 17 via US 158), this 3,200-acre park centers on a millpond built in 1811 to power a sawmill; it proved so successful that a variety of merchants grouped around it (hence its name), staying in operation until the mid-1940s. Today the 760-acre millpond has matured into an impressive cypress forest with open water at the very center. It's prime canoeing, and a concessionaire offers rentals. A cypress forest with some surprisingly ancient trees lines the upstream creek, and 11 miles of trail explore the backcountry. There's picnicking and family camping, a canoe-only campsite, and a backpack-only campsite.

College of the Albemarle Wetlands Boardwalk, Elizabeth City. Located on the campus of this community college, this 0.5-mile boardwalk wanders through marsh-forests to reach and follow a canal. When this empties into the Pasquotank River the boardwalk swerves over the river water and stays there, for 0.25 mile, then swerves back into the park at the rear of the campus. Along the way are benches, viewing platforms, and a gazebo (where barn swallows nest during the summer). You'll find it 3 miles north of the city via US Bus 17 to a right turn into the college at Coa Drive; the paved trailhead parking is 0.2 mile ahead on the left.

Pettigrew State Park and Lake Phelps (252-797-4475; ncparks.gov/Visit/parks/pett/main.php; pettigrew@ncmail.net), 2252 Lake Shore Rd., Creswell 27928. Admission is free. This large park in the middle of the Albemarle Peninsula includes 5,000 land acres, and the entire 16,600-acre surface of Lake Phelps. This natural lake is unusual for the area in having clear water, all of it furnished from rainfall; its surface, at 10 feet above sea level, is a local high point. Parklands largely encircle the lake, with hiking and bike-hike trails following the shoreline for 8.5

miles. The main park headquarters, at the lake's northernmost point, has picnicking, camping, and a fishing pier and boardwalk. There are several overlooks around the lake, including one at a remote southern tract, reachable from Shore Road, which branches right from Newland Road 6.9 miles east from Roper.

RIVERS Scuppernong River. One of two North Carolina rivers to give its name to a major plant species (the Scuppernong grape, the other being the Catawba rhododendron), the Scuppernong provides more than 14 miles of beautifully forested blackwater paddling, lined by hardwood marsh-forests. Amazingly, this twisty little wonder was used as a navigable stream during antebellum days, delivering goods and picking up crops from the plantations along it. Pettigrew State Park owns much of its banks, and maintains it as a water trail. Canoe and kayak access is at Newland Road and Spruill Bridge, and at Cross Landing Road farther downstream. Take-out is at the visitors center in Columbia, where the river becomes a tidal inlet.

ESTUARIES Albemarle Sound. Formed by the flooded mouth of the Roanoke River, Albemarle Sound stretches inland for 55 miles, ranging from 5 to 20 miles wide. Its northern shore is broken by three major inlets, each a mile wide, and on each a large town with some seriously good recreational boating facilities: Elizabeth City at the head of the Pasquotank River Inlet (where it passes the Intracoastal Waterway); Hertford at the head of the Perquimans River Inlet; and Edenton at the mouth of the Chowan River Inlet. Plymouth sets at the head of Albemarle Sound a short distance up the Roanoke River, and Columbia at the head of the (comparatively) small inlet of the Scuppernong River. Finally, the massive Alligator River, wholly wild, is the name given to the sound's southeastern inlet. There are many lesser inlets scattered about, and some narrow sand beaches as well; wild lands dominate, particularly along the southern shore.

✷ To See

CULTURAL SITES Arts of the Albemarle, Elizabeth City (252-338-6455; artsofthealbemarle.com; info@artsaoa.com), 516 E. Main St., P.O. Box 11, Elizabeth City 27907. This art center occupies an 1895 department store at the center of Elizabeth City's downtown, recently renovated and repurposed. Its gallery features works (including works for sale) from local and regional artists, plus solo and shared exhibits once a month. Also in the building is the Maguire Theater, with 250 seats, the home of Encore Theater Company, a community group.

The North Carolina Estuarium (252-948-0000; partnershipforthesounds.org; Estuarium@embarqmail.com), 223 E. Water St., Washington 27889. Open Tue.–Sat., 10–4. $. Anchoring the eastern end of Washington's waterfront is this newly built science and nature museum. Facing the massive estuary of Pamlico Inlet—itself only a branch off an even larger estuary—the Estuarium is dedicated to letting visitors explore these inland coastal waters, the marshes that border them, and the way humans depend on them. More than 200 artifacts include works of art, aquariums and terrariums with live estuary creatures, and historic boats. There's a 0.7-mile boardwalk along the estuary, and pontoon boat tours of the Pamlico waters (included in the admission).

HISTORIC SITES **Historic Edenton State Historic Site** (252-482-2637; Edenton State Historic Site: nchistoricsites.org/iredell; harrietjacobs.org; edenton @ncdcr.gov), 108 N. Broad St., Edenton 27932. Open daily; trolleys run Tue.–Sat. $–$$, depending on how many buildings you choose to visit. Noted for the stunning harbor views from its historic center, Edenton is home to a number of significant historic structures open to the public. These have been loosely organized into the Edenton State Historic Site, with an interpretive center and tours that visit five colonial and early republic buildings. The interpretive center occupies the restored Ziegler House on the north edge of downtown, built in 1892 and positively modern by Edenton standards. It has exhibits and an AV feature, as well as a gift shop. From there you can choose a walking tour to any or all of the five buildings they present, including the interiors, with the price varying in proportion; tours go out three times a day (once on Sunday). Trolley tours are available as well, visiting only the outsides of the buildings but covering more of this beautiful little town; these have six departures a day, Tue.–Sat. Two self-directed walking tours are also available, visiting exteriors only, one concentrating on architecture, and the other presenting the town from the point of view of escaped Edenton slave Harriet Jacobs, who wrote of her life in Edenton in her 1861 memoir *Incidents in the Life of a Slave Girl, as Told by Herself.*

CHOWAN COUNTY'S COLONIAL COURTHOUSE IN EDENTON, BUILT IN 1767 AND STILL IN USE

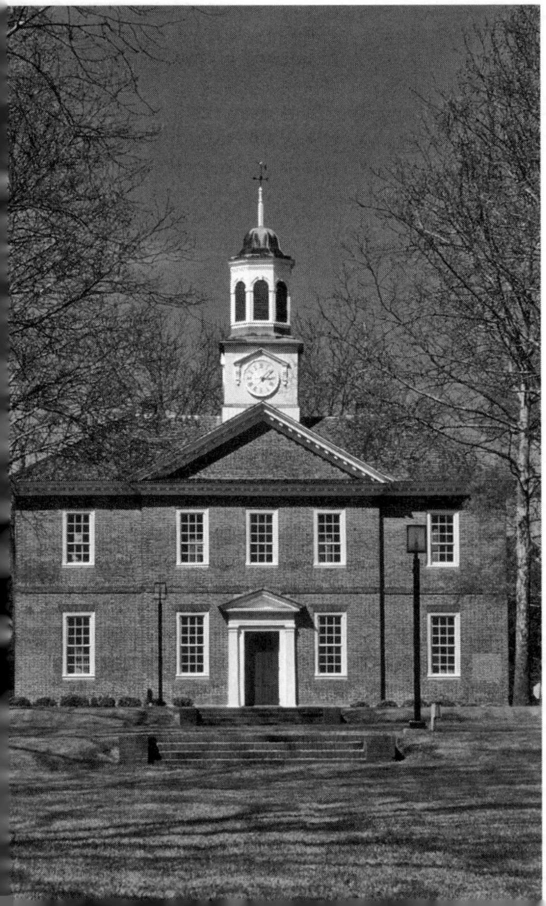

Here are the five buildings:

The **Iredell House**, whose oldest wing dates from 1756, was the home of early Supreme Court Justice James Iredell, whose opinions on judicial review and press freedom have influenced court opinions ever since. The house is fully furnished in Iredell's period, and has a number of outbuildings, including a kitchen and a one-room schoolhouse.

The elegant red-brick **Chowan County Courthouse**, set in its own large park across from the waterfront, has been cited as the finest Georgian public structure in the East. Built in 1755, it is still occasionally used as a courthouse.

The **Barker House**, built in 1782, stands catawampus across the street from the courthouse, its two story porches facing the sound. Owned and operated by the Edenton Historic Commission, it is fully restored inside and has a fine gift shop. It is the only one of the five whose interior can be visited without arranging a tour; it's open daily, with free admission, and its porches become a local gathering place on a fine day.

The 1736 **St. Paul's Episcopal Church** is a beautiful little brick structure set in a large churchyard, at what was then the northern edge of town. It is dwarfed by its tower and steeple—added in 1809, at the same time that it acquired the woodwork you see today. It's an active church with a congregation of 700.

The luxurious 1758 **Cupola House** was one of the nation's earlier public historic restorations, saved in 1918 and still run by the group that saved it, the Cupola House Association. Named after its odd rooftop ornament, it's furnished as an early republic great house. It's best known for its elaborate Georgian vernacular woodwork, and for its stunning gardens, created in the 1970s as a careful re-creation of colonial practices.

The Newbold-White House, Hertford (252-426-7567; perquimansrestoration.org), 151 Newbold-White Rd., P.O. Box 103, Hertford 27944. The oldest surviving house in North Carolina, the 1730 Newbold-White House sits in farmland along the wide Perquimans River Inlet, 2.5 miles south of the center of Hertford via US Bus 17, becoming Harvey Point Road as it crosses US 17. It's a simple brick structure with little decoration—not surprising, given that its builders were Quakers. Indeed, this site had already been at the center of a Quaker farming community for 60 years when it was built, and its solid construction shows how well its owners had prospered. The interior is fully furnished as its original family would have known it, and has a period kitchen garden in front. The site also includes a re-creation of the vineyard known to have existed here, growing the muscadine grapes first discovered in the Albemarle region. A 0.5-mile trail leads between forests and fields to the wide inlet of the Perquimans, ending at a pier.

The Museum of the Albemarle, Elizabeth City (252-335-1453; moa@ncdcr.gov), 501 S. Water St., Elizabeth City 27909. Open Tue.–Sat. 9–5, Sun. 2–5. This attractive new history museum sits directly opposite Elizabeth City's waterfront park. Its 700 artifacts tell the story of the counties of the Albemarle Sound, including two complete buildings, a 1755 smallholder's planked log farmhouse, and an antebellum smokehouse, fully furnished.

Historic Hope Plantation, Windsor (252-794-3140; hopeplantation.org; hopeplantation@coastalnet.com), 132 Hope House Rd., Windsor 27983. Open Mon.–Sat. 10–3:30. $$. Wealthy and precocious, Tidewater plantation heir David Stone graduated from Princeton in 1788, a rising star of a new generation after the lions of the Revolution. Hope Plantation, which he designed and built in 1803, expresses his academic interests in architecture, a fusion of Georgian and classical styles not unlike the more grandiose structures of the later antebellum age. Stone would become governor of North Carolina only five years later, and go on to be a U.S. senator. Owned and operated by the not-for-profit Historic Hope Foundation, the mansion is carefully furnished to its original period, closely following the inventory made of Stone's estate upon his death in 1818. Also on-site is a vernacular farmer's house from 1763, known as the King-Brazmore House, an unusual and attractive structure furnished from the inventory of its 1778 owner. There are nature trails and picnic tables on the 45-acre site.

Roanoke River Lighthouse and Maritime Museum, Plymouth (252-217-2204; roanokeriverlighthouse.org), W. Water St., Plymouth 27962. Open Tue.–Sat. 11–3. Located in a riverside park by downtown Plymouth, this is a full-sized, authentic replica of a manned channel light, once common on the inland waters of North Carolina. It's a cottage on stilts, with a light atop its gabled red roof—a very

THE PALMER-MARSH HOUSE IN HISTORIC BATH

striking sight, even when land-bound. Inside are exhibits on Plymouth's booming port in the 19th century. Across the street, the same local not-for-profit runs the fine Maritime Museum, whose many exhibits center on a locally built 1889 vernacular fishing boat.

Port o' Plymouth Museum (252-793-1377; porto@plymouthnc.com), 302 E. Water St., P.O. Box 296, Plymouth 27962. Open Tue.–Sat. 9–4. This delightful little museum occupies Plymouth's 1923 brick railroad depot, on the Roanoke River waterfront. Outside are restored railroad cars, and a riverside boardwalk to which is moored a working replica of the CSS *Albemarle*, an ironclad proto-submarine known as a "ram ship." Inside, the museum is dedicated to the April 1864 Battle of Plymouth, a Confederate naval victory at the nearby head of the Albemarle Sound.

Somerset Place State Historic Site (252-797-4560; nchistoricsites.org/somerset; somerset@ncdcr.gov), 2572 Lake Shore Rd., Creswell 27928. Open daily, Mon.–Sat. 9–5, Sun. 1–5; shorter hours in winter. Admission is free. This ambitious state historic site presents an entire plantation erected on the shores of Lake Phelps in 1785; you'll find it adjacent to Pettigrew State Park. It centers on the lakeside Collins House, a classic Big House with nearly 7,000 square feet of living space behind its columned double porch, carefully furnished to period. To its side is its formal garden, laid out as it might have been around 1810. The site goes well beyond that, however, with a dozen or so outbuildings, some reconstructed, showing the farmyard that always sat behind the Big House. This would be a busy and squalid zone, the domain of the farm's enslaved labor, with slave quarters, laundry, smokehouse, and central kitchen grouped around a yard of stamped dirt, where chores would be done and pigs slaughtered. It also included a slave hospital, a common feature of the largest plantations as a good slave could cost as much as a racehorse. This yard had to be sited carefully, concealing its sights, smells, and sounds from the family's elegant visitors, yet near enough to be kept under constant and careful surveillance. Indeed, this plantation would have been a brutal place for all but the owners and their friends, 100,000 acres hacked out of the dense marsh-forests by slave labor, including a navigable canal nearly 6 miles long. The rich peat soils grew rice, corn, oats, wheat, beans, peas, and flax, while the constant work of tree felling not only expanded the fields but also fed the plantation's sawmills.

✷ To Do

BICYCLE RENTALS Inner Banks Outfitters, Washington (252-975-3006), 1050 E. Main St., Washington 27889. Located by Washington's waterfront park on the eastern edge of town, this outfitter rents bicycles and kayaks all year, and offer bike and kayak tours during the summer.

BOAT RENTALS Edenton Harbor Kayak Rentals (252-482-2832). Open May–Sept., daily 9–9; Oct.–Apr., Mon.–Fri. 8–5. This concessionaire offers kayak and canoe rentals from the town of Edenton's harbor, at the foot of Broad Street.

Bath Harbor Marina (252-923-5711; bathharbor.com; Bathsail@aol.com), 101 Carteret St., Bath 27808. This busy little marina at the center of the quaint colonial village of Bath rents kayaks and canoes, sailboats, and powerboats, as well as offering sailing instructions.

Pungo Creek Marina, Belhaven (252-964-3777; pungocreekmarina.com; Randy@PungoCreekMarina.com), 1056 Hubs Rec Rd., Belhaven 27810. This marina, down a quite back road 3.4 miles east of Belhaven, offer kayak trips, and rents kayaks and sailboats.

BOATS MOORED IN THE PERQUIMANS RIVER AT HERTFORD

✷ Lodgings

BED & BREAKFASTS The Granville Queen Inn, Edenton (866-482-8534; 252-482-5296; granvillequeen.com; stay@granvillequeen.com), 108 S. Granville St., Edenton 27932. $$–$$$. Sitting in the middle of colonial Edenton's historic district, this 1907 mansion mirrors the grand appearance of an antebellum plantation house, with two-story columns, a wraparound porch, and second-story balconies. It has seven large and tastefully furnished rooms, with a choice of twins, queen, or king beds. WiFi is available. The gourmet breakfast, included in the tariff, is served 7–9, either in the elegant dining room on the enclosed sunporch.

The Trestle House Inn, Edenton (252-482-2282; trestlehouseinn.com; peter@trestlehouseinn.com), 632 Southside Rd., Edenton 27932. $$–$$$. Built as a retreat in 1972, this waterfront B&B is noted for being encircled on three sides by a landscaped wildlife pond, and for its beams made from California redwoods recovered from a railroad trestle. The 5-acre property is beautifully landscaped, with walking paths and a footbridge over the pond; canoes are available for exploring the small, wild lake that adjoins the property. The five rooms are spacious, with seating areas and exposed redwood beams. WiFi is available. The ample southern-style breakfast, included in the tariff, is served at 8:30, although business travelers can be accommodated with earlier times by prior arrangement.

COASTAL MARSH FARMLAND ALONG AN UNFENCED ROAD NORTH OF BELHAVEN

The Pack House Inn, Edenton (252-482-3641; thepackhouse.com; info@thepackhouse.com), 103 E. Albemarle St., Edenton 27932. $$–$$$. This striking B&B in a residential neighborhood of Edenton's historic district is a converted and restored tobacco packing house from 1915, moved to this spot in 1987. The two-story structure is long and low, with a full-length porch and an impressive mezzanine inside, over the common area. Decor has a homespun, country feel, with antiques and art from local artists. The eight rooms are very large, with spacious sitting areas. WiFi is available. A separate cottage in the back is the pet-friendly quarters; call ahead to make sure it's available. A full breakfast, included in the tariff, is served 8–9:30.

The Springfield Bed and Breakfast, Hertford (252-426-8471; springfieldbb.com; springfield@springfieldbb.com), 932 S. Edenton Road St., Hertford 27944. $$. This classic Victorian home, built in 1896 on the southern outskirts of pretty little Hertford, is run by the descendants of its original builder, who has carefully restored it to the look and feel of a country farmhouse. It sits on a working farm, and its barn contains a collection of turn-of-the-century farm equipment. The three large rooms have sitting areas, and have a choice of twin or queen beds. WiFi is available. The large country breakfast is served at 8 (8:30 on Sundays). If you are traveling with a pet you must call ahead to make arrangements.

The Pond House Inn, Elizabeth City (888-335-9834; 252-335-

9834; thepondhouseinn.com; innkeeper@thepondhouseinn.com), 915 Rivershore Rd., Elizabeth City 27909. $$–$$$. Built in 1941 in the European Manor House style, the Pond House sits on its own 6 acres in the middle of Elizabethton's finest residential section, surrounded by ponds. The ponds are dotted with islands that are linked by footbridges, a lovely garden touch. It has four large rooms with sitting areas and either queen or king beds, plus a pet-friendly suite with two queen beds and a micro fridge. Breakfast, included in the tariff, is chosen from a menu the night before and served 7–9, with a continental breakfast available for early risers.

The Four Gables Bed and Breakfast, Plymouth (252-202-5492; fourgablesbandb.com; requests@fourgablesbandb.com), 109 W. Main St., Plymouth 27962. $$. This 1870 house, built by a returning Civil War officer as a present for his bride, sits just behind downtown Plymouth a block off its scenic waterfront. Built in a cross between Gothic and neoclassical, it has a wide porch and a grassy back lawn facing a little goldfish pond with a trickling waterfall. Its three bedrooms, tastefully decorated with Victorian antiques, are large enough for sitting areas, and feature queen or double beds. A full breakfast, served at 8:30, is included in the tariff.

The Pamlico House, Washington (252-946-5001; pamlicohousebb.com; info@PamlicoHouseBB.com), 400 E. Main St., Washington 27889. $$$. This splendid late-Victorian (c. 1906) mansion combines wide wraparound porches with two corner turrets and neoclassical details, an exuberant architectural mash-up in the heart of Washington's historic district. The five rooms range from large to spacious, and all have sitting areas and either king or queen beds. WiFi is available. The breakfast, included in the tariff, is a continental buffet on weekdays, and a full savory or sweet breakfast on weekends. Children over 6 are welcome; contact the landlords about younger children.

The Carolina House Bed and Breakfast, Washington (252-975-1382; carolinahousebnb.com; info@carolinahousebnb.com), 227 E. 2nd St., Washington 27889. $$–$$$. Located two blocks from Washington's attractive waterfront, and a block from its gentrifying red-brick downtown, this 1880 Victorian house has a straightforward farmhouse appearance, framed by picket fences. Its four rooms all have sitting areas (one is a two-room suite), and are furnished with both family antiques and period reproductions; twin, queen, and king beds are available, as is WiFi. The suite is en suite; the other rooms have baths in the rooms (with privacy curtains) or a private bath across the hall. A full breakfast is served at the guest's preferred time, generally 7–9. Children over 6 are welcome.

The Inn on Bath Creek, Bath (252-923-9571; innonbathcreek.com; info@innonbathcreek.com), 116 S. Main St., Bath 27808. $$$ (rooms)–$$$$ (suite). While this inn, just across the street from historic Bath's waterfront, looks like a historic structure, it was in fact purpose-built as a B&B in 1999, with all the modern amenities planned from the beginning. It looks like an early farmhouse, with wide porches, high ceilings, and dormers, and its interior is furnished accordingly. Its five rooms are all large, with sitting areas and individual heating and cooling controls; beds are queens and kings, and WiFi is available. A full breakfast is served, typically at 8:30, but other times will be accommodated upon request.

The Belhaven Water Street Bed and Breakfast (866-338-2825; 252-943-2825; belhavenwaterstreetbandb.com; ahfisher@embarqmail.com), 567 E. Water St., Belhaven 27810. $$. This century-old house at the center of Belhaven, a block from the water, has the neoclassical appearance of an antebellum plantation house. Its three rooms are all large, with sitting areas, water views, zone heating and cooling, gas log fireplaces. queen beds, and WiFi. Breakfast, included in the tariff, is either full or continental according to the guest's preference, and served at the guest's time.

✷ Where to Eat

DINING OUT **Pia's, Washington** (252-940-0600; chefpias.com), 156 W. Main St., Washington 27889. Open for lunch and dinner, Tue.–Sat. $$–$$$$. Chef and owner Pia Van Coutren, of Greek descent and raised in Sudan, presents New American cuisine with the world influences from her background in this downtown Washington restaurant. The substantial menu of tapas, seafood, steaks, and pasta offers imaginative approaches to familiar dishes. A more limited lunch menu offers soups, salads, sandwiches, and burgers at competitive prices, but with the same international flair.

EATING OUT **Chero's Market Café, Edenton** (252-482-5525), 112 W. Water St., Edenton 27932. Open daily for lunch, and Wed.–Sun. for dinner. $$. Located on historic Edenton's town harbor in a fine old brick building, this lunch and dinner spot is bright and pleasant, with eclectic antique decor. Its food features Carolina favorites made from scratch, and offered at surprisingly reasonable prices. It occasionally offers live entertainment in the evening, featuring local artists on acoustic instruments.

Waterman's Grill, Edenton (252-482-7733; watermansgrill.com), 427 S. Broad St., Edenton 27932. Open for dinner, Mon.–Sat. $$–$$$. Located in downtown Edenton's historic fish market, this informal eatery offers a wide range of fresh seafood, much of it local, in it two dining rooms and raw bar. There's a good selection of steak, chicken, pasta, and sandwiches as well on the large menu, and the excellent beers of Asheville's Highlands Brewing Company are available.

Kathy's Kreations and The Wildflower Café, Elizabeth City (252-331-1888; kathyskreationsonline.com; kathy@kathyskreationsonline.com), 422 S. Hughes Blvd., Elizabeth City 27909. Open for lunch weekdays. $$. Located in a cedar-sided cottage-like building on US 17 at the western edge of town, this lunch spot (whose owner-chef is a professional nutritionist) features healthy, delicious food made from fresh ingredients. The menu has burgers and grilled chicken offerings as well as sandwiches and salads, plus a special menu of items under 500 calories. A sister restaurant is nearby, in Kenyon Bailey Garden Supply, offering sandwiches, wraps, and panini from a brick courtyard.

Cypress Creek Grill, Elizabeth City (252-334-9915; cypresscreekgrill.com), 113 S. Water St., Elizabeth City 27909. Open for lunch and dinner, Mon.–Sat. $$–$$. This seafood restaurant occupies a brick storefront in downtown Elizabeth City, directly across from the harborside city park. The menu mixes traditional Carolina seafood with Texas, Creole, and Gulf Coast favorites, reflecting the owner-chef's Texas coast origins. There's a "petite portions" menu for those who want less than Texas-sized servings.

Mama's Pizza, Plymouth (252-793-4773), 416 US 64 E., Plymouth 27962. Open for lunch and dinner, Mon.–Sat. $$–$$$. Opened in 1986 by two brothers from Sicily, this modest-looking eatery by a Piggly Wiggly on US 64 features true Italian food. The owners prepare their red sauce on the premises and cook it the way their mama did, for many hours. In addition to pizzas and deep-dish pizzas, they have a good range of Italian entrées: Alfredo and red-sauce pastas, baked pastas (including manicottis and raviolis), and veal, eggplant, and chicken parmigianas.

Down on Mainstreet, Washington (252-940-1988; citylivenc.com:9090/nc/foodDining/clientPage.html?id=57&cid=1&city=7; downonmainstreet@embarqmail.com), 107 W. Main St., Washington 27889. Open daily for lunch and dinner. $$–$$$. Located in downtown Washington a block from the yacht-lined waterfront, this pleasant storefront café has a patio on its water side. The dishes center on traditional American fare, with a dash of originality, as well as scratch cooking from fresh ingredients, to raise them above the small-town norm.

Blackbeard's Slices and Ices, Bath (252-923-9444), 101 N. Main St., Bath 27808. Open for lunch and dinner, Tue.–Sun. $$–$$$. Set in an old schoolhouse at the center of this historic village (and named after its most famous resident), this is a pleasant and airy place with some serious culinary muscle hidden in the kitchen—an owner and chief pizza maker who learned his craft under a famed New York restaurateur, and a chef trained in a leading New England culinary school. Apart from pizzas and ice creams, expect excellent Italian entrées from fresh ingredients, and house-made baked desserts.

The Back Bay Café at Wine and Words, Belhaven (252-944-2870; wineandwords.biz; info@wineandwords.biz), 413 Pamlico St., Belhaven 27810. Open for lunch, Thu.–Sun., and dinner, Fri.–Sat. $$–$$$. The tiny, remote fishing village of Belhaven would probably be the last place you'd look for a sophisticated eatery inside a bookstore and wine shop. And yet, here it is, in an old farmhouse on the east edge of town, still going strong a decade after its founding. Their ever-changing menu centers on seasonal items from local farms and fishing boats.

THE TIDEWATER REGION: NEW BERN AND BEAUFORT

The southern half of the North Carolina Tidewater centers on the colonial capital of New Bern on the Neuse River's flooded tidal inlet, extending eastward to the coast, with the small adjacent ports of Beaufort and Morehead City, and 85 miles of beach. This district ends at a series of massive inland wooded marshes, including the Croatan National Forest, with the Wilmington urban area and Cape Fear lying to its south and west.

GUIDANCE **New Bern** (800-437-5767; visitnewbern.com; info@visitnewbern.com), 203 S. Front St., New Bern 28563. The New Bern/Craven County Convention and Visitors Center covers the south bank of the Neuse River Inlet, including the large U.S. Marine base at Havelock. They run an information desk inside the convention center (in downtown New Bern at the foot of the US Bus 17 bridge), and an excellent website.

Beaufort, Morehead City, and Emerald Isle (800-786-6962; 252-726-8148; crystalcoastnc.org; brochure@sunnync.com), 3409 Arendell St., Morehead City 28557. The Crystal Coast Tourism Authority covers beachfront Carteret County, with its two small towns. Its large and attractive visitors center sits on US 70 at the center of Morehead City, with a large public boat ramp at its rear.

GETTING THERE *By car:* From most directions you'll want to take US 70, an expressway for much of its length, eastward into this area. From Wilmington, take US 17 north. These two highways form the backbone of this region, crossing each other at New Bern.

By air: Wilmington's airport (ILM), full-service with a good choice of flights, is 90 miles to the south. Raleigh-Durham's airport (RDU) is the closest major hub, 130 miles to the west.

By bus or train: **Greyhound** (greyhound.com) buses run twice a day between Raleigh and New Bern, then continue on to Jacksonville and Wilmington. This area has no train service.

MEDICAL EMERGENCIES **Carolina East Medical Center, New Bern** (252-633-8111; carolinaeasthealth.com), 2000 Neuse Blvd., New Bern 28560. This 350-bed facility, run by an independent foundation, is in the center of New Bern on NC 55, 2 miles west of downtown.

Carteret General Hospital (252-808-6000; ccgh.org), 3500 Arendell St., Morehead City 28557. The local not-for-profit hospital, with 240 beds, is located at the center of Morehead City on US 70.

✷ Exploring the Area

EXPLORING ON FOOT **The Neusiok Trail** (triangleoutdoors.com/trails/Neusiok.htm). The 20-mile Neusiok Trail, traversing the eastern edge of the Croatan National Forest, yields the most prolonged and intimate view of an inland coastal marsh-forest in the state. Ideal for backpacking, it runs from the south shore of the Neuse River Inlet at Cherry Point Recreation Area (near the ferry), southward to Oyster Point Recreation Area, just north of Morehead City, with three shelters with pump water supplies equally spaced along the way. (Boil the water before drinking.) The northern segment is the most scenic, with a prolonged walk along the shores of the Neuse, first on a sand beach, and then on bluffs above it. From there it turns southward, crossing through open grassy pinelands and tunneling through thick pocosin jungles, crossing streams and marshes on boardwalks (one over 0.4 mile long).

FEEDING THE GULLS FROM THE CHERRY BRANCH FERRY

EXPLORING BY BOAT **The Intracoastal Waterway in the Southern Tidewaters**. In this 83-mile section the Intracoastal Waterway completes its overland shortcut through the inland marshes of the Tidewater Region, to find its final home in the narrow gap between the mainland and its barrier islands. After the 5-mile crossing of Pamlico River Inlet it once again uses a narrow tidal stream, Goose Creek, to cut overland through farmland and marsh, reaching the Neuse River Inlet (via Bay River, a substantial tidal inlet) in 11 miles. It spends the next 22 miles in the mouth of the Neuse, here up to 7 miles wide, passing the superb recreational port of **Oriental** about halfway (and 48 miles from the previous port of Belhaven). From here another 18 miles cross-country brings you to the dual harbor

WHY DON'T THEY FINISH THE INTRACOASTAL WATERWAY?
Basically, things changed between the Intracoastal Waterway's conception in 1919 and the abandonment of its construction in 1971. Originally it was meant to be a protected inland route for commercial shipping—protected from both bad weather and enemy submarines. This became less important after the 1940s; we had no enemies brazen enough to threaten our shipping, and improved weather forecasting (starting with the invention of radar during World War II) made storms less of a problem. This left the waterway's commercial shippers dealing with interminable waits at a seemingly never-ending series of drawbridges, many of which opened on a fixed schedule as seldom as once an hour. Hit a drawbridge at the wrong time and you cool your heels for 59 minutes, burning diesel and paying your crew the whole time; then you putter along for a mile or two, and stop at another bridge. When satellites allowed really accurate storm tracking in the 1970s, commercial carriers abandoned the drawbridge-strewn canal for all but the shortest hauls or the worst weather. There are fewer drawbridges today, and they (like modern traffic lights) are better timed, but the problem remains, and has been compounded by shoaling. Because commercial traffic taxes pay for the canal's upkeep, low traffic means poor maintenance, and sand is allowed to drift into the canal. This is irritating for recreationists, but fatal to commercial carriers, who can't sit around waiting for the tide to add another 2 feet of water so they can float over a shoal (to the next drawbridge).

The two missing segments are both in Florida. The first is the most famous: The Cross Florida Barge Canal would have connected the Gulf and

of **Morehead City** and **Beaufort**, with every service imaginable. Now the canal follows the lagoon between the mainland and **Emerald Isle**, fully developed yet blessedly free of drawbridges, for 26 miles to swerve past the attractive and historic village of **Swansboro**, with full yacht facilities. In the next 4 miles it runs well behind wilderness **Hammock Beach State Park**, separated from its superb sands by a maze of twisting creeks and shifting shoals. Beyond here it enters the Wilmington area, described in the next chapter.

✷ Towns

Oriental. This attractive little village, commanding the mouth of the Neuse River Inlet, boasts that it has more boats than people. This is probably accurate, as Oriental, with fewer than 900 permanent residents, has several large and busy marinas, as well as an active seafood dock thick with shrimpers and other small commercial fishers. The main docks are on its southern end by a long bridge, a county road that links it with the **Cherry Point free ferry**.

Atlantic Intracoastals straight across the peninsula. It would've been a boon for shipping in 1919. However, by the time funding finally started in the late 1960s, scientists had learned that the water supplies of Orlando and Tampa (both insignificant towns in 1919) depended on underground water flows from the Okeefenokee area, which would be disrupted or destroyed by the deep channel. What's more, economic analysis showed only one large commercial user left standing after the massive changes since 1919 (that being Jacksonville's coal-fired power plant operator). President Richard Nixon ordered the waterway's defunding in 1971, after all its right-of-way had been purchased and about a third of it constructed; Congress made this official almost exactly 20 years later. The state of Florida is now converting this corridor into the Marjorie Harris Carr Cross Florida Greenway, named after one of the canal's opponents.

The other missing link would have cut along the marshy northwestern edge of the Florida peninsula, a nearly uninhabited area known as the Big Bend. Geologically it is the end of the coastal South's inland marsh belt, which starts far to the north at Virginia's Dismal Swamp; it's extremely environmentally sensitive, and now nearly completely protected by a series of national and state wildernesses, which would have to be explicitly disestablished by acts of Congress before a canal could be built. While Congress did authorize a canal through here in 1967 (to connect with the Cross Florida), it was never funded, studied, or plotted on the ground. It would have probably been 250 miles long, stretching between the current Intracoastal termini behind St. George Island on the north and at the Anclote River (Tarpon Springs) to the south.

New Bern. Located at the head of the Neuse River Inlet, this historic little city of 30,000 came to brief prominence as North Carolina's capital from 1770 to the mid-1794. Its capitol building, **Tryon Palace**, has been accurately and completely rebuilt on its original foundations, and is the centerpiece of one of the state's finest historic districts. New Bern faces a large, newly rebuilt yacht-lined harbor on the Neuse, with hotels, parks, and a convention center along the water. Its traditional downtown, filled with nice shops and restaurants, fills a six-block area adjacent to the waterfront, and includes the pharmacy where Pepsi-Cola was invented in 1898 (now a museum). Although US 17 and 70 once went directly through the center of town, in the last two decades these highways have been rebuilt as expressways that bypass the town to its west and south.

Beaufort and Morehead City. These two towns face each other across the Newport River, a tidal inlet about 1.5 miles wide, connected by a bridge and causeway carrying US 70. Beaufort (pronounced *BOE-fort*), on the eastern side, is the older, smaller, and more historic of the two. Now a town of about 5,000, it was founded in the early colonial era as a fishing port, and retains the atmosphere of an old sea town. Its main street directly faces the harbor, now filled with yachts, and old captains' homes line the western edge of the waterfront. Here you'll find **North Carolina's Maritime Museum**, dedicated to the history of the state's contact with the sea. Morehead City, on the opposite side of the inlet, is twice as large and much busier. Founded in the early 1850s as the sea terminus of the North Carolina Railroad (then one of the longest in the world), it continues its original function as a deepwater, container-friendly port. It has a sizable fishing fleet, and a group of seafood restaurants group around it on the far eastern edge of town, facing the water.

Swansboro. This pretty little town of 1,500 occupies a bluff above the tidal inlet known as White Oak River, about halfway between Jacksonville and Morehead City. It is known for its fine historic district, centered on a one-block downtown facing its waterfront, a block off the main highway, NC 24. The landward headquarters and ferry station for wilderness **Hammock Beach State Park** is just outside town.

* Green Spaces

PUBLIC LANDS **Croatan National Forest**. This 250-square-mile tract forms a large inland crescent stretching from New Bern to Morehead City and Beaufort. Its scenery is dominated by open, grassy pine forests (called savannas) and the dense and impenetrable pocosin marshes, but it has five natural lakes as well, all

SUNRISE OVER EMERALD ISLE

very wild in character. Like other national forests in the Atlantic coastal plains, the Croatan has long been managed for timber and hunting, but in the last few decades recreation and conservation have slowly emerged as priorities, and good opportunities are available. Chief among these are the 2 miles of trail and boardwalk through the coastal marshes of **Cedar Landing**, and the 20-mile-long **Neusiok Trail** along its eastern edge. The largest of the lakes, Great Lake, has a good boat ramp suitable for small boats, while remote Catfish Lake has a semi-developed boat ramp down a sand road. The forest has a respectable frontage along the Neuse River Inlet and has created three picnic areas fronting the water, with narrow but natural sand beaches.

Cape Lookout National Seashore (252-728-2250; nps.gov/calo), 131 Charles St., Harkers Island 28531. A visitors center on Harkers Island is open daily all year, 9–5. Ferries run Mar.–Dec. This national park preserves 58 miles of wild beach on two uninhabited islands. Core Banks runs nearly 45 miles southward from a point just across from Ocracoke to Cape Lookout itself, then doubles back to add another 4 miles of beach behind the cape. This is separated from east–west Shackleford Banks, with another 9 miles of beach, by narrow Barden Inlet, a scant 0.5 mile wide and shoaling up. (Core Banks itself is now split in half by New Drum Inlet, which opened in the mid-20th century.) Both islands can be reached by ferries under concession from the National Park Service.

Core Banks is the most visited and has the most to do. Its three historic districts include the reconstructed Banker village of Portsmouth on its extreme north, the stunning Cape Lookout Lighthouse, and the ruins of a Coast Guard station a mile south of the lighthouse. The cape itself is about 3 miles south of the lighthouse—the actual distance depending on your map, as the cape has been growing rapidly seaward during the last few decades. Even though Core Banks is uninhabited, it isn't completely wild. You can have your four-wheel-drive vehicle, and even a trailer, ferried over; and you can rent one of several (very primitive) cabins. The immense length of the beach, and the limited number of auto slots on the ferries, keep the island wild and empty in character.

Shackleford Banks, shorter and much less visited, is the home of the Outer Banks' largest remaining herd of wild horses. It is truly wild in character, with no structures and no vehicles. The western half of Shackleford has remarkable dunes, some up to 35 feet high, in contrast with Core Banks where dunes over 6 feet are largely lacking.

Facilities: There's an auto-accessible visitors center at the farthest end of Harkers Island, 20 miles east of Beaufort via US 70 and Harkers Island Road, but there's not much there besides an information desk and a museum. The main action is on the islands. Core Banks has four developed areas. Portsmouth, a completely reconstructed Banker town from the 19th century, is described in the Outer Banks chapter. Then, about a third of the way down, comes Long Point, reachable by vehicle ferry from the village of Atlantic; it has cabins, water, and gasoline. Two-thirds of the way down (and on the other side of New Drum Inlet) is Great Island, reached by vehicle ferry from Davis, also with cabins, water, and gasoline. Finally, at the southern end of the island, is the lighthouse and Coast Guard station; there is no potable water, and vehicle access requires an 11-mile beach drive from Great Island. You can camp anywhere you want on the beach, but there is nearly no shade and no potable water except at Long Point and Great Island. The only facilities on Shackleford Banks are toilets at the two ferry landings at the back of the island; once you're there it's just you and the horses.

PARKS AND GARDENS Hammock Beach State Park (910-326-4881; ncparks.gov/Visit/parks/habe/main.php; hammocks.beach@ncmail.net), 1572 Hammocks Beach Rd., Swansboro 28584. The office is open 8–6 daily in summer, 8–5 daily the rest of the year. The ferry runs Apr.–Oct. While the park remains open to boaters while the ferry isn't running, it winterizes in November, making water unavailable until March. $. This 1,100-acre state park centers on Bear Island, a 4-mile-long barrier island noted for its stunning wilderness beach. Unlike other wild beaches in this chapter, Hammock Beach is easily reached via a 15-minute ferry; it also has a full range of facilities including flush toilets, bathhouses, and showers, as well as a beach-side tent campground, and a second creek-side campground that's accessible only by kayak or canoe. The island was originally a private preserve owned by pioneer neurosurgeon Dr. William Sharpe. At the behest of his caretaker and friend John Hurst, Dr. Sharpe willed the island to North Carolina's African American teachers association, which maintained it as a minority-only beach under the segregation laws of the era. It became a state park in 1961, and, along with other segregated parks in the state, opened to all in 1964. Park headquarters, and the ferry dock, are located 2 miles west of Swansboro via Hammock Beach Road.

Cedar Point Recreation Area (cs.unca.edu/nfsnc/recreation/cedar_point.pdf). This Croatan National Forest picnic area, boat ramp, and campground is located on White Oak River, a very large tidal inlet just east of Swansboro off NC 58. It is best known for the 1.9-mile Tideland National Recreation Trail. This consists of two loops, an inner one 0.6 mile long that's disabled-accessible, and an outer one 1.3 miles long. These penetrate deep into the reedy coastal marshes on long boardwalks, with handsome little bridges over tidal creeks and wide views. The longer loop also penetrates deep into the adjacent forest on level, graded gravel trails, and reaches the shores of White Oak River.

Carrot Island (Rachel Carson Estuarine Preserve) (nccoastalreserve.net/About-The-Reserve/Reserve-Sites/Rachel-Carson/58.aspx). This 2,700-acre tract, part of the North Carolina National Estuarine Research Reserve, consists of a series of islands, marshes, and spoil banks immediately opposite Beaufort's harbor. It's best known for its population of wild horses, said to be descended from domestic horses placed here in the 1940s by a local resident. There are nature trails at its western end (the end closest to Beaufort's harbor), and a boardwalk opposite the boat ramp at the eastern end of Front Street. Private ferry services are available in Beaufort; inquire at the Maritime Museum.

ESTUARIES Core Sound. The northernmost of the coastal lagoons in this chapter, Core Sound marks the point where the backwaters of the Outer Banks suddenly narrow. Gone are the bays reaching up to 25 miles in width; from here down to Miami, a mile-wide lagoon will be unusually large. This, the first of the narrow backwaters, is somewhere in between, ranging between 2 and 3 miles wide in most places. The Core Banks portion of Cape Lookout National Seashore, the longest wild beach on the eastern seaboard, divides it from the sea. Its landward side is formed by low marshy ground, a peninsula that sits between Core Sound and the Neuse River Inlet. Here the high ground—a series of low sand hills and ridges—lines the sound, providing a platform for a series of small fishing ports: Smyrna,

WILD HORSE GRAZING ON CARROT ISLAND, IN THE RACHEL CARSON ESTUARINE PRESERVE, BEAUFORT

Davis, Sealevel, and Atlantic. These are all linked by US 70 (which terminates in Atlantic), and all have boat ramps and docks.

Bogue Sound. At the southern end of Core Sound, opposite Cape Lookout itself, the coast makes a sudden 90-degree turn west, and this turn marks a change in name: Back Sound as far as Beaufort, then Bogue Sound from Morehead City to Swansboro at the western end of this chapter. Apart from a sudden narrowing (to 0.25 mile) at Morehead City's busy commercial port, this remains an open, unobstructed water between 1 and 3 miles in width. Emerald Island, completely developed, divides it from the ocean, and residential development lines the sand hills of its landward side as well. The Intracoastal Waterway enters at Morehead City, to form a wide, marked channel along its landward coast.

Core and Bogue Sounds mark a sudden and dramatic change in the Atlantic coast's geology. North of here, the huge bays and sounds, all the way north as far as Philadelphia, are the result of the continent's edge sinking (holding sea level constant), literally bowing under the weight of the material eroded off the Appalachian Mountains. At Bogue Sound, however, the land begins to bow upward, emerging from the sea at the top of this enormous fold. From here to Charleston, South Carolina, you'll find high sandy shores and (starting in the next chapter) increasingly narrow lagoons; indeed, in places the open water disappears altogether, leaving only a narrow marsh. Maps trying to predict global warming's sea-level rise show the areas north of Bogue Sound sinking farther and faster than normal—but also show the areas west of it hardly sinking at all, as the natural continental rise keeps pace with the ocean-level rise.

BEACHES Cape Lookout National Seashore: Core Banks. The Atlantic coast's longest wild barrier island stretches for almost 45 miles, from Ocracoke

Inlet on the north to Cape Lookout on the south; there are, in fact, 49 miles of beach, due to the strand doubling back on itself for 4 miles at the cape. It breaks into two islands, and sometimes three islands, somewhere at the middle, a point known as New Drum Inlet. This inlet formed in the mid-20th century, replacing Old Drum Inlet 3 miles to its north. However, Old Drum Inlet occasionally reopens then shoals shut, and has repeated this several times in the last few decades; at press time it's open again. Both North and South Core Banks are narrow, with low dunes (less than 5 feet for the most part), and little by the way of trees or shade. The National Park Service (which owns and runs the island) allows private ferry concessionaires to carry vehicles over (for a very stiff price), so you can drive along the beach, and even bring over a camping trailer; potable water, however, can be found only at the two vehicle ferry termini.

Cape Lookout National Seashore: Cape Lookout. Much like Cape Fear to its south, Cape Lookout gets its dramatic name from its sinister reputation as the Graveyard of the Atlantic, a zone of unpredictably shifting shoals that has destroyed hundreds of ships and killed thousands of mariners. The cape itself illustrates this, having grown 0.5 mile south in the last century while shifting 400 feet west; air photos show more shoals being deposited for another 2 miles south. Diamond-shaped, the extreme tip sits 3 miles south of the Cape Lookout Lighthouse. The wide part of the diamond shelters a thinly treed maritime forest that extends as far as the lighthouse; here you'll find the stabilized remains of a Coast Guard base, slated for restoration as a historic district by 2016. The far end of the cape is particularly fascinating on a calm day, as the sand stretches far into the sea, so gradually losing its height and width that the point at which it finally disappears under the water can be difficult to determine, and changes quickly as the 2-foot tide ebbs and flows.

Cape Lookout National Seashore: Shackleford Banks (shacklefordhorses.org). Unlike Core Banks, east–west trending Shackleford Banks has no vehicles, no historic districts, no water, and no structures apart from the toilets at two ferry landings. What it has is true wilderness, including a large and well-developed maritime forest, and dunes that can reach 35 feet in height. It also has wild horses, the largest herd in the Outer Banks, healthy and people-shy.

Emerald Isle. Traditionally named Bogue Banks, this fully developed beach island stretches 25 miles westward from Morehead City. As its old name indicates, it's the last (or the first, depending on your direction) of the Outer Banks, but it is seldom now referred to as such, and an attempt during the 1990s to brand it as the "South Outer Banks" wrecked on the shoals of its initials. Except for a state natural area at its center (preserving a maritime forest) and a wild beach at its eastern tip, it is now wholly developed, a typical beach community with cottages, motels, resorts, condos, time-shares, and several fishing piers. It's broken into four small municipalities: Atlantic Beach on its eastern end, then Pine Knoll Shores, then an unincorporated area known as Salter Path, then Indian Beach, and finally Emerald Isle at its western end. Commercial facilities are scattered along its backbone highway, NC 58, which stretches for 19 miles along the back of the island, always two or three blocks away from the beach. Along this you'll find two major sites: **Fort Macon**, a perfectly preserved pre–Civil War brick fort at the east tip; and the **North Carolina Aquarium at Pine Knoll Shores** (see *To See* for both). The entire beach is wide and beautiful, and access points are plentiful. The far eastern end offers the best day access, 1.7 miles of wild beach with a fine dune line, bathhouses, summer lifeguards, and plentiful parking, part of Fort Macon State Park.

Emerald Isle Pier (ncaquariums.com/aquarium-piers/emerald-isle). Part of North Carolina's commitment to connect each of its three aquariums with beach piers, this pier will be located off Islander Drive, just east of the NC 58 bridge to the island. The tract will stretch from the beach to a canal leading to the lagoon, giving access to kayakers and sunbathers alike. At press time the plans had not been completed; look for a 2013 or 2014 opening.

✷ To See

CULTURAL SITES **Aurora Fossil Museum** (252-322-4238; aurorafossilmuseum.com; aurfosmus@yahoo.com), 400 Main St., P.O. Box 352, Aurora 27806. Open Mon.–Sat. 9–4:30; the fossil pit is open for collecting daily from sunrise to sunset. Admission is free. The village of Aurora (population about 500) sits at the center of a major mining district, where phosphates are extracted from large open-pit mines. These phosphate formations are rich in fossils, and the Aurora Fossil Museum presents the extraordinary richness and variety of these finds. It's a large facility in a restored red-brick downtown building, and its collections center on subtropical Atlantic specimens, including some monster sharks and whales. Its most popular feature, however, is a large pile of fresh fossil sands and clays, deposited in the front of the museum at regular intervals by the local phosphate mine, in which visitors may look for fossils without restriction. The Aurora fossils cover a period from about 20 million years ago to the present; dinosaurs, as a comparison, died out about 65 million years go. This means that the Aurora collections paint a picture of

SEARCHING FOR FOSSILS AT THE AURORA FOSSIL MUSEUM

the period that immediately led to the modern era, the configuration of land and water, plants and animals that we now recognize.

North Carolina Aquarium at Pine Knoll Shores (252-247-4003; ncaquariums .com/pine-knoll-shores; pksmail@ncaquariums.com), 1 Roosevelt Blvd., Pine Knoll Shores 28512. Open daily 9–5. $$. Like the other two state aquariums (at Fort Fisher and Roanoke Island), Pine Knoll Shores displays all the water-based wildlife of North Carolina, from river otters to sharks. In this case, the concentration is on those parts of the state through which the Neuse River and its tributaries run, from the mountains through the inlets and sounds of the coast, and out to the deep Atlantic. The 40 exhibits (one is a touching pool whose residents include a stingray) climax at a giant ocean tank centering on a shipwreck, with a number of sharks. The aquarium sits at the center of a 300-acre conservation site, the Theodore Roosevelt Natural Area, donated by President Roosevelt's grandson in honor of his grandfather's conservation efforts. This includes a marsh boardwalk and a 0.5-mile nature trail that crosses a pond on a pontoon bridge (part of the aquarium admission), and a mile-long nature trail that follows a relic sand dune through the heart of the natural area (and is free).

HISTORIC SITES **Tryon Palace, New Bern** (252-639-3500; tryonpalace.org), Open Mon.–Sat. 9–4, Sun. 1–4. $$$; a second day, however, can be added for $. The state's largest and most visually impressive historic site centers on an accurate and complete reproduction of the colonial capitol, a stunning red-brick mansion built by Governor William Tryon in 1770. Faced with a restive, rebellious populace, this newly appointed English aristocrat made it his first order of business to construct for himself one of the grandest mansions in North America—and raised taxes to pay for it. This was the proximate cause of the War of the Regulation, an armed uprising that Tryon suppressed with remarkable brutality. For this he was

TRYON PALACE, NEW BERN

BLACKSMITH WORKING AT TRYON PALACE STATE HISTORIC SITE

promoted to governor of New York. His successor also lived in the Palace, but enjoyed it only a few years before being run out of the colony at the start of the Revolution in 1775. From then it functioned as the capitol of an independent North Carolina, until the capital was shifted to Raleigh in 1794; the Palace burned to the ground four years later, with only a stable block surviving into the 20th century. The current grand structure, along with its stunning gardens, was built in the 1950s after its original plans were discovered and detailed archaeology had been performed.

The site you visit today occupies two entire blocks just west of downtown New Bern, and spills over into adjacent historic homes and buildings. The Palace itself is an elegant Georgian building with wide curving wings facing a courtyard, frankly meant to impress. Behind it stretch 16 acres of formal and informal gardens in the colonial style, reaching almost to the river; it is especially noted for its tulip displays in late March. The palace itself is furnished as in Governor Tryon's day, and is viewed on guided tours. Other Palace structures include the kitchens, stables, and blacksmith's shop, all staffed with costumed interpreters performing period tasks; these can be visited by either guided or self-guided tours. Also on the grounds is the 1830 Dixon House, fully restored; the grand Stanly House (c. 1780), where George Washington is said to have slept, is a few doors down. The most interesting of the separate houses is the most modest—the adjacent Hay House, recently restored to its exact 1835 condition and staffed by living history interpreters who portray the family and its neighbors.

The Tryon Palace experience has been significantly upgraded and expanded in recent years—first by the addition of the Hays House, then, in 2010, by the opening of a major new history museum, the North Carolina History Center. Built on a Superfund industrial site on the river, in a block between the Palace and downtown, this 6-acre, 60,000-square-foot complex is now the ticket office and introduction to the site. It is designed to look like a rebuilt harbor warehouse, but is completely new construction, purpose-built as a technologically advanced museum, centered on hands-on multimedia explorations of the New Bern area in 1835.

New Bern Firemen's Museum (252-636-4087; newbernfiremuseum.com), 408 Hancock St., New Bern 28560. Open Mon.–Sat. 10–4. $$. This museum, housed in a 1928 firehouse, shows what early firefighting was like in a small town, with displays of period fire equipment and trucks. New Bern's firefighting had a particularly raucous history. In the last year of the Civil War the town had both a Confederate and a Union fire company, and these two competing entities survived for decade after decade. Even the 1928 unified firehouse failed to join the two companies; each occupied its own end and had its own equipment. The rivalry between the two volunteer companies did not completely end until 2001, when the city hired its first full-time fire chief. This museum, first opened in 1955, was completely renovated in 2010.

Birthplace of Pepsi-Cola (252-636-5898; pepsistore.com), 256 Middle St., New Bern 28560. Open Mon.–Sat. 10–6. Admission is free. In this downtown New Bern storefront, pharmacist Caleb Bradham invented Pepsi-Cola in 1893—as a cure for an upset stomach. In 1902 he launched the Pepsi-Cola Company, then just a back room of this store, to manufacture and distribute his pepsin and kola nut syrup to soda fountains ("exhilarating, invigorating, aids digestion"). By 1910 he had franchised bottling rights to 250 companies in 24 states, and was on his way to creating a national brand. This came crashing down, however, in 1923, when he disastrously speculated in sugar futures and lost the entire shebang. The current Pepsico corporation, founded by Wall Street investors, purchased Bradham's routes and goodwill for $30,000, and Bradham went back to being a druggist. The Birthplace, run by the local Pepsi bottler, consists of history exhibits, memorabilia, and stuff for sale.

NORTH CAROLINA MARITIME MUSEUM IN BEAUFORT

North Carolina Maritime Museum, Beaufort (252-728-7317; ncmaritime.org; maritime@ncdcr.gov), 315 Front St., Beaufort 28516. Open Mon.–Fri. 9–5, Sat. 10–5, Sun. 1–5. Admission is free. This state-run museum in the center of Beaufort, facing the waterfront, occupies an attractive purpose-built structure designed to look like an old harbor building. It started in 1898 as an exhibit promoting North Carolina fisheries, taken to the International Fisheries Exposition in Norway; after that it ended up on display at the state's fisheries laboratory on Priver's Island, part of Beaufort's harbor. It expanded slowly over the decades and moved several times, becoming an official state museum in 1959 and getting its first curator in 1975. From then it quickly grew into an important historical museum and resource, moving into its current building in 1985. The museum is particularly noted for its exhibits on the U.S. Life-saving Service, on coastal watermen and how they earned their living, and most especially on its working watercraft. The latter includes a workshop, directly across the street, in which historic watercraft are made by hand, using traditional tools.

Fort Macon State Park (252-726-3775; ncparks.gov/Visit/parks/foma/main.php; fort.macon@ncmail.net), 2300 E. Fort Macon Rd., P.O. Box 127, Atlantic Beach 28512. Open daily 9–5:30. Admission is free. Built between 1826 and 1834, Fort Macon is an exceptionally well-preserved example of a series of coastal fortifications built in this period, a response to the near-drubbing the United States received during the War of 1812. Like other forts of the period, Fort Macon is a brick pentagon surrounded by a moat, with an earth-packed inner rampart protecting 26 brick-lined buried cylindrical rooms called "casements"; many of these have been furnished to their original occupied appearance, and the inner courtyard is the scene for historic reenactments. The mile-long beach along the Atlantic has a wild character, and is open for swimming with a bathhouse, lifeguard, and snack bar (in-season); the inlet-side beach, 0.5 mile long, is good for strolling and birdwatching, but is closed to swimming.

✷ To Do

BICYCLE AND KAYAK RENTALS **Rentals in Beaufort and Emerald Isle** (crystalcoastnc.org). Tourist-oriented Beaufort and the 25 miles of beach at Emerald Isle offer a wide selection of bicycle, kayak, and motorboat rentals—too many to list here. Consult the Crystal Coast website for a complete list with contact information.

MOTORBOATING **Galley Stores and Marina at Skipjack Landing** (252-633-4648; galleystores.com), 300 E. Front St., New Bern 28560. Located on the east side of downtown New Bern, this 25-slip marina caters to transient boaters, with fuel, a good restaurant, and a gourmet food store on premises; you can also rent bicycles.

Barnacle Bob's Boat and Jetski Rentals (252-634-4100; boatandjetskinewbern.com), New Bern Sheraton Marina, Dock F, New Bern 28560. Open Mon.–Sat. 9–7. Located in the downtown New Bern marina behind the Sheraton Hotel, this company rents pontoon boats and Jet Skis.

✷ Lodgings

HOTELS AND RESORTS

Broad Creek Guest Quarters, Fairfax Harbour, New Bern Area (252-474-5329; broadcreekguestquarters.com; broadcreekguestquarters@yahoo.com), 6111 Harbourside Dr., New Bern 28560. $$–$$$. These are marina-side condos on the Neuse River Inlet run as a small hotel, within a gated subdivision 15 minutes from New Bern. The six rooms are all full-sized studio apartments, individually furnished, with airy living rooms, seating areas, and dining areas; all have full kitchenette, WiFi, and queen bed (plus a sleeper sofa), and some have washer-dryer and/or screened porches. All guests have access to the harbor (of course), tennis and basketball courts, a campfire area, a sand volleyball pitch, a game room, a sauna and Jacuzzi, and a swimming pool. Continental breakfast makings are included in the kitchenette, and a fresh "pastry of the day" is included in the daily housekeeping. Pet fees apply.

BED & BREAKFASTS 🐾 **The Cartwright House Bed and Breakfast, Oriental, Neuse River Area** (888-726-9384; 252-249-1337; cartwrighthouse.com; innkeeper@cartwrighthouse.com), 301 Freemason St., P.O. Box 869, Oriental 28571. $–$$. This handsome historic home, built in 1903 with wraparound porches, sits in a quiet residential neighborhood a block from the waterfront of this remote village on the Neuse, where boats are said to outnumber residents. Each of its five rooms has enough space for a seating area, along with a gas fireplace, WiFi, and either a king or a queen bed. Breakfast, included in the tariff, comes in the form of a certificate (called "Cartwright currency") that can be redeemed at the pier-side Deli Bistro a few blocks away.

The Harmony House Inn, New Bern (800-636-3113; harmonyhouseinn.com; innkeeper215@yahoo.com), 215 Pollock St., New Bern 28560. $$–$$$$. Located on the edge of downtown New Bern, four blocks from the Tryon Palace, the 1809 Harmony House is unusual in that, in 1850, the feuding brothers who owned it sawed it in half and moved the two halves 9 feet apart, creating a center dividing hall between. And so it remains to this day, although the dividing walls have since had doors cut into them. It's a large and elegant home in a countrified neoclassical style, with a nice sitting porch. Its seven rooms and three suites are spacious and individually furnished, with WiFi and a choice of king, queen, or two twin beds. Breakfast, included in the tariff and always including a hot dish, is served buffet-style, 8–9 on weekdays and 8–9:30 on weekends. The tariff also includes wine and cheese in the evening.

The Pecan Tree Inn, Beaufort (800-728-7871; 252-728-6733; pecantree.com; innkeeper@pecantree.com), 116 Queen St., Beaufort 28516. $$–$$$$. This stunning Victorian mansion sits half a block off Beaufort's waterfront on a residential street. Built as a Masonic lodge in 1866, its elaborate first- and second-story porches were added when it was converted to a private home in 1900. Its backyard has been converted into a 5,000-square-foot English flower and herb garden, with stone paths that invite strolling. Its five rooms and two suites are spacious and airy, and some have bay windows; the suites are very large, with king beds. WiFi is available. The included continental breakfast is served buffet-style, 8–9:30.

✷ Where to Eat

DINING OUT The Chelsea, New Bern (252-637-5469; thechelsea.com; greatfood@thechelsea.com), 335 Middle St., New Bern 28560. Open for lunch and dinner Mon.–Sat. $$–$$$$. In the downtown New Bern red-brick building where Pepsi founder Caleb Bradham located his second pharmacy, the Chelsea is noted for an ambitious and innovative menu that takes a different slant on traditional dishes. The menu features fresh local seafood as well as beef and pasta dishes inspired by French, German, Italian, Asian, and Cajun originals. Casual dining and a bar are found downstairs, with a more elegant experience upstairs (accessible by elevator). Inexpensive sandwiches and burgers are available at dinner alongside the upscale and sophisticated entrées, a nice touch.

EATING OUT M&M's, Oriental, Neuse River Area (252-249-2000; pamlico-nc.com/restaurants/mandms.htm), 205 S. Water St., Oriental 28571. Open for breakfast, lunch, and dinner Wed.–Mon. (closed Tue.). $$–$$$. Listed as one of *Coastal Living*'s Top Ten Sailor's Hangouts, this attractive little restaurant sits across the street from Oriental's large and active fishery, a block east of NC 55. Not surprisingly it specializes in just-off-the-boat local seafood. The menu has all the old favorites, but goes well beyond them to feature intelligent and imaginative specials with seasonal local ingredients.

Morgan's Tavern, New Bern (252-636-2430; morganstavernnewbern.com), 235 Craven St., New Bern 28560. Open daily for lunch and dinner. $$–$$$. Located in a fine old redbrick Italianate building at the center of downtown New Bern, this pubby restaurant features exposed wood beams, hardwood floors, brick walls, and wooden pub tables, grouped around a large columned clock of the sort jewelers used to put in front of their shops 100 years ago. The expansive menu offers fresh local seafood, steaks, juicy burgers, sandwiches, and sophisticated dinner entrées, all made from scratch on the premises (including the croissants). Lunch features a large selection at a bargain price.

The Spouter Inn, Beaufort (252-728-5190; spouterinn.net; spouter@spouterinn.net), 218 Front St., Beaufort 28516. Open daily for lunch and dinner. $$–$$$$. This modest building, easily overlooked, sits quite literally on the Beaufort waterfront, overhanging the water with dock seating in the back. It combines a bakery, which opens every day for over-the-counter service for breads and pastries, with a full-service restaurant noted (natch) for its desserts. The inexpensive lunch menu has a fine selection of soups, salads, sandwiches, and pastas, while the more ambitious dinner menu always features fresh local fish.

WILMINGTON AND CAPE FEAR

Wilmington and the Cape Fear region offer the best of coastal tourism: fine beaches with stunning historic attractions. Most famous of the beaches is Cape Fear itself, so named for the danger it posed to mariners well into the 20th century, its shifting shoals part of the Graveyard of the Atlantic. Of course, when those shifting shoals wash up on shore they become beaches—wide and fluffy white, with handsome dunes. The Cape Fear region has a dozen different beaches, equally split between wild beaches and attractive old-fashioned beach towns.

Historic travel centers on Wilmington, a sophisticated little city facing the estuarine port of the Cape Fear River. A major shipping center since the early days of the Republic, Wilmington has a large and beautiful historic center, with antebellum mansions, museums, and a lively downtown that retains its red-brick charm. Wilmington's riverfront, its original port, is now the linear park Riverwalk, lined with stores on its landward side and yachts on its river side; its sunset views are not to be missed. To Wilmington's south, Southport has a colonial-era core behind its waterfront, and nearby Brunswick Town, a state archaeological site, preserves the impressive remains of Wilmington's early colonial competitor.

GUIDANCE Wilmington/Cape Fear Coast Convention and Visitors Bureau (877-406-2356; 910-341-4030; capefearcoast.com; wilmingtondowntown.com; visit@capefearcoast.com), 24 N. 3rd St., Wilmington 28401. The official tourism development authority for Wilmington and the surrounding New Hanover County offers information from their website, and from their visitors information center in the historic County Courthouse, downtown, on the corner of 3rd (US Bus 74) and Princess Streets. The organization Wilmington Downtown Inc. also has a good website.

Topsail (910-329-4446; topsailcoc.com; info@topsailcoc.com), 13775 NC 50, Suite 101, Surf City 28445. Remote Topsail Island's chamber of commerce website offers good information on visiting the island, from attractions and accommodations to avoiding traffic queues on a busy summer weekend.

Jacksonville (800-932-2144; onslowcountytourism.com), 1099 Gum Branch Rd., Jacksonville 28540. This agency and its website cover the northernmost part of this chapter's area. The visitors center, shared between the Tourism Development Authority and the chamber of commerce, sits in an area of recent development to

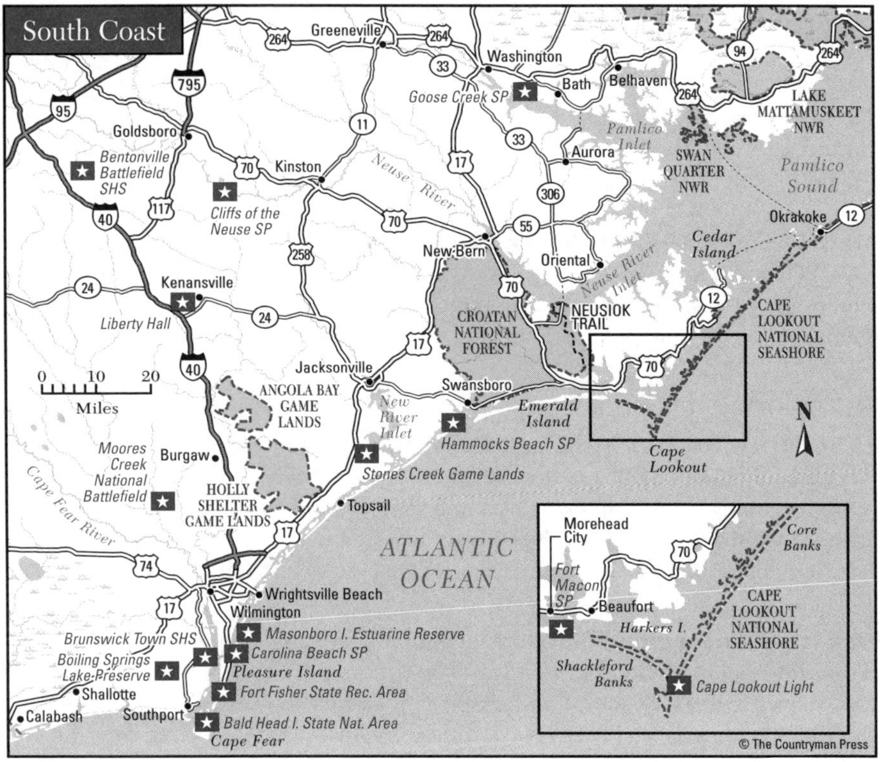

the northeast of town center; take US Bus 17 (Marine Boulevard) north to a right onto Gum Branch Road.

Southport and the Brunswick Islands (910-755-5517; official tourism site: ncbrunswick.com; chamber of commerce: brunswickcountychamber.org), P.O. Box 1186, Shallot 28459. The Brunswick County Tourism Development Authority promotes travel to the areas south of Wilmington. While it does not provide a walk-in visitors center, its website offers very thorough information.

GETTING THERE *By car:* America's great east–west interstate, I-40, starts on the northern edge of Wilmington, then runs northwest to reach Raleigh in 120 miles. US 74, four-lane and occasionally expressway, heads due west to link Wilmington with Charlotte. When approaching from the north or northwest, take I-95 to I-40; when approaching from the south or southwest, take I-95 to US 74. US 17 parallels the coast a short distance inland, and provides the backbone highway for this chapter's area.

By air: **Wilmington International Airport (ILM)** (910-341-4125; flyilm.com; info@flyilm.com), 1740 Airport Blvd., Suite 12, Wilmington 28405. Always open; two restaurants, a bar, and rental cars are open daily 5 AM–11 PM. This full-service airport on the north side of town is served by three airlines, with nonstop flights to five cities. It was founded as an Army Air Corps base during World War II, and its runways are so long that it was designated as an emergency landing site for the space shuttle. Its code *ILM* is from "wILMington," as airport codes are not allowed to start with *W*.

By train or bus: Wilmington has no train service. It has bus service from **Greyhound** (greyhound.com), which connects to Raleigh and Richmond, Virginia, to the north, and Myrtle Beach, South Carolina, to the south.

MEDICAL EMERGENCIES **New Hanover Regional Medical Center** (910-343-7000; nhhn.org), 2131 S. 17th St., Wilmington 28401. This 628-bed hospital, run by a not-for-profit, serves this entire chapter's area. You'll find it about 4 miles south and east of downtown Wilmington, with its entrance on South 17th Street.

✱ Exploring the Area

EXPLORING BY CAR **Wilmington's Port Loop**. This 66-mile route circles the large tidal mouth of the Cape Fear River, the state's primary seaport, stretching south from the city of Wilmington. On the way, it passes a number of fine beaches, crosses the mouth of the Cape Fear River on a free ferry, explores the quaintly historic burg of Southport, and ends at the colonial archaeological park at Brunswick Town.

Start at the **Wilmington Railroad Museum** in a freight depot at the north end of downtown—all that is left of the national headquarters of Atlantic Coast Line Railroad (now CSX), which moved to Jacksonville, Florida, in 1960. This is the only surviving building of what was once a stunning 19th-century industrial site (which included a six-story passenger station), all replaced by the modern buildings of the Cape Fear Technical Institute. From here *take Front Street south for 2.0 miles*, passing through the heart of downtown. Market Street (at 0.4 mile) leads right one block to the Cape Fear River and the **Riverwalk**, while Castle Street (at 0.9 mile) leads two blocks to a small riverside park with good views of the Cape Fear Bridge. *Bear right onto Burnette Boulevard for 1.6 miles*, marking the landward boundary of Wilmington's container port, the state's largest. *Turn right onto Shipyard Boulevard and go one block* to the gate of this port and shipyard, *then turn left onto River Road (SSR 1100), which you follow for the next 12.0 miles*. You have now entered an area of relic sand dunes with some fine views over the Cape Fear River as you skirt some marshes; pine trees and xeric oak forests line the road. After 6.7 miles small, wooded **River Road Park** on your right gives good views over the river from a small fishing dock; then, near the end of River Road (which by now has become suburban in character), **Snows Cut Park** has boardwalks along the steep sandy bluffs of Snows Cut, a canal that's part of the **Intracoastal Waterway**.

Turn right onto US 421 (Carolina Beach Road) to cross Snows Cut on an impressive high bridge and enter **"Pleasure Island,"** the beaches that string southward from Wilmington. *In 1.0 mile turn right onto Dow Road* to visit **Carolina Beach State Park** for a rare look at preserved nature behind the dune line—nearly the only place in America where you can view Venus flytraps in the wild. *From the park gate turn right onto Dow Road and go 0.2 mile, then turn left onto Harper Road and go 0.9 mile to its end at US 421, then turn right and go 6.3 miles to the Fort Fisher Ferry*. You are now in **Carolina Beach**, surprisingly retro with a funky, sprawling old center and a nice boardwalk, followed by equally old-

KURE BEACH, NEAR WILMINGTON

fashioned **Kure Beach**. Now the route enters public land with a series of worthwhile sites, starting with **Fort Fisher**, a reconstructed Civil War–era wooden fort and museum, then **Fort Fisher State Recreation Area** with 6 miles of wild beach and a wildlife center, and finally the **North Carolina State Aquarium** at Fort Fisher, the crown jewel of this route.

Now *cross the wide, tidal* ***Cape Fear River*** *on the free 4.2-mile* ***state ferry*** (see the introduction to this part), with glorious sightseeing from both open and closed observation decks. You can feed the gulls from the upper deck—quite a sight as these noisy, cheeky birds flock about you by the hundreds. Be sure to pick up a loaf of bread in Kure Beach. Go straight on NC 211 into the lovely and historic village of **Southport**, with a beautiful waterfront, fine old homes, and a colonial-era park with a gorgeous azalea display.

From town center continue on NC 211 (by turning right onto Howe Street) and go 1.5 miles to a right turn onto NC 87 (River Road). In 1.1 mile you'll pass the **Brunswick Nuclear Power Plant**, which has a visitors center. The next dozen miles are deeply rural for a reason—the road borders one of the US military's secure ports, Sunny Point Military Ocean Terminal. *After 3.2 miles from NC 211, take the right fork onto NC 133 (still River Road).* The left fork, NC 87, leads 3.3 miles to 6,000-acre **Boiling Spring Lakes Preserve**, a huge tract of this unusual ecosystem. In 8.1 miles a very sharp right onto Plantation Road takes you to **Orton Plantation**, one of the South's premier plantation homes and gardens (closed indefinitely in 2010, but possibly open if you visit after 2012), and then to **Brunswick Town State Historic Site**, preserving the ruins of a colonial port. Another 5.1 miles up NC 133 is **Town Creek County Park**, a 900-acre nature preserve in its earliest stages of development, combining estuary forests with abandoned antebellum rice fields; at press time it had only a canoe launch and a picnic shelter, but may have walking paths by the time you read this. *Another 10.0 miles (a total of 23.1 miles since NC 87) brings you to a right onto US 17/74/76, which will take you over the Cape Fear River and into downtown in 2.8 miles.*

EXPLORING ON FOOT: BEACH HIKES For those times when a mere stroll isn't enough, and only serious exploration and exertion will do, here are the best of the South Coast's beach hikes.

Topsail Island, with its three town centers, offers the best developed beach hiking. Not only is the beach excellent and the scenery interesting, but you can arrange a car shuttle and end your journey at a café.

Masonboro Island is the best alternative for backpacking, as this scenic state preserve, more than 8 miles long, allows camping.

Carolina Beach's Freeman Park, with 2.6 miles of wilderness beach, also allows backpack camping (with a permit); the good news is that you don't need a boat to reach it, but the bad news is you have to share the experience with four-wheelers.

Cape Fear, on an island until the late 1990s, is now the southern terminus of a 10-mile hike that starts at the Fort Fisher State Recreation Area's visitors center.

Sunset Beach's Bird Island offers a 2-mile wilderness hike that passes a hiker-maintained beach journal in a mailbox to end at a jetty in South Carolina.

For more details on these walks, see their listings under *Green Spaces*.

Bicycling the Cape Fear Coast (Blue Clay Bike Park info: sirbikesalot.com/entry.php?fid=218). Given the many square miles of publicly owned land in this area (*Green Spaces* lists the larger and more significant tracts), you'd think that this'd be a great region for off-roading. Unfortunately, all of these tracts are managed for wildlife rather than recreation, and off-road bicycling is generally prohibited. For off-road pedaling, the county maintains Blue Clay Bike Park on the north end of town, on Juvenile Center Road. Instead, this is the region of the beach cyclist, done on salt-tolerant "cruiser" bikes not unlike the paper-boy Western Flyers of half a century ago. *Green Spaces* includes information on places where beach cycling is permitted.

EXPLORING BY BOAT The Intracoastal Waterway through the South Coast (waterwayguide.com/navupdate.php?area=5). The Intracoastal Waterway spends 106 miles within this chapter's area. For the most part it cuts through the narrow, marshy lagoon that once connected the beaches to the mainland here, creating a belt of open water about 1,000 feet wide. It is supposed to be 12 feet deep; however, its owners, the U.S. Army Corps of Engineers, has officially put a low priority on channel maintenance, due to the scanty commercial barge traffic caused by poor channel maintenance. The practical result of this is that low tide depth might be as bad as half the project depth; the website waterwayguide.com has detailed information on recent shoaling and dredging. Its northernmost 11 miles furnish the only civilian access to Camp Lejeune, the huge U.S. Marine base that specializes in live-fire amphibious landing training—and yes, the beaches here are strictly off-limits. The next 48 miles of lagoon cutting are surprisingly remote, even wild, in character, despite being in the Wilmington urban area; the next large area of canal-side services is at **Wrightsville Beach**, 36 miles into this section. This lagoonal section ends at Snows Cut, a massive canal dredged in 1929, with a full-service recreation marina at its far end, in **Carolina Beach State Park**. Now it follows the main ship channel of the **mouth of the Cape Fear River**, a busy commercial port, for the next 12 miles, to reenter the back lagoons at the lovely historic town of Southport, with full marina services. The final 32 miles cut behind the four **Brunswick Island** beaches, with full services at or near most of the five bridges.

✷ Towns

Wilmington. With an metropolitan area population of 150,000, Wilmington is an urban island surrounded by miles of nearly empty rural lands. It sits on a peninsula formed where the drowned mouth of the Cape Fear River parallels the Atlantic coast for 27 miles—a major seaport, shared by a large container port just south of downtown and an even larger (and completely closed to the public) military port on the other side of the river. It's a prosperous city, well kept and handsome, and far more cosmopolitan than its small population and isolated location would indicate. Its historic downtown fills a seven-by-four-block grid attached to the riverfront, with handsome old buildings, mostly between two and six stories tall. This is followed, on the river side, by the mile-long Riverwalk, a boardwalk with stunning views that gives access to a wide range of shopping and cafés. More restaurants and shops can be found in the four blocks to the east, with a number offering live entertainment well into the night. At the far eastern end sits the impressive County Courthouse and the Thalian Hall, a combination opera house and city hall, surely one of the most eccentric and delightful government structures in America. As

FLAGS FLY OVER THE COUNTY COURTHOUSE IN WILMINGTON.

large as it is, this downtown is ringed by a 300-block historic district with several museums. From here the city stretches for nine miles east to the Intracoastal Waterway, with several worthwhile gardens sprinkled around. Immediately beyond this, and outside the city limits, sit the beaches, stretching 35 miles to the north and 27 miles to the south, ranging from highly developed to complete wilderness.

Pleasure Island. South of Wilmington stretches a long, thin peninsula with lovely sand beaches lining its ocean side, correctly (if not very commonly) known as Federal Point. In 1929 port authorities turned it into an island by slicing a canal, Snows Cut, across it, and its boosters have succeeded in renaming it "Pleasure Island." Its older name hints at its history: It was a military base from Revolutionary days until World War II, and a large tract remains in military hands. You'll find the rest of it to be an enjoyable mix of old-fashioned beach resort and public wild lands. Two beach towns make up its seaward side. On the north Carolina Beach centers on a large public park with a lake, from which extends its odd and colorful tourist district, and from there the beach itself. To its south, Kure Beach offers a small, colorful, town center. Both these towns are wonderful places to look for beach vacation rentals, both for the high quality of the beach and for their convenience to Wilmington's restaurants and sights. Behind these two towns sits beachless Carolina Beach State Park, which preserves a large area of natural lagoon-side ecology, and furnishes an attractive marina on the Cape Fear River.

To the south of the two towns are 6 miles of public lands that stretch from beach to river and include two major attractions, the North Carolina State Aquarium at Fort Fisher as well as Fort Fisher State Historic Site and Museum, a reconstructed Civil War site. The rest of the land is Fort Fisher State Recreation Area, with many miles of wild beaches. At the far end of the pavement sits one of the state of North Carolina's seven large auto ferries, this one linking the peninsula with the pretty little town of Southport.

Jacksonville and Camp Lejeune. For most of its history Jacksonville was a tiny, isolated county seat, a place where the railroad met navigable New Inlet, a shipping point for pine logs and naval stores. Then the Marines Corps invaded. In 1940, during the remilitarization that was going on (mainly in secret) while Europe and the Pacific sank into World War II, the navy quietly purchased vast tracts of the empty pocosin swamps and pine forests. When the United States finally entered the war in December 1941 the 250-square-mile New River Marine Corps Base had already been erected as a major training center for beach assault troops. Renamed Camp Lejeune in 1942, the base remains a major training facility—and strictly off-limits to civilian visitors. Its 14 miles of beaches can be used for live-fire amphibious training.

Now Jacksonville is a military town, its population swollen to 90,000. Despite being (on paper) nearly as large as Wilmington, Jacksonville is very much a small town with a deeply historic core surrounding a two-block downtown. Its old waterfront has a small but attractive park, and a good boat ramp for the New River Inlet; across the street is the historic 1942 USO Club, still operating and the oldest in America. Most services string out eastward from the old town center along NC 24 (Lejeune Boulevard) as it connects with the marine base 5 miles away. Just outside the base entrance is a small garden park, containing a moving memorial to the 270 marines killed in the 1982 terrorist attack in Beirut—particularly beautiful in spring, when the azaleas bloom.

Southport. Thirty miles (by car) south of Wilmington, this sleepy fishing village of 2,500 sits at the mouth of the Cape Fear River. In antebellum times Southport was an important fishing port, but as railroads improved it lost ground to Wilmington, and its last major packing plant burned to the ground over a century ago. Today it's noted for its historic charm, with two museums, a colonial-era park, and a beautiful waterfront with extensive parks and two marinas. The state's free auto ferry across the mouth of the Cape Fear River terminates just north of town, and the private pay pedestrian ferry to Bald Head Island (which contains Cape Fear) terminates at one of its marinas.

Bald Head Island (myreporter.com/?p=1597). This large landform (it stopped being an island in 1998, when the inlet separating it from Fort Fisher's beaches shoaled closed) sits opposite Southport, separating the mouth of the Cape Fear River from the Atlantic. Its southeastern point is none other than Cape Fear itself, named by mariners for its shifting shoals, notorious for wrecking hundreds of ships and drowning thousands of sailors. It consists of a series of low sand hills running east–west along the Cape Fear River's inlet for 4 miles, separated from each other by marshes and creeks, with the southernmost one being the modern beach. Since 1980 these dune-hills have been the site of a highly successful resort development, now nearing build-out, noted for its openness to the visiting public and its environmental sensitivity. Indeed, most of the land (and all of the lowlands) is owned by either the state or a local land conservation charity, and managed as a nature preserve.

Bald Head Island is reached by boat, with a pedestrian ferry available from Southport; day visitors are welcome. The ferry lands at a small town center and marina on the western end of the island, with shops, a hotel, and several restaurants—the only commercial development open to the public on this tightly managed island. (There are two members-only country clubs as well.) Here you can rent a golf cart or bicycle; no cars are allowed on the island. Nearby is the state's oldest lighthouse, Old Baldy, now a historic site with a museum adjacent. From here historic Federal Road heads eastward for 4 miles, leading to a state maritime forest preserve and an old Coast Guard station, to end at Cape Fear. Narrow lanes lead away from this to the developed areas (including a golf course), mainly detached and attached single-family homes.

The Brunswick Islands. Beyond the Cape Fear River, the coast curves westward for its last 31 miles before entering South Carolina. This stretch consists of four beach islands, each its own municipality. From east to west these are Holden Beach, Oak Island Beach, Ocean Isle Beach, and Sunset Beach. Each consists of a small center, a lot of vacation homes (almost all of them single-family detached stilt homes), and (more often than not) a length of wild beach. All four beaches are excellent, with fine sand, well-formed dunes, lots of access points, and plenty of parking. And all four come with a special treat: the ability to enjoy a sunrise and a sunset from the same beach. Each of these has its own listing under *Green Spaces—The Beaches* below, where you'll find enough information to choose the one that fits you best.

✷ Green Spaces

PUBLIC LANDS Angola Bay and Holly Shelter Game Lands, near Jacksonville (ncwildlife.org/Hunting/GameLand_Maps/Coastal/Angola_Bay.pdf;

ncwildlife.org/Hunting/GameLand_Maps/Coastal/Holly_Shelter.pdf). These two massive tracts of state-owned hunting lands form a figure-8 centered on NC 53, 33 miles north of Wilmington and 32 miles west of Jacksonville—Angola Bay being the bulge to the north of the highway, and Holly Shelter being the bulge to the south. Together they make up nearly 90,000 acres of pocosin and pine, 140 square miles of undeveloped natural environment ready to be explored. Angola Bay centers on the vast pocosin known as Angola Swamp. The northern half of this thickly wooded swamp remains wild and roadless, while the southern half was gridded into parallel tracks by past owners, to permit logging. Most of these roads remain open to vehicles, and some are passable without four-wheel drive; you'll find the scenery a blend of old forests, new plantations, and open meadows, a good mix for observing wildlife. Tot the south, the Holly Shelter portion protects the equally vast Holly Shelter Swamp, and is laced with open roads of varying quality (including paved). Holly Shelter also includes several lengths of the Northeast Cape Fear River, and supplies three wildlife boat ramps, open 24/7. Birders should note that Holly Shelter has a substantial waterfowl impoundment, little-visited although accessible by most ordinary vehicles, reached by taking maintained dirt-surfaced Lodge Road for 4.4 miles east of its intersection with paved Shaw Highway (SSR 1520); in another 1.1 miles on the left, a short jeep track leads to Back Island, a prime birding and wildlife location with ponds and fields.

Bald Head Island State Natural Area (bhic.org). This state-owned preserve includes 1,260 land acres and about eight times that amount in marshes and tidal waters—essentially everything on Bald Head Island apart from the development itself. Its most accessible tract is the remarkable Maritime Forest, 180 acres of virgin climax dune forest, explored by a nature trail; you'll find it along Federal Road, 2 miles east of the ferry terminal. Then, at the far eastern end of Federal Road, the preserve includes nearly all of the Atlantic beach and dunes, starting at Cape Fear and stretching northward for 6 miles (where it merges with the state-owned **Fort Fisher Recreation Area**). Finally, the preserve includes all of the marshland behind the dune line and north of the development, an area laced with narrow, twisting inlets and a delight to explore with a canoe or kayak.

Boiling Spring Lakes Preserve, near Southport (nature.org/wherewework/northamerica/states/northcarolina/preserves/art12787.html). This 6,200-acre state-owned preserve forms a crescent around the village of Boiling Springs Lakes in the otherwise empty pinelands of inland Brunswick County, 22 miles south of Wilmington. Boiling Springs Lakes is a 1960s-era development, now an incorporated municipality, centered on a series of small artificial lakes and a golf course. Less than half of it was ever completed, and the preserve is made up of much of the unbuilt platted lands. It is ecologically important as prime habitat for the endangered red-cockaded woodpecker, which nests and feeds only in old forests, and passes its nests down for generations. The tract is also known for its rich variety of carnivorous plants, including Venus flytraps, trumpet pitchers, purple pitchers, and sundews. A nature trail (3 miles round-trip), starting from the town's community center, explores a variety of the preserve's habitats.

PARKS AND GARDENS **Greenfield Park and Gardens, Wilmington**. Open daily, 6 AM–11 PM. Admission is free. A hundred acres of stunning azalea gardens surround 150-acre Greenfield Lake, just 2.0 miles south of downtown Wilmington via US 421. The lake is an antebellum millpond, turned into a garden by the Works Progress Administration (WPA) during the Depression; it extends for 1.3 miles into residential neighborhoods, sending out several arms along the way. Today it's a city park, kept in excellent condition, noted for its views through azalea blossoms, framed by cypress, into the lake. The official main entrance is left off US 421 at Willard Street, then one block to a left onto 3rd Street. Here you'll find the main picnic area, tennis courts, paddleboat rentals, and a canoe launch. Here also is the start of 5 miles of paths that circle the lake, with a stunning wood footbridge about a mile south, and several more picnic sites. East Shore Drive, a residential street, circles the entire lake, and you can park anywhere along it.

The Arboretum at New Hanover County, Wilmington (910-798-7660; gardeningnhc.org), 6206 Oleander Dr., Wilmington 28403. Located 7.2 miles east of downtown Wilmington via US 76 (Oleander Drive), the arboretum occupies 7 acres on the campus of the New Hanover County Extension Service. It's a demonstration garden at heart with a very complete collection of native plants and trees, aimed at helping landscapers and homeowners find native landscape plants to suit their needs; but underneath this seriousness of purpose is a broad streak of whimsy and creativity, most notably in the copper dragon that erupts from the middle of its pond. This is the garden to visit if you are here in any of the 10 months when azaleas are *not* in bloom.

AZALEAS BLOOM IN WILMINGTON'S GREENFIELD PARK.

Airlie Gardens, Wilmington (910-798-7700; airliegardens.org; airleeinfo@nhcgov.com), 300 Airlee Rd., Wilmington 28403. Open daily 9–5. $$. This 67-acre azalea garden, now a county park, fronts a wide tidal inlet 8.1 miles east of downtown via US 76, then right on Airlie Road. It was formed by Gilded Age industrialist Pembroke Jones and his wife, Sadie, part of an estate that centered on their 133-room mansion; at their height in the 1920s the gardens covered 155 acres and had over half a million azalea bushes. In 1930 Sadie Jones started opening the gardens as an admission-charging tourist attraction, as did her heirs, the Corbett family, who continued to live on the estate. Their long-time admission-taker was none other than the visionary folk artist Minnie Evans, who would sell her elaborate, colorful drawings from the entrance stand. Today's gardens still feature prolific azaleas framing beautiful views, and a camellia garden over 100 years old. Other landmarks include a sculpture garden dedicated to Minnie Evans, an 1836 church (still in use), and a 1902 freshwater lake that borders on the tidal Bradley Creek.

Carolina Beach State Park, Pleasure Island (910-458-8206; ncparks.gov/Visit/parks/cabe/main.php; carolina.beach@ncmail.net), 1010 State Park Rd., P.O. Box 475, Carolina Beach 28428. Open daylight hours. The visitors center is open daily 8–5:45. Admission is free. Despite its name, Carolina Beach State Park has no beach; it's named, instead, after the town to its immediate east. Located 14.5 miles south of Wilmington via US 421, this park protects more than 760 acres of back-island environment, mostly an open pine savanna on an old flat-topped sand dune, interspersed with natural ponds and marshes. Those ponds and marshes are home to a wide variety of natural carnivorous plants, easily reached by nature trails. Other trails in its 6-mile network explore forests, follow the Intracoastal Waterway's Snows Cut canal, and parallel the bank of the Cape Fear River to reach 50-foot-tall Sugarloaf Dune. The park has a nice full-service marina as well.

Fort Fisher State Recreation Area, Pleasure Island. The southernmost tip of Pleasure Island, long protected as a military base, is now a recreation area dedicated to its 4 miles of beaches, starting at its large new visitors center 4.5 miles south of Wilmington via US 421. This is one of the finest wild beaches in the state, with a wide, clean beach and dramatic dunes. It's also open to four-wheel-drive vehicles, which require a permit from the visitors center. A footpath, the Basin Trail, avoids the four-wheel areas to explore the marshes behind, passing a World War II bunker to end at an observation deck over the Cape Fear River in 1.1 miles. A second interesting site is best reached by driving past down US 421 to its end, then a short distance left past the ferry entrance. Here you will find a second abandoned bunker, and from it, extending for 3.2 miles into the water, an amazing seawall to nowhere known as "The Rocks," built in the 1870s to encourage the beach line to shoal up and so protect the shipping channel. It finally succeeded 110 years later, when the Fort Fisher beaches completely and seamlessly merged with those of Bald Head Island. Today, this 10 miles of wilderness beach makes a fine beach hike, ending at Cape Fear.

Oak Island Nature Center (910-278-5518; oakislandnc.com/Recreation/nature_center.htm). Town government address: 4601 E. Oak Island Dr., Oak Island 28465. Nature center open Memorial Day–Labor Day, Wed.–Sun. noon–5; rest of year, Fri–Sun. noon–5. Admission to all sites is free. The town of Oak Island, local government for the easternmost 13 miles of the Brunswick Island beaches, maintains a parks department that would be the pride of a midsized city. Along with the usual urban necessities of athletic fields and recreation centers, it has developed a range of environmental parks, giving remarkable access to the full variety of coastal island ecologies.

Start at the Oak Island Nature Center, which explains the coastal environment, including live animal exhibits; it's at the back of the island, at the corner of Yacht Drive and Northeast 52nd Street. Adjacent to it is a block of maritime forest bordering the Intracoastal Waterway, with attractive boardwalks to protect the delicate environment, a fishing pier, and a boardwalk over to a spoil bank on the canal itself. Also on the lagoon side of the island is little May Moore Park at the north end of Barbee Boulevard, with nice views.

Interior to the island, in its western half, is 2.4-mile-long Davis Creek, preserved when the original developers created the dry land and street grid in 1938. It's now a canoe trail, surprisingly wild looking and scenic, with launch points at Southeast 40th Street, Southeast 31st Street, and West 30th Place (off W. Beach Drive); if you are shuttling cars, launch at 9th Place and paddle to the right to avoid getting lost. For the land-bound, there's views at Heron's Lookout Park at its head at Southeast 40th Street; a canoe launch, bridge, and nature trail at Tidewaves Park (southern terminus of Southeast 31st Street, a remarkable bridge and boardwalk at Scenic Trail (southern terminus of Southeast 19th Street); and another bridge and boardwalk—0.25 mile long—known simply as Crossover at the southern terminus of Southeast 9th Street, connecting with the beach.

Finally, the town-maintained access to the far western end of the beach (at the terminus of West Beach Drive) lets visitors explore 0.75 mile of new beach that has emerged from the sea as natural currents move the sand.

Bird Island State Preserve (nccoastalreserve.net/About-The-Reserve/Reserve-Sites/Bird-Island/87.aspx), 40th Street Beach Access, Sunset Beach. Always open. Admission is free. The southernmost beach in North Carolina (and overlapping 0.25 mile into South Carolina), 1,300-acre Bird Island is named after its abundant and varied wildlife. The state purchased it in 2001 to protect it from development—evidently not an idle threat, as air photos show an earlier attempt to dredge a causeway to it from Sunset Beach. Like the southern end of many North Carolina barrier islands, it has been growing as ocean currents wash sand upon it. In 1997 this process closed off the shallow inlet dividing it from Sunset Beach; it's now a continuous wilderness beach walk of 1.3 miles from the southernmost beach access to its tippy end, at a 0.5-mile-long riprap jetty. Of particular note is the Kindred Spirit Mailbox, a mailbox placed about 0.75 mile from 40th Street, just off the beach, in which beachwalkers record their thoughts. Nude sunbathers sometimes use the island, but this seems to be illegal; public nudity is forbidden everywhere in North Carolina, and its South Carolina section is owned and regulated by the U.S. Army Corps of Engineers, which also prohibits it. The police of Sunset Beach regularly patrol the entire tract.

RIVERS AND ESTUARIES Mouth of the Cape Fear River. The drowned mouth of the Cape Fear River forms a tidal inlet 26 miles long and a mile wide that parallels the Atlantic, running nearly due south from Wilmington to finally enter the ocean in a 1.4-mile-wide inlet between Oak Island Beach and Bald Head Island. The head of this inlet is only 9 miles from the ocean, and during this entire southward detour it stays within 2 miles of its goal. Indeed, rather than finally reaching the coast, the coast swerves westward to reach it, so that the river mouth forms the boundary between east- and south-facing beaches.

The mouth of the Cape Fear River provides North Carolina's most important commercial port, with a container point just south of downtown Wilmington and a large military port just north of Southport. There's also an attractive wharf adjacent to downtown Wilmington and several marinas, including two at downtown Southport and one at Carolina Beach State Park. The Intracoastal Waterway shares the commercial shipping channel for its southernmost dozen miles, and the busy

Southport–Fort Fisher Auto Ferry crosses the channel at right angles. Despite its busy-ness and urban location, its size guarantees that pleasure boaters have plenty of room and lots of interesting places to explore.

Freshwater canoeing on the Black River. Wilmington's major freshwater streams are the Cape Fear River (see "The Coastal Plains") and its tributary, the Northeast Cape Fear River, large enough for powerboats as well as canoes and kayaks. A number of small rivers provide paddlers with better alternatives—wilder, narrower, shadier—including Town Creek and Rice Creek (11 miles south of Wilmington via US 17) and Lockwood Folly River (on the mainland behind Oak Island). The finest of these, however, is the Black River, a 60-mile tributary that empties into the Cape Fear River 15 miles north of downtown Wilmington. The Nature Conservancy, which has been working to preserve this river with conservation easements, states that the Black has the oldest known trees east of the Rockies, and is one of the cleanest waterways in North Carolina. Those ancient trees—some as much as 1,700 years old—are found in a stand of virgin southern bald cypress named the Three Sisters, where the oldest trees have immense buttresses and flattened, distorted crowns, torn apart by countless hurricanes. The river itself is almost completely wild along its entire length, with no towns and only a scattering of houses; there is no development, or landward access of any sort, along its lowermost 19 miles. The river has four ramps, all in its middle section. You'll find the ancient trees of the Three Sisters in the 2-mile segment between the lowermost ramps, with the upstream ramp off NC 11/53 and the downstream ramp just off Longview Road (SSR 1547). The next downstream boat ramp is in downtown Wilmington at the end of Castle Street, an amazing 34 miles away. There are no legal camping areas along the river, and virtually no dry land along the banks downstream from the last ramp.

New River Inlet, south of Jacksonville. Twenty-two-mile-long New River Inlet curves through rural pinelands between the north end of Topsail Island and the attractive downtown wharfs of Jacksonville, its widths varying from less than 800 feet to more than 2.5 miles. Its Atlantic mouth is 1,500 feet wide, drifting southward, and given to shifting shoals. In 2 miles it crosses the Intracoastal Waterway, and from there has a dredged channel for the next 19.4 miles to Jacksonville, with a project depth of 8 feet but shoaling possible. This is a remote and scenic locale for pleasure boating, noted for its high bluffs, which sometimes form cliffs as high as 25 feet. Its eastern bank, for its lowermost 19 miles, is within Camp Lejeune, a Marine Corps training base that's strictly off-limits to civilians. On its western bank 2 miles north of the Intracoastal Waterway is the fishing village of Sneads Ferry, where you'll find marine services and a restaurant.

Little River Inlet, Brunswick Islands. A mere 5 miles long and between 1,000 and 1,500 feet wide, Little River Inlet gains significance by roughly marking the boundary between North and South Carolina. It's S-shaped, with most of its waters on the South Carolina side of the boundary (one of those straight lines drawn with a ruler by aristocrats on another continent). A channel links it with Calabash, a fishing village noted for its seafood restaurants. This inlet is popular with pleasure boaters, being at the far northern end of South Carolina's Myrtle Beach resort area.

BEACHES (beach access points: dcm3.enr.state.nc.us/website/nccoastal_access/viewer.htm). The public beaches of the South Coast consist of 10 barrier islands connected to the mainland by a thick band of salt marsh. They look like true islands, however, as the Intracoastal Waterway forms a deepwater barrier to the mainland, typically 1,000 or so feet wide and requiring very high and impressive bridges. These 10 beaches come in two sections: an east-facing section northward from the mouth of the Cape Fear River, and a south-facing section between the Cape Fear River and the South Carolina border.

In general, beach quality is excellent, with a wide strand of quartz "sugar sand," white and billowy, in front of a well-defined dune line. The north end of each island tends to show erosion, sometimes very extreme (a number of houses have dropped into the ocean), but always balanced by deposition at the south end. Actually, this is a landlubber's view; if you were a local boatman, you would say that the inlets are shifting southward. Indeed, several inlets have sanded up altogether; 20 years ago there were 12 sand barriers (one a true island) instead of today's 10.

Five of the islands (Lea, Masonboro, Carolina Beach, Fort Fisher/Cape Fear Beaches, and Sunset Beach) have multi-mile wilderness beaches, and the others tend to have smaller wild tracts at their extremities. Seven of the beaches have extensive developed areas; these developed areas are continuously built up (or nearly so), but mainly in beach cottages and luxury second homes. Big condo projects, common in other states, are comparatively rare here. Motels are less common than you'd expect; most visitors rent private homes, with beachfront going from $1,500 to $4,500 a week and middle-of-the-island as low as $500. Commercial areas are typically limited to small, old-fashioned beach town centers, frequently grouped around a long wooden fishing pier; long Topsail Island has three such centers. Parking varies from island to island and from year to year; check the municipal sites for information.

Developed or undeveloped, all 10 beaches are teeming with wildlife. The clean and healthy waters have excellent fishing—which attracts birds as well as humans, making this a superb area for birders, both along the beaches and in the marshes behind. (Fishers and birders can easily enter the marshes by canoeing the many short tidal inlets.) Best of all, this is a major nesting region for sea turtles, which can be found on all 10 beaches. Hard-shelled loggerheads (which weigh up to 300 pounds and live up to 60 years) are surprisingly common despite their endangered status, while the critically endangered leatherbacks (frequently over 1,000 pounds) occasionally make an appearance. Nor is this just on the wilderness beaches; nests can appear in the dunes in front of vacation houses as well. All counties and municipalities maintain their own turtle-watch programs, which both protect the nests and help curious visitors enjoy this wonder from a safe distance; see the municipal websites for details.

Topsail Island's beaches (surfcity.govoffice.com; topsailbeach.org; North Topsail Beach: ntbnc.org). Topsail Island (pronounced *TOP-sul*) possesses the northernmost public beaches in this chapter, 34 miles from Wilmington and 21 miles from Jacksonville; there are additional beaches to its north, but as they are part of Camp Lejeune and are used for live-fire amphibious assault training, they are strictly off-limits. Topsail also has more beach than any other island in this chapter—22.5 miles of it. You reach the island via two bridges spaces 8 miles apart; NC 210 (see *Eccentric Highways of North Carolina* under "What's Where") crosses the southern bridge, goes up the island to the northern bridge, then crosses it as well. Topsail is split among three municipalities: North Topsail Beach at the northern bridge, then Surf City at the southern bridge, then Topsail Beach at the far southern end. In each of the three towns, a long wooden fishing pier marks a small commercial center. The southernmost commercial center is the most interesting, as it occupies the street grid (including two buildings) of a former top-secret rocket testing facility—America's first, used from 1946 to 1948. Beaches are smooth, typically with a reasonable width above high tide, and almost continuously, but modestly, built up; the characteristic view is that of a narrow dune line bridged by an endless series of boardwalks extending from a tightly packed line of stilt cottages. Apart from the major beach access points at the three town centers, there are a large number of well-spaced access points with small lots all along the island, and street parking is allowed in at least some areas. There has, however, been significant beach erosion in parts of the far north of the island, so much so that houses

LEA ISLAND

(audubon.org/chapter/nc/nc/IBAs/Coast/lea.htm; to compare maps, see mapper.acme.com and type "Lea Island, NC" in the search box). We are used to thinking of geological changes taking eons; in terms of human life spans, landforms are permanent. Not so on the beach! A barrier island takes dozens, not millions, of years to change—and no place demonstrates how rapidly beaches can change better than Lea Island, a 4-mile strip of wilderness between Topsail Island and Figure Eight Island, accessible by boat only.

You can get a good idea of what it looked like very recently from its USGS topographic map, last updated in 1970. New Topsail Inlet, deep and narrow, is shown as separating Lea Island (unnamed on the map) from Topsail Island, and shallow, little Old Topsail Inlet is separating Lea Island from Hutaff Island (also unnamed on the map). Yes, there were two islands then, not one. What's more, the combined island has drifted landward by several hundred feet. These, however, are not the big changes: New Topsail Inlet has moved southward by nearly a mile, obliterating the north end of the island. In 1975 Lea Island was surveyed for a subdivision and divided into 56 lots, each about 50 feet wide. Since then, the inlet's move southward has put 28 of those lots underwater, and drowned three of the four houses built. (The fourth is still standing, the only surviving structure on the island.) And yes, these very damp lots are still owned by the people who bought them to build beach cabins. One, now in the deepest water at the center of the sound, was purchased in 1999; the county lists "beach erosion" on its tax record. In fact, the outermost two lots have begun to reemerge on the other side, becoming valuable Topsail Island real estate.

At press time, Lea Island was still privately owned, but the Audubon Society was working with the 30 or so owners of dry land to convert it into a bird sanctuary. It has wide beaches, and is popular with boaters.

have been lost to the sea. In contrast, its far southern tip has been growing, with purely natural causes extending the beach for 0.7 mile since 1970, creating an attractive stretch of wilderness.

Figure Eight Island (developer/Realtor site: figure8island.com). Located just north of Wrightsville Beach and south of Lea Island, this 5-mile-long privately owned island is not accessible to the general public, but contains a number of summer homes that can be rented. Access is by a drawbridge over the Intracoastal Waterway, with a guarded gate at the landward end. The island, much favored by the wealthy, has more than 440 homes, all of them large and many of them mansions; it has no condos and no commercial structures other than the island's private yacht club. Part of the northern end of the beach is suffering from erosion so heavy that sandbags protect houses from high tide; the far northern point, however, has very wide beaches. The rest of the beach is very wide and smooth. Lagoon and inland renters should inquire about how far they must travel for beach access.

Wrightsville Beach, Wilmington (municipal site: townofwrightsvillebeach.com). Located on the eastern edge of the city of Wilmington, Wrightsville Beach is an independent municipality with 5 miles of shoreline. It's the most developed of the South Coast beaches; continuously built up, it's the only beach to have major condos and yacht basins as well as the large number of more ordinary beach cottages found on the other islands. The beach quality is excellent throughout, with wide sands available above high tide; the dunes are thick along the northernmost mile and the southernmost 1.6 mile, where development was most recent, but virtually nonexistent at its center. Both beach access points and parking spaces (including street parking, except at the northern end) are plentiful, but on parking meters; you either have to bring enough change to plug a meter—you'll need four quarters for every hour you want to park—or sign up for pay-by-phone at park-by-phone.com. Check the town website for details.

Mason Inlet, Wrightsville Beach's Northern End (nc.audubon.org/birds-science-education/education/free-mason-inlet-field-trips-offered-every-friday). As late as 1970, Wrightsville Beach had miles of wilderness shore on its western half. Then during the next three decades, development crept *north* while erosion crept *south*. Around 2000, they met. Two years later the U.S. Army Corps of Engineers moved the beach back to its 1970 location, creating more than 0.5 mile of empty beach in a massive dredge-and-fill project. Since then the re-created lands have been gaining dunes and plant life—and abundant bird life. There's a parking lot at the far north end of Lumina Avenue, and all you need for solitude is a good, long walk. The Audubon Society offers weekly birding walks, free, to anyone who cares to meet them by the parking lot information kiosk, at 9 AM Fri., Apr.–Sept.

Masonboro Island, Wilmington (nccoastalreserve.net/About-The-Reserve/Reserve-Sites/Masonboro-Island/59.aspx). This 8.4-mile-long wilderness beach, accessible only by boat, is located just south of Wrightsville Beach, adjacent to the city of Wilmington's southeastern residential areas. It's protected as an estuarine reserve, jointly owned by the state and the feds, with few if any private inholdings. It consists of a stunning white sand beach, perhaps 200 yards across at high tide, behind which are about 4,000 acres of wetlands. If you have access to a boat, this is your best wilderness experience in the area—you can even camp (with some restrictions—check the website).

Carolina Beach, Pleasure Island (municipal site: carolinabeach.org; official tourism site: carolinabeachgetaway.com). Located just south of Wilmington via US 421, this is the first of Pleasure Island's two municipalities. It's notable for its particularly nice small-beach-town type of downtown—older and modest, but brightly colored and well kept, with good beachy shops and restaurants. It's also pedestrianized, and a great place to stroll. A long wooden boardwalk, between downtown and its handsome dune line, links it all together. Parking is plentiful at the town center, and sparse elsewhere; there are limited free spaces, and many metered and pay station spaces at $1.25 per hour, or $7 a day. The 3.5-mile beach itself (with another 1.6 miles in Freeman Park; see below) is of very high quality, with a pronounced dune line and about 75 yards of sand above high tide.

Freeman Park, north end of Carolina Beach, Pleasure Island (carolina beach.org/site_new/pages/freeman_park.html). Always open. $$; a permit *must* be obtained at a local store before entering. At its northern end, Carolina Beach's Canal Drive dead-ends into deep, rutted sand. Beyond this is Freeman Park, a four-wheel-drive beach stretching 1.6 miles to Carolina Beach Inlet. Although any street-legal automobile is allowed (no motorcycles or ATVs), this is definitely for serious four-wheelers; even the parking area is soft and deeply rutted. You can camp on the beach and build fires in the northernmost mile (past marker 6). You can also ride your horse on the beach, or run your dog without a leash—but only during winter months, Oct.–Mar.

If you wish to walk into the park (or just explore the north end of the beach) there's a paved public parking lot on Canal Drive, 0.2 mile south of the park entrance.

Kure Beach and Kure Beach Pier, Pleasure Island (910-458-5524; municipal site: townofkurebeach.org; official tourist site: visitkure.com; pier site:kurebeach fishingpier.com), K Ave., P.O. Box 150, Kure Beach 28449. Open Apr.–Nov., all day. $$. Located 18 miles south of Wilmington via US 421, Kure Beach features a small, old-fashioned downtown with a pier, and wide beaches. Central Kure, lined up along Avenue K (which dead-ends at the pier), has free diagonal street parking—about 100 spaces stretching three blocks inland, and another 50 free spaces along the beach itself. The beach is shielded by small, attractive dunes, crossed by boardwalks. There's about 50 to 100 feet of fine sand above the high-tide line.

From this center Kure Beach stretches for about a mile north (to Carolina Beach) and 1.6 miles south (to Fort Fisher); there is regular public access along these outer stretches, but no public parking. Nearly all of these beaches are excellent, with dunes and significant sand above high tide, but continuously lined by vacation houses. The final 0.25 mile, however, is lined by condos, and suffers from increasing beach erosion southward, with the final few hundred yards having no high-tide beach.

Built in 1923, Kure Beach Pier sits downtown, at the center of the public beach. It claims to be the oldest surviving pier on the Atlantic coast—"oldest" here being a term of art, as this pier has been completely blown down by numerous hurricanes over the years. Nevertheless it has been rebuilt every time, and has remained in the ownership of the family of its founder, L. C. Kure. It's 711 feet long (from the high-tide line) with a T at the end for kingfishermen, 32 feet wide, and 26 feet above normal high tide. Read the "history" page on its website for a fascinating account of the life of a wooden pier in Hurricane Alley.

Proposed Carolina Beach Pier (ncaquariums.com/aquarium-piers/carolina-beach). The state of North Carolina is committed to creating old-fashioned beach fishing piers, linked to all three of its state aquariums. While the **Roanoke Island Aquarium's** pier at **Nags Head** (see "The Outer Banks") is scheduled to open by this book's publishing date, and the **Pine Shore Knoll's Aquarium** at **Emerald Isle** (see "New Bern and Beaufort") is to open a couple of years later, **Fort Fisher Aquarium**'s pier is, at press time, still in its early funding and planning stages. It will be located at the center of Carolina Beach, anchoring the western end of its boardwalk, giving yet another reason to visit this attractive, old-fashioned downtown beach.

Beaches of Fort Fisher (ncparks.gov/Visit/parks/fofi/main.php). The southernmost tip of Pleasure Island, also known as Federal Point, has been government land throughout North Carolina's history, and functioned as one of the area's many military bases during World War II. Indeed, part of it is still a military base, on the lagoon side opposite Kure Beach. The tip, however, has now passed into state hands and is split among a historic site (**Fort Fisher**), an aquarium (**Fort Fisher State Aquarium**), a state park (**Fort Fisher State Recreation Area**), and an estuarine preserve, to the south of the state park. To reach it, take US 421 for 19 miles south of Wilmington.

All in all there are 4.2 miles of public beach in the Fort Fisher area, ending at New Inlet, which forms the northern point of Bald Head Island. This inlet, however, only exists on old maps, having sanded up in the late 1990s. That's right: You have continuous undeveloped beach stretching from Fort Fisher to Cape Fear itself, a barefoot beach walk of 9.8 miles.

During the first few hundred yards, part of the Fort Fisher State Historic Site, the beach is spoiled by extensive riprap (which protects historic sites threatened by erosion). Beyond this stretches mile after mile of wide, billowy, duned beach, with nary a building in site. There's parking off Battle Acre Drive, but this first stretch of real beach is noted for its rip currents, and swimming is dangerous. Instead, go down Loggerhead Drive about 200 yards to the recreation area's visitors center, with ample parking, restrooms, showers, a canteen, and 200 feet of boardwalk crossing the dunes to the beach. From here south the beach widens, reaching 500 feet with a primary and secondary dune line; then these dune lines merge to become a sandy, grassy backcountry. Four-wheel-drive vehicles are allowed on the beach for the first 4 miles south of the visitors center. Beyond that point (well marked) is a true wilderness beach, 6 miles long, protected by state nature preserves all the way to Cape Fear.

Beaches of Cape Fear (developer site: baldheadisland.com). With a name that reflects the dread it brought to mariners, Cape Fear's shifting shoals and sudden storms have caused hundreds of wrecks with many thousands of lives lost. On a mild, warm day, however, it's a delightful beach, on the far southeastern corner of boat-access-only Bald Head Island. Here the high inland areas are an expensive residential resort, open to the public and reached by a regular passenger ferry to its southwestern point; once you're there, you can either bicycle (rent or bring your own) or rent a golf cart, to travel the additional 3.8 miles to the cape (automobiles are prohibited on the island). Up to the turn of the millennium Cape Fear was a wild beach; now, however, large mansions hover just behind 100 feet of dunes, and a luxurious country club, the Shoals Club, sits beside the cape itself—quite a comedown for such a fearsome place.

The beach itself is superb. It comes in two sections, each about 4 miles long: an Atlantic section stretching north from the cape (blending into the Fort Fisher Beaches), and an inlet section stretching west. Both sections feature well-defined dune lines and wide sands above high tide. The Atlantic section (after 0.5 mile of mansions poking up from behind the dunes) is a wilderness beach, owned and protected by the state as part of Smith Island Natural Area; only that first 0.5 mile can be reached by golf cart. In contrast, the inlet section starts right at the ferry terminal at the western end of the island and is followed by houses and many access points for most of the way to the cape. Apart from accessibility, the inlet beaches are calmer, while the Atlantic beaches have better surf. Day visitors should note that all public dining is at the little commercial center by the ferry port; the Shoals Club is members and guests only.

Oak Island Beach, Brunswick Islands (municipal site: oakislandnc.com). The easternmost of the Brunswick Islands, Oak Island stretches for 13.8 miles. It's the widest of this chapter's beaches, with an odd shape that can be confusing. It has two bridges: NC 133 at its eastern end, and a brand-new bridge (its street unnamed at press time) at the western. Its easternmost end, known as Caswell Beach, is the normal thin barrier island with marshes behind; its single road, lined by vacation cottages, goes past Oak Island Lighthouse to end at Fort Caswell, now a Baptist camp, whose historic ruins (including a 19th-century brick fort and later concrete shore batteries) are unfortunately off-limits to the general public. To the west of this stretches Oak Island proper, a gridiron of blocks 8.8 miles long and 0.8 mile thick, mainly built up. For the first 1.9 miles westward Oak Island Drive is the main road, running one or two blocks north of the beach. Then (at Southeast 58th Street) Beach Drive begins a block south of Oak Island Drive, and follows the beach all the way to its end 7.0 miles later. At Southeast 40th Street, Oak Island Drive swerves inland, and a tidal inlet blocks it off from the beach. Your last chance to cut over to the beach comes at Middleton Drive, where a new automobile bridge has been built. If you are approaching the beach by foot from a rental house on the north side of the island, you'll have two additional pedestrian crossover points between Southeast 40th Street and Middleton, but nothing farther west. This peculiar layout means not only that it's easy to lose your way to the beach, but also that some houses on Oak Island are as far as 2.4 miles from the nearest beach access. Be sure to check before you rent.

Oak Island's long beach is uniformly excellent, with no significant erosion, a wide strand above high tide, and a well-defined dune line. Unlike most of the other developed beaches it has no downtown by the beach; instead, commercial development straggles along Oak Island Drive from NC 133 west to Southeast 40th Street. It does, however, has two fishing piers, one at the end of Womble Street (which is the seventh block west of NC 133) and the other just west of 16th Place East. Nearly all of the beach is lined with homes (around 500 are available for rent); the far western end has a very nice wild area. The town government maintains a network of boardwalks and nature sites, which nicely complement the beach experience.

Holden Beach, Brunswick Islands (municipal site: hbtownhall.com; merchants' association: hbmerchants.com). Sitting at the end of NC 130, 8.9-mile-long Holden Beach is noted for its quiet character and appeal to families. Its tiny downtown centers on the bridge end, with a wooden fishing pier 1.6 miles to the west on Ocean Boulevard, and rather more commercial development on the landward side of the bridge. The beach is very good with a nice dune line, if a bit narrow in parts at high tide. Its easternmost tip, however is extremely wide, with multiple dune lines and a wild character, best reached by parking at the end of McCray Street and walking. The beach becomes very wide on its westernmost 2 miles as well, but this entire section has neither public access points nor parking.

To reach Holden Beach from the south or west simply take NC 130; this, however, is considerably out of the way when approaching from Wilmington. Instead, take US 17 south for 27 miles to a left turn onto Stone Chimney Road (becoming Old Ferry Connection, both SSR 1115), then go 7.0 miles to a right turn onto Sabbath Home Road (SSR 1120), then go 0.7 mile to a left turn (at a traffic light) onto NC 130; the bridge to the island is 0.8 mile ahead.

Ocean Isle Beach, Brunswick Islands (municipal site: oibgov.com; pier site: oibpier.com). This quiet, lightly developed island has 6.1 miles of excellent beach, stretching in equal directions from its one access bridge; to reach it take US 17 for 38 miles south of Wilmington to a left onto Ocean Isle Beach Road (SSR 1184), which you follow to its end. Town center consists of a handful of commercial buildings just after the bridge, ending at the wooden fishing pier, with 200 parking spaces. There are more beach access points, typically every couple of blocks in each direction, with about half of these having parking. The beach itself is wide along nearly its entire length, except for a very short distance at the extreme eastern end (where the sea is trying to claim several houses). The eastern tip has a wild character; to visit it, park along the western end of 3rd Street and walk the two blocks to where the sea has wiped out the eastern end of the street (a fine place to observe the effects of beach erosion). The western tip has no public access.

Sunset Beach, Brunswick Islands (municipal site: sunsetbeachnc.gov). The westernmost beach in the Brunswick Islands and the southernmost in North Carolina, 4.0-mile-long Sunset Beach overhangs 0.5 mile into South Carolina. This is the quietest of the developed public beaches, its built-up area fronting on less than half of its length; the rest is wilderness, including the entire 2-mile-long western end, owned by the state as the **Bird Island Estuarine Preserve** (it used to be a separate island). Its tiny downtown (a block long and only half developed) sits between the island's entrance and its wooden fishing pier, which has the only large parking lot on the beach. Not to worry—street parking is everywhere, legal and free, and access points are typically only 200 feet apart. The beach itself is amazingly wide and sandy, with a heavily vegetated dune line 500 feet wide isolating you from what development exists. The frequent access points all provide long, scenic boardwalks through untrammeled dune environments. But if this isn't wild enough for you, head west on Main Street to its end, and use the last access boardwalk to start on the two mile beach hike through true wilderness to the end of North Carolina.

If you're traveling to Sunset Beach from points west or south (basically, from South Carolina), leave US 17 to go to Calabash (signposted), then go east out of town on NC 179 (Beach Drive Southwest) for 1.0 mile, then go right (at the traffic light) onto NC Bus 179 (still Beach Drive Southwest), which you follow for 3.5 miles to a right turn back onto NC 179 just before the bridge to the island. From Wilmington, follow US 17 south for 41 miles to a left turn (at a traffic light) onto NC 904, which becomes NC 179/904 in 2.2 miles; continue straight, staying on NC 179 to reach the island bridge in 3.3 miles.

✱ To See

CULTURAL SITES **Cameron Art Museum, Wilmington** (910-395-5999; cameronartmuseum.com), 3201 S. 17th St., Wilmington 28412. Open Tue.–Sun. 11–5, Thu. 11–9. $$. Founded in 1964, this large museum occupies a 40,000-square-foot modernist edifice in a park-like campus 4.7 miles southeast of downtown. Its three major exhibit halls feature two temporary exhibitions, plus a thematic selection from the permanent collection that rotates several times a year. In general the displays are eclectic, emphasizing North Carolina artists and concerns but including regional and national figures as well. It has an attractive café and a museum shop.

HISTORIC SITES **Wilmington Railroad Museum, downtown Wilmington** (910-763-2634; wrrm.org), 505 Nutt St., Wilmington 28401. Open Apr.–Sept., Mon–Sat. 10–5, Sun. 1–5; Oct.–Mar., Mon.–Sat. 10–4. $$. In 1840 Wilmington emerged as one of the nation's great rail cities, the headquarters and terminus of the Wilmington & Weldon Railroad, then the longest continuous rail line in the world (at 161 miles). In 1872 this morphed into the Atlantic Coast Line Railroad, one of the great railroads of the South, and its corporate offices spread over the whole northern end of Wilmington's downtown. These offices included the full range of railroad functions, from simple warehouses, to repair yards and roundhouses, to a spectacular six-story passenger depot with corporate offices in the upper floors.

Then in 1961 it all ended, when Atlantic Coast Line moved, lock, stock, and barrel, to Jacksonville, Florida. Wilmington's government, faced with the huge and wholly abandoned railroad site sprawling across six downtown blocks, tore the entire thing down and replaced it with a community college. The only surviving buildings are among the most modest: two brick-built freight depots facing the river. These now house the Wilmington Railroad Museum, dedicated to the glory days of Wilmington railroading and the great steam-powered rail lines of the South. There is a limited collection of rolling stock (including a fine steam engine and a caboose) in the yard between. Of particular interest is the largest model railroad in the state, which includes an accurate reconstruction of the Wilmington Atlantic Coast Line headquarters and yard c. 1950, and shows how this related to its hinterland as far as Wilson.

The Bellamy Mansion Museum of History and Design Arts, downtown Wilmington (910-251-3700; bellamymansion.org; info@bellamymansion.org), 503 Market St., Wilmington 28402. Open for tours on the hour, Tue.–Sat. 10–4, Sun. 1–4. $$$. John Dillard Bellamy built this exuberantly columned antebellum mansion on the edge of downtown Wilmington in 1859–61, surely a candidate for worst timing ever. Elaborate Corinthian columns surround the building, extending in front of both floors to form a wide porch—a house Scarlett O'Hara would have appreciated. Inside are restored rooms and a museum of design arts; outside, the surviving narrow lot is planted in formal gardens. In the back the original slave quarters survive, a remarkable two-story brick structure, long and skinny, along the back alley of what was already an urban neighborhood when the house was built; it's being restored, and may be open by the time you read this.

The Latimer House, downtown Wilmington (910-762-0492; hslcf.org), 126 S. 3rd St., Wilmington 28401. Open weekdays 10–4, Sat. noon–5. $$. This Italianate mansion was built in 1852 in what was then the residential section of the village of Wilmington, and is now downtown. The home of the Historical Society of the Lower Cape Fear River, it has been furnished as a museum of the upper-class Victorian lifestyle, with more than 600 items on display in its 14 rooms.

The Burgwin-Wright House, downtown Wilmington (910-762-0570; burgwinwrighthouse.com; info@burgwinwrighthouse.com), 224 Market St., Wilmington 28401. Open Tue.–Sat. 10–3. $$. Built in 1770, this colonial-era mansion was occupied by British commander Cornwallis as he retreated toward his final defeat at Yorktown. It's a large, elegantly Georgian manor with classical elements. Interior furnishings cover the 18th through the late 19th century, while the extensive formal gardens reflect antebellum tastes. It has been owned and run by the Colonial Dames of North Carolina since 1963.

Battleship *North Carolina*, Wilmington (910-251-5797; battleshipnc.com; ncbb55@battleshipnc.com), 1 Battleship Rd., Wilmington 28402. Open daily, 8–8 from Memorial Day to Labor Day, 8–5 the rest of the year. $$$. Launched in 1941, the Battleship *North Carolina* was America's first new battleship in 20 years, and the greatest sea weapon in the world. Classed as a "fast battleship," her 16-inch guns cluster 3 at a time in 3 turrets, with 20 more 5-inch guns in 10 turrets. At her peak during World War II she had 2,300 sailors and officers, and participated in

THE BELLAMY MANSION MUSEUM OF HISTORY AND DESIGN ARTS, WILMINGTON

every major naval offensive in the Pacific, earning 15 battle stars. The Japanese claimed to have sunk her on six different occasions (including a direct hit with a torpedo)—but here she is, in her own berth directly across from downtown Wilmington, where she's rested since 1961. Today's ship is a memorial to North Carolina's 10,000 war dead during World War II, and a museum with thousands of items, dedicated to showing what a battleship did and what it was like to live in one. There's a lot to explore, with 5 decks and platforms below the main deck, and 10 levels above the main deck.

Cape Fear Museum, Wilmington (910-798-4350; capefearmuseum.com), 814 Market St., Wilmington 28401. Open Mon.–Sat. 9–5, Sun. 1–5; closed on Mon., Labor Day–Memorial Day. $$. This large museum is located four blocks east of downtown, in an attractive modern building. Its rotating and permanent exhibits deal with both the history and the environment of the Cape Fear region, an interesting combination that yields more than usual interest.

Poplar Grove Plantation, north of Wilmington (910-686-9518; poplargrove.com), 10200 US 17 N., Wilmington 28411. Open Mon.–Sat. 9–5, Sun. noon–5. $$. This plantation house, 16 miles northeast of Wilmington on US 17, was built in 1850 as the seat of the Foy family, who started farming these lands in 1795 and lived here until well into the 1970s. Its modestly elegant front, a subdued Classical Revival, gives little hint of its true size of nearly 4,500 square feet. This becomes apparent from the back, where wide, massive two-story porches loom over its farmyard high atop its walk-out basement, with a large wing framing it on the side. In antebellum times this yard would have been where its 22 slaves did the household chores, from laundry to blacksmithing; a postbellum "tenant's house" frames the yard, showing where the slave housing would have been. Slave treatment varied widely in North Carolina (as elsewhere), including plantations that were little more than farms for breeding humans; but the Foys were among the more humane slave owners, refusing to split families (or indeed to sell slaves, even though a healthy field hand cost as much as a racehorse), and allowing slaves to worship, obtain education, own property, and run side jobs. (The family explored freeing their slaves in 1861, but this was foiled by draconian North Carolina laws that would have forced the freemen from their homes and expelled them from the state.) Inside, the house is as elegant as its front suggests, with wood details made of black walnut from the plantation, and furnishings from the late antebellum period; interior lighting is by carbide gas. The Foy family has recently donated an additional 67 acres, now explored by a delightful nature trail, one of the few opportunities to experience the lands and woodlots of actively farmed areas.

Missiles and More Museum, Topsail Island (910-328-2488; topsailmissilesmuseum.org), 720 Channel Blvd., Topsail Beach 28445. Summer season (Memorial Day–Labor Day): Mon.–Sat. 2–5; shoulder season (six weeks before and after summer season): Mon.–Fri. 2–5. In 1946 Topsail Beach, isolated and uninhabited, became the site of the U.S. Navy's guided missile testing program, Operation Bumblebee—one of NASA's ancestors. Of the bits and pieces of this pioneer in early rocketry scattered about the island, the largest by far is its original Assembly Building (where the rockets were assembled), a cavernous hall on the lagoon side of Topsail's tiny downtown (the camp's original center), 6.1 miles south of the island's south (NC 50) bridge, and 40 miles from Wilmington. It's owned by the Topsail Historical Society, and part of it is dedicated to the Missiles and More

Museum, with exhibits on Operation Bumblebee and Camp Davis (of which this was a secret part), including declassified archives and mock-ups of the missiles.

Despite the obviously military architecture, the existence of this site was denied for decades. Yet pay a little attention and you can spot other buildings from this top-secret base nearby. A block toward the beach stands an observation tower, and a similar building stands abandoned a mile or so to its south. Directly across on the beach side, the Jolly Rodger Motel's concrete patio is said to be a former rocket launching pad.

Moores Creek National Battlefield, northwest of Wilmington (910-283-5591; nps.gov/mocr), 40 Patriots Hall Dr., Currie 28435. Open daily 9–5. Admission is free. Located 21 miles northwest of Wilmington on NC 210 (take US 421 north from town for 17 miles to a left turn), this 88-acre national park commemorates the odd but important Revolutionary War Battle of Moores Creek, fought here in February 1776. At that time North Carolina had already been in a state of insurrection for a year, so much so that its colony's royal governor, Josiah Martin, had been forced to flee Tryon Palace in New Bern (see "New Bern and Beaufort")—first for the cramped safety of the palisaded walls of Fort Johnston (now a waterfront park in Southport), and then to an offshore British sloop-of-war. From there Martin organized a counter-insurgency consisting mainly of Scottish Highlanders who, for reasons now hard to understand, were loyal to the Crown that had destroyed their land within living memory. (Combatants included the husband of Flora McDonald, who had, in 1746, gained fame for hiding Scotland's would-be liberator Bonnie Prince Charlie in her Hebridean home.) An army of 1,000 Highlander Loyalists started their attempt to regain the important Cape Fear River harbors by advancing on a bridge over Moores Creek, which they believed to be lightly held. They were wrong; an army of 1,600 Patriots was guarding the far side. Worse (for the Loyalists), most of the Highlanders were armed with claymores, the massive broadswords they had brought with them from Scotland, while the Patriots were plentifully supplied with muskets and small cannons. Before the battle the Patriots removed the planks from the bridge and smeared the cross-beams with lard, but this didn't stop the Highlanders. Swords in hand, the Scots jumped, unbalanced, from beam to beam, many slipping into the flood-swollen creek; when they bunched up at the end of the bridge the Patriots opened fire. It was a rout. The Loyalist army was completely destroyed, and all their equipment captured; Governor Martin fled to New York, never to return. Four months before the Declaration of Independence, North Carolina's government was in Patriot hands and would remain so until the end of war.

Today's park has the normal panoply of national battlefield items: a visitors center with a fine museum, a number of stone monuments (including one to the sacrifice of women during the Revolution, believed to be only such monument in America), reconstructed Patriot earthworks, and plentiful interpretive placards. The original road survives and bisects the park, and its colonial bridge has been reconstructed with its planks missing, so you can see just how hard it was to jump over. A boardwalk leads across the stream and through its marshes, and two other trails explore the Patriot side of the park. There's a reenactment encampment every February, although for safety reasons no one tries to leap the bridge in Highlands regalia.

Old Baldy Lighthouse and Smith Island Museum of History, Bald Head Island (910-457-7481; oldbaldy.org; info@oldbaldy.org), 101 Lighthouse Wynd, Bald Head Island 28461. Open Mon.–Sat. 9–5, Sun. 11–5. $$. Built in 1817 to replace an 18th-century structure, Old Baldy (as it is known) is the oldest lighthouse in North Carolina. You'll find it on Bald Head Island; take the passenger ferry from Southport, then go 0.2 mile south of the ferry terminal on Federal Road. This octagonal structure is 110 feet tall, built of brick coated with lime plaster, and topped with a peculiarly tiny lamp house. It seems too short to do any good for ocean shipping, and it is—it was built to help navigation in the mouth of the Cape Fear River, rather than the treacherous Frying Pan Shoals off Cape Fear. It was decommissioned in 1934. Inside are wooden steps, which you can climb all the way to the top, with some fine views. Adjacent to it is the reconstructed lightkeeper's house, which is now home to the Smith Island Museum of History (*Smith Island* being an older name for Bald Head Island).

There are other relics of pre-development days. Straight-as-a-stick Federal Road is one of them. It led to a Coast Guard station that once was located 0.5 mile north of Cape Fear, but was destroyed by beach erosion in 1914. The old station may be gone, but Federal Road is a fine, scenic drive by bicycle or golf cart, with good views of tidal inlets and maritime forests that make up the Bald Head Island State Natural Area. And yes, there used to be a lighthouse for Cape Fear and its shoals on the Atlantic side of the island, a slender concrete tower braced by a steel lattice, built in 1903. Although the Coast Guard tore it down when Oak Island Lighthouse replaced it in 1958, it left behind the three lightkeepers' cottages, now known as Captain Charlie's Station, which have been restored as historic vacation rentals. Perched within high dunes, this is one of the most scenic and photographable spots in all of North Carolina's beaches.

CAPTAIN CHARLIE'S STATION, NEAR CAPE FEAR, ON BALD HEAD ISLAND

Southport's Maritime Museum and Colonial District (910-457-0003; ncmaritime.org/branches/southport_default.htm), 116 N. Howe St., Southport 28461. Open Tue.–Sat. 9–5. Admission is free. This branch of the state-run North Carolina Maritime Museum (see "New Bern and Beaufort") covers the maritime history and ecology of the Cape Fear region from its storefront location in downtown Southport. Pirates, shipwrecks, naval stores, Civil War trade and blockade—these are the stories of port lands along the mouth of the Cape Fear River told in this museum. Of special note is a collection of ship models, and a scale replica of a commercial shrimp net, made by a local expert.

One block to its north is colonial-era Franklin Square Park, its entrance nestled between early republic buildings—a Greek Revival Masonic hall and a Carpenter Gothic Methodist church, both still in use. Azaleas line the main walk, and landscaped glades head off on either side.

Old Jail Museum, Southport (910-457-0579; southporthistoricalsociety.com/old jail.html), corner of Nash and Rhett Sts., P.O. Box 10014, Southport 28461. Open May–Oct., Wed. and Sat. 12:30–3:30. Admission is free. Built in 1904, this attractive red-brick structure in a residential area has housed such notorious prisoners as Sissy Spacek, when she filmed prison scenes for the movie *Crimes of the Heart*. Other than that, it's a typical southern sheriff's jail, used to hold drunks, vagrants, and other criminals for trial, restored to its early-20th-century appearance (complete with prisoner graffiti). It's been the headquarters of the Southport Historic Society since 1984, and they are happy to show you around, and answer your questions about this beautiful little colonial town.

Brunswick Town/Fort Anderson State Historic Site, north of Southport (910-371-6613; nchistoricsites.org/brunswic; brunswick@ncdcr.gov), 8884 St. Philip's Rd. SE, Winnabow 28479. Open Tue.–Sat. 9–5. Admission is free. This archaeological site presents the ruins of Brunswick Town, a major colonial port on the Cape Fear River, 19 miles south of Wilmington via NC 133 to Plantation Rd., and 15 miles north of Southport via NC 87 to NC 133 to Plantation Rd. Founded as the seat of newly created New Hanover County in 1726, it lost this economically important distinction to Wilmington in 1740. During this short heyday Brunswick Town was the center of a vital and rapidly expanding plantation economy, based not on tobacco or cotton as elsewhere, but on rice in the coastal marshes and naval stores extracted from the longleaf pine forests on the high ground. Like many among the first wave of settlements, however, Brunswick Town was not particularly well sited. While its harbor was exceptionally deep, and therefore excellent for receiving ships from the mother country, it was disease-prone, surrounded by swamps, and in a poor location for receiving goods from the many plantations being quickly established throughout the region. Wilmington, on the other hand, was located on a high, wide ridge, at the convergence of roads and river channels. Brunswick Town slowly faded, and when a British raiding party burned it to the ground in 1776, no one bothered to rebuild it.

Today's Brunswick Town is a handsome site shaded by live oaks, with a number of ruins, mainly stone foundations for wooden buildings, exposed by archaeologists and interpreted with placards. Its most interesting ruin is the intact walls of its church, St. Phillips, a massive Gothic brick structure whose 2-foot-thick walls survived bombardment during the Civil War. The reason for this bombardment was Fort Anderson, a large earthwork fortification built by the Confederates as part of an elaborate system guarding the mouth of the Cape Fear River. It was successful in this, surviving until February 1865, only two months before General Lee's surrender at Appomattox. Some of its earthworks can still be seen.

Orton Plantation, north of Southport (ortongardens.com). Open to the public since 1910, North Carolina's premier historic plantation and garden closed indefinitely in June 2010, upon being sold to a billionaire hedge fund manager. The new owner, said to be restoring the site, has not announced when, or even if, it will open again. In any case there is no chance of it being reopened during 2011, and little chance for 2012.

Oak Island Lighthouse, Brunswick Islands (oakislandlighthouse.org; light house-tours@caswellbeach.org), 1100 Caswell Beach Rd., Caswell Beach 28465. Open for tours Memorial Day–Labor Day, Wed. and Sat. 10–2. Tours to the top by appointment only. Tours are free. Erected in 1958, this most modern of all North Carolina lighthouses stands on the eastern end of Oak Island, 2.8 miles east of the terminus of NC 133 via Caswell Beach Road (SSR 1100). It's a concrete cylinder 15 stories high, its alternate white and black coloring due to dyes placed in the concrete itself. Inside, access to the narrow, vertiginous viewing platform directly below the light is by a series of ships ladders with 131 steps and no handrails. The twice-weekly tour includes the ground level and the first ship's ladder—but you can climb all the way to the top, by making an appointment at least two weeks in advance. Across the street from the lighthouse, a long boardwalk leads over the dunes to a fine beach with a wild character.

SPECIAL SITES **Cape Fear Serpentarium, downtown Wilmington** (910-762-1669; capefearserpentarium.com), 20 Orange St., Wilmington 28401. Open weekdays 11–5, weekends 11–6; feedings Sat. and Sun. at 3. $$. Located on the south edge of downtown, the serpentarium occupies an attractive purpose-built brick structure that blends nicely with the historic buildings around it. This is not your old-fashioned roadside-on-the-highway-to-Florida tourist attraction. Rather, it features the large private collection of herpetologist Dean Ripa, who holds the uncoveted world record for surviving the most bushmaster bites (seven). The 10,000-square-foot facility has 54 displays that together house more than 40 species of venomous snakes, plus three full-sized habitat exhibits of crocodiles, and five large bays featuring constrictors.

EUE/Screen Gems Studio Tours, Wilmington (910-343-3433; screengems studios.com/nc/tours.html; info@screengemsstudios.com; movies filmed in Wilmington: myreporter.com/?p=3938), 1223 23rd St. N., Wilmington 28405. Sat. 11:45 and 1:45. America's largest film studio east of California is located just off the US 74 freeway on the north end of town. Since being built in the 1980s it's cranked out an impressive array of movies, television shows, and commercials, starting with *Firestarters* in 1984, with *Dawson's Creek* and *One Tree Hill* generating the most fan interest. Wilmington locations feature prominently in a large number of movies, including the rolling hula hoop in *The Hudsucker Proxy* (downtown Wilmington) and the back-home segments of *The Butcher's Wife* (Captain Charlie's Station on Bald Head Island).

Fort Fisher State Aquarium, Pleasure Island (866-301-3476; ncaquariums .com/fort-fisher; ffmail@ncaquariums.com), 900 Loggerhead Rd., Kure Beach 28449. Open daily 9–5. $$. Located at the far southern end of Pleasure Island, 20 miles south of Wilmington via US 421, the southernmost of the state's three aquariums explores the waters of the Cape Fear River from far upstream to the open ocean. A freshwater, tree-filled atrium features an albino alligator among the fish, turtles, frogs, and reptiles, and a coastal waters gallery includes a touching pond, plus displays of salt marsh animals, jetty environment animals, sea turtles, and seahorses. From there check out the quarter-million-gallon shoals tank with sharks, stingrays, groupers, and moray eels, including a dramatic reef display.

✱ To Do

BICYCLE RENTALS **Cape Fear Cyclists** (capefearcyclists.org). This 500-member local cyclists' club is a good resource for traveling bicyclers. They sponsor regular bike rides open to the public, and their website has an extensive list of recommended road routes. They also have information on off-road biking.

Bike Cycles, Wilmington (910-256-2545; bikecycleshop.com; info@bikecycleshop.com), 6801 Parker Farm Rd., Wilmington 28405. Open Mon.–Sat. 10–6. This bicycle shop is located in the far northeastern of town, just off Military Cutoff Rd., 0.5 mile north of the intersection of US 74 and US 76. They rent a variety of road bikes and cruisers, including tandems.

Wrightsville Beach Supply Company (910-256-8821; wbsupplyco.com; contact@wbsupplyco.com), 1 N. Lumina Ave., Wrightsville Beach 28480. This beach supply company rents bicycles as well as surfboards and beach chairs.

Wheel Fun Rentals, Carolina Beach, Pleasure Island (910-458-4545; wheelfunrentals.com), 107 Carolina Beach Ave. N., Carolina Beach 28428. This national chain rents bikes as well as beach stuff such as surfboards and umbrellas. Choices range from beach cruisers to road bikes to odd "surrey" bikes that look like golf carts and seat up to eight people.

Julie's Rentals and Sweet Shop, Sunset Beach, Brunswick Islands (910-269-8646; juliesrentals.com), 2 W. Main St., Sunset Beach 28467. Located across from the pier, this beach rental offers bicycles as well as a range of fun beach stuff. They have kayaks as well, and sponsor kayak tours of the salt marshes.

CANOES AND KAYAKS **Paddling on Greenfield Lake, Wilmington** (910-762-5606; cfrw.us/greenfieldlake.html). Open daily 11–6. Local environmental not-for-profit Cape Fear River Watch runs the boat concession on 90-acre Greenfield Lake, Wilmington's fine old public garden, off US 421 2.0 miles south of downtown. They rent canoes and kayaks for use on the lake, and run birding tours during migration season.

Coastal Urge, Wilmington (800-383-4443; sup.coastalurge.com; info@coastalurge.com), 86 Keelson Row, Bald Head Island 28461. This company has introduced to the Wilmington area stand-up paddleboarding (SUP)—where you stand upright on a device that looks like a cross between a surfboard and a kayak, and paddle it around. The boards are stable and great fun, and can be used in both the lagoon and ocean waters. They are, however, particularly well suited for the tiny tidal inlets of the back marshes, where standing will give you an entirely different perspective from a canoe or kayak. While they have several beach apparel stores in the Wilmington area, their SUP rental outlet is on Bald Head Island, the best place in this region for exploring the marshes. They sponsor lessons and tours, and if you are renting a home on the island they will deliver rented boards to you free of charge. They also have kiteboarding lessons and coaching.

Hook, Line, and Paddle, Wilmington (hooklineandpaddle.com). This outfitter offers canoe and kayak rentals, sales, and repairs from a shop on US 74, 5 miles east of downtown. They offer tours and instruction as well as rentals, and have

SPORTFISHING BOATS ALONG THE INTRACOASTAL WATERWAY, WILMINGTON

specialized fishing tours and fishing kayaks. They also have a branch on the Intracoastal Waterway, at Wrightsville Beach's Blockade Runner Beach Resort.

Carolina Coastal Adventures, Pleasure Island (910-458-9171; carolinacoastaladventures.com), 306 N. Lake Park Blvd., Carolina Beach 28428. This Carolina Beach outfitter specializes in kayak rentals and tours throughout the marshes and along the coast. Fishing kayaks are available, as are surfboards.

The Adventure Company, Southport (910-454-0607; theadventurecompany.net; theadventurecompany@earthlink.net), 807-A Howe St., Southport 28461. Located on the northern edge of downtown, this company rents several types of kayaks, and offers kayak lessons and tours. They also rent bicycles, and sponsor bike tours of historic Southport.

MOTORBOAT RENTALS **NC Boat Rentals** (910-279-2355; ncboatrentals.com; info@ncboatrentals.com), 600 W. Brunswick St., Unit 1, Southport 28461. This Southport-based company rents Boston Whaler fishing boats in a variety of lengths and types from five different local marinas: downtown Wilmington's City Docks, Airlie Marina on Wrightsville Beach, Southport Marina just west of town center (their headquarters), the marina on Bald Head Island, and the marina within the gated residential development known as St. James Plantation, on the mainland opposite Oak Island.

Entropy Boats, Wilmington (910-675-1877; entropyboats.com; PeteK123@aol.com). This custom boatbuilder rents the 17- to 20-foot fishing boats that they make.

✱ Lodging

HOTELS AND RESORTS 🐾 **Front Street Inn, downtown Wilmington** (800-336-8184; 910-762-6442; frontstreetinn.com; richard@frontstreetinn.com), 215 S. Front St., Wilmington 28401. $$$–$$$$. This 12-room bed & breakfast occupies the historic, brick-built former home of the Salvation Army of the Carolinas, retaining its arched windows, thick walls, and maple floors. American art gathered from galleries, fairs, auctions, and attics gives it a bohemian flavor, and its 12 large suite-rooms are eclectically decorated. WiFi is available. Its breakfast buffet, served 7–11, features fresh-made pastries, breads, granola, and quiches. Only one of the suites is designated for pets, so make arrangements in advance.

✐ 🐾 **The Winds Resort Beach Club, Ocean Isle, Brunswick Islands** (800-334-3581; thewinds.com), 310 E. 1st St., Ocean Isle Beach 28469. $$–$$$$$. Still owned and operated by the family of its founder, this hotel spreads across four adjacent beachfront buildings, with 10 full-sized cottages directly across the street. Rooms, suites, and cottages have open and airy floor plans, with comfortable and stylish decor; rooms have wet bars and micro fridges, while suites have kitchenettes. There's a large beach-side swimming pool with a tiki bar, and a second pool across the street for the cottages. WiFi is available, and the tariff includes a full breakfast buffet. Call ahead if you are traveling with a pet, as pet-friendly rooms are limited in number.

✐ **The Sunset Inn, Sunset Beach, Brunswick Islands** (888-575-1001; 910-575-1000; thesunsetinn.net), 9 North Shore Dr., Sunset Beach 28468. $$–$$$$. This newly built hotel sits on the sound side of Sunset Beach adjacent to the causeway to the mainland. Its 14 rooms (4 of them extra-large) all have private screened porches overlooking the sound, with a wet bar and mini fridge. WiFi is available, and the tariff includes a full buffet breakfast. Children under 12 are allowed only with prior approval, and child-friendly rooms are limited.

BED & BREAKFASTS 🐾 **Camillia Cottage Bed and Breakfast, downtown Wilmington** (866-728-5272; 910-763-9171; camelliacottage.net; info@camelliacottage.net), 118 S. 4th St., Wilmington 28401. $$–$$$. A stunning 1889 Queen Anne home with wraparound porches houses this five-room B&B in a residential neighborhood just east of downtown, and four blocks from the riverfront. It is surrounded by a lush perennial garden filled with azaleas, magnolias, roses, and camellias. Rooms are attractively furnished and range in size from standard to large; the second floor consists of one entire room with kitchenette and private entrance, which rents by the month. WiFi is available, and a full three-course breakfast is included (which includes pastries made by the innkeeper, a former pastry chef).

Greystone Inn, downtown Wilmington (888-763-4773; 910-763-2000; graystoneinn.com), 100 S. 3rd St., Wilmington 28401. $$$$–$$$$$. Located on the southern end of downtown, three blocks from the river, this stone-built 1905 mansion was once home to some of the richest people in Wilmington; its projecting, half-round two-story porch, framed by massive Ionic columns, gives it more of the look of a courthouse than a private home. It is now a nine-room B&B, carefully restored inside and out to its original period appearance, with an emphasis on luxury. Rooms are large to very large, elegantly furnished with antiques, and feature the building's original exquisite architectural details. WiFi is available, and a full breakfast is included in the tariff.

✐ **Taylor House Bed and Breakfast, Wilmington** (800-382-9982; 910-763-7581; taylorhousebb.com; Info@TaylorHouseBB.com), 14 N. 7th St., Wilmington 28401. $$–$$$. This pleasant Victorian home on a residential block sits four blocks east of downtown, and within two blocks of both the Bellamy Mansion Museum and the Cape Fear Museum. The attractive furnishings are those of a comfortable family home of a century ago, and the five guest rooms are airy and large. A full breakfast, included in the tariff, is served at a common table at 9 AM, and changes daily.

✐ 🐾 **Beacon House Bed & Breakfast and Cottages, Carolina Beach, Pleasure Island** (877-232-2666; 910-458-6244; beaconhouseinnb-b.com; innkeeper@beaconhouseinnb-b.com), 715 Carolina Beach Ave. N., Carolina Beach 28428. $$$–$$$$. This old-fashioned boardinghouse, located across the street from the beach and 0.6 mile north of the boardwalk, dates from the 1950s, but has the look and feel of an earlier age. You'll find it a plain but attractive (and well-kept) building, with two-story verandas facing the narrow residential street. It retains this old-fashioned atmosphere throughout, a casually cultivated retro feel. Its seven rooms are standard-sized, furnished in a straightforward manner, with queen beds; like most B&Bs, this is for adults who like their peace and quiet. Adjacent cottages, with kitchens, accommodate families with younger children or pets. WiFi is available in the main inn building, and a full southern breakfast (for inn guests only) is served 9–10.

The Colonel's Lady Bed and Breakfast, Jacksonville (910-937-7718; bbonline.com/nc/colonelslady; mdgnon@yahoo.com), 215 Mill Ave., Jacksonville 28754. $$. Nestled adjacent to the old town center, in the village's original residential district, this 1901 home (typical of the rural southern middle class of the era) features wide wraparound verandas. Neither the house nor its neighborhood gives any hint that you are staying in anything other than a sleepy, small riverside town; the postmilitary scrum that makes Jacksonville into a full-fledged city is convenient, yet invisible. Its three rooms are large, furnished with antiques and quilts. WiFi is available, and a full southern breakfast, served at the time of your choosing (up to 10 AM), is included.

Robert Ruark Inn Bed and Breakfast, Southport (910-363-4169; robertruarkinn.com; info@robertruarkinn.com), 119 N. Lord St., Southport 28461. $$$–$$$$. This elegant Victorian home, named after an early-20th-century writer who lived here, sits in Southport's historic district only two blocks from the waterfront. Its four large rooms are tastefully decorated in period, with king or queen bed; three of the four have gas fireplace as well. A southern-style full breakfast, included in the tariff, is served 8–10.

The Rose Bed and Breakfast, Calabash, Brunswick Islands (mainland) (866-340-0139; 910-575-2880; therosebandb.com; rosebb2005@yahoo.com), 545 Hickman Rd. NW, Calabash 28467. $$. Located in a formerly rural area 3 miles north of Calabash, this purpose-built B&B has an appearance inspired by the South's Victorian farmhouses, with Doric-columned wraparound porches set off by a turret and a second-story balcony. The innkeepers offer you homemade treats upon arrival, and keep a guest refrigerator stocked with soft drinks. Decor is modern, themed around bright colors; the rooms are large, with king beds that can be converted into twins. WiFi is available. A four-course breakfast, included in the tariff, is served 8–10. The location may seem remote, but "remote" is relative; there are 63 holes of golf (open to the public) on three separate courses within only 2 miles.

✷ Where to Eat

DINING OUT Circa 1922 Tapas Restaurant and Bar, downtown Wilmington (910-762-1922; circa1922.com; circa1922nc@yahoo.com), 8 N. Front St., Wilmington 28401. Open daily for dinner. $$–$$$$. Located at the center of downtown, a block off the waterfront, this restaurant-bar has a decor based on old brick, high ceilings, and polished wood. It specializes in tapas, small plates, of which it offers a good variety; it also offers traditional full meals, as creative as the tapas. Happy hour runs 5–7 daily, and features $3 tapas and $5 pub grub; there's also a three-course prix fixe served Sun.–Thu. ($$$).

🐾 **Caffe Phoenix, downtown Wilmington** (910-343-1395; thecaffephoenix.com; caffephoenix@mac.com), 35 N. Front St., Wilmington 28401. Open daily for lunch and dinner. $$$–$$$$. At the heart of downtown Wilmington's restaurant district (and a block from the waterfront), this restaurant features fresh local food, including vegetables grown by the chef himself. You'll find it in a fine old brick storefront, built in 1899 for a dry-goods store, with high ceilings and polished wood floors; its walls serve as an exhibit space for local artists, rotating every six weeks. The menu emphasizes Mediterranean flavors, and has a good selection of lunch sandwiches; there's also a four-course prix fixe ($$$$). The *Wine Spectator* Award wine list has a decent selection of bottles under $30, and numerous wines by the glass. Dogs are permitted on their outside patio.

EATING OUT Front Street Brewery, downtown Wilmington (910-251-1935; frontstreetbrewery.com; FrontStreetBrewery@gmail.com), 9 N. Front St., Wilmington 28401. Open daily for lunch and dinner. $$–$$$. Wilmington's long-established brewpub occupies a handsome brick storefront at the heart of its downtown restaurant district, a block off the waterfront. Its award-winning brews range across all popular styles, from weissbier to IPA to stout. The ambience is very pubby, with brick and old wood and a long bar. The menu is pubby as well, but distinguished by fresh preparation and a fair amount of creativity, influenced by the Tidewater South, Britain, and their own beer; their routine pricing in the $$ to low $$$ range (when you add a beer) is a real bargain. A daily 4–7 happy hour features half-priced appetizers. Local musicians may entertain on weekends.

🐾 **Stone Crab Oyster Bar, Wilmington** (910-256-5435; stonecraboysterbar.com), 1900 Eastwood Rd., Wilmington 28403. Open daily for lunch and dinner. $$–$$$$. Located within the upscale Lumina Station shopping center, on US 74/76 on the eastern side of town, this seafood restaurant has a good variety of well-prepared non-seafood dishes as well. It centers on its steamer bar, offering a wide variety of crabs, clams, mussels, shrimp, oysters, and lobster—local, when available. The regular menu offers a variety of fried, broiled, and grilled seafood as well, including fish and scallops as well as the steamer bar items. Dogs are welcome in its patio area.

Havana's Fresh Island Seafood, Carolina Beach, Pleasure Island (910-458-2822; havanasrestaurant.com; pete@havanasrestaurant.com), 1 N. Lake Park Blvd., Carolina Beach 28428. Open for dinner Mon.–Sat., and Sun. brunch. $$$–$$$$. Located in a restored bungalow on US 421 at the center of Carolina Beach, this attractively laid-out seafood restaurant is two blocks from the beach. Its handsome interior, bright and airy, has small rooms for quiet, big rooms for larger parties, and a large, tented and screened, patio. Despite its name and Caribbean decor, the menu features good-quality American cuisine, distinguished from the crowd by being made from scratch using fresh ingredients wherever possible. The wine list is good, with many choices under $30, but the beer choice is limited to mass-produced lagers. They offer weekly live acoustic entertainment.

Freddie's Restaurante, Kure Beach, Pleasure Island (910-458-5979; freddieskurebeach.com; info@freddieskurebeach.com), 111 K Ave., Kure Beach 28449. Open daily for dinner. $$–$$$$. Located in Kure Beach's town center, two doors down from the pier, Freddie's specializes in Italian cuisine, made from scratch using fresh ingredients. Inside its plain but well-kept commercial building it has a casual, pubby decor and atmosphere, with a friendly little bar. The extensive menu features fresh pasta and red sauces made in the kitchen; the most remarkable entrées, however, are a set of special pork chop creations, in which the chop is grilled with a balsamic reduction, then married with various toppings. As to price, only the steak menu pushes into the $$$$ range, with most meal-and-drink prices hovering around the border between $$ and $$$.

Duck's Grille and Bar, Jacksonville (910-455-9128; ducksgrilleandbar.com), 1207 Gum Branch Rd., Jacksonville 28540. Open for lunch and dinner daily. $$–$$$$. You'll find this pleasant surprise in a nondescript suburban shopping district a mile north of town; to find it take US Bus 17 (Marine Boulevard) north out of town center to a left onto Gum Branch

SEAFOOD RESTAURANTS OF CALABASH, BRUNSWICK ISLANDS (MAINLAND)

Throughout this region you will find references to "Calabash-style" seafood. Calabash is a small village on the Little River Inlet, south of US 17 and almost on the South Carolina border. The home of a small fishing and shrimping fleet, it has become home to seafood restaurants as well—at last count over a dozen of them, some very large. They specialize in breading (presumably) local fish, and then plunging it into a deep fryer. Honestly, I am taste-deaf to this sort of fried seafood, and cannot tell a superb product worth the $$$–$$$$ typically charged in Calabash (a price normally associated chef-prepared dishes from original recipes) from Long John Silver's. If you want to try Calabash-style at its source, the **Dockside Seafood House** (9955 Nance St., 910-579-6775) gets rave Internet reviews from those who like it, and is one of four dockside restaurants with excellent views.

Road. Inside the plain brick building you'll find polished hardwood trim and wooden tables and chairs with white linen tablecloths and napkins. The large and varied menu features Italian, seafood, steaks, chicken, pork, and lamb, all prepared from fresh ingredients. An inexpensive bar meal has the usual suspects—but all items are hand-breaded, prepared to order, and served with the house's original dipping sauces. The wine list is good, with choices under $20; single-malt scotches are featured as well.

Captain Pete's Seafood Restaurant, Holden Beach, Brunswick Islands (910-846-9988; captpeteshb.com), 103 Southshore Dr., Holden Beach 28462. Open Mon.–Sat. for dinner. $$$–$$$$. Located next to a shrimp dock, facing the lagoon at the base of the NC 130 bridge, this restaurant features fresh seafood, with a good selection of chicken and steak as well. The menu mixes original recipes with old standards, and offers a good variety of seafood dishes well beyond the "Calabash-style" of other nearby eateries.

Purple Onion Café, Shallote, Brunswick Islands (mainland) (910-775-6071; purpleonioncafe.com; purple onion@atmc.net), 4647 Main St., Suite 1, Shallotte 28470. Open daily for breakfast and lunch; open for dinner, in the summer season, Wed.–Sat. $$–$$$. Coupled with a bakery next door, Shallotte's Purple Onion is noted for its freshly baked breads and original pastries. Beyond that, you'll find a full menu of hot breakfast items (including some excellent omelets), excellent sandwiches, and (when open for dinner) a good entrée list as well. You'll it in a modest shopping center to the north of Shallotte's center; from Wilmington take US 17 south for 33 miles to a left onto US Bus 17, which leads into Shallotte.

✷ Entertainment

CLASSICAL **Thalian Hall, downtown Wilmington** (800-523-2820; 910-343-3660; thalianhall.org), 310 Chestnut St., Wilmington 28401. This spectacular neoclassical building marks the traditional center of downtown Wilmington. The city built it in 1858 to promote itself as an emerging cotton port and railroad center, and to this end they combined in it an opera house with city hall. And so it remains today, one of the oddest and most beautiful combination buildings in the state, if not the South; as part of this combination, it may well be the only city hall with a liquor license. The current beautiful restoration has turned it into a modern performing arts hall with a full schedule of theatrical and musical events. When not in use (Tue.–Fri.) private tours can be arranged by appointment only ($$–$$$).

POPULAR **Downtown Wilmington** at night is pleasant, rather than lively. Two distinct areas carry the focus of nightlife. The first is the Riverwalk, particularly along its southern end as it goes over the water. There are bars and restaurants along the way, but generally this is a place for dusk strolling, talking and meeting with friends. The second is the Front Street restaurant district, three blocks from Chestnut Street south to Dock Street, plus a block of Market Street connecting Front with the Riverwalk. Here you will find between one and two dozen cafés and bars, many with live music; several of these are listed under *Where to Eat*.

WILMINGTON'S RIVERWALK

✷ Selective Shopping

Wilmington is, of course, the shopping destination of this region. Downtown is your best bet, concentrating on the Riverwalk and Front Street Districts described under *Entertainment.* Downtown's best boutique shopping venue, however, is the **Cotton Exchange** (shopcottonexchange.com) at the northern end of Front Street, with 25 independent shops and four restaurants housed in a handsome group of mid- to late-19th-century brick buildings.

Elsewhere, try poking around the many beach town centers (see *Green Spaces* for a complete listing). While these mini CBDs range from small to very small, they tend to attract the eccentric and original that make a shopping experience unique.

✷ Special Events

First full week in April: **The Azalea Festival, Wilmington** (910-794-4650; ncazaleafestival.org; info@ncazaleafestival.org). Admission is free. Since 1948 the people of Wilmington have celebrated the brilliant masses of azalea flowers that bedeck the city every spring with a weeklong festival that includes a street fair, parade, and historic home and garden tours. It's one of the South's premier festivals, attracting 300,000 visitors every year.

Every Thursday night all summer: **Fireworks by the Sea, Pleasure Island** (pleasureislandnc.org/fireworksbythesea.asp). Carolina Beach gets a jump on the weekend with live music from the gazebo on the boardwalk at 6:30, followed by fireworks viewable from its boardwalk at dusk (sometime after 8).

First Saturday in June: **North Carolina Blueberry Festival** (910-259-9817; ncblueberryfestival.com; info@ncblueberryfestival.com). Blueberries abound at the lovely brick courthouse at the center of Burgaw, a quaint rural town 24 miles north of Wilmington via US 117. Apart from the products of half a dozen local blueberry farms, you'll find blueberry food contests, arts and crafts booths, food vendors, bake sales from 10 local churches (more blueberries!), antiques sales (at the town's historic depot), a car show, a model train show, and live music. Eight blocks of downtown Burgaw close as 30,000 people descend upon the town, increasing its population for this single day by 650 percent; trolleys will ferry you from remote parking areas to the courthouse.

Second weekend in October: **Kure Beach Seafood, Blues, and Jazz Festival, Pleasure Island** (910-458-8434; pleasureislandnc.org/seafoodbluesandjazzfestival.asp). $$$–$$$$. The Pleasure Island Chamber of Commerce sponsors this annual celebration of music and seafood at the Fort Fisher Military Recreation Area, on the northern side of Kure Beach fronting on US 421.

Third weekend in October: **North Carolina Oyster Fest, Brunswick Islands** (brunswickcountychamber.org/OF-nc-oyster-festival.cfm). This annual celebration of Brunswick County's abundant oyster fisheries is held on Ocean Isle, and features live entertainment, art and crafts tents, shucking and stew contests, and of course plenty of local oysters.

Last Saturday in November: **North Carolina Holiday Flotilla, Wrightsville Beach** (ncholidayflotilla.org). Every year 50,000 visitors descend upon Wrightsville Beach, on the east side of Wilmington, to enjoy this unique night parade of decorated and lighted boats. The day starts with a Festival in the Park, with music, arts, crafts, and food. Then comes the parade—up the Intracoastal Waterway (on the Wilmington side) to the bridge, then down the back side of the island paralleling US 76 (whose right-of-way creates a long thin park along the channel). Fireworks serve to climax the event.

THE COASTAL PLAINS

The coastal plains of North Carolina form a crescent, curving parallel to the coast, 180 miles long and typically 60 miles wide. Geologically, they are formed from sand eroded off the Appalachian Mountains eons ago, and deposited in what was then shallow offshore waters. Falling sea levels (or rising continents—it's hard to tell them apart) have left former estuaries as wide and marshy valleys, former tidal whirls as oval lakes, and former sand dunes as hills. The poor, sandy soil turns out to be superb for raising brightleaf tobacco (see "The Raleigh-Durham Area"); you easily spot the white sand in the rows between tobacco plants.

This has never been a region noted for tourism, yet it has a surprising range of truly high-quality sites. Historic sites predominate, including colonial towns, a number of antebellum plantations, reconstructed farms of all eras, an early canal, and lovely small towns with intact 19th-century cores. Outdoor recreation is also plentiful, with the large reservoir Lake Gaston, four major rivers, the high-end golf resorts of Pinehurst, and the odd natural lakes of Bladen County. Seven state parks and an important wildfowl zoo furnish trails and nature appreciation, while two vast and unblazed game lands allow a more free-form and adventurous experience. The city of Fayetteville, home of the U.S. Army's headquarters at Fort Bragg, offers an impressive range of military tourism, ranging from Civil War sites (including the battle that ended the war, at Bentonville), to museums dedicated to the distinguished histories of Fort Bragg's divisions.

GUIDANCE Roanoke Rapids and Halifax (800-522-4282; 252-535-1687; visithalifax.com), 260 Premier Blvd., Roanoke Rapids 27870. The Halifax County Convention and Visitors Bureau runs an excellent website covering the northernmost parts of this chapter. Their headquarters are located near the Walmart just off I-95's exit 173, US 158 at Roanoke Rapids.

Rocky Mount and Tarboro (rockymounttravel.com; tarboro-nc.com). The north-central part of this chapter's area, following the corridor formed by the US 64 expressway, centers on the two towns of Rocky Mount and Tarboro. The two websites of their tourist authorities cover this area very nicely.

Greenville and Wilson (visitgreenvillenc.com; wilson-nc.com). The small university city of Greenville dominates this area's central part, defined by the US 264 expressway corridor. To its west, the town of Wilson and its surrounding county have their own website for additional details.

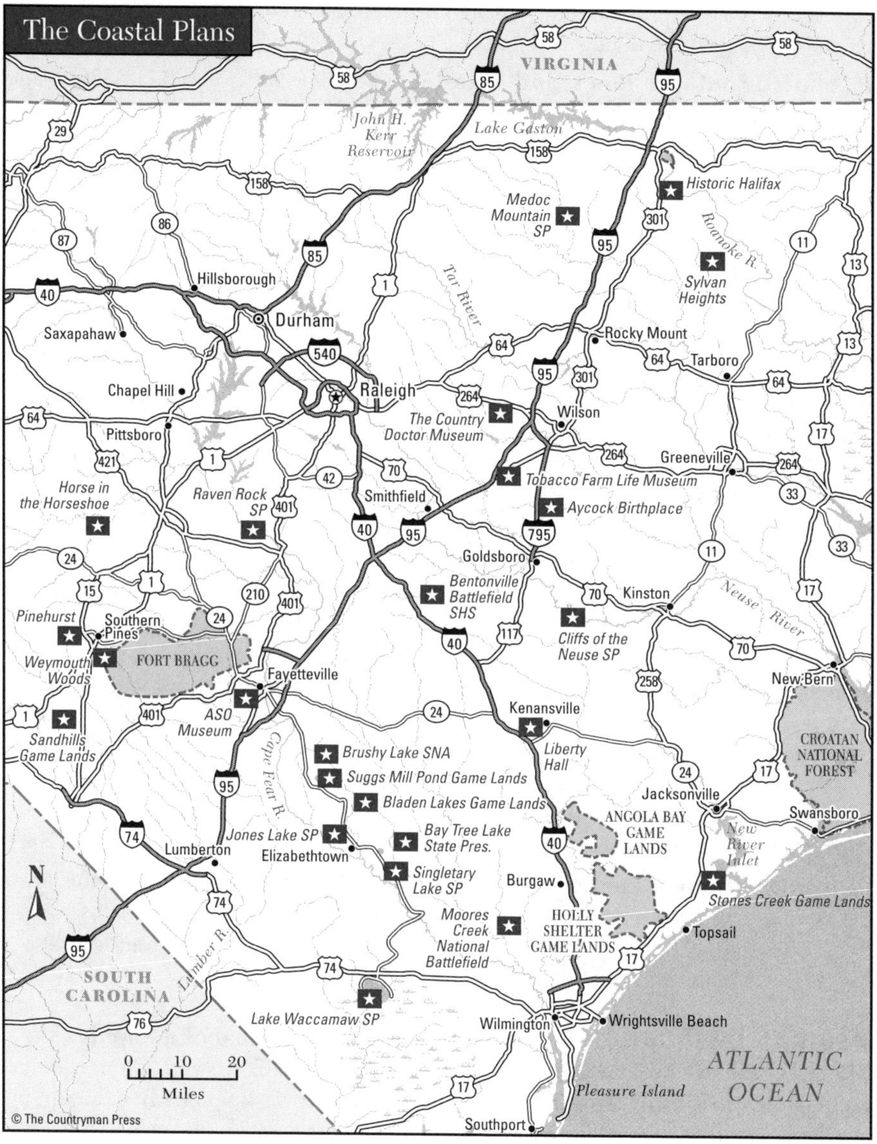

Goldsboro, Smithfield, and Kinston (greatergoldsboro.com; johnstoncountync.org; visitkinston.com). This town of 40,000 sits at the center of this chapter's area, a service center for the surrounding countryside astride the US 70 expressway. Goldsboro-Wayne County Travel & Tourism runs a good website for the area. Johnson County and Smithfield form a sizable independent area to its west, with its own website, while Kinston to its east has a separate website as well.

Fayetteville (800-255-8217; 910-483-5311; visitfayettevillenc.com), 245 Person St., Fayetteville 28301. Open weekdays during business hours. The coastal plain's largest city is a center for military-related tourism, based on adjacent Fort Bragg. Its website has all the details.

Pinehurst, Southern Pines, and Aberdeen (800-346-5362; 910-692-3330; homeofgolf.com), 10677 US 15/501, Southern Pines 28388. The three towns of North Carolina's golf region share the same tourism authority, which has an excellent website.

GETTING THERE *By car:* I-95 stretches north–south through the center of this region for 181 miles, linking the area with New York and Florida. Four expressways radiate eastward from Raleigh, providing east–west access: US 64 (Rocky Mount), US 264 (Greenville), US 70 (Goldsboro), and I-40 (Wilmington). The US 74 expressway runs through the southernmost parts of this region.

By air: Both Fayetteville and Greenville have regular passenger air service. City-owned **Fayetteville Regional Airport (FAY)** (flyfay.ci.fayetteville.nc.us) is served by two airlines, which connect it with Atlanta and Charlotte. The **Pitt County–City of Greenville Airport (PGV)** (pitt-greenvilleairport.com) has one airline, with daily flights to Charlotte. Raleigh (see "The Raleigh-Durham Area") is the closest airport for all points north of Greenville.

By train: This region may well be unique in the South for having better train service than air service, with five **Amtrak** (amtrak.com) routes linking six coastal plains towns to one another and the outside world. Selma (near Smithfield) is the major junction, serving the Carolinian and Piedmont (linking Rocky Mount with Charlotte and Raleigh) and the Palmetto and two Silver Service routes (which shuttle between New York and Florida). The other towns with stops are Rocky Mount, Wilson, Fayetteville, Southern Pines, and the tiny hamlet of Hamlet, whose enormous restored passenger depot (built into a 90-degree track intersection) is perhaps the finest in the state.

By bus: **Greyhound** (greyhound.com) maintains a complex network of routes in the coastal plains, with a number of different roads traversed. Coastal plains stations are found at Ahoskie, Fayetteville, Goldsboro, Greenville, Kinston, Lumberton, Rocky Mount, Smithfield, Wallace, and Wilson.

MEDICAL EMERGENCIES **Halifax Medical Center, Roanoke Rapids** (252-535-8011; halifaxmedicalcenter.org; info@halifaxrmc.org), 250 Smith Church Rd., Roanoke Rapids 27870. This 204-bed facility in downtown Roanoke Rapids, run by a local nonprofit corporation, serves the northernmost areas of this chapter.

Nash Health Care Systems, Rocky Mount (252-443-8000; nhcs.org), 2460 Curtis Ellis Dr., Rocky Mount 27804. Located off the US 64 expressway's exit 466, this 282-bed facility offers emergency services to the Rocky Mount–Tarboro area.

Pitt County Memorial Hospital, Greenville (252-847-4100; uhseast.com), 2100 Stantonsburg Rd., Greenville 27834. This 739-bed hospital, located just off the US 264 expressway's exit 73 and adjacent to East Carolina State University, is a teaching hospital affiliated with that college's Brody School of Medicine.

Wayne Memorial Hospital, Goldsboro (919-736-1110; waynehealth.org), 2700 Wayne Memorial Dr., Goldsboro 27534. This 316-bed facility located on the north side of town, just off US 70, serves the south-central area of this chapter.

Cape Fear Valley Health System, Fayetteville (910-615-4000; capefearvalley

.com; info@capefearvalley.com), 1638 Owen Dr., Fayetteville 28304. This 614-bed facility is located in the city's western suburbs, at the corner of Owen and Village Drives. From downtown, follow US 401westward as it leaves an expressway to become Robeson Street, then go 1.3 miles to a left onto Village Drive, then go another 1.3 miles to the entrance. From Fort Bragg take the All-American Expressway south, which becomes Owen Drive with a right-turn-only entrance.

FirstHealth Moore Regional Hospital, Pinehurst (910-715-1000; firsthealth .org), 155 Memorial Dr., Pinehurst 28374. This 315-bed hospital is located on the northeast edge of the village, on NC 211 two blocks west of the US 15/501 roundabout.

Southeastern Regional Medical Center, Lumberton (910-671-5000; srmc.org), 300 W. 27th St., Lumberton 28358. This 337-bed facility serves the southernmost part of this chapter's area from a campus that spreads across six city blocks in the northwestern portion of the county seat of Lumberton. From I-95's exit 20 take NC 211 (North Roberts Avenue) east 0.4 mile to a right onto Elm Street, then go 0.3 mile to a right onto 28th Street.

✷ Exploring the Area

EXPLORING BY CAR Along the Cape Fear River. This 136-mile drive explores three distinct areas in the Cape Fear River drainage: the exclusive golf resorts of the sandhills along its headwaters, the military city of Fayetteville, and the Bladen Lakes, the strange natural lakes that line up in the flatlands along its left bank. Although the river dominates and organizes this region, this drive visits it twice only.

Starting at the center of Pinehurst, go east on NC 12 (Midlands Drive), whose median preserves the route of the trolley that once linked the Southern Pines passenger depot with the **Pinehurst Resort**. This 6 miles of four-lane (very likely the first such highway in North Carolina) passes 15 golf courses, including Donald Ross's famous **Pinehurst #2**. This ends after 6.4 miles at Broad Street, downtown Southern Pines's main drag. *Your route proceeds to the center of town to turn left opposite the Amtrak station onto East Pennsylvania Avenue, then goes two blocks to another left onto May Street.* **Downtown Southern Pines** is handsome and shop-filled, a traditional red-brick center complete with its original train depot, still in use. Two blocks north on May, a short trip right on Connecticut Avenue takes you

COTTON READY FOR HARVEST, IN THE COASTAL PLAINS, NEAR FARMVILLE

to the **Weymouth Center**, a nicely restored early-20th-century vacation mansion with stunning gardens; farther on is **Weymouth Woods**, once part of the estate, now a state-owned nature preserve whose extensive trails explore the unique sandhills environment. *Seven blocks north on May from Pennsylvania (0.8 mile) make a right onto Delaware Avenue, continuing diagonally after one block as Youngs Road (SSR 2026).* For the next few miles you'll be wandering through horse-and-hounds country, with handsome large horse farms along the way—for the Pinehurst area is a center for all the favored pastimes of America's aristocracy. *After 5.3 miles from May Street (13.1 miles from Pinehurst Resort) turn left onto Lakebay Road (SSR 2023).* Just before this turn a sharp curve bends around Lake Bay on your left, a former millpond now completely grown over in bottomland forest. Lakebay Road takes you slowly out of horse country and into more typical coastal plains scenery, *ending after 6.7 miles at NC 690; turn right.*

As you follow NC 690 east you'll enjoy a large stretch of forest, once a Rockefeller family preserve named Overhills and since 1999 part of Fort Bragg. *In 13.5 miles (33.3 miles from Pinehurst) turn right onto NC 24* and follow it into the military gate town of Spring Lake and through **Fort Bragg**, with views of the fort. While this major army base is a secure area, you can get permission to view its two excellent on-base **museums** at any gate; be prepared for the guard to search your car, including closed boxes. *In 9.3 miles following NC 24 take a right fork onto Fort Bragg Road.* Follow the flow toward downtown Fayetteville, through the sprawling outskirts of this low-built city. You'll pass the turnoff to **Fayetteville Museum of Art**, set on a lovely lake, in 0.5 mile. *Your road passes under an expressway and becomes Hay Street,* and you enter something of a museum district. **The Museum of the Cape Fear Historical Complex** is just beyond the expressway, a right onto Bradford Street. Next up is the giant **Airborne and Special Operations Museum** on your left, with the city's handsome old Amtrak depot beside it. In another long block Fayetteville's **Transportation Museum** is a block south. Now your road narrows as you enter downtown Fayetteville—modest, attractive, and old-fashioned, with wide sidewalks, trees, and a good choice of restaurants. The English-style Market Square marks the center of downtown; *continue straight, your road's name changing to Person Street.* In six more blocks you can find the 79-acre **Fayetteville Botanical Gardens**, with a long frontage on the Cape Fear River, a short distance to your left along US 301. You leave Fayetteville as Person Street crosses the Cape Fear River, 47.2 miles from your start. *In 0.4 mile turn right onto NC 53.*

Below Fayetteville the Cape Fear River flows along the southern escarpment of what was once, not too long ago geologically speaking, a large tidal inlet. Your road will follow the flat, sandy, swampy floor of this inlet. Its main feature is a series of oval indentations known as Carolina bays, all shaped and oriented exactly the same way, fancifully credited to meteors but actually caused by ancient tidal currents. While most of these are so shallow as to contain only the dense woody swamp community known as pocosin, some are deep enough to be proper lakes, and give the name **Bladen Lakes** to this district. After 15.9 miles, Jessup Pond on your left (an old millpond with good bird-watching) marks the start of 40,000 or so acres of state-owned lands, in this case the wonderfully named Suggs Mill Pond Game Lands. *After 18.0 miles on NC 53 turn left onto Live Oak Methodist Church Road (SSR 1327), becoming sand-surfaced after 0.9 mile.* At 1.6 miles from NC 53 an inconspicuous orange gate on your left marks an 0.8-mile trail to Little Singletary Lake, little-visited and otherwise inaccessible. At 5.3 miles you can see Suggs Mill Pond itself, by taking the sand-surfaced forest road on your left for 1.9 miles. Here you can see one of the Bladen Lakes being taken over by pocosin, with a horseshoe of open water surviving on its southeast edge. It's excellent for fishing and bird-watching, best explored with a canoe. *After 6.1 miles turn left onto paved Gum Springs Road (SSR 1325) and go 3.7 miles to a right onto NC 242.* In another 3.2 miles you enter Bladen Lakes State Forest. In 6.2 miles you reach Jones Lake State Park, with picnicking, sand beach swimming, a fishing pier, and a small boat launch; 6 miles of hiking trails encircle the lake, explore the pocosin surrounding it, and even reach remote Salters Lake. *After 9.3 miles NC 242 ends at a confusing intersection; go left onto NC 53, then immediately left onto US 701/NC 53. After 4.1 miles turn right onto NC 53.* In 1.0 mile you'll reach White Lake, completely ringed by private homes whose docks are nearly as close together as teeth in a comb. At 6.7 miles Singletary Lake State Park is primarily a group camp.

After 16.4 miles turn right onto Elwell Ferry Road (SSR 1730), reaching the ferry after 1.2 miles. Elwell Ferry is an old-fashioned cable ferry over the Cape Fear River, one of three cable ferries still in operation in North Carolina; this two-car, 110-yard free ferry has been here since 1905. *After the ferry continue on Elwell Ferry Road for another 7.1 miles to a left onto NC 211, then go 3.6 miles to a right onto Old Lake Road (SSR 1740).* This will end in 6.1 miles at the largest of the Carolina bay lakes, Lake Waccamaw. The 12.7-mile road along its edge gives many wide and interesting views over this lake, with its thick crust of lake houses and bristling with piers. The 1.4 miles to your right are the most interesting, with some fine old architecture, and ending at town center, where there's a nice museum in a train depot. Both ends of the lakeside road dead-end at Lake Waccamaw State Park, preserving 4 miles of shoreline.

EXPLORING BY BICYCLE **The Roanoke Canal Trail** (roanokecanal.com/pdf/CanalBrochure.pdf). For most of the 19th century, a canal allowed small river barges to pass beyond the impressive rapids of the Roanoke River to the stillwaters behind, fostering trade far upstream along the NC–VA state line. Today a footpath follows the canal's lowermost 7.8 miles (the upper 2 miles being sunk under **Roanoke Rapids Lake**), from the Roanoke Rapids Dam to a riverside park in the town of Weldon. Scenery is varied and always fascinating, with long walks through riverine forests, views over this strange stretch of river, and back-lot insight into a couple of nice southern towns. Highlights include a stone aqueduct just upstream from Weldon that once carried canal boats above Chockoyotte Creek, and a brick generator building c. 1900, from an era when the canal was used for early hydropower, now the **Roanoke Canal Museum**.

RIVERINE GREENWAYS The state of North Carolina intends to build a hike-bike greenway that follows the Neuse River for nearly 200 miles, from **Falls Lake** to **New Bern**—part of the 900-mile **Mountain-to-Sea Trail** linking the Smokies with Cape Hatteras. The 30-mile Piedmont section, looping around the eastern edge of Raleigh (see "The Raleigh-Durham Area"), is nearing completion at press time. The coastal plains section, 165 miles or so, is still on the drawing board. Several small towns, however, have constructed significant riverside greenways on their own, along a number of rivers.

Smithfield Riverwalk. This 2.8-mile paved trail starts south of downtown and heads along the left bank of the Neuse as far as Buffalo Creek, then turns up a side creek to end at a local park.

Rocky Mount's Tar River Trail. This 3.9-mile paved greenway follows the Tar River through town, using a series of riverside city parks. There's a fine wood arch bridge over the river, which makes the claim of being the longest single-span wooden bridge in the world.

Fayetteville's Cape Fear River Trail. This paved greenway follows the Cape Fear River for 4.2 miles, running a mile to the east of US 401 from Treetops Drive to Clark Park on Sherman Drive. Apart from nearly undisturbed river forests, it offers a remarkable collection of bridges and boardwalks. Its southern end is within a 76-acre nature park with a variety of walking trails.

Lumberton Riverwalk. This 2.5-mile paved trail follows a flood-control berm on the right bank of this twisting, sluggish river, starting at Luther Britt Park's Crystal Road parking lot on the north, and ending at South Chestnut Street on the south.

✷ Towns

Roanoke Rapids and Halifax. With 17,000 inhabitants, **Roanoke Rapids** is the major service center of the northern part of the coastal plains. As its name implies, it formed at the Roanoke River's fall line, where a major set of rapids forced goods to be transferred from large steamboats to small canal boats before continuing upstream. It has a traditional red-brick downtown four blocks long, on NC 48, and roadside services at I-95's exit 173, east of town. To visitors its main interest is its two large hydro-lakes upstream, Roanoke Rapids Lake and Lake Gaston, and the remains of its 19th-century canal, followed by a path and interpreted by a museum in one of its structures. A dozen miles to its south, the tiny village of **Halifax**, with only 350 people, is the county seat and possesses an impressive collection of colonial architecture, preserved and interpreted by the Halifax State Historic Site.

Rocky Mount and Tarboro. The seats for adjacent counties along the US 64 expressway corridor, Rocky Mount and Tarboro furnish services to the north-central coastal plains. Contemporary **Rocky Mount** is a quiet place, looking very small-town despite a metro population approaching 150,000, whose old-fashioned downtown has rather more buildings than tenants—certainly not what you would expect for a city that, from 1990 to 2001, was home to one of America's top 20 financial corporations, Centura Banks. Beyond that, it has a number of well-kept historic areas, ranging from the villas of the wealthy to a riverside mill town; details are on the town's website (see *Guidance*). Rocky Mount has a full range of traveler's services.

Sixteen miles to the east sits the small town of **Tarboro**, where you can find a large historic district (with 300 listed homes) centering on its 15-acre oak-shaded town common, stretching for four blocks along the north edge of downtown. On the south side, a 25-acre park winds along the banks of the Tar River, with landscaped gardens and paths.

Greenville. This pleasant small city, with a metro population over 180,000, sits by the Tar River in the center-east of this chapter's area. It had a brief brush with potential fame when local entrepreneur Walter Hardee founded Hardee's Hamburgers here in 1960—but Hardee lost control of his creation to his partners (in a poker game, he claimed), and the chain moved elsewhere. Founded as an antebellum cotton-loading town on a steamboat stop, it now centers on its large state university and medical school, East Carolina State University, along with a significant clean industry base ranging from pharmaceuticals to the world's largest hammock manufacturer. Its downtown is attractive but small, and it has a nice riverside park.

Fayetteville. With 350,000 people in its metropolitan area, Fayetteville is the fifth largest city in the state and the largest city in the coastal plains. It was formed in early colonial times as an upriver trading post on the Cape Fear River, acquiring its current name during the Revolution in honor of General Lafayette. Its landmark Market House, at the center of its downtown, dates from 1832 and was originally used as a farmer's market and for slave auctions. Since 1918 its economy has been dominated by the huge adjacent army base, Fort Bragg, and the related Pope Air Force Base, and it is this massive military presence that has driven Fayetteville's contemporary growth. The military presence has lately become the basis of a thriving military tourism centered on its three major military museums, as well as tours of the historic sites and memorial statuary on the base. Its downtown has been steadily improving, and is now an attractive and strollable place with landscaped streets, museums, shops, and cafés, set off by Cross-Creek Linear Park along its northern edge.

Pinehurst, Southern Pines, and Aberdeen. With an international reputation for fine golf, this small resort city consists of 40,000 inhabitants in three separate, but adjacent, towns. **Pinehurst** is the resort center; founded in 1895, its original wooden hotel is still the center of town, and is still the most prominent of the many resorts in the area. Its compact and historic retail district, hidden away a few blocks to the northeast, has the finest shopping in this chapter. Founded in 1885, **Southern Pines** also began as a resort, but its rail-side location quickly turned it into the area's service center; its traditional red-brick downtown faces the tracks, with some worthwhile shopping and cafés. **Aberdeen** is the oldest and most modest of the three, formed in the 1870s as a turpentine depot along the railroad; it has a one-block downtown by the railroad. Town-owned Aberdeen Lake Park, at the center of Aberdeen off US 1, is very attractive and a good place to picnic.

✷ Green Spaces

PUBLIC LANDS: THE BLADEN LAKES (Suggs Mill Pond Game Lands: ncwildlife.org/Hunting/GameLand_Maps/Coastal/Suggs_Mill_Pond.pdf; Bladen Lake Game Lands: ncwildlife.org/Hunting/GameLand_Maps/Coastal/Bladen_Lakes.pdf; Jones Lake State Park: ncparks.gov/Visit/parks/jone/main.php; Lake Waccamaw State Park: ncparks.gov/Visit/parks/lawa/main.php; White Lake: whitelakenc.com). These natural lakes are found in the southernmost part of this chapter's area, with the majority in Bladen County—hence their most common name, although they are also known as Carolina bays, a more generic term (as these oddities can be found widely scattered throughout the coastal plains, in both Carolinas). They are all oval, with the same shape and orientation, and they all have a slight sandbar on their southeastern edge. Travel writers have fancifully attributed them to meteors, but geologists are united in their belief that these are tidal features, formed not too long ago when these sandy flats were the floor of a coastal inlet. Most are no longer lakes, but have become filled with organic material, and are now impenetrable brush-covered swamps known as pocosins. The ones that remain lakes are, of course, priceless resources, both for recreation and for wildlife.

The state owns 40,000 acres or more in the heart of the Bladen Lakes, split between two state parks (Jones Lake and Singletary Lake), two giant game lands (Bladen Lakes and the wonderfully named Suggs Mill Pond), and a couple of undeveloped preserves (Brushy Lake and Bay Tree Lake). This entire area is open to day hiking, but backpacking trips are not allowed, and Jones Lake has the only formally blazed trails. As you might expect, bird-watching is superb.

Here are all of the publicly accessible Bladen Lakes, from north to south.

Jessups Pond is not a Carolina bay, but rather a small millpond on NC 53 noted for its birding, in Suggs Mill Pond Game Lands.

Little Singletary Lake is a wholly undeveloped natural lake on the Suggs Mill Pond Game Lands, reached only by a 0.75-mile hike from Live Oak Methodist Church Road.

Suggs Mill Pond, also known as Horseshoe Lake, is reachable by dirt forest roads from Live Oak Methodist Church Road; it's mainly grown over by pocosin, but has a horseshoe of open water famed for its birding.

Jones Lake, perhaps the most scenic of the lakes and the centerpiece of Jones Lake State Park, has natural sand beach swimming, fishing from shore and small boats, camping, and hiking.

Salters Lake is part of Jones Lake State Park and can be reached only by a 2.7-mile (one-way) hike, ending at its sandy southeastern shore.

White Lake, off US 701 and NC 53, is completely ringed by cottages and bristles with piers; this is a good place to look for vacation rentals.

Bay Tree Lake has a gated subdivision taking up its northern third, and the state's undeveloped Bay Tree Lake Preserve on its western third, where an unblazed track leads 1.1 miles from NC 41 to a sandy stretch of shore.

WHEAT FIELDS IN THE COASTAL PLAINS

Singletary Lake, inside Singletary Lake State Park, is a group camp and not open to casual visitors.

Lake Waccamaw, the largest of these lakes and the only one outside Bladen County, is well to the south, off US 74/76; half of its shore is protected by Lake Waccamaw State Park, while the other (northern) half is encrusted with cabins and piers, with a nice village, complete with historic buildings and a museum, on its northern tip.

PUBLIC LANDS: THE SAND HILLS (Weymouth Woods Preserve: ncparks.gov/Visit/parks/wewo/main.php; Sandhills Game Lands: ncwildlife.org/Hunting/GameLand_Maps/Piedmont/Sandhills.pdf). These hills, located in the southwestern part of this area from Fort Bragg to Pinehurst and down to the South Carolina line, were formed in the not-too-distant past when this area was just offshore and caught the sand being washed down from the Piedmont. The 420-foot hilltops are flat, washed level by ancient waves; the sides have been carved down about 200 feet from that, by the streams that have washed over them since becoming dry land.

This means that each hill has nearly 200 feet of sand between its top and the local water table. The deep sandy soil dries out between rains, killing the roots of any plant not adapted to this soil-induced dryness. The resulting ecosystem is unusual, and surprisingly attractive—tall longleaf pines, widely spaced, frequently with an open understory. With such dryness and lots of summer lightning, the environment is fire-dependent, with many species requiring burning to reproduce; "old growth" here is either a small, rare, and very temporary island, or human-induced through fire control. The Weymouth Woods–Sandhills State Nature Preserve gives easy views of this environment through 4.6 miles of blazed, looping trails; its detached Boyd Tract, immediately behind the Weymouth Center, contains forests undisturbed by logging or fire control. The 60,000-acre Sandhills Game Lands, in state ownership, has many opportunities for day hiking and nature observation. Chief among these is a 5,600-acre tract immediately south of Hoffman, heavily managed for songbird habitat, including the endangered red-cockaded woodpecker; the tract extends between, and for a mile on either side, of Watson Road (SSR 1828) and Marston Road (SSR 1346) (watch for drifting sand on these dirt-surfaced roads). Within the game lands north of Hoffman is the J. Robert Gordon Sandhills Field Trial Grounds, covering 15 square miles, where sporting dogs train and compete over a 31-mile course.

PARKS AND GARDENS Sylvan Heights Waterfowl Park, between Halifax and Tarboro (252-826-3186; shwpark.com; info@shwpark.com), 4963 US 258, Scotland Neck 27874. Open Tue.–Sun.: Apr.–Sept., 9–5; Oct.–Mar., 9–4. $$. Founded in 1989 by English ornithologist Mike Lubbock as a breeding center for rare and endangered waterfowl, Sylvan Heights has had extraordinary success; the center holds 17 world and 15 North American First Breeding Awards, and is home to almost a third of the planet's white wing wood duck population (which the center is using to restore wild populations in the species' native Sumatra and Cambodia). In 2006 Sylvan Heights opened its large aviary to the public, with over 1,500 birds, representing 170 species from five continents, from kookaburras to flamingos. There's a handicapped-accessible tree house overlooking the site's wetlands, and future plans include a blind for viewing a working beaver dam.

Medoc Mountain State Park, between Roanoke Rapids and Rocky Mount (252-586-6588; ncparks.gov/Visit/parks/memo/main.php; medoc.mountain@ncmail.net), 1541 Medoc State Park Rd., Hollister 27844. Medoc Mountain towers 225 feet above the valley below, reaching a height of 325 feet above sea level—about the same as the hills around Orlando, Florida, for those into cross-state comparisons. The centers on the valley carved by Little Fishing Creek as it meanders for 2.5 miles past the "mountain," a pleasant and rewarding canoe paddle. The park's 10 miles of hiking trails explore all aspects of the fall-line forest, with 10 more miles of bridle paths in the park's newly added southern area.

Cliffs of the Neuse State Park, south of Goldsboro (919-778-6234; ncparks.gov/Visit/parks/clne/main.php; cliffs.neuse@ncmail.net), 345-A Park Entrance Rd., Seven Springs 28578. This 900-acre park preserves that rarest of natural sites in the coastal plains: a cliff, standing 90 feet vertically above the Neuse River. Views are lovely, and the cliff itself is fascinating. To the south of the cliff, two loop trails explore tree-covered bluffs. A millpond furnishes swimming and picnicking.

Cape Fear Botanical Gardens, Fayetteville (910-486-0221; capefearbg.org; info@capefearbg.org), 536 N. Eastern Blvd., Fayetteville 28305. Open Mon.–Sat. 10–5, Sun. noon–5; closed on Sun. during winter. $$. Located along the banks of the Cape Fear River where it's bridged by US 301 on the north side of town, this 79-acre garden features 2,000 varieties of ornamental plants, including camellia, daylily, and hosta specialty gardens. Several miles of paths explore the largely wooded site, including a riverside walk. An ambitious new visitors center, nearly 30,000 square feet in size, is under way at the entrance, along with improvements to its surrounding gardens.

Raven Rock State Park, near Sanford (910-893-4888; ncparks.gov/Visit/parks/raro/main.php; info.ravenrock@ncmail.net), 3009 Raven Rock Rd., Lillington 27546. This 4,700-acre park sits athwart the place where the Piedmont meets the coastal plains, known as the fall line. The lowermost waterfall on the Cape Fear River, Lanier Falls, marks the upstream boundary of the park; below here, the river is a coastal plains stream. But not the surrounding lands, for the river has eroded backward, upstream, into the tough Piedmont granites and schists. Raven Rock itself is a mile-long granitic prominence exposed by the river, largely covered by trees but with numerous outcrops, with some giving good views across the river. A variety of trails explore the rock, and there's a network of horse trails across the river.

RIVERS **Cape Fear River**. Formed south of Raleigh at the confluence of the Haw and Deep Rivers, the Cape Fear River wanders through the coastal plains for 157 miles before emptying into an estuary at Wilmington formed by its own drowned mouth. Up to a few decades ago the river was navigable by commercial craft as far as Fayetteville, and while this trade has stopped, the abandoned locks and their weirs continue to impound the river; expect it to be wide, smooth-surfaced, calm, and deep. Unlike other coastal plains rivers it has carved a fairly pronounced trench for itself, typically 75 feet below the surrounding sands; these flat sandlands represent the bottom of the river's ancient inlet, and a dozen natural lakes, the Bladen Lakes, have been swirled into them by the tides that once ran through here. The river has been declared a state paddle trail (see "What's Where").

Neuse River. The longest river entirely within North Carolina, the Neuse spends 160 of its 275 miles wandering through the coastal plains. Here it occupies a great flat plain of its own—another raised estuary bottom, whose shores form the bluffs revealed at **Cliffs of the Neuse State Park**. For most of its length it remains narrow enough to be tree-shaded, and it tends to form broad meander loops, making for a fine paddling stream. Because of frequent flooding the state owns rights to most of its banks, and intends to build the **Mountains-to-Sea Trail** along it as a hike-bike greenway. The towns of Smithfield, Goldsboro, and Kinston sit along its banks.

Lumber River. Perhaps the most important recreational river in the coastal plains, the quiet and remote Lumber River flows in tight meanders for 115 miles, from the **Sandhills Game Lands** to the South Carolina border. The only National Wild and Scenic River in the coastal plains, the Lumber is actively managed by the state as a scenic canoe trail, its corridor kept a little-visited wilderness. The Lumber River State Park includes over 9,000 acres along its banks, and has developed canoe launches and camps along its length.

TRUCK IN FRONT OF TOBACCO AUCTION HOUSE, WITH BUMPER STICKER, "TOBACCO MONEY PAYS MY BILLS," FARMVILLE

Roanoke River (dom.com/about/stations/hydro/roanoke-river-whitewater.jsp). The fall line becomes most apparent at Roanoke Rapids, where the Roanoke River flows over 5 miles of whitewater, from NC 48 in the town of Roanoke Rapids to the town of Weldon's River Rapid's Park. In this section the river breaks and braids around a series of islands, and the rapids you reach depend on which channel you take. Paddling ranges from flatwater to Class II or III, with the final fall (just after the US 301 bridge) being the biggest. This, however, can vary; the river level is regulated by the Roanoke Rapids Dam, and medium flows make the best paddling—higher flows simply cover the rocks. The Dominion Power website publishes a release schedule.

Beneath Weldon, the Roanoke flows swift, straight, and true through coastal plains for another 100 miles before finally sinking into the wide marshes at the head of Albemarle Sound. Altogether it offers 131 miles of canoeing, and is designated a state paddle trail (see "What's Where").

LAKES Lake Gaston and Roanoke Rapids Lake (lakegastonchamber

.com; lake-gaston-properties.com/marinas.htm). Constructed in 1963, Lake Gaston covers 20,000 acres over the flooded Roanoke River upstream from Roanoke Rapids, straddling the Virginia state line. Despite its remoteness its shoreline is heavily developed with second homes. It has seven public boat ramps, and eight marinas. Just below it, the Roanoke Rapids Dam floods another 8 miles of river, covering 4,500 acres. Its single public boat ramp is on the south side of the lake; go 5.8 miles west of Roanoke Rapids on Thelma Avenue, then turn right onto Van Warren Road, which ends at the ramp.

✷ To See

FAYETTEVILLE'S MILITARY SITES Massive **Fort Bragg**, at 250 square miles, stretches westward from Fayetteville for 26 miles, nearly reaching Southern Pines. It has long been the home of several U.S. Army units, most notably the XVIII Airborne Corps headquarters and its subordinate unit, the 82nd Airborne Division, as well as the army's Special Operations Commands. By press time, Fort Bragg will also be the headquarters of the uppermost army command, FORSCOM (United States Army Forces Command). Unusual for such a large and important military base, Fort Bragg is also open to all U.S. citizens with two museums, a fair amount of statuary, and some historic sites all available on a self-guided auto tour. (Foreign nationals must write ahead for permission.) Along with a third museum on civilian land inside Fayetteville, this makes the Fayetteville area one of your best chances to experience a contemporary military site, important and in active operation, with high-quality interpretation provided by multiple museums. Think of it as history, but still in the present.

DUSK OVER JONES LAKE STATE PARK, IN THE BLADEN LAKES

To enter Fort Bragg go to the west side of Fayetteville on any main road and proceed north on the All-American Expressway. Present yourself at the gates during normal business hours (except Monday) and tell the guard that you want to visit the museums. If you are a U.S. civilian you will have to furnish identification in the form of a driver's license and automobile registration. If you are a foreign national, expect to show your written permission to enter the base, previously acquired, as well. The guard will probably inspect your car, including a look inside boxes. When you are cleared the guard will give you directions on how to find your destination.

The Airborne and Special Operations Museum (910-643-2766; asomf.org), 100 Bragg Blvd., Fayetteville 28301. Open Tue.–Sat. 10–5, Sun. noon–5. Admission to museum and exhibits is free; simulator and theater: $$. Located in Fayetteville on the western edge of downtown, this large (60,000 square feet), new museum commemorates all the airborne and special forces troops of the U.S. Army—long the cutting edge of unconventional warfare. Exhibits highlight the museum's large collection of military artifacts in chronological displays, starting with the birth of airborne operations in 1940 and continuing through today's actions. There's a movie theater and a motion simulation experience, as well as a memorial garden.

John F. Kennedy Special Warfare Museum (910-432-4272). Open Tue.–Sat. 10–4. Admission is free. Sometimes called the Spy Museum, this institution on the Fort Bragg army base is so secret that viewing its web page requires a security clearance (which is why it's not listed here). Fortunately, *visiting* it is much easier; just present yourself at the All-American Expressway gate, allow your car to be inspected, and get directions. Once there you'll find a set of fascinating displays on special operations from World War II through the present. It's affiliated with the nearby John F. Kennedy Special Warfare Center and School (known as "Swick"), the army's special ops training command.

The 82nd Airborne Museum (910-432-3443; 82ndairbornedivisionmuseum .com), Bldg. C-6841, Ardennes St., Fort Bragg 28307. Open Tue.–Sat. 10–4. Admission is free. Located across from the JFK Special Warfare Museum, this large, modern facility commemorates the 82nd Airborne, known as the "All Americans" since their founding in 1917. The grounds include a number of aircraft on display.

Auto Tours of Fort Bragg. Giant Fort Bragg contains a number of historic sites, dating back as far as Sherman's March in 1865, as well as commemorative statues and monuments. An auto tour is available to visitors; visit the 82nd Airborne Museum for details.

Sicily Drop Zone (910-396-6366). You can witness an airborne practice jump as part of your Fort Bragg experience, if one happens to be going on during your visit—and it probably will be, as this is a major training base. It's an amazing sight. Any U.S. citizen, or foreign national with written permission, can enjoy it simply by calling the phone number for a recording that gives scheduled jumps, then presenting yourself at the All-American Expressway gate. The guard will give you instructions on how to find the viewing site, which will be on the north side of the base 6 to 7 miles west of the end of the expressway, either on Manchester or Longstreet Road.

General William C. Lee Airborne Museum, Dunn, north of Fayetteville (910-892-1947; generalleeairbornemuseum.org; info@GeneralLeeAirborne Museum.org), 209 W. Divine St., P.O. Box 1111, Dunn 28334. Open weekdays 10–4, Sat. 11–4. This museum, located 25 miles north of Fayetteville in the town of Dunn, preserves the 1906 Greek Revival home of General William C. Lee, "Father of the American Airborne." Exhibits detail his military career, from discovering the abilities of a parachute attack while acting as U.S. military observer to Nazi Germany in 1935, to planning the airborne attack at D-Day.

CULTURAL SITES The Imperial Centre for the Arts and Sciences, Rocky Mount (imperialcentre.org), 270 Gay St., Rocky Mount 27804. Open hours vary; see the website for specifics. Admission to the art center is free; science center: $. Run by the city of Rocky Mount, this converted tobacco factory occupies an entire city block on the north edge of downtown. It houses an arts center with permanent and rotating displays, a science and children's museum with a planetarium, and a theater, venue for Rocky Mount's half-century-old community theater. It includes an exhibit on Rocky Mount native and longtime resident Buck Leonard, a star of the Negro National League from 1933 to 1950, admitted to the Baseball Hall of Fame in 1972. The city's new Veterans Memorial is directly across the street.

Greenville Museum of Art (252-758-1946; gmoa.org), 802 S. Evans St., Greenville 27834. Open Tue.–Fri. 10–4:30, Sat.–Sun. 1–4. Admission is free. Located in a beautiful historic mansion just south of downtown, this museum specializes in permanent and rotating exhibitions that highlight North Carolina artists, including prominent local artists Francis Speight and Sarah Blakeslee. A student gallery displays works from East Carolina University School of Arts and Design seniors, just two blocks away.

Ava Gardner Museum, Smithfield (919-934-5830; avagardner.org), 325 E. Market St., Smithfield 27577. Open Mon.–Sat. 9–5, Sun. 2–5. $$. The daughter of a poor tobacco farmer, Ava Gardner was born and raised in the countryside outside Smithfield, where she is buried. She became one of Hollywood's most glamorous stars when her brother-in-law, a New York photographer, started promoting the portraits he had taken of her. She never lost touch with her family here, and came to Smithfield frequently to visit them; but that's not why the museum is here. This museum on the western edge of downtown presents the huge collection of Gardner memorabilia collected by Tom Banks, a fan who credited his obsession to having teased Ava (then just a pretty local girl) when he was 12, and gotten kissed in retaliation. As memories of Gardner fade, the museum continues to vividly re-create a glamorous international culture that once gently brushed this North Carolina town.

Weymouth Center for the Arts and Humanities, Southern Pines (910-692-6261; weymouthcenter.org), 555 E. Connecticut Ave., Southern Pines 28387. The grounds and garden are open daily. The house is open weekdays, 10–2. Admission is free. This early-20th-century mansion on the eastern edge of town was the home of James Boyd, a critically acclaimed historic novelist of the 1920s and '30s, and a literary figure whose visitors included Thomas Wolfe, F. Scott Fitzgerald, and Sherwood Anderson. Parts of the house are furnished as in Boyd's day; other portions function as a cultural center, including a residency program for writers and the North Carolina Literary Hall of Fame. The gardens, originally laid out by Boyd's wife, Katharine, are reminiscent of an English cottage garden, a jumble of color from March to November. Katharine Boyd donated nearby **Weymouth Woods** to the state as a nature preserve in 1963.

HISTORIC SITES Historic Halifax State Historic Site, near Roanoke Rapids (252-583-7191; nchistoricsites.com/halifax; halifax@ncdcr.gov), 25 St. David St., Halifax 27839. Open Tue.–Sat. 9–5. Admission is free. In April 1776 the Provincial Congress of the Colony of North Carolina met in the village of Halifax (the capital of New Bern being controlled by British troops) to formally declare independence from Britain. Known as the Halifax Resolves, this declaration helped precipitate events that resulted in the Declaration of Independence three months later. Modern Halifax isn't much bigger than colonial Halifax, and a core of seven historic buildings makes up Historic Halifax State Historic Site. The buildings range from a 1760s merchant's home, to a 1790 tavern, to an 1838 jail; all are authentically restored, and three are furnished. Of particular interest is the Montfort Archeological Exhibit, a building constructed over the foundations of an early mansion, whose walkways and exhibits show how archaeologists have been able to reconstruct the way people lived and worked there. A visitors center has a small museum, and offers guided and self-guided exhibits.

Roanoke Canal Museum, Roanoke Rapids (252-537-2769; roanokecanal.com; canalmuseum@roanokerapidsnc.com), 15 Jackson St. Extension, Roanoke Rapids 27870. Open Tue.–Sat. 9–4. $. Completed in 1823, the 9-mile-long Roanoke Canal allowed narrow canal boats to float above the treacherous **Roanoke River Rapids** to reach hundreds of miles upstream into North Carolina and Virginia. It thrived at first, and its wharf at Weldon attracted one of the region's earliest railroads, but by 1880 it was out of date and abandoned. From 1882 to 1912 its uppermost, steepest section was used to transmit water to an electric generator—and this early hydroelectric plant now houses a museum dedicated to the canal. Integral to the museum is the 7.2-mile-long **Roanoke Canal Trail**, following the tow path with interpretive boards; its major site is a massive brick aqueduct that carried canal boats over a stream.

Murfreesboro Historic District (252-398-5922; murfreesboronc.org). Museums are open on weekends, and guided tours are on Saturdays; call for times. Guided tour of six sites: $$; self-guided tour booklet: $. This sleepy little town of 2,000, located in remote farmland in the northeast corner of this chapter's area, is notable for having no fewer than 11 historic museums and venues, all within a few blocks of one another, created and maintained by the Murfreesboro Historic Association. These include three museums: a historical museum of coastal plains life in their headquarters, a 1790 brick mansion; a museum of agricultural and transportation equipment; and a museum of household artifacts from the late 19th to mid-20th century. In addition there's a working smithy, a tin shop (common in small southern towns through the 1920s), a law office, a country store, and a plantation house museum furnished in period.

Stonewall Manor, Rocky Mount (252-442-0063; stonewallmanornc.org), 1331 Stone Wall Lane, Rocky Mount 27804. $–$$. This large, elegant antebellum mansion sits just off NC 43 at its intersection with US Byp 64 on the north edge of town. Run by a local historical society, it's attractively furnished in period to give an accurate picture of the life of a wealthy coastal planter. This does not, unfortunately, extend into the back of the big house; the outbuildings and slave quarters upon which this lifestyle depended have long since vanished, the lands alienated when the plantation broke up at the close of the Civil War.

Tobacco Farmlife Museum, near Wilson (919-284-3431; tobaccofarmlifemuseum.org; groups@tobaccofarmlifemuseum.org), US 301 N., P.O. Box 88, Kenly 27542. Open Tue.–Sat. 9:30–5. $$. Located on the northern edge of small tobacco town of Kenly, 0.8 mile north of I-95's exit 107 on US 301, this 2-acre museum recreates an early-20th-century golden leaf tobacco farm. A visit starts at the modern visitors center with 4,000 square feet of exhibits explaining East Carolina tobacco culture, then proceeds to the fully furnished farmstead consisting of the farmhouse, its detached kitchen, smokehouse, and log tobacco barn.

TOBACCO IN BLOOM

The Country Doctor Museum, near Wilson (252-235-4165; countrydoctormuseum.org), 6642 Peele Rd., Bailey 27807. Open Tue.–Sat. 10–4. $. Located 13 miles west of Wilson in the little town of Bailey, this fascinating museum explores the practice of a early- to mid-20th-century country doctor. It was founded in 1967 by a group of locals inspired by Bailey's Dr. Josephine E. Newell, herself the seventh in a line of rural practitioners; it is now part of East Carolina State's William E. Laurus Health Sciences Library. The museum wanders through three 19th-century buildings, with two re-created doctor's offices, an apothecary, a transportation exhibit, and a tribute to nurses, as well as other exhibits.

Aycock Birthplace State Historic Site, near Goldsboro (nchistoricsites.com/aycock), 264 Gov. Aycock Rd., Fremont 27830. Open Mon.–Sat. 9–5. Admission is free. This open-air museum preserves the poor dirt farm where North Carolina's "education governor," Charles B. Aycock, was born in 1859. Aycock, a Democrat, rode into office in 1900 on a white supremacy platform that swept out a Republican-led biracial government known as the Fusionists (using force in Wilmington, a Fusionist stronghold). While governor, however, Aycock pushed public education relentlessly, and opened 1,100 new schools during his four-year term, one for every day in office. The site is interesting as presenting the sort of small, independent, but impoverished farm that was common in this period. It is doubly interesting for including an 1892 one-room schoolhouse, restored to the way it would have looked in Aycock's day, including a dunce's cap.

SHEEP GRAZE AT THE CHARLES B. AYCOCK BIRTHPLACE

Waynesborough Historical Village, Goldsboro (919-731-1653; waynesborough historicalvillage.com; waynesborough@earthlink.net). Located on the western edge of town off US 13, this open-air museum, established and run by a local group, has re-created a 19th-century rural village by moving historic structures onto this site. Its 13 buildings include a modern visitors center, two farmhouses, lawyer's and doctor's offices, a print shop, a smithy, a school, a church, and a general store. All buildings are furnished and filled with exhibits. The surrounding Waynesboro Park preserves a large tract of wild land along the Neuse River, with walking trails that explore its extensive river frontage and forests.

Bentonville Battlefield State Historic Site, south of Goldsboro (910-594-0789; nchistoricsites.com/bentonvi; bentonville@ncdcr.gov), 5466 Harper House Rd., Four Oaks 27524. Open Mon.–Sat. 9–5; closed Mon. during winter. Admission is free. Fought in late March 1865 on flat plantation lands 20 miles southwest of Goldsboro, the Battle of Bentonville marked the last time a Confederate army was able to launch an attack on a Union army, in this case General William T. Sherman's army completing its "March to the Sea" with a sweep up the Atlantic coast. It was an act of desperation. Sherman's 60,000 troops already outnumbered Confederate general Joe Johnson's army by three to one and were marching to the Goldsboro railhead for major reinforcements; this chance, as bad as it was, would be the last. Unfortunately for Johnson, to succeed in cutting Sherman from Goldsboro he had to place the entire Union army between his own and its escape route to Raleigh. Initial Confederate successes during the three-day battle were not decisive enough to overcome the Union force's considerable advantage. Johnston was finally forced to move his tattered forces around Sherman's in a retreat to safer ground at Smithfield, and Sherman, anxious to unite with his reinforcements to the east, let him go. It was a wise move. Robert E. Lee's Army of Virginia, not far to the north, was running out of steam, and the creation of this huge enemy force to Lee's rear forced him to retreat to Appomattox, where he surrendered 18 days later—followed by Johnston, now encamped at Durham, 8 days after that, to end the Civil War.

ONE-ROOM SCHOOLHOUSE AT CHARLES B. AYCOCK BIRTHPLACE

For Bentonville planters John and Amy Harper this was a terrible end to the war; the main battle raged around their plantation house. Nevertheless the Harpers and seven of their children stayed, and tended the wounded of both sides in their home. Now completely restored, its ground floor is furnished as a Civil War field hospital, and its top floor is furnished as a period planter's home. A Confederate mass grave, marked by the battlefield's largest monument, is near the Harper family cemetery. At the newly refurbished visitors center, exhibits and an interactive map explain the 900-acre battlefield, and an auto tour leads to the various battle sites, each explained by interpretive boards.

CSS *Neuse* and Governor Caswell Memorial (252-522-2091; nchistoricsites.org/neuse; cssneuse@ncdcr.gov), 100 N. Queen St., Kinston 28502. Open Tue.–Sat. 9–5. Admission is free. This early ironclad river warship was built by the Confederate navy in early 1863 as part of a plan to regain control of the entire Neuse River and the port of New Bern from Union forces. Confederate forces sunk it off a river bend in Kinston two years later, as Sherman's army occupied the coastal plains and massed for their final defeat of the state's forces at nearby Bentonville only a few days later. And there it sat, covered by sand and easily found at low water, for the next 96 years. Then in 1961 three businessmen decided to raise it, something they expected to take two weeks and ended up consuming two years. The raised hull, and the many artifacts found with it, have long since been properly studied by archaeologists, and have now been conserved as part of a new museum in downtown Kinston, which should be open by the time you read this. Also part of the site is a memorial to Richard Caswell, a Revolutionary War general, the commander of the Patriot forces at the Battle of Moores Creek Bridge, and the first governor of an independent North Carolina, serving six one-year terms between 1776 and 1787.

Liberty Hall, Kenansville, south of Goldsboro (910-296-2175; libertyhallnc.org), 409 Main St., Kenansville 28349. Open Tue.–Sat. 10–4. $. During antebellum times the town of Kenansville formed the center of a major growing region noted for its wealthy plantations reliant on large slave labor forces. The ironically named Liberty Hall, located on the southern edge of town, was home to the Kenan family, among the district's most important planters. It's an elaborate Greek Revival mansion, preserved with its outbuildings to show both the luxurious lifestyle of the planters and the working farm that surrounded it on all sides. Adjacent to Liberty Hall is the Cowan Museum in an 1848 farmhouse, a local history museum (open Tue.–Sat. 10–4; admission is free) whose thousands of artifacts portray early rural life in coastal North Carolina.

Two other Kenansville planters' mansions are open to viewing by the public, although only by appointment. The **Murray House** (910-296-1000; murrayhouseinn.com) is an 1853 Greek Revival structure with that classic plantation look; it is now a bed & breakfast. A few miles out of town to the west is the **Buckner Hill Plantation** (910-293-3001; carolinaplantation.com), one of the grandest in the state and surviving nearly unchanged since its 1855 construction; scenes from the 2002 movie *The Divine Secrets of the Ya-Ya Sisterhood* were shot there. Finally, one of North Carolina's oldest and most successful wineries, **Duplin Winery** (800-774-9634; duplinwinery.com), is nearby at Rose Hill, with wine tastings as well as lunches served in its own café, **The Bistro**.

Museum of the Cape Fear Historical Complex, Fayetteville (910-486-1330; museumofthecapefear.ncdcr.gov), 801 Arsenal Ave., Fayetteville 28305. Open Tue.–Sat. 10–5, Sun. 1–5. Admission is free. This complex, located on a residential street on the western side of town, has extensive exhibits on the southern coastal plains in its 1988 museum building. Adjacent is the 1897 Poe House, furnished in late-Victorian period, with tours by costumed docents. Behind the museum (and across the US 401 expressway on a handsome pedestrian bridge) is the 4-acre **Arsenal Park**, preserving the ruins of the Confederate arsenal destroyed by Sherman in 1865.

Fayetteville Area Transportation and Local History Museum (910-433-1455; fcpr.us/transportation_museum.aspx), 325 Franklin St., Fayetteville 28301. Open Tue.–Sat. 10–4. Admission is free. Edgar Allen Poe made the bricks for this stunningly beautiful Victorian passenger depot—not that one, the Fayetteville brickmaker. Located downtown, its two floors of exhibits chronicle coastal plain transportation from plank roads to interstates.

House in the Horseshoe State Historic Site, north of Pinehurst (910-947-2051; nchistoricsites.org/horsesho; horseshoe@ncdcr.gov), 288 Alston House Rd., Sanford 27330. This colonial-era farmhouse, deep in the countryside 20 miles north of Pinehurst, was the site of a skirmish between Patriot and Loyalist bands in 1781; bullet holes from that encounter still pepper the walls. It has been restored and furnished to its Revolutionary War appearance. While it gives the appearance of a prosperous little independent farm, it was in fact the center of a plantation, with 50 slaves by 1803.

✷ To Do

BICYCLE RENTALS Revolution Cycles, Greensboro (336-852-3972; revolutioncyclesnc.com; revolutioncyclesnc@gmail.com), The Shoppes at Lindey Park, 2823 Spring Garden St., Greensboro 27403. This local bicycle shop, located on the western side of town, rents a range of town and trail bikes, and will help you find local trails.

CANOES AND KAYAKS Tar River Paddle Sports, Rocky Mount (252-883-2441; tarriverpaddlesports.com; rockymountnc.gov/parks/paddletrail.html; frank@tarriverpaddlesports.com), Rocky Mount 27804. This dealership specializes in the NuCanoe, a kayak-canoe hybrid that's 10 to 12 feet long, 42 inches wide, seats two, and is stable enough to stand up in. While they do not sponsor trips or provide transport at this time, they will rent you a NuCanoe, which will easily ride on your car's rooftop rack or in the bed of your pickup. Nor will you have to drive far to find some fine canoeing. The nearby city of Rocky Mount has developed three separate lengths of the nearby Tar River as canoe trails, as well as Stony Creek, a rare opportunity to explore a small stream.

Riverside Bicycles and Outdoor Sports, Kinston (252-520-9400; riversideofkinston.com), 210 W. Gordon St., Kinston 28501. This local bicycle, canoe, and kayak dealer offers canoe and kayak rentals from its shop outside downtown on the Neuse River.

LAKE BOAT RENTALS Lake Gaston Water Sports (434-636-2175; corky@lakegastonwatersports.com), 183 Hendricks Mill Rd., Bracey, VA 23919. Located on the north side of Lake Gaston, this boat dealer rents pontoon boats from an attractive lake-side facility one step over the line in Virginia; they also have a dry-land sales outlet in nearby Henrico, North Carolina.

GOLF AT SOUTHERN PINES

(homeofgolf.com/golf; pinehurst.com/north-carolina-golf-resorts.php). In 1895 a Boston soda-fountain magnate named James Walker Tufts decided to create a resort in the remote, sandy hills of North Carolina. To this end he purchased 5,800 acres of logged-out land, built a nice big hotel (now the Holly Inn), and platted the curving streets of a village around it—Pinehurst. He evidently believed that the "pine ozone" had a salubrious effect on tuberculosis, but quickly discovered that tuberculosis was highly contagious and a giant health spa built around it was probably not going to work. In 1898 Tufts hit upon the idea of adding golf, building a clubhouse and the Pinehurst #1 course. This was a success, and in 1900 Tufts hired Donald Ross, a young Scotsman at the start of his career, to direct the effort. Ross, who stayed with Pinehurst until his death in 1948, established himself as one of the greatest course architects in the history of golf, and gave Pinehurst its international reputation. His Pinehurst #2, opened in 1907, will be the site of the U.S. Open and U.S. Women's Open in 2014; a major project, ongoing at press time, is restoring #2 to Ross's concept and aesthetics, of a course that seems to be laid casually across natural lands.

In fact, there are plenty of golf choices at Pinehurst. The resort itself has eight courses. The surrounding region has another 35. And the play is as good as you would expect for a place that has had to live up to Donald Ross's standards; *Golf Digest* has rated 23 of them at four stars or better, with Pinehurst #2 getting the only five-star rating in the state.

STATUES OF DONALD ROSS (R) AND RICHARD TUFTS (L) LOOK OUT OVER PINEHURST #2.

Stonehouse Timber Lodge (877-846-2379; 252-586-3012; lakegastonfun.com; stllg@lakegastonfun.com), 154 Stonehouse Lodge Dr., Littleton 27850. This resort on the south side of Lake Gaston rents pontoons, fishing boats, and canoes from their full-feature marina.

Eaton Ferry Marina (919-267-3868; morningstarmarinas.com), 1865 Eaton Ferry Rd., Littleton 27850. Located at the southwest corner of Lake Gaston, this member of the Morningstar Marina franchise rents deck boats, pontoons, skiffs, and Jet Skis.

✷ Lodging

HOTELS AND RESORTS ✐ **Pinehurst Resort** (800-487-4653; 910-235-8507; pinehurst.com; pinehurst.info@pinehurst.com), 80 Carolina Vista Dr., Pinehurst 28374. $$$$–$$$$$$. Since its founding in 1895, Pinehurst Resort has been the center of the Pinehurst community—its founder, the creator of the village, and the reason this has long been one of America's leading golf destinations. Its original inn is the 82-room Holly, an architectural oddity combining neoclassical detail with Dutch roofs. Its main inn is the 1901 Carolina, a grand and rambling structure with 226 rooms, whose verandas face its landscaped grounds. The Manor, with 42 rooms, has the personality of a hunting lodge. Villa and condo units are also available. A full range of resort activities is available as well as golf, including a large spa and a 200-acre lake. WiFi is available. Rooms are priced as packages, with the least expensive being a "Social Package" that includes breakfast, dinner, and use of the lake, starting around $300; packages that include golf start at around $600.

✐ 🐾 **Pine Needles and Mid-Pines, Southern Pines** (800-747-7272; 910-692-7111; pineneedles-midpines.com), 1005 Midland Rd., Southern Pines 28387. $$$–$$$$. Pinehurst is by no means the only resort in the Southern Pines area. These two resorts, under the same ownership, sit across Midland Road from each other, on the west side of Southern Pines. Both are the result of the 1920s tourism boom, and both feature Donald Ross–designed courses. The 1921 Mid-Pines Inn and Golf Club features an elegant hotel, with rooms decorated in a Georgian style. The 1928 Pine Needles Lodge and Golf Club is more casual in tone, with country decor in its chalet-style lodges, connected with covered walkways. WiFi is available. Small pets are allowed in some rooms; call ahead.

The Jefferson Inn, Southern Pines (910-692-9911; jeffersoninnsouthernpines.com), 150 W. New Hampshire Ave., Southern Pines 28387. $$$$. This boutique hotel, completely renovated in 2007, has been in continuous operation at the center of downtown Southern Pines since the late 19th century. The straightforward Italianate structure forms an el around a tiny courtyard, faced by verandas; the 15 rooms range from cozy to large, and have WiFi. The on-site restaurant is open daily for dinner; you may wish to note that there may be live entertainment in the courtyard, which some rooms overlook—a plus for some, a minus for others.

BED & BREAKFASTS ✐ 🐾 **Heathsville Haven Bed and Breakfast, south of Roanoke Rapids** (252-445-5448; heathsvillehaven.com; heathsvillehaven@touchnc.net), 25560 NC 561, Enfield 27823. $–$$. Located deep in rural countryside, this three-room B&B in a modern Colonial-style home is convenient to the northern part of this chapter's area, being less than 2 miles from I-95's exit 160. Common areas and all three rooms are tastefully furnished in antiques, and its executive suite has a living area as well as a bedroom and two baths. WiFi is available, and a full breakfast is included in the tariffs.

Cutawhiskey Bed and Breakfast, south of Murfreesboro (252-587-3667; cutawhiskeybb.com; contact@cutawhiskeybb.com), 913 Menola St. John Rd., Woodland 27897. $$. This antebellum farmhouse is strikingly remote, located in deep countryside in the northeastern part of this chapter's area. The three rooms are roomy and furnished in antiques, and high-speed Internet is available. A full breakfast is included.

🐾 **The Whitehead Inn, Wilson** (252-243-4447; whiteheadinn.com; reservations1@whiteheadinn.com), 600 Nash St. NE, Wilson 27893. $$–$$$. This unusual bed & breakfast near the center of Wilson consists of four adjacent historic homes, dating between 1858 and 1911, and accurately restored to their original period. Each house has two or three rooms and its own large veranda, and is furnished in antiques. WiFi is available, and a full three-course breakfast is included in the tariff. Two of the rooms are pet-friendly, with a size limit and an extra fee.

The 5th Street Inn, Greenville (252-355-0699; the5thstreetinn.com; innkeeper@the5thstreetinn.com), 1105 E. 5th St., Greenville 27858. $$. This four-room bed & breakfast occupies a 1924 Colonial-style house in a historic residential district directly across from East Carolina State University. Interiors are attractive and home-like, with furnishings consistent with the period. Rooms range from cozy to very large.

Plum Tree Gardens Bed and Breakfast, Goldsboro (919-736-3356; plumtreegardens.com; plumtreegardens@earthlink.net), 109 S. George St., Goldsboro 27530. $$–$$$. This handsome Victorian home sits in Goldboro's historic district at the edge of downtown. You'll find it decorated in a country antique manner, and exhibiting art and fine crafts from local artists, with a large veranda and handsome gardens. The five rooms are good-sized, and include a two-room suite in the Victorian house across the street; two of the rooms in the main house share a bath. WiFi is available. The tariff includes a three-course breakfast and an evening wine-and-cheese social; this may be reduced to an in-room continental breakfast for a $20 savings.

The Graham House Inn, Kenansville, south of Goldsboro (910-375-5865; grahamhouseinn.com; innkeeper@grahamhouseinn.com), 406 S. Main St., Kenansville 28349. $$–$$$. Located in the center of Kenansville across the street from the historic plantation house of Liberty Hall, this fine old Victorian house features a veranda and balcony framed by columns in a carpenter Greek Revival style. Inside, the house and its four rooms are furnished in period with antiques and reproductions. WiFi is available, and a full breakfast is included in the tariff.

🖉 🐾 **Simply Divine Bed and Breakfast, Dunn, north of Fayetteville** (910-892-2296; simplydivinebedandbreakfast.com; cr.forrester@gmail.com), 309 W. Divine St., Dunn 28334. $$. Located in a historic residential neighborhood of the pleasant small town of Dunn, this 1906 mansion, built by a congressman, is surrounded by handsomely landscaped grounds. The four rooms are all large and bright, and furnished in period. WiFi is available, and a three-course breakfast is included. Children under 12 and pets require prior approval, and a pet fee applies.

Knollwood House, Southern Pines (910-692-9390; knollwoodhouse.com; innkeeper@knollwoodhouse.com), 1495 W. Connecticut Ave., Southern Pines 28387. $$$. Located in an exclusive residential section of Southern Pines, this 1927 English Manor–style mansion sits on landscaped grounds adjacent to the Donald Ross–designed golf course at Mid-Pines. Common areas are spacious and bright, and the five rooms are large; four are suites with separate sitting rooms, and two of these have sleeping porches. WiFi is available, and a full breakfast is included.

The Old Buggy Inn, Carthage, north of Pinehurst (910-947-1901; oldbuggyinn.com), 301 McReynolds St., Carthage 28327. $$. This four-room B&B occupies a turreted Queen Anne home (one of the rooms is in the turret). The inn has wraparound rocking porches and a swimming pool, while a buggy commemorates the fact that this tidy, historic town was once America's greatest buggy manufacturer. Rooms are standard to large in size, furnished in antiques, and have working gas fireplace; all rooms have private bath, but two of them are down a hall. Breakfast, evening wine, and hors d'oeuvres are included in the tariff.

The Inn at Bryant House, near Pinehurst (800-453-4019; 910-944-3300; innatbryanthouse.com; innatbryanthouse@yahoo.com), 214 N. Poplar St., Aberdeen 28315. $$. This beautiful 1900 mansion sits near the center of sleepy little Aberdeen, surrounded by gardens. It's been an inn since 1913—a traditional southern boardinghouse for 75 years, then a luxurious bed & breakfast after a thorough modernization. You'll find it furnished in antiques reminiscent of its early-20th-century origin. It's eight rooms can sometimes be cozy. WiFi is available, and a full breakfast is included. There is a size limit and a fee on pets.

CABINS Stonehouse Timber Lodge, west of Roanoke Rapids (877-846-2379; 252-586-3012; lakegastonfun.com; stllg@lakegastonfun.com), 154 Stonehouse Lodge Dr., Littleton 27850. $$–$$$$. Built around a 1962 fish camp on the southern shore of Lake Gaston, this highly renovated fishing resort offers a variety of lakeside cabin and house accommodations as well as a full-service marina. Boat launching is free to tenants, slips are available, and a variety of boats can be rented if you don't want to tow your own. There's a sand beach as well. All rental cabins and houses have kitchens and living areas, with the price reflecting size and sophistication. The camp's original log cabins, small but well furnished, are the cheapest, a series of full-sized houses the dearest, and a set of well-kept mobile homes make up the middle.

* Where to Eat

DINING OUT Chef and the Farmer, Kinston (252-208-2433; chefandthefarmer.com), 120 W. Gordon St., Kinston 28501. Open for dinner Tue.–Sat. $$$–$$$$. Chef and founder Vivian Howard was born and raised in the coastal plains, then worked her way up through the restaurant trade in the exclusive eateries of Manhattan, to finally return to downtown Kinston. Her restaurant marries locally grown food with big-city sophistication. The menu, which changes daily, is eclectic, but features a good selection of North Carolina– and southern-inspired dishes.

The 1895 Grille, Pinehurst (910-235-8434; pinehurst.com), 145 Cherokee Rd., Pinehurst 28374. Open for breakfast daily, and for dinner Wed.–Sun. The Tavern is open daily for lunch and dinner. $$$$–$$$$$; Tavern: $$$–$$$$. Part of the Pinehurst Resort, this formal dining room is located in the Holly, the resort's original inn. Its menu is elegant and upscale, featuring a variety of North Carolina seafood, southern-inspired dishes, and steaks. Gentlemen are expected to wear shirts with collars, and denim is not allowed. For a more casual experience the attached Tavern offers a simpler and less expensive menu in a pub-like atmosphere.

EATING OUT

On the Square, Tarboro (252-823-8268; onthesquarenc.com), 115 E. St. James St., Tarboro 27886. Open for lunch, weekdays, and for dinner Thu.–Sat. Lunch: $$; dinner: $$$–$$$$. A Manhattan couple brings a big-city bistro experience to downtown Tarboro (he's the chef; she's the sommelier) while leaving big-city prices behind. Lunch offers soups, salads, and some lovely sandwiches. Dinner is more of a fine-dining experience, featuring local vegetables and a distinct southern inspiration. North Carolina craft beers are available on tap. The vast wine list, winner of *Wine Spectator's* Best of Award of Excellence, contains many choices under $20.

EAST CAROLINA BARBEQUE

(ncbbqsociety.com). North Carolina has two very distinct regional styles of barbeque. In the Eastern Style, a whole hog is cooked over greenwood and basted with a vinegar-pepper sauce—a more traditionally southern approach. The meat is served chopped, and there is controversy over whether this should be coarse or the texture of hash, and over whether skin and gristle should be left in or cut out. This contrasts with the Western (or Lexington) Style, where only the shoulder is cooked over hickory coals, basted with a combination of vinegar and ketchup, and sliced or pulled (see Lexington Barbeque in "The Mill Belt").

Partisanship runs high, with one Eastern Style backer saying, "People who would put ketchup in the sauce they feed to innocent children are capable of most anything." Fortunately the North Carolina Barbeque Society is nonpartisan, and a reliable guide to the best. Their recommended Eastern Style restaurants cook their meat for 8 to 16 hours over traditional wood pits, have been in business for at least 15 years, have covered seating, and have earned the respect of their community and of barbeque aficionados. Atmosphere is *not* judged, and the exteriors of these restaurants range from straightforward to downright dingy. Expect eccentricity and character, rather than "atmosphere," with Wilber's being the least eccentric of the bunch.

Starlight Café, Greenville (252-707-9033; starlightcafe.org; starlightcafe@suddenlink.net), 104 5th St., Greenville 27858. Open for lunch, dinner, and Sunday brunch. $$$–$$$$. This downtown café offers an exciting and eccentric menu, varying from familiar items such as local catfish and fries to such exotica as Middle Eastern lamb. Its attractive interior highlights the building's original brick, and two bars (upstairs and down) complement the dining, with oysters and jazz featured upstairs. All food is prepared fresh from scratch, frequently using meat and produce from local farmers.

McDuff's Tea Room & Emporium (910-488-0328; mcduffstearoom.com), 114 Gillespie St., Fayetteville 28301. Open for lunch and tea. Lunch: $$; tea: $$$. Established in 1999, this classic English tearoom offers an appealingly frilly atmosphere in the center of downtown, and an inexpensive menu of original sandwiches, soups, salads, and an extensive list of handmade desserts. A daily specials menu offers hot food as well, such as shepherd's pie. At 3 the restaurant stops serving lunch and switches to tea, by reservation only—an amazing presentation of tea, salad, quiche, and a three-tiered server with tea sandwiches, cookies and pastries, scones, and chocolate-covered strawberries.

Pierro's Italian Bistro (910-678-8885; pierrositalianbistro.com), 217 Hay St., Fayetteville 28301. Open daily

Skylight Inn, Ayden (south of Greenville) (252-746-4113), 4618 Lee St. Open for lunch and dinner. Very traditional; uses 19th-century recipes.

B's Barbeque, Greenville (no phone), 751 B's Barbecue Rd. (corner with NC 43, west of town). Open for lunch; closes when the barbeque runs out. Crowded and popular; don't let the shabby exterior put you off.

Jack Cobb and Son Barbecue Place, Farmville (west of Greenville) (252-753-5128), 3883 S. Main St. (US 258, just south of downtown). Open for lunch on Wed., Fri., Sat.; picnic table seating on a screened patio. This second-generation restaurant, opened in the 1940s, reflects the African American tradition in East Carolina barbeque.

Wilber's Barbecue, Goldsboro (919-778-5218; wilbersbarbecue.com), 4172 US 70 E. Open every day for breakfast, lunch, and dinner. This large restaurant is the archetype of Eastern Style barbeque.

Grady's Barbecue, Dudley (southern edge of Goldsboro) (919-735-7243), 3096 Arrington Bridge Rd. Open for lunch. A small, plain restaurant at a rural crossroads, noted for its sparkling kitchen and perfect state health rating.

for lunch and dinner. $$$–$$$$. This popular downtown eatery features a handsome exterior with sidewalk seating, and an equally appealing interior. The menu is large, and much more original than you would expect in a small rural city. Pizzas are baked in a brick oven, and the wine list gives you some good choices.

The Bakehouse, Aberdeen (910-944-9204; thebakehouse.biz; thebakehouse@yahoo.com), 120 N. Poplar St., Aberdeen 28315. Open for breakfast and lunch Mon.–Sat., and Sun. brunch. $$. Located at the center of Aberdeen, this Austrian-style bakery (in business here for more than 60 years) serves stunning burgers and homemade bratwurst on their own artisan breads. Their café area is attractive, bright, and roomy. And just try to resist their fancy European pastries!

✷ Entertainment

POPULAR Huske Hardware House Restaurant and Brewery (910-437-9905; huskehardware.com), 405 Hay St., Fayetteville 28301. Open daily for lunch and dinner. $$–$$$; may have a cover charge at night. This downtown brewpub occupies a beautifully renovated historic hardware building. It offers a fine lunch and dinner—but gets moved to our *Entertainment* column for its lively music on Tue.–Sat. nights, with live bands on Tue.–Thu., and a DJ and dancing on Fri.–Sat. Discounts are offered to military ID holders. Check their website for details.

✷ Selective Shopping

Pinehurst Village. Three winding blocks, hidden away from both highways and Pinehurst's main resort, the Carolina, have furnished exclusive shopping to wealthy golfers and horsers since the 1890s. It's charming and fun, no matter what your price range.

✷ Special Events

Special events in the coastal plains all seem to bunch up in spring, particularly in April and May. This not only reflects the beauty of freshly leafed trees and abundant blooms, and relief at the end of winter, but also coincides with pleasant temperatures, even in the midafternoon. If you can break free for a spring visit, these festivals give yet another good reason to spend it in the coastal plains.

Mid-April: **Halifax Day, Halifax**. Up through the 1980s, April 12—"Halifax Day," the day when North Carolina declared its independence from Britain in 1776—was an official holiday. In the little village of Halifax it still is, a celebration of the start of colonial independence. It's led by Historic Halifax State Historic Site, which has costumed docents in its seven buildings, and craft demonstrations; if you're lucky, the local colonial militia will show up as well.

Grifton Shad Festival, Grifton, east of Kinston (grifton.com/shadfest.html). Admission is free. For more than 40 years this remote town has celebrated the shad, a 1- to 3-pound saltwater fish that migrates up Carolina rivers every spring to breed. While its edibility is debated, a former mayor observed, "They don't eat azaleas at the Azalea Festival or mules at Mule Day." This small-town celebration features food, crafts, art, a parade, a shad fishing tourney, fish fries, barbeques, and, as a finale, a shad tossing contest.

Last weekend in April: **North Carolina Pickle Festival, Mount Olive, south of Goldsboro** (919-658-3113; ncpicklefest.org; moacc@bellsouth.net). The small town of Mount Olive, home of Mount Olive Pickle Company (founded here in 1926 and America's largest independent pickle producer), has hosted this pickle-saturated street fair every year since 1987. Apart from lots of pickles, the festival features non-pickle food vendors, antique cars, the "Tour de Pickle" bike race, and petting animals.

First weekend in May: **Buggy Festival, Carthage, north of Southern Pines** (thebuggyfestival.com). From the mid-19th century through the 1920s Carthage was home to America's largest carriage manufacturer, the Tyson and Jones Buggy Factory. This handsome little county seat celebrates its horse-drawn heritage with buggies to view and ride, as well as craft and food vendors, competitions, music, and antique cars.

2 The Piedmont

INTRODUCTION

Occupying the entire center portion of the state, the Piedmont consists of rolling hills, with rapid-strewn rivers. It had begun to industrialize in the earliest ante-bellum days, with water-powered mills springing up where roads crossed streams. This accelerated with a vengeance when the state of North Carolina built the North Carolina Railroad (1842–52) in a big arc between Raleigh and Charlotte. Every place the railroad crossed a good, strong stream became a candidate for industrial development, and a whole string of cities sprang up around the mills. The biggest of these are (from east to west) Raleigh (the capital), Durham (where the cigarette industry was invented), Chapel Hill (the seat of the state's university system), Burlington (of textile fame), Greensboro (textiles and tobacco), Winston-Salem (textiles and tobacco), High Point (furniture), Hickory (furniture), and Charlotte (banking and other corporate headquarters). Even with the retreat of the textile industry the region continues with strong growth into the 21st century.

With so many industries, there have been a great many industrialists feeling the need to be good guys who support the community rather than exploit it. Titans of industry being who they are, this takes the form of excellent museums, fine arts, and first-rate historic restoration.

All those industries need electrical power, and in the Piedmont this means giant hydroelectric dams. This leads to the region's other great recreation resource: its huge lakes. You'll find all of them described in the next few chapters, along with listings for places where you can rent a boat.

THE RALEIGH-DURHAM AREA

The new state of North Carolina created its capital on the eastern edge of the Piedmont, 5 miles west of the Neuse River, in 1792—for no particular reason, other than the fact that the bickering legislators couldn't agree on anyplace else. At about the same time the legislature founded the nation's first state-sponsored and -funded university, the University of North Carolina, 25 miles to the west, at a site with a hilltop chapel; by 1820 the town of Chapel Hill had grown up to service the thriving university. Durham, located 21 miles northwest of Raleigh, emerged around a railhead as the early center of North Carolina's tobacco industry. Together these three cities make up the Triangle, an urban area of 1.7 million people.

With over a million residents Raleigh dominates the area, showing the ascendancy of government as the 21st century begins. As late as the 1980s the I-440 ring defined its outermost limits, but now the city sprawls for miles beyond it in all directions, and a new outer ring, I-540, is being built to encircle its latest edge. Its state-dependent economy, aided by research firms linked to the Triangle's three world-class universities, has been on a 70-year tear, and the result has been a glorious selection of museums, galleries, historic sites, and parks.

Durham was less lucky. At one time the headquarters of a worldwide tobacco monopoly, it lost its tobacco factories in the 1980s and suffered the inevitable decline. Since then, however, it's been rebuilding its economic base, becoming more like its big sister to the south with technological and medical companies taking advantage of Duke University (within its limits). Its vast 19th-century tobacco factories and warehouses are now venues for living, working, shopping, and dining, while its historic sites highlight early tobacco, antebellum farming, and the end of the Civil War. Durham and its suburbs now have about 500,000 residents.

This area, taken together, presents the most concentrated and rewarding historic and cultural zone in the state, and one of the finest in the South. Major fine art museums can be found in all three cities, and the state's official (and excellent) history and science museums are adjacent to the capitol building. The 1840 State Capitol itself is largely given over to historic interpretation, although it remains the official seat of government by housing the office of the governor. Historic houses, sites, and plantations are abundant; there are even two wonderful old watermills. The art and theater scene is lively and varied. Outdoor recreation is also plentiful, with a number of major lakes, superb river canoeing, and a vast network of hiking trails and hiking-biking greenways.

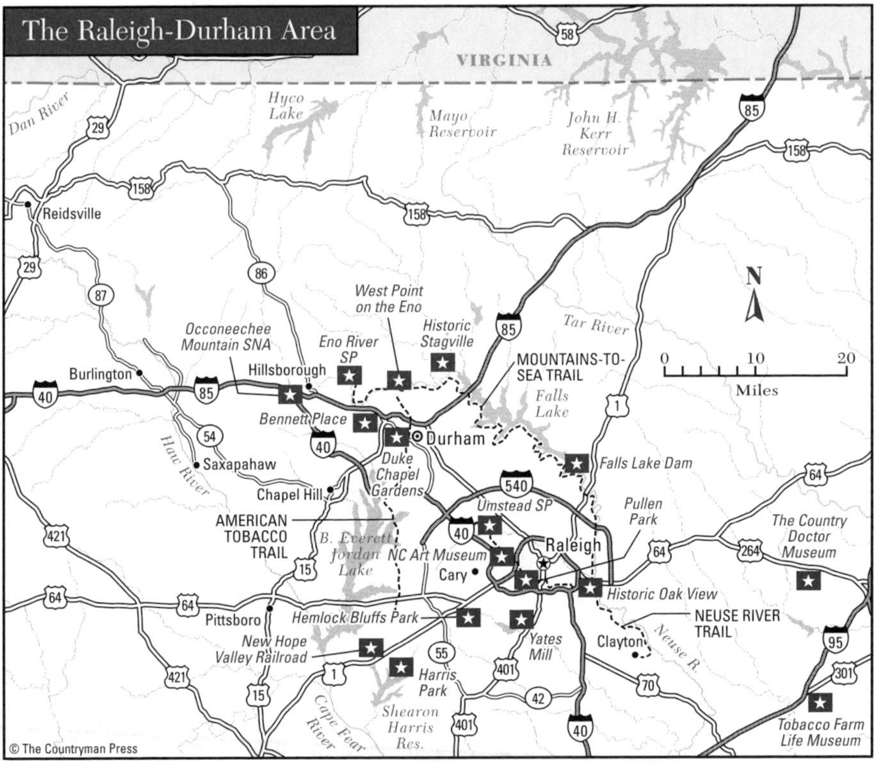

GUIDANCE Greater Raleigh Convention and Visitors Bureau (800-849-8499; 919-834-5900; visitraleigh.com), 220 Fayetteville St., Raleigh 27601. This is your primary source of travel information for the city of Raleigh and the surrounding towns of Wake County. Their visitors center is downtown, inside the Raleigh City Museum, a block south of the capitol on Salisbury Street.

Capitol Area Visitors Services, Raleigh (866-724-8687; 919-807-7950; ncmuseumofhistory.org/vs). This small state agency, located in the lobby of the North Carolina Museum of History, offers information on visiting the major government sites of the Capitol District.

Durham Convention and Visitors Bureau (800-446-8604; 919-687-0288; durham-nc.com), 101 E. Morgan St., Durham 27701. This agency serves travelers to the city of Durham and the surrounding Durham County, from their visitors center at the northern edge of downtown, on the corner of US 70 (Morgan Street) and US 15/501 South (Magnum Street).

Chapel Hill/Orange County Visitors Bureau (888-968-2060; 919-968-2060; visitchapelhill.org; info@visitchapelhill.org), 501 W. Franklin St., Chapel Hill 27516. The third of the tri-cities, Chapel Hill, and surrounding Orange County support visitors through this organization, which maintains a visitors bureau on the western edge of downtown Chapel Hill; they'll help you with Hillsborough as well.

GETTING THERE *By car:* Two of the East's long-distance interstates make a fork on the western edge of this area, just outside Durham. I-85, which has come up from Atlanta and Charlotte, forks northward to merge with I-95 south of Richmond, Virginia, which links with all the major cities of the Atlantic seaboard. I-95 itself has dropped eastward of this area, to meander through Tobacco Country (see "The Coastal Plains"). From the west, I-40 has come through Memphis, Nashville, Knoxville, Asheville, Winston-Salem, and Greensboro—an almost straight east–west line. Here, however, it starts curving southeast, passes around the southern edge of Raleigh, and then heads south to Wilmington (see "Albemarle Sound").

Within the urban area, I-440 makes a full circle around Raleigh's central city, and I-540 makes a half circle through its northern suburbs (giving access to its airport, which lies midway between Raleigh and Durham). Durham's downtown (along with Duke University) is reached via I-85 from points west and north, or via the NC 147 expressway from points east and south (including Raleigh). Chapel Hill lies 10 miles southwest of Durham via US 15, although you need to take a side road (NC 86 or NC 54) to reach town center.

By air: **Raleigh-Durham International Airport (RDU)** (rdu.com). This important regional airport is located almost exactly between Raleigh and Durham, just off the I-540 beltway, one exit east of I-40's exit 283. It has two long, skinny terminals, each facing the central parking garage, each with its own runway behind; despite this split there's enough traffic to support a range of dining and shopping services in each. Nine airlines serve this airport, with flights to 38 cities in all regions of the United States plus Canada, Mexico, and Great Britain.

By train: Raleigh is a major passenger rail hub, with three trains making daily stops (in each direction) at its modest c. 1950 station on the southwestern edge of downtown. The *Silver Star* runs along the coast to link with New York, Washington, and the Florida cities. The *Carolinian* stops at Raleigh on its run between New York and Charlotte. The *Piedmont* shuffles between Charlotte and Raleigh. All three trains stop at Cary, while the Carolinian and the Piedmont stop at Durham as well.

By bus: **Greyhound** (greyhound.com) stops in Raleigh and Durham. In Raleigh it maintains a fairly large terminal downtown at 314 West Jones Street, about four blocks northwest of the Capitol Building, with many daily departures.

Each of the four major cities—Raleigh, Durham, Chapel Hill, and Cary—maintains its own bus system. The **Triangle Transit Authority** (triangletransit.org) maintains a system of routes that link these four systems together. Triangle Transit offers a series of passes good on the entire regional system.

MEDICAL EMERGENCIES **Wake Medical Center, Raleigh** (919-350-8000; wakemed.org), 3000 New Bern Ave., Raleigh 27610. This 870-bed facility, run by its own not-for-profit organization, is the largest in the area and handles by far the most emergencies, having a Level 1 trauma center. It's located on the far east end of Raleigh, a block west (toward town) of I-440's exit 13.

Rex Healthcare, Raleigh (919-784-3100; rexhealth.com), 4420 Lake Boone Trail, Raleigh 27607. This 665-bed hospital sits on the western edge of Raleigh, on the opposite side from Wake Medical, off I-440's exit 5 then west (away from town) three blocks. It's run by UNC Health Care, a not-for-profit established by the state of North Carolina for the University of North Carolina's large medical school at nearby Chapel Hill.

Duke University Hospital, Durham (919-684-8111; dukehealth.org), 2301 Erwin Rd., Durham 27710. This 788-bed facility is run by Duke University (which has a very large medical school), and is located at the northern end of its campus, on the western edge of the city of Durham. It has a Level 1 trauma center. To find it, take NC 147 (the Durham Freeway) to its Fulton Street exit, and go south one block.

University of North Carolina Hospitals (unchealthcare.org), 101 Manning Dr., Chapel Hill 27514. Run by the University of North Carolina's medical school and owned by the state of North Carolina, this 719-bed facility, with a Level 1 trauma center, is located at the southern end of the Chapel Hill campus. To find it, leave I-40 at exit 270 and go south on US 15/501 (Fordham Boulevard) for 5 miles to a right turn onto Manning Drive, then continue for a mile.

✷ Exploring the Area

Centered on a densely populated and rapidly growing urban conglomerate, this area isn't the best for exploring by car. To make up for it, however, it has a spectacular system of greenways, connecting virtually all major sites and districts and extending deep into the most scenic parts of the countryside. So get yourself a bike (see *To Do* for rentals) and enjoy!

EXPLORING ON FOOT **The Mountains-to-Sea Trail** (919-698-9024; ncmst .org), A 100-mile segment of the Mountains-to-Sea Trail through this area nears completion at press time. By 2012 it should form a continuous half loop around the north of Durham following the **Eno River**, then turn to follow the **Neuse River** southward around the entire Raleigh urban area, ending (for the time being) at the town of Clayton in Johnson County. Uncompleted sections are 100 percent funded and all rights-of-way and permissions obtained, and at this writing the construction of the remaining gaps is under way.

Excellent day hikes and overnight trips have been available for a while, on two long sections following the west bank of Falls Lake, separated by the lack of a single bridge, now under construction. Its extension southward along the Neuse is already partially completed as the Neuse River Greenway, whose southernmost sections are scheduled for completion by 2012. Looking westward, the superb, but disconnected, system of walking paths in Eno River State Park and West Bend on the Eno should be linked by the time you have this book in your hands. This leaves only the 10-mile gap between the two sections, following the lower Eno to the swampy head of Falls Lake; this section is fully permissioned, and will hopefully be open by 2012. These Eno River sections depend on volunteer teams from the Friends of the Mountains-to-Sea Trail for their construction; if you feel you can do something to help speed its completion, you might drop them a line.

EXPLORING BY BICYCLE **Raleigh's Greenways** (tinyurl.com/20zu84 links to the city of Raleigh website). Most American cities now have a few disconnected miles of greenway (paths, separated from roadways, built for both walkers and bicyclers), along with an ambitious but wholly unfunded plan to connect them someday in the indefinite future. Raleigh is different. Raleigh actually has 63 miles of high-quality greenways, with long sections of continuous path between major landmarks, and many more miles under construction. The glory of the urban system is a 20-mile path that runs through the center of **Umstead State Park**, then heads through the art gardens of the **North Carolina Museum of Art**, passes through the campus of North Carolina State University, goes past **Pullen Park**, then follows Walnut Creek along the south edge of town to end at **Walnut Creek Amphitheater**. A side greenway links it with **downtown**. Long-range plans, unfunded at press time, call for it to be linked with the **Neuse River Greenway**, less than 3 miles away. To cycle the whole 20 miles, start at Umstead State Park's Old Reedy Creek Trailhead (see its website for directions) and follow Old Reedy Creek Trail to its end at Reedy Creek Greenway at the park edge; this goes for 5.0 miles, then becomes Gorman Street Connector for 0.4 mile, which becomes Rocky Creek Branch Trail for 4.5 miles, which becomes Lower Walnut Creek Trail to its current end in 4.2 miles. It's a really good idea to have a copy of the city's greenway map (on its website), plus a good street map, when you try this.

The Neuse River Trail (tinyurl.com/yln7kfw links to city of Raleigh website). Part of the city of Raleigh's greenway system, this paved hike-bike trail will follow the banks of the Neuse River along the eastern edge of the urban area for 30 miles, from **Falls Lake** in the north to the town of Clayton in the south. It will feature near-constant access and views of the river, which it will cross several times. The northern half should be completed by the time you get this book, with the southern half scheduled to be finished by mid-2012.

The American Tobacco Trail (triangletrails.org/ATT.HTM—capitalization required). No, it's not a memorial to the tobacco industry. The American Tobacco Trail is a 22-mile rail-to-trail project that follows the old spur line to the giant **American Tobacco Factory** on the south edge of downtown Durham. The trail is gloriously rural as it passes quietly through urban and suburban areas to reach countryside and a southern terminus near **Jordan Lake**. A little more than 6 miles south of its Durham terminus is a large gap, awaiting the completion of a graceful new pedestrian bridge over I-40, as early as 2011. For an even longer biking experience, you can tack on the city of Durham's 6-mile North–South Greenway, through downtown to the northern edge of town, by simply ducking under the NC 147 overpass on half a block of surface street.

✷ Towns

Raleigh (godowntownraleigh.com). In 1789 an exhausted state legislature, unable to come to an agreement on where to put the new state's capital, decided on an empty hilltop above the River Neuse. To this end they purchased 1,000 acres from planter Joel Lane, whose **house** survives as a museum and garden, and laid out a grid centered on a square, upon which they built the capitol itself. The capitol, rebuilt in 1840, still occupies that square; the government-dominated **Capitol District** stretches northward from there on the old grid streets, and Raleigh's modern downtown stretches southward.

And what a downtown it is. Since the financial collapse of 2008, Raleigh has emerged as one of the fastest-growing cities in America, a testament to the strength of an economy based on government and research. Plentiful money has made this a city of museums and galleries, restaurants and nightspots, parks and greenways. Keeping cool under a thick canopy of trees that extend even into downtown's core, Raleigh is a pleasant and entertaining place to visit.

There is free street parking near the capitol, limited to two hours, but it can be very hard to find a space during the week. There are two parking garages immediately south of the capitol, a third just to the east of the History Museum, and several others within a block or two; rates vary but $2 an hour is typical, and all are free on weekends.

Durham has traditionally been the factory-based, working-class city of the Triangle. It dates from an 1840s railroad depot, Durham Station, named after the local doctor who furnished the land for it. After the Civil War, local tobacco farmer Washington Duke set up a small factory for processing brightleaf tobacco, first in his barn, and later by the depot; by 1890 Duke and his sons had built this into an international tobacco monopoly, American Tobacco Company, headquartered in a massive brick complex by the station, now a center for entertainment, restaurants, and the arts. Other factories quickly followed, and Durham's population exploded. A large African American community supplied workers for these factories, centered on the Hayti historic district to the south of downtown, and as this community joined in the prosperity Durham emerged as America's leading center of African-American-owned financial institutions. Meanwhile, the incredibly rich Dukes decided to add a bit of tone to their hometown by founding Duke University, now a world-class innovator in science and medical research. This burst of prosperity was not to last. In 1911 the American Tobacco monopoly was broken up into several pieces, only two of which, American Tobacco and Liggett & Myers, remained in Durham. Textile plants started to close in the 1930s, American Tobacco disbanded in the 1980s, and Liggett moved out of town in 2000.

Modern Durham has shed its factory dependence to prosper in the glow of the Triangle's massive research industry. Its fine old brick factories have been redeveloped—not just American Tobacco, but also Brightleaf District, Golden Belt, and West Village (in the Liggett & Myers factory complex). Duke University, perhaps the handsomest campus in the South, anchors its western edge, and a belt of historic and natural sites rings it to the north. It has about half a million residents.

Downtown on-street parking is free, but time-limited. City-owned garages typically cost 75 cents an hour.

Chapel Hill evolved around the University of North Carolina's original campus, 25 miles west of Raleigh. You'll find it a charming, very walkable town of about 50,000 residents, with a low-slung five-block downtown, dominated by traditional southern red brick, that stretches westward from the campus's northwestern edge. Apart from the campus itself, Chapel Hill offers a stunning choice of places to eat, and a good variety of lodging as well. Despite its huge student population you'll find it a quiet and well-mannered town—unless the UNC Tar Heels have beaten one of their cross-town rivals, the Duke Blue Devils or the North Carolina State University Wolfpack, in which case expect an enormous, screaming street party. Downtown street parking is free.

Hillsborough. Located 13 miles west of Durham, this tiny town (fewer than 6,000 residents) almost became one of North Carolina's great cities. Already an established village in the 1780s, Hillsborough repeatedly missed being declared the state capital by one or two votes, with a plurality of legislators favoring it because it had a great inn. It lost, however, to an empty field 35 miles to the southwest (the future Raleigh), and sank into quiet oblivion. Today it has a superb collection of colonial and antebellum houses, with several good restaurants.

Cary. Once a railroad siding town 9 miles west of Raleigh, since 1970 Cary has exploded into a small city with well over 120,000 inhabitants. Due to the magic of annexation, modern Cary now stretches from I-40 in the north to well below US 1 in the south, a wide swath of suburbia. Indeed, it has overtaken Chapel Hill in size, and some assume it's the third point in the Triangle Cities. It is wealthy, low-crime, and almost formless, with its old town center (at NC 54 and Academy Street) now little more than one of its smaller and less fashionable commercial strips. Like neighboring Raleigh, Cary has extensive greenways and at least one exceptional park, **Hemlock Bluffs**.

✷ Green Spaces

PARKS AND GARDENS **William B. Umstead State Park, Raleigh** (ncparks.gov/Visit/parks/wium/main.php). Developed by the CCC during the Depression, this 5,600-acre park occupies a series of wooded hills directly between Raleigh and Durham. It was originally developed around two unconnected lake-side recreation areas—one for whites on the northeast, and one for blacks on the southwest—and it retains this structure, with its two old centers (both feature CCC architecture) separated by forest-covered hills laced with walking, horseback, and bicycling paths. One of these, **Reedy Creek Trail**, links the greenway systems of Cary and Raleigh and forms part of a 20-mile continuous off-road walk-bike path through the heart of Raleigh. Also of note is Airport Overlook, easily reached from the northeastern section, with wide hilltop views over the adjacent **Raleigh-Durham Airport**.

Pullen Park, Raleigh. In 1887 Richard Stanhope Pullen donated, designed, and ran this 72-acre park, sandwiched between downtown Raleigh and North Carolina State University, binding it up with covenants that would strip the city of this valuable tract if they dared to use it for anything other than recreation. The result is a delight, a classic Victorian park centered on a small lake, whose handsome landscaping sets off its various attractions. First among these is its 1900 carousel, its hand-carved animals gorgeously restored to their original colors. You'll also find a 1950 miniature railroad that toots through the park, paddleboats, a theater, and an arts complex, as well as the other things you associate with a really good city park: picnicking, tennis, swimming, and baseball. A statue of North Carolina–born Andy Griffith memorializes the TV show *Andy of Mayberry*, contributed in 2003 by cable channel TV Land (much to the horror of Mount Airy, where Griffith was raised).

Sarah P. Duke Gardens, Durham (919-684-3698; hr.duke.edu/dukegardens), 426 Anderson St., Durham 27705. Open daily 8–dusk. Admission is free. This 55-acre landscaped garden occupies a steep defile on the eastern edge of the main Duke University campus. It's large and intricate, with 5 miles of paths looping through its three main sections. The steep southern end of the ravine is taken up by terrace gardens, with the Bloomquist Garden of Native Plants taking up the opposite side, and the Culberson Asiatic Arboretum to the north. It's a wonderful place to explore, particularly in April and May when the azaleas are at their peak. To find it, take US 70 (West Main Street) west from downtown to a right turn onto

SARAH P. DUKE GARDENS AT DUKE UNIVERSITY, DURHAM

Campus Drive, then go 1.2 miles to a right turn onto Anderson Street; the Duke Gardens parking lot is a block farther on your left.

Eno River State Park, Durham (ncparks.gov/Visit/parks/enri/main.php). Just shy of 4,000 acres, the Eno River State Park protects 13 continuous miles of this Piedmont stream as it curves around the northern edge of the Durham urban area. Once heavily exploited for waterpower, the Eno's rugged stone bluffs have discouraged 20th-century loggers and developers, allowing a varied and beautiful forest to grow up around the ruins of old mills. A series of loop trails from various trailheads allow for easy foot exploration, and the stream itself is floatable by kayak. By the time you have this book in your hand, the **Mountains-to-Sea Trail** should run along all 13 miles, linking the various loops into a variety of possible explorations.

Occoneechee Mountain State Natural Area, Hillsborough (ncparks.gov/Visit/parks/ocmo/main.php). This small (190-acre) state park on the southern edge of Hillsborough, just off I-85's exit 164, preserves a 900-foot-tall monadnock, a granitic dome intruding upward through the deep soil beneath your feet. Despite its tiny size it has 3 miles of trails, up to the top, around to the Eno River on its northern flank, and past a small abandoned granite quarry. Unlike more famous monadnocks elsewhere, Occoneechee Mountain is completely covered in hardwood forests, and its only wide view is from a railed overlook at the top of the tiny quarry; this makes the trails to its northern flank, rather than to its tree-covered top, the better choice for a short visit. Several rare species live on this tiny mountain, including the brown elfin butterfly—marooned here when the retreating glaciers of the last ice age warmed the climate.

Hemlock Bluffs Nature Preserve, Cary (919-387-5980; tinyurl.com/hemlockbl opens the town of Cary website), 2616 Kildaire Farm Rd., Cary 27512. The preserve is open daily 9–sunset. The nature center is open daily 10–5 (Sun. 1–5), with lengthened evening hours in summer. Admission is free. Situated within Cary, this 80-acre town park preserves a mature forest rich in hemlocks, along the steep bluffs and rich bottomland of little Swift Creek. The 3 miles of trail include wood steps, boardwalks, and viewing platforms to protect the forest. At the top is the Stevens Nature Center, with exhibits on the park's unique habitat, a wildflower garden, and a gift shop.

RIVERS Cape Fear River. One of the great rivers of North Carolina, the 202-mile long Cape Fear starts at the confluence of the Haw and Deep Rivers, 4 miles south of Jordan Lake and 29 miles south of Raleigh. Only the uppermost 7 miles are in this chapter's area, all of it wide Class I water. Although it's seldom paddled, you can put in at the base of Jordan Dam, canoe the lowermost 4 miles of the Haw River, then continue on the 7 miles of the Cape Fear to small Buckhorn Dam, a good take-out point at the end of Buckhorn Road (SSR 1921), reached from NC 42 30 miles south of Raleigh. You'll find this section to be wooded, with a fair amount of industry. The best paddling is downstream from here as the river flows into, and through, the **coastal plains**.

Neuse River. At 275 miles the Neuse is the longest river wholly within North Carolina—and a pleasant, leisurely float along its entire length. Technically the Neuse starts at the uppermost end of **Falls Lake**, at the confluence of the Eno and Flat Rivers. For practical paddling, however, it starts at the Falls Lake Dam, where the city of Raleigh has created the first of five canoe-launch sites. From here the Neuse loops gently through the western edge of the Raleigh area, lined by trees and with few hints of the urban areas nearby, a very scenic 35 miles. Nor do you need a boat to explore this river; by the end of 2012 the **Neuse River Greenway** should be completed along this entire section. The water is Class I, and surprisingly narrow for such a major stream. It continues to be a fine canoe river, narrow and wooded, as it flows through the **coastal plains** to New Bern.

Eno River (enoriver.org). The 38-mile Eno River cuts through the edge of the Piedmont in a long series of bluffs and rapids. Heavily forested, all but the uppermost 12 miles are under public protection, most notably **Eno River State Park** and **West Point on the Eno**, a Durham city park. It is a very narrow river—hardly more than a stream—and requires high water to fill its Class I to III rapids before it can be paddled. It can be hiked at any time, however: The entire 26-mile public length should be lined by the Mountains-to-Sea Trail by 2012.

LAKES B. Everett Jordan Lake (Cape Fear River) (ncparks.gov/Visit/parks/jord/main.php; saw.usace.army.mil/JORDAN; epec.saw.usace.army.mil/jord.htm). $–$$ for access to state recreation areas. The Corps of Engineers built this 14,000-acre lake between 1967 and 1982 (slowed by multiple lawsuits) for the purpose of flood control on the Cape Fear River, downstream. Its earthen dam, 113 feet high and 1,330 feet long, has a small visitors center and a fishing platform at its base. Virtually the entire lakeshore is wooded and in public ownership, most of it split between Jordan Lake State Recreation Area, which has nine developed sites, and Jordan Lake State Game Lands, which maintains the bulk of the wild lakefront for hunting and fishing. The state recreation area (which charges an entrance fee) has boat ramps (two of them open 24 hours), camping (hookups as well as primitive), swimming, picnicking, and a good selection of walking paths. The game lands are completely undeveloped, and furnish a home for a large bald eagle population. There are 10 boat ramps on the lake, most of them large and well developed, and boat rentals at private **Crosswinds Marina**.

Falls Lake (Neuse River) (ncparks.gov/Visit/parks/fala/main.php; saw.usace.army.mil/falls). $–$$ for access to state recreation areas. Flooding the uppermost 28 miles of the Neuse River, Falls Dam is an earthen structure 1,915 feet long and 92 feet high, created by the Corp of Engineers in 1981 for flood control and water supply. It has a visitors center, a road across its top that's open to the public, and fishing access to its race. The reservoir it creates forms a great arc between Raleigh and Durham, just outside the urban area, with 12,500 acres of water. The 175 miles of shore are owned by the state of North Carolina, split between the seven developed recreation sites of Falls Lake State Recreation Area and the wild lands of the Butner-Falls of Neuse Game Lands. The Mountains-to-Sea Trail follows its western bank closely, linking the Neuse River with the Eno River for 100 miles of continuous hiking.

Shearon Harris Reservoir (Harris Lake) (wakegov.com/parks/harrislake). Progress Energy (then known as Carolina Power & Light) created this 4,100-acre lake 20 miles south of Raleigh to furnish cooling water for a nuclear power plant on its northern shore. Apart from the large area taken up by the nuclear power plant, the lakeshore is wild and heavily forested. A 680-acre peninsula between two arms contains a county park with picnicking, a fishing pier, a stocked fishing pond, hiking trails, disk golf, and a canoe launch. The remainder of the lake is owned by Progress Energy but under state management as the Harris Game Lands, with two large, well-developed boat ramps.

John H. Kerr Reservoir (Roanoke River) (saw.usace.army.mil/jhkerr; ncparks.gov/Visit/parks/kela/main.php; dcr.virginia.gov/state_parks/sta.shtml; dcr.virginia.gov/state_parks/occ.shtml). $–$$ admission to state parks in both states. The Corp of Engineers created this 50,000-acre lake, straddling the state line with Virginia, in 1952, for flood control and hydropower. It's impounded by a concrete dam over the Roanoke River in Virginia, almost 150 feet high and 0.5 mile long, and crossed by VA 4 for some good views. Congress named both the dam and the lake after a North Carolina congressman while the project was still under construction; the state of Virginia has never recovered from this insult to its honor, and still insists on calling it by its original name, Buggs Island Lake. The lake has 800 miles of wooded shore, the large majority of it in public ownership. About 25 percent of the lake is within North Carolina, consisting of a single long arm extending southward, 12 miles long and somewhere over a mile wide at its top. On this section are eight recreation areas, all with boat ramps and picnic areas, several with campgrounds, and two with marinas; these are organized as Kerr Lake State Recreation Area, which charges an entrance fee for each area. In between these recreation areas are state game lands, with four 24-hour-access boat ramps. On the Virginia side there are major recreation developments at two state parks, Occoneechee and Staunton River (both of which have cabins and allow pets), and a number of smaller recreation areas and boat ramps. The pretty little town of Clarksville, Virginia, sits on the lakeshore, its handsome old red-brick downtown straddling US 58.

✷ To See

THE CAPITOL DISTRICT, DOWNTOWN RALEIGH The State Capitol (919-733-4994; nchistoricsites.org/capitol; state.capitol@ncdcr.gov), 1 E. Edenton St., Raleigh 27601. Open daily; Mon.–Sat. 9–5, Sun. 1–5. Guided tours are Sat. at 11 and 2, and Sun. at 2. Admission is free. Located in a square at the center of downtown Raleigh, North Carolina's capitol building dates from 1840. It's a handsome Greek Revival structure with a columned front and wings spreading out from a domed rotunda, clad in granitic gneiss mined locally. Inside, the original plan design remains, carefully patterned on classical themes. Touring is easy because the courts moved out in 1888, and the legislature left to its new digs in the marble-clad **State Legislative Building** in 1963. The capitol remains the seat of government, however, as the governor, the lieutenant governor, and their staff have their offices on the first floor. The rest of the building is a historic site, and open to self-guided tours. Of particular note is the careful reconstruction of the famous Italian sculptor Antonio Canova's marble statue of George Washington, prepared for the original capitol building and destroyed when it burned down in 1832. On the second floor, the House and Senate chambers have been restored to their 19th-century glory, one modeled after a Grecian amphitheater and the other a Grecian temple. The third floor offers the official state library, restored to its 1859 appearance, and a fascinating look at the state geologist's office of the same period.

VIETNAM WAR MEMORIAL, IN FRONT OF THE STATE CAPITOL, RALEIGH

North Carolina State Museum of History (ncmuseumofhistory.org), 5 E. Edenton St., Raleigh 27601. Open daily; Mon.–Sat. 9–5, Sun. 1–5. Admission is free. This attractive modern building, clad in polished granite, sits across the street from the capitol and across a small pedestrian mall from the Museum of Natural Science. Established in 1902, the museum preserves more than 150,000 artifacts from six centuries of history, and features two floors of permanent and temporary exhibits. Permanent exhibits include an entertaining collection of unusual objects called Museum Sleuths, a 1920s drugstore, a section devoted to the state's military history, a NASCAR exhibit, and the North Carolina Sports Hall of Fame. Recent temporary exhibits have included Core Sound fishing boats, New Deal photographs, the 100th anniversary of the Boy Scouts, and the 50th anniversary of Barbie.

North Carolina Museum of Natural Science (919-733-7450; naturalsciences .org), 5 E. Edenton St., Raleigh 27601. Open daily; Mon.–Sat. 9–5, Sun. noon–5. Admission is free; special exhibits, $$. The largest natural science museum in the South, the state's official museum is housed in a large modern building, clad in granite and with classical details that blend with the adjacent government buildings—but with an impressive domed glass turret jutting from a corner. Here a pedestrian in the little mall in front of it, linking it with the capitol and the Museum of History, can catch glimpses of its biggest exhibit, the dramatic Terror of the South dinosaurs. As its name indicates, this museum is dedicated to the zoology, geology, and paleontology of the state, with 1.8 million specimens in its collection. Exhibits are large and impressive, a successful cross between the fun of a hands-on museum for kids and the high seriousness of the Smithsonian. Permanent displays include Coastal North Carolina (two stories, to house the giant whale specimens), Mountains-to-Sea (also two stories, including a re-created waterfall), Underground North Carolina, and more. It has a large and well-stocked museum store on the first floor, and a café on the fourth.

IN RALEIGH'S CAPITOL DISTRICT

A major expansion, known as the Nature Research Center, is under construction at press time and scheduled to open during 2011. It will be a long, glass-clad building, devoted to exhibits on how science works.

State Legislative Building (919-839-6262; ncga.state.nc.us), 16 W. Jones St., Raleigh 27607. Open daily; Mon.–Fri. 8–5, Sat. 9–5, Sun. 1–5. Admission is free. Completed in 1962, this handsome marble-clad building, set in pleasant plazas with fountains and oaks, houses both chambers of North Carolina's legislature. The interior is open to the public with both self-guided and guided tours, even when the legislature is in session. You can also observe a legislative session from the galleries, and even take pictures. The third floor contains displays and opens onto rooftop gardens. The cafeteria in the basement is open for lunch, weekdays. It's located one block north of the capitol, opposite the Museums of History and of Natural Science.

Haywood Hall Museum House and Garden (919-832-8357; haywoodhall .org; manager@haywoodhall.org), 211 New Bern Place, Raleigh 27601. Open

Thu. 10–1:30, Mar.–Dec. Admission is free. Located one block east of the capitol, this is the home of one of the first state legislators in Raleigh, a wealthy plantation owner who set out to duplicate both the architecture and the lifestyle of his family seat. In 1977 the Colonial Dames of America obtained it from the original family and restored it to its early republic grandeur, including a garden restored to its original condition.

CULTURAL SITES **North Carolina Museum of Art, Raleigh** (ncartmuseum.org), 2110 Blue Ridge Rd., Raleigh 27601. Founded in 1947 as the first state-funded art museum in America, NCMA occupies a 160-acre campus about 4 miles east of downtown. In 2010 the museum added a spectacular 127,000-square-foot structure, lit by skylights and clad in aluminum, to greatly expand the permanent collection on display. Its old building, a 180,000-square-foot 1983 brick-clad block whose recessed second-story windows give it a bunker-like appearance, now houses temporary exhibits, educational programs, and public events. Of special note is NCMA's museum garden, said to be the largest in the nation, whose 2 miles of trails, including a **greenway**, are lined with outdoor art; this now extends right up to the walls of the new building, where a special garden area features large works and reflecting pools.

The Contemporary Art Museum, Raleigh (cam.ncsu.edu), 409 W. Martin St., Raleigh 27603. Admission is free. CAM's new museum on the western edge of downtown is under construction at press time, and slated to be opened during 2011. Affiliated with North Carolina State University's Department of Design, CAM promises us innovated exhibits on the ways that contemporary art and design interact with all aspects of ordinary life.

Artspace, Raleigh (919-821-2787; artspacenc.org), 201 E. Davie St., Raleigh 27601. Open Tue.–Sat. 10–6. Admission is free. Located in downtown's **City Market**, the restored 1914 farmer's market two blocks south of the capitol via Blount Street, this art museum seeks to involve the visitor by combining exhibitions with open studios for the artists being exhibited.

Nasher Museum of Art at Duke University, Durham (919-684-5135; nasher.duke.edu), 2001 Campus Dr., Durham 27705. Open Tue.–Sun.; Tue., Wed., Fri., Sat. 10–5; Thu. 10–9; Sun. noon–5. Last admission is 20 minutes before closing. $$; admission is free on Thu., 5–8:40. Parking, adjacent to the museum, is $2 an hour. Located on the campus of Duke University, the Nasher occupies a purpose-built 60,000-square-foot facility designed in the traditional mode (for contemporary art galleries) of a blankly anonymous block. Oddly enough, this strongly modernist facility, now wholly dedicated to contemporary art, started as the permanent house of the 13,000-piece Brummer Collection of Medieval and Renaissance Art, a few pieces of which are on display. Its **café**, which does not require an admission ticket, is reasonably priced ($$) and a good place for lunch as you explore the Duke campus.

North Carolina Central University Art Museum, Durham (web.nccu.edu/artmuseum), 1801 Fayetteville St., Durham 27707. Open Tue.–Fri. 9–5, Sun. 2–5. Admission is free. Located a mile south of downtown via Fayetteville Road on the campus of historically black NCCU, this museum features extensive collections and exhibits of African American art from the 19th and 20th centuries, as well as art from the African continent.

Ackland Art Museum, Chapel Hill (919-966-5736; ackland.org), 101 S. Columbia St., Chapel Hill 27599. Open daily except Tue.; Mon., Wed., Sat. 10–5; Thu. 10–8; Sun. 1–5. Admission is free. Part of the University of North Carolina at Chapel Hill and located on its campus, the Ackland features a 15,000-work collection that's particularly strong in Asian art and art on paper (including photographs), as well as European masterworks, contemporary art, African art, and North Carolina pottery.

Morehead Planetarium, Chapel Hill (919-962-1236; moreheadplanetarium.org; mhplanet@unc.edu), University of North Carolina, 250 E. Franklin St., Chapel Hill 27599. Open summers, Tue.–Thu. 10–3:30, Fri.–Sat. 10–3:30 and 6:30–9, Sun. 1–4:30. Weekend hours only during the academic year. Consult the website for current schedule. $$; the NASA Digital Theater is free. This lovely Georgian red-brick structure, built in 1949, fronts on downtown's Franklin Street just two blocks from town center. The first planetarium in the South and the first on a university campus, the Morehead features a variety of shows each weekend, and on weekdays (except Monday) during the summer. Look for "Carolina Skies," based on tonight's sky and guided live by a staff member; one version or another has been presented for 60 years. In addition there are free multimedia shows in their Science 360 program, shown in the NASA Digital Theater, and a child-oriented interactive science exhibition (also free).

HISTORIC SITES **Joel Lane Museum House, Raleigh** (919-833-3431; joellane.org), 160 S. Saint Marys St., Raleigh 27605. Tours on the hour; Mon.–Fri. 10–1, Sat. 1–3. $$. Located in downtown's southwest corner, this museum presents the 1770 plantation home of one of Raleigh's principal founders. Accurate in every detail, the handsome house, modest by today's standards, would have been considered stately by the frontier standards of its day. It is surrounded by lovely formal gardens, duplicating what a wealthy grandee of the era might have planted; Lane himself more likely had a clean-swept chicken yard that separated his house from his 30 slaves' work and living quarters, with a detached kitchen representing this on the present site.

Mordecai Historic Park, Raleigh (919-857-4364; tinyurl.com/6xtafa links to city of Raleigh website), 1 Mimosa St., Raleigh 27604. Open for tours on the hour, Tue.–Sat. 10–3, Sun. 1–3. $$. This small city of Raleigh historic park, located just north of downtown via Pearson Street (becoming Mordacai Drive), consists of a square city block containing a number of early-19th-century buildings moved in from other sites. The highlight is a 1785 plantation house, expanded into a mansion in 1826 by wealthy planter Moses Mordecai, original to the spot (which was out in the country back then). It was grandiose by the standards of its day and place, but surprisingly modest to modern visitors expecting something from *Gone with the Wind.* Also on the site is the original birth home of President Andrew Johnson, the Ellen Mordecai Garden, a law office, a kitchen, and a church.

✐ **Historic Oak View County Park, Raleigh** (919-250-1013; wakegov.com/parks/oakview; oakview@wakegov.com), 4028 Carya Dr., Raleigh 27610. Open Mon.–Sat. 8:30–5, Sun. 1–5. The grounds are open daily, 8–one hour before sunset. Admission is free. Located on Raleigh's eastern edge, this 27-acre park preserves a prosperous farm with its outbuildings (except for slave quarters) intact, for a rare look at an operating farm from antebellum times to the 1950s. It preserves five buildings: a handsome 1855 plantation house, the 1822 detached kitchen, the 1900 carriage house, the 1900 livestock barn, and an early-20th-century cotton gin (a substantial mini factory). The recently built Farm History Center tells the story of this site, and includes the interactive Farmer's Corner for little kids. The site includes ponds, an herb garden, and a 1911 pecan grove.

Yates Mill County Park, Raleigh (919-856-6675; wakegov.com/parks/yatesmill), 4620 Lake Wheeler Rd., Raleigh 27603. Open daily, 8 AM–sunset. Admission to the park is free; mill tours: $$. This 174-acre county park on Raleigh's southwestern edge features a classic overshot gristmill, fully restored and operating, on a large millpond. The massive structure you see is older than it looks; it was probably built after a flood in the 1840s wiped out its predecessor. Closed in the 1950s, it has been fully restored, and operates the third weekend of every month, when there are half-hour and hour mill tours. There are environmental exhibits at the handsome Park Center, with boardwalks and views over the pond, and 3 miles of hiking trails.

Wake Forest College Birthplace Museum, north of Raleigh (919-556-2911; wakeforestbirthplace.org; birthplace@wfu.edu), 414 N. Main St., Wake Forest 27587. Open Tue.–Fri. 10:30–noon and 1:30–4:30, Sun. 3–5. Admission is free. It is one of the oddities of North Carolina history that Wake Forest University is not located in Wake Forest. This, however, was not always the case. Wake Forest University was founded in 1833 when the North Carolina Baptist Convention purchased the plantation known as Forest of Wake from Dr. Calvin Jones, to be converted into a school to educate ministers and laymen. By 1934 Wake Forest College had 41 faculty members, with both a law school and a medical school. Then in 1941 the Baptist Convention decided to move the medical school to its large teaching hospital in Winston-Salem, and the die was cast. In 1956, lured by great pots of R. J. Reynolds tobacco money, Wake Forest College moved to its current campus in Winston-Salem, leaving its home of 123 years for good; it is now the home of the Southeast Baptist Theological Seminary. The Birthplace Museum occupies the original plantation home of Dr. Price, and tells the full story. It's off US Bus 1, three blocks north of the old campus, which is worth a stroll while you're there.

North Carolina Railroad Museum, south of Raleigh (919-362-5416; nhvry.org; info@nhvry.org), 5121 Daisey St., New Hill 27562. Open weekends. Admission is free; train excursions, $$; operate a locomotive, $$$$$. Owned and operated by a local railroad club, this open-air museum features original rail equipment and a large, outdoor model railroad. On the first Sunday of each month the club offers a 5.5-mile rail excursion up and back along the historic line. Serious rail fans will note that you can, by reservation, operate either a steam or diesel locomotive for an hour. You'll find it 24 miles south of Raleigh at the old Bonsal rail yard; take US 1 south to Apex, then from downtown Apex take Salem Street (SSR 1011) south for 8.5 miles.

Duke University Chapel, Durham (919-681-1704), 401 Chapel Dr., Durham 27708. Open during the academic year 8 AM–10 PM, and during the summer 8–8; closes at 5 on holidays. Admission is free. A masterpiece of Gothic Revival architecture, Duke Chapel is a cathedral-sized structure clad in local bluestone, and much influenced by the soaring Late Gothic style known as Perpendicular, found only in England. Designed by the great African American architect Julian Abele in

1931, it glories in its soaring airiness as the great stone pillars vault lightly overhead. There's a 50-bell carillon concert weekdays at 5 PM, and an organ concert weekdays 12:30–1:30. Set in the beautifully landscaped heart of Duke University, it is the centerpiece and main destination for a campus stroll. Please remember that this is a church with services and prayer at all times. Because of weddings, weekend visits are chancy. Park at Bryan Center, either at the visitors lot or in Garage IV. To find it, take US 70 (West Main Street) west from downtown to a right turn onto Campus Drive, which you take to its end in 1.6 miles.

INTERIOR OF DUKE UNIVERSITY CHAPEL

Duke Homestead State Historic Site, Durham (919-477-5498; nchistoricsites.org/duke; duke@ncdcr.gov), 2828 Duke Homestead Rd., Durham 27705. Open Tue.–Sat. 9–5. Admission is free. This 43-acre site on the north side of Durham, just off I-85's exit 175, preserves the farm of Washington Duke, patriarch of the most important and influential family in the state's history. It was here, after the Civil War, that Duke both cultivated brightleaf tobacco and manufactured it, in farm outbuildings, into smoking tobacco suitable for hand-rolled cigarettes. In 1866 Duke produced 15,000 pounds of smoking tobacco; by 1873 he had a good-sized factory on his property and his three sons had built another in Durham, together producing 125,000 pounds. From then on Washington became the point man for the family, going on the road to sell the product that his sons made. Everyone got very rich indeed; in 1892 Washington founded Duke University. By 1902 the Dukes had established themselves as the rulers of an international tobacco cartel, the American Tobacco Company.

Today's Duke Homestead preserves Washington's surprisingly modest vernacular farmhouse and several outbuildings, including his third and largest factory, along with a visitors center with interpretive exhibits.

Historic Stagville State Historic Site, Durham (919-620-0120; stagville.org; info@stagville.org), 5828 Old Oxford Hwy., Durham 27712. Open Tue.–Sat. 10–4. Admission is free. One of the largest plantations of the antebellum Piedmont, Stagville at its peak comprised 30,000 acres and 900 slaves. Today's historic site is remarkable in preserving not only the plantation house but also its slave quarters. Located in farmland 11 miles north of Durham, the site consists of 73 acres in two

SLAVE QUARTERS AT HISTORIC STAGVILLE, DURHAM

tracts. The main tract contains the plantation house, a surprisingly plain white clapboard building from 1789, whose wealth shows in its exquisite (and carefully restored) furnishings. Nearby is Horton Grove, a set of two-story, four-room slave apartments from the 1850s; family records show that these were built to provide healthier living conditions for the slaves, in order to protect the owner's sizable investment. Next door is the colonial-era Horton Home, built by a poor white farmer, then sold to Stagville in 1823, when it became slave quarters. Also of note is the large barn, built in 1860 as a sign of optimism about the future—misplaced as it turned out. The owners of Stagville went from being the wealthiest family in North Carolina to just another bunch of farmers, as their poor tobacco-growing neighbors the Dukes (who opposed slavery) went on to found monopolies and endow universities.

Bennett Place State Historic Site, Durham (nchistoricsites.org/bennett).

SEAGROVE POTTER SID LUCK DEMONSTATES THROWING A POT AT DUKE HOMESTEAD STATE HISTORIC SITE.

BRIGHTLEAF TOBACCO

Washington Duke was an early cultivator of *brightleaf tobacco*, a mild and aromatic tobacco that forms the main ingredient of cigarettes and is the mainstay of North Carolina tobacco farming. Brightleaf was not a cultivar or variety. Rather, it was (and is) a method of agriculture, a way of cultivating ordinary dark tobacco to make it consistently light golden in color, thin and fine in texture, and mild yet flavorful. Brightleaf was always grown on poor, worn-out soils (plentiful in post-cotton North Carolina), from which it derived its thinness and fine texture. Despite the poorness of the soil, the ground had to be carefully prepared, and the growing tobacco required a number of labor-intensive steps before harvest. The harvested leaves would be hung in a special curing barn, where a hot fire finished the conversion to brightleaf, giving the tobacco its characteristic light golden color. During the last 50 years these curing barns were replaced with more modern methods, and can be seen, abandoned, dotting fields throughout the state.

The coming of brightleaf cultivation around 1860 could not have been more fortuitous. Soils in the Piedmont and the coastal plains had been completely worn out by cotton agriculture, dependent on slavery. However, large plantations such as nearby Stagville did not rely merely on cotton sales for wealth. With the end of slave imports in 1808, American plantations were the only source of supply and the price of a healthy young worker rose above $1,000, comparable to a thoroughbred horse. The dirty little secret of large plantations such as Stagville was that they had become primarily human stud farms. This ended with the Civil War, and brightleaf tobacco thrived on the lands destroyed by plantation slavery.

Nor was it a complete coincidence that Durham became the center for brightleaf cultivation and cigarette manufacturing. It was here, at the Bennett Place, that General Tecumseh Sherman formally accepted the surrender of the Confederate army and demobbed his 60,000 Yankee troops. Sherman's Union soldiers had spent their downtime sampling the local brightleaf products, and liked it. Washington Duke noted the northerners' strong preference for mild tobacco, and reckoned there might be a good market for it.

At the end of the Civil War, General Tecumseh Sherman was continuing his March through Georgia by turning northward into the Carolinas. On March 25, 1865, he met a large Confederate army under General Joseph Johnson at Bentonville Battlefield (see "The Coastal Plains") and defeated it. Two weeks later, in a wholly separate action, Union troops defeated the other large Confederate army under General Robert E. Lee at Appomattox Court House, Virginia, forcing Lee's surrender. Johnson's force, larger than Lee's, was the last hope of the Confederacy, and three days after the Appomattox surrender the president of the Confederacy, Jefferson Davis, traveled to Greensboro to confer with General Johnson on their next move. They could find no reasonable strategy, and decided to surrender.

On April 17 (three days after Lincoln's assassination), Johnson and Sherman met at a modest farmhouse 6 miles west of Durham Station (as Durham was then known) to negotiate, using the generous terms granted at Appomattox as a guide. The formal surrender occurred the next day. The Civil War was over.

The spot on which the Civil War ended is now part of Durham's western suburbs just off US 70 at I-85's exit 172. It is commemorated with a carefully reconstructed replica of the Bennitt (the correct spelling) farmhouse framed by split-rail fences, an incongruously elegant classical marble monument, and a visitors center with interpretive exhibits.

West Point on the Eno, Durham (919-471-1623), 5101 N. Roxboro Rd. (US 501), Durham 27704. Grounds open daily 8–dusk; buildings open weekends 1–5, Apr.–Dec. Admission is free. This 404-acre city park preserves 2 miles of the Eno River, here filled with rapids and lined with rock bluffs. On its banks sits the impressive West Point Mill, an accurate reproduction (on the original foundations) of the mill that operated at this site from 1778 to 1942. It's fully operational and grinds corn every weekend. Adjacent to it is the McCown-Mangum House, an 1848 vernacular farmhouse furnished as it would have been in the late 19th century. The Tobacco Packhouse, original to this site, now displays the early-20th-century photography of Hugh Mangum, who used it as a darkroom.

University of North Carolina at Chapel Hill (919-962-1630; unc.edu/visitors), 250 E. Franklin St., Chapel Hill 27599. The campus is always open; the visitors center is open weekdays, 9–5, during which student-led tours are available by appointment. Founded in 1789 and opening six years later, UNC–Chapel Hill is the oldest state-chartered university in America. Its original campus is extraordinarily beautiful and historic, and welcomes visitors. Now occupying over 700 acres, the original core takes up a five-by-three-block area immediately east and south of downtown's center at Franklin Street (NC 54) and Columbia Street (NC 86). This core centers on a north–south quadrangle park, named McCorkle Place, on which the old campus faces. As you enter this, the **Morehead Planetarium** will be on your right, and inside it is the visitors center; here you can get complete information on a walking tour. Exiting

THE OLD WELL AT THE UNIVERSITY OF NORTH CAROLINA–CHAPEL HILL

it onto McCorkle Place you'll come to two memorials, ***The Unsung Founders*** (2003) commemorating the African Americans, slave and free, who built the campus, and ***Silent Sam*** (1913), a memorial to the 321 university alumni killed in the Civil War. Just ahead is the **Old Well** (1897) with its justly famous classical temple structure, the symbol for the university. Across to the left is the university's first building, **Old East** (1792), still in use as a residence hall. Immediately across the street, the historic core continues with several more historic structures grouped around a second quadrangle, Polk Place, with the university's 1931 **Memorial Bell Tower**, whose 14-bell carillon summons students to class, behind and to the south. A block east of Old East lies the 1903 **Coker Arboretum**, a beautiful spot whose specimens demonstrate the evolutionary link between North Carolina and East Asia.

Historic Hillsborough (919-732-7741; historichillsborough.org; alliance@historichillsborough.org), Alexander Dickson House Visitors Center, 150 E. King St., Hillsborough 27278. Open Mon.–Sat. 10–4, Sun. noon–4. Admission is free. The Piedmont's finest historic town has a center filled with colonial and early republic structures, beautifully preserved, with several open to the public with no admission fee. The core of the old town consists of a three-block stretch of US Bus 70 (Churton Street), extending one block on either side; covering the best parts of the district requires only an eight-block stroll totaling 1.2 miles (1.8 miles including the return walk to your car). Start at the visitors center in the restored **Colonial Alexander Dickson House** at the southeastern edge of the district (the corner of King and Cameron Streets), where you can get a brochure, view the house, and enjoy the adjacent **Helen's Garden,** a 19th-century herb garden. A block west along King Street brings you to the 1844 **Old Orange County Courthouse**, with a courtroom still in use and the 1769 Town Clock. You pass a number of handsome privately owned period structures as you continue across Churton Street for a block, then turn for a block to double back on Tryon Street. Here you find the 1816 **Presbyterian church**, beautiful and rewarding in its own right, on the site where the state legislature met before Raleigh became the capital. Beside it is the **Orange County Historical Museum** (free, open afternoons Tue.–Sun.) in the handsome 1935 old town library, with interesting exhibits and a craft shop. The next open building is the **Old Burwell School**, a block north on Churton Street (free, open afternoons Wed.–Sun.), a fully restored antebellum house with 2 acres of gardens. Finally, the 1820s **Town Hall**, two blocks north at the corner of Churton and Orange Streets (free, open weekday business hours), is notable for its interior woodworking and its well-preserved outbuildings.

Ayr Mount, Hillsborough (919-732-6886; ayrmount.com; ayrmount@classicalamericanhomes.org), 376 St. Mary's Rd., Hillsborough 27278. Grounds open daily, 9–sunset (approximately). House open Wed. 11, Thu.–Sat. 11 and 2, Sun. 2. House: $$$; admission to the grounds is free. This elegant 1815 brick plantation home, 0.8 mile east of town center, is as close to grand as you're going to get in the North Carolina Piedmont. Its exterior, although austere, hints at restrained wealth, probably due to the extensive elegant gardens that surround it. Its true glories are inside—a stunning collection of period antiques and art pieces that reflect the lifestyle of a wealthy planter. The home of its original family until 1984, the outbuildings and slave quarters of its antebellum days have long since been stripped away, replaced by 265 acres of gardens and strolling lands.

Historic Occoneechee Speedway, Hillsborough (presnc.org/Travel/Ayr-Mount-Hillsborough). Open daily during daylight. Admission is free. This 44-acre tract on the Eno River preserves the only surviving track from NASCAR's first season. This dirt oval was long famous for its treacherous mud and a long slide off a curve that could (and did) land unwary drivers in the river. The last race, won by Richard Petty, was held in 1968. The track has since grown up in trees, but many traces remain and can be explored from the trail maintained by the preservation society that owns it (as part of adjacent Mount Ayr). It's south of town, off Elizabeth Brady Drive, reached via US Bus 70.

✷ To Do

BICYCLE RENTALS **The Bicycle Chain** (thebicyclechain.com/articles/rentals-and-demos-pg170.htm; sales@thecleanmachine.com). Open Mon.–Sat. 10–7, Sun. noon–5. As its name implies, this is a chain of five bicycle shops spread throughout the area. Each one has a different selection of rentals, and each is happy to help you find your way on the local greenways. The locations are:

Raleigh: 9000 Glenwood Ave., 919-782-1000. (This is right outside Umstead State Park, with its many bicycle paths.)

Durham: 639 Broad St., 919-286-2453.

Chapel Hill: 210 W. Franklin St., 919-929-0213.

Cary: 1791 W. Williams St., 919-362-4900.

Carrboro: 104 W. Main St., 919-967-5104. (Carrboro is a mile west of Chapel Hill.)

CANOES AND KAYAKS **Paddle Creek, Raleigh** (888-794-4459; 919-866-1954; paddlecreeknc.com; info@paddlecreeknc.com), 9745 Fonville Rd., Wake Forest 27587. Despite its mailing address, Paddle Creek is located on Falls of Neuse Road in far northeastern Raleigh, on the Neuse River at the base of Falls Dam, the river's head of navigation. It's a retailer as well as a rental store, with more than 75 rental kayaks and canoes available. You can take your rental where you want, or paddle down the Neuse with them arranging a pickup (1½- and 5-hour trips). There are specialty trips as well.

Frog Hollow Outdoors, Durham (919-949-4315; froghollowoutdoors.com; info@froghollowoutdoors.com), 805 Iredell St., Durham 27705. This outfitter rents canoes and kayaks, with or without shuttle service, and offers a wide variety of paddle trips on regional rivers.

HORSES **Dead Broke Farm** (919-596-8975; deadbrokehorsefarm.com; ride@deadbrokehorsefarm.com), 6921 Wildlife Trail, Raleigh 27613. Set on their own 91 wooded acres halfway between Durham and Raleigh, Dead Broke offers one- and two-hour trail rides on the 10 miles of trail on their own property, as well as boarding facilities for those who travel with their own horses.

LAKE BOATING **Crosswinds Marina** (919-362-5391; crosswindsmarina.com), 565 Farrington Rd., Apex 27523. Located on US 64 as it reaches the east shore of Jordan Lake, this marina rents 16-foot aluminum fishing boats and 25-foot pontoon boats.

Clarksville Marina (434-374-8501; clarksvillevamarina.com), 411 4th St., Clarksville 23927. Located in Clarksville, Virginia, 53 miles north of Durham via US 15, this marina rents pontoon boats for use on Kerr Lake.

✱ Lodging

RESORTS AND HOTELS

Washington Duke Inn and Golf Club, Durham (800-443-3853; 919-490-0999; washingtondukeinn.com), 3001 Cameron Blvd., Durham 27705. $$$–$$$$. Built in 1988 in the style of an English country inn, this 271-room hotel sits on the Duke University campus, adjacent to the university's 1957 Trent Jones golf course, the site of numerous championships. Rooms are comfortable and elegantly furnished, and include WiFi, laundry and valet service, and room service. Family suites have a king bed with bunk beds separated by a hallway, and cost little or no extra.

Duke Hotel Towers, Durham (866-385-3869; 919-687-4444; duketower.com), 807 W. Trinity Ave., Durham 27701. $–$$. Located on the northwest corner of downtown, this condominium hotel combines a modest appearance and low prices with luxury amenities. It occupies the grounds of an 1892 cotton mill, of which only its four-story brick tower survives. The hotel itself was built as an apartment complex in the 1970s using bricks from the mill, unfortunately using the flat, long, mansard roof design popular at the time. Converted into a hotel, each unit is a nicely furnished full two-room apartment with living area, kitchen, and separate bedroom—very large compared with standard hotel rooms. The courtyard, built from old brick and with a pool, is particularly nice. WiFi is available in all rooms, and a basic continental breakfast is available for a small fee. Premium rooms are the same size, but have more amenities and allow pets. A free 24-hour shuttle is available to Duke University and local hospitals and restaurants, and bicycles can be rented. Very low rates are available for long-term rentals, people on hospital business for any amount of time, and Duke families on student interviews.

The Carolina Inn, Chapel Hill (800-962-8519; carolinainn.com), 211 Pittsboro St., Chapel Hill 27516. $$$$. This 180-room hotel, styled after Mount Vernon, has graced downtown Chapel Hill since 1924; it's owned by the University of North Carolina, and profits support the campus library. The foyer is large and impressive, and the furnishings throughout are elegant, old-fashioned, and homey. It offers room service, valet service, and valet parking, as well as multiple in-room phone lines and free WiFi; some rooms are small. Its highly rated restaurant, **Crossroads**, features seasonal dishes made from fresh local ingredients; it's a great place for a superb, if expensive, breakfast.

The Franklin Hotel, Chapel Hill (866-831-5999; 919-442-9000; franklinhotelnc.com; reservations@franklinhotelnc.com), 311 W. Franklin St., Chapel Hill 27516. $$$–$$$$. This elegant small luxury hotel, newly built in a classical late-19th-century style, sits at the center of downtown Chapel Hill. It is particularly noted for its modern interior design and 67 comfortable guest rooms, with personalized telephone numbers, WiFi, valet service, and room service. The handsome lobby bar has good, moderately priced bar meals and a good wine list; on the second floor, **Windows Restaurant** offers fine, but very expensive, breakfasts 7–11 AM daily. Parking is on-site, in an underground garage.

The Fearrington House Country Inn, Pittsboro (919-542-2121; fearrington.com/house; fhouse@fearrington.com), 2000 Fearrington Village Center, Pittsboro 27312. $$$$–$$$$$. Located halfway between Chapel Hill and Pittsboro off US 15/501, this Relais

& Châteaux property, rated 5 Diamonds by AAA, has 35 individually decorated rooms in its farmhouse-style lodge. All rooms are spacious, and are reached through private garden entrances; the more expensive rooms have separate seating areas and additional amenities. WiFi is available. Tariff includes full breakfast, afternoon tea, and evening port and chocolate. The inn's restaurant, also 5 Diamond, is consistently rated one of the best in the nation.

BED & BREAKFASTS **Oakwood Inn Bed and Breakfast, Raleigh** (800-267-9712; 919-832-9712; oakwoodinnbb.com; Innkeepers@OakwoodInnBB.com), 411 N. Bloodworth St., Raleigh 27604. $$$. This classic bed & breakfast occupies an elegant 1871 Victorian home with wide porches in the Oakwood Historic District, just four blocks from the capitol. Its six rooms are elegantly furnished in antiques and come with phones, dial-up plugs, and WiFi, making it ideal for visitors with downtown business. A full breakfast is included.

Cameron Park Inn Bed and Breakfast (888-257-2171; 919-835-2171; cameronparkinn.com; innkeeper@cameronparkinn.com), 211 Groveland Ave., Raleigh 27605. $$$–$$$$. This large 1912 house in Raleigh's Cameron Park historic district, 1.6 miles west of downtown via NC 54, features a wide front porch and a shady oak lawn. Located in a residential neighborhood, it has the feel of a traditional B&B, with handsomely decorated common rooms that you'd find in comfortable large house, and five guest rooms ranging in size from normal bedrooms to suites with separate sitting rooms. WiFi is available, and a full breakfast is included in the tariff.

Arrowhead Inn Bed and Breakfast, Durham (800-528-2207; 919-477-8430; arrowheadinn.com; info@arrowheadinn.com), 106 Mason Rd., Durham 27712. $$$–$$$$. This inn, a beautiful, sprawling frame plantation house from 1775, occupies 6 acres of land adjacent to US 501, 9 miles north of Durham. Rooms are elegantly furnished with gas or log fireplace, and even the least expensive have room for a sitting area; the largest (and most expensive) are full-sized cabins (without kitchens) in the garden, one a log cabin and the other a converted carriage house. All rooms have WiFi. The tariff includes a full breakfast, afternoon refreshments, and a beverage center.

Morehead Manor Bed and Breakfast, Durham (888-437-6333; 919-687-4366; moreheadmanor.com; info@moreheadmanor.com), 914 Vickers Ave., Durham 27701. $$$–$$$$. The four-room B&B occupies an 8,000-square-foot Colonial Revival mansion built for the CEO of Liggett and Myers, just outside downtown and two blocks from the American Tobacco retail complex. The craftsmanship and elegance of such a house hardly needs description. The rooms are all spacious, with sitting areas; WiFi is available. A full breakfast is included in the tariff.

Chapel Hill Bed and Breakfast (919-967-3745; chapelhillbandb.com), 4421 Manns Chapel Rd., Chapel Hill 27516. $$–$$$. Located in rural countryside 6 miles south of Chapel Hill, this modern brick home with full-length first- and second-floor porches sits on 6 landscaped acres in front of a pond. The four rooms are very large and nicely furnished; three are suites with separate sitting areas, porch access, and marble-clad whirlpool baths. WiFi is available, and a full breakfast is included in the tariff.

✷ Where to Eat

DINING OUT Bu-ku Global Street Food, Raleigh (919-834-6963; bukuraleigh.com), 110 E. Davie St., Raleigh 27601. Open Mon.–Fri. for lunch and dinner, and Sat. for dinner only. $$$–$$$$. This downtown restaurant, located three blocks south of the capitol via Fayetteville Street, offers a vast and changing choice of small plates based on street food from around the world. It's the successor to long-popular Fins, at the same location and with the same chef.

Poole's Diner, Raleigh (919-832-4477; poolesdowntowndiner.com), 426 S. McDowell St., Raleigh 27601. Open for dinner Wed.–Sat., and for Sun. brunch. $$$$$. The successor to old-time downtown favorite Poole's Pie Shop, this modern restaurant with a full bar features a changing menu of locally focused offerings, while preserving some of the feel of its predecessor. An ever-changing (and strictly à la carte) menu of about five entrées features new takes on traditional diner items. On the minus side, expect long waits and noise on Friday and Saturday. Reservations are not taken, and children are not welcome.

Magnolia Grille, Durham (919-286-3609; magnoliagrill.net), 1002 9th St., Durham 27705. Open for dinner Tue.–Sat. $$$$$. Part of Durham's emerging 9th Street shopping district, this small and unassuming restaurant has garnered repeated national citations for its rather daring New South cuisine, featuring fresh ingredients, from local farms wherever possible. Chef-owners Ben and Karen Barker collaborate on the inventive offerings, Ben doing the entrées and Karen the desserts. Its wine list is excellent, with a small number of choices under $30, but craft brew lovers be warned: Their website boasts of their poor beer selection.

Elaine's on Franklin, Chapel Hill (919-960-2770; elainesonfranklin.com; info@elainesonfranklin.com), 454 W. Franklin St., Chapel Hill 27516. Dinner; closed Mon. $$$$$. This elegant little restaurant on the western end of downtown Chapel Hill features the inventive cuisine of owner-chef Bret Jennings, once named Best Chef in the Southeast by the James Beard Foundation. The food mixes farm-fresh local ingredients with an eclectic blend of approaches from the Deep South, Europe, and the Mediterranean. The wine list has received the *Wine Spectator* Award of Excellence from 2001 to 2008; nevertheless, there are good selections of both reds and whites at $25 a bottle and under.

La Residence Restaurant and Bar, Chapel Hill (919-967-2506; laresidencedining.com; laresidence@gmail.com), 202 W. Rosemary St., Chapel Hill 27516. Open Tue.–Sun. for dinner. $$$$. This elegant little restaurant occupies a saltbox house at the center of downtown Chapel Hill; it's been owned by the same family since 1976. Seating is scattered about the rooms of the old house, on the enclosed front porch, and in the covered (and, in winter, enclosed) patio. The varied menu offers a wide variety of North Carolina meat, seafood, and offal combined with local farm vegetables, typically with straightforward presentations. In addition to their full menu, offered well past midnight, they have a Cafe Menu, simpler and lower priced, 6–9 PM. The wine list is good, with nearly every bottle priced between $25 and $40.

Panciuto, Hillsboro (919-732-6261; panciuto.com), 110 S. Churton St., Hillsborough 27278. Open for dinner Wed.–Sat. $$$$. This attractive restaurant in Hillsborough's historic district features imaginative and elegant Italian fare made almost exclusively from locally farmed vegetables and meats; chef-owner Aaron Vandemark calls it "recognizably Italian with a measure of southern inflection." Menus change quickly, but are always short—a few first courses, a few entrées, and a couple of desserts—as the chef concentrates on what he can get from local farms that week.

The Fearrington House Restaurant, Pittsboro (919-542-2121; fearrington.com/house/restaurant.asp; fhouse@fearrington.com), 2000 Fearrington Village Center, Pittsboro 27312. Open for dinner Tue.–Sun. $$$$$. Consistently ranking as one of the finest restaurants in America, this Relais & Châteaux property, with 5 Diamonds from AAA, is part of the Fearrington House Country Inn, halfway between Chapel Hill and Pittsboro off US 15/501. You'll find it in the former homestead of the Fearrington complex, with elegant small dining rooms. The food is described as contemporary American cuisine, and relies on local products from the rich agricultural lands of the Piedmont. Dinner is served in either three or four courses, with a flat rate for choosing what you will for each course. Wine pairings are available, adjusted to the guests' tastes, and add $35 to $45 to the tariff. (The cost rating, above, includes this pairing.)

EATING OUT The City Market, Raleigh (citymarketraleigh.com), 214 E. Martin St., Raleigh 27601. $–$$$$. This handsome red-brick farmer's market, built in 1914 just three blocks south of the Capitol on Blount Street, has been beautifully restored. While its owners call it a shopping plaza, the majority of its tenants are small restaurateurs catering to the downtown crowd. You'll have a choice of all three meals, and Greek, Italian, German, Caribbean, southern, and Cajun cuisine. Daytime visitors to the downtown capitol district should particularly note **Big Ed's City Market Restaurant**, open for breakfast and lunch ($$), and featuring authentic country food made from scratch.

Boylan Bridge Brewpub, Raleigh (919-803-8927; boylanbridge.com; info@boylanbridge.com), 201 S. Boylan Ave., Raleigh 27603. Daily, lunch and dinner. $$. This pub on the southwest edge of downtown has an extensive beer list, with pub food to complement it. Its attractive modernist building has a large glass front to let in plenty of light, a large deck outside, and fine woodworking inside thanks to its owner, an architectural cabinetmaker. The short menu emphasizes pub grub and comfort food, with a good southern selection. The historic Joel Lane House is a block west.

Toast at Five Points, Durham (919-683-2183; toast-fivepoints.com), 345 W. Main St., Durham 27701. Open for lunch and dinner on weekdays, and lunch on Sat. $$. With prices comparable to a Subway, this brick storefront in downtown Durham (near both the Carolina Theater and American Tobacco) specializes in sandwiches and soups the way they are made in Italy, a "paninoteca." They use local produce and cheeses, breads from a small nearby bakery, and meats that they cure themselves; items they cannot find locally are imported from Italy. There are daily specials, and Italian wine and North Carolina craft beers are available. *Five Points* refers to the five-way intersection of Main Street (US 70), Chapel Hill Street, and Morris Street, another of the nice small café and shopping blocks that seem to be springing up in Durham.

Top of the Hill Restaurant and Brewery, Chapel Hill (919-929-8676;

topofthehillrestaurant.com), 100 E. Franklin St., 3rd Floor, Chapel Hill 27514. Open daily for lunch and dinner. $$–$$$$. Top of the Hill is not so much a brewpub as it is a casual dining spot and meeting place that brews its own (excellent) beer. It's open, attractive upstairs space flows into balconies that overlook the center of downtown Chapel Hill. Its dinner menu features distinctive takes (sometimes adventurous) on American fare, including pub menu favorites; the lunch menu is a shorter version with lower prices. It has a good wine list, with many choices below $30.

Carolina Brewery, Chapel Hill (919-942-1800; carolinabrewery.com), 460 W. Franklin St., Chapel Hill 27516. Open daily for lunch and dinner. $$. This downtown Chapel Hill microbrew produces some of the state's most popular craft ales. It's pleasant and pubby, with an interesting menu that combines bar favorites with more exciting dishes based on contemporary American cuisine. Their main brewery is now in the handsome little county seat of Pittsboro, 17 miles south via US 15 and very convenient for Lake Jordan; it has a small café that serves a limited menu.

Crooks Corner Café and Bar, Chapel Hill (919-929-7643; crookscorner.com), 610 W. Franklin St., Chapel Hill 27516. Open Tue.–Sun. for dinner, and Sun. for brunch. $$$. Founded and still run by cookbook author Bill Neal, Crooks has been anchoring the far western end of downtown Chapel Hill for over a quarter century. It occupies a modest 1960s-style structure with casual decor and a nice patio. It's well known for its take on southern food, with dishes both traditional and adventuresome; a signature meal is shrimp and grits.

Mama Dip's Traditional Country Cooking, Chapel Hill (919-942-5837; mamadips.com; info@mamadips.com), 408 W. Rosemary St., Chapel Hill 27514. Open daily for breakfast, lunch, and dinner. $$. This downtown Chapel Hill fixture has been serving traditional African-southern food since 1976. It is owned by its founder, noted cookbook writer Mildred Edna Cotton Council, known as Mama Dip. The large menu, based on the food found in the rural districts around Chapel Hill, is heavy on favorites featuring chicken and pork, but has less common fare as well, such as chitlins and fried green tomatoes.

Tupelo's, Hillsboro (919-643-7722; tupelos.com), 101 N. Churton St., Hillsborough 27278. Open Mon.–Sat. for lunch and dinner. $$–$$$$. Located in an old brick storefront in Hillsborough's historic district, Tupelo's features Gulf Coast specialties with a Louisiana emphasis. The dinner menu has all the dishes you'd expect, plus a few surprises; lunch offers a large choice of sandwiches, soups, and salads with a New Orleans slant, plus a few favorites from the dinner entrée menu. They have a good selection of microbrews on tap, and the wine list has many choices under $25 a bottle.

✷ Entertainment

CLASSICAL There are amazing numbers of venues and performing companies in an urban area with three major universities and lots of tobacco money. Here is just a sampling.

Progress Energy Center for the Performing Arts, Raleigh (919-831-6060; progressenergycenter.com; info@progressenergycenter.com), 2 E. South St., Raleigh 27601. Located on the southern edge of downtown facing US 70 East, the Progress Energy Center is the premier theater venue for the Raleigh area. Its original core was built in 1932 as an elegant Greek Revival structure intentionally echoing the capitol just four blocks north, and named Raleigh Memorial Auditorium to commemorate those who fell during World War I. The current structure is boldly postmodernist in all respects, flanking the distinguished central building with long low glass facades reminiscent of an airport terminal, and selling its name to the highest corporate bidder. It is the home of the major musical and theatrical companies for the area, including the Raleigh Symphony (the area's only fully professional symphony), the Opera Company of North Carolina, the Carolina Ballet, the North Carolina Theatre (an Actors' Equity company unaffiliated with the Durham theater building), and the Raleigh Dance Theater.

The Carolina Theatre. This gorgeous 1926 Beaux-Arts structure, built as the city auditorium in 1926, shows live performances and movies in the center of downtown. It's the home of the Full Frame Documentary Film Festival each April, one of the nation's premier documentary film festivals.

Playmakers Repertory Company, Chapel Hill (919-962-7529; playmakersrep.org; prcboxoffice@unc.edu), Center for Dramatic Art, Chapel Hill 27599. Founded in 1918, this company performs classic and contemporary works from its home at the Center for Dramatic Art on the campus of the University of North Carolina–Chapel Hill (on Country Club Road, east of Raleigh Street). Productions involve their full-time professional staff mentoring graduate students in the university's Dramatic Art MFA program.

POPULAR ***Raleigh Downtowner*** (raleighdowntowner.com). This free monthly newspaper is a great guide to what's going on in downtown Raleigh, and especially for its active music and bar scene. Its website is updated weekly.

The Walnut Creek Amphitheater (Time Warner Cable Amphitheater at Walnut Creek) (livenation.com/venue/time-warner-cable-music-pavilion-at-walnut-creek-tickets). Built by the city of Raleigh in 1991, this large open theater sits in park-like grounds on the southeast edge of the city, south from I-40's exit 300 off Rock Quarry Road (follow the signs). There's about 3,400 covered seats, another 3,400 open-air seats, and room for 13,000 more on the open lawn.

✷ Selective Shopping

Fearrington Village (919-542-2121; fearrington.com/village; fhouse@fearrington.com), 2000 Fearrington Village Center, Pittsboro 27312. Located halfway between Chapel Hill and Pittsboro off US 15/501, this elegant little destination centers on the world-class Fearrington House Inn. Here you'll find a number of offbeat shops set in a brilliant garden, with a couple of lunch places whose food is prepared by the AAA 5 Diamond Fearrington House Restaurant.

DURHAM'S SHOPPING VENUES
Surprisingly, working-class Durham is emerging as the best place in the area to stroll and shop. Although Raleigh and Chapel Hill both have pleasant and worthwhile downtowns, Durham has something they lack: fine old factory buildings of great charm, built in the 19th century of red brick, cast iron, and giant timbers. At this writing these still class as emerging shopping districts, particularly as the financial collapse of 2008 continues to bounce along the bottom at press time. However, they are all quite close together on the southern and western edges of

downtown, they all have good parking, and they all have enough independent shops, cafés, or entertainment to be interesting.

Brightleaf Square (historicbrightleaf.com), 905 W. Main St., Durham 27701. On US 70 West as it leaves downtown, this 1900 American Tobacco Company warehouse was Durham's first retail conversion, and remains the best, with a good selection of shops and restaurants.

West Village (westvillagedurham.com), 604 W. Morgan St., Durham 27701. Located in the handsome brick Liggett & Myers factory a block northeast of Brightleaf Square, this new development (opening in 2008) is finding some interesting tenants for its 50,000 square feet of retail and restaurant space.

American Tobacco (americantobaccohistoricdistrict.com), 210 W. Pettigrew St., Durham 27701. The late 19th century's largest tobacco company in the world, on the south edge of downtown, houses this complex. Shopping is poor, but entertainment is great with restaurants, a large outdoor amphitheater, a brand-new performing arts hall, and the Durham Bulls superb minor-league baseball.

Golden Belt (goldenbeltarts.com), 807 E. Main St., Durham 27701. In 1901 Bull Durham built this factory on downtown's southeast corner to make those little cloth pouches for their chewing tobacco. It now houses artists' studios, retail space, and restaurants.

✷ Special Events

Second weekend in July: **Duke Homestead Home, Garden, and Craft Festival, Durham**. The Duke Homestead State Historic Site sponsors this annual festival with craft demonstrations, costumed docents, 19th-century games for children, herb vendors, and craft vendors.

Third weekend in July: **Virginia Lake Festival** (clarksvilleva.com). This Clarksville, Virginia, street festival celebrates the state-line-straddling Kerr Lake (which Virginians call Buggs Island Lake, as Kerr was a North Carolinian) with hot-air balloons, antique cars, a shoreline boat gathering and fireworks show, 200-plus vendors, a juried arts show, and of course lots of food and live music. Clarksville is 53 miles north of Durham via US 15.

THE MILL BELT

In 1856 a brand-new North Carolina Railroad Company (NCRR) started service between the deepwater coastal port of Morehead City and the city of Charlotte. Its route made (and still makes) a giant arc through the Piedmont, a crescent along which North Carolina's industrial cities align. After the Civil War, North Carolina's economy increasingly turned to industry, and mills grouped wherever the NCRR passed over a stream suitable for a water mill. (Of course they could've used steam engines instead of waterpower, but why pay for something that's free?) Textile mills migrated from the North to take advantage of cheap labor; furniture mills emerged where Appalachian hardwood timber met the railheads; tobacco mills sprang up to take advantage of the new cigarette technology invented in Durham. Many of the early Tarheel entrepreneurs remain household names to this day: Broyhill, Hanes, Cannon, Reynolds, Duke—even Stanback.

The easternmost cities of the NCRR have been described in the "Raleigh-Durham Area" chapter. As the rail line heads west from Durham it passes the cities of the Mill Belt: Burlington, Greensboro, High Point, Salisbury, and Charlotte (discussed in the next chapter). These cities, along with Winston-Salem and Hickory (on westward spurs), owe their existence to the NCRR, and they share the same story—that of railhead manufacturing along the Mill Belt.

The very words *mill town* seem uninviting, but do not be deceived. These are not dirty little towns with ramshackle mill housing covered in coal dust. These cities are large and vital, brought alive by the sort of money that comes from having scores of America's most important and wealthiest companies founded in their back yard. With the philanthropy of old money flowing through, it could just as easily be called Museum Row.

GUIDANCE **Greensboro Area Convention & Visitors Bureau** (800-344-2282; 336-274-2282; greensboronc.org), 2200 Pinecroft Rd., Suite 200, Greensboro 27407. This organization maintains a visitors center three blocks south of the intersection of US 70 and the US 421 expressway; go south one block on US 29, then left for two blocks on Pinecroft Road. Their website is extensive and very helpful.

Winston-Salem Visitors Center (866-728-4200; 336-728-4200; visitwinstonsalem.com; nfo@visitwinstonsalem.com), 200 Brookstown Ave., Winston-Salem 27101. Open daily 8:30–5. This visitors center is located a block south of downtown

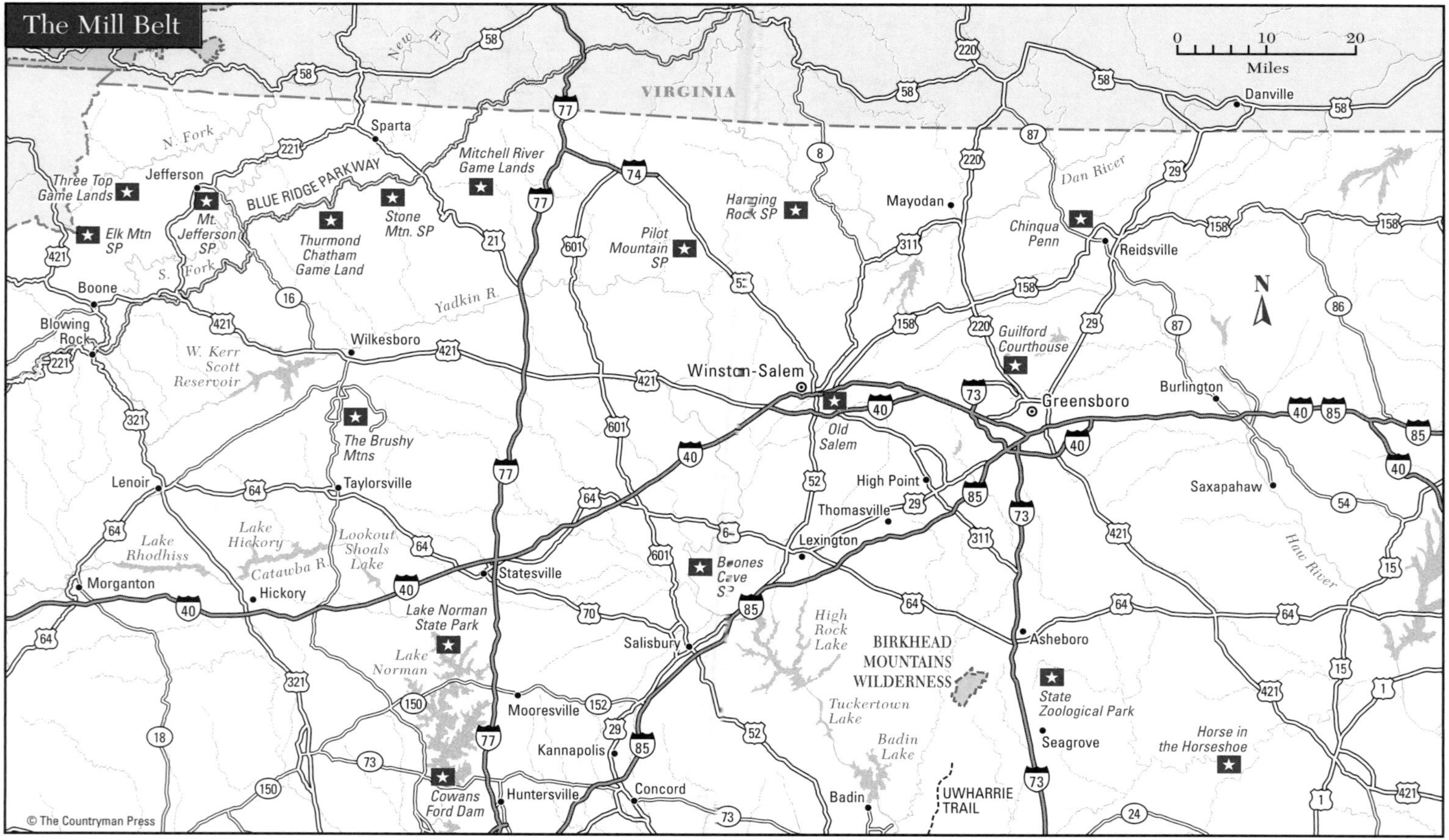
The Mill Belt
0
10
20
Miles
N
VIRGINIA
Danville
Sparta
N. Fork
Jefferson
Three Top Game Lands
Elk Mtn SP
Mt. Jefferson SP
BLUE RIDGE PARKWAY
Thurmond Chatham Game Land
Stone Mtn. SP
Mitchell River Game Lands
S. Fork
Boone
Blowing Rock
W. Kerr Scott Reservoir
Wilkesboro
Yadkin R.
Pilot Mountain SP
Hanging Rock SP
Mayodan
Chinqua Penn
Dan River
Reidsville
Guilford Courthouse
Burlington
Winston-Salem
Greensboro
Old Salem
High Point
Thomasville
Lexington
Saxapahaw
Haw River
The Brushy Mtns
Taylorsville
Lenoir
Lake Hickory
Lookout Shoals Lake
Lake Rhodhiss
Catawba R.
Morganton
Hickory
Statesville
Lake Norman State Park
Lake Norman
Salisbury
High Rock Lake
BIRKHEAD MOUNTAINS WILDERNESS
Asheboro
State Zoological Park
Seagrove
Horse in the Horseshoe
Tuckertown Lake
Badin Lake
Badin
UWHARRIE TRAIL
Mooresville
Kannapolis
Concord
Huntersville
Cowans Ford Dam
© The Countryman Press

Winston-Salem on Cherry Street, just off the US 421 expressway (Bus I-40); Old Salem is two blocks farther south. Their website is very good.

High Point Convention and Visitors Bureau (800-720-5255; highpoint.org; info@highpoint.org), 300 S. Main St., High Point 27260. Their visitors center is located at the center of downtown High Point, on NC 311. Their website is very thorough.

Hickory Metro Convention & Visitors Bureau (800-509-2444; 828-322-1335; fax: 828-322-8983; hickorymetro.com; info@hickorymetro.com), 1960-A 13th Ave. Dr. SE, Hickory 28602. Headquartered in Hickory's convention center, this agency's website gives a thorough-going guide to the Hickory area.

NCFurnitureStores.com. This advertising-supported website helps connect shoppers with stores and outlets. If you are confused by this region's massive furniture scene, it might help clear away the clutter.

GETTING THERE *By car:* I-85 follows the corridor of the North Carolina Railroad as it marches from Atlanta to Richmond. America's great east–west interstate, I-40, passes through Burlington, Greensboro, Winston-Salem, and Hickory before continuing on to Asheville and points west.

If you take I-40 through Winston-Salem, you will note that it loops several miles to the south of its city center. US 421 supplies an expressway link through downtown, coming within three blocks of Old Salem.

By air: **Piedmont Triad International Airport, Greensboro (GSO)** (336-665-5600; flyfrompti.com), 6415 Bryan Blvd., Greensboro 27409. Established in 1919 and one of the South's oldest airports, this large Greensboro facility emplanes over a million passengers a year, making it the third largest in North Carolina. It's also a major FedEx hub, and the corporate headquarters for Honda Jet. It is served by seven carriers with flights to 19 eastern cities, and has all the services you would expect in a large airport. You'll find it on the northwestern side of the city, 3.5 miles north of I-40's exit 210 via US 68 North.

By train: Three **Amtrak** (800-872-7245; amtrak.com) passenger trains make daily runs through this district: the Piedmont, the Carolinian, and the Crescent. All three stop at Greensboro, High Point, and Salisbury, and the first two stop at Burlington as well. The Piedmont is a business shuttle between Raleigh and Charlotte. The Carolinian and the Crescent connect with New York and Washington; the Carolinian terminates in Charlotte, while the Crescent goes on to Atlanta and New Orleans.

So what this means is: three trains daily (each direction) along the crescent of the Mill Belt between Raleigh and Charlotte, with two of these trains continuing on to New York, and one continuing to Atlanta and New Orleans.

By bus: **Greyhound Bus Lines** (800-231-2222; greyhound.com) operates routes along both I-85 and I-40. While the I-85 route connects with both Atlanta and Richmond, the I-40 route turns north onto I-77 at Statesville, missing Hickory and failing to connect to Asheville. Asheville can be reached in a roundabout way by transferring at Charlotte, but Hickory has no bus service.

MEDICAL EMERGENCIES **Greensboro: Moses Cone Health System** (336-832-7000; mosescone.com), 1200 N. Elm St., Greensboro 27401. This 1,300-bed hospital, operated by a local not-for-profit, sits to the north of downtown, a block north of US 220 (Wendover Avenue).

Winston-Salem: Forsyth Medical Center (336-718-5000; forsythmedicalcenter .org), 3333 Silas Creek Pkwy., Winston-Salem 27103. This 740-bed hospital, run by the giant regional not-for-profit Novant, is west of downtown at the corner of US 158 (Stratford Road) and NC 67 (Silas Creek Parkway).

Winston-Salem: Wake Forest University Baptist Medical Center (336-716-2011; wfubmc.edu), Medical Center Blvd., Winston-Salem 27157. This 950-bed hospital, associated with the Wake Forest University School of Medicine, is on the western edge of downtown Winston-Salem beside the US 421 expressway (Bus I-40).

High Point Regional Health System (336-878-6000; highpointregional.com), 601 N. Elm St., High Point 27262. This 350-bed facility, run by a local not-for-profit, is on NC 311 at the northern end of High Point's sprawling downtown.

Hickory: Catawba Valley Medical Center (828-326-3000; catawbavalleymedical .org), 810 Fairgrove Church Rd. SE, Hickory 28602. This 250-bed county hospital sits three blocks north of I-40's exit 128.

✷ Exploring the Area

EXPLORING BY CAR **Water mills of Burlington**. This 20.5-mile drive follows Burlington's scenic Haw River—which happens to be one of the state's finest waterpower streams as well as a popular **canoe trail**—and concentrates on exploring the Mill Belt's real history, the history of the industries that brought it into being. *Start by taking NC 87 south from I-40's exit 147 at Graham for 10.1 miles to a left onto Church Road (SSR 2171), then 1.2 miles to Saxapahaw, the start of this drive.* This mill town has a particularly lovely location, almost gorge-like, with public walking trails on the island crossed by this road. Here the old mill has achieved the best of fates, conversion to lofts in a pleasant development called Rivermill Village (rivermillvillage.com) that welcomes strolling and features a farmer's market and live music every summer Saturday. Amazingly, this water-driven plant produced textiles from antebellum days until 1994. The cute town center (one block long) is on a terrace above the modern road. *Take Swepsonville-Saxapahaw Road (SSR 2158) north for 6.4 miles.* In Swepsonville you'll see a more common fate for a 19th-century water-powered mill; on your right is a large slab and scattered bricks, and little else. Curiously, a brand-new Honda plant manufactures small engines only three blocks north on NC 119; not even another manufacturer wants such a constricted, flood-prone site. *Turn right onto George Bason Road (SSR 2156), then go 1.0 mile to a left onto NC 54, then go 1.2 miles to a right onto Jimmie Kerr Road (SSR 1928), then go 3.5 miles to a left onto Stone Street (SSR 1935), which takes you 1.2 miles into the village of Haw River on Old US 70.* The region's oldest mill town has had a mill here since 1745. The current mill, down the old U.S. highway to your left, dates from 1844, and it is no coincidence that the 1856 railroad passes right by it; three of its owners have become governors of North Carolina. Expect this spot to be more interesting than pretty.

At this point Old US 70, left, will take you back into **Burlington**. The best of this drive, however, is still ahead. *Go right on Old US 70 (NC 49) for 0.6 mile, then turn left onto Roma Road, then go 0.5 mile to a left onto Haw River Hopewell Road*

(SSR 1737), then go 2.6 miles to a left onto Sandy Cross Road, then go 0.8 mile to a left onto Carolina Mill Road at a T-intersection in the center of Hopewell. Continue along the river, through the Copland plant. This 1832 water-driven mill (surrounded by more modern additions) is the oldest operating plant in the state, and manufactures fibers for the ready-made curtain market. You'll see the reason for the success of this family-owned factory on your right: A hydroelectric facility has long since replaced the water mill, using the old millpond to generate electricity. *Continue for 0.9 mile along the river.* As you turn sharply uphill note the handsome small plant on your left, another water-driven mill now abandoned. The pipe-like water tower at the top of the hill is its surge tank, equalizing pressure from its large millpond. *Go left onto Carolina Road (SSR 1730) for 1.1 miles, then cross NC 62 onto Union Ridge Road (SSR 1001), to a left in 0.1 mile onto Glencoe Street (SSR 1600). Glencoe, the end of this drive, is 0.6 mile ahead.* **Glencoe** (see *To See*)

EXPLORING THE WATER-DRIVEN MILLS OF THE MILL BELT

We are used to thinking of water mills as premodern technology, something you might find in the medieval era or on the frontier. After all, steam engines started the Industrial Revolution, right? So you'd certainly never expect a water mill in a major industrial district founded at the height of the Industrial Revolution. But when you think about it, why not? Power from a water mill is free, and you can't get any cheaper than that. No wonder some Piedmont factories were still using direct water power into the 1950s!

And these weren't little factories, mind you. These were the same sorts of mills you'd normally power with a steam engine—multistoried brick buildings that were long, tall, and skinny. The power source (a steam engine, or a waterwheel, or an improved sort of waterwheel called a water turbine) would sit either at one end (common for steam engines) or in the middle (preferred for waterwheels) and power a turning rod that ran along the ceiling on each floor; equipment would connect to these rods with leather belts. Raw materials would enter the factory at the top floor at one end, and flow through to emerge as product at the ground floor. That spinning central rod, rather than any particular engine or machine, turns out to mark the real source of the Industrial Revolution.

Of course steam engines were important in the Piedmont; the railroad couldn't exist without them, and there were a number of steam-powered mills even in the early days. The Piedmont's mill industry, however, depended on the steam-powered railroad meeting sources of old-fashioned waterpower. In this way it combined cheap power with cheap labor and cheap transport, and dealt a death blow to its New England–based competition. Today nearly all of those original mills are deserted or converted to different uses, as cheap-labor industries have moved on to other places, but the cities they left behind still thrive.

is the reward at end of this drive, a 19th-century mill town completely restored by private developers, with a museum and thorough-going interpretive placards. Be sure to walk the short distance to the mill dam; it dates from 1951 (yes, that's a 19, not an 18), showing how long waterpower survived into the modern era. NC 62, a short distance to your left, will bring you back to Burlington.

A Brushy Mountain drive. This nearly circular drive explores the remote and beautiful Brushy Mountains, a little-visited miniature of the Blue Ridge—mainly from narrow gravel roads, so roadaphobes beware. Although it is only 21.5 miles long, expect it to take several hours on these twisting back roads. It's worth it despite the road quality; this drive is about the only way to see this unique and beautiful area, full of visual interest while nearly empty of tourists.

From US 64 0.5 mile west of the county seat of Taylorsville, take NC 16 north for 8.8 miles to Moore Mountain Road (SSR 1334), just before the highway crests out. As you approach 1,700-foot Kilby Gap in the Brushy Mountains, you will come upon a group of fruit stands, all of them outlets for the local orchards on the hill-tops above you and open to the public in-season. *Turn left on Moore Mountain Road (SSR 1334, becoming narrow gravel SSR 1110 at a county line) for 6.6 miles, where it returns to NC 16.* You'll start this drive with an impressive forested climb up the steep flank of Moore Mountain, gaining 700 feet in elevation with eight switchbacks. As you break upon the crest you enter wide orchards, where old peach and apple trees form bonsai shapes in rolling fields. The scenery only becomes better as the road narrows to the point where you can almost reach out your window and grab fruit off the trees; then the road dives into a fine old forest, only to twist out again into wide meadows with exceptional views toward the Blue Ridge and along the crest of the Brushies. *Go catawampus left across NC 16 to West Meadows Road (SSR 2486), a very narrow and steep gravel road, and follow it to its end in 1.7 miles.* West Meadows Road is a scary delight, twisting steeply uphill through heavy forests, then dropping down to open meadows and isolated farms in a narrow defile. *Turn left onto paved East Brocktown Road (SSR 2483) for 0.9 mile to a right onto paved Lithia Springs Road (SSR 2484), then go 2.2 miles to a right onto paved Brushy Mountain Road (SSR 1001).* Once the pavement is regained, the scenery becomes increasingly civilized before this route turns once again up into the Brushies—this time following a steep ridgeline with some good views. *Go 2.0 miles to a right onto Bethany Church Road (SSR 2480), which becomes Gilreath Road (SSR 1436) at the county line, and follow it for 8.1 miles to its end at Vashti Road (SSR 1403).* Here this route goes farther up and into the Brushies to explore the mountaintop community of Old Gilreath. You'll pass through more orchard country—old orchards that have been abandoned or grubbed up to form meadows, and new orchards resplendent with their handsome young trees. Before turning onto Bethany Church Road, continue 0.25 mile down Brushy Creek Road to find a small fruit stand selling apples and peaches picked in the surrounding orchards. Your final drive, Bethany Church Road, gradually descends the mountain, passing through forests in which islands of meadows with their modest farmsteads become increasingly rare. *A right turn on excellent Vashti Road will take you back to NC 16 in 5.0 miles; US 64 at Taylorsville is 4.7 miles to your left.* After all this driving, you've arrived only 4 miles away from where you started!

EXPLORING ON FOOT **Hiking the Sauratown Mountains** (sauratowntrails.org), Sauratown Trails Association, P.O. Box 42, Tobaccoville 27050. Located halfway between the Greensboro-Winston-Salem urban area and the Blue Ridge, this 15-mile-long outlier range is noted for peaks well above 2,000 feet, ringed with shining quartzite cliffs. With the Piedmont floor at elevations below 800 feet, views can be very impressive.

The eastern end is anchored by 6,000-acre Hanging Rock State Park. Here you'll find 18 miles of trail looping through a circle of miniature Blue Ridge mountains, visiting cliffs, rock formations, waterfalls, and wide views. Most trails start in the perched valley that forms the park's main area, with a visitors center and a fine little lake. From here, a variety of trailheads let you climb to the cliff-ringed peaks on all sides, an uphill pull as little as 300 feet to Hanging Rock, a breathtaking and appropriately named summit, and as much as 800 feet to the wide panoramic views from Moores Knob, the range's high point. Disabled-accessible paths lead to a rock outcrop and a lovely waterfall. Elsewhere in the park, short trails off country lanes lead to dramatic Lower Cascades Falls, Tory's Den Falls (perhaps the prettiest in the Piedmont), and along the lowermost section of Indian Creek as it flows into the Dan River. Equestrian trails loop through the park's remote western sector.

Pilot Mountain State Park anchors the western end with mesa-like Pilot Mountain, 2,421 feet high. Nine miles of trails circle and climb this isolated peak, allowing you to explore the summit from a high overlook on the park road, or do it the hard way, a 1,400-foot slog up from its base. From there the 6.6-mile Corridor Trail (open to horses and hikers) leads past private farmlands to the Yadkin River, where another 9 miles of trail (much of it open to horses) explore both sides of the Yadkin and the islands in the middle.

The 22-mile Sauratown Trail explores the private lands between the parks, and is open to all riders and hikers from January through October. This amazing bridle path, a collaborative effort between a local equestrian group and the private landowners who contribute access, allows riders to enjoy 35 miles of continuous trail (including the loops through the Hanging Rock State Park backcountry), and hikers to backpack up to 40 miles from the Yadkin to the Dan Rivers. (Be aware that there is no camping outside the state parks.) The Sauratown Trail is co-signed with the 1,000-mile (and 50 percent completed) Mountains-to-Sea Trail connecting the Smokies with the Outer Banks. For information and maps, contact the Sauratown Trails Association.

EXPLORING ON FOOT AND BICYCLE **Greensboro's City Trails** (336-373-3816; greensboro-nc.gov/departments/Parks/facilities/trails). Most large cities nowadays have some sort of rudimentary trail system, along with a promise to do better should they ever find the money. Greensboro goes far beyond this modest standard. The city of Greensboro's Trails Division maintains over 80 miles of walking and biking trails, ranging from primitive treadways to paved greenways, that form into two rough groups. The larger concentration forms an interconnected arc along the far northern edge of the city, starting at **Guildford Courthouse National Military Park** and the adjacent Country Park, then linking to its arc of **water supply reservoirs** via a fine rail-trail. The trails range from interpretive walks to garden strolls and on to wild forest paths, and allow a broad range of loops for foot and bike. Closer in, more trails interconnect in the **Greensboro Garden District** on the western edge of the traditional city center along Wendover Avenue, now a major office and commercial zone. Here good-quality greenways connect a series of creekside parks, giving walkers and joggers several miles of gardens to explore.

✷ Towns

Burlington. Anyone over 40 will probably remember the famed Burlington Mills, once one of America's largest textile companies and a heavy advertiser on national television in the 1970s and '80s. Yes, this is *that* Burlington. Local businessmen, led by the Burlington Chamber of Commerce, founded Burlington Mills just south of town center in 1924 to manufacture and weave rayon rather than the traditional cotton—a good move, as rayon manufacturing was about to go on an international tear, and Burlington Mills would become a household name. Alas, Burlington Mills (by then named Burlington Industries) went bankrupt in 2001, to be absorbed by giant ITG (International Textile Group) in neighboring Greensboro, which shuttered it.

When Burlington Mills closed, Burlington went into its second depression. It hit its first depression in 1886, when the North Carolina Railroad closed its major rail yard there. Up to that time the town so identified with the railroad it was officially named Company Shops, and the rail yard was the only employer. The townspeople responded by changing their name and going on a successful hunt for mills, including the remarkable Glencoe Mill, now restored and a wonderful place to explore.

At this writing, Burlington is down but not, by any stretch of the imagination, out. The last remaining building of the original Company Shops is now its Amtrak depot, beautifully restored with excellent exhibits in its lobby. Downtown stretches southward, of a size reflecting its 1950s heyday; it recently received a shot in the arm with the 2008 opening of the national corporate headquarters of LabCorp, a Fortune 500 company and one of the largest clinical laboratories in the world.

The Piedmont Triad. The North Carolina Railroad, the antebellum line that formed the backbone of the Mill Belt, met and merged with the vast Southern Railway system at a set of sleepy county seats: Greensborough, Winston, High Point. Today these form a single huge urban area, which the U.S. Census calls the Greensboro–Winston-Salem–High Point Combined Statistical Area, and everyone else calls the Piedmont Triad. With 1.8 million residents, it's the nation's 30th largest metropolitan area.

The Triad grew from textiles, tobacco, furniture, and the banks that financed all of these enterprises. R. J. Reynolds and Lorillard Tobacco still headquarter here, as do such textile giants as Hanes, Sealy, ITG (a fabric maker), and VF (Wrangler and Lee jeans). The late, great Wachovia Bank was founded in the Triad (*Wachovia* being an 18th-century name for the area), and BB&T Bank remains here. High Point continues to host the world's largest furniture market. The Triad's 11 undergraduate and graduate institutes include law, medicine, and the arts. And last (but certainly not first), it hosts the corporate headquarters of Gilbarco (of gasoline pump fame) and Krispy Kreme Donuts.

Greensboro, the easternmost of the three cities, has long been an international center of the textile industry. Its handsome 16-block downtown groups around its original courthouse square, a spot selected in 1808 as the geographic center of Guilford County. When local resident John Morehead was elected governor in 1841 he made sure that the North Carolina Railroad—which he championed and later ran—had a depot a few blocks from his house, and the town grew from there; Morehead's Blandwood Mansion, an impressive oddity, is open to the public. Apart from Blandwood, downtown has an attractive grouping of skyscrapers, a striking monument to writer O. Henry, and major art and history museums. It was the location of the first sit-in of the civil rights movement, and that original Woolworths is under renovation as a museum.

Winston-Salem, merging seamlessly with Greensboro to its west, is the oldest of the three cities. It was founded as Salem (meaning "peace") by Moravians migrating south from Pennsylvania on the Great Wagon Road in 1753, and their original settlement survives as Old Salem, three blocks southeast of downtown. When Southern Railway built a line through this area it missed Salem to its north, and the town of Winston formed around its depot; not surprisingly, Winston, not Salem, became the downtown. Today's downtown is dominated by Winston's biggest corporate successes. The Wachovia Bank built the gleaming marble skyscraper just before being taken over and moved to Charlotte; it's now owned by Wells Fargo. Even more impressive is the massive Reynolds Building, clad in red stone and the headquarters of R. J. Reynolds for the last 80 years.

High Point is the third of the triad, smaller than the others and located between them to the south. It, too, formed as a railhead on the NCRR, where it met the Southern Railway line from the hardwood forests of the mountains. When hardwood meets the railroad you get furniture mills, and High Point remains one of the most important furniture centers on the globe. The High Point Furniture Market, founded in 1909, is the largest in the world, held mid-April and mid-October for the industry only. The rest of downtown (as large as Charlotte's with a tenth the population) is testimony to this market dominance, with exclusive showcases dedicated to the world's finest brands. Thomasville, a quaint little town in its southern suburbs, has the world's largest chair.

THE TOWERS OF DOWNTOWN WINSTON-SALEM ARE VISIBLE FROM THE STREETS OF HISTORIC OLD SALEM.

Salisbury and Lexington. These two county seats hug the North Carolina Railroad as it turns southwest from Greensboro to head toward Charlotte; both are near I-85, as that highway follows the railroad as well. Lexington is a small place with a four-block downtown of brick storefronts and a gorgeous classical courthouse; it gains mention here for its distinctive **barbeque**, which it modestly claims to be the finest in the world. Salisbury is much more extensive, with a very large and beautiful historic district; it's a fine place to stay if you are history-minded. Salisbury's suburb of Spencer was at one time host to the North Carolina Railroad's largest repair yard; that yard is now home to the North Carolina State Transportation Museum, better known as Spencer Shops.

Hickory. This furniture town sits on the western edge of this chapter's area, nestling under the massive escarpment of the Blue Ridge Mountains. Like High Point to its east and Morganton to its west, Hickory formed as the break-in-bulk point where Blue Ridge hardwood destined for furniture manufacture met the railroad. As tropical rain forests, often harvested illegally and at great environmental cost, undercut domestic supplies, towns like Hickory go into decline. Nevertheless you'll find it a pleasant, if sleepy, place with a handsome downtown and some nice museums.

✷ Green Spaces

This chapter's area contains no giant tract of public land, no national forest or state-owned game land. It does, however, have nice parks, some quite large.

PARKS AND GARDENS Hanging Rock State Park (336-593-8480; ncparks.gov/Visit/parks/haro/main.php; hanging.rock@ncmail.net), 1790 Hanging Rock Park Rd., Danbury 27016. Admission is free. The Blue Ridge looms above the settled valleys of the Piedmont, a gapless wall 300 miles in length. It looks as if the granitic bedrock broke along a vast crack and heaved itself upward—and that's pretty much what happened. More specifically, the bedrock on the west heaved *upward* while the bedrock on the east sank *downward.* Then, on the eastern edge of that downward drop, a line of bedrock broke, irregularly and unpredictably, into an up-pointed edge. Much of this is buried, but parts stick above the soil, sometimes dramatically so, as outliers of the Blue Ridge.

TORY FALLS, IN HANGING ROCK STATE PARK

Hanging Rock State Park protects one of the larger and more visually impressive of these outliers. Founded in 1936, this 7,000-acre preserve is located 30 miles north of Winston-Salem just west of the tiny county seat of Danbury. The park centers on a small valley perched just below the highest peaks, perhaps 40 acres in extent, with a lovely little lake and the characteristic architecture of the Civilian Conservation Corp (CCC) (see "What's Where"). The surrounding peaks form a U, almost closed, with cliff-lined slopes named Cook's Wall, Moore's Wall (which holds the park's high point, at 2,579 feet), and Hanging Rock. Views are frequent and spectacular. Immediately down from the valley are a series of waterfalls, easily reached from the picnic area, with more waterfalls farther down in other parts of the park. The parklands continue to drop to the banks of the Dan River, where a canoe launch and a hiking trail mark the park's low point at 700 feet.

Pilot Mountain State Park (336-325-2355; pilot.mountain@ncmail.net), 1792 Pilot Knob Park Rd., Pinnacle 27043. Admission is free. This 3,700-acre state park, located 22 miles northwest of Winston-Salem via US 52 (future I-74), has two distinct areas. Its original and namesake section protects Pilot Mountain, an isolated peak at the western end of the Sauratown Mountains, ringed by precipitous cliffs. A park road climbs to a saddle just below the cliff ring, with wide views and a picnic area; from there, hiking paths circle the cliffs and pick their way to the top. The second area, 6 miles to the south, preserves 2 miles of the Yadkin River, a stretch with several large islands. There are hiking and horse trails on both sides of the river and on the islands, and a picnic area on the south bank. The **Horne Creek Living Historical Farm**, a living history museum depicting a 1900 Piedmont farm, is adjacent on the north bank. Connecting the two areas is a hiking and horse trail on a narrow corridor of state land, winding through the Piedmont farms.

Mayo River State Park (336-427-2530; ncparks.gov/Visit/parks/mari/main.php; mayo.river@ncmail.net), 2341 US Bus 220, Mayodan 27027. Admission is free. Established in 2003, this 2,000-acre park protects a section of the Mayo River just north of the town of Mayodan, along US 220 30 miles north of Greensboro. At press time it had not yet opened to the public, but interim facilities were under construction. By the time you read this there should be picnicking, a hiking trail, and a "visitor contact station," presumably at or near the lovely little Mayo River.

Haw River State Park (336-342-6163; ncparks.gov/Visit/parks/hari/main.php; haw.river@ncmail.net), 339 Conference Center Dr., Browns Summit 27214. Admission is free. Authorized in 2003, this park encompasses 1,300 acres of the swampy headwaters of the Haw River. At press time it is largely undeveloped, consisting only of an environmental education center (open by reservation only); its master plan shows day-use areas, hiking paths, and possible expansion downstream along the Haw River.

The North Carolina Zoo, Asheboro (800-488-0444; 336-879-7000; nczoo.org), 4401 Zoo Pkwy., Asheboro 27205. Open daily, Apr.–Oct. 9–5, Nov.–Mar. 9–4. $$$. Owned and operated by the state of North Carolina, this 500-acre habitat zoo boasts of more than 1,100 animals on display along its 5 miles of beautifully landscaped paths. That's right: *5 miles* of walking to take in all the animals. I get tired just writing it.

It turns out that you don't actually have to hike that entire distance. The zoo is arranged in a line, with parking lots at each end and a free shuttle from one lot to the other. Within the zoo, open trams and air-conditioned buses run on their own roadways, stopping roughly every 20 minutes at each of four places; these are disabled-accessible, but animal exhibits are not visible from them.

The zoo is divided into two zones: Africa on the east and North America on the west. The North American area starts with a large marsh exhibit near the parking lot with alligators and cougars among the larger species. After that is an arctic environment (polar bears, sea lions, puffins), followed by Nathan's Hot Dogs (not technically zoo animals), then a streamside exhibit with otters and bobcats. Then comes a large prairie exhibit with elk and bison, and exhibits of black bears and grizzlies. As you hike toward the center of the park you find straggling exhibits of wolves and the Sonoran Desert (ocelots and roadrunners). Then comes Africa.

Start at the other parking lot and Africa comes first. Here the trail takes the form of a figure-8. The large Forest Edge exhibit makes for a spectacular start with giraffes, zebras, and ostriches. Walking clockwise, you pass four widely separated views of the Forest Edge to reach a side trail that leads to an equally large area of elephants and rhinos. Back to the main trail, the Africa Pavilion features meerkats along with snakes and tropical plants; behind it, a long side trail leads to the antelopes and gazelles. Here the inside of the upper loop holds baboons, then gorillas; the outside leads to the Aviary and the patas monkeys. Now back at the lower loop, you pass separate habitats for chimps, lions, and (grand finale) red river hogs.

You'll find places to eat, rest, and use the toilet, as well as buy souvenirs, at each gate, at the center of North America, and at the far end of Africa. If you visit in winter you'll find the Africa parking lot closed (use the internal tram); some of the animals are kept inside when temperatures fall below 45 degrees.

Tanglewood Park, Winston-Salem (336-778-6300; co.forsyth.nc.us/Tanglewood), 4061 Clemmons Rd., Clemmons 27012. Open daily 7–sunset. $. This

OLD MILL OF GUILFORD, GREENSBORO

1,000-acre county park is located on the western edge of Winston-Salem on the left bank of the Yadkin River, just off I-40. It centers on the estate of William Neal Reynolds, of the R. J. Reynolds tobacco family, which he purchased in 1921 and left to the county as a recreation park upon his death in 1951. Its centerpiece is the Manor House, constructed in 1856 as an 18-room mansion, expanded by Reynolds to 28 rooms; it's now a bed & breakfast in the middle of the park. Surrounding it are Reynolds's gardens, including a rose garden, an arboretum, and a fragrance garden. Reynolds, a horse lover, had full stable facilities including a harness racing track, and these continue as part of the park, with trail rides available. The park has three golf courses, two of them championship. There are trails for hikers, bicyclers, and mountain bikers, as well as the standard range of local park recreation. It's a lovely park, and worth exploring.

The Gardens of Greensboro (336-373-2199; greensborobeautiful.org), P.O. Box 3136, Greensboro 27402. Open sunrise–sunset. Admission is free. Private organization Greensboro Beautiful works with the city of Greensboro to support a series of remarkable urban gardens, grouped northwest of downtown along or near Wendover Avenue. The largest of these is the Greensboro Arboretum, on the west side of Wendover between Market Street and Walker Avenue, where paths lead through broad fields and forest glades; within it are 18 separate areas, each with its own theme. Next to the north, the Bog Garden (Starmount Farms Road at Hobbes Road) features two city blocks of nature preserve, explored by boardwalks. Then a block north (1105 Hobbes Road) come the intimate flower gardens of Bicentennial Park.

RIVERS Yadkin River. Flowing eastward from the Blue Ridge's escarpment, the Yadkin forms one of the state's longest stretches of continuous rural river—124 miles of Class I and (very occasional) Class II water between W. Scott Kerr Reservoir at Wilkesboro and High Rock Lake at Salisbury. Between these two lakes you'll find nearly unbroken farmland and forest; apart from a 6-mile stretch through the small town of Elkin (by no means ugly), this river is devoid of development. Even as it passes through Winston-Salem's urban area, Forsythe County's large and beautiful Tanglewood Park shields it. High Rock Lake ends this blessed state, and for the next 52 miles the Yadkin becomes drowned under a series of four reservoirs set so close that each backs up to the foot of the next dam. This chapter ends after the second of these, Tuckertown Lake.

Catawba River (duke-energy.com/lakes). North Carolina's most important hydro-river, the Catawba was targeted as an electrical power producer by tobacco monopolist James Buchanan Duke in 1905. Today Duke Power has seven hydropower reservoirs on North Carolina's Catawba, two on South Carolina's section of the river, and five on tributaries. In this chapter's region you'll find Lake Rhodhiss, Lake Hickory, and Lookout Shoals Lake flooding all but a single 5-mile section of the Catawba.

Dan River (danriver.org). Virginians claim the Dan as their own; after all, the Dan starts in Virginia, spends most of its life in Virginia, and ends in Virginia. North Carolina, however, has 91 miles of the Dan as it flows southward, only to leisurely loop back across the state line. Like the Yadkin, North Carolina's Dan is noted for its rural scenery, overwhelmingly farm and forest; but unlike the Yadkin, it's comparatively narrow and winding, for a more intimate boating experience. This section of the Dan is free flowing, and no lakes obstruct it (although there are a few old milldams that require portaging). The Dan River Basin Association's website includes extremely detailed information on the river, including an excellent guide for boaters.

Haw River (hawrivertrail.org; thehaw.org). This 100-mile stream runs past Burlington, then through rural Piedmont countryside, blocked only by an occasional milldam. It's noted for its water-powered mills (see *Exploring by Car*), and for its canoeing. The state has declared 70 miles of it a State Paddle Trail, with Class I and Class II waters and some nice countryside scenery. In addition, the state intends to parallel the paddle trail with a hiking trail, part of the 1,000-mile Mountains-to-Sea long-distance path. When completed, this Haw River Hiking Trail will run from Haw River State Park to Lake Jordan; 10 miles have been completed at press time.

LAKES **W. Kerr Scott Reservoir (Yadkin River)** (336-921-3390; saw.usace.army.mil/WKScott), 499 Reservoir Rd., Wilkesboro 28697. The U.S. Army Corps of Engineers operates this 1,400-acre lake at the base of the Blue Ridge, 18 miles south of the Blue Ridge Parkway via NC 16. Its earthen dam, built in 1962 for flood control on the Yadkin River, is 150 feet high and 1,750 feet long. The lake itself is surrounded by 2,500 acres of government land, managed for recreation. Roughly a dozen sites offer picnicking, camping, boat ramps and docks, swimming, fishing, and trails. Overall, it's a handsome and well-maintained area.

High Rock Lake (Yadkin River) (hrla.com). This massive lake marks the uphill start of a 56-mile stretch of continuous flooding of the Yadkin. This has been done by the Alcoa Corporation, to supply power for their aluminum smelter in Badin, on Badin Lake—close to a quarter of a gigawatt in total. Constructed by Alcoa in 1924, High Rock Lake covers 23 square miles, with 365 miles of shoreline. It's extremely indented, with individual arms extending up to 4 miles from the main lake body. Despite strict access rules from Alcoa it has a large number of subdivisions along its shore, along with a good supply of marinas and boat ramps.

Tuckertown Reservoir (Yadkin River). Built in 1962 by Alcoa, Tuckertown Dam is a low, long concrete structure creating a "run of the river" hydroelectric operation. Its lake, covering a scant 4 square miles of surface, is long and skinny, following 9.5 miles of the Yadkin River with few side arms. Its banks are almost completely free of residential or industrial development, making this a long, leisurely boat trip through fields and forests, with some pleasant low "mountains" (offshoots of the nearby Uwharries) to break up the scenery. Recreational facilities consist of two boat ramps, of which the larger and easier to find is on NC 8/49, just west of the bridge over the lake.

Lake Rhodhiss (Catawba River) (duke-energy.com/lakes/facts-and-maps/lake-rhodiss.asp). The original Rhodhiss Dam was built in 1902 by local factory owners John Rhodes and George Hiss to provide electricity for their adjacent Rhodhiss Mill. Duke Power bought them out and replaced their early hydropower dam with the present 65-foot structure in 1925. Modern Lake Rhodhiss is long, narrow, and without arms of any size, an east–west strip of water 13 miles long and 0.25 mile wide. Even though residential development was heavy during the Housing Boom of the Noughts, forests still dominate its 90 miles of shoreline scenery, particularly along its upriver half. Duke Energy provides four excellent boat ramps, and a private marina gives additional access and services.

Lake Hickory (Catawba River) (duke-energy.com/lakes/facts-and-maps/lake-hickory.asp). Like its partner Lake Rhodhiss immediately upstream, Lake Hickory is a string bean of a lake, only a bit longer and larger even though its 1927 dam is almost double the height of Rhodhiss Dam. Lake Hickory cuts directly through the Hickory urban area, and its 105 miles of shoreline are heavily dominated by lakeside homes. Nevertheless, boating access is excellent, with owner Duke Energy providing five first-rate boat ramps, two city of Hickory parks providing additional access, and five private marinas offering a full range of services.

Lookout Shoals Lake (Catawba River) (duke-energy.com/lakes/facts-and-maps/lookout-shoals.asp). Immediately downstream from Lake Hickory is Duke Energy's oldest and smallest Catawba River hydropower facility, the 1915 Lookout Shoals Dam and its linear lake, 10 miles long but so narrow that it covers only 2 square miles of surface and 37 miles of shoreline. Its upper half, extremely narrow and so shallow that the old river shoals are exposed at low water, has lovely rural scenery, while its lower half is dominated by lakeside residences. Duke Energy provides two boat ramps, one on each shore above the dam.

Greensboro Watershed Lakes (336-373-2574; greensboro-nc.gov/departments/Parks/Facilities/regionalparks/watershed), 1001 4th St., Greensboro 27405. The city of Greensboro maintains a series of three midsized watershed lakes to the northeast of its urban area, with complete ownership of the surrounding lands. The city has now organized this into Watershed Park, with fishing, sailing, canoeing, and kayaking, as well as 42 miles of hiking trails (with about half of them open to bicyclists as well).

A PIEDMONT FARM, NEAR STATES

✷ To See

MUSEUM ROW North Carolina's Mill Belt has brought forward a slew of major corporations, along with their multimillionaire owners. As you drive through this area note the civic monuments that preserve the names of these early entrepreneurs, the state's commercial aristocracy: Duke, Reynolds, Broyhill, Hanes, Cone. These parks and museums give a note of refinement to this string of mill towns.

Blandwood Mansion, Greensboro (336-272-5003; blandwood.org), 447 W. Washington St., Greensboro 27401. Open Tue.–Sat. 11–4, Sun. 2–5. $$.

Located on the western edge of downtown Greensboro, Blandwood is the home of the first, indeed the founding, aristocrat of the Mill Belt: John Motley Morehead. As governor from 1841 to 1845 Morehead pushed through an aggressive program of wide-ranging improvements to education and transportation. This most definitely included railroads; Morehead had the state of North Carolina create the semi-private North Carolina Railroad (NCRR) and insisted that it place a major station near Blandwood. After finishing his term as governor, Morehead became president of the NCRR.

Blandwood is a strange and fascinating structure. It was built in 1795 (13 years before Greensboro was founded five blocks north) as a modest farmhouse, and when Morehead (then a newly married young lawyer) bought it in 1827 it had only six rooms. When he became governor, however, he somehow sensed that his financial future was brightening. He commissioned the great architect A. J. Davis (whose work already included New York's Federal Hall) to modernize Blandwood. Davis more than doubled its size and remodeled it as an exquisite Tuscan villa, the oldest such example in North America. But Blandwood is a Tuscan villa only in front; it's back remains a colonial wood farmhouse. This seems curious, but is readily understood when you remember that, on a slave-owning estate, the rear yard of the big house was given over to slave activities, so that Morehead would have seen no point in making it pretty or fashionable. The gardens exhibit North Carolina native plants in a design partly based on a description published in 1844.

Reynolda House Museum of American Art, Winston-Salem (888-663-1149; 336-758-5150; reynoldahouse.org; reynolda@reynoldahouse.org), 2250 Reynolda Rd., Winston-Salem 27106. Open Tue.–Sat. 9:30–4:30, Sun. 1:30–4:30. $$$. Between 1906 and 1923, tobacco baron R. J. Reynolds lived on a 1,067-acre private estate just north of downtown Winston-Salem, which he dubbed Reynolda. The son of a Virginia plantation owner, Reynolds founded his eponymous firm in 1875, and later thrived on Prince Albert tobacco and Camel cigarettes. He built Reynolda House as his primary home in 1917; it's long, low, and elegant, exuding comfort and wealth even as it eschews ostentation. Since 1967 the house has been open to the public as a museum of American art, exhibiting its wide collection throughout the house. The former boiler room houses a French restaurant, and more services are nearby in the old servants' village, now the exclusive shopping district known as Reynolda Village.

Southeastern Center for Contemporary Art (SECCA), Winston-Salem (336-725-1904; secca.org; general@secca.org), 750 Marguerite Dr., Winston-Salem 27106. Founded in 1956, this large museum now occupies underwear king James G. Hanes's 32-acre estate across just across the street from Reynolda, then west down side street Marguerite Drive. About a third of the museum occupies Hanes's English Hunt–style mansion, with the rest in a modernist, predictably bunker-like, expansion in the back. Now part of the North Carolina Museum of Art, SECCA concentrates on contemporary southeastern artists acting within their communities.

Weatherspoon Art Museum, University of North Carolina at Greensboro (336-334-5770; weatherspoon.uncg.edu; weatherspoon@uncg.edu), corner of Spring Garden St. and State St., P.O. Box 26170, Greensboro 27402. Open Tue.–Fri. 10–5 (later on Thu.), Sat.–Sun. 1–5. Admission is free. Part of the University of North Carolina at Greensboro and named after a respected educator, the Mill

Belt's other modern art museum is largely the result of the philanthropy of the Cone family, relatives of the early denim entrepreneur. The extensive collection includes Matisse, Picasso, de Kooning, and other modern masters, as well as specialized collections of American 20th-century art, art on paper, and (surprisingly) a fine collection of 18th-century Japanese prints. The building itself is one of the more breathtaking exhibits, a massive freestanding sculpture of a structure by Romaldo Giurgola.

Chinqua Penn Plantation, Greensboro Area (336-349-4576; chinquapenn.com; cppinfo@chinquapenn.com), 2138 Wentworth St., Reidsville 27320. Open Wed.–Sat. 10–5, Sun. 1–5. $$$. Not all of the Mill Belt barons were giants. Thomas Jefferson Penn made a modest fortune by founding a small cigarette factory and then selling it to giant American Tobacco Company. He then retired to the good life of a gentleman farmer on 1,000 acres of beautiful rolling piedmont, and built his elaborate and eccentric home, Chinqua Penn. Dating to 1926, 27-room Chinqua Penn sits in romantic gardens, clad in native stone, with an interior vaguely modeled on a European country house. Its vast "living room"—more of a great hall at 35 by 55 feet and two stories high—is particularly worthwhile. There is no better place to see what life was like for the mill elite.

INSIDE THE GREENSBORO HISTORICAL MUSEUM

Greensboro Historical Museum (336-373-2043; greensborohistory.org), 130 Summit Ave., Greensboro 27401. Open Tue.–Sat. 10–5, Sun. 2–5. Admission is free. This attractively designed 17,000-square-foot museum on the northeast edge of downtown Greensboro has special exhibits on local residents Dolley Madison and O. Henry, a re-creation of the Greensboro Sit-In of 1960, and rooms from an elegant local mansion destroyed in 1954. Upstairs, a large exhibition re-creates the Greensboro of the late 19th century, while a second exhibit features Civil War firearms. In the back are two 18th-century farmhouses moved in from other locations.

CULTURAL SITES North Carolina Vietnam Veterans Memorial. The state's memorial to its Vietnam war dead and missing is set in a forested park created in a 400-yard gap between the north- and southbound lanes of I-85 near Thomasville, at mile marker 100 (between exit 96, US 64, and exit 103, NC 109). Sunken into a large grassy amphitheater, a red-brick wall contains the names of the 1,647 men and women from North Carolina who were fallen or lost. A paved, disabled-accessible path links the two sides of the interstate through a riverine forest and over pretty little Hamby Creek.

The O. Henry statues in downtown Greensboro (336-373-2043; greensboronc.org/attraction_details.cfm?AttractionID=7), corner of N. Elm St. and Bellemeade St., Greensboro. This downtown pocket park features one of the most enchanting urban bronze sculptures in the state. At the center of it, a huge book is open to the O. Henry story "The Gift of the Magi," with an illustration on the left page; Red Chief mischievously hides between the pages. O. Henry himself stands to one side, on the sidewalk, quietly observing them (and you), and taking notes. Born William Sydney Porter, Greensboro native O. Henry was the master of the short story, writing optimistic tales of ordinary folk at the beginning of the 20th century.

The Three College Observatory (uncg.edu/phy/tco). Open times vary; consult their website. Admission is free but reservations are required. This large optical telescope, operated by three Greensboro universities, sits isolated on its own 60-acre tract atop Cane Creek Mountain, an 850-foot-tall Blue Ridge outlier just west of Saxapahaw. It keeps several days a month open for the public to come and look through the 32-inch reflecting telescope—the largest in North Carolina, and one of the largest in the South.

Thomasville's Big Chair, near High Point. Thomasville, located 7 miles southwest of High Point via NC 68, put itself on tourism map in 1922 when it erected a

O. HENRY MEMORIAL, GREENSBORO

THE BIG CHAIR, IN DOWNTOWN THOMASVILLE

30-foot chair in the middle of downtown. Rebuilt in 1951, it's a Duncan Phyfe reproduction that for many years could make the claim of being the largest chair in the world. You'll find it, surrounded by flowers, in an attractive small park between the railroad tracks and the small red-brick downtown. Thomasville Furniture Industries (which was founded here in 1904 and built the original chair) still maintains its corporate headquarters and showroom four blocks east on Main Street.

HISTORIC SITES

Old Salem (888-653-7253; 336-721-7300; oldsalem.org), 600 S. Main St., Winston-Salem 27101. Open Mar.–Dec.: Mon.–Sat. 9:30–4:30, Sun. 1–5; Jan.–Feb.: same hours, but closed Mon. $$$. A quietly pastoral village sits two blocks south of Winston-Salem's downtown, just off Bus I-40's South Liberty Street exit. It's not a fenced-off museum, admission required and empty after five; instead it's a living neighborhood, 16 blocks in extent, beautifully gardened and lively with people strolling past the two-century-old buildings. If you want to see inside some of those buildings—about 20 of them, including some impressive museums—you can pay admission. But you don't have to. The Old Salem National Landmark Historic District is an actual city neighborhood, open to all. And it really does look like an 18th-century country village.

Old Salem, Inc., a private not-for-profit, created this village between 1950 and 1966 out of the colonial core of Winston-Salem, and continues to run it as a large open-air museum. They have around two dozen properties open to the public and staffed with interpreters in period costumes: a gunsmith, printer, tinsmith, baker (who'll sell you bread and cookies), a tavern, the Single Brothers Hall, several homes, many gardens . . . you get the idea. Across from the village they have a handsome new visitors center with interpretive exhibits, deli, and bookstore;

WACHOVIA

A hundred years before Martin Luther, Czech priest Jan Hus tried to reform the Roman Catholic Church, and got himself burned at the stake for it. This set off 20 years of war in Bohemia (today's Czech Republic), followed by almost two centuries of religious toleration. During this period Hus's followers, the *Unitas Fratrum* or "United Brethren," prospered. This happy state, however, did not survive the Thirty Years War, when the Bohemian army had their clock cleaned and the Roman Catholic Church could again impose itself by force on the Czech populace. Nevertheless, a group of Brethren survived as an underground movement in Moravia for another century, and so became known to this day as Moravians. Later on, many Moravians migrated to Pennsylvania, and founded the city of Bethlehem (of steel fame).

Got that? Okay, let's move on to North Carolina.

Around 1750 (we're now more than 300 years from Jan Hus), the leaders of the Moravian Church in Bethlehem decided to found a new settlement on the southern frontier. To this end they purchased 100,000 acres of land on what was then the North Carolina frontier and what is now the city of Winston-Salem. They named their land Wachovia to honor a count from Wachau, Austria, who had sheltered and supported them. In 1753 a dozen Moravians started settling the area, creating the village they named Bethabara (House of Passage), now a city park and historic site. It was the Moravians who created the Great Wagon Road along the route of their pioneer trek—one of the most important early roads in colonial America.

In 1766 the Moravian Church created the town of Salem (peace) 8 miles to the south, and placed their Home Church facing the town square (where its successor still stands). They designed the town to reflect Moravian religious practices, organized around "choirs," groups of church people of the same age and gender. In this system, children would live with their parents until reaching the age of 13, then go to live with their choir, either in the Single Brothers House or the Single Sisters House. Living in dorms and eating communally, the boys would apprentice to a trade, while the girls would learn how to manage a household. A lad would stay in the Single Brothers

there's also a huge 1800 organ in full working order, beautifully restored, and the second oldest on their property. It's linked with the village proper by an arched truss wood bridge, covered of course, built in 1998.

On the village side of the bridge, Old Salem, Inc., runs the Horton Museum Center, which combines the Museum of Early Southern Decorative Arts (MESDA) with the Old Salem Toy Museum. The two-level toy museum is a delight, jammed full of 18th- and 19th-century playthings, including a very large display of fur-

House until he had mastered his trade and accumulated enough money to justify marriage to one of the single sisters.

Church control started to slip after 1820, and was complete enough by 1849 that the state of North Carolina organized Wachovia (with some adjacent lands) as Forsyth County. The church sold the new county a substantial tract just to the north of Salem, and this became the county seat of Winston. (Winston's local bank, Wachovia Bank, would become one of the largest in the nation before being destroyed by the 2008 credit crisis.) The two towns merged to form the city of Winston-Salem in 1913, although Winston, glutting on tobacco money, was already much larger and Salem was deep into a long slide into insignificance.

In 1950 local historic conservationists started working to preserve Salem's original core and restore it to its colonial appearance. By 1966 they had succeeded beyond all expectation, and Old Salem National Landmark Historic District is now a world-class destination.

LOG CABIN, C. 1816, BETHABARA PARK

nished dollhouses. MESDA exposes Old Salem's vast collection of 18th- and early-19th-century southern antiques, displayed in period rooms, most of which were removed from historic houses slated for demolition; these range from the high-ceilinged elegance of a Charleston town house to the single rough room of a Piedmont log cabin. Old Salem, Inc., also runs several shops and a restaurant in the village, the Old Salem Tavern.

The Old Salem, Inc., properties only take up a quarter or so of Old Salem. Across from the town square is the Moravian Home Church, the headquarters for the Moravian Church Southern Province. Impressive with its gargantuan organ, modestly elegant chancel, and stunning curved balcony, the Home Church is open for tours most afternoons, and is free. Next to it is Salem Academy and College, founded in 1772 and the oldest women's college in America. It maintains a small but worthwhile (and free) museum in what was once the Single Sisters House, now long since absorbed into its fabric.

One of Old Salem's finest delights, however, is simply staying there at the privately owned **August Zevely Inn**, across the street from the restaurant. From there you can enjoy an after-hours stroll along the brick sidewalks, and appreciate this island in time as one of the neighbors.

Guilford Courthouse District, Greensboro (nps.gov/guco; greensboro-nc.gov/departments/Parks/Facilities). In March 1781 the Revolutionary War came to an end in the fields north of modern-day Greensboro. No one knew it at the time—the British thought they had won—but the Battle of Guilford Courthouse left the British forces in the South so weakened that their campaign was over. That October, the decimated British army surrendered at Yorktown, Virginia.

R. J. REYNOLDS CO. CORPORATE HEADQUARTRERS IN DOWNTOWN WINSTON-SALEM

New Englander Nathanael Greene commanded an American force that was far larger than Lord Cornwallis's highly trained regulars, but mostly made up of untrained and undisciplined local recruits. Cornwallis had already lost a significant proportion of his troops when the bulk of his German mercenaries, called Hessians, defected as they marched through the lands of their fellow Germans, the friendly, peace-loving Moravians. Nevertheless, Cornwallis was convinced that his troops, with their strategy of rapid volleys from massed muskets, would tear through the backwoodsmen. Greene, however, had no intent of asking his raw recruits to hold ground against British regulars. Instead, Greene put his least experienced locals in a straggling front line in the midst of a large field, then a line of semi-trained recruits behind that, and his battle-hardened regulars in a third line, hidden in the forests along the field. He instructed each of the two front lines to fire a single volley, then go home—which they did, dropping their personal gear and running. As Greene expected, this sent the British into a charge, right into the third line. Facing the vastly more accurate American long rifles in a heavy wood, the British were unable to effectively use either volleys or bayonets, and suffered 25 percent losses before driving the Americans from the field. At this point the British army charged with conquering and holding the Carolinas was down to a scant 1,200 regulars, at the start of the campaign season. Their retreat into Virginia sealed their fate. Carolinians named four cities and two counties after General Greene (some now in Tennessee, at the time part of North Carolina).

This important site offers a variety of ways to explore history and enjoy some outdoor recreation to boot. You'll find the actual battlefield restored and interpreted in the National Park Service's (NPS) Guilford Courthouse National Military Park. A block to its west, tiny Tannenbaum Park (jointly run by Greensboro City Parks and the NPS) presents a Piedmont farm as it would appear during the Revolution, with furnished log cabins and outbuildings. Country Park, a Greensboro city park, occupies 300 acres of land adjacent to the national park, with trails, lakes, picnicking, a science center, and off-trail biking. And lastly, a rail-trail, the 4.9-mile Lake Brandt Greenway, links the Guildford Courthouse district with the city's Watershed Lakes, crossing two of the lakes in the process.

✐ **Horne Creek Farm State Historic Site** (336-325-2298; nchistoricsites.org/horne; hornecreek@ncdcr.gov), 308 Horne Creek Farm Rd., Pinnacle 27043. Open Tue.–Sat. 9–5. Admission is free. Located 22 miles northwest of Winston-Salem via US 52 (future I-74), this living history museum re-creates a Piedmont farm c. 1900. It centers on the 1875 Hauser Farm and its seven outbuildings, all restored to the way they had been in the early 20th century. The farm is active, with crops, animals, and a heritage apple orchard, and visitors are welcome to join in. Ongoing events are patterned after those that would have occurred on such a farm: ice cream socials, corn shucking, musical afternoons, and plowing with draft animals. The site is adjacent to Pilot Mountain State Park.

✐ **Charlotte Hawkins Brown Museum, Greensboro Area** (336-449-4846; nchistoricsites.org/chb; chb@ncmail.net), P.O. Box B, Sedalia 27342. Open Mon.–Sat. 9–5. Admission is free. This 40-acre state historic site, located midway between Greensboro and Burlington on US 70, preserves and exhibits the Palmer Institute, an African American residential prep school that operated from 1902 to 1971. It serves as a memorial to its founder, Dr. Charlotte Hawkins Brown, an important and influential African American educator. About 10 buildings are restored and open to visitors, most built in the 1920s. The visitors center occupies a handsome brick teacher's cottage, and houses a museum (including a video) that interprets the site. Dr. Brown's home, Canary Cottage, is furnished as her students would have seen it in the 1940s and '50s. Elsewhere on campus, several dormitories and teachers' cottages, the dining hall, and the bell tower are open, and the teahouse serves as the museum store. Alas, the original schoolhouse is gone, but interpretive plaques mark its location and explain its significance. More plaques line the trails through this extensive site, and there's a pleasant, shaded picnic area.

Glencoe Village (336-260-0038; textileheritagemuseum.org; textileheritage@triad.rr.com). The museum is open weekend afternoons 1–4. Admission is free. To find it drive 3.7 miles north of Burlington off NC 62 (just north of the Haw River), then left onto Union Ridge Road (SSR 1001) for a block, then left onto Glencoe

Street (SSR 1600) to its end. No place captures the feel of the early Mill Belt better than this private restoration of a postbellum mill town. Founded in 1889, Glencoe was a typical mill for its time—a long, tall brick structure by a river, powered by running water, with a company-owned mill town adjacent. It closed in 1954, and the entire complex sat abandoned for 44 years, preserved by neglect. Today you'll find it intact and largely restored, nearly all the company housing brightly painted and occupied, a museum in the company store, and interpretive plaques everywhere. It's a wonderful place to stroll. Of particular interest are the milldam and millrace upstream from the factory, now a county park and easily reached by short, level paths. You'll find picnic tables scattered along the river up and down from the dam, and some nice places to fish.

✐ **Spencer Shops—The North Carolina Museum of Transportation** (877-688-6386; 704-636-2889; nctrans.org; nctrans@nctrans.org), 411 S. Salisbury Ave., Spencer 28159. Open May–Oct.: Mon.–Sat. 9–5, Sun. 1–5; Nov.–Apr.: same hours, but closed Mon. Admission, free; train rides $$, turntable rides $. In 1891 the North Carolina Railroad (NCRR) opened this huge repair yard just north of Salisbury, at the halfway point between Washington and Atlanta, to replace the recently closed yard at Company Shops (modern Burlington). Spencer Shops functioned as the main facility for the semi-merged NCRR and Southern Railroad (they've since come unmerged) as long as steam ruled the rails—but when low-maintenance diesel engines took over, this yard slowly became redundant. By the 1970s, it was abandoned.

LOCOMOTIVE ON DISPLAY IN THE SPENCER SHOPS ROUNDHOUSE OF THE NORTH CAROLINA STATE TRANSPORTATION MUSEUM

Today the Spencer Shops houses the massive collections of the North Carolina State Transportation Museum in a series of 15 buildings on 57 acres, including the town's 1898 passenger depot, the vast 1902 Back Shop (used to repair entire steam locomotives), and a 1924 roundhouse. The tour starts with the passenger depot, which holds the visitors center; here you can ride through the site on vintage rolling stock pulled by one of the historic diesel engines, and (for only $4 more) even ride with the engineer. A longish walk (a shuttle runs on weekends) brings you to the track-side Master Mechanics Office (1911) with general exhibits, and the Flue Shop (1928), holding the collection of antique automobiles. Across the tracks are the gargantuan Back Shops, now under restoration, that will one day hold a mixed display of aircraft, train engines, and automobiles. The highlight of the museum comes last: the 37-bay roundhouse. Here you'll find the museum's collection of rolling stock: 21 steam and diesel locomotives, as well as many passenger cars, freight cars, private cars, baggage cars, mail cars, even a World War II hospital car, all fully restored. The last few bays hold current restoration projects, and are open to view. At the center of the roundhouse is the turntable, 100 feet in diameter, used to rotate the giant steam locomotives to their proper bays; it's completely functional, and you can ride on it.

Bunker Hill Covered Bridge, Hickory Area (828-465-0383; catawbahistory.org; info@catawbahistory.org). Open daily, sunrise–sunset. Admission is free. Located west of Hickory just off US 70, the Bunker Hill bridge is the only surviving historic covered bridge in the state—that is, the only historic bridge whose cover was an integral part of its structure, and not just added to look pretty. The Bunker Hill bridge carried heavy wagon traffic over flood-prone Lyle Creek on the predecessor of US 70. A more normal bridge design, where beams rested on piers, would have required a pier in the riverbed, and this could easily have been wiped out during a flood. Instead, its 1895 builder chose a wood truss design, capable of carrying very heavy loads over long distances without intermediate supports. When the slanting wood trusses started to show signs of decay after only five years of exposure to rain, the builder covered them with clapboard and a wood shingle roof. Like all such bridges of this period, its attractiveness was merely an accidental by-product of a decision to reduce repair bills. Bridge fans will want to examine the truss itself, as it's the world's only surviving example of the Haupt Truss, a scientifically designed improvement over folk methods that reduced wood while increasing strength. To reach this county park, leave I-40 at Oxford Street/Claremont (exit 135), then go 0.7 mile south to a left onto US 70; the bridge's parking area is 2.0 miles farther on the left.

Hickory History Center (828-324-7294; catawbahistory.org; historicharper@bellsouth.net), 310 N. Center St., Hickory 28601. Open Thu.–Sat. 9–4, Sun. 1:30–4:30. Harper House, $$; the Bonniwell-Lyerly House is free. The Hickory History Center, only one of four major sites run by the amazing Catawba County Historical Society, consists of two historic homes on the north side of downtown Hickory on 3rd Avenue NE. The stunning 1887 Harper House, with its turret, arched balcony, and wraparound porches, claims to have the finest Queen Anne interior in the state. Adjacent is the Lyerly House, a fine 1912 Craftsman structure that sports a 1930s remodeling in the Tudor Revival style. It holds museum exhibits on Hickory's history, as well as a conference facility.

✐ **Murray's Mill National Historic District, Hickory area** (828-241-4299; catawbahistory.org; info@catawbahistory.org). Open Thu.–Sat. 9–4, Sun. 1:30–4:30. Closed in winter. $. One of four major sites run by the Catawba County Historical Association, this remarkable complex preserves a traditional gristmill with a large overshot wheel, an impressive millpond and dam, an earlier wheathouse, a miller's house, and a general store, all *in situ*. The mill is the centerpiece, a large white clapboard structure with a 28-foot wheel, built in 1913 and still grinding corn with its original equipment. Adjacent is the contemporaneous miller's house, furnished in period. Also adjacent is the 1880s wheathouse, a two-story structure that used to store raw grain and now holds collections of architectural miniatures and local historic architecture. Across the street, the 1890s Murray and Minges General Store holds nostalgia items from old-fashioned bottled Coke, to candy, to wooden toys—

all for sale. The site itself is very handsome, deep in a rural district, about 10 minutes from I-40 between Hickory and Statesville. Leave I-40 at NC 10 (exit 138) and head south for 4.8 miles to a left onto SSR 1003 (Murray's Mill Road), then go 0.6 mile to the site.

VINEYARDS AND ORCHARDS **Yadkin Valley Appellation** (yadkinvalleywine trail.com). Located west of Winston-Salem, the Yadkin Valley became North Carolina's first American Viticulture Area in 2005. Wineries and vineyards occupy moderate elevations, with long, warm growing seasons and sharp winter chills. There are 23 wineries within this appellation, producing 118 wines—too many to list here. The Yadkin Valley Wine Trail website will give you complete details.

Swan Creek Appellation (swancreekvineyards.com). Tiny (at 96,000 acres) as appellations go, the Swan Creek American Viticulture Appellation (AVA) nestles in the upper Piedmont, just under the Blue Ridge. It's cooler, drier, and higher than the adjoining Yadkin Valley AVA, yet not so extreme as the mountain regions to its north.

GOLD, EMERALDS, AND HIDDENITE **Gold Hill Mines Historic Park**, 735 St Stephens Church Rd., Gold Hill 28071. This local park preserves the remains of a large 19th-century gold mine. It's a fun place to explore while on a picnic. The surrounding rural area is worthwhile as well, with a number of historic homes set in handsome scenery.

The Hiddenite Center (the Lucas House) (828-632-6966; hiddenitecenter .com; info@hiddenitecenter.com), 316 Church St., Hiddenite 28636. Open weekdays 9–4:30. Free admission; house tours, $. Located in rural Alexander County, 33 miles northeast of Hickory, the village of Hiddenite gets its name from a rare gemstone, discovered here in 1879 and first brought to geologists' attention by mineralogist William Earl Hidden. The Hiddenite Center promotes the history and arts in this area from its headquarters in a 22-room, three-story mansion at the village's center, known as the Lucas House. Built in 1900 as a two-story Victorian home, its second owner, James "Diamond Jim" Lucas, expanded it in 1915 by cutting it in half horizontally and inserting a new, full-sized floor between the original first and second stories. The Hiddenite Center maintains the first floor as a history museum, furnished in period, but with exhibits on the village's namesake mineral. The second and third floors (which can be toured free) contain an art museum and a large doll collection.

Emerald Hollow Mine at Hiddenite (866-600-4367; 828-632-3394; hiddenite gems.com; info@hiddenitegems.com), 484 Emerald Hollow Mine Dr., Hiddenite 28636. Open daily 8–sunset. $$. Claiming to be the only emerald mine open to the public in the world, Emerald Hollow offers buckets of unsalted, virgin soil from its 70-acre mine, as well as salted buckets for higher amounts. Panning can be done on a covered sluiceway or directly from one of several mineral-rich creeks on the property. They also allow you to dig in their mine, for an extra fee.

* To Do

CANOES, KAYAKS, AND RAFTS **Yadkin River Adventures** (336-374-5318; yadkinriveradventures.com; paddle@yadkinriveradventures.com), 104 Old Rockford Rd., Rockford 27017. This outfitter offers half-day and full-day canoe

NEARBY . . .

There are two gold mines open to the public, and not too far away. Both offer panning in unsalted local alluvium. **Reed Gold Mine State Historic Site** (see "The Charlotte Region") lets you tour the East's first gold mine, including underground tunnels and authentic period processing equipment, as well as pan for gold. In contrast, **Thermal City Gold Mine** (see "The Northern Mountains") has been in continuous production for 150 years, and is strongly oriented toward those who are serious about panning.

and kayak trips on the unspoiled Yadkin River, as well as shuttle services and rentals.

✐ **Dan River: Three Rivers Outfitters** (336-627-6215; 3-r-o.com; info@3-r-o.com), 413-B Church St., Eden 27288. This retail store offers kayak, canoe, and batteau rentals, shuttle services, and guided rides on the eastern half of Dan River and its tributaries, the Mayo and Smith Rivers.

✐ **Dan River Adventures** (336-427-8530; danriveradventures.com; danrivercampground@hotmail.com), 724 Webster Rd., Stoneville 27048. This outfitter offers canoe, kayak, and tubing rentals and shuttles on the eastern half of the river. They will also shuttle your own boat for you.

The Haw River Canoe and Kayak Company (336-260-6465; hawrivercanoe.com; info@hawrivercanoe.com), P.O. Box 22, Saxapahaw 27340. Located in the terraced riverside village of Saxapahaw, this outfitter offers canoe and kayak rentals and shuttle services on the Haw River, as well as an intriguing selection of guided trips (one includes local wines).

LAKE BOATING Marinas on the Big Lakes (pilotmedia.us/Piedmont/plfeatures.htm, and click on "Marina Guide"). There are too many marinas on this chapter's seven big lakes to list separately. Fortunately, the magazine *Piedmont Lakes Pilot* keeps track of all the services available to boaters (both paddle and motor), and keeps them up to date on their website.

✷ Lodging

HOTELS ✐ **The Historic Brookstone Inn, Winston-Salem** (800-845-4262; 336-725-1120; brookstowninn.com; Info@brookstowninn.com), 200 Brookstown Ave, Winston-Salem 27101. $$–$$$$. Located in Winston-Salem's first factory, the 1836 Brookstown Inn is a full-service 71-room hotel, three blocks from the giant tin coffeepot that marks the northern limit of historic Old Salem. Rooms are good-sized and handsome, with free WiFi; smoking rooms are available. Continental breakfast, evening wine and cheese, and bedtime cookies and milk are included in the tariff.

BED & BREAKFASTS ✐ 🐾 **August T. Zevely Inn, Winston-Salem** (800-928-9299; 336-748-9299; winston-salem-inn.com; Reservations@winston-salem-inn.com), 803 S. Main St., Winston-Salem 27101. $$–$$$$. This 1842 brick house sits in the middle of Old Salem, Winston-Salem's beautifully restored colonial district. It's furnished completely in period, in the rooms as well as common areas. Common areas include a dining room, breakfast room, and sitting room. The 12 bedrooms are all comfortably roomy, with TV and telephones, and spread over four floors (stairs only); they include pet rooms, ADA-approved rooms, and micro-fridge rooms. An expanded continental breakfast is served, along with afternoon wine and cheese and an evening treat.

The Henry F. Shaffner Inn, Winston-Salem (800-952-2256; 336-777-0052; shaffnerhouse.com; info@shaffnerhouse.com), 150 S. Marshall St., Winston-Salem 27101. $$–$$$$. The grandiose home of one of Wachovia Bank's founders, the 1907 Shaffner House combines Queen Anne styling with Tudoresque half timbers. Inside, it's furnished in period antiques, with nine rooms ranging from cozy to large, including some with separate sitting rooms; all have free WiFi, and all are nonsmoking. The tariff includes a full hot breakfast, and wine and cheese in the evening. It's about three blocks from the center of downtown, and about five blocks from the northern edge of Old Salem.

Tanglewood Park Manor House Bed & Breakfast, Winston-Salem (336-778-6300; manorhouse.tanglewoodpark.org), 4061 Clemmons Rd., Winston-Salem 27012. $$–$$$. This 10-room B&B sits in the middle of Forsyth County's 1,000-acre Tanglewood Park, tucked between the western edge of Winston-Salem and the unspoiled Yadkin River. The manor itself dates back to an 1859 plantation house—but most of its present form comes from a Reynolds scion who bought it in 1921, and donated it to the county upon his death. Rooms are individually furnished with antiques and reproductions, and breakfast is included. The surrounding park is well kept and handsomely landscaped, with full recreation facilities including tennis and three golf courses. Housekeeping cottages are also available.

Twin Lakes Lodge, Greensboro (888-484-5253; 336-852-6968; thetwinlakeslodge.com; anita@thetwinlakeslodge.com), 2700 Twin Lakes Dr., Greensboro 27407. $$$–$$$$. This large modern property, built in the Colonial Revival style, sits on a small lake on the southern edge of Greensboro, on a large, landscaped property. Only somewhat more expensive than other such inns, it emphasizes comfort and privacy. All four rooms are very large, with two-person whirlpool tub, fireplace, refrigerator, WiFi, and outside entrance. The full breakfast is served in-room. All guests must be 18 or older.

Rowan Oak House Bed and Breakfast, Salisbury (800-786-0437; rowanoakbb.com; info@rowanoakbb.com), 208 S. Fulton St., Salisbury 28144. $$$–$$$$. The Rowan Oak occupies an overwhelmingly Victorian mansion, complete with turret and wraparound veranda, in the heart of Salisbury's lovely historic district. Outside are well-kept gardens; inside, the public areas and four large guest rooms are decorated in high-Victorian style. The tariff includes WiFi, evening wine, and full breakfast served in the dining room.

🐾 **The Inn at Hickory** (828-431-4425; theinnathickory.com; relax@theinnathickory.com), 464 7th St. SW, Hickory 28602. $–$$; pet fee. This 1908 Colonial house sits in a residential neighborhood on the south edge of downtown Hickory, on 2 acres of landscaped grounds. One of the four attractively decorated rooms is pet-friendly, with a single small dog or cat allowed. WiFi is available. Breakfasts are made to your order, and can be delivered to your room or enjoyed in the dining room.

River Landing Inn, Saxapahaw (336-376-1502; riverlandinginn.com; matt@riverlandinginn.com), 5942 Whitney Rd., Graham 27253. $$. Set on 20 acres of land that back onto the scenic Haw River, noted for its canoeing, this four-room inn offers rural quiet, river access, and on-site walking paths as well as WiFi and a full breakfast.

✷ Where to Eat

DINING OUT **Old Salem Tavern, Winston-Salem** (336-748-8585; oldsalemtavern.com), 736 S. Main, Winston-Salem 27101. Lunch daily; dinner Mon.–Sat. $$–$$$$. The only restaurant in Old Salem sits deep in the village beside the 1784 tavern that forms part of the open air museum. The restaurant occupies an 1816 annex to the original tavern, and is carefully designed and staffed to reflect its origins. Lunch is busy and fast, emphasizing 18th-century Moravian foods and modern sandwiches. Dinner is leisurely and quiet, with a gourmet menu more modern in its approach, though Moravian and southern influences make their appearance. It has a good wine list with a number of choices under $25, and about a dozen wines available by the glass.

Christopher's, Winston-Salem (336-724-1395; christophersngc.com; info@christophersngc.com), 712 Brookstown Ave., Winston-Salem 27101. Open for dinner Mon.–Sat., and for Sun. brunch. $$$–$$$$. Located in a large late-Victorian house on the western edge of downtown, Christopher's offers novel recipes with fresh local ingredients, frequently with a southern twist. There's a piano bar and patio dining; the good wine list has one or two entries under $25 in nearly every category.

Ryan's Restaurant, Winston-Salem (336-724-6132; ryansrestaurant.com), 719 Coliseum Dr., Winston-Salem 27106. Dinner only, closed Sun. $$$$. Noted for its handsome wooded location with good views from the dining area's large windows, this high-end eatery is best noted for its steaks and seafood. Its wine list has received *Wine Spectator*'s Award of Excellence, with one or two wines under $25 in most categories. Casual dress is fine; reservations are not required, but are a good idea.

EATING OUT

Stamey's Old-Fashioned Barbeque, Greensboro (336-299-9888; stameys.com; feedback@stameys.com), 2206 High Point Rd., Greensboro 28754. Lunch and dinner. $. Warner Stamey was one of those folk selling barbeque from a tent outside the courthouse in the early years of the Depression. He got his own restaurant in 1938, and moved it to its present location in Greensboro in 1953; his grandchildren still run it, as well as another location near the Guildford Courthouse National Military Site on US 220. They remain the classic, standard Lexington Style, slow-cooked over hickory coals for 10 hours.

Lexington Barbeque (336-249-9814), 10 US 29/70 S., Lexington 27295. Lunch and dinner. $. Founded in 1962 by an apprentice of Warner Stamey named Wayne Monk, Lexington Barbeque is the main cathedral of the Western Style. It's a big white barn-like building on a hill. They let you specify which part of the pork shoulder you want. Despite its large size and rural location, lines are long on Friday and Saturday nights.

LEXINGTON-STYLE BARBEQUE

(barbecuefestival.com/history.html). The small county seat of Lexington has somewhere over 20 barbeque restaurants, or more than 1 per 1,000 residents. It isn't just this, however, that leads Lexington to declare itself the "Barbeque Capital of the World," nor is it the eight-block-long **Barbeque Festival** in October that draws 150,000 people in a single day. It's the distinctive Lexington (also called Western or Piedmont) method. Lexington barbeque cooks the pork shoulder—and only the shoulder—over hickory coals, so that the dripping fat is the only source of smoke. Some claim it must be unbasted, but others baste it with a sauce made from cider vinegar and ketchup. The pork is served chopped with no sauce on it, and the vinegar-ketchup is served on the side. The coleslaw is also made from the baste, and has no mayo in it.

There is also an Eastern barbeque, and no topic is more highly contested in North Carolina than the merits and shortcomings of these two competing regional styles. In the Eastern Style, a whole hog is cooked over greenwood and basted with a vinegar-pepper sauce—a more traditionally southern approach. The Lexington Style traces back only to the 1920s, when entrepreneurs sold it out of tents in front of the courthouse on court days, using only ingredients (including pork shoulder) they could get cheaply.

Well, there's only one way to find out which is better . . .

The Barbeque Center, Lexington (336-248-4633; barbecuecenter.com), 900 N. Main St., Lexington 27292. Lunch and dinner. $$. The only barbeque place on downtown Lexington's Main Street to use pit smoking over hickory wood has been in business at this location since the 1950s. It's a power behind the mammoth Lexington Barbeque Festival (held in the street in front), and a stalwart supporter of Western Style Barbeque Purity.

Liberty Oak, Greensboro (336-273-7057; libertyoakrestaurant.com), 100 W. Washington St. #D, Greensboro 27401. Lunch and dinner. $$–$$$. This attractive downtown café and bar blurs the line between our *Eating Out* and *Dining Out* categories. It has the ambience, quality, and exciting menu to justify a special occasion, while having plenty of low-cost choices, including comfort foods (labeled "Blue Plate Specials") and sandwiches on the dinner menu. Its large wine list has a number of good choices under $25.

Sweet Potatoes, Winston-Salem (336-727-4844; sweetpotatoes-arestaurant.com), 529 N. Trade St., Winston-Salem 27101. Lunch and dinner. $$. This downtown Winston-Salem favorite features inspired entrées based on Old South favorites. Lunch is down-home, with regional sandwiches and old-school dishes such as meat loaf, while the dinner menu is filled with colorful riffs on the old standards. The wine menu is imaginative and informative, with a good choice of local wines; its low prices push dinner into the "inexpensive" column.

Foothills Brewery, Winston-Salem (336-777-3348; foothillsbrewing.com; info@foothillsbrewing.com), 638 W. 4th St., Winston-Salem 27101. Lunch and dinner. $$. This is a good downtown bar, large and clean, with very decent pub grub. But the reason to go here, rather than nearby Sweet Potatoes with its superior menu, is its beer, brewed on the spot—some of the best in the state.

Old Hickory Tap Room (828-322-1965; oldehickorybrewery.com; agagner@webtv.net), 22 Union Square, Hickory 28601. Lunch and dinner. $$. This pleasant pub in downtown Hickory has a standard pub menu, well prepared, and the full selection of microbrews from local Olde Hickory Brewery, its owner.

✷ Entertainment

CLASSICAL Greensboro Symphony Orchestra (336-335-5456; greensborosymphony.org), 200 N. Davie St., Suite 328, Greensboro 27401. Founded in 1939, the Greensboro Symphony has 80 musicians performing at War Memorial Auditorium in the Greensboro Coliseum Complex at 1921 W. Lee St.

Winston-Salem Symphony (336-725-1035; wssymphony.org), 201 N. Broad St., Suite 200, Winston-Salem 27101. This 80-musician orchestra holds most of its concerts in downtown's Stevens Convention Center, at the corner of 4th and Marshall Streets.

Western Piedmont Symphony Orchestra (wpsymphony.org). Founded in 1964 and conducted by John Gordon Ross, Hickory's philharmonic orchestra has 70 musicians performing an eight-concert season.

POPULAR Greensboro's nightlife (greensboronc.org/nightlife.cfm). Here's a pleasant surprise—the Greensboro Convention and Visitors Bureau has extensive listings of places that offer live entertainment after dark. There's enough information here to make an intelligent choice, then actually find the place.

Winston-Salem's nightlife (visitwinstonsalem.com/visitor_center/vis_nightlife.html). Winston-Salem's club web page is also sponsored by its official tourism promoters, and the place to look for the venue you want. Downtown is where to find the most action. Check out **Foothills Brewery** for live local bands; two blocks east, **Speakeasy Jazz** offers live jazz and tapas.

Hickory Alive! (828-322-1121; downtownhickory.com, and click on "Festivals"; info@downtownhickory.com), Union Square, Hickory 28601. Performing June–July, Fri. nights 7–10. Free. The Hickory Downtown Development Association and the Jaycees usher in the weekends with live bands at downtown Union Square. Beer, wine, and food are available, and families with children are welcome.

✷ Selective Shopping

Reynolda Village (336-758-5584; reynoldavillage.com), 2201 Reynolda Rd., Winston-Salem 27106. The servants' quarters of R. J. Reynolds's once-huge estate of Reynolda, sandwiched between the Reynolda House Museum and Wake Forest University, now house a large and intriguing collection of fashionable shops and cafés. It's quite large, and worth visiting for the history and architecture alone (as well as the perspective on just how many employees it took to keep Reynolds's family comfy).

Hickory Furniture Mart (800-462-6278; 828-322-3510; hickoryfurniture.com; info@hickoryfurniture.com), 2220 US 70 SE, Hickory 28602. This huge indoor mall, located southeast of Hickory on US 70, has over 100 shops, representing more than 1,000 manufacturers, spread over four levels. Guest Services at each entrance help you plan your shopping, and there's a consolidated freight handler on-site to get all your purchases home. Other on-site services include a restaurant, a WiFi coffee bar, and the pet-friendly **Holiday Inn Express** hotel; there's even a furniture museum. For the truly committed, they offer combination shopping and hotel discounts, and a personal shopper program. Their parking lot can accommodate Class A RVs and tour buses. The "Shopping Tips" section on their website is worth a gander.

✷ Special Events

Mid-March: **Battle of Guilford Courthouse Reenactment**. This annual event takes place in the city of Greensboro's Country Park, adjacent to the actual battlefield.

Mid-April: **Hickory Hops Brew Festival** (828-322-1121; hickoryhops.com), downtown Hickory. This annual event, sponsored by downtown microbrewery Olde Hickory, features the products of 30 craft brewers, mainly from North Carolina—a good place to enjoy the start of spring and see what the region has to offer.

Last Saturday in October: **The Lexington Barbeque Festival** (barbecuefestival.com). Admission is free. Lexington, the self-appointed Barbeque Capital of the World, has been holding this eight-block festival every year since 1984, attracting 150,000 visitors to this tiny county seat.

Carolina Balloon Fest, Statesville Regional Airport, Statesville. Balloon festivals are always colorful fun, and worth a visit if you're in the area. This one is held at Statesville's small regional airport, between Winston-Salem and Hickory off I-40.

Christmas holidays: **Tanglewood Park Festival of Lights** (336-778-6300; co.forsyth.nc.us/Tanglewood), 4061 Clemmons Rd., Clemmons 27012. $$$. One of the South's largest Christmas lights festivals with 300,000 visitors, this annual drive-through has nearly 200 illuminations, more than 70 of them animated, along its 4-mile course. There are over 100 craft booths as well, and a 110-foot Christmas tree. It starts in early November.

THE CHARLOTTE REGION

Charlotte sits at the center of North Carolina's largest urban area, just north of the South Carolina state line, a sprawling metropolis extending 25 miles in all directions from town center. It was founded in 1755 by the uncle of future president James K. Polk (who was born nearby), and named after King George III's wife, Charlotte of Mecklenburg—thus its nickname, the Queen City. It came to prominence during the early 1800s as the site of America's first gold rush, when a young boy found a 17-pound gold nugget in a creek 24 miles east of town. Charlotte became a major city, however, in the period after the Civil War, as a place where the burgeoning textile industry could gain ready access to a major rail hub. In the late 20th century Charlotte became the headquarters of the nation's largest and fourth largest banks, Bank of America and Wachovia, respectively. Wachovia, however, failed to survive the 2008 credit collapse and was absorbed by Wells Fargo, so that Charlotte's brief reign as America's second largest financial center may well be over.

Charlotte is best known for its handsome and lively downtown, which the local tourism promoters insist on calling "uptown" as it sounds snazzier. (This chapter will use both terms interchangeably.) It is small but densely built, and filled with nightclubs, restaurants, galleries, and museums. Charlotte is also the heart and soul of NASCAR, America's professional stock-car racing circuit, with a large concentration of pro shops and museums around Lowe's Motor Speedway (formerly Concord Motor Speedway) in the city's northern suburbs. Historical sites are limited, but make up for it in quality—the boyhood log farmstead of James K. Polk, the early gold rush at Reed Gold Mine, and a reconstructed village of the pre-Columbian Mound Builders culture. Far to the east of Charlotte, the Seagrove Potteries continue two centuries of tradition.

Despite the area's massive sprawl, outdoor recreation is excellent. Three major reservoirs surround it on its west, with three more in wilder lands 50 miles to its east. The Blue Ridge Mountains reemerge as two sets of outliers: the Uwharrie Mountains, massive but low, 50 miles east of town, and Crowders Mountain, small but tall, 30 miles west of town. Both of these mountain-like areas have large trail networks in their extensive publicly owned lands. A city-bound visitor, however, doesn't have to travel that far to enjoy the outdoors, as Charlotte has a system of large urban nature preserves.

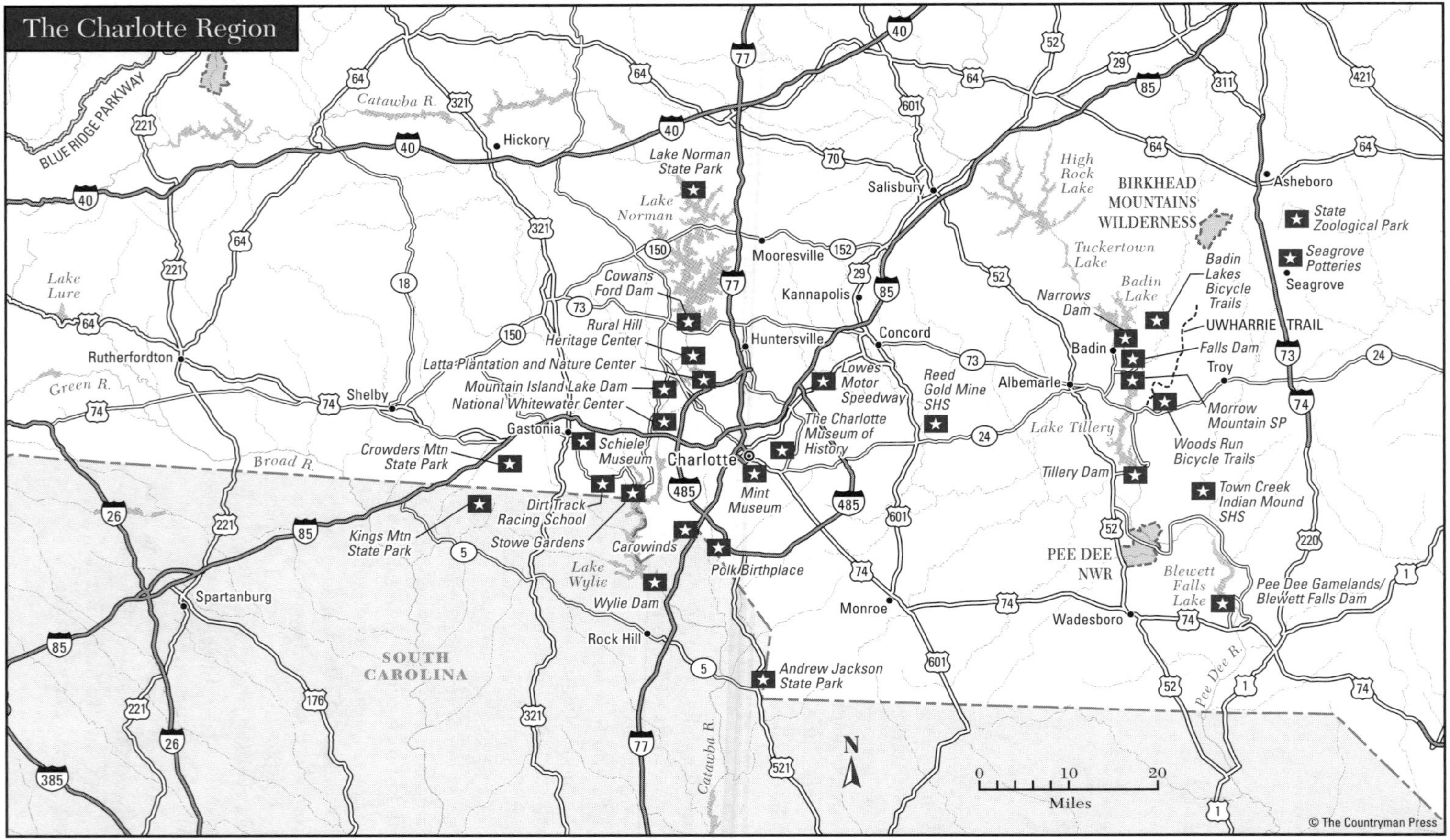
The Charlotte Region
BLUE RIDGE PARKWAY
Catawba R.
Hickory
Lake Norman State Park
Lake Norman
Salisbury
Asheboro
High Rock Lake
BIRKHEAD MOUNTAINS WILDERNESS
State Zoological Park
Seagrove Potteries
Seagrove
Tuckertown Lake
Badin Lake
Badin Lakes Bicycle Trails
UWHARRIE TRAIL
Narrows Dam
Badin
Falls Dam
Troy
Lake Lure
Rutherfordton
Mooresville
Kannapolis
Cowans Ford Dam
Rural Hill Heritage Center
Huntersville
Concord
Latta Plantation and Nature Center
Mountain Island Lake Dam
National Whitewater Center
Lowes Motor Speedway
Reed Gold Mine SHS
Albemarle
Morrow Mountain SP
Green R.
Shelby
Gastonia
The Charlotte Museum of History
Lake Tillery
Woods Run Bicycle Trails
Crowders Mtn State Park
Schiele Museum
Charlotte
Tillery Dam
Broad R.
Mint Museum
Town Creek Indian Mound SHS
Dirt Track Racing School
Kings Mtn State Park
Stowe Gardens
Carowinds
PEE DEE NWR
Polk Birthplace
Blewett Falls Lake
Pee Dee Gamelands/ Blewett Falls Dam
Lake Wylie
Spartanburg
Wylie Dam
Monroe
Wadesboro
Rock Hill
SOUTH CAROLINA
Andrew Jackson State Park
Pee Dee R.
Catawba R.
N
0 10 20
Miles
© The Countryman Press

GUIDANCE Visit Charlotte (800-231-4636; 704-331-2753; charlottesgotalot.com; info@visitcharlotte.com), 330 S. Tryon St., Charlotte 28202. Mon.–Fri. 8:30–5, Sat. 9–3. Once known as the Charlotte Convention and Visitors Bureau, Visit Charlotte promotes tourism in the urban area. Their visitors center is at the center of downtown.

Central Park, NC (910-428-9001; centralparknc.org), P.O. Box 159, Star 27356. Originally known as the Yadkin-Pee Dee Lakes Project, this organization promotes tourism and business in the extremely rural counties to the west of the Charlotte urban area. Although they do not operate a walk-in visitors center, their website is excellent.

GETTING THERE *By car:* Charlotte sits at the intersection of I-85 and I-77. US 74 links Charlotte with Wilmington and the coast; while much of it remains substandard (as of 2010), it is slowly being upgraded to expressway quality, one segment at a time.

By air: **Charlotte Douglas International Airport (CLT)** (704-359-4000; charmeck.org/Departments/Airport; info@charlotteairport.com), 5501 Josh Birmingham Pkwy., Charlotte 28208. This major airport is US Airways' largest hub, the 16th busiest airport in America, and the 28th busiest in the world. Its 11 airlines serve 134 nonstop destinations, including cities in Canada, Mexico, the Caribbean, Central America, and Europe.

By train: **Amtrak** (704-330-4667; amtrak.com), 1914 N. Tryon St., Charlotte 28206. Charlotte has some of the best Amtrak service in the South, with three separate trains, each running through town once a day in each direction: The Crescent (New Orleans to New York), the Carolinian (Charlotte to New York), and the Piedmont (Charlotte to Raleigh). So, you get three trains a day northward as far as Raleigh, with two of them continuing to New York, plus one train a day southward to Atlanta and New Orleans. The depot is a squat 1960s structure in a rail yard 1.5 miles northeast of downtown.

By bus: Charlotte's **Greyhound** (greyhound.com) bus terminal is located downtown, two blocks north of the football stadium. Bus routes extend north toward Greensboro and Washington; south to Columbia, Charleston, Savannah, and Florida; southwest to Greenville and Atlanta; and west to Asheville and points beyond.

Local bus service, run by the Charlotte Area Transit System, hubs out of a huge, newly built covered bus shed on the eastern edge of downtown. Across the street from it sits the main terminal for Lynx, a commuter light rail system. At this time (2010), Lynx consists of the Blue Line, which runs southward about 10 miles to a large mall at I-485's exit 65, with 15 stations along the way. In addition, a historic-style streetcar uses the Lynx tracks on weekends, shuttling up and down along downtown's eastern edge with 11 stops. Plans to expand Lynx are being made, but are unfunded.

MEDICAL EMERGENCIES Carolina Medical Center (704-355-2000; carolinasmedicalcenter.org), 1000 Blythe Blvd., Charlotte 2820. Located on the eastern edge of downtown Charlotte, this 861-bed hospital has a Level 1 trauma center. It is the flagship campus of Carolina Healthcare Systems, with 23 hospitals the third largest public health care system in the nation.

✷ Exploring the Area

EXPLORING BY CAR A Pee Dee River drive. The Piedmont countryside can be lovely, but it unfortunately tends to lack the sort of travel destinations that get listed in a guide like this. This 82-mile drive makes the scenery itself the destination—some of the finest between the mountains and the coast. There are some neat places to stop along the way as well. It parallels the beautiful and remote **Pee Dee River**, starting 64 miles east of downtown Charlotte as US 74 crosses the Pee Dee. You'll view this beautiful river, see some impressive dams, get a chance to explore riverine forests and look for wildlife, drive up the tallest peak in the Uwharrie Mountains, and visit an unusual small town. At its finish, you'll be 57 miles northeast of Charlotte.

As you drive out from Charlotte you'll get no view over the Pee Dee River—a terrible way to start a river drive. *So go across the Pee Dee on US 74, then in 0.2 mile turn left onto Old Charlotte Highway (SSR 1140) and retrace your steps over the river* for some good views upstream. After the bridge *make a right turn onto Power Plant Road (SSR 1748) to its end in 2.7 miles.* Here you will find the business end of the large **Blewett Falls Lake Dam**, where the hydroelectric station sits over the dam outfall. Catwalks provide access to fishermen and sightseers along this impressive structure, while paths lead through trees to the riverbank. *Retrace your steps and take a left onto Old Charlotte Highway, then go 2.3 miles to a right onto Blewett Falls Road (SSR 1141) and take it to its end in 4.7 miles.* Now you are at the opposite end of the dam, with superb views unobstructed by fences, with a rough boat ramp on the downstream side. *Retrace your steps for 1.7 miles to a left onto Ford Hill Road (SSR 1144)*, an exceptionally beautiful forest drive with some impressive views. *In 2.8 miles turn left onto Holly Grove Church Road (SSR 1146) for 1.9 miles, then turn left onto Grassy Island Road for 12.6 miles to a left onto NC 109.* This fine section continues through forests, with some good views as you gain Grassy Island Road, then some very attractive riverside scenery as you reach and pass the Grassy Islands of the Pee Dee, now open public lands. Beyond, the forests very gradually give way to farmlands, with large unfenced fields of cotton and wheat. *Follow NC 109 for 3.5 miles*, crossing the Pee Dee with more river views, then *turn right onto SSR 1634 (also named Grassy Island Road but a different road) for 4.6 miles.* This traverses the 8,400-acre **Pee Dee National Wildlife Refuge**, created in 1963 from Piedmont farmland, some of it still in grain crops for the benefit of migrating birds—a fine place to explore, with dirt roads and hiking paths galore. *Turn right onto Pinkston River Road (SSR 1627)*, a stunning rural drive marked as a state scenic byway, and the visual climax of this drive. *This ends in 4.8 miles, at US 52.*

The second half, while less continuously stunning than the first, has its points. *Turn right onto US 52, and go north 4.1 miles to a right onto NC 731; proceed 3.2 miles, crossing the Pee Dee River, to a left onto Tillery Dam Road (SSR 1187).* Once again your Pee Dee crossing will give you good river views, with a bonus of being able to see **Norwood Dam** as well, as it creates long, skinny **Lake Tillery**. *Take Tillery Dam Road uphill for 0.7 mile, crossing a railroad and passing through an open yellow gate.* As you approach the railroad, a left turn will take you 0.25 mile to the base of this imposing cement structure, where fishermen's access again gives you good views. *Turn right onto Hydro Road (SSR 1188), then go 1.2 miles to a right onto Lilys Bridge Road (SSR 1110), then go 6.3 miles to a left onto NC 73,*

This pleasant stretch is unremarkable, except for a handsome spot where the road crosses an arm of the lake. *Go 1.1 miles to a left onto NC 24.* Here you'll get another bridge view of the Pee Dee, this time over Lake Tillery. The **Uwharrie National Scenic Trail**'s southern terminus is just 2 miles to your right on NC 24. *Go 3.8 miles to a right onto Valley Drive (SSR 1720),* passing over the Pee Dee River with more good views from the bridge. *Take Valley Drive 3.3 miles,* a very pretty drive through farmland, *to a right onto Morrow Mountain Road (SSR 1798).* You are now in **Morrow Mountain State Park**, which preserves a small group of Blue Ridge outliers. Park roads lead to the highest point, 936-foot Morrow Mountain with rustic picnic shelters and wide views, then around to the Pee Dee River with paths and a boat launch, finally reaching a restored farmstead and historic museum. *This totals 11.1 miles before you return to Valley Drive and turn right, then go 2.6 miles to Badin and NC 740, the end of the drive.* **Badin** is an Alcoa company town built in 1913, very attractive and charming; its unusual architecture comes from its original owner, a large French conglomerate, and reflects continental European approaches. Ahead on NC 740 are views over **Lake Badin**; behind, on Falls Road (SSR 1719), you can reach **Falls Lake**, the Piedmont's most beautiful reservoir, in a 2.3-mile dead end.

EXPLORING ON FOOT **The Uwharrie National Recreation Trail**. Created by a local Boy Scout troop in 1975, this 20-mile trail explores the backbone of the Uwharrie Mountains, the Blue Ridge's easternmost outlier, through the center of the Uwharrie National Forest. Don't start this trail expecting a mountain experience, however, as the worn-down peaks along this path struggle to reach 900 feet in elevation and can't ever seem to gain as much as 500 feet of climb. Its main fascination is the peculiar geology and environment found on these broken stubs, and the remarkably steep, rocky, and broken terrain found in a number of sections. Nearly the entire trail is forest-covered, dominated by young pines; look for subtle differences in short distances, environments changing with geology. While a strong walker might be able to complete the trail in a day (with a car shuttle), it's better enjoyed as an overnighter.

Its southern and northern endpoints offer some good opportunities for short exploratory walks. From its southern end, 60 miles east of Charlotte via NC 24 (and 11 miles east of Albemarle), the trail leads directly into an unusual broken land of very steep, but small, peaks separated by narrow defiles, with about 400 feet of relief from bottom to top. The path immediately drops into one such defile, skirts around into a second, then climbs 300 feet to the top of one of the little "mountains" before dropping (just as steeply) into a third defile—all in the first 4 miles. The northern end, at Flint Hill Road (SSR 1306) (consult a local map for directions), leads very steeply uphill to the top of 953-foot Dark Mountain, a 0.6-mile (one-way) climb with a good view along the way.

Hiking Crowders Mountain (ncparks.gov/Visit/parks/crmo/main.php; southcarolinaparks.com/park-finder/state-park/945.aspx). This Blue Ridge outlier 30 miles west of Charlotte is called Crowders Mountain, then Kings Mountain as it extends a short distance into South Carolina. It consists of a single ridgeline, very steep and with a number of cliffs, that extends southwest from Gastonia, 12 miles long and 2 miles wide. Its peaks reach as high as 1,700 feet above sea level, but are separated by deep gaps; local relief ranges from 200 feet in the gaps to 1,000 feet

CROWDERS MOUNTAIN STATE PARK

at the tallest peak, Kings Pinnacle. The entire arc is protected by a series of public lands, **Crowders Mountain State Park** in North Carolina, and **Kings Mountain National Military Park** and **Kings Mountain State Park** in South Carolina.

Hiking trails follow the ridgeline from one end to another for a continuous hiking experience up to 30 miles long. The northern end, in Crowders Mountain State Park, is the most mountainous and the most popular, starting with an 800-foot climb in only 0.5 mile on Backside Trail to gain the narrow ridge. From there it continues with rocky clambers and great views along Rocktop Trail, Crowders Trail, and Pinnacle Trail—all the same crestline trail, really—to reach Ridgeline Trail, completed in 2009 specifically to link with the South Carolina parks. By late 2010 or so, the final missing link should take you across the border to the 16-mile Kings Mountain Loop Trail, passing through both South Carolina parks. If you're looking for a good day hike with stunning views, however, the northernmost mile makes a fine choice.

EXPLORING BY BICYCLE **Bicycle paths in the Charlotte area** (parkandrec.com/greenways; tarheeltrailblazers.com). There are a variety of dedicated trails within the Charlotte urban area. For street bicyclists, a network of greenways now exceeds 30 miles in more than a dozen separate places, and will eventually interconnect to form a 190-mile network; while no segment is now long enough to rate a separate mention in this book, construction to link various segments is actively under way and the situation may be better when you visit. For mountain bikers, the **U.S. National Whitewater Center** has an extensive system of free trails, plus bike rentals (see *To Do*). In addition, mountain bike trails are found in a number of Mecklenburg County's nature preserves (see *Green Spaces*). Charlotte's mountain bike club the Tarheel Trailblazers has complete details on their website.

Mountain biking in the Uwharrie National Forest (sorbauwharrie.org). Farther afield, the Uwharrie National Forest offers two large areas with extensive mountain bike trails; local relief here is only a few hundred feet at a time, but can be extremely steep. The **Badin Lake Trails** wind through a large (perhaps 30-square-mile) area to the immediate west of Badin Lake. Trails tend to be easy to moderate, with 10 of the 40 miles of blazed mountain bike trail rated as difficult or very difficult; while there is plenty of steep terrain, most of it is reserved for ATVers. While you have to share the Bladen Lakes Trails with horses and hikers, the **Woods Run Bike Trails**, with 11 miles of blazed trail, are bicycle-only. These explore the same broken area as the southern terminus of the **Uwharrie National Recreation Trail**, and share the same trailhead. The local mountain biking club, SORBA Uwharrie, has a good website with trail information and downloadable maps.

✷ Towns and Villages

Charlotte, North Carolina's largest city, is a giant circular splat on the landscape, 2,000 square miles of late-20th-century sprawl. There are some real gems embedded in this distinctly bland matrix—museums, nature parks, historic sites, and a humongous motor speedway—but downtown remains its chief treasure. Relabeled "uptown" about 20 years ago by tourism promoters, it hardly needs any such verbal gilding. It's the home of a dozen major corporations, starting with a bunch on the Fortune 500 list and going down to such southern favorites as Bojangles, Lance, and Carolina Beverage, makers of Cheer Wine and Sun Drop sodas. Not surprisingly, uptown Charlotte is an agglomeration of very large and very showy skyscrapers, dominated by the 60-story Bank of America Corporate Center, an omigosh postmodern Industrial Gothic structure topped with a huge glass crown illuminated internally. Walk into the lobby to admire the fresco by Ben Long, and then wander the streets for a truly stunning succession of public art pieces. Uptown really comes alive after dark, however, as its large assortment of trendy (and very pricey) restaurants and nightclubs start to fill up. None of this takes up a lot of space—just three blocks along Tryon Street both north and south of Trade Street (the center of town since its founding in 1755), plus the parallel six blocks to the east. These 14 blocks have an amazing number of things to do and buildings to gawk at; to really appreciate it, get the walking guide from **Visit Charlotte** on Tryon Street, three blocks south of Trade Street.

Concord and Kannapolis. These adjacent towns sit 20 miles northeast of Charlotte, astride the historic railroad corridor that arcs from Charlotte to Greensboro, Burlington, and Durham, the center of the once-mighty southern textile industry. They both date from the late 1880s when entrepreneur James William Cannon founded the Cannon Mills Company, leading maker of terry cloth until its takeover and bankruptcy in the early 21st century. The massive mills, one of which was larger than the Pentagon, have now mainly been torn down. Concord is the site of Lowes Motor Speedway.

Albemarle. This attractive small town will be your gateway to the Uwharrie Mountains. Its downtown is very attractive, a classic small town. However, you will mainly be interested in it when you are exploring the nearby scenic and outdoor attractions: the Uwharrie Mountains, and the lakes of the Pee Dee River. It has all the normal franchise restaurants and motels.

✱ Green Spaces

PUBLIC LANDS The Uwharrie Mountains. The last and lowest of the Blue Ridge outliers, the Uwharries nevertheless cover a very large area, much of it public land in the form of Uwharrie National Forest and Morrow Mountain State Park. They were formed about half a billion years ago as a string of coastal volcanoes, rather like Japan today, but with peaks up to 20,000 feet. Today, however, they are mere stumps, struggling to reach 1,000 feet and never more than about 500 feet above their valleys. While there are some broad views, most notably from the picnic area atop Murrow Mountain, the Uwharries are best explored for their diverse environments and strangely broken geology. The 5,025-acre **Birkhead Mountain Wilderness**, created by Congress in 1984, preserves a large area of old-growth forest, a good place for hiking and camping. The larger mountains, and more dramatic geological formations, are farther south in the national forest, reachable via the Uwharrie National Recreation Trail.

Pee Dee National Wildlife Refuge (704-694-4424; fws.gov/peedee), 5770 US 52 N., Wadesboro 28170. Open daily, from an hour before sunrise to an hour after sunset. Admission is free. This intriguing tract, created by the federal government in 1963, preserves more than 8,000 acres of mixed Piedmont ecosystems. Unlike the nearby Uwharrie National Forest, much of this land has been kept in crops to better support the wildlife; from an automobile, this yields the sort of open scenery that was common half a century ago. Trails and jeep tracks lead to the Pee Dee River, impounded streams, Piedmont brooks with their unique forests intact, and upland forests. Hikers and other recreationalists are welcome during the off-season, and on Sundays during the hunting season (October to December; wear hunter orange in case poachers are present). Their brochure, downloadable from their website, has a map of the refuge's roads, trails, and points of interest.

Morrow Mountain State Park (704-982-4402; ncparks.gov/Visit/parks/momo/main.php; morrow.mountain@ncmail.net), 49104 Morrow Mountain Rd., Albemarle 28001. Open daily, Nov.–Feb, 8–6; Mar.–May, 8–8; Jun.–Aug., 8–9; Sept.–Oct., 8–8. Admission is free. This state park, founded in 1939, protects the westernmost extension of the Uwharrie Mountains, a group of four low peaks isolated from the bulk of the range by a curve of the Pee Dee River. For the most part this is a mature mixed forest over steep sloped hills, explored by a network of trails and 5.5 miles of paved scenic road. The top attraction (literally as well as figuratively) is the peak of Morrow Mountain, the highest in the park. Its views are far more impressive than you would expect from its 936 feet, as they extend far out over the Piedmont, and are beautifully framed by trees and boulders. The summit is topped by a classic CCC (Civilian Conservation Corps) picnic area built when the park was first opened. At the base of the mountain a large boat ramp gives access to (and views of) Lake Tillery's upper reaches, here set in a mountain gorge. Finally, the park holds the farmstead of pioneer doctor Francis Kron, including his home, office, and infirmary restored to their 1870 appearance.

Crowders Mountain State Park (704-853-5375; ncparks.gov/Visit/parks/crmo/main.php; crowders.mountain@ncmail.net), 522 Park Office Lane, Kings Mountain 28086. Open daily, Nov.–Feb, 8–6; Mar.–Apr., 8–8; May–Aug., 8–9; Sept.–Oct., 8–8. Admission is free. This 6,800-acre park protects the North Carolina portions of Kings Mountain, a prominent Blue Ridge outlier, located some 30 miles west of Charlotte. Unlike the Uwharries, these look like proper mountains with cliff-sided peaks that climb as much as 1,000 feet above the surrounding valleys. The northern portion is the most rugged, with 100 climbing routes as well as wide views from the network of hiking trails; it's also very popular, and the lookout at the peak of Crowders Mountain can become crowded. The central portion contains the picnic area on a small fishing lake, and more views from King's Pinnacle. South of that the mountains become shorter and more stump-like, as the park continues southward to the state line, abutting South Carolina's King Mountain State Park. The **Ridgeline Trail** follows the entire ridgeline and (by the time you read this) should extend deep into the South Carolina portion of the mountains. If you're interested in climbing, check out CrowdersMountain.com, an enthusiast's site.

PARKS AND GARDENS **Carolina Raptor Center** (704-875-6521; carolinaraptorcenter.org), 6000 Sample Rd., Huntersville 28078. Open Mon.–Sat. 10–5, Sun. noon–5; hours may be restricted during winter. $$. Founded in 1980 by faculty and students of the University of North Carolina–Charlotte's Biology Department, this rescue organization has grown and thrived at its dedicated 57-acre facility within the **Latta Plantation Nature Preserve**. While rescue-and-release remains one of their primary concerns, they display unreleasable birds along a network of trails as an educational exhibit. This is not a small facility; the twisting trails pass by around 20 different species of hawks, owls, and vultures, allowing close viewing and photography; in all, more than 100 injured or imprinted individuals are housed here at any one time. Their website is filled with information on raptors, including the two bald eaglets they proudly raised and released, the first in North Carolina.

Daniel Stowe Botanical Garden (704-825-4490; dsbg.org; info@dsbg.org), 6500 S. New Hope Rd., Belmont 28012. Open daily, 9–5. $$$. This very large garden sits by Lake Wylie, 22 miles east of Charlotte on NC 279 (best reached, however, via NC 273, from I-85's exit 27 to its end at NC 279, then right). It's comparatively new and still adding new features, but already well justifies its admission. Dedicated to preserving and highlighting the Piedmont environment, it features elaborate fountains, a canal-side garden, and a first-class orchid conservatory. They welcome picnickers to spread a blanket anywhere on the grounds, which is just as well as there is no restaurant.

Mecklenburg County Nature Preserves (parkandrec.com/Parks). Open sunrise–sunset; gates open by 7:30 AM. Admission is free. Mecklenburg County's Division of Parks and Recreation maintains an amazing 6,000 acres of nature preserves within the city of Charlotte's immediate urban area, including a campground, and three nature centers. The 12 tracts are widely spread and extremely varied, ranging in size from a couple of dozen acres up to 1,300 acres. Access is by formal trail only, but with 30 miles of trail you'll have plenty of choices. Consult their website for maps and trails of the park nearest you.

RIVERS **Pee Dee River**. When the Yadkin River merges with the Uwharrie River, its name changes to the Pee Dee. From here the river flows another 56 miles to the South Carolina state line, then continues another 150 miles to the Atlantic Ocean near Georgetown, South Carolina. Interestingly, it has run through three names since 1891(as determined by the U.S. Board on Geographic Names), starting with Pedee in 1891, then Peedee in 1912, and finally settling on Pee Dee only in 1928 (and its South Carolina portion has changed a fourth time, to Great Pee Dee in 1979). Its namesake is the Pee Dee (or Pedee or Peedee) tribe, local to this area.

This is a beautiful, large river, and makes for fine canoeing. You can launch at the upstream end from Murrow Mountain State Park for a 2-mile float to the head of Tillery Lake; this first 10 miles takes you through a gorge carved into the Uwharrie Mountains. A developed portage trail eases you over Lake Tillery's dam, and this is followed by 20 miles of superb Piedmont rural scenery, including a 4-mile passage through the Pee Dee National Wildlife Refuge, to the head of Blewett Falls Lake. Here the riverbanks become gorge-like and forested once more. A developed portage trail takes you over Blewett Falls Dam, to the final section of the Pee Dee in North Carolina, 15 miles of beautiful Piedmont countryside. Your next take-out spot is 8 miles farther down, at Cheraw, South Carolina.

The **Catawba River** flows through the western, urbanized section of this chapter, reaching within 9 miles of the city of Charlotte. Like the Pee Dee River, the Catawba is named after a local tribe—but there the similarity ends. Within this chapter only 1 mile of the Catawba flows freely; the rest of the river is impounded in three large reservoirs created and owned by Charlotte-based Duke Energy (founded in 1905 specifically for that purpose). The scenery is overwhelmingly residential and industrial, except for several miles at the head of Lake Norman, kept in forest as Lake Norman State Park, and a forested stretch of Mountain Island Lake, much of which is protected in two large Mecklenburg County nature preserves. This is a wonderful river for powerboaters, fishermen, and skiers, but not so great for canoeists, sightseers, or nature lovers.

LAKES Lake Norman (Catawba River) (lakenormansweb.com; duke-energy.com/lakes/facts-and-maps/lake-norman.asp). The largest lake wholly within North Carolina, Lake Norman has more than 50 square miles of surface and 520 miles of shoreline. It's a hydropower lake, held back by Cowans Ford Dam, a 1963 concrete structure that's 130 feet high and 0.25 mile long, clearly visible from NC 73, 5.4 miles west of I-77's exit 25. Apart from the hydroelectric station by the dam, there's also a nuclear station just to the east on NC 73 (with a visitors center), and a coal-fired generator (called a "steam station") at the northern end of the lake.

In all, the lake is 34 miles long and up to 8 miles wide, with a shoreline that's hilly and deeply indented. Once very rural in character, it's now entirely inside the Charlotte urban area, and what lakeshore hasn't been covered with suburbs is lined by second homes. The exception: 13 miles of heavily forested shoreline are protected within Lake Norman State Park (once known as Duke Power State Park), with hiking and biking trails, picnicking, camping, swimming, canoe rentals, and boat launching. For the automobile-bound the lake can be quite a barrier, its first crossing being 15 miles upstream from its dam, and its next crossing another 9 miles above that. If you have a boat, though, it's great fun, as the many marinas testify. It has 28 access points, 13 of them in public parks, all listed in the website above.

Mountain Island Lake (Catawba River) (duke-energy.com/lakes/facts-and-maps/mountain-island.asp). Built in 1924, this hydropower lake sits immediately downstream from Lake Norman, its concrete dam and hydro station not accessible to the public. You'll find it to be a thin ribbon, 12 miles long and 0.25 mile wide, with steeply sloping banks mostly covered in forests. This is the wildest (or perhaps "least urban") of the three Catawba lakes in this region, as about a third of its shoreline is protected in Mecklenburg County nature preserves. There are five access points, all of them in public parks.

Lake Wylie (Catawba River) (duke-energy.com/lakes/facts-and-maps/lake-wylie.asp). First built in 1904, the was rebuilt (and the lake expanded) in 1928 by Duke Energy (then Duke Power). Smaller than Lake Norman yet still very large, Lake Wylie covers 21 square miles astride the South Carolina state line, with 325 miles of shoreline. The lake is long and skinny, sending several arms deep into the Carolina countryside. Shoreline scenery tends to be forests mixed with homes in its northern, upstream reaches, becoming mostly residential as the lake pokes southward into South Carolina. It has 15 access points, of which 6 are in North Carolina. The impressive dam, 1,200 feet across with a right-angled bend in the middle, is not open to the public but can be viewed from an informal fisherman's access point. (Take I-77 south into South Carolina to its exit 85, then go west on SC 160 to a left onto SC 49, then go 1.2 miles to a right onto New Gray Rock Road; the access point is left at the right-angled curve in 1.6 miles.)

Badin Lake (Yadkin River) (alcoa.com/yadkin/en/lakes/narrows.asp). Alcoa constructed this 8-square-mile reservoir in 1917, one of four still owned by them and until very recently used to power their smelter at Badin on the lake's downstream end. It's officially named Narrows Reservoir, but only Alcoa seems to use that name. Badin Lake is vaguely Y-shaped, typically 0.5 mile to 1 mile wide, with 115 miles of largely forested shoreline. The Uwharrie Mountains adjoin its eastern shore, making for some very attractive scenery. Its dam, named Narrows Dam, is a 216-foot-high concrete structure, visually impressive but with land access closed to the public; to see it, canoe to it from Falls Lake. You can access Badin Lake on its west side at the town of Badin, or on its east side at the USDA Forest Service's Arrowhead Campground in the Uwharrie National Forest.

Falls Reservoir (Yadkin River) (alcoa.com/yadkin/en/lakes/falls.asp). This region's smallest and most scenic reservoir (one of the prettiest man-made lakes in the state) sits immediately below Badin Lake and its Narrows Dam in a deep and constricted mountain gorge. Built by Alcoa in 1919, this lake is 2.6 miles long and from 100 to 300 yards wide, for a total surface of only 204 acres and a shoreline of 6 miles. Here the river cuts cleanly through the Uwharrie Mountains, so that the lake is lined by cliffs and near-cliffs up to 500 feet in height. Access is via a boat ramp at the end of Falls Road (SSR 1719), which starts at Badin's town center. As with Badin Lake's dam, Falls Reservoir's dam has no land access, but can be reached by canoeing a mile upstream from Murrow Mountain State Park.

Blewett Falls Lake (Pee Dee River). This long, narrow lake stretches for 11 miles through a very remote area, with typical widths of 0.25 to 0.5 mile. It breaks through Pea Ridge and Ingram Mountain, a low Blue Ridge outlier related to the Uwharries, creating some stunning scenery. Its shoreline is almost completely undeveloped and largely public, run by the state as the Pee Dee Game Lands, with numerous lakeside campsites and four boat ramps. Snags are common even at full pool, making this lake more appropriate for canoes and johnboats than for larger powerboats. The huge dam, built in 1912 by a predecessor company of its current owner, Progress Energy, is 0.6 mile long with a Gothic-style hydroplant perched over the spillway, an impressive sight and easily visited (see *Exploring by Car*).

Lake Tillery (Pee Dee River) (ncwildlife.org/Boating_Waterways/BAA_West_Piedmont_Region.htm). Progress Energy (then called Carolina Power and Light) created Lake Tillery in 1928 by constructing Tillery Dam, a 0.5-mile-long concrete-and-earth structure. It's a very skinny lake, covering 8.2 square miles with 104 miles of shoreline. Lake Tillery fills the same mountain gorge as Falls Reservoir and floods all the way to the foot of Falls Dam, but has a much lower and more rolling shoreline. Consequently, Lake Tillery has a considerable amount of second-home development along its shoreline, making it a good place to look for a vacation rental. The lake has seven public access points (including two private marinas), as well as canoe portage around the dam; the website gives directions to the four large paved ramps maintained by the state.

✷ To See

The Wells Fargo Cultural Campus. Started in 2005 by the now-defunct Wachovia Bank and then called the First Street Cultural Campus, this one-block area, completed as this book hits the stands, contains three major museums and a dance theater, centered on a 48-story glass tower, the Duke Energy Center. A 46-story condominium tower was planned and is still possible, but has been put on indefinite hold after the 2008 collapse of the economy (as well as its developer, Wachovia). The complex is adjacent to the NASCAR Hall of Fame as well as the city's civic center. It's worth visiting just for the architecture, stunningly postmodern from the most exuberant heights of the bubble.

The Harvey B. Gantt Center for African American Arts + Culture (704-547-3700; ganttcenter.org), 551 S. Tryon St., Charlotte 28202. Tue.–Sat. 10–5, Sun. 1–5. $$. Named after Charlotte's first African American mayor, the Gantt Center (as it is commonly known) moved into its stunning new building in 2009, the first building to open as part of the Wells Fargo Cultural Campus. It features three inside galleries, centering on the amazing John and Vivian Hewitt Collection, amassed by a middle-class Pennsylvania couple who simply fell in love with this art and discovered (in the 1960s and '70s) that they could afford it; Gantt Center will now be its permanent home. There are also two areas of outdoor galleries, as well as a regular schedule of dance, theater, and workshops. The Gantt Center is part of the Wells Fargo Cultural Campus.

The Mint Museum (704-337-2000; mintmuseum.org), 2730 Randolph Rd., Charlotte 28207. Open Tue. 10–9, Wed.–Sat. 10–5. $$; admission is free on Tue., and includes all museums on the same day. Charlotte's major art museum has three distinct campuses. The original Mint Museum was built in 1836 as part of the U.S. Mint, striking coins made from the region's vast gold deposits. One century later this handsome early Federalist building was slated for demolition; Charlotte art lovers purchased it, moved it from downtown to its present spot 2.7 miles east, and reopened it as an art museum. This original campus remains dedicated to fine arts, while the museum has opened a new facility uptown that it dedicates to regional craft and design specialties. The newly opened Mint Museum of Craft + Design presents five stories and 145,000 square feet dedicated to American and contemporary art, as well as fine crafts and design in the heart of the southern textile belt.

The Mint's third museum opened in the Wells Fargo Cultural Campus in late 2010. You'll find it a large modernist structure whose four-story slabs of yellow concrete are pierced by glass balconies and a 60-foot atrium. Its third and fourth floor expand the exhibits at the other two museums.

The Bechtler Museum of Modern Art (bechtler.org; info@bechtler.org), 420 S. Tryon St., Charlotte 28202. Open Mon. 10–6, Wed.–Sat 10–6, Sun. noon–5. $$. This museum features the mid-20th-century art collection of Andreas Bechtler, with more than 1,400 items including works by Picasso, Miró, Calder, Le Corbusier, and Warhol. The terra-cotta-clad building features a fourth-story gallery cantilevered over a plaza, with a glass atrium extending through its core.

The Knight Theater (blumenthalcenter.org, choose "Visiting," then "Theaters"). One of the **Blumenthal Center**'s six venues, the 1,100-seat glass-clad Knight specializes in dance and music, and is the permanent home of the North Carolina Dance Theater.

CULTURAL SITES **NoDa—North Davidson Street Art District** (noda.org). In 1903 Charlotte's first electrified mill opened alongside a railroad yard 3 miles north of downtown. Other mills followed, and a thriving working-class district was in full swing by the 1920s. Today this district is emerging as the center of a thriving art community, centered on the historic mills and modest shopping district of the old mill workers' neighborhood. You'll find about a dozen studios and galleries, and about the same number of cafés, music, and theater venues. A number of the mills survive as well, converted into apartments and condos. It's a good place to spend a pleasant afternoon, followed by a nice dinner.

The Light Factory (704-333-9755; lightfactory.org; info@lightfactory.org), Spirit Square, Suite 211, 345 N. College St., Charlotte 28202. Open Mon.–Sat. 9–6, Sun. 1–6. Admission is free. Founded in 1972 as a professional photographers' cooperative, this gallery presents fine photography prints from regional artists, traveling exhibitions, and independent cinema.

The Scheile Museum of Natural History (704-866-6900; schielemuseum.org), 1500 E. Garrison Blvd., Gastonia 28054. Open Mon.–Sat. 9–5, Sun. 1–5. $$. Located in a residential section of Gastonia, about 20 miles west of Charlotte, the Scheile goes far beyond what you would expect from a local nature museum. In its large modern building, dioramas present the stories of North Carolina's natural habitats and ocean floor, as well as the Everglades, the Sonoran Desert, and the Alaskan tundra. Other exhibits present North American wild animals in their context, and the extinct environments discovered by paleontologists. A final permanent exhibit explores American Indian culture. There's a planetarium, and changing special exhibits. Outside, a 0.75-mile nature trail leads through exhibits that re-create a pre-Columbian Catawba village and an 18th-century pioneer farm complete with sheep, chickens, and cattle.

HISTORIC SITES **Levine Museum of the New South** (704-333-1887; museumofthenewsouth.org), 200 E. 7th St., Charlotte 28202. Open Mon.–Sat 10–5, Sun. noon–5. $$. In 1865 the people of a destroyed South, mired in a ruined economy and a lawless countryside, faced one another across racial and class divides. Within a generation, however, the southern people had begun inventing an entirely new economy for themselves, and with it a new social order. Boosters dubbed it "the

THE SEAGROVE POTTERY DISTRICT

(seagrovepotteryheritage.com; discoverseagrove.com; ncpotterycenter.com). Located 75 miles east of Charlotte off I-73's exit 45, Seagrove has been a center of handmade pottery since colonial times. The continuity is remarkable; original pre-Revolutionary potter families—the Owenses, the Lucks, the Leagues—have produced Seagrove wares without any break for well over two centuries. Excellent local clays and good access to local markets kept them in business throughout the 19th century. Then, in the early 20th century, New York folk art specialists opened Jugtown Pottery (which still exists) to produce wares for northern collectors. As the fame of Seagrove ware spread, the area has attracted outside potters as well, and today more than 100 potters call it home.

SEAGROVE POTTER BOYD OWENS MIXES LOCAL CLAYS BY HAND

Nearly without exception, these potters welcome the public into their studios, a unique experience for casual shoppers and an invaluable aid to the serious collector. The town itself is hardly more than a wide spot in NC 705 a mile west of I-73; nearly all of the potteries are scattered about the area on back roads. At the town center are two pottery museums, the **North Carolina Pottery Center** (which is larger and charges a $2 admission) and the **North Carolina Museum of Traditional Pottery** (which is smaller and free). Either will get you properly oriented and pointed toward the potters you find most interesting. In addition, two of Seagrove's potteries sponsor their own on-property museums, **Ben Owen Pottery** (2199 NC 705, benowenpottery.com), and **Jugtown Pottery** (330 Jugtown Rd., jugtownware.com). Splitting the distance between these two is the area's oldest pottery, **the Original Owens Pottery** (3728 Busbee Rd., originalowenspottery.com), operated by the same family in the same buildings since 1895.

New South," and the phrase remains a useful term for describing the period. And when did it end? Well, it hasn't, yet.

Founded in 1990, the Levine Museum presents the experience of the southern people during this transformation—poor as well as rich, black as well as white—from their newly built 40,000-square-foot facility in downtown Charlotte. Their permanent exhibit, Cotton Fields to Skyscrapers, features interactive exhibits including a tenant farmer's cabin, an early Belks department store, and a lunch counter from the civil rights era.

Historic Latta Plantation (704-875-2312; lattaplantation.org), 5225 Sample Rd., Huntersville 28078. Open Tue.–Sat. 10–5, Sun. 1–5. House tours at the top of the hour, starting an hour after opening. $$. This early antebellum cotton plantation sits in the middle of Mecklenburg County's largest nature preserve. This living history farm is one of the few that presents a balanced picture, not just the Big House of the owner's family, but also the lives of the slave families that supported it. To those weaned on movies, the Big House itself is a bit of a surprise. This is not Scarlett O'Hara's home; while Latta was large by the standards of 1800 (when it was built), to us it seems like a big wooden farmhouse. Instead of elaborate wallpaper and sweeping stairways, you'll find painted wood planks and simple, narrow steps in the back. Of particular interest is the fully reconstructed plantation yard, with slave quarters and outbuildings, where slaves would perform both household and farm chores within close eye of the Big House—a typical feature of the slave-dependent farm. Be sure to save time for the nearby nature center, which offers Segway tours of the 1,300-acre preserve ($35 per person).

The Charlotte Museum of History (704-568-1774; charlottemuseum.org; info@charlottemuseum.org), 3500 Shamrock Dr., Charlotte 28215. Open Tue.–Sat. 10–5, Sun. 1–5; tours of the Hezekiah Alexander Homesite at 1:15 and 3:15. $$. Set on an 8-acre tract in Charlotte's inner suburbs, 6 miles east of downtown, this museum complex centers on the Hezekiah Alexander House, a lovely stone-built colonial house of a prosperous farmer, built in 1774. The 5,000-square-foot house, which includes a log-built kitchen wing, is furnished with period antiques; there's also an herb garden and springhouse, and tours are led by costumed docents. You'll get the impression of a well-kept independent farm much like the ones in the Alexander's home state of Pennsylvania—but the slave quarters have never been reconstructed, so that the role of the 13 humans owned by the Alexanders is slighted. Adjacent, a 36,000-square-foot museum (built in 1999) holds three permanent galleries that trace Charlotte's history from the 18th century to the present, plus a fourth gallery for temporary exhibits.

President James K. Polk State Historic Site (704-889-7145; nchistoricsites.org/polk), 12031 Lancaster Hwy., Pineville 28134. Open Tue.–Sat. 9–5. Admission is free. This collection of log buildings reconstructs a very typical, yet very special pioneer-era farmstead: the one in which future president James K. Polk was born and raised. Polk's uncle had founded the village of Charlotte some decades before, with a log cabin at what is now uptown's center, Tryon and Trade Streets. He convinced Polk's dad to migrate south and carve out a farm at this spot—at the time a far piece from Charlotte, but now adjacent to one of its biggest malls. (That mall, thank goodness, is invisible from the Polk farmstead, shielded from it by a thick tree screen.) Within the compound you'll find a nice small museum about Polk (who turns out to have had an important and successful presidency), plus a num-

BOYHOOD HOME OF PRESIDENT JAMES K. POLK, NEAR CHARLOTTE

ber of log farm structures in period furnishings. It's a lovely little island of early history.

Andrew Jackson State Park (SC) (803-285-3344; southcarolinaparks .com/park-finder/state-park/1797.aspx; andrewjackson@scprt.com), 196 Andrew Jackson Park Rd., Lancaster, SC 29720. Open daily 8–6 when on Standard Time, 9–9 when on Daylight Saving Time. $. America's future seventh president was born in 1767 within a couple of miles of the NC–SC state line—but no one knows which side. North Carolina stakes its claim to Old Hickory on its large capitol statue, *Presidents North Carolina Gave the Nation*; South Carolina competes with this 360-acre state park, 36 miles south of Charlotte via US 521. The park (which makes no claim to be the actual birthplace) has a museum and a one-room schoolhouse, with living history interpretation; there's also picnicking and a little fishing lake.

The village of Badin (badin.org). Located 57 miles east of Charlotte, and 7 miles northeast of Albemarle, along NC 740, the village of Badin sits on the banks of its namesake, Badin Lake. It's an odd little place, and worth your while if you value either lakefronts or curiosities. First the lakefront—perhaps the best in the state, 0.5 mile long with beaches, picnic tables, and boat ramps all easily reached from the highway. Across the street sits the silent hulk of the Alcoa aluminum smelter, the original reason for the town's construction, now closed. Alcoa built four of the Catawba River dams to power this factory, including the two nearby, **Falls Dam** and **Narrows Dam**. But Alcoa didn't build the smelter or the town; this was done in 1913 by a French company which went broke during World War I. The decidedly French construction methods of the workers' housing give the village an odd, and oddly charming, appearance; history buffs will enjoy touring the unusually twisted streets of this continental-style company town, enjoying the contrast with typical southern company towns in the nearby Mill Belt (see *Water Mills of Burlington* in that chapter). There's a local museum at the town's center (one block south of NC 740) to help you understand the town's history, and a handsome historic golf resort at the town's center, originally built by Alcoa for visiting executives, with a restaurant open to the public.

Carolina Aviation Museum (704-359-8442; carolinasaviation.org; info@carolinas aviation.org), 4108 Minuteman Way, Charlotte 28202. Open Tue.–Fri. 10–4, Sat. 10–5, Sun. noon–5. $$. Set in a corner of Charlotte's massive jetport, this museum presents 45 major aircraft as well as a wealth of other artifacts. Their centerpiece is a fully operational Douglas DC-3 painted in the livery of the late, lamented Piedmont Airlines, one of the last airlines to keep these Depression-era workhorses in regular passenger service. Its two hangars include the first one built in 1937 for Charlotte's brand-new airport, now restored to its full glory.

Kings Mountain National Military Park (864-936-7921; nps.gov/kimo), 2625 Park Rd., Blacksburg, SC 29702. Open daily 9–6. Admission is free. In 1780 British colonel Patrick Ferguson, commanding a force of 1,000 Loyalists, called for Patriot mountain forces to surrender, using language widely interpreted as a threat of genocide. Patriot forces rallied on both sides of Smoky Mountains, and organized a secret march and rendezvous to oppose Ferguson. Ferguson had sufficient warning to dig in along the top of Kings Mountain just over the line in South Carolina, a position he considered impregnable. It wasn't; the frontiersmen attacked straight up the heavily forested side, shooting from behind trees and rocks, decimating the Loyalist forces and killing Ferguson. The 65-minute battle ended with a third of the Loyalists dead and the remainder captured. Cornwallis at this time had a large British force encamped in Charlotte, only 30 miles east, and one of the mysteries of the war was why he didn't help Ferguson; the best guess is that Cornwallis just didn't like him very much. Whatever his reason, it was a disastrous mistake. With a large, fierce Patriot force on his flank, Cornwallis was forced to retreat to Charleston for the winter, ceding the Carolina backcountry to the Patriots. This marked the turning point of the Revolutionary War in the South; within a year, Carolinians and Virginians would expel the British force and end the war.

Today's battlefield is well interpreted and crowned with the requisite number of impressive monuments. Ferguson had no view of the surrounding countryside through the woods and neither will you, as the National Park Service has long worked to restore the battlefield to its original appearance. Footpaths lead through the woods, and connect with adjacent Kings Mountain State Park in South Carolina and Crowder Mountain State Park in North Carolina.

Rural Hill Center of Scottish Heritage (704-875-3113; ruralhill.net; office@ruralhill.net), 4431 Neck Rd., Huntersville 28070. Open weekdays 9–4, by appointment only. $$. This fascinating, and exceptionally beautiful, 265-acre site north of Charlotte preserves the farmstead of one of the district's oldest families, which held it from 1760 to 1989. Here you can trace a single family from a pioneer cabin to one of the largest slaveholdings in the Charlotte area, then into the modern era. Unlike nearby Latta Plantation, its Big House was quite impressive—and burned to the ground in 1886, leaving only a few columns to evoke its splendor. Much reduced, the family replaced it with a substantial but unadorned farmhouse in the local style. A full range of outbuildings make up the farm, including some awaiting restoration. Best of all it's a working farm, with crops, cattle, sheep, and bison. Rural Hill is owned by Mecklenburg County, but operated by a private Scottish heritage foundation, which holds the Loch Norman Highland Games (see *Special Events*) on its grounds. One of Mecklenburg County's largest nature preserves is at the end of the road, and worth a visit when you are in the area.

✐ **Reed Gold Mine State Historic Site** (704-721-4653; nchistoricsites.org/Reed/reed.htm; reed@ncmail.net), 9621 Reed Mine Rd., Midland 28107. Open Tue.–Sat. 9–5. Entry is free; $ for gold panning. This has got to be the funnest state park in the region—an underground gold mine and gold panning park, with some stunning history to boot. This is the place where, 200 years ago, the Reed family found a 17-pound gold nugget (no, that's not a misprint), and used it for a doorstop. They found out its worth when, three years later, a smooth-talking stranger talked them into selling it for $3.50—and that was the last time this pioneer family lost money on gold. Located 25 miles east of Charlotte via NC 24, this site preserves the first gold mine in America, founded in 1803 by John Reed, who found the nugget. By 1824 the Reeds had earned $100,000 from their backyard gold mine, including a 28-pound nugget found by one of their slaves; the mine stayed in operation until it finally played out in 1912. Set in a lovely forest, this park lets you go underground into 400 feet of restored early tunnel, then pan for gold in the adjacent creek. Its stamping mill has been restored to operating condition, and the visitors center contains a nice museum.

Town Creek Indian Mound State Historic Site (910-439-6802; nchistoricsites.org/town/Town.htm; towncreek@ncmail.net), 509 Town Creek Mound Rd., Mount Gilead 27306. Open Tue.–Sat. 9–5, Sun. 1–5. Entry is free. This site, located 70 miles east of Charlotte via NC 73, re-creates an 11th-century ceremonial site of the Pee Dee culture, based on an archaeological dig that started in 1937 and continued intermittently to 1977. Here you'll find palisade walls with lookout towers surrounding the central mound topped with a temple, with other structures at its foot. The structures are furnished inside, and the temple is particularly interesting. The culture it portrays, part of the larger Mississippian culture, was complex and sophisticated, a pre-literate agricultural civilization on a par with the builders of Stonehenge. It was, however, already under deep stress by the cooling climate brought on by the Little Ice Age (c. 1400), when diseases inadvertently introduced by the de Soto expedition decimated the population and destroyed their way of life. When Europeans reappeared 150 years later, they found only mounds abandoned in the forests.

UNDERGROUND IN THE REED GOLD MINE

NASCAR TOURISM While Daytona Beach may have the headquarters of NASCAR, Charlotte has its heart and soul, with more race teams than any other area. Charlotte offers quite a choice of things to see and do for the NASCAR fan; this section gathers them together, including items that would normally appear under *To Do* or *Special Events.*

Lowe's Motor Speedway (800-455-3267; 704-455-3200; lowesmotorspeedway.com; tickets@lowesmotorspeedway.com), 5555 Concord Pkwy. S., Concord 28027. Formerly known as Charlotte Motor Speedway, this 1.5-mile

TOWN CREEK INDIAN MOUND STATE HISTORIC SITE

oval track forms the center of Charlotte's large NASCAR industry. Built in 1959, it has seating for 165,000 spectators with an additional 50,000 in the infield. Major events include three NASCAR Sprint Cup races, two NASCAR Nationwide Series races, and a NASCAR Craftsman Truck race. In addition to the famous oval track, there is a 2.25-mile road course and a 0.6-mile karting course in the infield and two smaller ovals using part of the main oval, plus a dirt track and a drag strip across from the main speedway. As you might expect, this is a major landmark, starkly isolated on its 2,000-acre tract on the south edge of Concord, 17 miles north of Charlotte via i-85's exit 49, Speedway Boulevard.

NASCAR Hall of Fame (nascarhall.com), 501 S. College St., Charlotte 28202. Open Mon.–Sat. 10–6, Sun. noon–6; hours may vary. $$$. Ground broke on the 130,000-square-foot NASCAR Hall of Fame in downtown Charlotte in January 2007, and it opened its doors in May 2010. Although NASCAR's head offices are elsewhere, Charlotte has long been considered the unofficial center of the sport, with 80 percent of the Sprint Cup and 70 percent of the Nationwide Cup teams headquartered there, and the Hall of Fame plays tribute to Charlotte's role. It's a streamlined modern building, gleaming in chrome; inside, the "Glory Road" curves gently upward past winning autos of the past to reach the Hall of Honor. Displays include a transporter simulator that duplicates a crew's experience and a racing simulator that shows you what a driver goes through on racing day, as well as galleries on NASCAR history. There's a 250-seat theater, a restaurant, and, of course, plenty of chances to buy NASCAR memorabilia. Adjacent buildings, part of the Hall of Fame complex, link the Hall to the Charlotte Convention Center, and add a 19-story glass office building whose major tenant will be NASCAR and NASCAR Images.

Hendrick Motorsports Museum Complex (hendrickmotorsports.com/hendrick-motorsports-shops-museum-complex.asp). Open weekdays 9–5. Admission is free.

The headquarters and shops of eight-time NASCAR Sprint Cup winner Hendrick Motorsports, located near Lowe's Motor Speedway in Concord, are open to the public. While there are no guided tours, people are welcome to view the two separate team workshops, as well as the 16,000-square-foot museum. This is your premier opportunity to see inside an actual working NASCAR ownership.

Richard Petty Driving Experience (800-237-3889; 704-455-9443; 1800bepetty.com), 6022 Victory Lane, Concord 28027. $$$$$–$$$$$$. The ultimate thrill for any race fan is experiencing the race from inside the car. The Richard Petty Driving Experience allows you to ride alongside a professional driver for three laps on Lowes Motor Speedway, and even get behind the wheel yourself.

Dirt Track Racing School (704-728-2969; driveondirt.com; info@driveondirt.com), Carolina Speedway, 6335 Union Rd., Gastonia 28506. Saturdays, one to three times a month; reservations are not required but are highly recommended. $$$$–$$$$$. Short oval dirt tracks are NASCAR's roots, and remain the proving grounds of new drivers. Gastonia's Dirt Track Racing School offers a range of experiences from ride-alongs and simple driving to in-depth instruction, on the 0.4-mile Carolina Speedway.

THEME PARK ✐ **Carowinds** (800-888-4386; 704-588-2600; carowinds.com; guestrelations@carowinds.com). Opening days and hours vary; generally, Carowinds is open daily spring through fall, but call ahead or consult their website. $$$$. Owned by California's Cedar Fair company, Carowinds features a large number of thrill rides and children's rides. Originally founded as a Carolina theme park on the state border, off I-85's exit 90, it has slowly converted to a straight-up amusement park under a variety of owners. Its new (since 2006) owner is a special-

WINNING NASCAR AUTOS AT HENDRICK MOTORSPORTS COMPLEX IN CONCORD'S MOTOR SPEEDWAY DISTRICT

ist in such parks with a sterling track record, so upgrades and improvements are in the works. It's a very big amusement park; Carowinds tightly packs its 122-acre site with 13 roller coasters, two water rides, and 11 other major rides, plus a children's section now themed on Snoopy (until 2010 based on Nickelodeon), a big water park, and live shows. There are 30 places to grab a bite inside, but food cannot be brought in.

✷ To Do

OUTFITTERS God's Country Outfitters (704-983-7373; godscountryoutfitters .org; info@godscountryoutfitters.org), 1454 US 52 N., Albemarle 28001. This outdoors retailer on the western edge of the Uwharrie Mountains rents canoes and kayaks for the Uwharrie River as well as four local lakes.

Uwharrie Tours (704-463-0768; uwharrietours.com), 15750 Matton Grove Church Rd., Gold Hill 28071. Run by the Bed and Bike Inn near Gold Hill at the western edge of the Uwharrie Mountains (see *Lodging*), this operator offers three bus tours of the local area: the Seagrove potteries, the wineries, and the remarkable local parks and museums. Of special note is their signature tour: a moonlight kayak float on the stillwaters of remote Falls Lake, in a mountain gorge.

✐ **Uwharrie Adventures and Stables** (910-572-1614; uwharriestables.com; Johnny@uwharriestables.com), 4084 NC 109 N., Troy 27371. Located in the center of the Uwharrie National Forest, this outfitter offers guided horseback rides within the forest, as well as canoe and kayak rentals. Stables and camping for those traveling with their horses is also available.

BOATS AND FISHING Kings Point Marina (Lake Norman) (704-892-3223; kingspoint@morningstarmarinas.com), 18020 Kings Point Dr., Cornelius 28031. This large, full-service marina on the south end of giant Lake Norman, off I-77's exit 28, rents both pontoon boats and bow riders.

Westport Marina (Lake Norman) (704-483-5172; boatwestportmarina.com; sales@boatwestportmarina.com), 7879 Water Oaks Dr., Denver 28037. This full-service marina on the southwestern shore of Lake Norman rents both pontoons and bow riders.

Tega Cay Marina (Lake Wylie, SC) (888-820-9329; tegacaymarina.com), 1 Marina Dr., Tega Cay, SC 29708. This full-service marina, just over the state line in South Carolina's section of Lake Wylie, offers pontoon boat rentals.

Fish Tales Marina & Grill (Badin Lake) (336-461-2565; fishtalesmarina.com), 700 Lake Forest Dr., Badin Lake 28127. This small marina on the north end of Badin Lake offers pontoon boat rentals.

BICYCLE RENTALS iRide Cycles (704-947-2865; iridecycles.com; info@iride cycles.com), 15906-B Old Statesville Rd., Huntersville 28078. This shop in the Lake Norman area rents mountain, street, and urban bikes for periods of up to one day.

Middle Ring Cycles (704-322-3559; middleringcycles.com), 1448 US 52 N., Albemarle 28001. This bicycle shop near Murrow Mountain State Park and the Uwharrie National Forest rents mountain bikes, with helmets, for half and full days.

OF SPECIAL INTEREST The National Whitewater Center (704-391-3900; usnwc.org), 820 Hawfield Rd., Charlotte 28214. Open daily 10–6. Hours for individual activities may vary. Parking: $5. A wide variety of activities and rentals are individually priced, which can vary by season and day of week; trail access is free. Run by a local not-for-profit, this 306-acre facility operates the world's largest and most complex recirculating artificial whitewater course. Rated at Class III, the multichannel course is 0.75 mile long, and has a conveyor to haul your boat back to the start. Its advantages over natural streams in the Blue Ridge are that it gives an absolutely consistent and reliable whitewater experience, and it's a not a 200-mile drive down mountain roads (the distance to the next nearest Olympic-quality whitewater facility). Its disadvantage is that it won't let you paddle about on your own on its artificial course unless you are an experienced Class III kayaker and bring your own boat. Kayak instructions, however, use the course and are open to anyone.

The center offers a lot of other outdoor recreation opportunities. It has stillwater kayaking and canoeing in the adjacent Catawba River (with rental boats in this case), climbing walls, a ropes course, a zipline 0.2 mile long overlooking the river, and a large network of walking and biking trails maintained by a local mountain biking club. There's climbing instruction as well, including a specific merit badge course. There's even a restaurant and bar on the campus. They offer full equipment rentals, including bikes.

✱ Lodging

RESORTS AND HOTELS ✐ **The Duke Mansion** (888-202-1009; 704-714-4400; dukemansion.com; info@dukemansion.org), 400 Hermitage Rd., Charlotte 28207. $$$$. Situated in Charlotte's historic Myers Park neighborhood only 2 miles from the city's center, this 1915 mansion has 20 rooms and is surrounded by almost 5 acres of gardens. It reached its current spectacular form when James B. Duke made it his home. Duke had made a fortune controlling America's cigarette monopoly until it was broken up in 1906; after that, Duke made a second fortune by founding Duke Energy, Inc. The mansion is currently owned and operated by a nonprofit that applies all proceeds to preserving the estate and running a leadership center. Because this is a mansion, rooms are varied and have a lot of character, including some with a sleeping porch; furnishings are elegant and simple, and high-speed Internet is available. The tariff includes a full breakfast, made to your order. The mansion is a Select Registry hotel with a AAA 4 Diamond rating; expect luxury.

The Dunhill Hotel (800-354-4141; 704-332-4141; dunhillhotel.com; dunhillreservations@shgltd.com), 237 N. Tryon St., Charlotte 28202. $$–$$$$. This 1929 10-story building at the center of downtown, built as an apartment hotel, is now a luxury boutique hotel with 60 recently renovated rooms. This is a full-service facility with an excellent restaurant and a piano bar, oriented toward business travelers and welcoming to families. The rooms have free wireless Internet, room service, and valet service. You can choose to include breakfast with your room for an additional fee.

The Morehead Inn (888-667-3432; 704-376-3357; moreheadinn.com), 1122 E. Morehead St., Charlotte 28204. $$$$. Located on the southeastern edge of downtown Charlotte, just a few blocks from the Carolinas Medical Center, this 13-room hotel offers accommodation both elegant and convenient, with free wireless Internet in all rooms. A full hot southern breakfast is served in the dining room. Its sister facility, the **Vanlandingham Estate Inn**, offers similar quality and facilities in its eight-room mansion 2 miles northeast of downtown.

BED & BREAKFASTS **The Victorian Villa Bed & Breakfast Inn** (704-394-5545; victorianvillainn.com; manager@victorianvillainn.com), 10925 Windy Grove Rd., Charlotte 28278. $$$–$$$$. This very large Victorian-style house sits facing Lake Wylie, within easy driving distance of Charlotte's international airport. Its five rooms are quite large, and furnished with antiques. A full breakfast is included.

Franklin Street Bed & Breakfast (800-560-6143; 704-436-7378; franklinstreetbandb.com), 8501 E. Franklin St., Mount Pleasant 28124. $$. This pleasantly country-style Victorian home sits at the center of the sleepy rural town of Mount Pleasant, about 16 miles east of Lowe's Motor Speedway and 20 miles west of the Uwharrie Mountains. The center of the home is a two-story log cabin that housed slaves before the Civil War; the Victorian parts, including its wide wraparound veranda with a witch-hat pavilion, were added by the local druggist in 1882. It has three rooms, and the tariff includes a full breakfast.

The White Oak Inn Bed and Breakfast (704-736-1944; whiteoakinnnc.com), 2641 Ivey Church Rd., Lincolnton 28092. $$–$$$. This traditional southern-style farmhouse has first- and second-story columned verandas on an 8-acre property that's only 8 miles from the northwestern shore of Lake Norman, near the pretty little county seat of Lincolnton. It has three rooms ranging in size from cozy to very large, and the full breakfast is prepared by its owner, a certified chef.

The Blair House Bed and Breakfast (866-572-2100; 910-572-2100; blairhousebb.com; innkeeper@blairhousebb.com), 105 Blair St., Troy 27371. $$–$$$. Located in the heart of the Uwharrie National Forest, in the small county seat of Troy, the 1893 Blair House is a red-brick classical manor in the plantation style, with wide verandas. Nearby, the 1839 **Arscott House** is a turreted, verandaed wood Victorian mansion. Together they are run by the same innkeepers, with a total of eight recently remodeled en suite rooms with individual climate control.

The Duck Smith House Bed & Breakfast (888-869-9018; 336-873-7099; ducksmithhouse.com; scmdaisy@aol.com), 465 N. Broad St., Seagrove 27341. $$$. This 1914 farmhouse sits in the shrunken village of Seagrove, central to the pottery district and convenient to both the Uwharrie Mountains and the North Carolina Zoo at Asheboro. Its four bedrooms all have their original paneling, and the house is faced with a nice veranda. Wireless Internet is available. A full breakfast is included.

The Forever Inn Bed & Breakfast (704-695-1304; theforeverinn.com; merrielynns.com; info@theforeverinn.com), 214 S. Greene St., Wadesboro 28170. $$. This handsome Victorian mansion, with wraparound verandas, sits near the center of the pleasant little county seat of Wadesboro, not very far from Blewitt Falls Lake and the Pee Dee National Wildlife Refuge. Despite the low tariff, the three rooms are ample in size and beautifully decorated, with free wireless Internet. On the premise is **MerrieLyn's Gourmet Pecans**, a gift shop featuring handmade pecan goodies. A full breakfast is included.

CABINS 🚲 🐾 **The Bed and Bike Inn** (704-463-0768; bedandbikeinn.com), 15750 Matton Grove Church Rd., Gold Hill 28071. $$–$$$; pet fee. Located at the edge of the Uwharrie Mountains, this group of three cabins and a meeting yurt is named for its planters made of old bicycles. The modern-built cabins are all different: a full-sized log home, a contemporary home, and a small cabin.

✱ Where to Eat

DINING OUT Monticello Uptown Restaurant and Bar (704-342-1193; dunhillhotel.com/monticello-restaurant), 235 N Tryon St., Charlotte 28202. Open daily for breakfast, lunch, and dinner. $$–$$$$. Part of the historic and luxurious Dunhill Hotel at the center of uptown Charlotte, the Monticello is quietly elegant, with a menu that emphasizes southern recipes and locally grown foods. Probably your best uptown bet, the Monticello is low-key and reliable.

Blue Restaurant and Bar (704-927-0553; bluerestaurantandbar.com), 214 N. Tryon St. #100, Charlotte 28202. Open Mon.–Thu. 5–10 PM, Fri.–Sat. 5–11. $$$$–$$$$$. Located in the Hearst Tower at the center of uptown, the Blue has an elegantly modernist interior and live jazz. It features imaginative takes on Mediterranean cuisine, with a wine list that has picked up a *Wine Spectator* Award of Excellence, but has no bottles under $35 and precious few under $50.

Cajun Queen (704-377-9017; cajunqueen.net; robineiden78@gmail.com), 1800 E. 7th St., Charlotte 28204. Open daily for dinner, and for brunch Sun. $$$. Improbably located in a staid brick manor from 1918, this New Orleans–style dinner place has attractive decor, live Dixieland jazz, and authentic cuisine. Located just three blocks southeast of uptown, it's a perfect place for those suffering from overly elegant and overly priced center city alternatives. Too bad they don't do lunch.

EATING OUT Mert's Heart and Soul (704-342-4222; mertsuptown.com), 214 N. College St., Charlotte 28202. Open daily for lunch, dinner Tue.–Sat., brunch Sat.–Sun. starting at 9. $$. Located in the center of uptown Charlotte, Mert's has a wide variety of authentic southern, Low Country, and Gullah food at very reasonable prices. This isn't fancy uptown cuisine, mind you, but the food your grandma in the country used to make on Sundays. If you're looking for a picnic, their website lets you put in a to-go order online.

Prices Chicken Coop (704-333-9866; priceschickencoop.com), 1614 Camden Rd., Charlotte 28203. Open Tue.–Sat. 10–6. $. This strictly take-out place, located in the gentrified south side of uptown, is renowned for having some of the finest fried chicken in the Carolinas. Expect a line, but lines move fast, and the chicken is made as fast as it's ordered. It comes out in boxes, and you pick up a dessert of either fried apple pie or sweet potato pie at the register; drinks consist of Cheer Wine from a machine. There is no seating, but many folk sit on the grassy berm across the street.

The Prickly Pear (704-799-0875; pricklypear.net; pricklypear1@alltel.net), 761 N. Main St., Mooresville 28115. Open for lunch Sun.–Fri. 11–2:30; open for dinner Sun.–Thu. 5–9:30, Fri.–Sat. 5–10:30. $$$. This café occupies a Jesuit mission near the center of Mooresville, near the northern end of Lake Norman. An attractive interior complements an ambitious menu; don't expect the usual burrito combos here.

The Fresh House (704-888-1460; oldschool.com; dave@oldschool.com), 805 Main St. W., Locust 28097. Open Tue.–Sat. for lunch and dinner, Sun. for lunch only. $$. This remote rural café and country store is located on NC 24 halfway between Charlotte and Albemarle. It's an outlet for Albemarle's Old School Mill, which re-creates historic foods and recipes and produces them using authentic methods. Expect to find traditional food with a flavor and freshness that's been missing for most of the last century—very far removed from the normal Kountry Kookin' diner.

Hillbilly's Barbeque and Steaks (704-824-8838; hillbillysbbqsteaks.com; hillbillysbarbeque@bellsouth.net), 720 McAdenville Rd., Lowell 28098. Open daily for lunch, Mon.–Sat. for dinner. $$–$$$. This straightforward barbeque has two locations in the Gastonia area; the easier one to find is just off I-85's exit 22 (NC 7). The barbeque is cooked over a wood pit fire and the sauce is on the side. They have a good list of side dishes, plus a salad bar.

✷ Entertainment

CLASSICAL The Charlotte Symphony (704-972-2003; charlottesymphony.org; info@charlottesymphony.org), 1300 Baxter St., Suite 300, Charlotte 28204. Founded in 1932, the Charlotte Symphony is led by Christof Perick and has 65 full-time musicians; its main venue is uptown's Blumenthal Performing Arts Center.

The Charlotte Philharmonic Orchestra (704-543-5551; charlottephilharmonic.org; info@charlottephilharmonic.org), P.O. Box 470987, Charlotte 28247. Founded by director Albert E. Moehring in the late 1980s, this full-sized orchestra uses part-time professional musicians to present a strongly pops-oriented season. Performances tend to be either at the

THE TREE-LINED STREETS OF CHARLOTTE

city's Owen Auditorium or at Central Piedmont Community College, both a short distance east of uptown. Their video programs appear on PBS stations throughout America.

POPULAR ***Creative Loafing*** (charlotte.creativeloafing.com). The Charlotte live music scene centers on **Uptown** and **NoDa**. For thorough coverage, grab a copy of the weekly tabloid *Creative Loafing*, distributed free throughout the urban area.

✷ Selective Shopping

Uptown Charlotte. In New York City "uptown" and "downtown" are separate skyscraper districts, kept apart by the seven-story tenements of Greenwich Village. Not so Charlotte: *Uptown* here is an honorific bestowed by its promoters upon downtown, an invitation to compare it with the New York neighborhood that contains Times Square and the Empire State Building.

Uptown Charlotte is smaller, of course; in fact, its area is small even by big-city standards. While maps may indicate an 11-block-by-11-block grid, most of this is parking lots, two-story apartments, a government complex, and other low, noncommercial structures. The actual skyscraper district consists of the blocks facing Tryon Street (US 29)—10 blocks long on the west side, and 8 blocks long on the east. To a lesser extent, the blocks facing College Street, one block east of Tryon, also have significant commercial development, and should also be explored.

One comparison with Uptown New York is valid: Charlotte contains an unusual concentration of corporate headquarters, from America's largest bank (Bank of America) to the Muzak elevator music company and Bojangles spicy fried chicken chain. As a result, uptown is filled with the triumphal architecture, pastimes, and charitable obsessions of the corporate elite. First and foremost it's an eye-catching conglomeration of omigod buildings, each one playing can-you-top-this with its predecessors. Next, it has a major concentration of high-end museums (see *To See*, above), a fine place to browse museum shops. Finally, it has a number of fine art and craft galleries. It has a lively night scene as well, with good restaurants and nightclubs.

Seagrove. Located in the far northeast of this chapter, Seagrove has already been described (in *To See*, above, which has directions and contact information); this is a brief mention in case you missed the main entry. In short, Seagrove is one of the best places anywhere to look for, and at, handcrafted pottery, with five dozen or more potters, nearly all with open studios. Even if you aren't a pottery fan, you will probably end up carefully stowing a bubble-wrapped piece or two in your luggage at the end of your trip.

✷ Special Events

Mid-April: **Loch Norman Scottish Festival and Highland Games** (ruralhillscottishfestivals.net), Rural Hill Heritage Center, 17 miles north of Charlotte. Now in its 17th year, the Festival and Games feature bagpipes, tossing rocks and telephone poles, eating Scottish food (yum!), Scottish dance, harps, fiddles, bagpipes, battle-ax throwing, longbow shooting, clan tents, and bagpipes. These things are always a blast, and the Rural Hill setting couldn't be lovelier.

Mid-November: **Festival in the Park** (704-338-1060; festival@FESTIVALinthePARK.org), 1409 East Blvd., Charlotte 28203. For nearly half a century Charlotteans have celebrated the arts in this four-day festival held in Freedom Park, 3 miles south of downtown. The art is juried and prizes are given; there are continuous live music performances; and a variety of activities keep the little ones from getting too restive. And, of course, there are lots of food vendors.

Late November: **Seagrove Pottery Festivals**. Yes, plural; there are *two* autumn art festivals on the same day, sponsored by dueling artists' organizations. (Seagrove also has two pottery museums.) Between the two of them, every potter in the Seagrove region is displaying and selling at the same time—plenty of reason to make the 75-mile trip from Charlotte.

3 The Mountains

INTRODUCTION

The Blue Ridge marks the beginning of the mountains. It makes for a dramatic start—an unbroken line of slopes and cliffs 316 miles long, typically looming 1,500 feet or more above the Piedmont immediately below, stretching from Virginia to Georgia. Surprisingly, it doesn't drop dramatically on its far side; instead, all the valley floors to its west are elevated by (at least) an extra 1,000 feet. Within this elevated district stand the tallest mountains in the East: the Smokies, the Blacks, and the Balsams, with 40 peaks that top 6,000 feet. (Only one other mountain in the East reaches this height, New Hampshire's Mount Washington, which ranks 17th on this list of 6'ers.) The mountains end as abruptly as they started, at the state line, dropping straight down into Tennessee. One of the most dramatic hikes anywhere follows this state line crest, with the sharp droop into the plains of the Mississippi on the one hand and the undulating peaks of North Carolina, like waves in a stormy sea, on the other.

THE NOLICHUCKY RIVER NEAR THE NC–TN STATE LINE

The chief mountain town is Asheville, an established tourist center since Cornelius Vanderbilt construct his baronial Biltmore House at the town limits in 1889, still the largest private house in the East. Here Vanderbilt brought into existence the early seeds of modern scientific forestry as well as the national forest system in the East—done to improve the view from his porch, which encompassed 125,000 acres that he purchased and revived. In this period Asheville became a center of wealth that attracted some of the most prominent architects in the country. Today, these give Asheville one of the most handsome, and funky, city centers anywhere, with the state's largest and most active arts colony (specializing in fine crafts), its liveliest night scene, and nine microbreweries (a per capita record that has earned it the title Beer City).

Of course the real attraction is the mountain scenery. Three enormous tracts of federal land—the Great Smoky Mountains National Park, the Nantahala National Forest, and the Pisgah National Forest—protect about half the high ridgelines and make them available to recreationists. Trails are many and excellent, whitewater rivers are managed for rafting and kayaking, campgrounds (both primitive and developed) are plentiful, and the scenery is remarkable. Three scenic highways have been intentionally constructed specifically for enjoying these mountains. The Blue Ridge Parkway, the National Park Service's most heavily visited property, follows the highest and most breathtaking mountain crests for more than 250 miles in this state (and another 216 in Virginia). Newfound Gap Road, in contrast, goes straight up and over the middle of the Great Smoky Mountains National Park at its highest point. Finally, the Cherohala Parkway, jointly built by Tennessee and North Carolina in the 1990s, penetrates some of the most remote and beautiful scenery on the western border.

THE NORTHERN MOUNTAINS

The Northern Mountains consist of two parallel ridges, running northeast–southwest, with a valley between them that's 10 to 20 miles wide. First comes the Blue Ridge, rising steeply from the broken lands of the upper Piedmont in a wall of granite. Behind it the terrain drops gently to high rolling farmland drained by powerful rivers. Then come more mountains—the tall peaks that mark the state line with Tennessee, known as the Roan Highlands to the south and Stone Mountain to the north, but really a northward extension of the Great Smoky Mountains. Both the Blue Ridge and the Roan Highlands produce peaks that reach above a mile, and several that top 6,000 feet; no taller elevations can be found between here and New England.

To help keep you oriented in this chapter's large area, we'll divide it into these zones:

1. The Catawba River Valley, at the foot of the Blue Ridge
2. The Blue Ridge itself, closely followed by the Blue Ridge Parkway
3. The valleys between the ridges, in three distinct parts:
   - The New River Valley, behind the Blue Ridge in the north
   - The Boone Area, behind the Blue Ridge in the center
   - Mayland Valley, behind the Blue Ridge in the south
4. The Roan Highlands, along the state line with Tennessee, edging the Mayland Valley

The Blue Ridge Parkway forms the main attraction in this chapter, hugging the crest of the Blue Ridge for 127 miles and giving easy access to its many wonders. Beneath it lies the Catawba River Valley, where mountains and Piedmont mix. Beyond the Blue Ridge, the little-visited New River Valley features stunning rural scenery, a quaint county seat, and first-rate recreation on its famous river. The Boone Area has a handsome university town, good restaurants and inns, and the best snow skiing in the state. Mayland Valley, ringed by 6,000-foot peaks, is a major center for fine crafts. And finally, the Roan Highlands rival even the Great Smokies for spectacular scenery.

GUIDANCE Ashe County Chamber of Commerce & Visitor's Center (888-343-2743; 336-246-9550; ashechamber.com; info@ashechamber.com), 303 E. 2nd St., P.O. Box 31, West Jefferson 28694. Located off the main highway in West Jef-

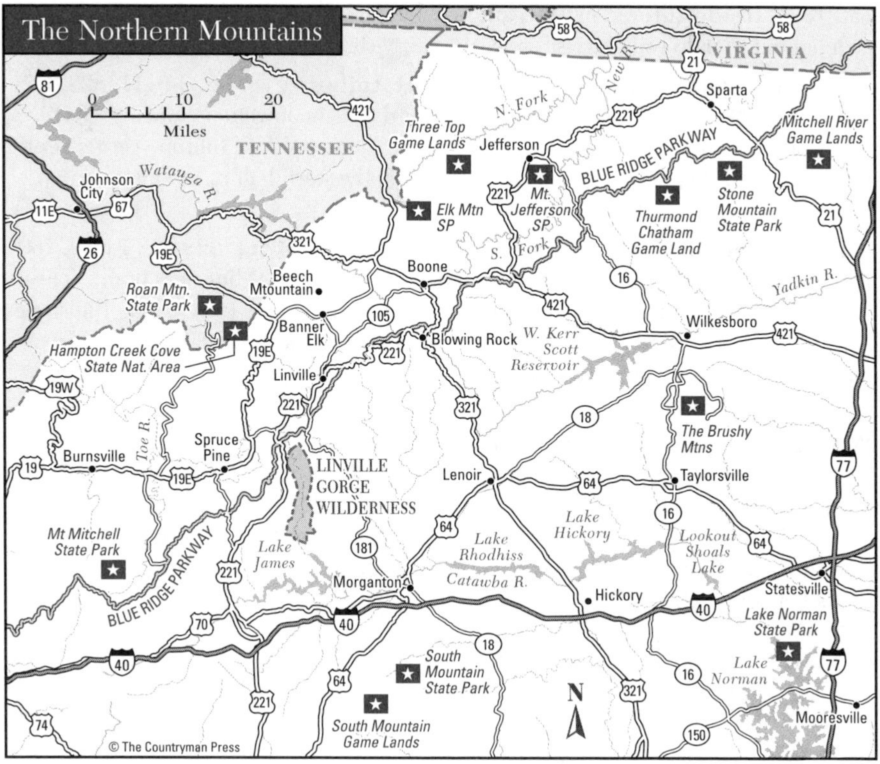

ferson's red-brick downtown, this visitors center offers help and advice for the rural New River Valley.

Boone Convention & Visitor's Bureau (800-852-9506; 828-262-3516; visit boonenc.com; info@VisitBooneNC.com), 208 Howard St., Boone 28607. Located in downtown Boone on a back street, this friendly information desk will help you with the central area of this chapter, including the ski slopes.

Yancey County Chamber of Commerce (800-948-1632; 828-682-7413; yancey chamber.com; info@yanceychamber.com), 106 W. Main St., Burnsville 28714. For the Mayland Valley, turn to the Yancey Chamber of Commerce, with its attractive visitors center on the western edge of downtown Burnsville. It has some historic exhibits, and a fine history museum, the **McElroy House**, is immediately behind it.

Burke County Travel & Tourism Commission (888-462-2921; 828-433-6793; fax: 828-433-6715; discoverburke county.com; rosemary@discoverburke county.com), 102 E. Union St., Morganton 28655. Open weekdays 9–4,

WANT MORE?
Countryman Press's *The Blue Ridge and Smoky Mountains: An Explorer's Guide* covers this area in far greater detail, with six chapters—117 fully illustrated pages—dedicated to this chapter's area alone.

Sat. 10–1. Headquartered in Morganton's fine Old Courthouse, this small agency is delighted to help walk-in visitors with their visits to the Catawba Valley.

McDowell County Tourism Development Authority (888-233-6111; 828-652-1103; fax: 828-652-3862; mcdowellnc.org; tourism@mcdowell.main.nc.us), P.O. Box 1028, Marion 28752. This authority runs a large, modern hilltop visitors center by US 221 as it bypasses Marion, and covers the western half of the Catawba Valley.

Pisgah National Forest, Grandfather Ranger District (828-652-2144), 109 E. Lawing Dr., Nebo 28761. Open weekdays during normal business hours. The Pisgah National Forest includes an arc of large mountainous tracts along the slopes and side ridges of the Blue Ridge, extending north to the Roan Highlands. The ranger station for these lands is a large, new building by exit 90 on I-40, in the Catawba Valley at Nebo.

Watauga Ranger District, Cherokee National Forest (423-735-1500), P.O. Box 400 (TN 173 north of town center), Unicoi, TN 37692. Open weekdays during normal business hours. If you're exploring the Roan Highlands in any depth, you will quickly notice that the beautiful scenery just refuses to stop at the state line. For information on the Tennessee side stop by this large modern office, just east of I-26's Unicoi exit (exit 23).

GETTING THERE *By car:* In the 19th century parts of this region were so hard to reach that they were known as the Lost Provinces. It's still not exactly the most accessible area of the state. The Catawba Valley is the exception, neatly bisected by I-40—your main entry highway for all directions except the north. From I-40, get to the **New River Valley** via four-lane US 421 (exit 188 in Winston-Salem, or via I-71's exit 73 north of Statesville), then via NC 16. Get to the **Boone Area** via either US 421 from Winston-Salem, or via US 321 (exit 122) from Hickory. Get to the **Mayland Valley** via either US 221 (exit 85) from Marion then west via NC 190 to US 19 (avoid NC 226, one of the worst highways in the South), or via I-26's exit 9, north of Asheville, to US 19, becoming US 19E.

The three central valleys have no coherent road system, and the road numbering is downright screwy. For instance, if you are driving southwest from Boone/Blowing Rock, US 221 is a horrid back road while NC 105, running parallel, is reasonably modernized. For the **New River Valley**, use US 221 as your backbone highway and avoid NC 88 or NC 194 (unless you wish a very scenic 25 mph countryside drive). The Blue Ridge Parkway is actually better than any parallel state or national highway, but it closes in winter. In the **Boone Area** US 321, US 421, and NC 105 are your best bets, along with US 211 in the Linville area (but not between Linville and Boone), again supplemented by the Blue Ridge Parkway in summer. In the **Mayland Valley** US 19/19E is your main highway between Spruce Pine, Burnsville, and points west, with a big blank area of bad roads between it and Linville.

The mountains along the state lines are pierced by three scenic, two-lane mountain highways: from north to south, US 421, US 321, and US 19A. If you are coming from the north, these will be your entry points.

By air: Your closest major airports are Charlotte (CLT), Asheville (AVL), and Tri-Cities in East Tennessee's Johnson City (TRI). Tri-Cities is the closest both in time and distance, at 70 miles and less than a two-hour drive from Boone, and closer than that to the Mayland Valley; it has a good choice of car rentals. Charlotte is 90 miles and about two hours away. Asheville is about the same distance, and your computer navigation software will tell you it's only a 2½-hour drive, but don't believe it. The roads between Asheville and Boone are very mountainous and very bad; while you might make it in three hours, allot four to be on the safe side.

By bus or train: There is no bus or train service in this area.

MEDICAL EMERGENCIES **Watauga Medical Center** (828-262-4100; apprhs .org, click on "Locations"), 336 Deerfield Rd., Boone 28607. This private, nonprofit regional hospital is the main facility for the high mountains of this chapter. It has a wide range of surgical and medical specialties as well as 24/7 emergency room services at its main building. It's located 2 miles south of Boone on US 221/321, then a block north on Deerfield Road.

Grace Hospital (828-580-5000; blueridgehealth.org/grace-hospital.html), 2201 S. Sterling St., Morganton 28655. This major regional hospital serves the I-40 corridor from its location at Morganton, by I-40 at the NC 18 exit.

Allegheny Memorial Hospital (336-372-5511; fax: 336-372-6032; amhsparta.org; info@amhsparta.org), 233 Doctors St., Sparta 28675. Located in Sparta, three blocks from downtown's US 21 via NC 18, this not-for-profit hospital offers full emergency services for the mountainous areas near the Virginia state line.

Blue Ridge Regional Hospital (877-777-8230; 828-765-4201; spchospital.org), 125 Hospital Dr., Spruce Pine 28714. Formerly known as Spruce Pine Community Hospital, this small regional hospital furnishes a 24/7 emergency room service for the Mayland Valley region. You'll find it off US 19E on the south edge of Spruce Pine.

The McDowell Hospital (828-659-5000; mcdhospital.org; jjudd@mcdhospital .org), 430 Rankin Dr., Marion 28752. If you get into trouble at Marion, between Morganton and Asheville on the I-40 corridor, this 65-bed local hospital with 24/7 emergency room service is where you'll go. It sits by I-40 at exit 81 (Sugar Hill Road).

✷ Exploring the Area

EXPLORE BY CAR **The Blue Ridge Parkway in the Northern Mountains.** The Blue Ridge Parkway, America's most popular national park, enters this chapter at the Virginia state line, 0.5 mile from NC 18 near Sparta. By this point it has already logged 217 miles of its 469-mile journey from Shenandoah National Park to the Great Smoky Mountains National Park—and in this chapter will knock off an additional 127 miles. Unless you drive straight through without stopping, expect this trip to take all day.

The parkway enters North Carolina at **Cumberland Knob Recreation Area**, where construction on the parkway started in 1933. At 12 miles a side trip onto US 21 takes you south 20 miles to **Stone Mountain State Park**, with a restored farm underneath massive granite cliffs. After 24 miles on the parkway you'll reach **Doughton Park**, with wide views from a mile of mountaintop meadows, and a log cabin at which weaving demonstrations are given. At 41 miles a paved lane (Trading Post Road, SSR 1632) leads 0.5 mile right to the **Church of the Frescoes** at Glendale Springs. At 55 miles the Cascades Overlook on your left has an excellent short path to a waterfall, and some interesting log cabins sit by the road a mile farther down.

After 60 miles the parkway sweeps over US 421, then swings around Boone; you'll find a marker at the place where Daniel Boone's road crossed the parkway. At 75 miles the parkway reaches the elegant resort village of **Blowing Rock**, known for its fine shopping. Just beyond is **Moses Cone Park**, where a mansion said to be the second largest in the state looks out over landscaped meadows laced with carriage paths. Then, at 80 miles, you'll swing around Prices Lake, the centerpiece of **Julian Price Park**. After that you'll slab around the middle slopes of **Grandfather Mountain**, soaring above sensitive high-altitude environments on the **Linville Cove Viaduct**, an engineering wonder. At 89 miles a right onto US 221 leads to **Grandfather Mountain Park**, the world's only privately owned International Biosphere Reserve. At 100 miles a spur leads left for 3 miles to **Linville Falls**, an impressive 90-foot straight drop into a cliff-sided bowl. At 112 miles the parkway passes by the historic **Altapass Orchards**, with tours, heritage apples, and live music. After 125 miles, **Black Mountain Overlook** on your right gives a 180-degree view toward **Mount Mitchell**, at 6,684 feet the highest mountain in the East.

Two miles farther, the parkway intersects with NC 80, our other scenic drive. Burnsville and the Mayland Valley are 19 miles north (left); Morganton and the Catawba Valley, 39 miles south (right).

NC 80, from the parkway to the Roan Highlands. This 54-mile drive crosses Mayland Valley through some of its most remote areas, featuring a great deal of beautiful mountain scenery and a surprising number of things to do. *Starting at the Blue Ridge Parkway, follow NC 80 north to its intersection with NC 226 in Bakersville, a distance of 30.6 miles.* From the parkway, your highway will quickly drop away from the high mountains, giving you fine views toward **Mount Mitchell**, the highest peak in the East. From here you'll wander through the scattered rural community of Celo, noted for its **fine crafts**; keep your eyes open for roadside galleries and workshops. In 15 miles NC 80 crosses US 19E, and the lovely county seat of **Burnsville**, with its town square shopping, is 5 miles to the left. After that you'll quickly reach the South Toe River as your road becomes a narrow country lane of astonishing twistiness, coiling past cemeteries and churches, through forests, and into fields with wide mountain views. If you wish, a pretty side trip down country lanes will lead you in 5 miles to the famous craft school and artists' colony at **Penland**. (Go right on Snow Hill Road, SSR 1170, 2.4 miles to a right on Conley Ridge Road, SSR 1164; the campus is 2 miles farther.) Then NC 80 reaches the attractive village of **Kona**, with excellent views and a museum dedicated to the state's most notorious female murderer, Frankie Silver. Seven twisty, view-studded miles later, NC 80 ends at the settlement of Loafers Glory, named after the gang of old-timers that once gathered in front of its (now defunct) general store.

Go north on NC 266 for 12.7 miles to the state line in a high gap; continue straight (as the road becomes TN 143) for 10.3 miles to Roan Mountain State Park, a total distance of 23.0 miles. The second leg starts at the tiny county seat of **Bakersville**, with a half-block downtown by its old courthouse; **Dellinger's Mill**, a 1901 overshot waterwheel still in operation, is 4 miles west. North of Bakersville, the route sweeps through lovely rural valleys, then climbs up to the mile-high Carvers Gap deep in the **Roan Highlands**. At the top, wide mountaintop meadows sweep uphill to the right, following the Appalachian Trail for a mile with **incredible panoramic views**. To the left, a paved side road leads 2.3 miles to **Roan Gardens**, a 600-acre natural rhododendron garden with wide views from two 6,000-foot peaks. Crossing into Tennessee, the highway becomes TN 143. This is the most spectacular part of the drive, as the highway becomes a narrow ledge carved into the cliff-like side of Roan Mountain, descending steeply with breathtaking views for 3.5 miles. Tennessee's **Roan Mountain State Park**, 8.5 miles from Carvers Gap, makes for a good final destination and turnaround point.

EXPLORE ON FOOT **Doughton Park Walks**. Doughton Park is part of the **Blue Ridge Parkway**, with its main entrance at milepost 241. It protects a mile or more of mountaintop meadows, with some wonderful places to walk—beautiful scenery, lots of wildflowers, magnificent views, and much easier than any Blue Ridge mountaintop deserves to be. The clifftop views at **Wildcat Cliffs** (only a short distance from the parking lot) give a wide sweep down the 2,000-foot escarpment of the Blue Ridge and over the wide plains of the Piedmont; at the base of the cliffs, a single log cabin breaks the forest. A gentle 1-mile round-trip leads from there to Fodderstack Knob, a rocky bald with the characteristic Japanese garden look framing another wide view. South from the lodge, a path is hardly needed through the wildflower meadows that crown the mountain for a mile—though one exists, just in case. On this long summit you will come across wide and ever-changing views, many wildflowers, rocky outcrops, and dwarfed and twisted trees. The picnic area's access road parallels the summit meadows on their western downhill side, allowing picnickers to stroll up from their tables into the meadows at any point.

The Tanawha Trail. The Linville Viaduct engineers built this 12-mile hiking trail as part of the bridge project in 1987, and to the same high standards. Staying on the National Park Service's Blue Ridge Parkway properties throughout, this moderately easy path wanders through every type of Blue Ridge scenery from rough crags to soft meadows. It starts at the **Linn Cove Viaduct Visitor's Center** (milepost 305.1), and then passes under the viaduct, giving a close view of the bridge and the ecology it protects. From there it climbs up to Rough Ridge and crosses its rare and fragile mountain heather ecology on a **200-foot boardwalk**, with continuous panoramic views off the Blue Ridge, over the viaduct and into the Piedmont. Beyond, the path goes through New England–style forests and Blue Ridge–style rhododendron tunnels as it approaches **Julian Price Park**, then passes through a long series of old meadows, fields, and apple orchards before ending at **Price Lake** (MP 297). This makes a fine one-day hike if you can arrange to be picked up.

The Roan Highlands. Starting at Carver Gap on NC 216, this walk goes eastward through the wide meadows of the Roan Highlands to the northernmost 6,000-foot summit in the South, Grassy Ridge Bald. This undulating trail is a 5-mile round-trip, with 1,000 feet of climbing (a third of it on the way back). Park in the Forest Service picnic area on the left side of the road, and take the Appalachian Trail across the road, through a split-rail fence, and into the mountaintop meadows. Both the views and the wind will increase steadily as you climb 300 feet up Round Bald, reaching the first of several 360-degree panoramas from its summit in 0.4

mile. The trail continues down to a small gap, then uphill to Jane Bald (1.1 miles), staying in grassy meadows with wildflowers and wide views the entire way. After a shallow gap, the trail starts on a long climb (600 feet in 0.7 mile) up Grassy Ridge Bald; when the Appalachian Trail slabs off the ridge crest to the left, continue on the side trail along the ridge. After passing through thick rhododendrons, the trail tops out on the 6,200-foot summit, with a full-circle view from the top of the world. Return the way you came.

Table Rock walks on the Linville Gorge rim. Table Rock Picnic Area gives access to one of the most interesting and spectacular day hikes in the area, following the rim of the Linville Gorge within the East's oldest wilderness. The drive to this picnic area is a bit of an adventure in itself. From Morganton in the Catawba Valley, take NC 181 north for 8.9 miles to a left onto Fish Hatchery Road (SSR 1240), then go 2.2 miles to a right onto gravel Old Table Rock Road (FS 99) and proceed to the end at the picnic area after 6.3 miles and seven switchbacks. The picnic area itself is hard by a cliff at 3,400 feet in elevation, but pleasant and tree-shaded nonetheless.

The Mountains-to-Sea Trail passes through as it follows the Linville Gorge's eastern edge, and you can take it in either direction. To the north, it climbs steeply (500 feet in 0.5 mile) up to the cliff-lined, flat-topped Table Rock, a remarkable mesa-like formation protruding 600 feet above the trees of the surrounding ridge. The clifftops give a sweeping view over the entire gorge and the Blue Ridge beyond, as well as out over the Catawba Valley. Southward from the picnic area, the trail heads to the rocky hoodoos known as the Chimneys. Much easier and only slightly longer (100 feet up in 0.7 mile), the path starts as a gentle ridgetop climb to an exposed rocky cliff with wide views, including one back toward Table Rock. From there the trail descends gently to a gap as the ridge becomes increasingly knife-like. More rocky cliffs give views over the gorge, with tall spires eroded along its edge. The trail continues along the knife ridge to the top of the Chimney, a phallic spire towering above the rest. Return the way you came.

✷ Towns

Jefferson and West Jefferson. Twenty-five miles north of Boone in the New River Valley, and far off the beaten tourist paths, these little-developed red-brick sister towns retain their old mountain look and feel. They complement each other; Jefferson, with 1,400 residents, has the government functions and the historic domed courthouse, while West Jefferson, with 1,000 residents, has the downtown main street (called Jefferson Street). Once a railroad depot on America's last steam railway, the Virginia Creeper, West Jefferson's old-fashioned red-brick downtown is surprisingly interesting with a scattering of galleries representing local artists. **Mount Jefferson** looms above both towns, a state park with magnificent views from four overlooks.

Blowing Rock. This village sits in a shallow bowl just behind the crest of the Blue Ridge, a short distance off the parkway. It's been around since the 1890s, a resort town from the first, and many of the buildings are very historic. The model for **Jan Karon's Mitford**, Blowing Rock's old village center remains attractive and busy, with a four-block downtown and a city park at its center. It has always been a gathering place for the wealthy so the shopping is excellent, and both quality and price tend to be high. Parking can be difficult, even in the off-season, and you may find yourself forced to walk a few blocks.

Boone. This college town and county seat sits in a high valley straddling the headwaters of the Watauga and New Rivers. Not that many years ago it was a sleepy mountain town, but the explosive growth of its local college, Appalachian State University, has left Boone bursting at the seams with 13,400 residents, its overflow sprawling down US 321 toward Blowing Rock and NC 105 toward Banner Elk. This is a lot of people for a mountain town that can only be reached by two-lane highways, and traffic can be bad. On the bright side, it has a neat downtown shopping district and plenty of interesting shops and restaurants. The compact university campus sits only two blocks from downtown, paralleling it along a stream and up the opposite mountain slope.

Beech Mountain. In all likelihood the highest town in the East, Beech Mountain's town hall sits just barely above 5,000 feet in elevation—and 0.3 mile higher into the sky than nearby Boone. This ski village in the Boone area is reached by taking NC 184 north from Banner Elk, then straight up five switchbacks and 1,500 feet. The village sits in a perched valley about 200 feet shy of the mile-high summit, a small scattering of modest shops and motels surrounded by condos and second homes. The ski slope starts some distance downhill (toward the back of the mountain) and rises directly behind the town hall, making it easy to watch the skiers from the little town square. In fact, the town government provides a children's sledding slope behind the town hall, complete with artificial snow. The temperature difference is very noticeable, with Beech Mountain being cool and breezy in the warmest of summer weather.

Burnsville. This beautiful little village in the center of Mayland Valley centers on its classic town square. The square is a large, well-kept strolling space with lawns, trees, flowers, and a statue of an early-19th-century sea captain (Otway Burns, the town's namesake). Grouped around the square are the county courthouse, city hall, public library, and a 170-year-old coaching inn. The shopping is surprisingly good, with a variety of craft galleries. Parking is free, with overflow parking two blocks west of the square.

Morganton. Founded in the late 1700s as the pioneer settlement of Morganborough in the Catawba Valley, Morganton gained its prosperity as a furniture mill town in the 19th century. The mountain hardwood forests furnished the raw material, and the railroad shipped out the final product. Morganton has several worthwhile historic sites and a lovely downtown, a classic small-town Main Street, anchored by a lovely Courthouse Square, dominated by its old square courthouse (now an historic museum). A good-quality shopping district, full of active, interesting stores and cafés, runs along the north side of the Courthouse Square, while two complexes of historic buildings are being renovated into more shops nearby. Parking is plentiful and free, with lots of street parking as well as large municipal lots behind the storefronts.

✷ Green Spaces

PUBLIC LANDS The Roan Highlands. The 15,000 protected acres of the Highlands of Roan contain the largest concentration of grassy mountaintop balds in the East, 600 acres of natural rhododendron gardens, large tracts of Canadian-style spruce-fir forests, and more rare species than the Great Smoky Mountains National Park. John Fraser discovered the Catawba rhododendron here in 1787, and great early scientists such as Asa Gray and Elisha Mitchell studied its unique environments. Gray called it "without doubt the most beautiful mountain east of the Rockies," while Mitchell wrote, "It is the most beautiful of all the high mountains."

The Roan Highlands consist of a single wall of remote, high mountains along the NC–TN state line, stretching from Hughes Gap (SSR 1330, Buladean Road) eastward to the deep gap that carries US 19E. Most of it is within the Pisgah National Forest and the Cherokee National Forest, with significant tracts protected by the Southern Appalachians Highlands Conservancy, The Nature Conservancy, and the state of Tennessee. Made up of hard old rocks, the crest of the Roan Highlands stays above 4,000 feet for nearly its entire length, with 5 miles more than a mile high. Its three peaks that top 6,000 feet are the last in the Appalachian Mountains until Mount Washington in New Hampshire, 800 miles to the north.

Despite heavy exploitation between 1890 and 1940, the Roan Highlands look much the same today as they did 160 years ago. In 1836 Mitchell wrote, "The top of the Roan may described as a vast meadow without a tree to obstruct this prospect, where a person may gallop his horse for a mile or two with Carolina at his feet on one side and Tennessee on the other, and a green ocean of mountains rising in tremendous billows immediately around him." Gray rocky crags stick out of the knee-high grasses; wildflowers form carpets whipped by winds that average 25 mph. Most astonishing are the panoramas, frequently extending in a complete circle around the viewer, continuing unbroken for mile after mile. Even the bureaucracy of the U.S. Department of Agriculture is impressed, writing in a 1974 planning document, "There is no other area that offers such extensive panoramic views of the high country of the Southern Appalachians. Unique is not, in this sense, misleading."

The Roan Highlands are crossed by only one road, NC 216/TN 143, which climbs up the ridge to mile-high Carver Gap. Carver Gap is the Roan's main access point for recreationalists, with a side road leading west to Roan Gardens, and the Appalachian Trail leading east through miles of open meadows.

The Black Mountains. South of Burnsville and Micaville looms the tallest summit in the East, **Mount Mitchell**, 1 of the 10 6,000-foot peaks in the Black Mountains. The eastern base of the Blacks, rising out of the South Toe River, is almost entirely owned by the Pisgah National Forest. The Blacks typically rise 3,800 feet above the Toe River in a linear distance of 3 miles, creating an unbroken barrier 7 miles long. This great steep slope is banded with forests, each band appropriate for the climate induced by its elevation and topography—the bands occasionally broken by great rockslides at the steepest slopes. While much of the area was logged, the very steepness spared large tracts along these slopes, and some trails climb through old-growth forests. Five paths make the climb up the face of the Blacks, all of them scenic, and all of them difficult all-day slogs. The whole wall of the Blacks can be admired from the South Toe River at Carolina Hemlocks Recreation Area, a great swimming hole.

Linville Gorge Wilderness. One of the earliest wilderness areas created by Congress, this 11,000-acre tract preserves a deep, 13-mile-long gorge cut into the face of the Blue Ridge. The gorge starts with the massive 90-foot plunge of the Linville

River over **Linville Falls**, then quickly drops away in near-vertical slopes to a river bottom that's 0.3 mile below the gorge edge. The fierce river and steep slopes have prevented logging, leaving the gorge in pristine shape—a rich, riverside old-growth forest. Access to the gorge bottom is by footpaths that go straight down the gorge sides, making for an extremely difficult return. Even the riverside trail can be difficult, finding its way along the rough, rocky gorge bottom. Nevertheless, the gorge bottom is reasonably popular with day hikers, backpackers, and fishermen. Fortunately for the less athletic, the gorge rims are easier to reach, and the finest viewpoint, **Wiseman's View**, is disabled-accessible.

South Mountains State Park (828-433-4772; fax: 828-433-4778; ncparks.gov/Visit/parks/somo/main.php; southmountains@connine.com), 3001 S. Mountain Park Ave., Connelly Springs 28612. Open daylight, all year. Admission is free. The 16,664-acre South Mountains State Park occupies the rugged central heart of the South Mountains, an outlier of the Blue Ridge that marks the southern edge of the Catawba Valley. With about 1,000 feet of valley-to-peak relief, the South Mountains are smaller than the other mountains in this chapter—but they more than make up for it with rugged scenery. Streams twist and dash through deep gorges; the sharp points of gray cliffs emerge from deep forests; truck-sized boulders litter the bottoms of steep gulches; great waterfalls plunge over cliff edges. The mixed forests are dominated by hemlocks, a conifer with pine-like bark and fir-like needles that grows rapidly to great sizes. On exposed cliffs, pines and hemlocks twist into bonsai shapes.

Heavily logged in the 20th century, South Mountains State Park is laced by a network of slide roads (used to skid timber downhill), jeep trails, and even automobile roads—nearly all now closed to vehicles. The best of these are marked as bicycle and/or horse trails, while other paths are strictly for foot travel only. The rugged topography makes nearly all paths difficult, but the short local relief limits the pain. The park has a new visitors center, two picnic areas, and an equestrian camping area.

The park's trail system is vast and complex, yet it occupies less than half of the park's total acreage; the western half, only recently purchased, is still in its planning stages. Nor is this all. To the immediate south of the park are the South Mountain Game Lands, with 19,781 acres and no official paths. The game lands are state-owned and open to hikers during the off-season and on Sundays. Together the two giant tracts encompass 57 square miles.

South Mountains State Park is 20 miles south of I-40, exit 104 (Enola Road). Take Enola Road south for 9 miles to its end at Old NC 18, then go right 5 miles. From here, large brown state park signs will guide you in for the remaining 6 miles.

PARKS AND GARDENS **Stone Mountain State Park** (336-957-8185; fax: 336-957-3985; ncparks.gov/Visit/parks/stmo/main.php; stone.mountain@ncmail.net), 3042 Frank Pkwy., Roaring Gap 28668. Open daylight, all year. Admission is free. This large state park has a common boundary with the **Blue Ridge Parkway**, and can be reached by exiting onto US 21 south, then driving south 4.6 miles to a right onto Stone Mountain Road (SSR 1100), then another 3.0 miles to the park. The park has a large amount of backcountry wilderness climbing the slopes to the parkway, and some fine historic sites in its central valley—but it's real fascination is its **unusual collection of granitic domes**, explored by a series of loop trails.

Formed as one large pluton, today this exposed granite mound rises up to 1,000 feet above its valley floor, appearing as a series of bare rock monadnocks broken by rugged little stream valleys. Even though these peaks aren't very high by North Carolina standards, their steep sides and rocky terrain can make the paths difficult and tiring. The most popular (and difficult) trail is the 4.5-mile loop that climbs **Stone Mountain** itself—the easternmost and largest of the three monadnocks. Beneath Stone Mountain is the park's largest historic site, the **Hutchinson Homestead**, where original *in situ* structures have been restored to a working 19th-century farm.

Mount Jefferson State Natural Area (336-246-9653; ncparks.gov/Visit/parks/moje/main.php; mount.jefferson@ncmail.net), P.O. Box 48, Jefferson 28640. Open daylight, all year. Admission is free. This isolated mountain rises just south of Jefferson, its peak 1,400 feet above the wide valleys that surround it. A paved lane climbs the west slope of Mount Jefferson in seven switchbacks, with two overlooks giving broad views over West Jefferson and Bluff Mountain. At the top is a tree-shaded picnic area, a nature trail, and walking paths along the narrow 0.5-mile-long summit to two more overlooks.

Broyhill Park and Annie Cannon Gardens. This large and attractive town park in central Blowing Rock (one block west of downtown) has informal gardens and a gazebo around a lovely lake. Below the dam lies Annie Cannon Gardens, a native flower garden. Downstream from Cannon Gardens, a hiking path leads steeply downhill to two large and beautiful waterfalls, a worthwhile if strenuous hike (3 miles round-trip, 800-foot climb).

Daniel Boone Native Gardens (828-264-6390; danielboonegardens.org; dbgardens@danielboonegardens.org), 651 Horn in the West Dr., Boone 28607. Open May–Oct., 10–6, closing later on days with *Horn in the West* performances. $. Owned and run by the nonprofit Garden Club of North Carolina on land contributed by Horn in the West (Southern Appalachian Historical Association) in Boone, the Daniel Boone Gardens presents native Appalachian plants in a free-flowing, informal landscape. First opened in 1966, the gardens have had more than three decades of growth and improvement, offering season-long displays of every native flower imaginable. The 3 acres of gardens now include a bog garden, a fern garden, a sunken rock garden with a tiny pond, a mountain spring, a reflecting pool, and a meditation garden. The large wrought-iron entrance gate with the initials DB was handmade by artist and Daniel Boone descendant Daniel Boone VI.

🐾 **Roan Gardens** (fs.fed.us/r8/cherokee/recreation/roz_nroan.shtml). Closed in winter. $. Six hundred acres of natural rhododendron gardens cover two 6,000-foot peaks deep within the Pisgah National Forest, the centerpiece of the Roan Highlands. Just off NC 216 on the state line, Roan Mountain Gardens offers a mile of high ridgetop meadows and rhododendron balds, with stunning views. Managed as a park by the USDA Forest Service (which levies an admissions charge), this site has three major activity areas. First after the entrance station is a ridgetop parking lot with picnic tables; a trail leads right over meadows to the site of a long-gone 1880s hotel, and left uphill to more meadow views. It is here that the Appalachian Trail climbs its last southern peak above 6,000 feet, Roan High Knob (6,285 feet). Half a mile up the road, a small information booth, toilets, and a picnic area on the left mark the center of the gardens. Here a disabled-accessible trail loops 0.3 mile through spectacular rhododendrons (blooming mid- to late June), with a platform

ONE STEP OVER THE LINE:
TENNESSEE'S PARKS IN THE ROAN HIGHLANDS

(800-250-8620; 423-772-0190; state.tn.us/environment/parks/RoanMtn—capitalization required), 1015 TN 143, Roan Mountain, TN 37687. Open Wed.–Sun. 8–4:30. Tennessee's **Roan Mountain State Park**, 9 miles north of Roan Gardens via TN 143, preserves 3 square miles of the middle slopes of the Roan Highlands. It has an attractive visitors center graced by an old-fashioned overshot wheel, a number of hiking trails, and several good picnic areas. Considered a "resort park," it also has a set of 30 cabins as well as tennis courts and a swimming pool. Within the park is the **Dave Miller Farmstead**. This lovely early-20th-century farmstead, immaculate white with stylish little gable dormers over its front porch, is the successor to two pioneer log cabins, the homes of the Millers since 1870. Now it's an open-air museum, demonstrating a turn-of-the-20th-century mountain farmstead. You'll find it adjacent to Roan Mountain State Park, on TN 143, 3 miles south of the village of Roan Mountain. Try to stop by on a summer's Saturday between noon and 2 PM, when artists and musicians are present.

Unique among the state of Tennessee's 60 natural areas, Hampton Creek Cove (3 miles from the park down back roads) contains a working farm, still run by the family that has farmed this land for the last century. A state-owned part of the 15,000-acre Highlands of Roan, Hampton Creek demonstrates mountain farming practices that conserve natural ecosystems and improve biodiversity. A track runs uphill through the farmlands and into the woods above, eventually reaching the famous ridgetop meadows of the Roan. You will find the natural area at the end of Hampton Creek Road, which starts at the village of Roan Mountain.

giving wide views across the Toe River Valley to the Black Mountains. Continuing to the end of the road and the park's third and final picnic area, an easy walking path leads 1.2 miles round-trip to Roan High Bluff, at 6,367 feet the 12th highest summit in the East. Here a platform overlook built over rocky crags gives a clifftop view over the broken mountains of the Toe Valley.

RIVERS New River (336-982-2587; ncparks.gov/Visit/parks/neri/main.php; new.river@ncmail.net), P.O. Box 48, Jefferson 28640. The most remarkable thing about the South Fork of the New River is the way it meanders, acting as if it's lazily wandering through a level plain. This is not the case. The New River sits more than 3,100 feet above sea level, just behind the Blue Ridge, and follows the Blue Ridge for nearly 90 miles. Of course, those are meandering river miles; the actual linear distance covered is 29.4 miles. Those distance-tripling meanders reduce the slope of the river to the point where canoes commonly replace kayaks; much of the river is flatwater, and none of its rapids is worse than a mild Class II. Despite their flatland shapes and slopes, these meanders have managed to cut straight down into the hard rock of the Blue Ridge, leaving the river surrounded by cliff-like slopes. Frequently the river will make a sharp 180-degree curve, cutting a gorge that doubles back on itself.

The easy paddling couples with the prime mountain scenery to offer 90 miles of day explorations and overnight adventures. The state sponsors formal canoe launching points at a number of places, and its 1,500-acre New River State Park is dedicated to supporting this river as a canoe trail. Private livery services offer guided and unguided rentals, and lots of information on river conditions and campsites.

This stretch of river has long enjoyed the reputation as the second oldest river in the world, and the oldest in North America—claims repeated by President Clinton when he declared it a National Heritage River from its banks near Jefferson in 1998. Some have objected to this, claiming that there is no agreed-upon measure of a river's age, and even if there was, it has never been used in a world survey. Well, picky, picky, picky. Those 90 miles of meanders formed when the New River flowed through a flat plain. The meanders cut into the rock as the mountains rose underneath them—in this case the Blue Ridge Mountains, 220 million years old. You do the math.

Catawba River (ncwaterfalls.com/catawba1.htm). The 220-mile Catawba River rises from the Blue Ridge above Old Fort to flow eastward through this chapter's area. Its uppermost section, noted for its fine forests and a striking waterfall, has recently been added to the Pisgah National Forest; the website gives directions (and impressive photos). For kayakers and canoeists, river access starts as the river emerges from the mountains at Old Fort. For the next 18 miles the river meanders through a 0.5-mile-wide floodplain as the mountains gradually recede on both sides, a nice canoe stream with Class I to II water. For the most part it's an attractive small river, with generally healthy environments and handsome riverside scenery, although it passes several factories and gravel pits along the way. This flows into **Lake James**; after that the river flows another 18 miles, passing Morganton, to leave this chapter's area as it enters another hydropower lake, **Lake Rhodhiss** (see "The Mill Belt"). Surprisingly, this section is more wild in character than the upstream one, and, except for Morganton itself, is mainly riverside forests and an occasional farm. Inside Morganton, a 3.8-mile greenway follows the river's right bank, giving continuous access and some canoe launches.

LAKES ✐ **Lake James (Catawba River)** (828-652-5047; ncparks.gov/Visit/parks/laja/main.php), P.O. Box 340, Nebo 28761. Giant electric utility Duke Power created this huge reservoir at the foot of the Blue Ridge between Marion and Morganton by damming two separate watersheds—the Catawba River and the Linville River—and linking them with a canal. They actually needed three dams to do this, with the third preventing the combined impoundments from slipping into a side stream. Like all such lakes, Lake James provides lots of room for motorboat-based sports, and lots of public and private boat launches. One of these is at **Lake James State Park**, along with a number of short walking trails, a sandy beach, and a very good picnic area.

Sitting at the foot of the Blue Ridge, Lake James gives exceptional mountain views—particularly toward the cliff-lined mouth of the Linville Gorge Wilderness. The easternmost dam, known as Bridgewater Dam, gives the best shore views; from the top of this tall earthen dam, traversed by a paved state road, you can see the sweep of the Blue Ridge curving in front of you, from the Linville Gorge cliffs on your right to the mile-high peaks of the Black Mountains on your left. This is a first-rate sunset spot, especially when the air is still and the water glassy. To reach this spot, take NC 126 west out of Morganton for 9 miles, then go left at a fork onto North Powerhouse Road; Bridgewater Dam is 3 miles farther on.

✱ To See

ALONG THE BLUE RIDGE PARKWAY Here in one place are the major sites that you will reach by traveling along the 127 segment of the Blue Ridge Parkway as it passes through this chapter. It is by no means an exhaustive list—just the don't-miss, cream-of-the-crop-places. The sites directly on the Blue Ridge Parkway are owned and operated by the National Park Service, and are free. Three adjacent, privately owned sites are listed as well, and their hours and charges are in their listings.

Cumberland Knob Recreation Area. The 1,000-acre Cumberland Knob Recreation Area was the first segment of the Blue Ridge Parkway opened to the public, and the site of the dedication ceremony in 1935. It's a forested knob located a mile south of the Virginia border, adjacent to the parkway's NC 18 exit. It has a visitors center with exhibits, and a very nice picnic area. It has two pleasant trails, a 1-mile stroll to the top of Cumberland Knob (only 2,840 feet, but the highest point in the area), and a more strenuous 2-mile loop down to Gully Creek—the latter an 800-foot return climb, offering mountain views, deep forests, attractive small waterfalls, and a log barn.

HORSEBACK RIDING AT MOSES CONE PARK ON THE BLUE RIDGE PARKWAY

Doughton Park. Originally named Bluff Mountain, this 6,000-acre Blue Ridge Parkway tract includes 6 miles of the Blue Ridge Crest and the watershed beneath it. Typical of the Blue Ridge, the Atlantic side is a rugged, broken drop of 2,000 feet, while the western side is little more than rolling hills. The crest is especially notable for its large **wildflower meadows** and **rocky outcrops** with wide views. Paths link the meadows and the outcrops, forming multiple loops that plummet into the stream basin beneath and climb back out again. At the center is a classic parkway recreation area—picnic area, camping area, store, coffee shop, and a motel-style lodge.

At the north end is the Brinager Cabin (milepost 238.5), built in 1885 and one of the loveliest log cabins in the region; it's the site of weaving demonstrations in summer. In 2 miles the parkway enters meadows, with an overlook and path on the left (milepost 240.6). You'll reach the main area of meadows, heaths, rocky outcrops, and grand views in another 0.5 mile, where a left on a spur leads to the lodge and picnic area. Here the meadows follow the Blue Ridge Crest for nearly a mile, while the parkway stays discreetly out of sight from the wild and windy views.

The Parish of the Holy Communion (Churches of the Frescoes) (336-982-3076; fax: 336-982-9870), 120 Glendale School Rd., Glendale Springs 28629. Open weekdays and Sat. during normal business hours; worship services on Sun., and occasionally other days. Admission is free. These two rural parish churches in the New River Valley are noted for their exquisite frescoes in the classic Italian Renaissance manner. These Episcopalian churches are simple wood buildings constructed between 1901 and 1905, still serving congregations in Ashe County. Artist Ben Long created the frescoes between 1971 and 1980, choosing themes that mirrored the annual cycle of Episcopalian liturgy. The larger of the two churches, St. Mary's Church in West Jefferson, has three frescoes, each depicting a stage in the life of Christ: *Mary Great with Child*, *John the Baptist*, and *The Mystery of Faith*. The tiny Holy Trinity Church in Glendale Springs, just west of the Blue Ridge Parkway via NC 16, is decorated with one giant fresco behind the alter, a moving and original interpretation of the Last Supper. These remarkable works of art have become an attraction—or perhaps a pilgrimage site—of great popularity, receiving 60,000 visitors a year.

🐾 **Moses Cone Park**. In the 1890s Greensboro denim manufacturer Moses Cone and his wife, Bertha, started to accumulate a large estate along the crest of the Blue Ridge above the new resort village of Blowing Rock. The Cones built a summer home for themselves second only to Biltmore (see "Asheville") in resplendence, with Grecian columns that framed a view not even the Vanderbilts could command. The Cones converted the tired old farmlands they had purchased into wildflower meadows and laced these meadows with miles of carriage paths. Without any close heirs they decided to will their estate to their favorite charity, a Greensboro hospital, under the condition that it remain intact, a recreation ground for the American people. In 1949 the hospital did the best thing for meeting the Cones' wishes: They donated it to the National Park Service to become part of the **Blue Ridge Parkway**—the present Moses Cone Park.

This is not a wild place. It is a cultured place, a cultivated place, a place where a man-made landscape of great beauty and richness spreads over thousands of acres. At its base, the lovely Bass Lake sits on the edge of Blowing Rock, ringed by carefully planned carriage paths. From it, meadowlands stretch uphill, broken and framed by forests and rhododendrons, woven by carriage paths, to reach the beautiful mansion, simple and elegant, now a craft center run by the Southern Highland Craft Guild. Crossing the parkway behind the manor, the meadows continue uphill, as the carriage path forks to two high peak views—a 3-mile switchback to Flat Top, and a 5-mile spiral to Rich Mountain.

Julian Price Park. Part of the Blue Ridge Parkway, 6.5-square-mile Julian Price Park fills the gap between **Moses Cone Park** and **Grandfather Mountain Park**. It does this in the most literal sense, filling in the mountainous spaces between these two better-known areas; and it does it in a more figurative sense as well,

THE LINN COVE VIADUCT ON THE BLUE RIDGE PARKWAY

being less civilized than Moses Cone Park, yet not so wild as the windswept cliffs of Grandfather Mountain. It is more of a typical Blue Ridge landscape, with fields left from grazing and woods left from logging, crossed by trails that are rough and steep. The middle of the park is taken up by a rolling plateau surrounded by slightly taller peaks, containing a pleasant lake, a large picnic area framed by split-rail fences, and a campground. The parkway runs close by the edge of the lake and over its stone dam—a popular and scenic stop. From the picnic area a path runs 2.5 miles (round-trip) along Boone's Fork to a pretty 25-foot waterfall, from there connecting to a number of rougher backcountry trails.

Linn Cove Viaduct. The last segment of the parkway to be built, Linn Cove Viaduct (along with four other nearby viaducts) flies over one of the Blue Ridge's most delicate environments in great, graceful curves. State of the art for its day, the five viaducts pioneered new bridge-building techniques now in common use. At 1/8 mile, Linn Cove is the longest of these viaducts, a breathtaking S hugging the mountain slope. To minimize environmental damage its seven piers were erected with no access road, and little ground construction beyond digging the foundations. Then its 153 segments, all curving and no two alike, were precast in concrete and fixed in place from the top, as cantilevers from the seven piers. It has won 11 design awards.

Like many spectacular bridges, you have to find a viewpoint to appreciate its beauty and its achievement; as you cross it, it'll just look like a roadway. Driving from Blowing Rock you will first see the Linn Cove Viaduct as you get beyond the Rough Ridge Overlook (MP 303); then, a mile later, you'll be on it with no opportunity to stop and admire it. To get a good look, stop at the Yonalossee Overlook

(MP 303.5), where a roadside path leads to its beginning. Once you've driven across it, you will reach the Linn Cove Viaduct Visitors Center on the left on the opposite side, with an information desk and exhibits. A disabled-accessible trail leads a short distance to an overlook. Finally, follow the Tanawha Trail to reach an overlook high above the viaduct, for the finest view of all.

Grandfather Mountain Park (800-468-7325; 828-733-4337; fax: 828-733-2608; grandfather.com; nature@grandfather.com), 2050 Blowing Rock Hwy., P.O. Box 129, Linville 28646. Open daily; summer 8–7; winter 8–5. $$$. Founded in the early 1950s by conservationist Hugh Norton, this self-styled "scenic travel attraction" centers on one of the most stunning and beautiful habitats of the East—the high peaks of Grandfather Mountain. It's a theme park where the theme is nature, the environment, and incredible natural beauty.

VIEW OF LINVILLE FALLS OFF THE BLUE RIDGE PARKWAY

The attraction area starts at the park entrance on US 221 (1 mile west of the Blue Ridge Parkway and 2 miles east of Linville), and centers on a 2.2-mile road that climbs 1,000 feet up the mountain in eight tight switchbacks. This section of the Blue Ridge Crest has spectacular, sheer cliffs facing west; the road gains views of these cliffs on its westward curves (including a clifftop picnic area), while eastward curves wander through lovely forests broken by large rock formations. The road's last 0.5 mile swags steeply up the mountain with wide views over high meadows.

Halfway up is the outstanding habitat zoo, which, like everything else in this park, is included in the admission. Grandfather's large animal enclosures feature native mountain fauna in their actual habitats, with the human visitors separated by moats or elevated walks. The adjacent Nature Center presents the history of Grandfather Mountain (both natural and human) in a museum designed by the Smithsonian's former chief of natural history exhibits. There's also a restaurant.

The road ends at almost exactly 1 mile in elevation, in an area of great open views, meadows, spruce-fir forests, cliffs, and strange rock formations. In the middle of it all is the Mile High

Swinging Bridge, a cable suspension footbridge almost 100 yards long, crossing a rocky chasm 80 feet deep. An easy 2.5-mile walk goes through the chasm under the bridge, then through boreal forests and across rocky outcrops to a viewpoint overlooking the Blue Ridge Parkway. A second, more challenging walk leads uphill, using cables and ladders to climb exposed rocks and skirt hoodoos, to the high point of 5,900 feet.

Behind the scenes, Grandfather Mountain Park has undergone big changes. The attraction and the auto-accessible area are now owned and operated by the Grandfather Mountain Stewardship Foundation, a not-for-profit that uses proceeds to ensure the future of the mountain. The rest of the area, known as "the backcountry," is now 2,700-acre Grandfather Mountain State Park, and its trails are free if you start outside the attraction. The Nature Conservancy owns or controls conservation easements on another 1,000 acres around the backcountry's perimeter.

Linville Falls Recreation Area. As the parkway approaches the Linville River, it enters lovely meadows with split-rail fences. A spur road to the left leads 1.5 miles to **Linville Falls**; just beyond, a side road leads right to the riverside picnic area, where you can get a good view of the parkway crossing the Linville River on a stone-clad arched bridge. The picnic area is nice, and the Linville River Bridge is impressive, but the waterfall is the real attraction.

The falls occur as the Linville River reaches the upper edge of Linville Gorge and plunges straight down into it. Trails to the waterfall spread out in fingers from a visitors center to various viewpoints. A path along the Linville River's left bank leads first to a ledge and pool at the top of the waterfall, with a view out over the gorge and a lovely little cascade upstream. Then the path continues to a view toward the falls from the gorge rim and two views over the gorge. A right bank path lead to a rim-top view toward the waterfall, then a drop to the bottom of the gorge for a view from beneath. The shortest walk is a level 1 mile round-trip, while visiting all six overlooks will require about 5 miles of strenuous climbing.

The Orchard at Altapass (888-765-9531; 828-765-9531; altapassorchard.com), P.O. Box 245, Little Switzerland 28749. Open daily, business hours, May–Nov. Admission is free. Weekend music is free. At the turn of the 20th century, the Clinchfield Railroad built an amazing grade up the face of the Blue Ridge, with 17 tunnels in 23 miles of hairpin loops. Above the last loop, the railroad planted an apple orchard that followed the crest of the Blue Ridge for 2 miles.

Today it's a wonderful place. Restored by its private owners in 1993, the heritage apple trees, nearly a century old, are again healthy and beautiful, framing unimaginable views from the parkway with bright red fruit in huge clusters. Hayride tours wind through the orchard, with orchard storytellers telling the lively history of this important pass. Behind the packinghouse you'll find a monarch butterfly garden (the staff hand-raises monarchs in a special area of the packinghouse), an herb garden, and a spring wetland. The packinghouse hosts live music and holds a remarkable gift shop, with apple products made in the orchard, local honeys and preserves, and local craft art. It also has a small café if you are feeling peckish.

CULTURAL SITES **Penland School of Crafts** (828-765-2359; fax: 828-765-7389; penland.org; office@penland.org), P.O. Box 37, Penland 28765. The grounds are open to strolling daily during normal business hours. The gallery and visitors center are open Tue.–Sat. 10–5, Sun. noon–5. Studios are not open to the public when classes are in session. Admission is free. One of the most distinguished craft schools in America, Penland (at the center of the Mayland Valley) was founded as a weavers' cooperative in 1923, by local schoolteacher Lucy Morgan. Miss Morgan brought in instructors to improve the weavers' skills—and was surprised by the outpouring of interest in professional-level craft instruction. In 1929 she formally opened the Penland School to offer regular schedules of instruction. Over the years nine other craft areas have been added: books & paper, clay, drawing, glass, iron, metals, photography, printmaking, and wood.

Then as now, Penland is a serious school for craft professionals and dedicated amateurs. Completely residential, its classes, studios, and student buildings wander over a pastoral 400-acre campus 5 miles northwest of Spruce Pine. Straddling both sides of a twisting country lane, the campus has an informal, genteel-shabby look, with buildings of every conceivable 20th-century style. Intense summer programs are one to two weeks in length, while autumn and spring see eight-week in-depth sessions in selected subjects. An old school houses the gallery and visitors center, with excellent rotating displays of affiliated artists. Campus tours are available, by appointment, on Tuesdays and Thursdays.

The Turchin Center for the Visual Arts (828-262-3017; fax: 828-262-2848; turchincenter.org; turchincenter@appstate.edu), 423 W. King St., Boone 28608. Open Tue.–Sat. 10–6. Admission is free. Affiliated with Appalachian State University, this arts center occupies the 100-year-old octagonal brick Methodist Church that has long been a prominent downtown Boone landmark. Meant as a center for campus–community interaction, it has a main gallery and six smaller galleries, plus two terraces for displaying sculpture, a lecture hall, and a wing for classrooms and studios.

HISTORIC SITES ***Horn in the West*** (828-262-2120; hornin thewest.com), P.O. Box 295, Boone 28607. Evening performances June 22–Aug. 11, Tue.–Sun. For over half a century, the Southern Appalachian Historical Association, headquartered in Boone, has presented Kermit Hunter's large-scale outdoor musical drama of the early settlement of the Watauga Valley, centering on Daniel Boone and the American Revolution. Held six evenings a week throughout the summer, the performance is preceded by an evening tour of the historically authentic reconstructed pioneer farmstead, Hickory Ridge Homestead—actually an extension of the performance, with period-costumed guides demonstrating the pioneer way of life. It's located on Horn in the West Drive, off US 321 south of Boone.

The adjacent living history museum, Hickory Ridge Homestead, can be visited by itself during the day. The buildings, sited on an attractive wooded slope below the amphitheater, are beautifully and authentically furnished, and have period vegetable and herb gardens. Guides in period clothing explain the pioneer way of life, demonstrate crafts, and perform authentic music. Visitors are invited to participate in activities such as carding and spinning wool, weaving on a 185-year-old loom, candle making, and cooking over an open hearth.

Village of Kona. The remote village of Kona, deep in the most rural section of the Mayland Valley, is best known as the home of North Carolina's most notorious female murderer, Frankie Silver (Mrs. Francis Stewart Silver). Three days before Christmas 1832, in her log cabin and with her infant daughter looking on, the petite 18-year-old chopped husband Charlie into pieces and burned him in the fireplace. The mountain folk song "Ballad of Frankie Silver" (not to be confused with the Delta blues song "Frankie and Johnny") attributed the murder to jealousy—but the real motive was Charlie's brutal abuse. Best-selling author Sharyn McCrumb, whose grandparents lived nearby, has written a fine (and very insightful) novel on the subject, *The Ballad of Frankie Silver.*

Modern-day Kona is an exceptionally pretty mountain settlement straddling scenic NC 80 6 miles north of US 19E. Kona occupies a set of meadowy hilltops that drop from the old Baptist church with its colonial-era graveyard, past the new Baptist church, then straight down to a gorge below. While the colonial graveyard gives pride of place to Revolutionary War veteran George Silver, most tourists will be interested in his grandson Charlie's graves—three of them, as they kept finding bits of Charlie hidden in the snow. The adjacent church is now a small museum for the Silver clan, and the views are spectacular.

Morganton's National Historic Districts (828-437-4104; historicburke.org), P.O. Box 915, Morganton 28680. In the Catawba Valley, Morganton's historic districts center on the tiny old Burke County Courthouse in the middle of downtown, on its nicely kept square with its Civil War statue out front. It's older than its Victorian trim; it was built in 1837 as a simple, elegant Federal-style structure, and served as the summer seat of the North Carolina Supreme Court until the Civil War. Inside, the Historic Burke Foundation maintains a small historic museum with exhibits that change annually.

Actually, Morganton has nine historic districts listed on the National Register of Historic Places. This adds up to a lot of old buildings. However, it means more than this; a historic district preserves the look and feel of the past, and is an experience in itself. The Historic Burke Foundation has an excellent color brochure listing all nine districts and giving details of the major buildings in each one. It's a good way to get a deep insight into the way an American small town used to be.

Just outside town, the 1812 McDowell House sits on the 6 remaining acres of the once-vast Quaker Meadows Plantation. It's a high-ceilinged two-story structure made of on-site red brick. The two front doors show a Pennsylvania Dutch influence (even though the McDowells were Scots-Irish). Despite encroaching urbanization the house remains beautifully situated amid rolling lawns. To reach the McDowell House, take NC 181 for 4 miles northwest from Morganton's town center to the end of the four-lane; then turn right onto St. Mary's Church Road.

Senator Sam J. Ervin Jr. Library (828-438-6000; fax: 828-438-6015; samervinlibrary.org; moreinfo@wp.cc.nc.us), 1001 Burkemont Ave., Morganton 28655. Open weekdays, business hours. Admission is free. Those of us old enough to remember Watergate will no doubt remember the late Senator Sam Ervin, chairman of the Nixon impeachment hearings, for his fairness, shrewdness, sharp intelligence, deep knowledge of the Constitution—and frequent protestations that he was just "a simple country lawyer." Senator Sam was a Morganton man, born and bred in the Catawba Valley, and Western Piedmont Community College has commemorated their local-boy-made-good in a most appropriate way: by preserving his large personal library. Western Piedmont Community College has gone well beyond saving the senator's personal papers and 7,500 books. It has faithfully recreated his large, wood-paneled library, every piece of furniture the way the senator left it, every book it its original place on the shelf. Located in its own room within the college's library, the Ervin Library offers a window into a great mind. Apart from the Ervin Library, Western Piedmont Community College is worth a visit for its wide views and handsome campus. To reach the Ervin Library, follow the signs from exit 103 on I-40; once on campus, you'll find the library on the second floor of the Phifer Learning Resource Center. Then explore the views by strolling this compact campus. Parking is ample and no permit is needed.

Andrews Geyser. Built as part of the Swannanoa Grade railroad in the 1870s, Andrews Geyser shoots 30 feet up in the air continuously—that is, as long as it's turned on. The geyser, located at the far upper end of the Catawba Valley, sits in a small park surrounded by railroad; it's in the crook of a hairpin turn that the railroad makes as it climbs the face of the Blue Ridge. In the early days, the geyser served as a scenic focal point for railroad passengers entering (or leaving) this spectacular mountain climb, impressing the passengers as their train circled it. Today it's a historic artifact from a bygone era, kept in loving repair by locals such as the innkeeper of the Inn on Mill Creek; the lovely little lake that feeds the geyser is on the inn's property, and the innkeeper is the one who turns the valve on and off daily. The geyser, shooting straight up in the middle of a pentagonal reflecting pond, is surrounded by shaded picnic tables. If you are lucky, a train will pass while you visit it, looping around you with half its cars going toward you and the other half away. To find Andrews Geyser take US 70 west from Old Fort and follow the signs, first onto Old US 70, then up Mill Creek Road.

MYSTERIOUS PHENOMENA **The Brown Mountain Lights**. Since 1900 (and perhaps earlier, according to local tales), mysterious lights have danced and flickered over the 2,725-foot peak of Brown Mountain, a side ridge off the Blue Ridge 13 miles north of Morganton. Attempts to explain them have all failed, including train lights (they appear when trains don't run), auto headlights (no autos), and swamp gas (no swamps). Most of the remaining explanations involve ghosts in some way. So find a good viewpoint and a clear night, bring to mind your favorite campfire tale, and wait for the lights to come out. With luck, you can view the Brown Mountain Lights from overlooks along NC 181 north of Morganton.

✷ To Do

BICYCLE RENTALS **Boone Bike and Touring** (828-262-5750; boonebike .com), 899 Blowing Rock Rd., Boone 28607. Open Mon.–Sat. 10–6. Located on US 321 on the south side of Boone, near the busy intersection with US 221 and NC 105, this bicycle shop rents high-quality touring and mountain bikes, along with trail maps and suggested destinations.

Cycle4Life (828-898-5445; cycle4lifebikeshop.com), 76 High Country Square, Banner Elk 28604. Open Mon.–Sat. 10–7. Owned by a former college cycling coach, this bike shop is located in Banner Elk's High Country Square shopping plaza on NC 184. It rents touring bikes, mountain bikes, and hybrids, and has plenty of info on local cycling sites. They sponsor a Sunday group bike during the season.

CANOES, KAYAKS, AND RAFTS **Zaloos Canoes** (800-535-4027; 336-246-3066; zaloos.com; zaloos@skybest.com), 3874 NC 16 S., Jefferson 28640. Located on the New River, at the corner of NC 16 and NC 88 (5 miles east of Jefferson),

Zaloos rents kayaks and canoes, and offers tubing and canoe trips (including camping trips) along the New River.

River Girl Fishing Company (336-877-8800; rivergirlfishing.com; rivergirl24@skybest.com), 4041 Todd Railroad Grade Rd., Todd 28684. Located in the 1888 train depot at the historic center of Todd, midway between Boone and Jefferson on NC 194, this company furnishes complete river outfitting—fly fishing, tubing, kayaking, and canoeing on the adjacent New River, as well as bicycling on the scenic lanes in the New River Valley. While you're there, check out the neat general store across the street.

High Mountain Expeditions (800-262-9036; 828-264-7368; fax: 828-262-0572; highmountainexpeditions.com; info@raftingnc.com), 1380 NC 105 S., Boone 28607. Located in downtown Blowing Rock, High Mountain Expeditions furnishes rafting trips—calm, family oriented floats on the Watauga River, or wild, whitewater trips on the Nolichucky River. They also offer a whole lot of other stuff: caving tours, hiking tours, mountain bike tours, mountain bike rentals, flatwater (mountain lake) kayaking tours, and—note this, hikers—shuttle services.

Wahoo's Adventures (800-444-7238; 828-262-5774; wahoosadventures.com), P.O. Box 3094, Boone 28607. Wahoo's offers a wide range of rafting experiences throughout the Smokies, with branches in Tennessee as well as their GHQ in Boone. In the Boone area, they offer both gentle family trips and fierce rapid-runners on a variety of nearby rivers.

MINING AND PANNING **Thermal City Gold Mine** (828-286-3016; huntforgold.com; info@thermalcitygoldmine.com), 5240 US 221 N., Union Mills 28167. Open Mar.–Oct., daily 8:30–5. The Catawba Valley's South Mountains were the site of America's first gold rush, when a 12-year-old boy picked up a 17-pound (yup, that's *pounds*, not ounces) gold nugget from a nearby creek. Gold was quickly found along the Second Broad River, 9 miles south of I-40 via US 276. One of the first gold mines, the 1830 Thermal City Mine, is still in operation, under the ownership of the same family since 1890. Owner Lloyd Nanney offers recreational gold miners 30 acres of unsalted on-site placer deposits along a scenic 0.5-mile section of the river. Lloyd has an on-site snack bar and café, and sells a full line of gold-mining equipment from a small store in the center of the mine.

SKIING **Ski Beech** (800-438-2093; skibeech.com; info@skibeech.com), 1007 Beech Mountain Pkwy., P.O. Box 1118, Beech Mountain 28604. Open in winter, 8:30 AM–10 PM. Located downhill behind the Beech Mountain village center in the Boone area, Ski Beech is clean and well kept, and popular with families; happy little children cover the bunny slope, giggling and screeching. Its run is 3,600 feet with a drop of 750 feet from a summit of 5,505 feet to a base of 4,700 feet, the highest ski elevations in North Carolina.

Sugar Mountain (800-784-2768; 828-898-4521; skisugar.com; info@skisugar.com), P.O. Box 369, Banner Elk 28604. The Sugar Mountain ski lodge, in the Boone area, is easily accessible from NC 184 in Banner Elk. It is busy with adults and families, but handles crowds well. It has the longest run and the farthest drop in the area—1.5 miles and 1,200 feet, from a summit at 5,300 feet to a base at 4,100 feet.

✷ Lodging

RESORTS AND HOTELS ✐ **The Mast Farm Inn** (888-963-5857; 828-963-5857; fax: 828-963-6404; mastfarminn.com; stay@mastfarminn.com), 2543 Broadstone Rd., P.O. Box 704, Valle Crucis 28691. Rooms, $$–$$$$; cottages, $$$–$$$$$. This popular and respected small country inn in a rural area near Boone has so many historic buildings that it's listed on the National Register as a Historic District. The grounds are beautifully landscaped, and the farmhouse's wide wraparound porch is a perfect place to sit and rock. Both rooms and cottages are available, all authentically furnished historic structures; young children are allowed in the cottages, but not the inn. A full breakfast is included. Their restaurant is noted for its organic gourmet regional cuisine.

✐ **Eseeola Lodge** (800-742-6717; 828-733-4311; eseeola.com), 175 Linville Ave., P.O. Box 99, Linville 28646. Open May–Oct. $$$$–$$$$$$. In existence since 1892, the Eseeola remains a summer playground for the wealthy in the village of Linville, on the Blue Ridge near Grandfather Mountain. The present lodge, dating from 1926 and on the National Register, has 24 elegant rooms with all amenities, including wireless Internet. The rates include breakfast and dinner (coat and tie required) at the lodge's gourmet restaurant. Guests have access to the 18-hole private golf course ($80 per round), little changed since Donald Ross designed it in 1924.

BED & BREAKFASTS Buffalo Tavern Bed and Breakfast (877-615-9678; 336-877-9080; fax: 336-877-9081; buffalotavern.com; DocAdams@BuffaloTavern.com), 958 W. Buffalo Rd., West Jefferson 28694. $$–$$$. Built in the 1870s, this large wooden house in the New River Valley (6 miles west of Jefferson) was a popular 19th-century coaching inn and Prohibition-era tavern. Today it's an elegant four-room B&B, surrounded by azaleas, its first- and second-story porches shaded by large old trees. A full breakfast is served by candlelight in the dining room.

THE MAST FARM INN, A NATIONAL REGISTER HISTORIC DISTRICT NEAR BOONE

Lovill House Inn (800-849-9466; 828-264-4204; lovillhouseinn.com; innkeeper@lovillhouseinn.com), 404 Old Bristol Rd., Boone 28607. Open all year. $$$–$$$$. This inn retains the look and feel of the mountain countryside while sitting on the edge of downtown Boone. The 1875 Victorian farmhouse with wraparound porches and rockers, built by one of Boone's most prominent citizens, sits on 11 acres of landscaped gardens and woods. The six rooms are large, with wireless Internet, fireplaces (half wood, half gas), and elegant antiques and reproductions; there's also a cabin. A full breakfast is served in the sunny dining room.

Fairway Oaks Bed & Breakfast (877-584-7611; 828-584-7677; fairwayoaksbandb.com; fairwayoaks@charter.net), 4640 Plantation Dr., Morganton 28655. $$. This purpose-built Catawba Valley B&B looks like a traditional southern farmhouse, with its wide wood porches and tall windows. Set inside the gated golf community of Silver Creek Plantation 10 miles west of Morganton, this course-side inn has sweeping views over the links toward the majestic South Mountains. Each of the five sizable guest rooms is furnished with wireless Internet, a phone, and a desk. Guests receive a discount on the semi-private Silver Creek Plantation Golf Club.

✐ 🐾 **The Inn on Mill Creek** (877-735-2964; 828-668-1115; fax: 828-668-8506; inn-on-mill-creek.com; info@innonmillcreek.com), P.O. Box 185, Ridgecrest 28770. $$$–$$$$. This peaceful, beautiful haven lies deep within the Pisgah National Forest, on the slopes of the Blue Ridge above the Catawba Valley, the only home on a country lane that winds up the mountain through 9 miles of forest. Beside the inn, a 1916 dam creates a small lake stocked with trout; its outfall, through a pipe regulated by the innkeepers, feeds Andrews Geyser. The home is a dramatic modernist structure from the early 1980s, with large, comfy common areas and seven rooms, moderate to large in size. Wireless Internet is available, and a full breakfast is included.

CABINS The Cottages at Glowing Hearth (888-232-5080; 828-963-8800; glowinghearth.com; glowingheart@skybest.com), 171 Glowing Hearth Lane, Vilas 28692. $$$$. Five luxurious cottages sit on 40 acres of mountaintop land, in the countryside near Boone, with sweeping views. The large, elegant cabins are modern, reminiscent of farmhouses with picket rails, but with an 18-foot peaked ceiling and broad windows facing the view. Each has a large living area with a stone fireplace, an excellent kitchen, and a master bedroom with a 100-gallon whirlpool bath in the master bath.

✐ **Clear Creek Guest Ranch** (800-651-4510; 828-675-4510; clearcreekranch.com; ccrdude@prodigy.net), 100 Clear Creek Rd./NC 80 S., Burnsville 28714. $$$–$$$$. This stunningly beautiful classic dude ranch sits in the shadows of Mount Mitchell, the tallest peak in the East, just off the Blue Ridge Parkway's NC 80 exit. The tariff includes a full slate of trail rides and ranch activities, both on the ranch and in the adjacent Pisgah National Forest. Accommodations are in log-sided cabins with full front porches. Hearty ranch meals are served three times a day, included in the tariff. This family-friendly resort offers a full program for children ages 5 and up.

🐾 **The Cottages at Spring House Farm** (877-738-9798; 828-738-9798; springhousefarm.com; thecottages@springhousefarm.com), 219 Haynes

Rd., Marion 28752. $$$$. This ecology-minded retreat has six widely spaced cabins on a wooded 92-acre farm in the Catawba Valley's South Mountains, 15 miles south of Marion. All cabins have private porches or decks, with full-sized outdoor hot tubs, and all cabins have either a wood-burning stone fireplace or stove. The Craftsman-style furniture is handmade locally from salvaged historic lumber. Kitchens are well furnished. Adult dogs are allowed in one of the cabins; no puppies or cats. The owners live on-site, in the 1836 Ledbetter House that retains its original interior paint—a worthy attraction in its own right.

✱ Where to Eat

DINING OUT **Crippen's Country Inn and Restaurant** (877-295-3487; 828-295-3487; fax: 828-295-0388; crippens.com; jimmycrippen@crippens.com), 239 Sunset Dr., P.O. Box 528, Blowing Rock 28605. Open daily for dinner, July–Oct.; may be closed on some days during the off-season. $$$–$$$$. Owner Jimmy Crippen and chef James Welch have created one of the finest and most exciting restaurants in the mountains in this beautifully restored boardinghouse off downtown Blowing Rock. Each evening's menu is unique, selected from a large repertoire of adventurous, boldly flavored creations. Desserts are decadent, and can be finished with fine brandies, single-malt scotches, ports and dessert wines, and fine cigars (smoking on the porch only). Crippen's is located on Sunset Drive, a side street running between downtown Blowing Rock and US 321.

The Jackalope View (888-827-6155; 828-898-9004; archersinn.com/jackalopes.htm; theinn@archersinn.com), 2489 Beech Mountain Pkwy., Beech Mountain 28604. $$$$. Located in the Boone ski area, halfway up Beech Mountain on NC 184, this casual fine-dining restaurant has glass walls and a deck hanging over a 180-degree open south-facing panorama. The three wine cellars offer 300 different wines, with a limited choice of bottles $25 or less. The menu presents exotic and original preparations of beef, trout, fresh seafood, and game. Upstairs is a large and comfortable bar, with even more great views, a wide selection of microbrews, and live jazz on weekends.

EATING OUT **Famous Louise's Rockhouse Restaurant** (828-765-2702), US 221 and NC 183, Linville Falls 28657. $$. This landmark stone building, by the Blue Ridge Parkway on US 221 in Linville Falls, once furnished a hearty good time to the parkway's WPA construction crews—an endeavor helped by its position straddling three county lines, discouraging unwanted snooping by county sheriffs. Now it's a popular southern-style restaurant serving good home-style food three meals a day. Cash and debit cards are accepted but not credit cards.

✐ **Dan'l Boone Inn** (828-264-8657; danlbooneinn.com; manager@danlbooneinn.com), 130 Hardin St., Boone 28607. Open daily, May–Oct., for lunch and dinner, and for breakfast on the weekends; off-season (Nov.–Apr.) weekdays are dinner only. $$. A popular family eatery since 1959, the Dan'l Boone Inn occupies a large former boardinghouse at the south edge of downtown Boone. Although seating is at individual tables, all food is served in bowls family-style—huge helpings of traditional southern fare, brought out until the large tables are full. You take what you want, and if the bowl goes empty they bring you some more.

✐ **Judges Riverside Barbeque** (828-433-5798; fax: 828-433-9842; judges riverside.com; judgesriverside@fulenwider.net), 128 Greenlee Ford Rd., Morganton 28680. Open daily, lunch and dinner. $$. This large restaurant sits on a remote, shaded spot on the south bank of the Catawba River, at the end of Greenlee Ford Road on the western edge of Morganton; its floor-to-ceiling windows give wide views over the Catawba, as does its multilevel deck. Judges serves classic Piedmont-style barbeque (see Lexington Barbeque "The Mill Belt")—fresh made, slow cooked over wood, mild, smoky, tender, and moist. They serve sauce on the side, not on the meat, and they make it themselves. The homemade sides include a wonderful cayenne-hot coleslaw made not with mayonnaise, but with the vinegar baste, a North Carolina tradition.

✷ Entertainment

CLASSICAL Parkway Playhouse (828-682-4285; parkwayplayhouse.com; info@parkwayplayhouse.com), 202 Green Mountain Dr., P.O. Box 1432, Burnsville 28714. Plays start at 8 PM, most summer weekends. Reservations are required; call on weekday afternoons. Founded in 1947 as a summer outlet for Greensboro university students, Mayland Valley's Parkway Playhouse is the state's oldest continuously operating theater. Now a semi-professional company, it features a combination of old Broadway standards, children's plays, and Appalachian-themed plays from its giant barn-like theater down a (well-signposted) back street in Burnsville, one of the prettiest small towns in the mountains.

POPULAR Old Fort Mountain Music. Performances every Friday, from 7 PM until late at night. Admission is free. Old Fort Mountain Music shares space with EMS in an old brick building at the center of town, at the western end of the Catawba Valley just off I-40's exit 73. Outside, the wide, empty EMS driveway provides a place for the musicians to tune up, practice, and talk. Inside, a long, narrow hall with folding chairs forms the venue for this free weekly mountain concert and jam session.

✷ Selective Shopping

Downtown Boone. Stretching four long blocks along US 321/421, downtown Boone is a classic turn-of-the-20th-century brickfront, lively and active with interesting shops. The main street is a simple two lanes with parallel parking, named King Street; behind it on the downhill side is alley-like Howard Street, where most of the off-street parking is to be found. With a 13,000-student university two blocks away, parking is highly regulated, but the chamber of commerce on the western end of Howard Avenue will give you a permit that lets you park to shop downtown.

Downtown Blowing Rock. Blowing Rock's elegant little downtown stretches along four blocks of US Bus 321, opposite the town park. It's built up from numerous small buildings—old brick fronts, houses, renovated gas stations—now given over to catering to the needs of the village's well-heeled visitors. Galleries, gift shops, antiques shops, and restaurants dominate the street.

✐ **Mast General Store** (828-963-6511; mastgeneralstore.com; info@mastgeneralstore.com), NC 194, Valle Crucis 28691. Open Mon.–Sat. 7–6, Sun. 1–5. Admission is free. You may have seen various Mast General Stores selling outdoor and gift items in downtown Boone, Hendersonville, Asheville, and Waynesville. Make no mistake: The 19th-century frame store in the remote countryside west of Boone is the *real* Mast General Store and always has been—the primary general store for the community of Valle Crucis since 1882. This National Register structure is really a collection of white clapboard buildings sort of stuck together, with doorways passing through common walls. Inside, it combines the items needed by the Valle Crucis community—groceries, mail, fishing licenses, burning permits, and a checkers set by a potbellied stove—with local canned jellies and honeys, barrels of marbles, bulk candy, local arts, outdoor products, and all sorts of other stuff. Its current owners have taken the Mast's longtime formula of "Everything from Cradles to Caskets" and used it to create a general store marketing powerhouse. However, they've kept the original Mast General Store true to its heritage, one of the few general stores to make it successfully into the 21st century.

Downtown Burnsville. This attractive county seat at the center of Mayland Valley has an impressive selection of small craft galleries clustered around its well-kept town square, then trailing westward along Main Street. The Garden Deli, on the square, is a good place for lunch.

✷ Special Events

First weekend in May: **Spring Studio Tour** (toeriverarts.org). Sponsored by the local non-profit Toe River Arts Council, this annual event opens more than 50 artists' studios and galleries to the public, spread throughout the Mayland Valley but centered on the Penland Craft School.

Second weekend in July: **Grandfather Mountain Highland Games and Gathering of the Clans** (828-733-1333; fax: 828-733-0092; gmhg.org), P.O. Box 1095, Linville 28646. $$$–$$$$. For over half a century, the Grandfather Mountain Highland Games have been held on MacRae Meadows at Grandfather Mountain Park. A highly popular five-day event with attendance in the tens of thousands, events include classic Scottish athletics, bagpipe demonstrations and competitions, Highland dancing, ceilidhs (Celtic jam sessions), Scottish harp and fiddling, Gaelic song, and sheep dog demonstrations. There are a large number of vendors and clan tents.

Third weekend in July: **Alleghany County Fiddler's Convention** (alleghanyfiddlers.com; savfd@skybest.com), 334 Reynolds Rd., Sparta 28675. $$. Third weekend in July. Old-time mountain and bluegrass bands come from all over to compete for cash prizes at the county fairgrounds at Sparta, at the far northern end of the New River Valley. There's also a dance competition.

First weekend in August: **Mount Mitchell Crafts Fair**. Admission is free. This Burnsville town square craft fair in Mayland Valley, founded in 1956, features over 200 local and regional craft artists, selected by the Crafts Fair Selection Committee for quality, originality, and variety. There is ongoing bandstand entertainment that emphasizes mountain music and dance, as well as a number of food vendors.

Mid-September weekend: **Cove Creek Farm Heritage Days** (828-297-2200; covecreek.net/wordpress), Historic Cove Creek High School, 207 Dale Adams Rd., Sugar Grove 28679. $. This annual fund-raiser, located at an old stone high school northwest of Boone, is patterned after the local agricultural fairs of 100 years ago. It has mountain music and clogging, farm exhibits, farm crafts, old-time games, a petting zoo, and canning judging. The day after the fair, local farms open their doors for afternoon farm tours.

Third weekend in September: **Banner Elk Woolly Worm Festival** (woolly worm.com). $$. Held in the Boone ski area for the last quarter century, this celebration of the furry caterpillar draws more than 15,000 people every year to the school grounds in Banner Elk. There are 50 heats of the worms racing up strings, bringing cash prizes to their owners. When a champion is finally declared, the festival's official forecaster uses its stripes to predict the coming winter weather.

Mid-November to mid-December: **Cut & Choose Christmas Tree Celebration** (828-264-3061; wataugachristmas trees.org; info@wataugachristmastrees .org). Each Christmas season, 16 or so Boone-area Christmas-tree growers organize an old-fashioned family Christmas-tree-cutting celebration, holding a special welcome for families coming from the warm flatlands to choose a tree and maybe see some pre-Christmas snow. A brochure describes each farm in detail, telling how to get to it and how you will be welcomed.

ASHEVILLE AND THE CENTRAL MOUNTAINS

Asheville, a city of about 200,000 people, occupies the center of the Blue Ridge's most peculiar elevated valley, a giant feature stretching 58 miles from north to south and typically 5 to 10 miles wide, drained by the French Broad River. Its 2,000-foot valley floor is ringed by some of the East's tallest and most rugged mountains, with many peaks over a mile above sea level and a number of 6,000-footers. On its southeastern corner, however, the valley floor is actually perched *above* the surrounding mountains, which drop steeply away to the Piedmont's 800-foot elevations.

The city of Asheville is surprisingly sophisticated, with a 60-block downtown that has more and better shops, art galleries, restaurants, and nightclubs than you'd expect from an urban area 10 times its size. It's had an active tourism industry since antebellum times, and this certainly helped, but much of the credit goes to its richest homeboy, George Vanderbilt, whose 1890 Biltmore Estate is the state's premier private tourist attraction. In the decades before World War I, society families flocked to Asheville to be near Vanderbilt, and society architects followed. A century later Asheville remains a striking early-20th-century city, resplendent in Craftsman and art deco architecture. Today these buildings host one of the South's largest artists' colonies, centering on the Fine Crafts Movement.

George Vanderbilt also built Asheville's wilderness and outdoor recreation. He didn't like the fact that his panoramic mountain view was spoiled by eroded, logged-out slopes, so he bought the view (totaling 125,000 acres) and hired top German-trained foresters to restore naming it Pisgah Forest. Upon his death his wife sold it to the US Forest Service (which his first forester, Gifford Pinchot, had gone on to establish); it is now the core holding of the huge Pisgah National Forest, and one of the East's great outdoor recreation tracts.

There are other great public tracts as well. West of the Pisgahs, the Great Balsam Mountains form a mile-high barrier with 17 peaks over 6,000 feet in elevation. Here you'll find wide mountaintop meadows that sprawl for miles, Canadian-style spruce-fir forests, waterfalls, and views, all easily reached from the Blue Ridge Parkway. Northeast of Asheville are the Craggy and the Black Mountains (one ridge with two names), also followed by the parkway, and whose 18 peaks above

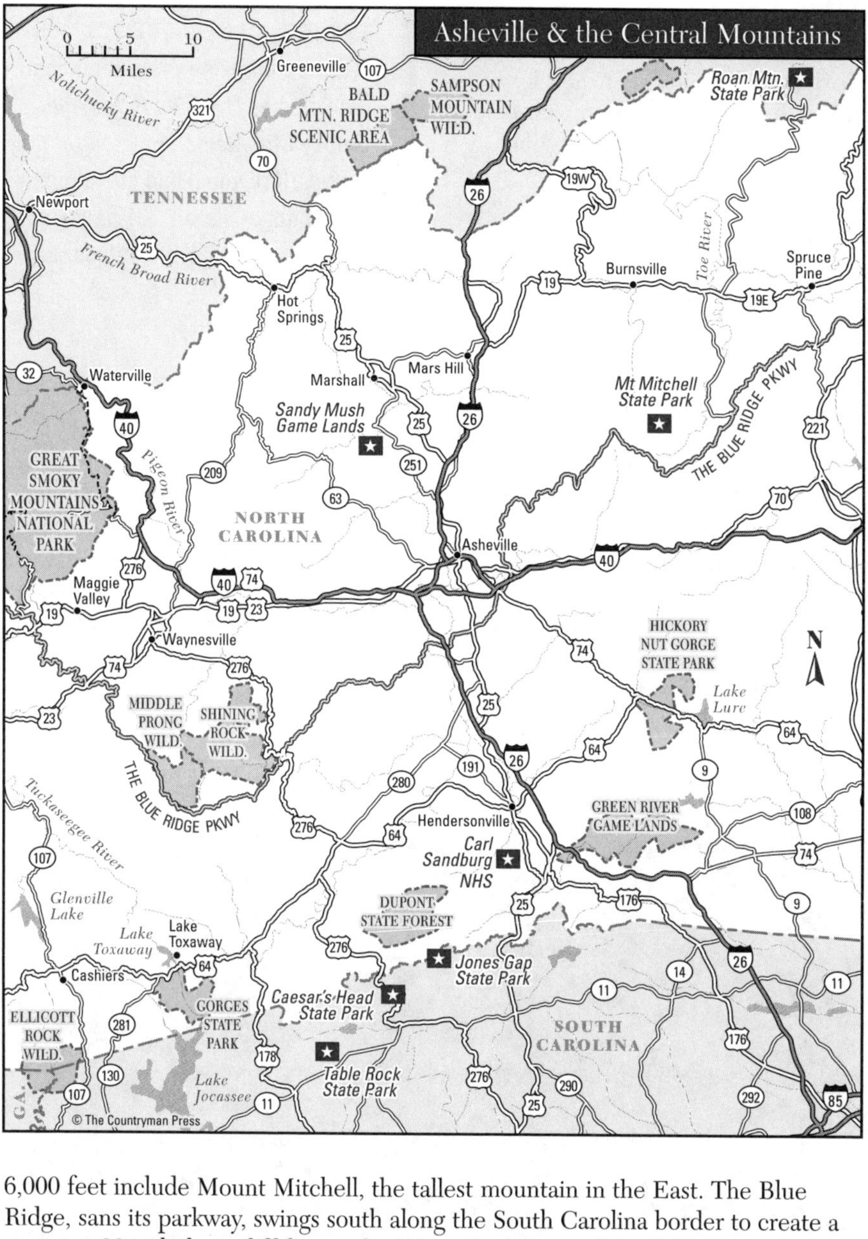

6,000 feet include Mount Mitchell, the tallest mountain in the East. The Blue Ridge, sans its parkway, swings south along the South Carolina border to create a stunning 32-mile-long cliff feature known as the Blue Wall. And finally, the little-visited Bald Mountains, blocking the northern end of Asheville's valley along the Tennessee line, offer their own set of wonders.

GUIDANCE Asheville Visitors Center (800-257-1300; 828-258-6101; fax: 828-254-6054; ashevillechamber.org; member@ashevillechamber.org), 36 Montford Ave., Asheville 28802. This chamber covers Asheville and the surrounding area. It runs a large and sophisticated visitors center (with a nice gift shop) just north of downtown Asheville, off I-240's Montford Avenue exit.

The Blue Ridge Parkway Headquarters (828-271-4779; nps.gov/blri), 99 Hemphill Knob Rd., Asheville 28754. Its street address notwithstanding, park headquarters for the Blue Ridge Parkway faces the parkway at milepost 382. Here you'll find a large new visitors center, with exhibits, information, gifts, and books. Opposite it, on the other side of the parking lot, are the administrative headquarters, with a very nice small garden behind.

THERE'S A LOT MORE . . .

. . . in Countryside Press's companion volume, *The Blue Ridge and Smoky Mountains: An Explorer's Guide.* Here you'll find five chapters about this area, 131 pages of additional listings and details.

Blue Ridge Mountain Host of North Carolina (828-285-9907; fax: 828-285-9908; ncblueridge.com; info@ncblueridge.com), P.O. Box 1806, Asheville 28802. This organization of independent hotels and B&Bs covers this chapter's entire area, along with the western half of the previous chapter. Its excellent website is a good resource, particularly for the remote mountainous areas.

Asheville Bed & Breakfast Association (ABBA) (877-262-6867; ashevillebba .com). This association is made up of 13 small B&Bs, all of them in private homes located in quiet neighborhoods in and around Asheville. You can use either their website or their toll-free number to find and reserve the room that's right for you. Highly recommended.

VIEW OF WAYNESVILLE SURROUNDED BY THE FORESTED SLOPES OF THE PISGAH RANGE, IN THE PISGAH NATIONAL FOREST

The Pisgah National Forest, Pisgah Ranger District (828-877-3265), 1001 Pisgah Hwy., Pisgah Forest 28768. Located on US 276 4 miles north of Brevard, this National Forest Service visitors center has interpretive displays, a bookstore, and an information desk as well as the administrative offices of the Pisgah District.

GETTING THERE *By car:* This area is crossed by I-40 running from east to west, and by I-26 running from north to south (and confusingly marked "East" and "West" on its signs); these intersect just south of downtown Asheville. Other highways in this region are scenic but slow; if you want to make tracks, stick to these interstates as long as you can. US 276 in particular is one of the most scenic, and worst-quality, highways around; if you need to travel quickly between Brevard and Waynesville you'll find the interstates faster, even though they add 16 miles to a 38-mile journey.

By air: **Asheville Regional Airport (AVL)** (828-684-2226; flyavl.com), 61 Terminal Dr., Suite 1, Fletcher 28732. Asheville's small regional airport is located 15 miles south of downtown off I-26, exit 40 (NC 280). It's an old-fashioned terminal from the 1950s, with a central one-story terminal and radiating gates, but has been remodeled and modernized in recent years—less quaint but more comfortable. It is served by five airlines, with daily service to Atlanta, Charlotte, Chicago, Detroit, Orlando, Houston, LaGuardia, and Newark. Several car rental agencies are located within or near the airport.

By bus or train: Asheville has regular bus service, several times a day, on routes that approach it from the south on I-26 and leave it to the north on I-40. The bus station is immediately east of downtown on US 70 (Tunnel Road), just after the tunnel. Asheville has no train service.

MEDICAL EMERGENCIES **Mission Hospital Complex, Asheville** (828-213-1111; msj.org), 509 Biltmore Ave., Asheville 28801. This 730-bed hospital complex, the center of the mountain's largest medical not-for-profit, has a huge double campus south of downtown Asheville, straddling Biltmore Avenue. It's made up of two former competitors, one on each side of the highway, and each has its own Level 2 trauma center. The easier one to find is on the left, 1 mile south of downtown's Patton Square via Biltmore Avenue; it has better visitor parking as well.

Margaret R. Pardee Memorial Hospital, Hendersonville (828-696-1000; pardeehospital.org), 715 Fleming St., Hendersonville 28791. This 222-bed regional hospital, run by a local not-for-profit, offers 24/7 emergency room service from its campus on the northwest edge of downtown Hendersonville.

✷ Exploring the Area

EXPLORING BY CAR **The Blue Ridge Parkway in the Black Mountains**. As with all other sections of the parkway, this 60-mile segment—from NC 80 in the boondocks south of **Burnsville** (see "The Northern Mountains") to NC 151 on the other side of Asheville—is described as for a through-traveler heading south. If you're staying in Asheville, however, this is best done there-and-back-again, first up to NC 80, then returning to go down to NC 151.

From NC 80 the parkway climbs uphill into increasingly rugged country. The road breaks out of the forest on both sides for frequent views; Mount Mitchell, the highest point in the East, can be clearly seen on the right, distinguishable by its tower. In 9 miles the mountain known as the Blue Ridge heads south into South Carolina and Georgia, and the parkway abandons it to climb northward into the **Black Mountains** (see "The Northern Mountains"). A mile later, the Mount Mitchell Spur Road heads 4.5 miles right to **Mount Mitchell State Park**, a remarkable drive that leads to wonderful views from the highest point anywhere east of the Rockies. Once inside the state park, the restaurant (run by a local family) offers good food (including fresh local farm trout) with wide views.

Back at the parkway, the road continues through high spruce-fir forests and frequent views. Along this stretch, any land that slopes downward to the left is part of the Asheville Watershed, where gray cliffs surround a pretty little lake, and stopping is prohibited. Ahead, an overlook on your left gives you a view over the watershed to Glassmine Falls far on the other side of the watershed, a contender for the title of "Highest in the East." After that, you've entered the **Craggy Gardens** area, noted for its views and its June rhododendron display.

From here the parkway drops 0.6 mile vertically, from the 5,520-foot Craggy Gardens Visitors Center to Asheville's Swannanoa River at 2,080 feet. Near the bottom of this stretch is the **Folk Art Center**, built to promote native mountain crafts. The parkway then bypasses Asheville to its south; as there are no intersections with any of the interstates, you need to plan your exits. The first intersection, US 70 (Tunnel Road), leads into eastern Asheville's mall district. In 2 miles there's an exit onto US 74A with access to I-40 and downtown Asheville, followed in 4 miles by the US 25 exit, the best approach to the **Biltmore Estate**. Five miles later you cross the **French Broad River** on a dramatic high bridge, then reach the fourth and last Asheville exit, NC 191, which leads to the **North Carolina Arboretum** and then to I-26 and I-40.

THE BLUE RIDGE PARKWAY VIEWED FROM CRAGGY PINNACLE

From here the parkway climbs steadily away from Asheville and into the wilderness. The views start immediately, over the gorge of the French Broad River. In 6.5 miles gravel Bent Creek Road gives access to Lake Powhatan Recreation Area. A series of tunnels brings you above 4,000 feet as you approach the NC 151 exit. Ahead are the Pisgah Mountains and the Great Balsam Mountains, the grand finale of the parkway, deserving their own entry. NC 151 provides a beautiful drive back to Asheville.

The Blue Ridge Parkway in the Pisgah Range. This parkway drive starts where the last one left off, at NC 151, 11 miles south of US 19 just west of Asheville, and a pleasant drive in itself. It ends at US 19 at Maggie Valley, which you take west to I-40 to return to Asheville. Although it's only 49 miles long, it's best to allot at least half a day.

This starting point, already 4,200 feet above sea level, is on the crest of the Pisgah Ridge, which you'll be following for the next 17 miles. Your first landmark will be the short dead-end Mount Pisgah Spur Road, on the left. Go down it a few hundred yards for a good view southward over the forests of the Mills River, then continue to the end if you want to pick up the justly popular (but steep) 2.5-mile round-trip hike to the 5,720-foot cone of **Mount Pisgah**. Back at the parkway, the Mount Pisgah Picnic Area is a short distance away, with the **Mount Pisgah Inn** (with a good restaurant) a bit farther on. From here the views open up to the south over the rhododendron-covered cove known as the Pink Beds, with the enormous rock dome of **Looking Glass Rock** behind it; then scenic US 276 furnishes an excellent side trip south to the **Cradle of Forestry in America**, an outstanding historic site. Now the parkway climbs to 5,000 feet through increasingly rugged and dramatic scenery, to **Graveyard Fields**, a meadow-covered cove perched high among mile-high peaks. In another mile Black Balsam Spur Road leads left to the trailhead for the **Shining Rock Wilderness**, and access to six peaks topping 6,000 feet. Back at the parkway, look for the great stone outcrop known as the **Devils Courthouse**, and don't miss the short, easy path to its top, with panoramic views. At the end of this leg you are 24 miles from Waynesville via NC 215 north to a right on US 276; there are no services (but lots of spectacular scenery) for the first 6.5 miles.

Now the parkway follows the crest of the **Great Balsam Mountains**, with seven more 6,000-foot peaks along its 32 miles of ridgetop wilderness. Built in the 1960s, this modern highway slashes through the wilderness landscape in huge cuts, with long sweeping views from its wide, clear shoulders. The views start suddenly as the parkway turns upward along the cliff-like flanks of 6,110-foot **Mount Hardy**, with continuous and wide panoramas southward. At Rough Butt Bald Overlook a short path leads to the **Mountains-to-Sea Trail**, which continues into the heart of the **Middle Prong Wilderness**. More views open up as the parkway sweeps toward 6,000 feet in elevation, with exceptional panoramas near **Caney Fork Overlook** and at **Cowee Mountain Overlook**. After that, the parkway reaches its highest elevation as it crests out at 6,190 feet at the **Richland Balsams Overlook**. From there it follows the mile-high meadows of the **Long Swag** before it starts its long drop to Balsam Gap. On this downward leg the parkway gives impressive views of itself as approaches the long, curving Pinnacle Ridge Tunnel; beyond, look for sunrise views at **Waynesville Overlook**.

The parkway dips into Balsam Gap, where it intersects with the four-lane US 23/74 and the first gas since you left Asheville (go right 1 mile; Waynesville is 7 miles east). After Balsam Gap the parkway climbs steadily for the next 8 miles, as good views open up. The parkway crests out as it crosses the massive side ridge known as **Plott Balsams**, at 5,710 feet. Here a spur road leads to the impressive **Waterrock Knob Overlook**, with a new visitors center, water, toilets, and picnic tables. As the parkway descends from Waterrock Knob it passes a series of good views west over the Cherokee lands, before dropping into the forests of **Soco Gap**. Waynesville is 13 miles east on US 19 to US 276.

US 276. The 61-mile scenic drive down US 276 is a perfect way to get acquainted with the Pisgah Range and the Blue Wall, with some fine old forests, good views, stunning waterfalls, unique geology, and quaint small towns along the way. *Start in downtown Waynesville*, a classic small town and very strollable, with some nice shops and galleries. The next 14 miles are a pleasant rural drive, and you might wonder at the warning sign prohibiting through-semi-trailers; then the mountains close in on the highway and you begin to climb. At 18 miles you reach the first of several 180-degree curves, with trail access to the **Shining Rock Wilderness** on your left. At 21 miles you top out, and cross the crest of the **Pisgah Range** at 4,533-foot Wagon Road Gap, where you'll find an intersection with the **Blue Ridge Parkway.**

At 4 miles from the parkway, the highway passes a Forest Service picnic area at the Pink Beds, named after its spectacular June rhododendron display, and the **Cradle of Forestry in America**. Here you'll find Vanderbilt's forestry school, the first in America, fully restored, with costumed docents and craft demonstrations. In the next 5 miles the highway drops into a gorge-like valley, passing **Slide Rock**, a popular swimming hole, and **Looking Glass Falls**, a classic river-over-a-cliff waterfall. A quarter mile later, a paved side road leads right to the Pisgah Center for Wildlife Education, a museum and fish hatchery. Here you'll find the trail up to the top of **Looking Glass Rock**, the spectacular 4,000-foot knob of exposed granite visible for miles along the Blue Ridge Parkway.

Leaving the national forest, US 276 immediately turns and follows four-lane US 64, reaching **Brevard's quaint downtown** in 3.4 miles—another good opportunity to stop, stroll, and shop. The highway quickly leaves Brevard to follow the old, slow, meandering **French Broad River** for 2 miles, then enters a long series of straight stretches through pastoral scenery; look for craft artists' studios and galleries scattered about. At 11 miles south of Brevard, a side road to the left (paved Cascade Lake Road) leads to the **DuPont State Forest**, with its first-rate waterfall walks.

Soon the highway crosses the **Blue Ridge** and suddenly tips over the edge of the world. No other road gets so up close and personal with **South Carolina's Blue Wall**. The highway follows the flat top of a side ridge for 3 miles out into the cliff lands, reaching **Caesars Head State Park** with its stunning panoramic views and walks to gorges and waterfalls. Then the highway drops down off the ridgetop and switchbacks wildly down the steep slopes of the Blue Wall to the floor of the South Carolina Piedmont. Five miles into this you will reach a graffiti-covered roadside rocky bald called Bald Rock, with wide views over the sudden end of the mountains to the endless flatness of the Deep South. In 2 more miles the highway reaches the flatlands, with views over fields toward the Blue Wall.

To return to Asheville, continue on US 276 to a left onto SC 11, then go 4.4 miles to a left onto US 25, then go 17.5 miles to I-26 west; Asheville is 26 miles farther.

EXPLORING ON FOOT **Downtown Asheville Urban Trail** (828-259-5855; fax: 828-259-5832), P.O. Box 7148, Asheville 28802. This 1.6-mile loop is not your ordinary downtown historic walk. A city of Asheville public art project, the Urban Trail marks each of its 30 interpretive stations with a unique work of art. Some are solemn historic statuary with explanatory plaques, such as the monument to Elizabeth Blackwell, MD, the Ashevillian who became the first American woman to get a medical degree. However, the most notable pieces are whimsical tributes to

Asheville's past. A little girl drinks from a fountain, a boy walks on stilts, a cat chases birds, and turkeys waddle along the **Buncombe Turnpike**. You might sit down on a bench to rest a spell only to find yourself facing dancers swirling to mountain music. Historic buildings, never completed due to timidity, rise in the glorious form imagined by their architects.

The Asheville Visitors Center is your headquarters for taped interpretive guides, guided walks, and even Segway tours. Amazingly, this treasure has no dedicated website.

Max Patch Walks. Dubbed the Jewel of the Blue Ridge by Appalachian Trail hikers, 4,630-foot Max Patch marks the western end of the Bald Mountains with easy and dramatic walking across mountaintop meadows. To reach it from Hot Springs take NC 209 south for 6.4 miles to a right onto Meadow Fork Road, then go 5.2 miles to a right onto Little Creek Road, then go 3.6 miles to its end at gravel Max Patch Road, then go right 1.5 miles to the trailhead parking lot.

Walk uphill through meadows, climbing 200 feet in a scant 0.5 mile, gaining increasingly spectacular views on the way up. At the top you will find a surveyor's monument marking the summit, and posts with white blazes marking the route of the **Appalachian Trail** through the grasses and flowers. Here the view is a complete circle of endlessly receding mountains. The Max Patch summit is a wonderful place for a sunset, and it's not uncommon to see people all over the ridge, picnicking and camping in an impromptu sunset party.

To extend the walk, follow the Appalachian Trail downhill to the left, dropping 400 feet. As the trail reaches a lower set of meadows, it briefly merges with an old farm track running along the ridge. Follow this track along the ridge for another mile of stunning meadow views. When you reach the end, return by following the farm track all the way back to Max Patch Road. When you reach the road, your car is parked 1,000 feet to the right.

ONE OF 30 SCULPTURES ALONG ASHEVILLE'S URBAN TRAIL

✷ Towns

Asheville sits at the center of its gigantic perched valley, the major urban center of the North Carolina mountains since the days of the early wagon road known as the **Buncombe Turnpike**. Already a center of tourism by antebellum times, Asheville became a major watering hole of 19th-century high society when George Vanderbilt constructed **Biltmore House**, still the largest private home in America, on the south end of town. Since then Asheville has been a center of history, architecture, and the arts. A 1920s land boom gave it a stunning **60-block downtown**, still mainly intact—one of the largest concentrations of shopping, dining, and art in the state. There's a second arts district in an area of riverside warehouses just southwest of downtown, and a third area of arts and shopping just outside the Biltmore House, in its old servants' quarters still called **Biltmore Village**. Bed & breakfasts proliferate in the city's historic mansions, and fine dining can be found in all sorts of odd corners. One measure of its sophisticated palate is its **nine microbreweries**, more than Charlotte and Atlanta combined. This is all particularly impressive given the city's small population. The U.S. Census overestimates it at 408,000 using flatlander assumptions about commuting patterns; a figure of about 200,000 is probably closer to the mark.

Weaverville. Located on the north edge of Asheville's urban area, Weaverville has managed to retain its small-town look and feel. Its two-block downtown lines the former US 19 with nice old brick-front stores and three good restaurants, with a fourth nearby. Its handsome residential districts, with houses dating to the 1840s, host several nice B&Bs that offer a small-town ambience within an easy drive of downtown Asheville. The handsome **Vance Birthplace** log farmstead is just outside of town.

Saluda and Tryon. These two small towns sit at the southern edge of Asheville's huge perched valley, at a point where the valley ends at sharp drop into the Piedmont. Saluda is at the top of the drop, and Tryon at the bottom, the two towns linked by the old main highway south, US 176. Tiny **Saluda**'s short downtown lines one side of US 176 with turn-of-the-20th-century brick buildings, facing the uphill end of the East's steepest mainline railroad, the Saluda Grade. Eight miles south and 1,000 feet down, **Tryon** has been a summer retreat for the South Carolina aristocracy since the turn of the last century. The rolling hills that extend from the end of the mountains had immediate appeal to the horse-and-hounds set, and Tryon has long been a center for hunt-oriented equestrian activities.

Hendersonville. This busy little city of 10,000 sits in a wide valley 20 miles south of Asheville via I-26. A successful small center of commerce, it's surrounded by a ring of modern, sprawling development, its highways busy and noisy. However, its quiet little downtown is a wonderful place. Almost completely preserved from the early 20th century, it has five blocks of Italianate red-brick storefronts, with wide, landscaped sidewalks and free street parking. The **Village of Flat Rock** sits 3 miles south via NC 225, noted for its old-style summer camps and inns, as well as the **NC State Theater** and the **Carl Sandburg Home**, a national park historic site.

Brevard. This small mountain town of 6,800 people, the seat of Transylvania County, sits on a hillside by the French Broad River, 20 miles west of Hendersonville via US 64. The main approach doesn't do it justice; leave the highway to explore the traditional center of town, and you will find a perfectly preserved red-brick downtown. Brevard gains a surprising level of cultural sophistication from its small Methodist liberal arts college (Brevard College), and its first-rate summer program for aspiring young professional musicians, the **Brevard Music Center**.

Waynesville. At first glance this mountain town 30 miles west of Asheville seems more sprawling and industrial than others nearby; however, attractive and genteel neighborhoods, rich in historic architecture, sit only a scant half block off the main drag. These historic neighborhoods have become a prime destination for knowledgeable visitors, as a number of bed & breakfast inns have moved in. Waynesville has a charming downtown, three blocks of historic red-brick structures with a good choice of interesting shops. Every July this Waynesville becomes the main venue for **Folkmoot**, a large-scale gathering of national dance troupes.

Hot Springs sits astride US 25 at the far northern end of this chapter's area, a small village whose old downtown tries to stretch itself to three blocks. This central business district, however, gets an unusual boost from its sidewalk: This particular stretch of concrete is known to the world as the **Appalachian Trail**, one of only two such "urban" stretches along its 2,000-mile length. You'll see hikers with backpacks walking the sidewalk, sitting and resting on a bench, or inside one of the stores with their gear stored neatly in a corner. The other notable thing about Hot Springs is its remoteness. It's 30 minutes to the nearest town in any direction, down twisting, two-lane highways. Hot Springs tends to attract people who like it quiet and isolated, making for a tightly knit community of mountain people, free spirits, and folk dedicated to some serious relaxing. Most services are available at Hot Springs, including beer and wine service in the restaurants.

* Green Spaces

PUBLIC TRACTS The tallest mountains in the East. In the mid-19th century, New Englanders were astonished to learn that **Mount Mitchell**, at 6,682 feet, was taller than New Hampshire's impressive Mount Washington (6,288 feet). By the end of that century, people knew that *eight* nearby peaks topped Mount Washington.

The tallest mountains in the East start just north of Asheville and run northward for about 25 miles, ending just south of Burnsville. Locals have seen fit to give this ridge two separate names: the Craggy Mountains near Asheville, then the Black Mountains farther north. Remarkably, paved, mile-high roadways run along the crest of this ridge for its first 15 miles, first the Blue Ridge Parkway, then the spur road to Mount Mitchell State Park. From the end of the paved road, a short, easy path leads to the Top of the East itself. There's even a good restaurant.

There's no reason, however, to confine yourself to a car, or limit yourself to short, easy walks. From the start of the spur road, the crest and much of the slope is owned by either Mount Mitchell State Park or Pisgah National Forest, and the trails are endless, beautiful, and (for the most part) famously difficult. The most notorious is the Black Mountain Crest Trail; starting at the Mount Mitchell parking lot, it ascends and descends 12 peaks over 6,000 feet along its 11.3-mile length, before dropping to a remote trailhead on a country lane south of Burnsville, with a final descent of 3,200 feet in 4.4 miles. Southward into the Craggies you'll find Craggy Gardens, where thick heath is broken by wide areas of grassy meadows and wildflowers, for wide views framed by deep purple rhododendrons. Here the Mountains-to-Sea Trail runs along the ridgetops, giving wide views from rock ledges and access to a network of little-visited paths in the Pisgah National Forest's Big Ivy Tract, whose waterfalls and old-growth forests form a recreation and conservation area important in its own right.

The Pisgah Forest. The Pisgah National Forest wanders through much of western North Carolina, with important tracts stretching from the eastern edge of the

Great Smoky Mountains National Park to Roan Mountain and on to the slopes of Grandfather Mountain. However, to the Asheville folk, "the Pisgah Forest" is the great stretch of wild lands straddling the Pisgah Ridge, north of Brevard and Hendersonville.

The area was originally part of George Vanderbilt's Biltmore Estate. Vanderbilt had carefully tended and restored its forests over a 30-year period. To do this, his foresters set up America's first forestry college in log cabins deep in the forest, now preserved as the Cradle of Forestry in America. More than a century later, Vanderbilt's Pisgah Forests are remarkably diverse and beautiful, with a network of gravel roads and hiking trails leading to scenic wonders.

The Pisgah Forest splits naturally into two halves along US 276. From it gravel forest roads run cross-grain through the area, giving ready access to most corners of the forest. The Blue Ridge Parkway follows the mile-high crest of the Pisgah Ridge through the center of the forest, allowing you to tackle a number of these trails from the top down.

The Shining Rock and Middle Prong Wildernesses. Adjacent to the Pisgah Forest to its west, the 18,400 acres of the **Shining Rock Wilderness** center on the high Shining Rock Ledge, a north-trending side ridge of the Pisgah Range with three 6,000-foot peaks. Just to the west of it sits the 7,900-acre **Middle Prong Wilderness**, separated by a deep gorge that carries scenic NC 215 to the **Blue Ridge Parkway**.

SPRING VIEW OVER THE BLACK MOUNTAINS FROM THE BLUE RIDGE PARKWAY

Champion Paper purchased all of these lands in 1906, building the huge paper mill still in use at Canton to exploit the spruces found in their high-altitude forests. In 1926 sparks from a logging train touched off a 25,000-acre wildfire in the clear-cut that denuded the high-altitude crests, creating the broad grassy meadows that remain these wilderness's most distinctive feature. Logging ceased after the fire, and the tract passed into the hands of the Pisgah National Forest in 1935. Congress created the Shining Rock Wilderness in 1964 and Middle Prong 20 years later.

Although both wildernesses are easily reached from the parkway, Shining Rock is by far the more popular and has the better trails. Its main destination is the large Shining Rock, a great mass of quartz that shines in the sun. From there the meadows extend southward all the way to the crest of the Pisgah Range and the parkway, and northward to 6,030-foot Cold Mountain—the same mountain used as the title for the movie and best-selling novel. Middle Prong's meadows are easily reached via the Mountains-to-Sea Trail, heading eastward from the parkway's Rough Butt Bald Overlook. Once within the Middle Prong, expect the trails to be difficult, obscure, and dangerous, as this is one of the steepest places in the Southern Appalachians with 3,000 feet of local relief in only 2 linear miles.

The Bald Mountains of Hot Springs. Lower and less visited than the Asheville area's other huge tracts of national forest, Hot Springs's tracts are nevertheless huge—completely surrounding the village for miles on all sides—and filled with interest. To its immediate north, gravel **Paint Gap Road** follows the **French Broad River** to an impressive hoodoo, then becomes a national forest recreation road noted for its fine waterfalls, fishing holes, and picnic areas. Farther east you'll find a vast tract along the Bald Mountains, split by the Appalachian Trail and the state line. Here the mountaintop meadows of Tennessee's **Bald Mountain Scenic Area** can be reached by car, while the adjacent **Sampson Wilderness Area** is noted for its waterfalls; on the North Carolina side, **Shelton Laurels Backcountry** has more waterfalls and an extensive trail system. During the Civil War, the Shelton Laurels Backcountry was settled by pro-Union folk, and was the sight of an infamous massacre of civilians by regular Confederate troops. Only the most sharp-eyed can now spot the signs of long-gone farms.

Elsewhere around Hot Springs the national forest lands are even less visited, the haunts of local hunters. The exception is Max Patch, a stunning sunset location with panoramic views, "the Jewel of the Blue Ridge."

DuPont State Forest (828-251-6509; fax: 828-251-6541; dupontforest.com; john.pearson@ncmail.net), 14 Gaston Mountain Rd., Asheville 28806. This 10,300-acre North Carolina state forest, purchased from the DuPont Corporation in 1997, lies in a high plateau 13 miles south of Brevard via US 276 and Cascade Road (SSR 1536). It's noted for its many waterfalls, and its excellent views from a number of exceptionally large rocky balds. Its forests are young and varied, and its slopes are much gentler and shorter than other mountain tracts. It has four lakes, one of them quite large—remnants of old real estate schemes and summer camps. It has nearly 100 named trails, most of them old roadbeds, and nearly all of these gentle old paths are open to bicyclers and horses as well as walkers. In the middle of this large, popular recreation site once sat a large film factory, like a hole in a doughnut. Although it was razed in 2003, it remains an environmental remediation site and access is strictly prohibited. Access to everything else is free and open.

PARKS AND GARDENS Pack Square Park (packsquarepark.org). This urban park covers four blocks of downtown Asheville, between Pack Square and the seats of local government, the Asheville City Hall and the Buncombe County Courthouse. It's a lovely place to stop and rest, with ample tree-shaded benches and well-kept flower beds. Its courthouse is an attractive 1927 neoclassical "skyscraper" of 17 stories, with an elaborately decorated interior. However, the real star of the square is the Asheville City Hall, a 1927 nine-story art deco masterpiece in rich gold brick, white limestone, and rose terra-cotta trim. Its architect, Ashevillian Douglas D. Ellington, designed several other stunners within an easy walking distance—the adjacent Fire Department, the octagonal First Baptist Church two blocks north, and the S&W Cafeteria Building two blocks south. The entire park complex was redesigned and expanded in 2010, eliminating a major highway in the process. The new version extends, unbroken, all the way to the center of downtown at Pack Place.

The North Carolina State Arboretum (828-665-2492; fax: 828-665-2371; ncarboretum.org), 100 Frederick Law Olmsted Way, Asheville 28806. Gardens are open 8–9 daily; buildings keep shorter hours. $$ (per-car parking fee). Founded in 1992, this 426-acre arboretum (part of the University of North Carolina) has 65 acres of formal and informal gardens, 10 miles of walking paths, greenhouses, and educational programs. The entrance drive, off the Blue Ridge Parkway at the NC

ONE STEP OVER THE LINE: THE BLUE WALL IN SOUTH CAROLINA

Rising 2,000 feet nearly straight up from the South Carolina piedmont, this cliff-like 35 miles of mountains straddles the border with North Carolina. The terrain is extraordinarily beautiful, with lush forests, deep gorges, huge waterfalls, and high cliffs. It's also very difficult, a rough and broken land with extreme elevation changes in short distances. Much of this wild territory is protected by the government of South Carolina in a series of state parks, game lands, and heritage preserves, while other large tracts are protected by private conservation foundations and city watersheds. Altogether these state, local, and private conservation tracts make up 40,000 acres of wild lands dubbed the Mountain Bridge Wilderness by the state of South Carolina.

Three South Carolina state parks make up the bulk of the recreational opportunities in this area. Table Rock State Park, on the western edge of this chapter's region off SC 11, centers on an outlying dome of hard gray rock that looms 2,000 feet above the park's lakeside picnic area; history buffs will want to check out its extensive CCC architecture, listed on the National Register. Caesar's Head State Park, bisected by US 276 in the center of the region, protects a long series of cliffs and waterfalls—the only place on the Blue Wall with clifftop views you can drive to. Jones Gap State Park protects the upper reaches of the Middle Saluda River, with some spectacular cliff scenery.

191 exit, is spectacular—beautifully landscaped in an unobtrusive style that blends in with the native habitats, including a viaduct over a delicate stream environment. The handsome main building of stone and gray wood combines contemporary architecture with such homey touches as a large porch with rocking chairs; it has an information desk, a café, and a gift shop, with the rest of the building given over to classrooms and offices. Outside stretch a series of contemporary formal gardens, designed by the original architect and rather severe. Adjacent to this is "Plants of Promise" (or POP), a riot of native garden plants, both showy and practical, in a setting designed by the arboretum staff and maintained with home garden equipment and methods. Behind the main building are the greenhouses, the source of the arboretum's seasonal and potted plants and an active participant in the campaign to conserve rare and endangered native species. Paths stretch downhill through forests to reach Bent Creek, where an old road has been converted to a walking and biking path. Here you'll find the National Azalea Repository, containing all but two of the native American azalea species. Picnicking is allowed, as are dogs on leashes. Segway tours are available.

Western North Carolina Nature Center (828-298-5600; fax: 828-298-2644; wildwnc.org), 75 Gashes Creek Rd., Asheville 28805. $$. Run by Buncombe County Parks and Recreation, this large and sophisticated nature study museum concentrates on the animals and plants of the western North Carolina mountains, occupying 42 acres on the east side of Asheville, off NC 81. Much of the museum is taken up with live animal and plant displays that put their subjects in their environmental context. Habitat displays include predators (red wolves, black wolves, cougars, and bobcats), river otters, turkeys, deer, and bears. A Nocturnal Hall displays animals found only at night—bats, owls, rabbits, flying squirrels. The Educational Farm has farm animals (including a petting area) and exhibits. The Main Hall has 75 live animal exhibits and encourages touching, except for the poisonous snakes and spiders. There are also raccoons, foxes, turtles, hawks, and eagles, as well as a log cabin, herb garden, and nature trail.

Chimney Rock State Park (800-277-9611; 828-625-9611; chimneyrockpark.com; ncparks.gov/Visit/parks/chro/main.php), US 64/74A, P.O. Box 39, Chimney Rock 28720. Open daily; ticket plaza 8:30–5:30, May–Oct,; 8:30–4:30, Nov.–Apr. $$$. Privately run from 1885 to 2007, Chimney Rock is a very old, very traditional, and very beautiful scenic attraction off US 74A in Hickory Nut Gorge. The park centers on a series of stunning cliffs along the south edge of the gorge, where unusual geological formations frame overwhelming panoramas of Lake Lure, Hickory Nut Gorge, and the Blue Ridge. Entering the park in the middle of Chimney Rock Village, you'll travel a mile through parklands before reaching the 1920 stone-built ticket booth. Two more miles brings you to the base of the cliffs, with views up to the Chimney Rock—a 300-foot rock tower with a flat top, crowned by a giant American flag. From here a 25-story elevator through the heart of the granite zooms you up to a cliff ledge large upon which is perched a gift shop and snack bar. Outside are wide views from large rock-floored balconies—views over to the Chimney Rock, now only a little way up, along the cliffs, and over Lake Lure. This is the end of the disabled-accessible area. Now steps climb up to a bridge across the chasm that separates the Chimney Rock from the cliff face; the wide top of the Chimney furnishes more views. From there the trail continues, climbing the cliffs in stairs, looking down on the Chimney Rock, getting even better views, cutting

CLIMBERS SCALE CHIMNEY ROCK IN CHIMNEY ROCK STATE PARK.

through the cliff face on a narrow ledge, and viewing the unique cliff-side forest stunted into bonsai shapes by harsh winds. The climax of the cliff walk: a huge, violent waterfall that plunges straight down for 400 feet without so much as a bounce off a ledge until it crashes to the bottom—the same waterfall featured in the 1992 movie *Last of the Mohicans.* A separate (much easier) path leads to the bottom of the falls, with astonishing views upward. The path from pre-elevator days, built in 1920, is still there, and a fun trip down. If you bring your dog, you are required to use the steps instead of the elevator.

Foothills Equestrian Nature Center (828-859-9021; fence.org; therapeuticriding@fence.org), 3381 Hunting Country Rd., Tryon 28782. Admission is free. This beautiful and unusual center (known as FENCE) sits in the foothills of the Blue Ridge near Tryon. It combines an educational nature center with a large, national-quality horse show and steeplechase venue. Best known as the host of Tryon's famous equestrian events, it also has 320 acres of picnic areas, walking paths, forests, and wildflower meadows. Its rolling foothills location provides an astonishing variety of environments for its 5 miles of paths—hardwood forests, pine forests, hilltops, open meadows (with lovely views), marshlands, and ponds. A historic building at the center, shaped like a stable, holds the offices and a shop; next door, an herb garden surrounds a log cabin. One of the trails is disabled accessible.

On the other side of I-26 sits the equestrian center, with an 8-furlong track and stalls for 200 horses. Some sort of equestrian event is scheduled for almost every weekend, and is worth looking into.

The Botanical Gardens at Asheville (828-252-5190; ashevillebotanicalgardens.org), 151 W. T. Weaver Blvd., Asheville 28804. Admission is free. This 10-acre garden in central Asheville is dedicated to preserving and exhibiting the native plants of the Western North Carolina Mountains in their natural surroundings. Designed in 1960 by Doan Ogden, the gardens follow a narrow draw formed by Reed Creek. Four bridges cross the creek, each with its own view. Special environments include a Sunshine Garden, a Woods Garden, a Rock Garden, a Heath and Azalea Garden, and a Garden for the Blind, emphasizing textures and smells. Also on the property are a historic log cabin, earthworks from a Civil War skirmish, and a length of the original **Buncombe Turnpike**, the historic road that opened up the mountains. This volunteer-run garden sponsors regular walks and talks. The gift shop sells a detailed guide to the garden, and sells native landscaping plants; their website is a good resource for native Blue Ridge gardening.

RIVERS French Broad River. For most of its 218-mile length, the French Broad River meanders lazily through a wide floodplain, the haunt of canoeists rather than kayakers or rafters. For its uppermost 60 miles it remains steadily Class I, then breaks into Class II as it passes through the Asheville area and reaches Marshall. Then it gets lively. For 8 miles, from the settlement of Barnard just north of Marshall to the US 25/70 bridge at Hot Springs, the French Broad bounces through a deep gorge, surrounded by national forest lands, with Class III to IV-plus rapids. Then, as it reaches Hot Springs, the river reverts to its old self, becoming once again a fine Class I to II canoe stream through the mountains with lots of fishing access.

LAKES Lake Lure. The Morse family, founders of Chimney Rock Park, built Lake Lure and its adjacent village in 1926, wishing to expand Chimney Rock's appeal by adding a scenic lake, recreational opportunities, and upscale vacation development. It was the Morses who created the vintage-1928 town center and the 1926 Donald Ross golf course, now open to the public. However, the Depression intervened, and Lake Lure was sold off in bankruptcy; most of Lake Lure is given to modern second homes. It's attractive nevertheless, with the towering cliffs of the Blue Ridge forming a crescent around the lake's western end. The lake itself is private and has no public ramps, but you can rent a boat or use a private ramp. A city-owned park at the western end gives great views over the lake toward the cliffs, and is a pleasant place to picnic. Access is via US 64/74A, a narrow prewar relic that hugs the lake's southern coastline.

✷ To See

ALONG THE BLUE RIDGE PARKWAY Mount Mitchell State Park (828-675-4611; ncparks.gov/Visit/parks/momi/main.php), Rt. 5, Box 700, Burnsville 28714. Open whenever the Blue Ridge Parkway is open, 8–9 in summer, shorter hours other times of the year. Admission is free. This 1,700-acre state park centers on the highest peak in the East—6,684-foot Mount Mitchell, more than 1.25 miles above sea level. A spur road runs from the **Blue Ridge Parkway** to the park, a 2.4-mile drive through Pisgah Forest lands, just below the crest of the Black Mountain. At the park entrance the road passes above 6,000 feet with wide meadow views, and stays above 6,000 feet to its end on Mount Mitchell, 2.5 miles later, only a bit downhill from the summit. Here you will find plenty of parking, a first-rate picnic area, a snack bar, and a small visitors center. Expect it to be cold and blowy, even in summer. The wide, easy path to the summit passes through forests and wildflower meadows to reach the peak in 0.2 mile. A newly constructed tower allows you to climb above the trees for a 360-degree view, with the entire eastern United States beneath your feet.

Nor is this an isolated high point; 80 percent of this 12-mile crest exceeds 6,000 feet in elevation. Of special note is the nearly flat path that follows the old toll road from Montreat, itself built on a logging railroad bed. After 1.2 miles of profuse wildflowers and dense fir forests it reaches Camp Alice, an early-20th-century lumber camp that became, for a while around World War I, a backcountry tourist attraction. Here you will find some scant ruins and a lovely waterfall.

Craggy Gardens (nps.gov/blri/craggy.htm). This recreation area on the Blue Ridge Parkway takes in the three highest peaks of the Craggy Mountains: 6,080-foot Craggy Dome, Craggy Pinnacle, and Craggy Gardens. Views are great—but there is more here than views from high mountains. Each June, the Craggies have one of the finest rhododendron displays in the mountains.

Driving up the parkway from Asheville, you enter the Craggies at Potato Field Gap, MP 368, with views left over the town of Woodfin's watershed. In 0.5 mile a paved spur road leads left 1.2 miles to Craggy Gardens Picnic Area, a lovely tree-shaded meadow. This is the lower end of the Craggy Gardens Trail, climbing 400 feet in 0.4 mile to Craggy Gardens, a stunning natural rhododendron garden. Craggy Gardens mixes clumps of June-flowering heath shrubs with expanses of grassy meadows. The grassy meadows give wide views over lush displays of perennial flowers, framed in June and July by huge mounds of purple Catawba rhododendrons, mixed with rosebay rhododendrons, flame azaleas, blueberries, and mountain laurels.

Back at the parkway, the road curves wide past Craggy Gardens on a breathtaking ledge. In 3 miles the road reaches Pinnacle Gap, with panoramic views in both directions. Here a tiny visitors center has several exhibits about the Craggy Mountains and a gift shop, as well as the uphill end of the Craggy Gardens Trail. The Craggy Pinnacle Overlook is 0.5 mile farther, with wide views that improve dramatically as you walk up the easy path to the rhododendron-covered summit. Here a clifftop overlook gives views back toward Craggy Gardens, with the parkway dramatically cut into the side of the mountain.

The Folk Art Center and Allanstand Craft Shop (828-298-7928; fax: 828-298-7962; southernhighlandguild.org; shcg@buncombe.main.nc.us), milepost 382, Blue Ridge Pkwy., Asheville 28805. Open daily all year, 9–6 (9–5 in winter). Admission is free. Founded in 1930 to help poor mountain folk refine their craft skills and find markets for their crafts, the Southern Highland Craft Guild has evolved into an juried membership organization of fine craft artists from a large area centered on the Southern Appalachian Mountains. In the 1970s the National Park Service collaborated with the SHCG to provide a facility to interpret Southern Appalachian mountain culture on the Blue Ridge Parkway. To achieve this, the Park Service built the present Folk Art Center, a large building on the Blue Ridge Parkway just north of US 70, and turned it over the SHCG. The Craft Guild has utilized this building by moving their Allanstand Craft Shop into it from downtown Asheville, and by installing a medium-sized gallery in an upstairs mezzanine. Although the gallery features items from the guild's collection of 3,500 mountain craft pieces, for the most part it displays contemporary art by its current members.

Mount Pisgah. This large recreation area has picnicking, camping, a camp store, a good restaurant, and a nice lodge, all at an elevation around 5,000 feet. Its centerpiece is 5,721-foot-tall Mount Pisgah, reached by a 2.6-mile (round-trip) trail that gains 700 feet in elevation. The path is a pleasant forest walk, fairly steep and generally busy; at its end is a large observation platform by an even larger TV tower, with a 360-degree view. Of special interest is the cable-driven railcar used by the television technicians to service the tower.

Looking Glass Rock. This giant granite dome sits off the main ridgeline, 2 miles south of the parkway. It's huge, rising 1,000 feet above the forests that completely surround it, and well over a mile long. As you drive west from the **Mount Pisgah** area it dominates the wide views to your left, and remains a prominent landmark as far west as **Devils Courthouse**. Its slopes are popular with rock climbers, and a hiking trail sneaks up its southern slope for fine views and a close-up look at a large rocky bald.

Graveyard Fields. This high perched valley sits nearly a mile above sea level, flanked by seven 6,000-foot peaks, 3 miles east of NC 215. Once covered by huge old-growth forests—the *graveyard* refers to the grave-like mounds left by fallen giant trees as they return to the soil—it was devastated by clear-cut fires in the early 20th century and remains meadow-covered to this day. A lovely system of hiking trails, most starting at the Graveyard Fields Overlook on the Blue Ridge Parkway, loops around the wildflower-carpeted meadows, along the clear mountain river that cuts through its center, down to the roaring waterfall that marks its foot, and up to the tall, graceful waterfall that sits at its head.

The Devils Courthouse. This classic Blue Ridge cliff projects out a bit from the main ridgeline, giving it an appearance a bit like a large, grotesquely proportioned building. A short, easy hiking trail leads to its top for spectacular views.

Caney Fork and Cowee Mountain Overlooks. Caney Fork Overlook marks the midpoint of a 2-mile stretch of the parkway that gives dramatic roadside views down a 3,000-foot drop into the valley of the Tuckaseegee River, with layered mountains that recede endlessly into the background. Sunset lovers will appreciate the way the sun dips down below the horizon into the lowest part of the deep valley, throwing orange sidelights on the tall ridges to its right and left. Two miles later Cowee Mountain Overlook gives a 270-degree view from a promontory, nearly 6,000 feet in elevation, that thrusts westward from the parkway over the deep valleys of the Balsams. A quarter mile north, the Haywood-Jackson Overlook supplies the missing 90-degree view, eastward over the deep gorge of the West Fork to the mountaintop meadows of the **Middle Prong and Shining Rock Wilderness**; fans of the best-selling novel *Cold Mountain* should look for this 6,030-foot peak in the far background.

Waynesville Overlook. At this point the north-to-south traveler is quickly descending from the rarefied heights of the Great Balsams along one of the parkway's most notorious grades, a steady drop of nearly 2,000 feet in 6 miles. The parkway has curved its closest to Waynesville, a crow's flight of 5 miles. This overlook gives a particularly good view eastward over the entire town—and incidentally, toward the rising sun on a summer's morning. The best place for a sunrise is the grassy verge immediately beyond the overlook.

Waterrock Knob. In its climb northward out of Balsam Gap, the parkway passes a number of good overlooks with views west and south. However, you might want to save your film for the top; as the parkway finally reaches the crest, it sends a 0.3-mile spur to a series of three overlooks with stunning 270-degree views. These overlooks occupy the high, grassy crest of a great wall-like side ridge known as Plott Balsams, after the local frontier family who bred the Plott bearhound for hunting these slopes. The collection of overlooks makes up a small recreation area, with a modest visitors center, water, toilets, several tables, many wildflowers, and large grassy verges perfect for picnic blankets or tossing a Frisbee. Beyond the overlooks a wide, heavily used trail climbs very steeply to the peak of Waterrock Knob, for some good views.

Soco Gap. The parkway intersects with US 19 in this high (4,345-foot) gap. It may well be the snowiest US highway in these mountains, and can have deep snow when other highways have had only a cold drizzle. This can be a good thing. Because US 19 gets winter salting and plowing you can drive up it to Soco Gap, park on the intersection verge, and join with the other families sledding, cross-country skiing, throwing snowballs, and building snowmen along the closed, snow-covered parkway. For other times of the year, if you need facilities at this exit drive 4 miles east on US 19.

MOUNTAIN SITES **The waterfalls of DuPont State Forest**. Three lovely waterfalls, each with its own unique personality, group tightly together at the center of the DuPont Forest. A single walk to all three, following a roaring mountain river most of the way, takes a total of 3.5 miles with 250 feet of climbing. To reach the trailhead parking, take US 276 for 11 miles south of Brevard to Cascade Lake Road; then take Cascade Lake Road north 2.4 miles to its fork with Staton Road; then take Staton Road 2.3 miles to a parking lot on the left just after a bridge.

Your first destination is **Hooker Falls**—through the gate at the end of the parking lot, then 0.35 mile along the river on a level old road. Here the Little River, 130 feet wide, pours straight down over a 13-foot ledge. Retrace your steps, then cross the river to continue upstream on the opposite bank. As the scenery becomes more mountainous, the trail ascends to a view of **Triple Falls** on the Little River—three separate cascades that together drop 120 feet. From here a path leads to the base of the fall, and a roadbed leads to a picnic shelter. Continue on the main trail to the base of **High Falls**, where the Little River slides straight down a 150-foot cliff. The main trail continues uphill to views from the top of High Falls, then more views from a picnic shelter.

Skytop Orchard (828-692-7930; skytoporchard.com), P.O. Box 302, Flat Rock 28731. Open Aug–Oct., daily 9–6. Located on a side road off US 25 near the center of Flat Rock, this U-pick apple orchard has stunning views from 50 acres of handsome orchards straddling the Blue Ridge. Pickers have 20 varieties of apples to choose from; there are also hayrides, farm animals to pet, picnicking, and a farm stand during the picking season. From US 25 turn west onto Pinnacle Mountain Road and follow the signs.

CULTURAL SITES Asheville's most impressive cultural places are not static museums of old art, but rather the vibrant contemporary art scene centered on fine crafts. You'll find details of this under *Selective Shopping*. Meanwhile, some of those static places are worth your time as well.

Pack Place (828-257-4500; fax: 828-251-5652; packplace.org; info@packplace.org), 2 S. Pack Square, Asheville 28801. Open Tue.–Sat. 10–5, Sun. 1–5. $$$. Located on downtown Asheville's Pack Square, this art and science center's small entrance is deceiving. Behind the entrance, a large complex of museums, public spaces, and the Diana Wortham Theater stretches back through several buildings, including the marble-clad 1920s neoclassical Public Library Building. Off the public area are three independent museums—the art museum, the gem and mineral museum, and the hands-on health museum—and the Diana Wortham Theater.

Behind this main structure in its own historic building is the YMI Cultural Center, a major part of Asheville's African American community. Pack Place will sell you combined tickets at various complex prices (every tenant sets its own price rules), or you can buy tickets at each venue separately. Combined tickets are cheaper.

Grovewood Galleries (877-622-7238; 828-253-7651; fax: 828-254-2489; grovewood.com; grovewood@grovewood.com), 111 Grovewood Rd., Asheville 28804. Open Mon.–Sat. 10–6, Sun. 11–5. This collection of two museums, a gallery, and a lovely little café occupies a group of historic buildings in their own little garden by the Grove Park Inn. This complex was erected by the Vanderbilts in 1901 as a training school for traditional mountain weavers and woodworkers, and the small complex produced fine homespun cloth for the craft market into the 1980s. Today its large fine craft gallery represents regional artists in a wide variety of media, including a large furniture gallery. Adjacent are two museums, one dedicated to the Vanderbilt's school and the homespun industry of the early 20th century, and the other with a collection of 30 antique cars. All these buildings front on a lovely tree-shaded garden, with sculptures scattered about, and a wide view over the Grove Park Inn and its golf course toward downtown Asheville. To find the Grovewood Galleries, go to the Grove Park Inn, enter its parking lot, and follow the signs.

Montreat (800-572-2257; 828-669-2911; fax: 828-669-2779; montreat.org), P.O. Box 969, Montreat 28757. This region has long been a center of religious retreats and conference centers, with 20 or so in current operation. Of these, Montreat is one of the more worthwhile for a casual visit, as well as friendly and open toward sightseers. Located at the end of NC 9, 2 miles north of Black Mountain, Montreat features a major concentration of early-20th-century resort architecture, from its impressive front gate (now permanently open) to the large and beautiful Assembly Inn, built of local stone. Historic stone and wood buildings face Lake Susan on one side; a garden-like park lines the other. Uphill, winding gravel roads lead past early-20th-century cottages to reach various hiking trails. The best-known and most popular trail follows the old Mount Mitchell Road, abandoned in 1940 in favor of the Blue Ridge Parkway.

The Museum of North Carolina Handicrafts (828-452-1551; blueridgeheritage.com/node/915), Shelton House, 49 Shelton St., Waynesville 28786. Open May–Oct., Tue.–Sat. 10–4; call for winter hours. $. Located on the south edge of Waynesville on US 276, the 1875 Shelton House is home to this extensive display of both home crafts and fine art crafts from the Smokies and other parts of North Carolina. This beautifully restored mountain farmhouse, surrounded by meadows, has two-story verandas along its front and walnut trim throughout its interior. Inside are traditional 19th-century farm furnishings and a wide array of mountain crafts—pottery, baskets, quilts, toys, and dulcimers. It has a large collection of Seagrove pottery, and items from fine craft artists throughout the state. A gift shop offers handmade craft items for sale.

Tryon Fine Arts Center (828-859-8322; fax: 828-859-0271; tryonarts.org; tfac@tryontfac.org), 34 Melrose Ave., Tryon 28782. Founded in the mid-1960s, the Tryon Fine Arts Center occupies a half-block campus a block away from downtown across the tracks, with several public gardens and art galleries. On-site is Tryon Crafts, a craft school and one of the founding members. Also on-site is the gallery for the Tryon Painters and Sculptors, a co-op made up of local professional artists.

HISTORIC SITES The Biltmore Estate (800-624-1575; fax: 828-255-1139; biltmore.com; happenings@biltmore.com), 1 Approach Rd., Asheville 28801. Open daily; 9–4, Jan.–Mar.; 8:30–5, Apr.–Dec.; sites within the estate have different hours. $$$$. In 1889, 28-year-old George Vanderbilt decided to become a medieval nobleman. Like many of the Victorian aristocracy, he looked back on medieval Europe as a happy, stable society where the laboring classes found satisfaction through fine craftsmanship while the nobility watched over all with fatherly concern. Vanderbilt wanted to create such a society with himself as the nobleman, and chose Asheville as his new demesne.

Vanderbilt had discovered Asheville on his many travels. He loved the mild climate and the scenic beauty, and appreciated the advantages of forming a great estate from cheap Appalachian land. And Vanderbilt had a very large estate in mind. Before he was done he had purchased 125,000 acres—nearly 200 square miles stretching from the southern edge of Asheville to the Pisgah Mountains on the far horizon. He then assembled a remarkable team of experts to convert this tired-out land into a noble domain: leading architect Richard Morris Hunt to design the house; Frederick Law Olmsted, the designer of Central Park and the U.S. Capitol grounds, to design the gardens and develop a management plan; and America's first forester, Gifford Pinchot, to restore and manage 100,000 acres of logged-out forest. He had Hunt build the largest house in America, a 250-room French château, and emparked this house with several hundred acres of Olmsted's gardens. Beyond the gardens he laid out 1,000 acres of farmland and dairy to establish the self-sufficiency of a great medieval estate. He built a medieval village at the estate gates, today's Biltmore Village, to provide his workers with housing and shops.

Vanderbilt's heirs ceased living at Biltmore in 1958, but have continued to run it as a self-sufficient estate; they proudly boast of being a profit-making, tax-paying enterprise. Currently possessing 8,000 acres, the estate continues its extensive farming and forestry operations as well as a distinguished winery and vineyard. But the core of the estate remains the house and gardens, carefully preserved and restored to reflect the way they looked to George and Edith Vanderbilt, an Appalachian lord and lady at the height of the Gilded Age.

The Biltmore Estate is located on US 25, 0.2 mile north of I 40, exit 50. The mailing address is for the administrative offices in downtown Asheville.

The Biltmore House. Famed architect Richard Morris Hunt personally supervised the construction of this 250-room French château from 1889 to 1895, and helped its owner, George Vanderbilt, pick out the furniture in a series of European buying sprees. Today, still fully furnished as in Vanderbilt's day and immaculately preserved by his heirs, the Biltmore House is completely overwhelming.

The front entrance is a delightful surprise—a bright, open place, where white marble floors surround a glass-roofed atrium, opening into arches that lead into great spaces. To one side of the entrance is the grandest room in the house, the baronial Banquet Hall with a barrel-vaulted wooden ceiling 70 feet high and a leaf table that expands to hold 64 guests. Opposite the hall, the Library has balconied two-story-tall walls, completely covered with 10,000 books (less than half of Vanderbilt's personal collection).

Walk onto any one of a series of terraces that line the rear of the house, and one of the grandest views in the region opens up. Meadows and glades drop away from the steep stone sides of the terraces to the farmland lining the French Broad River far below. Then, after miles of steeply rolling forestlands, the grand cliff-like sides of the Pisgah Range form a tall, unbroken wall along the horizon. Vanderbilt owned this view; every bit of land in this wide panorama was his.

Upstairs, on the second and third floor, are the family's private quarters and a very large number of guest rooms. Vanderbilt disliked formal entertainment but he enjoyed having house guests, informal house parties of the sort popular in the great houses of Europe. Downstairs, the basement housed servants' quarters, kitchens, and indoor recreation rooms including a swimming pool, bowling alley, and gymnasium.

In all, the self-guided house tour leads through 23 rooms upstairs and 11 rooms downstairs, and has disabled access. Guided tours, requiring advance registration and an additional fee, take visitors through closed portions of the house, from the servants' quarters up onto the roof for sweeping views.

The Biltmore Winery. Biltmore opened its ambitious winery in 1985, in a dairy barn designed by Hunt and built as part of the original estate construction. The short winery tour includes a seven-minute video and a self-guided walk through the winemaking areas and the basement. The tour ends with a delightful tasting in the old calf barn, where you can interact with wine-serving bartenders at U-shaped bars.

✐ **The Cradle of Forestry in America** (828-877-3130; fax: 828-884-5823; cradleofforestry.com; cfaia@citcom.net). Open May–Oct., daily 9–5. $. When George Vanderbilt founded Asheville's Biltmore Estate as his private residence in the 1880s he surrounded it with vast tracts of forestlands, including much of the Pisgah Ranger District of the Pisgah National Forest. With no scientific forestry in existence in America at the time, Vanderbilt imported professional foresters from Germany to manage his forests—first the German-trained American Gifford Pinchot, then the German scientist Carl A. Schenck. With no trained assistants or staff available in the United States, these scientists were forced to start a training school on Biltmore property. This training school is now preserved as the Cradle of Forestry in America, a beautiful and fascinating collection of historic log structures. The tour starts at the large modern museum, where historic and modern forestry practices are explained. Then a loop trail leads to the historic site, with a log schoolroom, store, and cabins (including some built in a properly German style by Dr. Schenck), where craft demonstrations are held. A second loop trail leads through a demonstration of historic forestry practices. Run by the National Forest Service, the Cradle of Forestry is on US 276, 14 miles north of Brevard and 3.5 miles south of the Blue Ridge Parkway.

Thomas Wolfe Memorial State Historic Site (828-253-8304; fax: 828-252-8171; wolfememorial.com; contactus@wolfememorial.com), 52 N. Market St., Asheville 28801. Open Mon.–Sat. 9–5, Sun. 1–5; shorter hours in winter. Admission is free. Author Thomas Wolfe, acclaimed for his autobiographical novels during the 1930s, spent his childhood in his mother's boardinghouse, My Old Kentucky Home, on the eastern edge of the Lexington Hill section of downtown Asheville. That boardinghouse and the town of Asheville became the thinly veiled subject of his most famous novel, *Look Homeward Angel: A Story of the Buried Life*, published in 1929 to high acclaim (and great embarrassment among Asheville's worthies). Today the boardinghouse and a modern visitors center make up the Thomas Wolfe

Memorial, furnished as it was when Wolfe lived there in the 1910s, and housing a considerable collection of Wolfe memorabilia and artifacts.

Vance Birthplace State Historic Site (828-645-6706; nchistoricsites.org/vance/vance.htm; vance@ncdcr.gov), 911 Reems Creek Rd., Weaverville 28787. Open Tue.–Sat. 9–5. Admission is free. This log farmstead east of Weaverville on Reems Creek Road accurately reconstructs the early-19th-century birthplace of Zebulon B. Vance, one of North Carolina's most beloved politicians. In the mid-19th century Vance led the movement to democratize North Carolina's patrician planter-controlled government; during the Civil War Governor Vance (in the nuanced politics of the era, an anti-secessionist but not a Unionist) protected North Carolina from lawlessness, preserved civil liberties, and sheltered his state from the Confederate government's worst excesses. This state historic site memorializes his life, and presents an accurate picture of the frontier mountain life that shaped his boyhood.

The farmstead is a well-crafted two-story log home, set on a grassy hill, shaded by large old trees, and surrounded by mountains. It has been carefully furnished to reflect the frontier period of Vance's boyhood. A vegetable garden separates the farmhouse from several log outbuildings—a weaving house with a period loom, a toolhouse, a smokehouse, a corncrib, a springhouse, and a slaves' house. Beautiful

THE BUNCOMBE TURNPIKE

(828-253-9231; wnchistory.org), 283 Victoria Rd., Asheville 28801. Open Wed.–Sat. 10–4, Sun. noon–4. $$. The true foundation of Asheville and its prosperity was the antebellum drover road, the Buncombe Turnpike.

Completed in 1827, the turnpike made a beeline from Charleston, South Carolina (the South's biggest city at the time), through the heart of the Blue Ridge Mountains, to the rich farmlands of Virginia, Tennessee, and Kentucky. Because the South Carolina slave plantations concentrated on cash crops such as cotton, rice, indigo, and slave breeding, they needed to import large amounts of food. The food came on the hoof, driven down from beyond the mountains: hogs above all, but also cattle, sheep, and turkeys. (And a turkey drive was truly a sight to behold.)

Hundreds of thousands, even millions, of animals walked and fluttered down the turnpike every fall of every year, from 1827 to 1860. And every last one of them had to pass in front of the Asheville County Courthouse, then cross the French Broad River at Smith's Ferry. In 1834 John Smith replaced his ferry with a bridge, and his wealth billowed. He grew feed corn for the animals all along the French Broad floodplain, and in the process prevented any competitors from building another bridge. This action probably did more than anything else to establish Asheville, as opposed to some other nearby crossroads settlement, as the mountains' major town. He died, rich as Croesus, in 1858; you can visit the splendid house he built, now fully restored and the headquarters of the Western North Carolina Historical Association.

views stretch from the split-rail worm fence, past the log buildings, and to the mountains beyond.

Throughout the season, this is a venue for various programs interpreting early life on the mountain frontier. There's a visitors center with a small museum on Vance's life. Only the visitors center, the restrooms, and the picnic area are fully disabled-accessible.

✐ **Carl Sandburg Home National Historic Site** (828-693-4178; fax: 828-693-4179; nps.gov/carl), 81 Carl Sandburg Lane, Flat Rock 28731. Open daily 9–5. Free admission to grounds and goat barn; $$ for house tours. In 1945 poet and scholar Carl Sandburg and his wife, Paula, moved from Michigan to Flat Rock, North Carolina. Mrs. Sandburg was a dedicated goat farmer and serious goat breeder, and the mild climate of Flat Rock was a superior place to raise goats. They purchased Connemara, a large farm with a beautiful antebellum house and a large pond, at the center of Flat Rock. Carl Sandburg remained at Connemara until his death in 1967; a year later Connemara became Carl Sandburg National Historic Site, part of America's national park system.

VANCE BIRTHPLACE STATE HISTORIC SITE NEAR ASHEVILLE

Connemara would have been worthy of preservation under any circumstances. One of the oldest farmsteads in this region, it was built in 1838 as a vacation home for a rich South Carolinian, Christopher Memminger, later Treasury secretary for the Confederate States of America. Despite this history, the National Park Service realized that nothing more distinguished has happened to this fine old house than the Sandburgs, and kept the estate the way Carl and Paula left it.

Connemara is an extraordinarily beautiful place. From the roadside parking lot, you walk along a lovely pond with views toward a meadow-covered hill and the columned old house. The path crosses a wooden bridge, then climbs along wood fences and through meadows for 0.25 mile to the surprisingly modest house, with its columned porch and lush azaleas. The basement visitors center has a small bookstore and information desk. From there you can tour the house, carefully preserved the way the Sandburgs left it, a slice from a warm and comfortable life in the 1940s. From the house, you continue up into the farm area with 21 buildings preserved from the Sandburg era. It's still a functioning goat farm, and your kids can pet their kids as they wander out from the giant red barn to great visitors. Beyond the goat dairy, walking paths lead through woods to mountaintop viewpoints.

MICROBREWERIES With nine microbreweries in the area, Asheville has more craft breweries than Atlanta and Charlotte combined—very likely some sort of per-capita record. Even better, five of them are downtown, within easy stumbling distance of one another.

Highlands Brewing Company (828-299-3370; highlandbrewing.com; info@highlandbrewing.com), 12 Old Charlotte Hwy., Suite H, Asheville 28803. Tasting room open Fri. 4–8; tours weekdays at 4. Founded in 1994, Highlands is Asheville's oldest and most popular microbrew. Their English-style Highland Gaelic Ale is ubiquitous in Asheville bars, restaurants, and supermarkets, and distributed throughout the South. For eight years they were located in a downtown basement; now they have their own factory in East Asheville, with a tasting room on-site.

Green Man Brewing and Tasting Room (828-252-5445; jackofthewood.com), 95 Patton Ave., Asheville 28801. Open daily noon–late. This is the beer made for downtown's popular Celtic-themed brewpub, **Jack of the Wood**. Brews are heavy and distinctive, and one of them is nearly always available as a cask ale, sitting on live yeast (a common English practice that greatly improves the subtlety). The brewery itself is in a modest building four blocks south at 23 Buxton Avenue, and has a tasting room open daily 4–9.

🐾 **Asheville Brewing Company** (ashevillebrewing.com), 77 Coxe Ave., Asheville 28801. Open for lunch and dinner. This downtown brewery has an old-fashioned neighborhood pub in front, where you can sample all of their many ales and enjoy the best pizza in town. It has outdoor seating as well, where your leashed dog is welcome.

French Broad Brewing Company (828-277-0222; frenchbroadbrewery.com; info@frenchbroadbrewery.com), 101 Fairview Rd., Asheville 28803. Open weekday evenings. This brewery, located just east of Biltmore Village, produces a range of Belgian- and German-inspired beers that are distributed at 75 Asheville area restaurants, pubs, and stores. They have a tasting room on-site, with live music in the evenings.

Craggie Brewing Company (828-254-0360; craggiebrewingco.com; contact@craggiebrewingco.com), 197 Hilliard Ave., Asheville 28801. Open Wed.–Sat. 4–10. Opened in 2009, this brewery is in a modest building on the south end of downtown, where it has a tasting room. It brews organic craft beers with European inspiration, using local ingredients where possible.

Lexington Avenue Brewery (828-252-0212; lexavebrew.com), 39 N. Lexington Ave., Asheville 28801. Open for lunch and dinner. Opened in 2010, this downtown gastropub features unfiltered beers brewed on the premises and an exciting menu that goes well beyond bar favorites.

Wedge Brewery (828-505-2792; wedgebrewing.com), 125 B Roberts St., Asheville 28801. Open weekdays 4–10, Sat. 2–10, Sun. 2–9. Opened in 2009, this brewery in the River Arts District, downstairs from an artists' studio, has a tasting room that opens early on weekends for gallery strollers, and a wild variety of beers, including an American (make that Czech) style pilsner, an IPA, and some nifty Belgians.

Oysterhouse Brewing Company (828-350-0505; oysterhousebeers.com; thelobstertrap.biz), 35 Patton Ave., Asheville 28801. Open for dinner Mon.–Sat. This small brewery is part of the Lobster Trap, downtown Asheville's fine seafood restaurant—the only place where its brews can be found. Its specialty is an oyster stout, an unusual Anglo-Irish concoction that contains, yep, oysters (including the shells).

Pisgah Brewing Company (pisgahbrewing.com; info@pisgahbrewing.com), 150 Eastside Dr., Black Mountain 28711. Open daily, afternoons and evenings. The South's first certified organic brewery, Pisgah distributes its products widely throughout Asheville, as well as serving them up in their own tap room attached to their headquarters in the town of Black Mountain, 10 miles east of Asheville off I-40.

✷ To Do

BICYCLING **Backcountry Outdoors** (828-884-4262; backcountryoutdoors.com), 18 Pisgah Hwy., Pisgah Forest 28768. This outdoors supply store, located north of Brevard on US 276, has trail bike rentals, trail maps, and guided trail bike trips for the Pisgah Forest, one of the region's finest trail biking destinations.

Bio-Wheels (828-236-2453; biowheels.com; asheville@biowheels.net), 81 Coxe Ave., Asheville 28801. This large bicycle shop on the south edge of downtown Asheville (on US 25) offers rentals and tours, with your choice of off-road mountain biking, road touring, or leisure biking.

CANOES, KAYAKS, AND RAFTS **Huck Finn River Adventures** (877-520-4658; huckfinnrafting.com; Rafting@HuckFinnRafting.com), P.O. Box 366, Hot Springs 28743. Headquartered in Hot Springs, this outfitter leads whitewater rafting trips on the remote and beautiful French Broad River upstream from Hot Springs, and float trips on the calm waters downstream from Hot Springs. Special trips include an evening float trip with a sunset steak dinner, and an overnight river camping trip with a steak dinner and pancake breakfast.

USA Raft French Broad (866-872-7238; 423-743-7111; mtnadventureguides.com). This affiliate of a West Virginia rafting operation offers a variety of rafting trips on the French Broad River from their location north of Asheville on US 25, near Marshall.

French Broad Rafting Company (800-570-7238; 828-649-3574; frenchbroadrafting.com), 7525 Unit 2, US 2570, Marshall 28753. Located between Asheville and Hot Springs, off US 25 near the French Broad River, this outfitter offers both whitewater and calm-water trips on different sections of the French Broad.

Southern Waterways (800-849-1970; 828-232-1970; fax: 828-232-1978; paddlewithus.com), 521 Amboy Rd., Asheville 28806. Southern Waterways offers gentle, self-guided trips on the French Broad River as it cuts through the Biltmore Estate—several miles of private wilderness, little changed since Frederick Law Olmsted designed its landscape in the 1880s. You have your choice of raft, canoe, or kayak, or they will shuttle your private boat for a modest fee. A guided sunset paddle goes down the same stretch in the twilight hours.

Headwaters Outfitters (828-877-3106; headwatersoutfitters.com; info@headwatersoutfitters.com), P.O. Box 145, Rosman 28772. Located at the start of 50 miles of serpentine flatwater on the French Broad River, Headwaters Outfitters offers canoe and kayak sales, rentals, and shuttled trips.

TOYMAKER DEMONSTRATES A TOP, CRADLE OF FORESTRY IN AMERICA.

HORSES AND LLAMAS English Mountain Llama Trekking (828-622-9686; hikinginthesmokies.com; info@hikinginthesmokies.com), 767 Little Creek Rd., Hot Springs 28743. This outfitter features llama treks in the Pisgah and Nantahala National Forests—hiking with a really cute animal instead of a backpack. Day treks include lunch; overnight treks include all gear and meals. You can plan your own camping trip as well.

Biltmore Estate Equestrian Center (828-277-4485), 1 Biltmore Estate Dr., Asheville 28803. The Biltmore Estate's stables offer riding on the 100 miles of estate trails that George Vanderbilt constructed in the 1890s.

Cedar Creek Riding Stables (877-625-6773; 828-625-2811; cedarcreekstables.com; hakbarnman@aol.com), 542 Cedar Creek Rd., Lake Lure 28746. Located deep in the mountains north of Lake Lure, Cedar Creek offers scenic one- and two-hour trail rides on their own 360-acre ranch. Two night pack trips in the Pisgah National Forest include all equipment and meals.

Sandy Bottom Trail Rides (800-959-3513; 828-649-9745; sandybottomtrailrides.net; info@sandybottomtrailrides.net), 155 Caney Fork Rd., Marshall 28753. This horse stable offers half- and full-day trail rides, as well as overnighters, from their location in a beautiful rural valley west of Marshall.

LAKE BOATING Lake Lure Marina (877-386-4255; 828-625-1373; fax: 828-625-2036; lakelure.com/tours.php; skipper@lakelure.com), 2930 Memorial Hwy., Lake Lure 28746. This marina on Lake Lure rents a variety of human- and machine-powered boats, including canoes and kayaks.

MINING AND PANNING Old Pressley Sapphire Mine (828-648-6320; oldpressleymine.com; cjohnboy2@aol.com), 240 Pressley Mine Rd., P.O. Box 263, Canton 28716. Open daily 9–6. This remote mine has produced record-setting sapphires in years past. It remains one of the few recreational gem mines in these mountains to be located at an authentic mine, using unsalted ore from on-site (which you can dig yourself). To find it, take exit 33 from I-40, then go north 1 mile on Newfound Road; from there, follow the signs for another 1.5 miles down back roads.

SKIING Wolf Laurel (800-817-4111; 828-689-4111; skiwolfridgenc.com; marketing@skiwolfridgenc.com), 578 Valley View Circle, P.O. Box 70, Mars Hill 28754. This ski slope is located on the leeward side of snow-magnet Bald Mountain, just below its crest. Maximum vertical drop is 700 feet from a high elevation of 4,650 feet, with 14 runs and four chair lifts. All runs have artificial snow and night lights.

OF SPECIAL INTEREST Asheville Hot Air Balloons (828-667-9943; ashevillehotairballoons.com), 1410 Pisgah Hwy. (NC 151), Asheville 28715. A hot-air balloon dealer and certified FAA repair shop with more than 25 years' experience, Mount Pisgah Balloons offers one-hour sunrise flights in one of the most beautiful corners of Asheville area. Reservations are necessary.

✷ Lodging

RESORTS AND HOTELS 🐾 Hotel Indigo (800-951-4667; 828-239-0239; ashevillehotellodgingdowntown.com; boutiquehotel@hlihotels.com), 151 Haywood St., Asheville 28801. $$$–$$$$. This new high-rise hotel, constructed in 2009 at the edge of downtown, is modern and snazzy, describing itself as a "boutique hotel." It has full room service, WiFi, and a restaurant that's open every day, late. Breakfast packages are available for an extra fee. The price range is for the hotel proper; two of the balconied upper floors are devoted to short-term apartments, very large and luxurious, and very expensive. It's within easy walking distance (a block or two) of the Thomas Wolfe Auditorium, the Grove Arcade, and a wide range of restaurants and shops.

✐ The Grove Park Inn Resort & Spa (800-438-5800; 828-252-2711; fax: 828-253-7053; groveparkinn.com; info@groveparkinn.com), 290 Macon Ave., Asheville 28804. $$$$–$$$$$. This impressive stone inn sits on a hillside above Asheville, just north of downtown. Built in 1913, it was a focal point for Asheville's early development; now it's at the center of an upscale historic neighborhood. The large old inn is built of huge granite stones and topped with a bright red roof—a grand sight viewed across its 1899 golf course (redesigned by Donald Ross in 1923). This old inn is flanked by two modern wings, built in the 1980s; together they offer 510 rooms. These rooms are all furnished in Arts-and-Crafts-style furniture—reproductions in the new wings, the hotel's custom-built original furniture in the old inn. Resort activities are extensive. This child-friendly inn offers fully supervised children's programs (ages 3–12) in a summer camp format for half days, full days, and (some) evenings. Child-averse adults can stay in the child-free (and very expensive) Club Floor, which has oversized rooms and its own private lounge. Apart from the Club Floor, breakfast is not included in the tariff.

Inn on Biltmore Estate (800-624-1575; biltmore.com, click on "Stay at Biltmore"; innsales@biltmore.com), 1 Antler Approach Rd., Asheville 28803. $$$$–$$$$$. This 213-room hotel stands six stories tall on a hillock within the Biltmore Estate, about 2 miles from the house and garden. A monolithic modern structure built in 2001, it has been given exterior decorative flourishes reminiscent of the Biltmore House's French château architecture. The same sort of decorated modern architecture carries on in the interior, where distinctly contemporary lines and room designs serve as backdrops for English and French country house furniture. The room rate does not include a ticket to the Biltmore House and Gardens, even though the hotel is on the estate grounds.

✐ **The Chalet Club** (800-336-3309; fax: 828-625-9373; chaletclub.com; reservations@chaletclub.com), P.O. Box 100, Lake Lure 28746. $$$–$$$$. The Washburn family has run this intimate resort above Lake Lure on the rim of Hickory Nut Gorge since they founded it in 1934. Even though classed as a private club, they welcome all visitors with no restrictions; the modest annual fee is used to maintain the surrounding wild lands. With five guest rooms and six cottages, it is nevertheless a traditional full-service resort, including all meals and all activities in the price; guests can also get a "bed & breakfast" limited to breakfast and only a few of the activities. The main lodge, built in 1927 as the family vacation retreat, is in a chalet style with plenty of period charm and panoramic views. It contains the five comfortable guest rooms and the large common areas. The cottages were all built as private houses, and range from a quaint 1927 log caretaker's cabin to a comfortable 1962 home. Meals are prepared from fresh ingredients, with breakfasts served from a menu, a simple lunch served buffet-style or taken as a picnic. Dinners are more formal, with gentlemen expected to wear a coat. Outdoor activities for which there is no extra charge include two tennis courts, a platform tennis court, 7 miles of hiking and biking trails, basketball, shuffleboard, and horseshoe courts, two swimming pools, lake swimming, waterskiing, canoeing, kayaking, electric boating (for lake fishing), and powerboating.

BED & BREAKFASTS 🐾 **1900 Inn on Montford** (800-254-9569; 828-254-9569; innonmontford.com), 296 Montford Ave., Asheville 28801. $$$–$$$$$. Tree lovers take note: The 1900 Inn on Montford has the North Carolina state-record Norway maple in its front yard. This fine old Victorian house in Asheville's Montford National Historic District, immediately north of downtown, is a classic of the Asheville Arts and Crafts style, with a barn-red shingle exterior, flanking front gables, and a huge wraparound porch overlooking its English garden landscaping. Common areas as well as the eight rooms are elegantly furnished in a turn-of-the-20th-century style, with fireplace, Jacuzzi, and WiFi. A full breakfast is included. The pet-friendly rooms are large suites, and more expensive than the standard no-pet rooms.

✐ 🐾 **WhiteGate Inn & Cottage** (800-485-3045; 828-253-2553; fax: 828-281-1883; whitegate.net; innkeeper@whitegate.net), 173 E. Chestnut St., Asheville 28801. $$$$–$$$$$. Located in Asheville's Chestnut Hill National Historic District, just three blocks north of downtown, the hilltop White-Gate is surrounded by gardens, with the tops of downtown Asheville's tallest buildings visible over the white picket fence. Gravel paths loop through its English-style gardens, with a 1,200-

square-foot greenhouse and conservatory holding an orchid garden. Inside, the common rooms are wood-paneled and decorated with Edwardian antiques. The four rooms in the main house are large, each theme-decorated with period antiques; two have separate sitting rooms. A small garden cottage, original to the house, makes up the fifth room in the inn. A full breakfast is included. Pets and children are restricted to certain rooms, so call ahead to ensure availability.

🐾 **Biltmore Village Inn** (866-274-8779; 828-274-8707; biltmorevillageinn.com), 119 Dodge St., Asheville 28803. $$$$. This elaborately Victorian 1892 mansion, built by the man who sold Biltmore to George Vanderbilt, is on a quiet street in Biltmore Village only a few blocks from the Biltmore House entrance and with easy walking to shops, cafés, and galleries. Its seven large rooms were redecorated with European antiques in 2006, and have WiFi. The tariff includes a full breakfast, and wine and cheese in the afternoon.

🖍 🐾 **The Blake House** (888-353-5227; 828-681-5227; fax: 828-681-0420; blakehouse.com; blakehouseinn@charterinternet.com), 150 Royal Pines Dr., Asheville 28704. $$–$$$. Built as a summer home in 1847, the Blake House sits in what is now a quiet southern suburb of Asheville, convenient to the airport. Built entirely of granite, it sports 22-inch-thick granite walls and 14-foothigh ornamental plaster ceilings, as well as a wide front porch with rocking chairs. The seven rooms, plus a family suite, are individually decorated, and have WiFi. A full breakfast is included. Pets and children are welcome.

🖍 🐾 **The Black Mountain Inn** (800-735-6128; 828-669-6528; blackmountaininn.com; jbergeron@mindspring.com), 1186 W. Old Hwy. 70, Black Mountain 28711. $$$. This historic inn sits on 3 wooded acres just west of Black Mountain, off Old Highway 70. Old Highway 70 is now a back lane, but it was once the main coach road over the Blue Ridge—and the Black Mountain Inn was built as a coaching inn in the 1830s. Today it has seven beautiful en suite rooms, all individually furnished in antiques. Unusually for a B&B, the Black Mountain welcomes well-behaved children and small pets, but you must make arrangements in advance. A full breakfast is included.

🖍 **Ox-Ford Farm Bed and Breakfast** (828-658-2500; ox-fordfarm.com), 75 Ox Creek Rd, Weaverville 28787. From I-26 north of Asheville, take exit 21 onto New Stock Road, then go east one block to US Bus 19; turn right and go 0.8 mile to a right fork onto Reems Creek Road (SSR 1003); then go 4.5 miles to a right fork onto Ox Creek Road (SSR 2109), and go about 2 miles. From the Blue Ridge Parkway, turn west at milepost 375.3 onto paved Ox Creek Road, then go about 2 miles. $$. This 1876 farmhouse sits on a working cattle and sheep farm in an exceptionally pretty valley above Weaverville, near the Blue Ridge Parkway and the Vance Birthplace. The four rooms share three baths. The included full breakfast features eggs from the farm and home-baked bread.

The Inn on Main Street (877-873-6074; 828-645-4935; innonmain.com; relax@innonmain.com), 88 S. Main St., Weaverville 28787. $$$. Built by a local doctor in 1900, this late-Victorian country house sits in the center of charming little Weaverville, two blocks south of its strollable downtown in a residential neighborhood. This seven-room Victorian B&B features tall bay windows and wide porches, and is furnished throughout with antiques.

Rooms tend to be normal to large in size, each theme-furnished, and with WiFi. A full breakfast is included, as well as afternoon hors d'oeuvres.

The Magnolia Mountain Inn (800-914-9306; 828-622-3543; fax: 828-622-9553; mountainmagnoliainn.com; innkeepers@magnoliamountaninn.com), 204 Lawson St., P.O. Box 6, Hot Springs 28743. $$–$$$$. This elaborate 130-year-old Victorian house in Hot Springs—built by a South Carolina Unionist who had to flee his home state during the Civil War—has been beautifully restored to a five-room B&B. It has 3 acres of gardens with a 100-year-old boxwood maze, vegetable and herb gardens (used in the food prepared for guests), and rhododendrons, all framed by spectacular mountain views. The 10 rooms range from cozy to large, each with its own personality. A full breakfast is included in the price. Dinner is available to guests and non-guests on Fridays and Saturdays, for an extra charge.

✐ **Stone Hedge Inn** (800-859-1974; stone-hedge-inn.com; stonehedgeinn@alltel.net), 222 Stone Hedge Lane, P.O. Box 366, Tryon, TN 28782. $$$. This 1934 mansion, made of stacked fieldstone taken from the property, makes a charming site for this small inn and restaurant. Located 3 miles north of Tryon in the shadow of the Blue Ridge, the original house combines its vernacular local stonework with elements of art deco and Mediterranean architecture, all framed by spectacular views over the 28-acre estate. All six guest rooms are large enough to have sitting areas. Its owners run a fine small restaurant in the main house; the tariff includes a full breakfast. Small children and infants are accepted, but you must call ahead to make arrangements.

The Yellow House (800-563-1236; 828-452-0991; fax: 828-452-1140; theyellowhouse.com; info@theyellowhouse.com), 89 Oakview Dr., Waynesville 28786. $$$–$$$$. This B&B occupies a century-old house on a pond, surrounded by beautiful gardens, in the pastoral Plott Creek Valley 3 miles from downtown Waynesville. Built by the prominent Lykes family of Tampa in the late 19th century, the Yellow House is a simple, elegant late-Victorian structure with wraparound porches and a second-story balcony. All of the 10 large guest rooms are individually theme-decorated, each reminiscent of a favorite place. A full breakfast is included.

Key Falls Bed & Breakfast (828-884-7559; fax: 828-884-8342; keyfallsinn.com; Keyfallsinn@brinet.com), 151 Everett Rd., Pisgah Forest 28768. $–$$. This large two-story farmhouse from the 1860s sits on 35 acres by the French Broad River, 3 miles east of Brevard. Its well-kept gardens and meadows give views toward the river and the mountains beyond, while the large property contains a pond, tennis courts, and hiking trails (including one to the lovely Key Falls, on-site). Comfortable common areas and five guest rooms are furnished with Victorian decor, including antiques. The room rate includes a full breakfast.

The Claddagh Inn (866-770-2999; 828-693-6737; claddaghinn.com; innkeepers@claddaghinn.com), 755 N. Main St., Hendersonville 28792. $$–$$$. This lovely old inn sits on downtown Hendersonville's Main Street, a large late-Victorian mansion surrounded by its own lawn and shaded by giant oak trees. The three-story Classical Revival house, listed on the National Register, features an extra-wide wraparound front porch and a cute second-story balcony. The 14 en suite guest rooms, all comfortable to large in size with telephone, television, and air-conditioning, are individually furnished in Victorian antiques and reproductions. Guests are treated to a hearty country breakfast and an evening light refreshments and wine.

CABINS Lakemont Cottages (800-597-0692; 828-693-5174; fax: 828-693-5174; lakemontcottages.com; reserva tions@lakemontcottages.com), 101 Lakemont Dr., Flat Rock 28731. $–$$. Lakemont features 14 pleasant modern cottages spread around a rolling, wooded tract south of Hendersonville, not far off US 176. A small lake (or large pond) makes up the centerpiece of this little village. Cottages have separate bedrooms and full kitchens, as well as enclosed porches.

🐾 **Oxglen Vacation Rentals** (800-326-2373; 828-645-2974; oxglen.com; jim@oxglen.com), 376 Ox Creek Rd., Weaverville 28787. From the Blue Ridge Parkway, turn west at milepost 375.3 onto paved Ox Creek Road, then go 2.2 miles. $$–$$$. This 13-acre forested tract sits just 2 miles off the Blue Ridge Parkway via paved road. Five chalet-style cottages, varying in size from one to four bedrooms, are comfortably furnished; each has a satellite TV, gas fireplace, private phone line, WiFi, porch and/or balcony, and washer-dryer, as well as a full kitchen.

✷ Where to Eat

DINING OUT The Market Place Restaurant and Wine Bar (828-252-4162; marketplace-restaurant.com; food&wine@marketplace-restaurant .com), 20 Wall St., Asheville 28801. Open for dinner, Mon.–Sat. $$$$. One of the attractive storefronts on Wall Street in downtown Asheville, the Market Place offers a fusion of Continental and global cuisine with fresh mountain ingredients. The dinner menu changes daily, depending on the fresh, seasonal fruits, vegetables, and seafood available. It may feature meats from local farms, perhaps smoked with applewood, or berries from the Biltmore Estate. The wine list includes hundreds of different bottles with many rare vintages, but a very limited choice of wines under $30.

Rezaz Mediterranean Cuisine (828-277-1510; rezaz.com; reza@rezaz.com), 28 Hendersonville Rd., Asheville 28803. Open Mon.–Sat, plus Sun. brunch; restaurant: lunch and dinner; Enoteca: 10–late. Lunch: $$; dinner: $$$$. Located in a large brick storefront on the northern edge of Biltmore Village, Rezaz has long been noted for its elegant and original cuisine from North Africa, the Middle East, Spain, and Italy. Its wine list is excellent, with a good choice for $30 or less. The adjacent building is **Rezaz Enoteca**, an Italian wine bar (*enoteca* translates as "wine library"), a very informal hangout that offers tapas and sandwiches along with dozens of Italian wines by the glass.

The Weaverville Milling Company (828-645-4700; weavervillemilling.com; Wmilling@aol.com), 1 Old Mill Lane, Weaverville 28787. Open for dinner, daily except Wed. This early-20th-century watermill, just off Reems Creek Road, continued in operation into the 1960s. Today it houses a fine restaurant, specializing in southern foods, imaginatively yet traditionally prepared. The exterior looks just the way it did a century ago; inside it's beautifully converted, with polished bare wood and open rafters, decorated with authentic country objects from the area. Some of the original machinery is still in place, and a loft houses a collection of quilts and other mountain antiques. To find it, go north on US Alt

APPLE ORCHARD ON THE BLUE RIDGE NEAR HENDERSONVILLE

19/23 at future I-26's exit 21 for 1.4 miles, to a right onto Reems Creek Road (SSR 1003); it's 0.6 mile farther on the right.

EATING OUT ✐ **Barley's Taproom and Pizzeria** (828-255-0504; barleys taproom.com), 42 Biltmore Ave., Asheville 28801. Daily, lunch and dinner. $$. This favorite downtown watering hole (located on Biltmore Avenue south of Pack Square) has long been noted for its huge selection of microbrews on tap—43 of them, with both regional and European breweries well represented and no taps wasted on the mass-market stuff. Barley's has the singular distinction of being the pub that introduced microbrews to Asheville audiences, who promptly went nuts; the Asheville urban area now has **10 craft breweries**. The Barley's downstairs is family-friendly, and nearly always has a lot of kids scarfing down pizza. Its upstairs (no elevator) is strictly grown-ups only, and has pool tables. The food is good, basic bar fare, and very reliable.

Jack of the Wood (828-252-5445; jackofthewood.com; jackwood@bell south.net), 95 Patton Ave., Asheville 28801. Open daily noon–late. $$. Unlike many "Irish pubs," this downtown Asheville storefront pub has a distinctly Celtic slant—and good beer, including their own brew, Green Man Ale. Simple bar meals of sandwiches, stew, curry, fish cakes, or chili complement the British-style ales. Sundays feature a Celtic ceilidh (jam session) starting at 5, and there's live music most other nights as well (starting between 9 and 10).

The Early Girl Eatery (828-259-9292; earlygirleatery.com), 8 Wall St., Asheville 28801. Open daily for breakfast, lunch, and dinner; breakfast is served all day. $$–$$$. This small storefront in downtown Asheville's Battery Hill shopping district specializes in original food with a southern twang, made fresh from locally grown ingredients. The hillside café is bright and airy, its back windows overlooking a downtown park two floors below. There are always vegetarian and vegan choices, and the extensive vegetable list will show you just what the mountain farms are harvesting right now. Beer and wine are available, with a good choice of microbrews and quality wines by the glass.

The Laughing Seed Café (828-252-3445; laughingseed.com; info@laughingseed.com), 40 Wall St., Asheville 28801. Open Wed.–Mon. for lunch and dinner. Lunch: $$; dinner: $$$. Any vegetable lover will enjoy this downtown Asheville vegetarian café for its wide choice of fresh, exotic produce, and its imaginative preparation that fuses a variety of ethnic themes and ideas. It occupies its own little building on Wall Street, bright and sparkling inside, with a big mural and lots of blond wood. The menu is varied and satisfying, even for the meat lovers in your group, with vegan choices clearly labeled. All food is prepared from scratch with fresh ingredients (including the bread), and they strive to find local organic suppliers for their huge selection of exotic produce. They offer a good choice of organic wines.

Blue Mountain Pizza (828-658-8777; bluemountainpizza.com), 55 N. Main St., Weaverville 28787. Open Tue.–Sun. for lunch and dinner. $$. This friendly neighborhood eatery, located in downtown Weaverville's oldest building, happens to make some of the best pizza in the Blue Ridge. They also have good salads and sandwiches, and the best cheesecake in the region (made by a local woman in her home). Local microbrews are on tap.

The Pisgah Inn (828-235-8228; fax: 828-648-9719; pisgahinn.com), P.O. Box 749, Waynesville 28786. Open daily, Apr.–Oct., for breakfast, lunch, and dinner. $$–$$$. This national park concessionaire sits by the side of the Blue Ridge Parkway, high and remote on the flanks of Mount Pisgah. The casual, simply furnished restaurant has dramatic views from huge windows that cover its entire southern side, flanked by large timber beams. The menu emphasizes fresh ingredients and mountain recipes, although there are plenty of old favorites available, too. Wine and beer are served.

Mount Mitchell State Park Restaurant (828-675-9545; fax: 828-682-6510), NC 128 (Mount Mitchell Spur Rd.), Burnsville. Open daily, May–Oct., for lunch and early dinner. In Mount Mitchell State Park. Access from the Blue Ridge Parkway, milepost 355, Mount Mitchell Spur Road. $$$. Run by a local family, this pleasant lodge-style restaurant sits on the crest of the Black Mountains inside Mount Mitchell State Park, with stunning vistas from its large windows. Inside, it's all native stone and polished wood, kept immaculately clean. The food is southern-style, well prepared and fresh; the trout is caught daily at a local trout farm. You choose a main dish, then sides from a list—two sides with a dinner, one with a sandwich. This lets you pick fried okra with your hamburger, a surprisingly good combination. Desserts are particularly worthwhile. Their somewhat higher prices reflect the difficulty both suppliers and employees must endure to reach this remote and beautiful spot.

Cypress Cellar (828-698-1005; cypresscellar.com), 321-C N. Main St., Hendersonville 28792. Open daily for lunch and dinner. Lunch: $$, dinner: $$$. Located in a roomy, airy space below sidewalk level in downtown Hendersonville, the Cypress Cellar features authentic dishes from southern Louisiana. The lunch menu features hot Cajun dishes and po-boys as well as sandwiches and burgers. The dinner menu drops the sandwiches, and adds a variety of steak, pasta, and seafood entrées. On weekend evenings, it's a popular venue for live music.

The Purple Onion Café and Coffee House (828-749-1179; purpleonion saluda.com), 16 Main St., Saluda 28773. Open Mon.–Tue. and Thu.–Sat. for lunch and dinner. Lunch: $$–$$$; dinner: $$$. This small upscale eatery occupies a well-kept storefront in downtown Saluda. Its menu offers California-style cuisine, with lots of fresh and exotic ingredients. It has a good wine list with a good selection under $30, and a large selection of microbrews on tap.

Rocky's Soda Shop & Grill (828-877-5375; ddbullwinkels.com/Rockys_.html), 38 S. Broad St., Brevard 28766. Open daily for lunch; extended hours in summer. In downtown Brevard, on US 64. $–$$. This nostalgic store, at the center of downtown Brevard since 1942, re-creates (or, perhaps, preserves) a 1950s soda fountain, with a menu of burgers, hot dogs, sandwiches, sundaes, and shakes. There are a few homey surprises as well, such as grilled pimiento cheese (I remember that!), and fried peanut butter and jelly. It's fun, cheap, and good.

✷ Entertainment

FREE CONCERTS Park Rhythms (828-669-2052). Held July–Aug., Thu. starting at 7. Admission is free. These free concerts at Black Mountain's Lake Tomahawk Park feature a variety of bluegrass and alternative music.

Mountain Street Dances (828-456-3517). Held July–Aug., every other Sat. 6:30–9. Admission is free. Clogging and square dancing to live bluegrass music on the front lawn of the county courthouse, in downtown Waynesville.

Shindig on the Green (828-259-6107). Held July–Aug., Sat. 7–10. Admission is free. Asheville sponsors this weekly outdoor musical get-together on the large green in front of the downtown city hall, featuring old-time mountain music, bluegrass, and dancing.

CLASSICAL Brevard Music Festival (888-384-8682; 828-884-2011; brevardmusic.org; brevardmusic@citcom.net), P.O. Box 312, Brevard 28712. Held June–Aug.; box office opens in Apr. Students at the Brevard Music Center combine with top-notch professional musicians to put on a summerlong series of performances—typically 50 or so—outdoors in their spacious and beautifully landscaped campus on the north edge of town. Events include symphony orchestras, chamber music, popular music, musicals, and fully staged operas.

Flat Rock Playhouse (828-693-0403; flatrockplayhouse.org; frp@flatrockplayhouse.org), P.O. Box 310, Flat Rock 28731. The State Theater of North Carolina, this professional Actors' Equity company performs nine or so productions at its barn-like theater on US 25 in Flat Rock. The town's namesake rock is on its property.

The Asheville Symphony Orchestra (888-860-7378; 828-254-7046; fax: 828-254-1761; ashevillesymphony.org; info@ashevillesymphony.org), P.O. Box 2852, Asheville 28802. Since 1960, the Asheville Symphony Orchestra has been bringing professional symphony to the mountains. Seasons typically include six masterworks concerts, two pops concerts, and a fully staged opera in conjunction with the Asheville Lyric Opera Company.

Hendersonville Symphony Orchestra (828-697-5884; hendersonvillesymphony.org), P.O. Box 1811, Hendersonville 28793. Hendersonville is probably the only small-town rural county seat with its own full-sized symphony orchestra. Made up of talented local musicians, it's led by Music Director and Conductor Thomas Joiner, professor of violin and orchestra activities at Furman University and co-concertmaster of the Brevard Music Festival. Performing at various local venues (including the high school auditorium), its typical concert season includes a pops concert, a Christmas concert, and a couple of traditional classical concerts with guest soloists.

The Diana Wortham Theatre (828-257-4530; dwtheatre.com; packplace@main.com), 2 S. Pack Square, Asheville 28801. This 500-seat theater, part of the Pack Place complex, hosts around 150 performances a year, of every conceivable type.

POPULAR ***Mountain Xpress*** (mountainx.com). Asheville's lively music and entertainment scene is far too large and quickly changing to describe here. Fortunately, it's brilliant described, fresh every Wednesday, in the *Mountain Xpress,* an excellent alternative newspaper distributed free at newsstands throughout the region.

The Orange Peel (828-225-5851; theorangepeel.net; info@theorangepeel.net), 101 Biltmore Ave., Asheville 28801. The box office is open Wed.–Sat. 12:30–5:30. Cost varies with the act. Located on Biltmore Avenue to the south of downtown, Asheville's Orange Peel is a state-of-the-art live music club whose ability to attract national acts has earned it inclusion in *Rolling Stone*'s Top Five Rock Clubs in the country for 2008. *Mountain Xpress* readers rate it Asheville's best dance spot as well. There's a full bar, and food is available. Most acts have a minimum age for admittance of 18; no smoking is allowed inside. For tickets by phone, contact Ticketweb at 866-466-7630.

✷ Selective Shopping

Downtown Asheville. Asheville's 1920s-era downtown spreads over a 60-block area just south of I-240 at US 25 (exit 5A). Frozen in time by the Great Depression, it somehow survived the modern era with its charm intact. Nearly all of the large downtown area is dominated by low buildings dating from the early 20th century. Southern red-brick Italianate is, of course, common, but this is Asheville; nearly as common are buildings with art deco industry-inspired decorations, or the elaborate fillips of the 19th-century Art Nouveau movement. Indeed, you will find only six modernist buildings in the entire district (one of them by I. M. Pei), and few buildings higher than 10 stories. Without glass towers to sterilize the streets below, downtown remains a walking district of charm and grace. Shoppers stroll past buildings crusted with fancy brickwork, colored tile, stone trim, and sculptures small and large. Sidewalks are filled with people, and storefronts filled with shops.

Asheville's downtown is large enough to split into four districts, each with its own distinct personality. To the west, Battery Hill has the largest concentrations of vintage-1920s architecture and small boutiques, including the spectacular 1925 Grove Arcade, the oldest indoor mall in America. Pack Square marks the busy heart of downtown, its banking and office district, and its arts district, all centered on a brand-new park. To the north of Pack Square, Lexington Park houses businesses and people pursuing alternate or New Age lifestyles. And to the east, the Courthouse Plaza area (heavily urban-renewed in the 1960s) holds the institutions of urban life—the city hall (a remarkable art deco classic), the courthouse, the glass-tower hotel, the YMCA, and lots of parking.

When visiting downtown Asheville, be sure to park in one of the city-owned garages for 50 to 75 cents an hour with the first hour free. On-street parking, always difficult, is $1 an hour with a two-hour maximum.

The River Arts District (riverarts district.com). In the early 20th century Asheville's industrial district trailed along the railroad tracks that hugged the banks of the French Broad River, swinging around town center in a broad semicircle. This was a common pattern in the industrializing South, as was its modern sequel of slow abandonment, leaving behind dozens of tall brick factories, semi-ruinous. Asheville, however, has an advantage over other small cities—a large population of artists, who need great amounts of very cheap square footage for studio and gallery space, and who easily fall in love with the bricks and timbers of the old factories. And so the old industrial district has been reborn as the River Arts District.

The River Arts District has reached critical mass, and is growing fast. Its website, maintained by one of the artists, lists 13 buildings open to the public, each with a variety of studios, galleries, and businesses, plus four cafés and a microbrewery. Some studios are open daily, others on Friday or Saturday, and some by appointment. Check the website before you visit, where you can download a map.

Biltmore Village (biltmorevillage .com). In the 1890s George Vanderbilt constructed Biltmore Village outside the gates of his Biltmore Estate as the home for his hundreds of workers. Frederick Law Olmsted planned the village and Richard Morris Hunt designed its buildings, giving it a unique appearance that survives to this day. Sold off after Vanderbilt's death in 1914, Hunt's handsome buildings and Olmsted's landscaping survive—now holding an upscale shopping district.

To understand the village, picture the idyllic rural world that Vanderbilt tried to create. Vanderbilt placed his village across from the main gate of his estate, separated from it by an old narrow coach road and an expanse of green lawn. On one side of the village he placed an elegant little train station to serve the needs of the estate. In the ensuing decades, a large industrial rail yard grew up beside the little depot. The narrow coach road became US 25 and slowly expanded to 10 lanes. The grassy lawn, sold off and divided into pieces, came to hold a 1950s motel, two gas stations, a fast-food franchise, and a modern hotel that spectacularly fails in its attempt to parrot Hunt's architectural style. Fortunately, the noise and ugliness stop as if cut off by a curtain as soon as you enter the tiny back streets of the village. The center of the village remains pretty much as Vanderbilt left it.

The large selection of independently owned shops include half a dozen antiques stores, several galleries, five clothiers, and a dozen or so gift shops. If you get a mite peckish, there are a number of small independent restaurants inside the village, including Rezaz for dinners both fancy and casual. The village features free street parking, usually (but not always) with enough spaces to handle all the shoppers.

The Grove Arcade (828-252-7799; fax: 828-255-7953; grovearcade.com; info@grovearcade.com), 29½ Page Ave, Asheville 28801. This astonishing 1920s downtown mall, said to be the oldest indoor mall in America, covers two entire city blocks in downtown Asheville. It's a five-story elaborately decorated structure; outer walls are covered with terra-cotta tiles and limestone, and stone-carved lions and gryphons guard the entrance. Built by the developer of the Grove Park Inn in 1929, it functioned successfully as an "indoor market" throughout the Depression, only to be taken over by the federal government in 1942 as part of the war effort. (Curiously, it was the home of the federal research effort into global warming until that agency moved to new digs a block away.) In 1995 the city of Asheville bought it from the feds with the intent of restoring it to its original glory. They've succeeded. There are about 70 stores, many specializing in unique local products.

Downtown Brevard (828-884-3278; brevard.org), 62 W. Main St., Brevard 28712. This four-block classic small-town Main Street centers on its beautiful and well-kept Transylvania County Courthouse. For the past decade it's been evolving from a rural downtown to an upscale shopping district; you can still get your hair cut and shoes repaired, but you can browse for art and antiques as well.

Downtown Waynesville (828-456-3517; downtownwaynesville.com; info@downtownwaynesville.com), 19 S. Main St., Waynesville 28786. Downtown Waynesville furnishes one of the more interesting and varied shopping districts in the Smokies. A classic small-town district, it stretches for three blocks along the former main highway, from the county courthouse to the city hall. Its 86 retailers and restaurants are dominated by small craft galleries and boutiques, but you'll also find antiques stores, kitchen supplies, books, cafés, wine sellers . . . almost anything except the franchised or the dull.

Downtown Hendersonville (downtownhendersonville.org). Hendersonville's five-block downtown remains dominated by turn-of-the-20th-century two- and three-story buildings, facing a landscaped Main Street dedicated to walkers. The old storefronts have a good selection art and fine craft galleries, antiques shops, gift shops, specialty shops, and restaurants—90 retailers and eateries in all. The Main Street shopping district is bordered on the north by US 64, and on the south by the old and distinguished Henderson County Courthouse. Parking is free along Main Street, and 25 cents for two hours on four metered lots along US 25.

✷ Special Events

It shouldn't be too surprising that the state's biggest tourism region has the most, and the most varied, special events. Here are a few of the best.

(Also see *Entertainment* for free summer concerts.)

Last weekend in April: **TrailFest at Hot Springs**. Admission is free. This celebration of the Appalachian Trail brings the entire town out to commemorate the first great long-distance path in the world, and to welcome the through-hikers just beginning to walk along the downtown sidewalk that the trail follows.

Early May: **Spring Herb Festival** (828-689-5974; ashevilleherbfestival .com), WNC Farmer's Market, NC 109 at I-26. Admission is free. This annual gathering brings together all of the region's many herb farmers, selling seedlings and meeting new customers. This is the place to see such unique Blue Ridge herbs as ginseng and galax, and to talk to the people who raise them.

Last weekend in May: ✐ **Lake Eden Arts Festival** (828-686-8742; the leaf.com; info@theLEAF.com), 377 Lake Eden Rd., Black Mountain 28711. $$$$–$$$$$. This twice-annual festival (it's repeated in mid-October) is an eclectic mix of New Age and traditional mountain elements, heavy on music and crafts, families and good times. Limited to 5,000 attendees at any one time, it's held at Camp Rockmont, a large and beautiful facility (formerly the campus of avant-garde Black Mountain College) in the mountains west of the town of Black Mountain.

Mid-June: **Tryon Riding and Hunt Club Horse Show** (800-438-3681; 828-859-6109; fax: 828-859-5598; fence.org, click "Calendar of Events"), P.O. Box 1095, Tryon 28782. $$$$–$$$$$. Mid-June. This hunter-jumper show has been held in Tryon since 1928. It's a four-day event at the FENCE equestrian center—one of a number of such events held throughout the spring and summer months.

Last two weeks in July: **Folkmoot USA** (877-365-5872; 828-452-2997; fax: 828-452-5762; folkmoot.com; folk moot@pobox.com), 112 Virginia Ave., P.O. Box 658, Waynesville 28786. $$. This major folk dance event brings 8 to 10 national dance troupes to the Smoky Mountains Region, with Waynesville at the center of the action. As many as 350 dancers and musicians perform folk music and dance in native costume, at venues scattered throughout the mountains.

Last weekend in July: **Belle Chere** (828-259-5800; belecherefestival.com). Admission is free. This annual street fest boasts of being the largest free outdoor festival in the South. Taking over most of downtown Asheville for three days, Belle Chere is best known for its multiple, ongoing music venues (featuring bluegrass, jazz, rock, pop, whatever), its street food, its copious beer sales, and its hundreds of art and craft vendors.

First weekend in August: **Village Art & Craft Fair** (newmorninggallerync .com/avacf.html), Asheville. Admission is free. This large fine craft and art show, held on the shaded grounds of the Cathedral of All Souls in Biltmore Village, attracts 140 or more artists from all over America. Held annually since 1972, its posters are notable for their original art, which always features cats. It's sponsored by the New Morning Gallery.

Labor Day weekend: **The North Carolina Apple Festival** (828-697-4557; ncapplefestival.org; ncapplefestival @yahoo.com), P.O. Box 886, Hendersonville 28793. Admission is free. This four-day festival in downtown Hendersonville celebrates the local apple industry. Six blocks of Main Street are filled with 150 vendors and two music stages. Prominence is given to local apple growers and their products, while apple-related activities and demonstrations go on throughout the county. The festival ends with a downtown Labor Day parade.

Mid-October: ✐ **Lake Eden Arts Festival** (828-686-8742; theleaf.com; info@theLEAF.com) See *Last weekend in May*, above.

First weekend in December: **Tryon Christmas Stroll**. Admission is free. Downtown Tryon celebrates Christmas with carriage rides, refreshments, an open house, carol singing, and a craft sale. The celebration extends to nearby towns; in the evening, Saluda has its Home Town Christmas open house and celebration, while nearby Columbus has a Christmas parade the next day.

THE GREAT SMOKY MOUNTAINS

The Great Smoky Mountains make up the craggy climax to the Southern Appalachians. While the nearby Black Mountains (see "The Northern Mountains") may be taller by a few dozens of feet, no other eastern range is steeper, more twisted and knotted, or more rugged. The Smokies run as an unbroken wall for 60 miles along the state line, blocking North Carolina from Tennessee with a cliff-walled edge that has mile-high gaps and 6,000-foot peaks. Then, at Tricorner Knob, the Smokies suddenly twist south, change their name to the Great Balsam Mountains, and run as a mile-high wall for another 45 miles. Behind this great L-shaped range (to its south and west) lies a tangle of tall knotted mountains with deep gaps and slashing narrow valleys.

Mountains this tall make their own climate. Valley floors as low as 800 feet above sea level have a warm southern climate with oak and pine forests. Looming above these valleys, the mile-high ridgelines extend into a subarctic climate zone typical of Canada, dominated by spruces and firs (known locally as a "balsam forest"), left behind by the last ice age. Between these two forest types are every type of hardwood forest imaginable, changing by slope, elevation, local rainfall, exposure to the sun, history, and pure luck. The trees cover nearly every slope, no matter how steep, with the most rugged slopes covered in "laurel hells," dense tangles of rhododendron and mountain laurel. High rainfall, on some ridges more than 100 inches a year, can bring about a lush temperate rain forest of wondrous variety and beauty, where springs ooze out of the rocks to become raging rivers within 3 miles. With all this variety, it comes as no surprise that the Great Smoky Mountains National Park is an International Biosphere Reserve, said to contain more tree species than Europe.

In these tangled ridges, away from the railroads and turnpikes, 19th-century settlements fanned out among the steep draws and coves as a thin cover of small subsistence farms. A high-mountain family would live in a one-crib log cabin and grow the food they planned to eat—mainly corn—in a small steep plot cleared by girdling trees. They would probably have a log barn with a horse or mule and a few cattle, as well as a corn crib, a chicken coop, and (perhaps) a springhouse. Uphill, where it was too steep to farm, the ancient forest spread to the ridgeline; the menfolk hunted the forest, but did not log it. These small plots spread up streams wherever there was enough land to grow a little corn. The Great Smoky Mountains National Park preserves quite a number of these high-mountain farmsteads, some as major open-air museums, others as cabins sitting by a path.

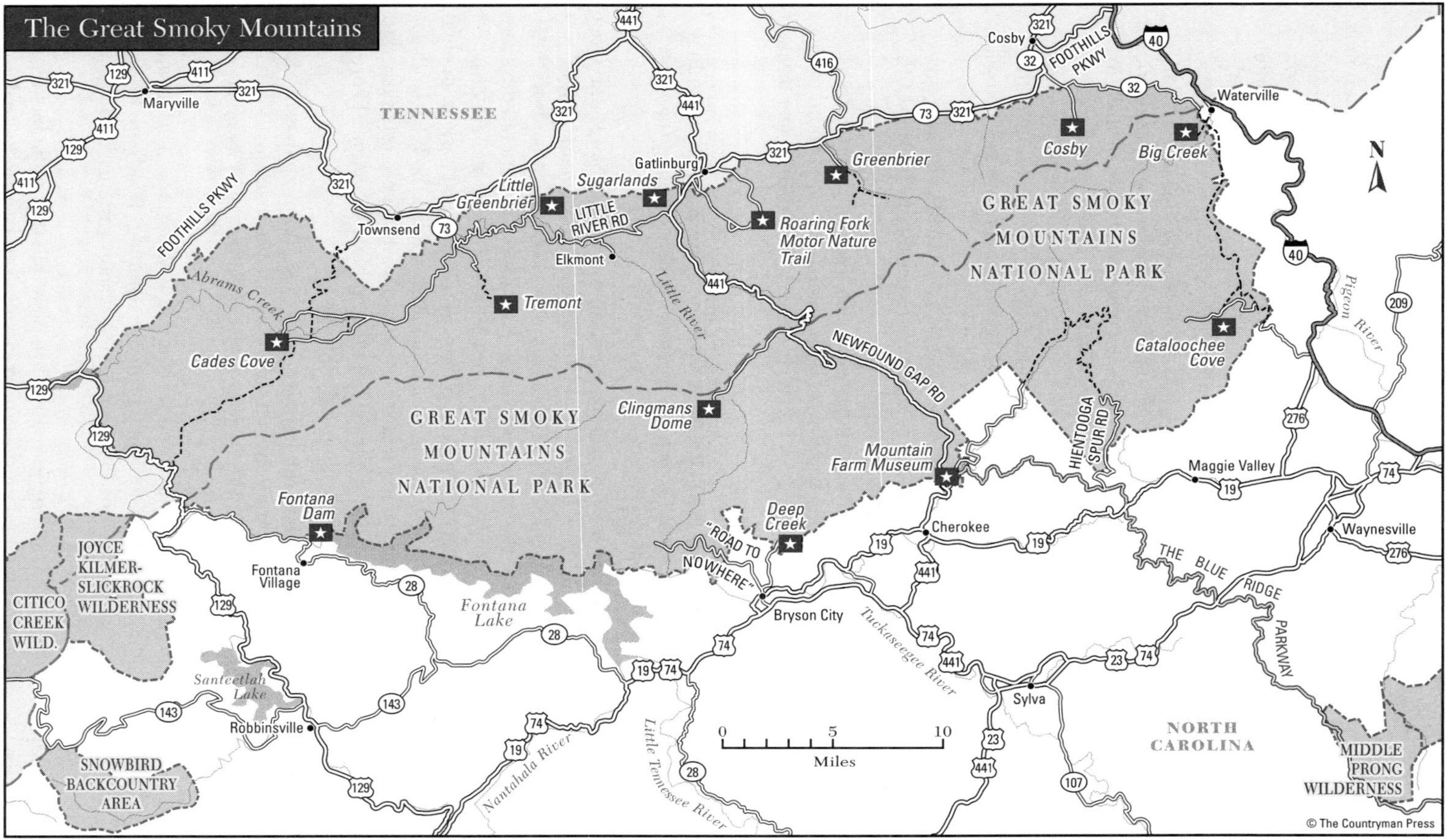
The Great Smoky Mountains
TENNESSEE
NORTH CAROLINA
GREAT SMOKY MOUNTAINS NATIONAL PARK
GREAT SMOKY MOUNTAINS NATIONAL PARK
Maryville
Townsend
Gatlinburg
Cosby
Waterville
Elkmont
Maggie Valley
Waynesville
Cherokee
Bryson City
Sylva
Fontana Village
Robbinsville
Little Greenbrier
Sugarlands
LITTLE RIVER RD
Greenbrier
Roaring Fork Motor Nature Trail
Cosby
Big Creek
Cataloochee Cove
Tremont
Cades Cove
Clingmans Dome
Mountain Farm Museum
Deep Creek
"ROAD TO NOWHERE"
Fontana Dam
NEWFOUND GAP RD
HIENTOOGA SPUR RD
FOOTHILLS PKWY
FOOTHILLS PKWY
THE BLUE RIDGE PARKWAY
Abrams Creek
Little River
Pigeon River
Tuckaseegee River
Little Tennessee River
Nantahala River
Fontana Lake
Santeetlah Lake
JOYCE KILMER-SLICKROCK WILDERNESS
CITICO CREEK WILD.
SNOWBIRD BACKCOUNTRY AREA
MIDDLE PRONG WILDERNESS
N
0 5 10
Miles
© The Countryman Press

Logging came in the last decades of the 19th century, and penetrated nearly everywhere, thanks to the Shay locomotive engine, a massive little workhorse designed for sharp curves and steep slopes. Logging companies would push a makeshift railroad track up a valley, clear-cut it as fast as they could, and then move the tracks to the next valley. As a result only a few limited stands of old growth are left; the forests you see are filled with handsome, straight trees in early maturity.

The Great Smoky Mountains National Park combines all these areas of interest—scenic grandeur, ecological diversity, pioneer history, and environmental upheaval. It forms a half-million-acre oval with the highest and most difficult ridges running lengthways along its center, and roads penetrating in from its periphery. Only one road, the popular Newfound Gap Road, penetrates deep into the park's interior to emerge on the other side. All other roads skitter along its edge, or run up valleys to dead-end at the mountain wall. Those roads lead to all sorts of places: wide views, deep forests, noisy rivers, beautiful waterfalls, and quaint log farmsteads. And footpaths—over 800 miles of foot and bridle paths wander through the national park's backcountry. If you stay in your car, you will miss most of the park.

Half of the national park flows over the state line into Tennessee—and this includes more than half of the food and lodging. You probably won't stop at the state line, and this book won't, either. Within this chapter you'll find evenhanded coverage of the entire national park area, based on quality rather than borders.

Finally, the Olympic-class whitewater river Nantahala Gorge is covered in this chapter, as it is best enjoyed from Bryson City, the lovely little county seat on the park's southwestern edge.

GETTING ALONG IN THE NATIONAL PARK Here you'll find some guidelines general to the Great Smoky Mountains National Park, including rules and regulations, as well as some dangers to look out for.

Who Runs the Parklands? Like all national parks in the United States, the Great Smoky Mountains National Park is owned and run by the U.S. Department of Interior's National Park Service (NPS). In contrast, the government lands to the south of the park, including the Nantahala Gorge, are owned and operated by the U.S. Department of Agriculture's National Forest Service (NFS), and are organized as the Nantahala National Forest. The NPS runs this national park as an environmental preserve and wilderness-style recreation area. Unlike the NFS lands to the south, these NPS parklands carry a large number of restrictions, established to preserve the character of the park while encouraging public enjoyment. There are good reasons for all of them. (Well, almost all of them.)

Cost and amenities. Entrance to the park is free, thanks to the Tennessee state legislature putting deed restrictions on land they donated way back in 1936. There are no charges for any of the historic sites inside the park, or any of its picnic grounds. Campgrounds, however, levy a fee.

The NPS has, from the first, administered this park as a wilderness. This means no gas stations, no cabins, no lodges, and only primitive camping. Roads are few and, apart from the Newfound Gap Road, penetrate only a short distance into the park. Some roads are gravel-surfaced.

Day hiking is unrestricted, and opportunities are plentiful; this guide includes some suggested paths. You'll find most of the park's trails to be high in quality, wide, and properly graded. Nearly all paths are forest walks, including those along ridgetops.

Two dangers confront even the casual walker. The first is bears, discussed below. The second, and by far the more deadly, is hypothermia, dehydration, and exhaustion. Hypothermia—sudden body cooling leading to disorientation—can occur in the hottest weather when altitudes exceed 5,000 feet and rainstorms blow up suddenly. Exhaustion and dehydration can occur whether or not a person is overcooled, particularly when pulling up a 25 percent gradient that stretches for miles without a break. In either case, a disoriented person can wander off the trail—a very dangerous place to be in this twisted, craggy land. The Park Service posts a daily web report on trail conditions, weather, trail closures, and bear problem locations.

Bicycling. For the most part, the National Park Service treats bicycles as vehicles on a par with autos, and requires them to follow the same rules. As a practical matter, this means that bicycling opportunities are limited, as the automobile roads are narrow, shoulderless, and crowded. The Park Service allows bicycles up the Deep Creek and Indian Creek Trails near Bryson City, even though these are closed to vehicles. In addition, the wonderful Cades Cove Loop Road is closed to automobiles Wednesday and Saturday mornings until 10, to allow bicyclists and walkers to enjoy it without noise and fumes. The park's three long gravel roads make for good biking, but cyclists must obey the one-way regulations just like other vehicles.

Backpacking (865-436-1297). Couch potatoes may be surprised to learn that backpacking in the Great Smoky Mountains National Park is so popular that it has had to be rationed for the last 35 years. The rationing system takes the shape of backcountry camping permits, required for all overnight trail use. The most popular backcountry areas require reservations and assigned camping spots, while the less visited areas have fewer restrictions. This system has succeeded in its goal of spreading backpackers throughout the park, instead of concentrating by the hundreds along the Appalachian Trail. You can get a permit from any of the ranger stations, or by calling in advance of your trip.

Backpacking on the Appalachian Trail. Many people are interested in hiking the Appalachian Trail as a special and famous place. Day hiking the trail is unrestricted, and this book describes one of the many great walks. However, the Appalachian Trail remains badly overcrowded by backpackers at all times of the year except the (very dangerous) dead of winter, and is strictly regulated by the permit system. Here as elsewhere along its 2,100-mile length, the trail has three-sided shelters with shelf bunks, but these are reserved for long-distance hikers and completely full nearly all the time. Overuse can make these camping spots unpleasant. In addition, there are bear problems, as bears have learned to raid the Appalachian Trail camping areas (and tents) for food. It's a good idea to backpack down other park trails, or on sections of the Appalachian Trail outside the park. Near the park, the Appalachian Trail at Max Patch (see Max Patch Walks in "Asheville") and Standing Indian are excellent alternatives.

Automobile camping (877-444-6777; recreation.gov). Most campgrounds close seasonally; ask in advance. Auto-based camping is allowed at 10 campgrounds, all of them scenic but primitive, with unheated toilet rooms, no hookups, no electricity, and no showers. Despite these conditions the national park campgrounds are extremely popular and fill up fast. You can get advance reservations at the most popular campgrounds—Cades Cove, Elkmont, and Smokemont. Of the remaining first-come, first-serve campgrounds, Deep Creek is an excellent alternative to the Big Three, with a convenient location right outside Bryson City, a fair amount of room at 92 spaces, and great waterfalls, fishing, and wading. But on a really hot summer's day, try to get into Balsam Mountain Campground on the Heintooga Spur Road—at 5,300 feet, one of the coolest places in the park. If you want remoteness, the 12-site Abrams Creek is hard to beat; you may be two hours from Gatlinburg or Cherokee, but the campground is lovely, the footpaths are some of the park's easiest and most beautiful, and the fishing is great.

Fishing. Inside the national park, fishing for rainbow and brown trout is allowed year-round; you must have a state license, use a single hook on an artificial lure, and not take brook trout (a native species the National Park Service is trying to restore). Despite the fact that the Park Service stopped stocking streams over 35 years ago, the fishing is excellent and most streams are at their trout population maximums. Fishing within the Qualla Boundary requires a tribal license but no state license; fishing on some streams is limited to tribal members.

Pets. The Great Smoky Mountains National Park is definitely not a pet-friendly place; the National Park Service sees them as an environmental risk, period. Pets are prohibited on all trails, to the extent that through-hikers on the Appalachian Trail are required to kennel their dogs until they clear the park. Dogs are allowed only in the overlooks and picnic areas, and they must be on leashes at all times.

Bears. The park's first-ever black bear fatality happened in March 2000, on the Little River Trail about 4 miles from Elkmont. In this incident, two bears attacked two adult hikers without apparent provocation, killing one and guarding the body as bears do a carcass they intend to eat, until rangers could arrive and kill the bears. Bears are extremely dangerous. They should never be approached or fed.

GUIDANCE **The National Park Service (NPS)** (865-436-1291; nps.gov/grsm), 107 Park Headquarters Rd., Gatlinburg, TN 37738. The NPS has a visitors center at both the Gatlinburg and the Cherokee entrances. The one near Gatlinburg is called **Sugarlands**, the name of the local community that existed here before the park. It is the larger of the two, a 1960s park-modern structure with natural history exhibits and a nature trail that leads a short distance to a log cabin. The one near Cherokee is called **Oconaluftee**, named after the adjacent river, a classic stone-and-wood ranger station with limited exhibits inside, but the stunning **Mountain Farm Museum** adjacent. Both have a bookstore whose profits benefit the park, and an information desk.

Smoky Mountain Convention & Visitors Bureau (TN) (800-525-6834; smokymountains.org), 7906 E. Lamar Alexander Pkwy., Townsend, TN 37882. Open normal business hours, every day. This nonprofit organization, dedicated to promoting economic growth and tourism in the northwestern area of the Smokies, maintains a visitors center in a modern log building in Townsend. This visitors center has a good gift shop and displays of local artists, as well as a staffed information desk.

Smoky Mountain Host of North Carolina (800-432-4678; 828-369-9606; visit smokies.org), 4437 Georgia Rd., Franklin 28734. This innkeepers organization will help you find a room throughout the North Carolina side of the Smoky Mountains. They run a large, friendly visitors center on US 441 south of Franklin, near the Georgia state line.

Gatlinburg Visitors Center (Chamber of Commerce) (800-900-4148; gatlinburg.com; info@gatlinburg.com), 811 East Pkwy., P.O. Box 527, Gatlinburg, TN 37738. The Gatlinburg Chamber of Commerce cooperates with the National Park Service to run this large welcome center on US 441 at the eastern entrance to the town. It's also a major terminus (with free parking) on Gatlinburg's elaborate trolley network, making it a good place to park while visiting the rest of the town.

GETTING THERE *By car:* US 441 bisects the Great Smoky Mountains National Park, running from Cherokee, North Carolina, northward to Gatlinburg, Tennessee; within the park, it's called the Newfound Gap Road. US 19 parallels the park's southern border, running from Maggie Valley to Cherokee to Bryson City, then turning south to enter the Nantahala Gorge. On the Tennessee side, US 321 roughly parallels the northern park border, running from I-40 near Newport to Gatlinburg to Townsend, then on to Maryville (a southern suburb of Knoxville) and I-75.

GPS routing is even more unreliable in these mountains than elsewhere, and is likely to send you down bad—or even nonexistent—roads. This is especially true when approaching the park from North Carolina; there's continuous expressway from I-40 West to US 74 West to US 441 North, but every GPS I've tested sends you down narrow, steep, twisting US 19 instead, for an 11-mile savings that'll cost you an hour in travel time.. In Tennessee use only US routes to reach the park, avoiding local and park roads.

By air: For visiting the Tennessee side, start at Knoxville's **McGhee Tyson Airport (TYS)** (865-970-2773; fax: 865-970-4113; tys.org; mcghee@tyson.org), 2055 Alcoa Hwy., Alcoa, TN 37701. It has seven airlines and plenty of car rentals; it's 21 miles from Townsend and 44 miles from Gatlinburg (down inferior roads). (Please note: Your GPS will probably give you bad routing advice; stick to US highways.) But you are probably visiting the North Carolina side first—so start at Asheville's airport (see "Asheville") and drive in via I-26 East to I-40 West to US 74 West to US 441 North (ignoring your GPS's suggestions) for a scenic and easy 67 miles of expressway driving.

By train or bus: There is no train or bus service to this area from the outside world. Once you are here, however, you'll find there's a regular bus service between Cherokee and Gatlinburg May–Oct., and excellent local transit within both Cherokee and Gatlinburg (cherokee-nc.com/index.php?page=170).

MEDICAL EMERGENCIES **Cherokee Urgent Care Clinic & Pharmacy** (828-497-9036), El Camino Plaza, US 19 N., P.O. Box 2039, Cherokee 28719. Open weekdays 9:30–4:30. This walk-in clinic welcomes travelers with non-life-threatening illnesses or injuries. It's located by Harrah's Casino, and must be accessed either through the Harrah's parking lot or the parking lot of the El Camino Motel.

Swain County Hospital (828-488-2155; westcare.org/for-patients-and-visitors/swain-county-hospital), 45 Plateau St., Bryson City 28713. A rare survival from earlier days, this fully accredited small-town hospital has 48 beds, general surgical facilities, and a fully staffed Level 3 24/7 emergency room. Formally a county hospital, it is now owned by nonprofit Westcare, whose primary hospital is in Sylva. You'll find it on an obscure residential side street uphill from the train depot; look for the blue hospital signs on the north side of the depot.

Fort Sanders Sevier Medical Center (TN) (865-429-6100; fssevier.com), 709 Middle Creek Rd, Sevierville, TN, 37864. Despite its Sevierville address, Sevier (pronounced *severe*) Medical Center is located in Pigeon Forge, 1.2 miles east of US 441 on Middle Creek Road; if you are coming from Gatlinburg, you will find this to be a right turn, 7 miles north of downtown. A branch of Knoxville's massive regional hospital company, Covenant Health, Sevier is a small, full-service local hospital with surgery facilities and a 24/7 emergency room.

Blount Memorial Hospital (TN) (865-983-7211; blountmemorial.org), 907 E. Lamar Alexander Pkwy., Maryville, TN 37804. Located 20 miles west of Townsend on US 321 in Maryville, Tennessee, this 250-bed regional hospital is the closest to the Cades Cove area.

✷ Exploring the Area

EXPLORING BY CAR The Great Smoky Mountains National Park, managed for its wilderness experience since it opened, has few roads. Nearly all of these, however, are incredibly scenic, and will make up the backbone of any sightseeing trip. Here are some descriptions to help you get the most out of the best drives.

Newfound Gap Road. At the northern end of Cherokee, US 441 hits the boundary of the Great Smoky Mountains National Park, and becomes the Newfound Gap Road, one of the great drives of the East. In this description, we'll follow it from Cherokee to Sugarlands, then continue on the NPS's Gatlinburg Bypass to its end at US 441 north of Gatlinburg, for a total of 34.5 miles.

For the first 8.8 miles you'll follow the Oconaluftee River upstream into the park. The early parts of this stretch will wind in and out of meadows and glades, a great drive in the early morning when the deer graze. At 0.8 mile you'll pass the southern terminus of the **Blue Ridge Parkway**, another world-class drive, then reach **Oconaluftee Visitors Center** at 1.7 miles. Here you will find the park's finest open-air museum, the **Mountain Farm Museum**, a full-sized restoration of a mountain log-built farmstead, with costumed docents, fully furnished buildings, and authentic crops and livestock. At 2.0 miles on your left is **Mingus Mill**, an operating gristmill and very photogenic. At 4.7 miles you'll pass the entrance to Smokemont Campground on your right, and at 6.8 miles you'll pass the Collins Creek Picnic Area on your left—your last opportunity to picnic for almost 20 miles. From here the Oconaluftee's valley narrows into a sharp defile, with some nice places to enjoy the cascading mountain stream running along the roadway to your right. At 8.8 miles a bridge on your right marks the Kephart Prong Trailhead, with the ruins of an old CCC camp a short distance up.

Now the road starts to climb in earnest with two hairpin turns, and the first of several spectacular views comes between them at 13.4 miles. At the second hairpin the road reaches the ridgeline known as Thomas Ridge, with a series of stunning views. The best of these is a 180-degree panorama over the ocean of wave-like ridges that recede into North Carolina, viewed from a boardwalk over a near-cliff, with parking at 15.0 and 15.4 miles. The overlook at 16.5 miles furnishes one of the park's best sunrise views. The road tops out at 17.1 miles, with the **Clingman's Dome Spur Road** going left and the impressive **Newfound Gap Overlook** just beyond on your right; you are now 5,046 feet above sea level.

The Tennessee side of the Smokies is more rugged, and the road down is more narrow and twisting, yet surprisingly there are fewer views. In fact, Morton Overlook at 17.9 miles on your left (watch for oncoming traffic!) is your last good mountaintop panorama. The justly popular **Alum Caves Trail** starts on your right at 21.5 miles; then, at 22.8 miles you reach an unusual pigtail loop in the road. At 25.7 miles you reach Chimneys Picnic Area, where you can usually find a table beside a stunning little mountain river. At 27.9 miles on your right, Campbell Overlook gives a stunning 180-degree panoramic view of Mount Le Conte and the Smoky Mountain Front, said to be the longest and steepest slope in the East.

At this point you are off the mountain and traveling through the old community of Sugarlands, where the **Sugarlands Visitors Center** is worthwhile for its museum and short, scenic path to a log cabin; you'll find the visitors center at the intersection with the Little River Road to Cades Cove, at 30.1 miles. Sugarlands was also known as Blockader's Heaven because of its moonshine production, which utilized the sorghum sugar that gave the valley its official name; the community was destroyed to make way for the national park, but its ruins (including an early motel) can by found along the Sugarlands Trail, which starts at 30.4 miles, at the far end of the bridge on the right.

At 30.9 miles the road forks, with the right fork leading straight into **Gatlinburg**, and the left fork continuing a scenic drive in the mountains above town. There are superb views over the town, with the mountains towering behind, at 31.6 and 32.4 miles. This scenic bypass end at 34.5 miles at four-lane US 441; a right turn takes you into Gatlinburg in 1.1 miles.

The Blue Ridge Parkway and the Heintooga Spur Road. The Blue Ridge Parkway's final 13-mile section runs from Soco Gap on US 19 to the Newfound Gap Road just inside the Great Smoky Mountains National Park. From Soco Gap, the parkway climbs uphill through forests for the next 3 miles—a particularly fine stretch for spring wildflowers—reaching the **Heintooga Spur Road** (described later) at Wolf Laurel Gap. From here the parkway picks its way down a side ridge, dropping 3,200 feet to reach the Oconaluftee River. Although heavily forested, the terrain is rough enough to require five

DRIVING ON THE NEWFOUND GAP ROAD IN NORTH CAROLINA, GREAT SMOKY MOUNTAINS NATIONAL PARK

tunnels, and the parkway gets its share of views. The best views are found on a 2-mile stretch between Big Witch Gap Overlook and Noland Divide Overlook, where the wall-like Great Smoky Mountains are framed in June by a stunning rhododendron display. The parkway ends at an intersection with US 441 just outside **Cherokee** and just inside the Great Smoky Mountains National Park.

Back on the parkway, the unusual and fascinating Heintooga Spur Road loops 27 miles through the park's backcountry, a leisurely forest drive that ends deep in the Qualla Boundary. The first of the spur's three views arrives quickly, at Mile High Overlook—as its name implies, a 5,280-foot overlook with a 180-degree view toward the Smoky Mountain Crest. At 3.6 miles the road reaches Black Camp Gap, where a pyramidal Masonic Monument sits a short distance off the road. From here the road is a pretty forest drive that climbs gently to Balsam Mountain Picnic Area on a high ridgetop. Here a short path leads to Heintooga Overlook, a broad view sideways over the high crest of the Smokies, renowned for its fine sunset.

From the picnic area, the road becomes a one-lane, one-way gravel road, of dependably good quality, a car path (with no oncoming traffic) through the great overhanging trees. Your final view comes 2 miles into this segment, a 90-degree southward look over the deep canyon-like valleys of the Smokies toward the Qualla Boundary. Six miles later the road reaches Pin Oak Gap, an important backcountry trailhead, and finally drops away from the high ridgeline into the stream valleys below. At 22 miles the road bottoms out at Round Bottom Horse Camp and becomes two-way again as it follows a lovely little stream to enter the Qualla Boundary. In 3.5 more miles it reaches Big Cove Road, its first real intersection since it left the Blue Ridge Parkway. A left turn will bring you to Cherokee in 11 miles.

Roaring Fork Motor Nature Trail (TN). This 9.8-mile nature trail for the auto-bound explores old farm roads that once wandered through the settlements south of Gatlinburg, leading to four historic sites, beautiful forests, several waterfalls, and a great view. It starts in downtown Gatlinburg, turning onto Historic Nature Trail (that's the name of the street) from US 441 at Light 8 (the number hangs from the light). Continue past the lovely little Mynant Park (good for picnics) to enter the national park just beyond. The road goes through gentle curves to climb through hardwood forests to the Bud Ogle Place, at 2.7 miles, a log cabin with running water in hollow logs, and a large barn behind. Just beyond, the road breaks into a mile-long one-way loop through Cherokee Orchards, an apple orchard and commercial nursery until 1940. At 3.7 miles, as the road loops uphill and around (to return to the Bud Ogle Place), turn onto the one-lane, one-way Roaring Fork Motor Nature Trail to the right. From here the road twists up to a ridge with a good view (4.2 miles), then twists around to a second ridgeline with a great view (4.9 miles). Passing the **Grotto Falls** trailhead (5.5 miles), the road twists through a hemlock forest, then follows a boisterous creek; look for the stone wall on its opposite side. At 6.6 miles a parking lot will mark the second historic site, a log cabin and outbuildings overlooking a small waterfall. Then, at 6.8 miles, the road reaches the Ephraim Bales Place, a modest dogtrot log cabin and barn with an impressive stone wall marking the location of the old farm road. At 7.3 miles the road passes the last and most colorful of the historic sites, the brightly painted Alfred Reagan Place, with a restored horizontal wheel "tub mill" by the stream.

ROARING FORK FALLS IN THE BLACK MOUNTAINS

Now the stream drops suddenly down into a small gorge with two wonderful waterfalls dripping down the rocks above the road at 8.4 miles. The road finally leaves the park at 8.9 miles, reentering Gatlinburg; return to downtown by taking the turn to the left.

Cades Cove Loop Road (TN). To reach the start of the 10.3-mile, one-way Cades Cove Loop Road, enter the park at Townsend and follow the signs 7.3 miles to Cades Cove. This one-lane loop furnishes a scenic ramble through the national park's most historic and beautiful corner. Meandering through forests and fields, with sweeping views toward the Smoky Mountains, this lane passes 10 separate historic sites, each one preserving one or more pioneer-era structures from the cove's past.

The loop road begins at a large meadow where grazing horses provide foreground for the wide view toward the Great Smoky Mountains; there is parking and an information kiosk. From there, the road wanders through forests and meadows for 1.1 miles, where gravel, two-way **Sparks Lane** on the left cuts straight across the width of the cove floor to meet the loop 1.7 miles from its end. Just beyond on the right is the parking lot and path for the **John Oliver Place**, the cove's oldest and most photogenic log cabin, set back 0.25 mile from the road. At 2.4 miles the narrow, winding lane takes you to a short, gravel side lane to the **Primitive Baptist Church**, during the Civil War a hotbed of Unionism and a stop on the Underground Railway. At 2.7 miles you reach the loveliest of the three surviving cove churches, the white clapboard **Methodist Church**. You'll find wide views from the wildflower meadows above the church.

At 3.1 miles, **Hyatt Lane** leads off to your left across the cove floor, a two-lane, two-way gravel road that regains the loop road at the far side of the cove in 1.3 miles. This tree-lined lane is your best place to admire the view from the middle of the cove, a substantially different perspective from the loop road. The lane is lined with wide meadows that invite wandering, and is full of wildlife, including deer and bears. If traffic has snarled beyond endurance (as sometimes happens on a fine fall weekend), this is your best escape route.

Next comes the **Missionary Baptist Church** at 3.2 miles, across the lane from the one-lane, one-way gravel Rich Mountain Road, which leads 10.9 miles out of the park to the village of Townsend. If you venture 1.1 miles up this road you will find the single best road view in the entire park, a spectacular 180-degree panorama over the whole cove, with the wall of the Great Smoky Mountains revealed in all its glory, and the tiny, white Methodist Church on a hill below. And from there, you have an achingly slow 9.8-mile drive through heavy forest, passing over two gaps with many switchbacks, all the way to Townsend; there is no return to the cove.

Now that you've reached the western end of the cove, the views reach their finest. At 4.6 miles there's parking for the 0.6-mile easy walk to the **Elijah Oliver Cabin**, a full-sized farmstead set in remote meadows. You are now driving along the "Hayfields" stretch of the loop road, a full mile of continuous views in all directions. Toward the end of the Hayfields, a split-rail fence on the right frames views over wildflower meadows toward a large farmstead—the **Cable Mill Area** (entrance at 5.6 miles), for many the high point of the loop with its visitors center, working watermill, restored farmhouse, cantilevered barn, collection of pioneer farm tools, and craft demonstrations. Another good reason to stop: Cable Mill has the only toilets on the loop road.

From Cable Mill, the loop road turns sharply left as the paved two-way Forge Creek Road goes 0.7 mile to the **Henry Whitehead Cabin**. Another 0.5 mile leads to the end of the two-way road and the start of Parsons Branch Road, a one-way, one-lane gravel road that preserves an antebellum wagon road, including a dozen stream fords; it ends at US 129 at the park's southern border.

Back at the loop, a long, twisty forest section passes the Cades Cove Nature Trail on the right at 6.0 miles, and then (at 6.8 miles) reaches the **Dan Lawson Place**, a log cabin behind split-rail fences. Hyatt Lane enters at this point, and a short jaunt up the lane will give you a good view over meadows to the Lawson Place nestled in the forests. At 7.4 miles on the right on sits the elaborate **Tipton Place**; its impressive cantilevered barn, a unique mountain feature, is the first building you'll see. The final cabin on the loop, the modest **Carter Shields Cabin** at 8.6 miles, sits in an open glade rich in spring dogwoods. From here you have 1.5 miles of pleasant, if anticlimactic, scenery before reaching the Cades Cove Recreation Area and two-way traffic; the ranger station is a short distance to your right. The loop's start and the road out of the Cove is 0.2 mile ahead on your left.

A final word of warning: Loop road traffic can be very bad. It's one lane wide with no passing, so you'll go no faster than the slowest car on the loop. On a weekend the road can become a parking lot, with traffic inching forward slower than a walking pace. That's right; if traffic is backed up to the entrance, it'll be faster to park and walk. There's a great alternative, though: On Wednesday and Saturday mornings (until 10:30 AM) the loop road is open to bicyclists and walkers only.

EXPLORING ON FOOT A High Ridge Walk on the Appalachian Trail. This 3-mile walk follows the Smoky Mountain Crest westward from Clingman's Dome, staying above 6,000 feet with stunning views into both Tennessee and North Carolina. Starting at the **Clingman's Dome Overlook** parking lot, go a short distance down the Forney Ridge Trail to the Clingman's Dome Bypass Trail. This little-used cutoff will save you some climbing while leading past some good meadow views into North Carolina. After 0.3 mile you gain the **Appalachian Trail** on the high, sharp ridge of the Smokies Crest. From here are first-rate views into Tennessee, toward **Elkmont** and over the side ridges that fall steeply downward to

FOR MORE INFORMATION

I find myself continually writing apologies for having to omit some of the most fascinating and rewarding mountain sites in order to fit everything into a single, statewide volume. The Cades Cove area is particularly painful in this regard; it's not even in North Carolina, yet any visitor to the North Carolina Smokies will want to see it. You'll find a great deal of extra coverage of the entire Smokies region—more exploring, more things to see, and more cafés and lodgings (particularly in the Tennessee side)—in the companion volume from Countryman Press, *The Blue Ridge and Smoky Mountains: An Explorer's Guide.*

the Foothills. Turn left onto the Appalachian Trail. You will be hiking along the razorbacked spine of a ridge, with grass growing between exposed rocks and long views over both North Carolina and Tennessee. The trail will remain more or less level to Mount Buckley, then start a moderate but inexorable drop, losing 1,000 feet in the next 2.5 miles. The trail remains scenic, passing through grassy areas and forests—but don't forget that going up this slope is going to be a lot more difficult than going down. When you decide to turn around, stay on the Appalachian Trail until it reaches the Clingman's Dome Observation Tower, to pick up a few good views you missed on the way out.

Noland Creek Trail. Up until 1942 Noland Creek was the site of a streamside settlement, 50 or so families in scattered farmhouses that ranged from log cabins to modern bungalows. Then the Tennessee Valley Authority built **Fontana Dam** and flooded their road access. Rather than rebuild the road, the TVA condemned the Noland Creek community, evicted its residents, and donated their land to the Great Smoky Mountains National Park. To visit their old community, take Lakeshore Drive (better known as the Road to Nowhere) to the trailhead at Noland Creek Overlook. Although the National Park Service demolished all of the structures in Noland Creek for safety reasons, signs of the settlement remain; boxwoods and roses grow rank around old homesites, where a set of steps or an old chimney might poke up through the trees. Because the valley was never logged the forests are extraordinarily beautiful, a combination of old woodlots and young trees growing in former farmland.

At 3.7 miles the track enters a flat-floored stretch known as Solola Valley, a heavily settled area that took its name from the Cherokee word for "squirrel." The remains of this settlement include the ruins of a large mill, its wheelhouse foundations emerging from the streambed. At 4.0 miles a side trail, the Springhouse Branch Trail, leads uphill to the left, passing house and field ruins to reach a large old-growth forest in 0.7 mile. At 4.2 miles an unmarked side trail leads uphill a short distance to a cemetery, still used by the families evicted from Noland Creek. Another 0.25 mile leads to a nice waterfall—a good place to turn around.

Three popular hikes near Gatlinburg (TN). These three hikes, all within 10 miles of Gatlinburg, are overwhelmingly popular. Each is extraordinary even by Smoky Mountain standards, with a magnificent view, remarkable feature, or beautiful waterfall. Each is well maintained (one is paved) and capable of handling its visitors, although parking can be a problem. In fact, the only thing wrong with any of these hikes is their lack of solitude. On a sunny weekend, expect these hikes to be more like a carnival than a wilderness experience.

1. *Laurel Falls Trail*, 4 miles west of Sugarlands Visitors Center on Little River Road. This 1.3-mile paved trail, partially blasted through solid rock by the CCC in 1935, leads past a view to a strong 75-foot waterfall.
2. *Alum Cave Trail*, 8.6 miles south of Sugarlands Visitors Center on Newfound Gap Road. The lowermost 2 miles of this Mount Le Conte access trail feature huge boulders, an interesting geological formation known as Arch Rock, old-growth forests, and spectacular views from exposed bluffs.
3. *Grotto Falls* (on Trillium Gap Trail), 3.5 miles from Gatlinburg on the Roaring Fork Motor Nature Trail. This easy 1-mile walk leads through mature forests to a large waterfall that you can walk behind—a good place for kids.

EXPLORING BY BICYCLE **Tsali Recreation Area**. This large National Forest Service recreation area, south of the national park on the shores of Fontana Reservoir, is devoted to off-road bicycling and horseback riding. It occupies the site where the Cherokee chief Tsali hid with his clan during the Trail of Tears—a tragic story and, as it happened, a turning point in the 1838 expulsion of the Cherokees from their homeland. Tsali's womenfolk had been attacked by federal troops, and the young men took murderous action to protect their family. Tsali voluntarily gave himself up to his tribal leaders, knowing he would be executed, to save the remainder of the Cherokees in North Carolina.

This large recreation area features 39 miles of marked bicycle and horse paths, ranging from old roads to rough tracks. Paths lead to lake and mountain views, wildflower meadows, and old homesites, through a predominantly pine forest. But don't expect to see the rugged gorges that sheltered Tsali's family; they are all under the waters of Fontana Reservoir. There's also a boat ramp and a small picnic area.

✱ Towns

Cherokee. The main administrative center of the Qualla Boundary since the 19th century, Cherokee sits astride US 19 and US 441, abutting the southern boundary of the Great Smoky Mountains National Park. It's much smaller and more modest than Gatlinburg, and its traffic isn't quite as bad. Much of its modest appearance is due to rules within the Qualla Boundary that restrict land possession to tribal members; this has discouraged outside business investment and kept Cherokee in sort of a 1950s time warp.

Here's the layout. US 441 goes north and south, while US 19 goes east and west. Cherokee sits at their intersection, with modest businesses stringing outward along these highways. The most densely developed area, called "Downtown Cherokee" on road signs, straddles US 19 just east of US 441. Compared with the Tennessee tourist towns, Downtown Cherokee" is startlingly retro, with a look and feel that's changed surprisingly little since the early days of park tourism, and old-fashioned open-front souvenir stands, bursting with an astonishing variety of trinkets, still dominate Downtown. At Downtown's far (eastern) end is the giant **Harrah's Cherokee Casino**, the only wet place in the Qualla Boundary.

The real center of Cherokee gathers around its government complex on US 441 about a mile north of Downtown. Here you'll find a riverside park with good picnicking, a first-rate **museum**, and the Eastern Band's **craft cooperative**, as well as the Cherokee Historical Association's outdoor drama ***Unto These Hills*** and 18th-century Cherokee village **Oconaluftee Village**.

Bryson City. Visitors to Bryson City will find it a handsome town of about 1,500 inhabitants, with an old-fashioned downtown stretched into a T-shape and possessing a full range of services. The Old Swain County Courthouse sits by the main downtown intersection and furnishes an unmissable landmark. It's guarded by a World War I doughboy statue instead of the traditional Confederate soldier, showing Swain County's post–Civil War origin. The town's Main Street follows US 19 east and west from the Old Courthouse, ending at the town's beautiful hilltop cemetery, with good views and a Thomas Wolfe angel (looking homeward, as described in his famous novel set in 1929 Asheville). Down from the courthouse, the downtown district crosses the Tuckaseegee River to reach the old railroad depot, now housing the **Great Smoky Mountain Railroad** with daily scenic excursions. Parking is ample and free. Bryson City offers some of the better lodging and dining in the mountains, and, for the serious traveler, offers the most authentic mountain experience.

Gatlinburg (TN). In the late 1920s Gatlinburg was just another poor mountain crossroads, a fork with a general store and a gas pump. The left fork (today's US 321) went to a Methodist mission, and the right fork (now US 441 and the **Newfound Gap Road**) went deep into the Smokies to dead-end at the poverty-stricken community of Sugarlands. Then came the park, and Gatlinburg found itself the main entrance to a site that was already attracting a million automobile-driving visitors by 1941. All those tourists quickly turned the mountains crossroads into a small city.

NEWFOUND GAP ROAD CLIMBS THE NORTH CAROLINA SLOPES OF THE GREAT SMOKY MOUNTAINS NATIONAL PARK.

Gatlinburg is still centered on that old fork in the road, but now the fork is a busy multilane intersection in the middle of a crowded downtown. Here two-story buildings, jammed against the sidewalk and one another, are filled with every sort of tourist enticement imaginable—gift shops, restaurants, candy shops, old-timey photo places, sideshows (labeled "museums" and "attractions"), amusement rides . . . you name it. It has more than a passing resemblance to a really large county fair, complete with bad parking, high prices, and a stiff dose of hucksterism. It's easy to complain about it, but it's a lot more fun to enjoy it.

Apart from this full-time street fair, Gatlinburg has a serious, mountain-oriented side. On the rural east side of town, the **Glades area** hosts a community of 100 craft artists, some newcomers, others from old mountain craft families. A series of crafter-owned shops string out along this scenic mountain cove, with members of the community proudly displaying a logo certifying that they make what they sell, in the shop, and usually open to view.

AUTUMN VIEW OVER CADES COVE, FROM THE RICH MOUNTAIN ROAD

Gatlinburg traffic is always slow, and can grind to a stop during the season. If you wish simply to get beyond Gatlinburg to the park on other side, take the **Gatlinburg Bypass**, a scenic road maintained by the National Park Service. Downtown parking is in a couple of expensive city garages. As an alternative, you can park for free at the **visitors center** at the north end of town or the city hall at the east end of town on US 321, and take a trolley (the cost ranges from 25 cents to $2.00).

Townsend (TN). Founded as a lumber mill town in 1901, Townsend sits on the first piece of flat land outside the national park boundaries, straddling the main road into this area of the park. This makes it the closest town to Cades Cove, and the closest collection of travel facilities (including food and gasoline) for the cove's two million annual visitors. Nevertheless, Townsend has always been dwarfed in popularity by Gatlinburg (23 miles east on US 321), and this has allowed it to retain some of the character of a quiet mountain cove. Today it consists of a scattered (but increasing) number of modest commercial buildings widely spread along a 2-mile stretch of four-lane US 321. It retains little of its past as a mill town apart from a worthwhile (and free) **historical museum**, and it lacks any real town center. However, views are good, and the town parallels the lovely Little River as it exits the Smokies. While Townsend is low on chains and franchises, it has a good selection of independent motels and restaurants as well as craft shops, antiques shops, and gift shops. It is an excellent place to find a rental cabin. Compared with the mess at Gatlinburg, traffic and parking pose few problems.

The Nantahala Gorge (nantahala-river.net). Located 13 miles southwest of Bryson City along US 19, this 8-mile-long gorge has acquired its own community of tourist-oriented businesses, drawn by the increasing popularity of rafting and kayaking on the Nantahala River. Most of it consists of roadside businesses of crude and recent architecture, separated by long stretches of beautiful national forest land. Traffic can be very slow on a warm summer weekend, with lots of pedestrians, cars entering from parking lots, and old repainted buses loaded high with inflated rafts.

✷ Green Spaces

PUBLIC LANDS The Smoky Mountains Front. A drop of rain, falling on the highest point of Mount Le Conte, travels through 7 miles of wilderness before it reaches the river in downtown Gatlinburg. It also drops 1 mile vertically—in all likelihood the longest and steepest slope in the eastern United States. This slope is wet as well as steep, with 7 *feet* of rainfall in a typical year. This combination of high rainfall and high, steep slopes does more than create big rivers and impressive waterfalls; it also creates one of the richest temperate forests in the world.

Start at the top, with that drop of water on the 6,593-foot peak of Mount Le Conte. You'll be in a boreal forest, an extension of the great subarctic forest that covers much of Canada, whose Christmas-tree species of spruce and fir form a forest canopy over thin, rocky soils. Below that will be a mosaic of forest types: New England–style hardwood forest, oak-hickory forests, beech-maple forests, pine-oak forests on warm, dry ridgelines, northern riverine forests along many streambanks. Unique to the Smokies and other nearby mountains is the cove hardwood forest, with the highest species richness in temperate North America. A cove forest can mix and match as many as 25 tree species in a single acre of old-growth forest, covering a thick shrubby understory that bursts into colorful blooms every spring—rhododendron, mountain laurel, flame azalea, dogwood, redbud, silverbell. These thick forests cover even the steepest slopes with trees that grow 6 to 10 stories high.

And there's a lot of slope that has to be covered. The front of the Smoky Mountains at Gatlinburg forms an unbroken wall 65 miles long. The central 56 miles of that wall, immediately behind Gatlinburg, stay continuously above 4,000 feet, with half of that length above a mile high. On the northwestern (Tennessee) side of the crest, the Smokies drop to a valley that appears flat-bottomed from a crest-top viewpoint, and stretches off to the horizon as far as the eye can see. On the southeastern (North Carolina) side, other mountains, nearly as tall, fill the view in a confused jumble.

Access to this great forest is either from the Newfound Gap Road, or from a series of trailheads that ring its perimeter. All these trailheads are gateways into rich and varied forests, with stunning wildflowers, roaring rivers, large waterfalls, and magnificent views. Almost without exception, the hiking and horse trails that lead from these trailheads are well built, well kept, and incredibly beautiful; it should go without saying that nearly all of them are very steep as well.

PARKS AND GARDENS The Greenbrier Cove area (TN). Six miles east of Gatlinburg on US 321, a right turn on a narrow paved lane leads 4 miles up a broad valley named Greenbrier Cove. Inhabited by scattered farms in the 1920s, Greenbrier Cove is now grown over by a young riverside forest along the noisy, boulder-strewn Middle Prong of the Little Pigeon River. The modest, pleasant picnic area is 2.5 miles up the lane. In another 0.5 mile, a side road crosses the Middle Prong at a particularly scenic spot, then winds through forests to the start of

DEVASTATION ALONG THE LITTLE RIVER

When the Tennessee National Park Commission started buying land for the Great Smoky Mountains National Park in 1925, the Little River Lumber Company owned the entire Little River Drainage, some 77,000 acres. The company agreed to sell the land for a national park, but only if they could retain logging rights for 15 years. The park commission agreed; after all, how many trees could they harvest in 15 years? The answer turned out to be "All of them." The company attacked the slopes, stripping them of every tree they could sell before the deadline came. They beat the deadline by a year, denuding the virgin forests of the Little River by 1939. Then they took up the last of the rails from the railbeds, disassembled the Townsend mill, and turned control of the wrecked Little River Basin over to the National Park Service. The logging company had purchased a huge tract of old-growth forest, removed every tree, left a destroyed land bereft of economic value—and sold it to the government for a 50 percent profit.

This was not unique. On the North Carolina side, Champion Paper stripped all the lands east of the future Newfound Gap Road by 1930, leaving an environment so devastated that at one point rainfall stripped the crest down to a bare cliff, named Charlie's Bunion after the foot problems of one of the hunters who discovered it. Charlie's Bunion remains one of the great sights of the Smokies, a full day's return walk eastward from Newfound Gap on the Appalachian Trail (round-trip: 8.6 miles, with 3,000 feet of total climb, half out and half back).

The forests you see along the Newfound Gap and Little River Roads are a product of this clear-cut logging, a forest of young, straight hardwoods 70 to 100 years old. You'll see the same along the deepest of backcountry trails as well; nearly all of the park was clear-cut between 1890 and 1940. Hikers gain some benefit, however, from all those old logging railroads with their wide, firm surfaces and steady 6 percent grades, following the streams to end at the great mountainous wall of the Smokies Crest.

the Ramsey Cascades Trail, one of the park's most popular hikes. Straight ahead, the road follows Porters Creek to end at a gate in 1 mile. You can park here and continue up the road on foot. This was once the road to a farming community; you will pass old stone walls, steps leading up hills, boxwoods and roses growing rank where houses once stood. At the end of the road, in a mile, a short path leads right to an old cantilevered barn in the woods, and a log cabin nearby.

The Cosby area (TN). Cosby Picnic Area is at the far northeast corner of the Tennessee Smokies; go 18 miles east of downtown Gatlinburg on US 321 to TN 73 at Cosby community, then right 0.4 mile to TN 32, then right 1.3 miles to a Park Service lane on the right. The picnic area at the end of the 2-mile paved road (there is also a campground here) is small and forest-covered, along the lovely Cosby Creek. Here you will find a trailhead to the Lower Mount Cammerer Trail—a lengthy trail that eventually climbs to the Smokies Crest. The first 1.5 miles, however, climb only 260 feet, following old roadbeds with stone walls indicating a formerly settled area. This ends at one of the best views in the park, with the Smoky Mountains Front towering over the flat lands below.

RIVERS **Little River (TN)**. This important tributary of the Tennessee River rises from the 6,000-foot slopes under **Clingman's Dome** to flow for 34 miles before leaving the mountains, with 21 of these miles within the Great Smoky Mountains National Park. Back in the early 20th century it was the main corridor for the lumber railroad used to clear-cut these slopes, and a railroad bed carries automobile traffic along its banks for 16 miles. Above this, the railbed continues as a hiking path, easy and level, giving good access for fishing.

Kayakers can join in the fun as far upstream as Elkmont, but the first 9 miles, rated Class II to III, are not favored. Instead, boaters flock to the 5.8 miles that start at the Sinks for a Class II to IV-plus thrill ride through some very beautiful scenery. The dramatic 10-foot waterfall at the Sinks always has plenty of sightseers on hand, for those who like a little theater. As the river approaches the park border it becomes slack, so that its final 11 miles before leaving the mountains have only occasional Class II rapids; there is a dam portage on this section, and a second, demolished dam provides some artificial Class III action. Handsome limestone bluffs add to the pastoral scenery.

The **Pigeon River (TN)** rises in North Carolina's **Shining Rock Wilderness** to drain northward, cutting a deep water gap through the Great Smoky Mountains to join the Tennessee River, 72 miles from its origin. An 8.9-mile stretch within this chapter's area has become particularly popular with kayakers and commercial rafters. The uppermost half, starting at the Waterville powerplant downhill from **Big Creek**, is the livelier of the two, with plentiful Class II to III-plus water. A midway take-out is the segue to a somewhat milder lower section, Class I to II-plus, ending in a Class III drop. The entire length is paralleled by I-40, so that all access points are easily reached.

Nantahala River. One of the South's most popular rivers, the Nantahala has produced a number of Olympians and several medals, thanks to the excellent facilities provided by the **Nantahala Outdoor Center (NOC)** at the river's outlet. On any given summer day the lowermost 8 miles, known as the Nantahala Gorge and followed by US 19, become a continuous parade of rafters and kayakers, its water levels controlled to perfection by an upstream dam. The water is nearly continuous

Class II, with some Class III thrown in for variety (including a startling set of rapids right after the put-in). Upstream from this put-in is a section of Class III to IV water for the more experienced. The gorge itself is beautiful, largely owned by the National Forest Service (NFS), with some private inholdings given over to outfitters and other visitors services. The NFS provides picnic areas, put-in and take-out points, and overlooks, as well as carefully keeping commercial and private boaters from tangling one another up. It charges a $5-per-boat fee, or $25 for a season pass, to help pay for all this; purchase your license at either NOC or Endless Rivers (see *To Do*).

LAKES **Fontana Lake (Little Tennessee River)**. The Tennessee Valley Authority (TVA) built the giant reservoir to provide World War II power for nearby Alcoa aluminum smelters. In doing so, they destroyed a dozen small mountain communities, cutting them off with rising floodwaters. The TVA handled this by condemning the hundreds of small farms, removing all the structures, then donating the land to the Great Smoky Mountains National Park.

The lake they created stretches for 25 miles to Bryson City, with many long side arms. It has 238 miles of shoreline, half of which is inside the national park and much of the rest owned by the National Forest Service. Despite this, it has only 16 square miles of surface; this is one long, skinny lake. There are several marinas along it, and you can rent a boat at the marina run by Fontana Village.

✷ To See

CULTURAL SITES **The Museum of the Cherokee Indian** (828-497-3481; cherokeemuseum.org; infocwy@cherokeemuseum.org), US 441 and Drama Rd., P.O. Box 1599, Cherokee 28719. Open daily 9–5, with extended summer hours. $$. The Museum of the Cherokee Indian is one of the most intriguing, involving, and moving museum experiences in the western mountains. Its displays mix carefully chosen artifacts with artworks and state-of-the-art museum technology to tell the story of the Cherokee clearly, simply, and beautifully. And storytelling is just what it does. Starting with the Cherokee creation myth, the museum leads visitors gently through the ages, from Archaic times, to the pre-Columbian Cherokee culture and way of life, through their contact with Europeans and the chaotic dislocations that ensued, and ending with an emotional account of the Trail of Tears, the violent relocation of most of the Cherokees to Oklahoma. The museum, which is a wholly independent not-for-profit, has a first-rate gift shop. You'll find the museum in a handsome 1970s wooden building constructed to remind one of the surrounding mountain peaks, in town at the intersection of Drama Road and US 441, 1.25 miles north of US 19.

The Qualla Arts and Crafts Mutual (828-497-3103; fax: 828-497-4841; qualla artsandcrafts.org), P.O. Box 310, Cherokee 28719. Open daily, 8–7 summer, 8–5 winter. The Qualla Mutual is a craft cooperative and gallery for several hundred crafters who are enrolled members of the Eastern Band. A museum area has a series of glass-case wall displays that explain the varieties of contemporary Cherokee crafts, including their history, style, materials, and methods: stone carving, basket weaving (several kinds), pottery, masks, dolls, wood carving, jewelry. The main area of the building contains a large shop that wanders through several rooms, offering every kind of Cherokee craft at a wide range of prices. All crafts for sale are handmade by members, and carry an authentication mark. The Qualla Mutual is in a low-slung 1960s-era building across the street from the Museum of the Cherokee.

Unto These Hills (866-554-4557; 828-497-2111; cherokee-nc.com; cheratt@dnet.net), P.O. Box 398, Cherokee 28719. Open mid-June–late Aug., daily except Sun.; pre-show entertainment starts around 7:45 PM. Founded in 1950 by the nonprofit Cherokee Historical Association, this large-scale outdoor pageant, performed by 100 actors and dancers over three stages, presents the history of the Cherokee people, from their contact with Hernando de Soto to the Trail of Tears.

Harrah's Cherokee Casino (828-497-7777; harrahscherokee.com), 777 Casino Dr., Cherokee 28719. Open all the time. Let's call this one "popular culture." The Eastern band owns, and Harrah's Entertainment operates, this large, luxurious video gaming emporium, a short distance east of Cherokee on US 19. The casino includes five restaurants (with alcohol service), a 1,500-seat theater, and a 576-room, 15-story high-rise hotel. At press time the casino was under a major expansion and refurbishment, expected to be completed by 2012.

The Glades Craft Community (TN) (artsandcraftscommunity.com). This scenic rural cove on the east side of Gatlinburg has been known as a center for mountain crafts since the 1930s. An 8-mile loop road, well signposted off US 321 3 miles east of town, runs through the center of this crafters' community, becoming increasingly beautiful as it draws away from Gatlinburg's center; along it, small craft shops sit in meadows with views over the low mountains of the foothills. In 1937 the craft artists of the Glades formed their own association, the Great Smoky Arts and Crafts Community, limited to crafters who feature their own work in their own studios. There are now more than 100 such studio-galleries displaying the ARTS & CRAFTS COMMUNITY logo. According to member and porcelain artist Judy Baily, "People feel free to take their time in our shops. Many times they ask us a lot of questions about what we do, and we are glad to spend time with them." These fine crafters are Gatlinburg's main attraction for serious shoppers.

A HORSE EATS SNOW FROM A SPLIT-RAIL FENCE AT THE MOUNTAIN FARM MUSEUM, GREAT SMOKY MOUNTAINS NATIONAL PARK.

HISTORIC SITES Mountain Farm Museum. Located just inside the park on the Newfound Gap Road, 1.35 miles outside Cherokee, the Mountain Farm Museum is one of the most complete, and one of the most handsome, exhibits on mountain farm life anywhere in the Southern Appalachians. Unlike sites in the more famous **Cades Cove**, the Mountain Farm Museum portrays a full-sized operating farm—furniture in the house, flowers along the porch, corn in the field, chickens in the coop, and a horse in the barn.

The farmstead consists of log structures, all built around 1900, moved in from remote areas of the park. The log farmhouse is a solid two-story structure with a kitchen wing and two porches, built in 1902 by local farmer John Davis. Today the farmhouse is furnished in late-19th-century style, and docents in period costume explain the way of life. The barn anchors the other end of the site. Original to this location, it's a large cantilevered log barn with an oversized clapboarded hayloft. Inside are examples of late-19th-century farm equipment, a horse, several stray chickens from the nearby coop, and a cat. The horse is a friendly old creature who loves to meet gentle and well-behaved children.

Between the two main structures lies a working late-19th-century farmstead. Corn grows behind high, strong split-rail fences; beans and squash grow among the corn, a standard mountain practice. A vegetable garden, protected by pickets, grows a riot of tomatoes, squash, beans, and peas, as well as flowers for the kitchen table. Gourd birdhouses provide natural insect control. Log outbuildings include a corncrib, a chicken house, a springhouse, a smokehouse, an apple house with a stone foundation, a gear shed, a blacksmith shop, a pigpen (with pig), hollow log beehives (with bees), and a sorghum press.

Adjacent to the farm museum is the modest Oconaluftee Visitors Center, with an information desk, bookshop, and interpretive exhibits housed in a classic 1930s stone building.

Mingus Mill (TN) (877-338-0652; 423-338-0652; info@MountainShadowCabins.com), 285 Locke Lane, Benton, TN 37307. Located just 2 miles from Cherokee (and 0.3 mile from the Mountain Farm Museum) on the Newfound Gap Road, Mingus Mill is a late-19th-century gristmill restored to operation. In its time it was a modern facility, with two grist stones powered by an efficient store-bought turbine instead of the old-fashioned hand-carpentered overshot wheel. You can scramble under this large clapboarded building to see the turbine in operation, then go inside to watch the miller operate the great grist stones, and then buy a pound of stone-ground cornmeal. However, its most impressive part is its elevated millrace, standing 20 feet off the ground as it passes into the building to fall into the turbine. There's a short, pleasant walk that follows the millrace to the mill's small log dam on Mingus Creek.

Elkmont National Historic District (TN). In 1908 the first logging train climbed up the Little River Gorge to the new lumber camp, Elkmont—a journey so scenic, to a site so cool and pleasant during the summer's heat, that tourists started coming up the rail line to stay at the modest little company hotel. By 1912 it had become a vacation development popular with Knoxville's powerful elite, and easily survived the lumber camp's closure in 1926. In fact, it survived until 1992, an enclave of privilege inside the national park.

The NPS had long planned to tear down these cottages when they finally obtained title. However, by then the vacation home subdivision had become Elkmont National Historic District with 69 of its structures on the National Register of Historic Places. This made the park's wholesale demolition plan illegal, leaving the

MINGUS MILL IN THE GREAT SMOKY MOUNTAINS NATIONAL PARK

NPS frustrated and furious; it took until 2009 for a compromise plan to be adopted. They will leave the most densely built area as a historic district interpreting the early tourism of the last century, preserving 18 cabins and a clubhouse, and restoring the environment of the rest of the site to that of a cove forest. As yet no timetable has been announced; in the meantime, you can wander through the unrestored site, staying out of the buildings.

SCHOOLTEACHER IN THE DOORWAY OF LITTLE GREENBRIER SCHOOL, IN THE GREAT SMOKY MOUNTAINS NATIONAL PARK

Little Greenbrier Community (TN). Little Greenbrier Community, one of the park's least-known and least-visited historic sites, is the place where the mountain folk lingered longest inside the park. To find it, take Wear Gap Road from the middle of the Metcalf Bottoms Picnic Area, 0.5 mile to a gravel road on the right, then another 0.5 mile up this narrow gravel road to its end.

You'll be parked by a one-room log schoolhouse that started life as a church—hence the incongruous presence of a pioneer cemetery on the hill above it. The Greenbrier schoolhouse is still in use, being the site of special classes for the schoolchildren of

Blount and Sevier Counties. With a bit of luck you'll find it open and class in session, hosting lessons to local schoolchildren on field trips. For years many of these classes were taught by retired teacher Miss Elsie Burrell (now no longer with us), who started her career in this schoolhouse, and went on to become one of the state's most prominent educators.

One of the Greenbrier community's cabins still survives, a remote 1.2-mile (one-way) walk from the school along the gated jeep track across from the cemetery. A lovely and nearly level walk, the track follows Little Brier Creek upstream to the Walker Cabin. This fine log cabin, set in a clearing with a springhouse and barn, was the home of the Walker sisters, who refused to move out of the park and continued to live in their family cabin until the 1960s. No other site in the park gives quite the feeling of remoteness, of quiet, and of simplicity.

Oconaluftee Indian Village (828-497-2315; fax: 828-497-6987; oconalufteevillage.com; cheratt@dnet.net), P.O. Box 398, Cherokee 28719. Open daily 9–5:30, May 15–Oct. 25. $$$. This living history museum, owned by the tribe, re-creates an authentic 18th-century village. The village itself is a simple grouping of log structures, as would be most such settlements in the early historic period. ("Downtown" aside, the Cherokees did not use tepees.) The main attraction is the costumed interpreters, who demonstrate a variety of period crafts and perform sacred dances. You start with a guided tour, after which you are free to wander around, talk with the crafters, and take photos. Adjacent is a botanical garden featuring native garden and medicinal plants.

Fontana Dam (TN) (423-988-2431; tva.com/sites/fontana.htm), 804 US 321 N., Suite 300, Lenoir City, TN 37771. Visitors center open May–Oct., daily 9–7; closed when the homeland security alert is orange or red. Admission is free. Sitting at the base of the Smoky Mountains 22 miles west of Bryson City, Fontana Dam is the tallest dam in the eastern United States, blocking the gorge of the Little Tennessee River with a concrete wall 480 feet high and over 0.5 mile long at the top. Built in a great hurry between 1942 and 1944, Fontana was an emergency wartime project, intended to ensure that the Knoxville area had enough electrical power for the strategically important Alcoa aluminum plant and the top-secret Oak Ridge Research Laboratory. Its impoundment created the 29-mile-long Fontana Lake, flooding the gorge of the Little Tennessee River and forcing the abandonment of half a dozen mountain communities.

Fontana Dam is an impressive sight, and well worth a visit. A modernist visitors center sits at its southern end, with a large observation deck giving fine views of the mammoth structure. From the center, those wanting to tour the dam take an inclined tram down the gorge wall to the generators at the base. A public road crosses the 2,600-foot dam top to national park trailheads on the opposite side—a fascinating drive.

The Great Smoky Mountain Railroad (800-872-4681; fax: 828-488-0427; gsmr.com; info@gsmr.com), 119 Front St., Dillsboro 28725. All year; schedule varies. $$$$. As a major visitor attraction, the Great Smoky Mountain Railroad takes second place only to the national park itself. Organized to save a dead-end freight spur line from closing, its management has revamped it into a touring excursion line by day, with 53 miles of spectacular mountain sightseeing, steam and diesel engines, and a wide variety of special events. The Bryson City depot hosts two basic excursions. The more common excursion (available all year) crosses Fontana Lake on a high old iron trestle, the follows the lakeshore up into the flooded lower reaches of the Nantahala Gorge. It stops for lunch at Nantahala Outdoor Center, then travels up the gorge to its end, returning the way it came. The second route (available in-season) runs eastward to the lovely little craft village of Dillsboro, with 1½ hours of excellent shopping; this is the track where the train wreck in the movie *The Fugitive* was staged, and you will pass the wrecked engine. You will have a choice of an open excursion car, an air-conditioned Crown Coach, or an adults-only Club Car—a beautifully restored historic lounge car with wine and beer service.

MOUNTAIN SCENERY Deep Creek waterfalls. Just north of Bryson City, the park's Deep Creek area offers streamside picnicking and camping—and a trailhead to one of the easiest places to spot waterfalls in the park. An old road, closed to traffic since the park came, follows the beautiful little creek, and is the only park path open to bicycles. Start with the 0.25-mile spur trail (walkers only) to Junywhank Falls, a thin trace of water that hurls itself over a 50-foot ledge, dashes under a log bridge, then bounces down another 30 feet of rock. Then follow the old roadbed 0.2 mile to view Tom Branch Falls, a side stream that enters Deep Creek by pouring over a 30-foot rock wall. At 0.7 mile the old road forks at a bridge where Indian Creek pours in from the side, through a chute into a still pool that throws rippling reflections onto the overhanging rocks. A short side trail leads to the base of the third and most impressive waterfall, Indian Creek Falls. Here a wide wall of water pours over a 50-foot ledge into a deep, still pool with a natural pebbly beach. A short distance beyond the side trail, the main path offers a good view over the top of the falls. Return the way you came.

Mingo Falls. One of the most beautiful waterfalls of the Smokies, Mingo Falls is the highlight of a tribal park and campground within the Qualla Boundary. A short, steep track leads 0.25 mile uphill to the base of the falls—a lacy curtain of water hung over a 100-foot cliff. You'll find it 6 miles north of Cherokee on Big Cove Road; turn left at Saunooke Village, then just keep going.

Newfound Gap. This high gap marks the point where the Newfound Gap Road crosses the crest of the Smokies. Not surprisingly, it's heavily visited, with a huge parking lot. A monumental stone platform at its eastern edge served as the site of the 1940 dedication ceremony, personally attended by President Franklin Roosevelt (who gave a speech from it). The Appalachian Trail runs by the dedication platform, and furnishes a steep but beautiful day hike (8.4 miles round-trip with 3,000 feet of climb) to Charlie's Bunion, a massive cliff with sweeping panoramic views. An overlook south of the platform has interpretive plaques and a handsome 180-degree sweep over the upper Oconaluftee drainage basin on the North Carolina side.

Clingman's Dome. At 6,643 feet, Clingman's Dome is the highest point in the national park and the second highest peak in the eastern United States. It offers some of the best views in the Smokies. Many of these views can be found at its large crescent-shaped parking lot, almost 0.2 mile long, with a continuous south-facing panorama so broad that you have to walk its entire length to take it all in. The rest of the views are from the dome's large, modern observation deck, a concrete pillar surrounded by a huge spiral ramp, a steep 0.25 mile up a paved trail from the parking lot. There are flush toilets and drinking water, but no picnic tables.

Access is by the Clingman's Dome Spur Road (closed in winter), a 6.9-mile paved road following the crest of the Smokies westward from Newfound Gap. It's narrow and twisting, shaded by the Canadian-style spruce-fir forest crowding its edge, with trimmed rock walls on the downhill side. Its cuts are too modest to provide the wide views of a more modern highway, and its shoulders are frequently too narrow to pull off and park. The first view (0.4 mile from the beginning) is one of the best, a 5,200-foot-high bird's-eye straight down to the Oconaluftee Valley, with the Newfound Gap Road curving away below. Then, at 5.3 miles, Webb Overlook gives another fine view eastward.

Foothills Parkway East (TN). In 1943 Congress authorized the Foothills Parkway to curve around the northern edge of the national park as a consolation prize to Tennessee, which had just lost their bid to get the Blue Ridge Parkway. Only two sections have ever been completed, with a third under intermittent construction since 1968. The eastern section links I-40 with US 321, a good shortcut (closed in winter) for people heading from Asheville to Gatlinburg. It's worth a visit, however, even if it's out of your way. This 5.9-mile section of parkway climbs to the 2,200-foot top of Green Mountain, the first foothill beyond the northeast end of the Smokies. Overlooks give panoramic views of the Great Smoky Mountains as they rise almost a mile above the valleys in front of you; other viewpoints look westward, over the foothills as they descend in waves into the Great Valley.

FALL IN THE VALLEY, WINTER ON THE PEAKS, AT CLINGMAN'S DOME IN THE GREAT SMOKY MOUNTAINS NATIONAL PARK

Foothills Parkway West (TN) (nature.nps.gov/air/WebCams; click on "Look Rock" for a webcam view). The other open section of the Foothills Parkway starts just west of Townsend on US 321, and follows the crest of 2,600-foot Chilhowee (*chill-HOW-ee*) Mountain southward for 17.0 miles to US 129. There are fine views all along the parkway, eastward toward the massive Smoky Mountains Front towering 0.5 mile above the Chilhowee ridgeline, and westward over the Great Valley of Tennessee, looking nearly flat and receding to the horizon. At the center of this stretch is Look Rock, with an observation tower and a dramatic, breezy picnic area.

✱ To Do

BICYCLE RENTALS ✐ **Cades Cove Bike Shop (TN)** (865-448-9034), P.O. Box 4923, Maryville, TN 37802. Open daily, Apr.–Oct. This national park concessionaire offers reasonable daylong rentals on sturdy, well-kept machines. They are located at the Cades Cove Camp Store at the start of the Cades Cove Loop Road.

CANOES, KAYAKS, AND RAFTS ✐ **Rafting in the Smokies (TN)** (800-776-7238; 865-436-5008; raftinginthesmokies.com; rafting@raftinginthesmokies.com), P.O. Box 592, Gatlinburg, TN 37738. Open Mar.–Oct. From their downtown Gatlinburg location, this company runs whitewater rafting trips and float trips on two different sections of the Pigeon River, a half-hour shuttle from town. The intermediate level rapids of the Pigeon are restricted to children over 8 who weigh more than 60 pounds, but the float trip is open to anyone over the age of 3.

✐ **Smoky Mountain Outdoors (TN)** (800-771-7238; 865-430-3838; smokymountainrafting.com), 453 Brookside Village Way, Gatlinburg, TN 37738. This outfitter offers Pigeon River whitewater rafting adventures and leisurely floats from their headquarters on the banks of the Pigeon River a mile down Hartford Road from I-40's exit 447, on the Tennessee side of the state line. They maintain a location in Gatlinburg as well, on the east side of town on US 321.

✐ **USA Raft (TN)** (800-872-7238; 423-487-4303; usaraft.com/pigeon-river; raft@usaraft.com), 3630 Hartford Rd., Hartford, TN 37753. This West Virginia rafting company maintains an outpost on the Pigeon River in the Hartford community, just off I-40's exit 447, just beyond the TN–NC state line.

Nantahala Outdoor Center (NOC) (888-905-7238; 828-488-2176; noc.com), 13077 US 19 W., Bryson City 28713. This complex of half a dozen handsome buildings straddles both the Nantahala River and the Appalachian Trail, and qualifies as a tourist attraction all by itself. The employee-owned NOC offers kayaking and rafting, bicycle rentals, instruction at a variety of levels, restaurants, cabin rentals, and an outdoor store. NOC also offers Pigeon River trips from an outpost at Hartford, Tennessee.

Endless Rivers Adventures (800-224-7238; 828-488-6199; endlessriveradventures.com; info@endlessriveradventures.com), 14157 US 19 W., P.O. Box 246, Bryson City 28713. This outfitter offers whitewater rafting on the Nantahala and other rivers, as well as workshops for kayaking and rock climbing, and fly-fishing guide service.

Rolling Thunder River Company (800-408-7238; rollingthunderriverco.com; rafting@RollingThunderRiverCo.com), 10160 US 19 W., Bryson City 28713. Rolling Thunder offers a variety of inflatable rentals as well as guided raft trips on the Nantahala and other rivers. They have on-site camping and bunkhouse lodging.

Wildwater Rafting (866-319-8870; 828-488-2384; wildwaterrafting.com), P.O. Box 190, Bryson City 28713. This outfitter offers a variety of guided and unguided rafting trips, as well as the popular Raft & Rail trip in association with the Great Smoky Mountain Railroad. In addition, they run an 11-section zipline (built in 2009) that offers half an hour of air time, and backcountry jeep tours.

HORSES AND LLAMAS Smokemont Riding Stables (828-497-2373), P.O. Box 72, Cherokee 28719. May–Oct. This national park concessionaire offers guided horseback rides in the Smokemont area.

McCarters Riding Stables (TN) (865-436-5354). One of two national park concessionaires operating in the Gatlinburg area, McCarters offers trail rides in the Sugarlands area of the park, near the Sugarlands Visitors Center.

Smoky Mountains Stables (TN) (865-436-5634). The second of two national park concessionaires in the Gatlinburg area, Smoky Mountain Stables offers trail rides up the little-visited Dudley Creek area of the national park from a stable on US 321, 4 miles east of downtown.

Cades Cove Riding Stables (TN) (865-448-6286; cadescove.net/horseback_riding.html), 4025 E. Lamar Alexander Pkwy., Walland, TN 37886. Daily 9–5, Apr.–Oct.; closed Nov.–Mar. This national park concessionaire operates guided trail rides within Cades Cove, from a well-kept stable across from the picnic area. They also offer carriage rides and hayrides inside Cades Cove.

FISHING Fishing on the Qualla Boundary (828-497-5201). North Carolina's record brown trout (at 15 pounds, 2 ounces) was caught on the Qualla Boundary in 1990. The boundary has 30 miles of trout streams open to visitors, plus several trout ponds. The tribe stocks these streams twice a week in-season, and has a creel limit of 10 fish per day. Unlike the national park, you need no state fishing license; however, you must have a Tribal Fishing Permit, which costs $7 per day (children under 11 free with permitted adult). Permits are sold in most campground stores, outfitters, tackle stores, and general stores within the boundary.

SKIING Ober Gatlinburg (TN) (865-436-5423; obergatlinburg.com; fun@obergatlinburg.com), 1001 Parkway, Gatlinburg, TN 37738. Open all year, except for the first two weeks in March (dates vary). Ski season runs Dec.–Feb.; summer amusement park, Apr.–Nov. You can drive to the ski slopes of Ober Gatlinburg, but it's a lot more fun to take the Swiss-made cable car from downtown Gatlinburg. The enclosed cars sweep over the Gatlinburg rooftops, up a hollow, and over a ridge to a wide panorama—Mount Le Conte towering on the right, the much lower hills of East Tennessee on the left, and Gatlinburg deep in the valley directly below. The ski hall (which doubles as a fun center in summer) is a wide-spanning metal building with exposed girders and a sloping floor of exposed concrete. Inside, county-fair-style concessions surround a skating rink, with the floor spiraling down. The eight ski trails have a longest run of 5,000 feet and a maximum drop of 600 feet, with a maximum elevation of 3,300 feet. A snow report can be obtained by dialing 800-251-9202.

ENVIRONMENTAL ACTIVITIES ✐ The Great Smoky Mountains Institute at Tremont (TN) (865-448-6709; gsmit.org; mail@gsmit.org), 9275 Tremont Rd., Townsend, TN 37882. Multiday programs run all year; reservations are required. For more than 30 years the Great Smoky Mountains Institute at Tremont has been giving youth and adult programs in environmental topics from their headquarters in an old YCC camp within the national park, near Townsend. The Tremont Institute offers an immersive experience with a great deal of group interaction, in the setting of a rustic camp surrounded by deep forest. Programs for the general public are typically three- to five-day residencies with extensive outdoor time, and meals are taken in a large mess hall. Youth and teen camps are scheduled throughout the summer, while adult multiday programs include nature observation, wildflowers, geology, fall colors, photography, backpacking, and elderhostels.

A Walk in the Woods (TN) (865-436-8283; awalkinthewoods.com; Erik@awalkinthewoods.com), 4413 Scenic Dr. E., Gatlinburg, TN 37738. Erik and Vesna Plakanis offer half- and whole-day guided nature walks within the Great Smoky Mountains National Park, as well as custom trips and backpacking trips. All walks include a guide, car shuttles, and a picnic lunch. They also rent camping equipment. Appalachian Trail hikers should note that the Plakanis offer through-hiker support.

The Smoky Mountains Field School (TN) (865-974-0150; fax: 865-974-0154; ce.utk.edu/Smoky; professionalpgms@utk.edu), University of Tennessee, 313 Conference Center Bldg., Knoxville, TN 37996. Courses run spring through late fall. This cooperative program between the National Park Service and the University of Tennessee offers outdoor walking-based courses, taught by experts. A typical course will meet in a picnic area inside the park, then travel (most likely, walk) to the course's various locations over a period of four to eight hours. Many of the courses are specifically structured for parents to share with their children, with separate courses aimed at parents with teens and parents with youngsters. The Field School's headquarters are far outside the park, at the University of Tennessee's Knoxville campus.

✷ Lodgings

HOTELS AND RESORTS **The Fryemont Inn, Bryson City** (800-845-4879; 828-488-2159; fryemontinn.com; fryemont@dnet.net), P.O. Box 459, Bryson City 28713. $$–$$$$. Built by timber baron Amos Frye in 1923, this National Registry lodge sits on a hill above downtown Bryson City, with sweeping views from its wide front porch. The inn's large grounds are beautifully landscaped with native rhododendrons and hemlocks, isolated and very quiet. The bark-clad lodge has a large, comfortable lobby, filled with original Craftsman-style furniture. The 37 en suite rooms in the main lodge all have wormy chestnut paneling and simple, comfortable furnishings in a country style. Room tariffs include a full breakfast and dinner, ordered from the menu, at the inn's excellent dining room (except in winter, when the tariff is lower). A separate building, constructed in 1940 as a recreation hall, has been redone into large and comfortable "fireplace suites," each with a living room with fireplace, a separate king bedroom, and a wet bar. There's also a cabin, in which pets are allowed.

Historic Calhoun Country Inn, Bryson City (828-488-1234; fax: 828-488-0488; calhouncountryinn.com; innkeeper@calhouncountryinn.com), 135 Everett St., Bryson City 28713. $$–$$$. Founded in the 1920s as the Calhoun Hotel, this historic depot-area inn has been restored to its glory days. Its extra-wide front porch has rockers facing downtown's Everett Street, and its public rooms are large, bright, and airy. The rooms are reminiscent of a fine old country hotel—small to medium in size, bright, with antiques mixed into the decor. Of the 23 rooms, 8 have shared baths. The price includes a hearty country breakfast served in the sunny dining room.

The Swag, Maggie Valley (800-789-7672; fax: 828-926-2036; theswag.com; letters@theswag.com), 2300 Swag Rd., Waynesville 28785. $$$$$. This large log inn sits in a grassy swale 5,000 feet high, at the end of a 2.5-mile driveway that climbs over 1,000 feet in elevation. Remote and quiet, the views from its wide porches and balconies are spectacular. Rooms range in size from cozy to huge, each distinctively decorated with antiques and heritage quilts. Three log cabins (one with its own billiard room) give additional choices. WiFi is available. The tariff includes a full breakfast, a picnic lunch, evening hors d'oeuvres, and an elegant, relaxed dinner. The 250-acre site includes a pond, a waterfall, a 3-mile nature trail with fine views, and four sheltered hideaways for a little private relaxing in the woods.

Eight Gables Inn, Gatlinburg (TN) (800-279-5716; 865-430-3344; eightgables.com; inquiries@eightgables.com), 219 North Mountain Trail, Gatlinburg, TN 37738. $$$–$$$$. The Eight Gables Inn sits in forests on the northern edge of Gatlinburg, 2 miles from downtown and a short distance off US 441. Built in the 1990s, the handsome, stylized exterior reminds one of a prosperous Victorian farmhouse, with wide porches, high windows, powder-blue clapboarding, and two gables on each side. Inside, a large common area occupies half or more of the first floor, with sofas and two wood-burning fireplaces. All rooms are comfortable and full-sized, theme-furnished with reproduction antiques. A full breakfast and evening dessert are included in the tariff.

The Buckhorn Inn, Gatlinburg (TN) (865-436-4668; fax: 865-436-5009; buckhorninn.com; buckhorninn@msn.com), 2140 Tudor Mountain Rd., Gatlinburg, TN 37738. $$–$$$$. Located in the beautiful, rural Glades craft district east of Gatlinburg, this historic 1930s resort is set in the midst of its own 25 private acres, surrounded by meadows and woodlands carefully set out by its original founder. From the approach road the inn appears as a simple, modest white-painted wood structure; it turns its more elegant side to the Smokies, with a lovely view over wildflower meadows and hemlock forests to the peak of Mount Le Conte. Rooms are theme-decorated with English country antiques and reproductions, and range in size from comfortable to large. Suites are available in a newer annex, and there's a range of quaint cottages (with kitchens) in a 1930s style. WiFi is available. A hearty, fresh breakfast from a menu is included in the tariff.

Dancing Bear Lodge, Townsend (TN) (800-369-0111; 865-488-6000; fax: 865-448-3075; dancingbearlodge.com; info@dancingbearlodge.com), 137 Apple Valley Way, Townsend, TN 37882. $$$–$$$$. Formerly known as the Maple Leaf Inn, this is a modern log-built lodge in the grand style, sitting on a large tract of woods and meadows adjacent to the center of Townsend. All of its 12 lodge rooms and 16 cabins are individually decorated, and the cabins have kitchens, wood-burning fireplaces, indoor whirlpool tubs, and porch hot tubs. A continental breakfast is served in the lodge restaurant, which offers a full menu and bar in the evenings. The property has 3 miles of nature trails and paved bicycle paths, with views over meadows toward the Smokies.

Blackberry Farm, Townsend (TN) (800-648-4252; 865-984-8166; fax: 865-977-4012; blackberryfarm.com; info@blackberryfarm.com), 1471 W. Millers Cove Road, Walland, TN 37886. $$$$$$. Formerly a 1920s-era summer estate on 4,200 acres adjacent to the national park, Blackberry Farm has evolved into a luxurious 63-room mountain resort. United by an architecture that combines the American Shingle Style of the original Main House with motifs from England's Cotswold District, the resort's facilities spread across 100 landscaped acres in groupings of large houses and small cottages. The landscaped grounds give the appearance of a thoroughbred horse farm through which guest can hike, bicycle, or jog on 7 miles of hiking paths and 3 miles of paved jogging trails; there are tennis, basketball, and shuffleboard courts, a swimming pool, and bicycles available to guests. All rooms are individual and unique, decorated in a simple, elegant country English style. The tariff includes all meals at the inn's internationally renowned dining room, open only to guests; dinner is a multicourse, fine-dining experience (gentlemen must wear coats) featuring a 200-page wine list with limited choices under $70.

MOTELS **Cherokee** has a wide choice in motel rooms (2,500 of them) and a good selection of cabins, but no B&Bs or country lodges. You can hire a private vacation home in the Cherokee area from any of several Realtors in Sylva and Bryson City.

Gatlinburg, Tennessee, has several thousand motel rooms, and Pigeon Forge (8 miles north) has several thousand more. Gatlinburg, squeezed into a gorge, tends toward independent motels set tightly on small pieces of property, frequently with unusual architectural flourishes. Pigeon Forge features sprawling interstate-style motels, mostly chains and of standard construction. See *Guidance* for sources of more information.

BED & BREAKFASTS ✐ **Charleston Inn Bed & Breakfast, Bryson City** (888-285-1555; charlestoninn.com; info@charlestoninn.com), 208 Arlington Ave., Bryson City 28713. $$$. Built by a local attorney in 1927, the large and beautiful house sits on a wooded piece of property on a hillside within the town on Bryson City. Beautifully renovated in 1997, the Charleston Inn has 12 rooms, carefully decorated with new furniture in an elegant English country style. WiFi is available, and a full breakfast is included in the tariff.

Folkestone Inn Bed and Breakfast, Bryson City (888-812-3385; 828-488-2730; fax: 828-488-0722; folkestone.com; innkeeper@folkestone.com), 101 Folkestone Rd., Bryson City 28713. $$–$$$. This beautifully restored 1920s farmhouse sits 0.25 mile from the Great Smoky Mountains National Park on Deep Creek Road. A wide full-front porch faces Deep Creek with comfortable chairs, with another porch on top serving the second floor. The 10 comfortable rooms feature Victorian and country reproductions, including 3 ground-floor rooms with stone flag floors; upstairs rooms have private balconies. A full breakfast is included in the tariff.

The Richmont Inn, Townsend (TN) (866-267-7086; 865-448-6751; richmontinn.com; info@richmontinn.com), 220 Winterberry Lane, Townsend, TN 37882. $$$–$$$$. Inspired by the unique barns found in nearby Cades Cove, this modern purpose-built small inn has a log ground floor and a much larger second and third floor cantilevered over it. Located on 11 wooded ridgeline acres, the Richmont's site combines spectacular views with lovely woodland walks. Its rooms, ranging in size from cozy to full-sized luxury suites, are individually decorated around a theme from Smoky Mountain history, and each has either a fireplace, a private balcony, or both. WiFi is available. Room rates include a full gourmet breakfast and a candlelight desert. Separate antique log buildings house the **Cove Café**, an intimate dinner place specializing in fondue, and a gift shop. Golfers receive a discount on the Laurel Valley golf course only a short walk away.

CABINS Ol' Smoky Log Cabins, Cherokee (olsmokylogcabins.com). $$. In a rural area within the Qualla Boundary, just north of Cherokee, these purpose-built riverside log cabins all have porches facing the Oconaluftee. Comparable in price to motel units a short distance away, these handsome cabins are attractively furnished. The cabins are fairly close to one another, but removed from the paved (and not particularly busy) access road, for a quiet stay.

Boyd Mountain Log Cabins, Maggie Valley (828-926-1575; boydmountain.com; betsy@boydmountain.com), 445 Boyd Farm Rd., Waynesville 28786. $$$. Set on a 150-acre private farm in Maggie Valley's scenic Hemphill Creek area, these six well-spaced log cabins are all authentic, restored pioneer structures ranging from 150 to 200 years old. They're cozy, comfortable, historic cabins set in beautiful meadows, by or near a fishing pond; all have full porch and fireplace, with upstairs bedroom(s). The Christmas-tree farm on-site offers cut-your-own in the holidays. WiFi is available.

Gatlinburg Cabins The Housing Bubble of the Noughts has left Gatlinburg with a vast inventory of second homes and condos, and a very large number of these are available for daily or weekly rent. "Resorts"—essentially second-home developments—seem to cost more and should offer additional amenities such as a pool or clubhouse. Independent agencies are more apt to list lower-priced units, spread over the area. In either case, avoid any agency that charges extra for housekeeping. Then there are the independent motels, many of them little changed from the heyday of road travel, with their tourist cabins and kitchenettes; a large number of these are right downtown. There are too many good choices to list here; see the *Guidance* section for help, or just open Google or Bing Maps to "Gatlinburg" and then type in "cottages."

Blue Smoke Cabins, Townsend (TN) (865-448-3068; bluesmokecabins.com; bradycabin@aol.com), 1233 Carrs Creek Rd., Townsend, TN 37882. $$–$$$. Retired fireman Ron Brady and his wife, Linda, run this collection of handsome log cabins high atop a pine ridge 3 miles north of town. These well-furnished and roomy cabins have fine views from the rocking chairs and hot tubs on their wide porches, yet each cabin is completely isolated from its neighbors. You'll find the site's roads to be mountainy verging on breathtaking, but well within the abilities of the family sedan.

Mountain Mist Cabins, Townsend (TN) (800-686-9288; 865-448-6650; mtnmistcabins.com; mistcabins@aol.com), P.O. Box 162, Townsend, TN 37882. $$. This small community of country-style log cabins, each set in its own woods separate from the others, is located in scenic Dry Valley just west of Townsend. Distinctive red tin roofs sit above full-sized wraparound porches; walls are sided with rough-cut 12-inch planks.

Each porch has rockers and a hot tub. Inside, doors are handmade, and on-site wood is used for decorative accents with the log country furnishings. Fireplaces are finished in local stone, with gas log insets.

BACKPACKERS' CABINS Le Conte Lodge (TN) (865-429-5704; fax: 865-774-0045; leconte-lodge.com; reservations@lecontelodge.com), 250 Apple Valley Rd., Sevierville, TN 37862. Open mid-Mar.–mid-Nov. $$. Deep within the national park's backcountry and accessible only by hikers, Le Conte Lodge sits just shy of the 6,593-foot peak of Mount Le Conte. This collection of log buildings and primitive cabins is surrounded by old balsam forests, with only a short walk to wide sunset and sunrise views off clifftops. Hikers stay in bunk beds (linens and blankets supplied) in tiny board-and-batten cabins, heated by propane and lighted by kerosene lamps; there's no electricity or running water at Le Conte Lodge. Meals, served in the rustic lodge and included in the price, are plain and hearty, not surprising as the food has to be packed in by llama; wine is available for a surcharge. On any given day it's the coolest place to stay in the South; it's typically 20 degrees cooler than nearby Knoxville, and daytime temperatures have *never* reached 80 degrees. It's also one of the rainiest and foggiest—and no, they won't give you a rain check. However, if the weather cooperates you will experience the finest sunrises and sunsets anywhere in the South, from clifftops 1.25 miles above sea level. Reservations are required, and very hard to get. Try calling the first week in October for the following year.

✱ Where to Eat

DINING OUT ✐ **The Fryemont Inn, Bryson City** (800-845-4879; 828-488-2159; fryemontinn.com/dining.htm; fryemont@dnet.net). Open to the public for breakfast and dinner, Apr.–Nov. $$$. The historic Fryemont Inn, on a hill overlooking Bryson City and the Great Smoky Mountains from its wide porch, opens its dining room to the public for breakfast and dinner from mid-April to late November. This large room is in keeping with a 1923 mountain lodge, with its wood rafters, polished hardwood floors, giant stone fireplace (with a wood fire cackling merrily away in chilly weather), and wormy chestnut paneling. Its full-service bar is comfortable and quiet, with lots of old wood and two pool tables. The dinner menu is noted for its local trout. Breakfasts emphasize simple country foods, well prepared: eggs, omelets, French toast, and pancakes.

The Buckhorn Inn, Gatlinburg (TN) (866-941-0460; 865-436-4668; buckhorninn.com; info@buckhorninn.com), 2140 Tudor Mountain Rd., Gatlinburg, TN 37738. Open all year. Gatlinburg's historic resort inn offers an elegant yet friendly dining experience. The Buckhorn offers only one seating for the small number of tables in its 1938 main lodge, so that service is attentive and food is prepared specifically for each table. All diners are seated at one time and presented with five courses of a fixed menu; reservations are required, as preparation starts long before the seating time. The imaginative and exquisitely prepared food varies daily, but tends to combine familiar favorites in new and exciting ways. Located in a dry area of the county, the Buckhorn has no wine list, but welcomes you to bring your own and charges nothing for corkage.

Trailhead Steak House, Townsend (TN) (865-448-0166), 7839 E. Lamar Alexander Pkwy. (US 321), Townsend, TN 37882. Open for dinner all year. $$$. A white-linen restaurant with casual dress, the Trailhead specializes in a wide variety of grilled favorites. Filets seem to be the favorite, but you'll also find wild seafood steaks, local trout, chicken breasts, kebabs, and shrimp, with game occasionally showing up when available.

VIEW OVER FARMLAND TO THE GREAT SMOKY MOUNTAINS NATIONAL PARK, NEAR BRYSON CITY

EATING OUT Brushy Mountain Smokehouse and Creamery, Cherokee (828-497-7675; brushymtnsmokehouse.com), 664 Casino Trail, Cherokee 28719. Open for lunch and dinner. $$. Located near the casino, this large new restaurant features good hickory-smoked barbeque and ice cream made on the premises. Food is laid out on a buffet, and features pulled pork, chicken, and (after 4 PM) barbequed ribs as well as smoked pork chops and roast pork, plus a large variety of vegetables and a salad bar. Desserts center on their homemade ice cream, with 23 choices that rotate regularly.

Everett Street Diner, Bryson City (828-488-0123), 52 Everett St., Bryson City 28713. Open for breakfast and lunch daily. $$. This busy café may occupy a brick storefront in downtown Bryson City, but it's no grits-and-ham small-town eatery; the Everett Street Diner offers an upscale menu filled with fresh foods and intelligent recipes. You'll find the prices remain downtown Bryson City, tightly grouped between $5 and $7.

Smoky Mountain Brewery and Restaurant, Gatlinburg (TN) (865-436-4200; Smoky-Mtn-Brewery.com), 1004 Parkway, Gatlinburg, TN 37738. Open for lunch and dinner. $$–$$$. This tavern and pizzeria has its own on-premises microbrewery, the only one in Gatlinburg. A two-story eatery toward the back of the Calhoun Village retail area, it's decorated in rough wood with 1950s-style furniture and flooring. It's immaculately clean, the atmosphere is neat, and the food is great. The pizza is excellent, and the sandwiches are made with bread baked fresh on the premises. Next door, **Calhoun's** is run by the same people and has the same high-quality food; it's more of a sit-down restaurant with ribs and steaks dominating the menu.

The Fox & Parrot Tavern, Gatlinburg (TN) (865-436-0677; fox-and-parrot.com; brian@foxandparrot.com), 1065 Glades Rd., Gatlinburg, TN 37738. $$. Gatlinburg's best place for a friendly meal won't be found among the tourist-crowded downtown shops; instead, it sits above photographer Brian Papsworth's first-rate gallery in the Glades Arts & Crafts Community. Brian's Fox & Parrot Tavern re-creates the atmosphere and spirit of a great village local in the heart of England. It's a place where townsfolk and visitors meet and talk over a game of darts while enjoying a locally brewed ale and a freshly prepared bar meal. Every item on the menu is made from scratch ingredients on the premises, featuring British pub fare made as authentically as possible.

✷ Entertainment

MOUNTAIN MUSIC ✐ **Appalachian Music at the Community Center, Walland (TN).** Every Friday night, year-round, local musicians come to the Walland Community Center, 8 miles west of Townsend on US 321. What happens next depends on who shows up; bluegrass musicians might be playing in one room, while old-time fiddlers hold court in another.

Mountain Music Program, Cades Cove (TN). The Great Smoky Mountains National Park sponsors a monthly program of authentic Appalachian mountain music at the Cades Cove Amphitheatre, next to the camp store. In these programs, skilled musicians perform the historic music and ballads of the Smokies, and talk about this heritage music. Traditional dance may also be performed. This event occurs on the third Saturday of every month, from June through October; for details, call the park office (see *Guidance*).

✷ Selective Shopping

The Drama Road Gift Shops, Cherokee. Not surprisingly, the first-rate **Museum of the Cherokee** has a first-rate gift shop. Spacious, handsome, and full of stuff, this museum gift shop has Cherokee art and crafts, books, children's toys and books related to the museum, as well as a fascinating selection of tasteful and relevant gewgaws and knickknacks. The **Qualla Mutual**, a Cherokee crafters' cooperative, is just across the street and simply bursting with even more good stuff—all of it handmade on the Qualla Boundary, and carrying a certificate of authenticity from the U.S. Bureau of Indian Affairs. You'll find these two locations on US 441 and Drama Road, 1.25 miles north of US 19.

The Depot Area, Bryson City. Bryson City's classic small-town depot, on the north edge of downtown, is once again lively with passenger traffic—this time on the Great Smoky Mountain Railroad. And just like in the old days, the depot area is coming alive with small shops. A quilt shop and discount bookshop occupy the old car dealership on one side, while the old brick buildings across the street hold a variety of shops, including one specializing in mountain fiddles. Sideways across the street are more old brick storefronts with antiques and collectibles.

Downtown Gatlinburg (TN). "We don't want to be noticed as T-shirt City, USA," the mayor of Gatlinburg once told a newspaper reporter, but "evidently it's easier to make a dollar selling T-shirts than anything else." Yes, downtown Gatlinburg has a lot of T-shirt shops. However, there are a lot of other downtown shops as well: old-timey photographs, tattoo parlors, NASCAR memorabilia, wedding chapels, souvenir stores, fudge shops, funnel cakes, gaudy jewelry, four different Thomas Kinkade stores (the California-based "painter of light"), museums of the curious and weird (filling the role of sideshows), amusement arcades, even carnival rides. It's easy enough to sneer at this "rundown, haphazard collection of buildings ranging from the good to the bad to the ugly," as did the **Sonoran Institute** in a report funded by the Gatlinburg Chamber of Commerce, no less; "Gatlinburg is widely viewed as one of the most unattractive and inappropriate gateways to a national park in the United States," the institute sniffed. But it's also easy to relax and have fun, at Tennessee's giant unofficial permanent state fair.

Of special note is the **Arrowcraft**, located at the center of downtown between Lights 5 and 6 (the numbers hang from the lights). This crafters' gallery predates the downtown area that crowds around it on all sides; its wandering log building has been selling fine crafts by local artists since 1926. Originally part of the adjacent Arrowmont School of Arts and Crafts, it's now run by the not-for-profit Southern Highland Craft Guild, and features only items handmade by Craft Guild artists.

Finally, be sure not to miss the Glades (See *To See*) with 100 craft artists selling their own creations from their studios.

✷ Special Events

Mid-March: **Honor the Elders Day, Cherokee**. Cherokee stickball, a ceremonial (and very exciting) sport, combines with traditional dances and food at the Cherokee Ceremonial Grounds.

Early April: **Ramp and Rainbow Festival, Cherokee**. The North Carolina side of the Smokies celebrates that pungent herald of spring, the ramp, at the Cherokee Ceremonial Grounds. A ramp is a type of wild onion also known as a wild leek. It has a sweet, mild taste with a hint of garlic, but is notorious for the strong odor it leaves behind. One of the first plants to emerge in spring, the ramp has traditionally been a center of community celebration in the mountains, typically a ramp supper given by the volunteer fire department. In this festival the tribe welcomes the coming of spring by combining ramps with rainbow trout, a natural combination.

Late April: **Annual Spring Smoky Mountain Wildflower Pilgrimage, Gatlinburg (TN)** (865-436-7318; springwildflowerpilgrimage.org), 115 Park Headquarters Rd., Gatlinburg, TN 37738. For over half a century a group of East Tennessee organizations has sponsored this weeklong exploration of the national park's spring wildflowers. There are exhibits and vendors at the Gatlinburg Convention Center, but the real action takes place in a long series of field trips into the park—by foot, bicycle, and automobile. Wildflower walks predominate, but there are daily field trips for birders, and specialized trips for geology, plant identification, medicinal plants, moss, algae, fungi, insects, spiders, salamanders, bats, bears, old-growth forests, second-growth forests, logging, history, folk art, plant sketching, photography . . .

Early May: **The Cosby Ramp Festival, Cosby (TN)** (cosbyrampfestival.org). Over on the Tennessee side of the Smokies you'll find the ramp festival at Cosby, 18 miles east of Gatlinburg via US 321 (check their website for directions). The Cosby Festival, held since 1954, has become the largest ramp celebration in the mountains, with a full slate of mountain and bluegrass music.

Memorial Day: **Heritage Day Festival, Bryson City** (800-867-9246; 828-488-3681). This annual celebration of mountain heritage features traditional food, music, and crafts, as well as a toy duck race on the Tuckaseegee River.

Fourth of July: **Fourth of July Powwow, Cherokee**. The tribe celebrates the Fourth of July with a powwow dance competition, art and craft displays, Native American foods, and a fireworks display, all at the Cherokee Ceremonial Grounds.

Late October: **Cades Cove Fall Harvest Hayride**. The National Park Service collaborates with the Cades Cove Stables concessionaire to offer this evening hayride around the Cades Cove Loop Road. As you progress around the cove you meet people from the cove's history: a cove farmer, a Cherokee, perhaps an escaping Union soldier or a Confederate raider.

New Year's: **New Year's Eve Space Needle Spectacular**. A New Year's street party centers on downtown Gatlinburg's Space Needle attraction, with a ball drop and a stunning display of fireworks launched from the 340-foot observation tower.

THE SOUTHERN MOUNTAINS

Mountains extend southward from the Great Smokies through North Carolina to meet the Blue Ridge near the Georgia state line. These ridges are high and steep-sided, with most peaks above 4,000 feet and many topping a mile high. They zig and zag with no obvious reason, hemming in narrow-bottomed little valleys. The major rivers—the Tuckaseegee, the Nantahala, the Little Tennessee, the Valley River, the Hiwassee, the Tellico—can run obediently through a wide valley between low ridges, then turn suddenly to cut a deep gorge straight through a high barrier.

Early roads and railroads tried to pick their ways through the least-difficult gaps and gorges, with settlements following. The state legislatures broke the mountains into increasingly small counties in a vain attempt to create courthouses within horseback distance of most of the settlers. Today these courthouses sit at the center of compact, old downtowns in small county seats: Sylva, Franklin, Robbinsville, Hayesville, and Murphy.

More than most other eastern mountains, these southern ridges are dominated by public ownership, with settled areas sometimes little more than islands in a sea of forest. More than any other chapter in this book, this chapter will be dominated by these vast public tracts, their incredible scenery, and their wealth of recreation opportunities. In North Carolina, the Nantahala National Forest owns the majority of the mountain slopes; in Tennessee, it's the Cherokee National Forest. Where the Blue Ridge overlaps into South Carolina, the Sumter National Forest takes over, and in Georgia the Chattahoochee National Forest rules the roost. All four of these national forests maintain ranger stations in the major towns throughout this area, and these stations always have staffed information desks, books, and maps. As with all national forests, public recreation (including hunting) is permitted nearly everywhere; however, these are not national parks or conservation areas, and active logging continues on many government-owned tracts.

GUIDANCE Jackson County Chamber of Commerce (800-962-1911; 828-586-2155; mountainlovers.com; jctta@nc-mountains.com), 773 W. Main St., Sylva 28779. This chamber covers the eastern part of this chapter's area, with a visitors center in downtown Sylva, in a restored house across from the Old Courthouse.

Franklin Area Chamber of Commerce (866-372-5546; 828-524-3161; fax: 828-369-7516; franklin-chamber.com; facc@franklin-chamber.com), 425 Porter St.,

OLD JACKSON COUNTY COURTHOUSE IN FRONT OF KING MOUNTAIN

Franklin 28734. The Franklin Chamber handles tourism promotion and visitor relations for all of Macon County, which takes up much of this chapter's center. Their visitors center is located south of downtown Franklin on US Bus 441.

Graham County Travel and Tourism Authority (800-470-3790; 828-479-3790; grahamcountytravel.com; info@GrahamCountyTravel.com), 12 N. Main St., Robbinsville 28771. Located in Robbinsville, this body is the official tourism promoter for the northwestern part of this chapter. They have a detailed website with many accommodations listings.

Cherokee County Chamber of Commerce (828-837-2242; fax: 828-837-6012; cherokeecountychamber.com; info@cherokeecountychamber.com), 805 W. US 64, Murphy 28906. The Cherokee County Chamber covers the southwestern part of this chapter from their headquarters and visitors center 3 miles southwest of Murphy via US 64.

Nantahala National Forest, Nantahala Ranger District (828-524-6441), 90 Sloan Rd., Franklin 28734. The ranger station for the Nantahala Mountains is located 1.6 miles west of downtown Franklin, just off Old US 64 (now known as Old Murphy Road, SSR 1442). They have a staffed information desk during business hours, and can help with maps of the Nantahala backcountry. The Nantahala National Forest does not have its own website (see *Public Lands: The National Forest Service* under "What's Where").

THE BLUE RIDGE PARKWAY

The Blue Ridge Parkway's highest and most breathtaking section hugs the eastern border of this chapter's area, and is easily reached from Sylva by taking four-lane US 74 east for 12 miles. It is described in "Asheville and the Central Mountains."

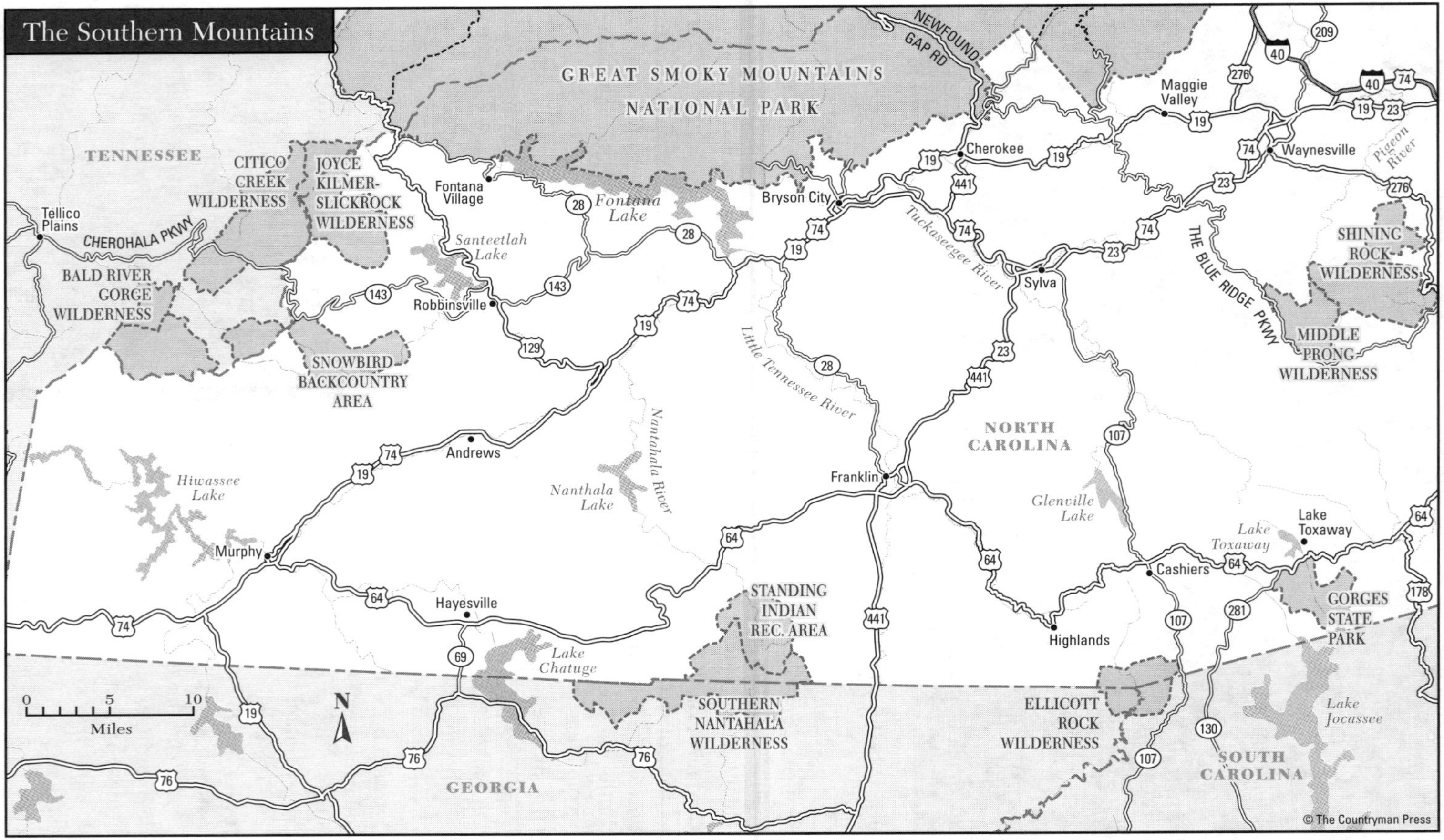

The Southern Mountains
GREAT SMOKY MOUNTAINS NATIONAL PARK
NEWFOUND GAP RD
TENNESSEE
CITICO CREEK WILDERNESS
JOYCE KILMER-SLICKROCK WILDERNESS
Tellico Plains
CHEROHALA PKWY
BALD RIVER GORGE WILDERNESS
SNOWBIRD BACKCOUNTRY AREA
Fontana Village
Fontana Lake
Santeetlah Lake
Robbinsville
Bryson City
Cherokee
Maggie Valley
Waynesville
Pigeon River
THE BLUE RIDGE PKWY
SHINING ROCK WILDERNESS
MIDDLE PRONG WILDERNESS
Tuckaseegee River
Sylva
Little Tennessee River
Nantahala River
Nanthala Lake
Andrews
Hiwassee Lake
Murphy
Hayesville
Lake Chatuge
Franklin
NORTH CAROLINA
Glenville Lake
Lake Toxaway
Cashiers
Highlands
STANDING INDIAN REC. AREA
SOUTHERN NANTAHALA WILDERNESS
ELLICOTT ROCK WILDERNESS
GORGES STATE PARK
Lake Jocassee
SOUTH CAROLINA
GEORGIA
0 5 10
Miles
N
© The Countryman Press

Nantahala National Forest, Cheoah Ranger District (828-479-6431; fax: 828-479-6784), Rt. 1, Box 16-A, Robbinsville 28771. Because of its great size, the Nantahala National Forest has a second ranger station that covers the westernmost parts of this chapter. It's located on NC 143 northwest of Robbinsville, near Santeetlah Lake, on the site of a historic CCC camp, with some interesting exhibits and a nature trail.

Cherokee National Forest, Tellico Plains Ranger Station (TN) (423-253-8400; fs.fed.us/r8/cherokee; mailroom_r8_cherokee@fs.fed.us), 250 Ranger Station Rd., Tellico Plains, TN 37385. As in the Smokies, the state line here follows a high mountain ridge, and the mountain wilderness continues on into Tennessee. On that side you'll find the Cherokee National Forest, whose ranger station is set in a lovely little cove off the Tellico River, in a historic CCC camp. It's located near the base of the **Cherohala Skyway**, 38.7 miles from its North Carolina terminus and 18.5 miles into Tennessee; turn left onto FS 240 (Tellico River Road), to a left after 0.4 mile.

GETTING THERE *By car:* People from the east or north will approach this area via Asheville and I-40 west, and then continue southward into the chapter following the US 74 expressway to either US 441 to Franklin or US 19 to Murphy. From Florida and points south, however, you'll want to use US 441 northward from I-85 from Atlanta. From southern Tennessee you'll take US 64 to Murphy. Other roads are very bad, and should be driven only for scenery.

Once you are in this chapter's area you'll find two north–south and two east–west backbone highways. First the east–west highways: US 74 becoming NC 28 hugs the top of this area, while US 64 goes through the lower portions. Both vary in quality from expressway to extremely bad; they're very scenic, though. The north–south highways are multilane US 441 running from Sylva-Dillsboro to Franklin and into Georgia; and variable-quality US 19/74 running between Bryson City and Murphy.

As with the other mountain chapters, do not let your GPS fool you into thinking that a back road is a shortcut. A number of back roads are not passable by passenger car, particularly in the Nantahala Mountains between Murphy and Franklin. Always have a paper map backup—and be ready to back out to a turnaround space when the road goes bad.

By air: **Greenville-Spartanburg International Airport (SC)** (864-877-7426; gspairport.com), 2000 GSP Dr., Suite 1, Greer, SC 29651. If your first stop is Cashiers or Highlands, your closest and most convenient airport will be Greenville-Spartanburg, located 78 miles away in Greer, South Carolina. Greenville-Spartanburg is served by six passenger airlines with direct flights to 15 cities. Asheville's airport (see "Asheville") is the better alternative for the rest of the chapter's area.

MEDICAL EMERGENCIES **Harris Regional Hospital** (828-586-7000; westcare.org), 68 Hospital Rd., Sylva 28779. Sylva's 86-bed regional hospital serves the northeast part of this chapter with 24/7 emergency room service. If you want to see what it looks like, rent the movie *The Fugitive*, in which it had a starring role. It is a mile east of town on US Bus 74, just off the easternmost of the three Sylva exits on US 23/74.

Angel Medical Center (828-524-8411; angelmed.org), 120 Riverview St., Franklin 28734. This independent not-for-profit 59-bed hospital has 24/7 emergency room service from its location a few blocks north of downtown Franklin on Riverview Street. It's been in business at this spot since 1923, when it was founded by Dr. Furman Angel; the current campus is quite modern.

Murphy Medical Center (828-837-8161; murphymedical.org), 4130 US 64 E., Murphy 28906. This 57-bed local hospital, renovated in 2002, is the closest 24/7 emergency facility for the Murphy area. It's a short distance east of town on US 64.

✷ Exploring the Area

EXPLORING BY CAR US 64: Cliffs and waterfalls of the Blue Ridge. This 33.6-mile drive follows US 64 along the Blue Ridge between Lake Toxaway and Franklin. It sounds short, but it's not. This is a difficult road, unimproved since it was paved in the era of the Model T, and this is made worse by fast growth in the Cashiers tourist district. Nevertheless there are enough beauty spots accessible from it (including the East's tallest cliff and tallest waterfall), along with one drop-dead gorgeous stretch west of Highlands, to be worth your while.

Start at **Lake Toxaway**, an early-20th-century resort settlement whose dam sits just above the highway, and blocks water from a once-enormous waterfall just below the highway. From here, back roads lead 6.4 miles north to **Panthertown Valley Backcountry** and an easy walk in to **Schoolhouse Falls**. Driving west on US 64, a left onto NC 281 leads to two remarkable sites: **Gorges State Park** with its views and waterfalls at 1.0 mile, and **Whitewater Falls**, reportedly the tallest

VIEW TOWARD THE SHINING ROCK WILDERNESS FROM THE MIDDLE PRONG WILDERNESS

waterfall in the East, at 8.4 miles. Back on US 64, at 10.6 miles from Lake Toxaway a side road left leads 5.6 incredibly scenic miles to the western edge of Panthertown Valley, with a short, easy walk to wide views from **Salt Rock**. Continuing on US 64, you'll find yourself at the center of the resort village of **Cashiers** at 12.5 miles; to the right up NC 107 you'll reach **Glenville Lake** in 4.2 miles.

Your next remarkable site comes up suddenly at 4.5 miles past NC 107; here, at Cowee Gap, a stunning view of retreating cliff faces opens without warning on your left, and just as suddenly disappears. There's parking on the left side, worth doubling back if you miss it. Just beyond is the left turn that leads to the **Whiteside Mountain** trailhead, for panoramic views from the top of the East's tallest cliff. You'll reach the center of Highlands in 9.9 miles from Cashiers. This beautiful little town offers fine shopping in its historic center, along with Blue Ridge cliff views from **Sunset Rock**, and a stunning native plant garden at the **Highlands Biological Station**. Beautiful **Glen Falls** is 3 miles southwest of town via NC 106.

West of Highlands, US 64 follows the bottom of the 8-mile-long Cullasaja (*cul-la-SAY-jah*) Gorge. The current roadway is utterly unchanged since the 1930s, when the CCC developed its scenic features for tourism—a mountain road built for tin lizzies, lined by classic national forest recreation sites. Leaving Highlands, you'll pass by **Lake Sequoyah**, one of the long lakes that meander through the town's neighborhoods, at 2.1 miles; look for the dam on your left. Half a mile farther, lacy **Bridal Veil Falls** drops 30 feet from an overhanging cliff. Modern US 64 passes in front of the falls (a concession to safety made in 1954), while the original highway's roadbed still goes underneath, maintained and drivable. In 3.5 miles from Highlands you'll reach the parking area for **Dry Falls**, so named because the footpath passes underneath the overhang, allowing walkers to pass dry (mostly) behind it. At 4.4 miles you reach **Cliffside Lake Recreation Area**, with lakeside and clifftop walks, and a CCC picnic area. The next 4 miles of road are particularly twisty; then, at 9.0 miles, it becomes a narrow ledge carved into a perpendicular granite cliff, with barely enough room for two cars to pass. Views over the gorge are spectacular. However, there is only one place to park, on the left, with room for only about four cars. Don't miss it—it's your only chance to view 200-foot **Cullasaja Falls**, a stunning double cataract. The gorge drive ends suddenly, dropping out onto flat farmlands in a suddenly widened valley. Franklin is an easy 6.0 miles ahead.

The Cherohala Skyway. This 50.6-mile drive between Robbinsville and Tellico Plains, Tennessee, crosses the Unicoi Mountains at their highest and most rugged point, via a state highway that intentionally copies the Blue Ridge Parkway as closely as possible. It's a stunning trip with views that rival the more famous parkways, and wildflowers, lakeshores, and rivers that surpass it.

Start by going west on NC 143, 1.6 miles north of Robbinsville via US 129. The highway roughly follows the **Santeetlah Lake**'s south shore for the first 4.6 miles, passing a **Forest Service headquarters** along the way with picnicking and historical exhibits at this old CCC camp. From there the road becomes twisting and intimate for 3 miles, then suddenly opens up to full modern standards as you approach the start of the Cherohala Skyway. Immediately at the start you'll find a first-rate view, with a 180-degree panorama northward toward the **Joyce Kilmer–Slickrock Wilderness**.

The next 26 miles feature sweeping and ever-changing views from a gently curving roadway with wide shoulders. The Cherohala slabs and switches up the great state-line ridge, the Unicoi Mountains, reaches the top, then runs from gap to gap along the crest. After 9.2 miles of steady climbing you'll reach 5,200 feet in elevation, with two scenic sites nearby. The first, on your right, is a trailhead for an easy walk of up to 3 miles (round-trip) to mile-high meadows on **Huckleberry Knob**, covered in wildflowers and berries. A short distance later on your left is a parking lot for trails to the top of **Hooper Bald**, with cliff views over the parkway and eastward toward the Smoky Mountains. You'll reach the crest of the Unicois at 11.6 miles, then turn north to follow the high ridge that carries the state line. At 14.2 miles you will reach Mud Gap and intersect with a long-distance footpath, the Benton MacKaye Trail, which follows the originally planned route of the Appalachian Trail. At 17.6 miles the parkway swerves west again and enters Tennessee for good, becoming TN 165. At this point the Benton MacKaye Trail continues north along the Unicoi Mountains, exploring the highest points of the **Citico and Kilmer-Slickrock Wildernesses**. From here the parkway follows **Sassafras Ridge** slowly downward. At 19.1 miles a parking lot on your right is the trailhead for lovely **Falls Creek Falls**.

At the bottom of the mountain a right turn will take you to **Indian Boundary Lake** as well as trailheads for Citico Creek Wilderness. The Skyway, however, continues left as TN 165 for a long, easy 12-mile ramble. The first 9 miles wander through the Unicoi foothills, an easy forest drive. Then the parkway meets the Tellico River, with **Tellico River Road** heading upstream to the left. TN 165 now follows the river closely for 3 miles, along the bottom of its gorge, ending at the attractive village of Tellico Plains, Tennessee, a fine little museum and visitors center marking its western end. Tellico Plains has several nice cafés.

EXPLORING ON FOOT A Slickrock Wilderness walk. Slickrock's isolation adds to its charm. Cut off from the rest of the world when **Calderwood Lake** flooded its entrance in 1928, Slickrock Creek has always been a difficult area to penetrate. Although it's been a national forest wilderness area since 1975, the Forest Service has long had a policy of doing nothing to improve its network of rough hunters' paths beyond assigning them numbers and showing them on a map. Even a level hike is tiring and difficult, because of the rough trail. It's incredibly scenic, though, and the very roughness makes the track more memorable.

This walk takes the only reasonably level path into Slickrock, starting at US 129 at the **Cheoah Dam**. From the south side of the highway bridge, a Forest Service trail heads west along the steep slopes above Calderwood Lake, hugging the top of the Little Tennessee River's drowned gorge. After 0.5 mile the trail climbs to an intersection; continue straight. When the trail starts to fall it is turning the bend to enter the Slickrock Creek basin; a sign marks the wilderness boundary. From here the trail follows the old lumber railroad along the creek, very rough from long abandonment, and a mere ledge in some places. Nevertheless, the forests are handsome and the stream is very beautiful. At 2.6 miles from the trailhead the path reaches **Lower Falls**, an attractive 20-foot waterfall with a high volume. This is a good destination for a 5-mile return trip. However, the creekside trail continues another 6 miles past a gorge and two more waterfalls. The many side trails lead high into the Unicoi Mountains, over into **Joyce Kilmer Forest** or the **Citico Wilderness**.

The Foothills Trail (foothillstrail.org). The 76-mile-long Foothills Trail crosses the deeply incised side ridges of the Blue Ridge, roughly following the NC–SC border. For years it was almost completely within the vast Duke Power lands that surrounded **Lake Jocassee**, and built with their help and support by the independent Foothills Trail Conference; now, with Duke's donation of this land to the public, the trail is mainly within a series of large state and federal tracts. The trail stretches from its western terminus 20.8 miles south of Cashiers (and outside this book's area), to follow the state line to South Carolina's **Mountain Bridge Wilderness**, with alternate eastern termini in two cliff-ringed state parks.

The trail begins in South Carolina's Oconee State Park, from where it saunters northward for 7 miles along a ridge with some nice views, to the Chattooga Wild and Scenic River of *Deliverance* fame, which it follows north to the state line. Along this stretch it hooks up with two other long-distance paths: the Palmetto Trail, which when finished will reach the Atlantic, and the Bartram Trail, which in turn links to the Appalachian Trail and the Benton MacKaye Trail for some remarkable loop backpacking. Once inside North Carolina the trail passes Whitewater Falls, reputedly the tallest in the East, plunges into its gorge, and follows the Whitewater River downstream to the Bad Creek Project and the spectacular Lower Whitewater Falls. From here the trail parallels the north shore of Jocassee Lake, going up and down a series of ridges. This section gives access to rough bushwhacks up gorges where rare plants thrive and waterfalls have yet to be named. This ends as the trail enters a long, leisurely climb up Laurel Fork Creek, with a truly fine waterfall along the way, to South Carolina's 1,000-acre Laurel Fork Creek Heritage Area, preserving half a dozen rare species in its cove and uplands forests. Beyond this, the main trail goes south to Table Rock State Park, an impressive monadnock, while an alternate branch continues along the state line to the cliffs known as the Blue Wall at Caesars Head State Park.

The Standing Indian Loop. Apart from all its many recreational and scenic glories, the Standing Indian area (see *Public Lands*, below) has one outstanding claim to fame among hikers: The Appalachian Trail makes almost a complete loop, typically running about 22 miles (depending on which side trails you use to reach it). You can set up a car camp at its excellent family campground and start hiking the next morning; two or three days later (depending on how relaxed your pace), you walk back into your car camp from the other direction. As far as I know, it's the only place along the Appalachian Trail's entire 2,100-mile length where you can do this. The loop climbs from the campground at 3,400 feet above sea level to the peak of Standing Indian, with its famously wide views from classic Blue Ridge balds (yes, it's on the Blue Ridge), a few inches shy of 5,500 feet, with lots of fine scenery along the way. Because of the way the trail follows ridgelines, the total climb is 5,100 feet.

Snowbird Creek waterfalls. North Carolina's 10,000-acre **Snowbird Creek Area** is popular for its remote beauty, its 37 miles of looping hiking trails, its fine fishing, but most of all its waterfalls. You'll find it within the Nantahala National Forest abutting the state line, west of Robbinsville in the Unicoi Mountains; follow NC 143 west of Robbinsville for 5.4 miles, then turn left onto Snowbird River Road (SSR 1115) and go 3.1 miles, then turn left onto SSR 1120 to its end at a Forest Service parking lot. From there you can hike in to four major waterfalls. Heading up Snowbird Creek along the old logging railroad grade that serves as the trail, the 10-foot double cascade misnamed **Big Falls** comes first at 3.9 miles. Then comes the most impressive of the four main falls, 20-foot **Middle Falls**, at 5.1 miles and a good turnaround. If you feel ambitious, however, **Upper Falls** is only 1.2 miles farther (6.3 miles from the trailhead), and your efforts will be rewarded by a 10-foot slide rock into a large swimming hole. Go ahead and jump in; you are probably already wet, as the trail loops repeatedly across torrential Snowbird Creek to get here. The fourth waterfall, **Sassafras Falls**, is a dramatic 50-foot plummet over hard gray rock on a side stream, Sassafras Creek. A cross-trail connects Snowbird Creek with Sassafras Creek just above Middle Falls, allowing a strong hiker to do all four in a day, a 12.8-mile round-trip with 1,330 feet of climbing and 13 major fords. Nor does this exhaust the hiking possibilities; the trails continue to the mile-high mountains on the state line, connecting with the **Cherohala Skyway** and the extensive trail system in Tennessee's adjacent **Tellico River backcountry**.

EXPLORING BY BICYCLE **Little Tennessee River Greenway** (828-369-8488; fax: 828-349-4119; littletennessee.org; frogquarters@verizon.net), 573 E. Main St., Franklin 28734. This paved 4-mile walk-bike path follows the **Little Tennessee River** from one end of Franklin to another. Apart from many views of this lovely river, it has four major bridges over the Little Tennessee (including one historic steel structure), canoe launch points, picnic areas, and a nice large playground with water features. Its **monarch butterfly garden** is certified as a monarch way station by the University of Kansas's Monarch Watch program (monarchwatch.org), a protected place for monarchs to regain their strength on their long migration to Mexico.

✷ Towns

Sylva. The county seat of Sylva snuggles in a narrow side valley of the Tuckaseegee River, under the mile-high peaks of Plott Balsams in the northeastern part of this chapter's area. Its four-block downtown hugs the hillside above Scotts Creek, so that each storefront on Main Street has a basement that comes out at street level on Mill Street. Its Main Street is not so much restored as unchanged, frozen in a time where people went downtown to shop in tiny old brick buildings. Main Street ends at a flight of steps climbing a tall green hill—past a fountain, then past a Confederate soldier statue, and on up to the column-and-dome Old Courthouse. With its exterior recently restored, the Old Courthouse makes a stunning landmark visible as far away as the Blue Ridge Parkway (from Grassy Mine Ridge Overlook, milepost 437). The Old Courthouse is especially beautiful in spring when framed by dogwoods, but is worth a visit at any time for its views over Main Street toward the Blue Ridge Parkway and the 6,000-foot peaks of the Great Balsam Mountains. Downtown street parking is free and plentiful.

Adjacent to Sylva on its west is **Dillsboro**, with its own downtown district, just as historic but in white wood frame instead of brick. Although Dillsboro is the smaller of the two its downtown is much larger, with a number of fine crafters' studios and galleries as well as gift shops and some miscellaneous surprises. The **Great Smoky Mountain Railroad** has a depot here (see *To See* in "The Great Smoky Mountains"), once a center for excursions but now only a destination for rides that start in Bryson City.

Cashiers. Pronounced *CASH-ers*, this town was until recently little more than a crossroads post office and general store at the intersection of US 64 and NC 107. Since 1845, when South Carolina's Hampton family established their High Hampton hunting lodge there, Cashiers has drawn wealthy South Carolina socialites, and in recent decades its popularity with the wealthy has increased. The low hills around High Hampton have become crossed with narrow roads and crusted with hidden mansions, and a downtown area has slowly grown up around the old crossroads. You will now find Cashiers a full-service town, although you might have to ask where to find something. There's an Ingles Supermarket a mile east of town on US 64, the only chain supermarket between Franklin and Brevard.

Highlands. The town of Highlands sits in a large bowl on the crest of the Blue Ridge, at an elevation above 4,000 feet; until the incorporation of **Beech Mountain** in 1981, Highlands was the highest town in the East. It's been a high-end resort, popular with Atlanta and Florida socialites, since it was founded in the 1870s, and much of its 19th-century core remains. Even better, strict zoning laws have kept out the worst modernist blight, so that it looks more like a New England village than a small southern town. You'll find it nearly free of chains and franchises, but rich in local independent shops, restaurants, and hotels. Parking is free and plentiful. Still true to its 19th-century origins, Highlands has quite a variety of small independent hotels, and almost no motels.

Franklin. An early pioneer town, Franklin has been a major market center for the surrounding mountains since stagecoach roads converged here in the 1850s. Today it has a handsome and shoppable downtown of three square blocks, with lots of businesses sprawling outward along its U.S. highways, US Byp 441, US Bus 441, and US 64. It sits in the middle of a broad flat valley, straddling the Little Tennessee River with low hills that wouldn't look out of place in the Piedmont. However, when the mountains get started they kick in with a vengeance, with all local ridgelines surpassing 4,000 feet and the Nantahalas to its west reaching a mile high.

SYLVA'S COUNTY COURTHOUSE, VIEWED FROM A BACK ROAD

Murphy. The market town for the western portion of this chapter, Murphy is a good size, somewhat sprawling place at the center of a very large valley. It has a lovely, well-developed old downtown that climbs a hill, making for interesting strolling. Within North Carolina it is famous for its early-20th-century courthouse, reputed to be the most beautiful in the state—a large and stately neoclassical structure completely clad in locally quarried marble. **Hiwassee Lake**, which starts 10 miles east of town, backs up into the village's downtown.

✷ Green Spaces

PUBLIC LANDS **Jocassee Gorges**. In this area the Blue Ridge shifts north, leaving a maze of hard rock side ridges and outliers extending deep into South Carolina. Duke Power acquired most of this area for its hydroelectric potential during the 1960s, building **Lake Jocassee** in the 1970s and the **Bad Creek Project** in the 1980s. In the 1990s Duke converted most of its undeveloped land into public conservation areas, with the remaining Duke properties having conservation easements and public access via wildlife management programs. By 2001 the conversion was complete, and the 60,000-acre Jocassee Gorges Tract had been created.

The tract possesses immense value for its biological diversity, rugged scenery, and many waterfalls. However, it is now split among six different entities in two states (NC State Parks, SC State Parks, NC Wildlife Resources, Nantahala National Forest, Sumter National Forest, and Duke Power); cooperation is less than perfect, and there is no comprehensive recreation or management plan. The best recreation facilities are at Gorges State Park (south of Lake Toxaway via NC 281), now being actively developed with trailheads, picnic areas, a scenic drive with views, and a major campground in the works. These developed areas, however, will always be a tiny portion of the total. The backcountry is reached from Auger Hole Trail, a former wagon road that cuts diagonally across the gorges and is reached from its own trailhead on the eastern end of the state park, and the Foothills Trail.

Panthertown Valley. Panthertown Valley (locals say "Painter-town") is a classic Blue Ridge perched valley, a wide, flat-bottomed bowl sitting just below the crest, between Cashiers and Lake Toxaway. Part of the Nantahala National Forest since 1989, it is noted for its high cliffs, waterfalls, sandy-beached swimming holes, and incredible biological diversity. The valley has two access points, one on each side. The **western gate** is reached from Cashiers, an interesting and beautiful drive that crosses the Blue Ridge Crest twice; take US 64 west 1.8 miles to a left onto Cedar Creek Road (SSR 1120), then climb 2.1 miles to a right onto Breedlove Road (SSR 1121), which you follow to its end in 3.5 miles. The **eastern gate** is reached from Lake Toxaway; take NC 281 north from US 64 for 0.8 mile to Cold Mountain Road (SSR 1301), which you follow to its end in 5.5 miles. The valley stretches between these two gates, closed to motor vehicles but easily traversed by foot or mountain bike.

Panthertown has been gaining a reputation among local outdoors enthusiasts for its amazing scenery and wide choice of recreational opportunities. Salt Rock offers great views from an exposed clifftop a short stroll from the western parking lot. From the eastern parking lot, a gravel road heads a mile downhill to Schoolhouse Falls, a popular swimming hole with its 20-foot cascade and sandy beach. From the same lot, a stepped footpath travels nearly 2 miles to the top of the granite dome named Little Green Mountain, with fine views over the entire valley. Panthertown's granite cliffs are becoming popular with rock climbers, with Black Rock Mountain, Big Green Mountain, and Laurel Knob being among the favorites.

Standing Indian and the Southern Nantahala Wilderness. Located 13 miles west of Franklin via US 64, this popular 20,000-acre national forest tract (surrounded by many more tens of thousand of public acres in all directions) offers waterfalls, clifftop views, fly fishing, family camping, and a wide choice of hiking trails, including the **Appalachian Trail**, which here forms a loop. It centers on the headwaters of the **Nantahala River** and is ringed by a dozen 5,000-foot peaks—the southernmost in the East, with the tallest being Standing Indian itself, at 5,499 feet. Forests are second growth from 70 to 100 years old, all very mature and handsome.

When you visit you'll find all of its attractions accessible from its scenic main road, FS 67—a fine drive that follows the Nantahala River, then turns uphill to climb to 4,800-foot Mooney Gap on the Blue Ridge. The first 2.1 miles are paved, a mildly attractive forest drive, passing the Appalachian Trail at 0.4 mile on your left. This paved section ends at the main recreation area, straddling the river—a good place to picnic or camp, and the area's main trailhead. From here a good-quality gravel road follows the river closely with some excellent scenery and more trailheads. As your road turns uphill and away from the river you'll reach easy walks to two lovely waterfalls: Laurel Creek Falls, a level 1.2-mile round-trip at 6.5 miles, and Moony Falls, a steep 0.2-mile round-trip at 6.7 miles. At 9.3 miles a side road leads off to the left (to reach a fire tower, now abandoned) and your road number changes to FS 83. You top out just beyond at 9.7 miles. The scenic drive continues to 10.4 miles, where gravel parking marks the trailhead to Pickens Nose remarkable both for its name and its views, a nearly level 1.2-mile round-trip. This is where you turn the family sedan around and head back. For the adventurous, however, FS 83 continues steeply downhill with 14 switchbacks to finally reach US 441 8.7 miles south of Franklin, a steep and twisting drop that may not be appropriate for the family sedan.

The southern half of the Standing Indian area is within the much larger Southern Nantahala Wilderness. Congress created this 24,500-acre wilderness to protect the great knot of mountains at the juncture of the Blue Ridge and the Nantahalas, extending from Standing Indian southward into Georgia and westward into some of North Carolina's least-visited mountains.

The Wayah Bald area. The highest peak in the northern Nantahalas is not Wayah Bald; it is Wine Springs Bald, a mile to the south and a good 100 feet higher. No one cares. Everything in this area is named after Wayah Bald, including (until 2007) the local ranger district. The bald has its own gravel road, 4.5 miles long, climbing 1,100 feet up from Wayah Gap just to reach it. It has one of the oldest ranger stations in the East on its slopes, preserved as the **Wilson Lick Historic Site**. It has a **stone lookout tower** that's been there since 1912 and is simply beautiful. And it has 360-degree panoramic views that just won't quit.

Wayah Bald marks a rough halfway point in the northward march of the Nantahala Mountains, one of the region's great barrier ranges. It's surrounded by huge expanses of the Nantahala National Forest, a lot of it purchased as soon as the Weeks Act established the national forest system in 1911. Nearly all the recreational development has centered on the Nantahala Crest, traversed by the Appalachian Trail from one end to the other. Downslope, the public lands roll on and on, cut by logging roads and open to those who don't mind entering trailless areas armed only with 50-year-old USGS maps.

Joyce Kilmer Memorial Forest and the Kilmer-Slickrock Wilderness. In the 1930s the National Forest Service decided to dedicate a large, virgin forest to the poet Joyce Kilmer, author of "Trees," who was killed in World War I. They chose the forests of Little Santeetlah Creek, northwest of Robbinsville, calling them "some of the finest original growth in the Appalachians." Today this watershed contains thousands of acres of never-cut old-growth forest, with trees reaching 20 feet in diameter. A 2-mile loop trail leads through some of the most dramatic forest, climaxing in a grove of champion trees that include 165-foot-tall tuliptrees (once known as yellow poplars). A separate trail follows the valley uphill to its end, reaching the Unicoi ridgeline in 5 miles after a 2,700-foot climb; at the crest, the path to the right leads another 2 miles to **stunning views** from Hangover Lead.

In 1975 Congress expanded the original "Memorial Forest" northward to become the 17,400-acre Kilmer-Slickrock Wilderness. This northern portion, centered on the Slickrock Creek basin, had only been partially logged when the 1928 impoundment of Calderwood Lake flooded the timber railroad and forced its abandonment. Today Slickrock retains its character of a remote land crossed only by hunters' trails, and the Slickrock experience remains one of deep and difficult backcountry.

Kilmer-Slickrock ends at the state line; just over the line, however, Tennessee's adjacent Citico Creek Wilderness doubles the size of this congressionally protected wilderness zone. Trails interconnect among Slickrock, Kilmer, and Citico Creek, creating a large number of possible ridge-and-valley trips that combine old-growth forests with waterfalls and mountaintop meadows. These include the newly completed Benton MacKaye Trail, a long-distance path whose connections with the Appalachian, Bartram, and Foothills Trails open up some unusual backpacking adventures.

Tennessee's Tellico River area. The upper reaches of the Tellico River are almost entirely owned and controlled by the National Forest Service, mostly within Tennessee's Cherokee National Forest and easily reached from the town of Tellico Springs. A paved scenic road, **Tellico River Road** (FS 210), runs along the riverbank, frequently flanked by gray cliffs as the Tellico digs its way deep into a gorge. At one point FS 210 passes immediately by a huge waterfall, 100 feet tall and carrying a huge volume of water. This is **Bald Creek Falls**, and behind it is the 3,700-acre **Bald Creek Gorge Wilderness**. Here you'll find a 4.3-mile trail that follows the gorge bottom upstream, gaining 500 feet in elevation before it reaches Bald Creek Road (FS 216), a good gravel road that forms the wilderness's upper boundary. Arrange a car shuttle and enjoy the many views of rapids and waterfalls on a downhill walk. The nearby Waucheesi Mountain Tower gives good views over the gorge.

The Bald River Gorge makes up only a third of the protected forests of the Tellico. Another 10,000 acres upstream from the Bald Creek Gorge Wilderness have received administrative protection as a series of primitive areas and provide some more remote opportunities for hiking, camping, and fishing. The Benton MacKaye Trail runs along through these protected areas, first following the Unicoi Mountain ridge, then descending to the remote upper reaches of the Bald River before climbing back up to the crest of the Unicois.

For many years this Tennessee scenic drive ended in a large off-highway vehicle area just over the state line in North Carolina. No longer—the Nantahala National Forest has permanently closed the Upper Tellico OHV area to all vehicles. It remains open to hikers (and hunters), and can now be explored on foot, in safety and quiet.

POTTER BRANT BARNS OUTSIDE HIS SHOP IN DILLSBORO

PARKS AND GARDENS Highlands Botanical Garden (828-526-2602; fax: 828-526-2797; wcu.edu/hbs/Garden.htm; ldavis@email.wcu.edu), 930 Horse Cove Rd., P.O. Box 580, Highlands 28714. Open daily, all year. Admission is free. At the center of Highlands sits a very special botanical garden. Run by the University of North Carolina, the 30-acre Highlands Botanical Garden is a biological reservoir of native species and a serious research station for mountain botany, ecology, and biology. The garden is highly informal in its design and layout, a skillful modification of the found environments that safeguards and showcases the specimens. Paths loop around a lakeshore thick with lily pads, climb along sheltered streambanks, and break into old cove forests. The gardens were established in 1962, but the research station has been there since the 1930s, and has the look and feel of an old-time ranger station. New additions include a Cherokee Garden and the William Bartram Trail, an interpretive trail that features 30 mountain species connected with the great early botanist. On-site, facing Horse Cove Road, is the Highland Nature Center, a nature museum open seasonally. Lovely lakeside Ravenel Park is adjacent, and **Sunset Rock** is an easy walk up a footpath.

Cliffside Lake Recreation Area. This Nantahala National Forest recreation area, inside the **Cullasaja Gorge**, has a lovely little lake underneath cliffs. Paths lead around the lakeshore and up the cliffs for some really excellent views. The park features classic **CCC architecture** from the 1930s, including a gazebo at the top of the cliff and a number of picnic shelters. The picnic area sits by the lake, under a canopy of tall old trees.

RIVERS Tuckaseegee River. People who know "the Tuck" can instantly recognize its appearance in the movie *The Fugitive*, where we see an obviously freezing Harrison Ford pulling himself out of the roiling brown water. Rising along the north slopes of the Blue Ridge around Glenville and Lake Toxaway, the Tuckaseegee (also spelled *Tuckaseigee*) flows for 40 miles northward through this chapter's area. In its headwaters, its East Fork and West Fork offer some superb gorge and waterfall scenery, but are mostly either flooded or dewatered by hydropower projects (including **Glenville Lake**). Then comes a 20-mile stretch of wide, clear, mainly calm water with stunning scenery, paralleled by NC 107 and several smaller lanes. As it passes Dillsboro, the Tuckaseegee picks up its characteristically brown color, along with several rafting outfitters. This final 10-mile section has numerous Class II and III rapids, a perfect venue for a family rafting trip. Minimum body weight for rafting on the Tuckaseegee is 40 pounds (compared with 60 pounds on the Nantahala), so all but the smallest children are welcome.

The **Little Tennessee River** is wide, smooth, and beautiful, passing through handsome farmland with wide views toward the Nantahala and Cowee Mountains. This Class I and II stream is popular with local canoeists, particularly now that 26 miles of it are state-owned downstream from Franklin. It is, however, an uncontrolled stream and subject to the vagaries of flood and drought. At this time, no raft trip operators offer tours along it, but the Smoky Mountain Fish Camp, on the riverbanks near Cowee Valley, will rent you a kayak, canoe, or tube.

The **Chattooga Wild and Scenic River** rises from waters that flow off the cliffs of **Whiteside Mountain**, then southward through deep, boulder-strewn gorges. It became notorious as the model for the 1970 book and 1972 movie *Deliverance.* However, when Congress declared it a Wild and Scenic River in 1974, they were more concerned with the four separate proposals to destroy this 57 miles of free-flowing wilderness river for hydropower. Today the USDA Forest Service holds 15,432 acres along its banks, very nearly its entire length. All but about 3 miles of this is paralleled by a footpath, the Chattooga River Trail.

The Forest Service divides the river into five sections, The uppermost two sections, upstream from US 28, have been closed to boaters since 1976, much to the consternation of whitewater enthusiasts, who have launched a lawsuit. For bankside travelers these are the most scenic sections, moving through a deep mountain gorge with numerous waterfalls, including the glorious swimming hole at Norton Mill Creek Falls and three different waterfalls at Burells Ford. Several Class V-plus rapids are on this closed section, including Big Bend Falls, a single 25-foot drop stretching across the entire river. Floating starts at the GA 28 bridge, on the GA/SC line, well outside the scope of this guide.

Cheoah River. After 1926, Alcoa's **Santeetlah Dam** dewatered the Cheoah River, leaving it a dry ribbon of boulders. No longer; starting in 2007, Alcoa has scheduled 18 recreational water releases each year, with a commitment to continue these releases through 2047 at a minimum. And how good is it? The Cheoah offers a steep, unchanging gradient where Class IV and V rapids abut each other almost continuously, with nearly no room for a breather between them. One section of Class V rapids lasts for a mile and a half! If this is your cup of tea, contact the Nantahala Outdoor Center for information.

LAKES Glenville Lake (Tuckaseegee River). This large lake, 3,500 feet in elevation, sends out long, thin arms into many former valleys in the Glenville area, north of Cashiers on NC 107. The highway skirts the lake for some distance before swerving away as it reaches what passes for central Glenville (still a dispersed mountain community). Lakeside scenery is very mixed, with much forest, a number of farms and meadows, and a steadily increasing number of subdivisions. A winding narrow lane (SSR 1157) turns left off NC 107 on the north end of Glenville, first reaching a nice county park with picnicking and a boat ramp, then crossing the impressive World War II–era dam (with a free boat launch on the other side). The lake is owned by Duke Power; its water flows through a giant pipeline to a hydropower station at Tuckaseegee. By the way, it's officially known as Thorpe Reservoir, but if you call it that no one will know what you're talking about.

Nantahala Lake (Nantahala River). One of the most remote and beautiful hydropower lakes in the region, Nantahala was built in the 1940s by this region's local power company, Nantahala Power and Light (now Duke Power). It floods a rugged mountain valley 17 miles west of Franklin via paved Wayah Road (SSR 1310), a rugged and scenic drive. Nantahala Lake is T-shaped, with each of its arms 2 or 3 miles long and 0.25 to 0.5 mile wide. It's surrounded by 4,000- and 5,000-foot peaks on all sides, which rise straight up out of the water; the west side, and nearly all of the surrounding mountains are primitive national forest lands. This makes the lakeside scenery very wild and remote, particularly when viewed from SSR 1310, which follows it for some length.

Release water from Nantahala Lake provides the dependable, high-quality white-water sports in the downstream Nantahala Gorge. Like several other hydropower sites in these mountains, Nantahala's power station is located some miles from the dam; the river water is carried to it through pipes, leaving the channel dewatered for some distance below the dam.

Santeetlah Lake (Cheoah River). Alcoa built this huge lake just north of Robbinsville in 1926 as part of its Tapoco Project, which created enough hydropower between 1917 and 1957 to supply half the needs of its aluminum plant near Knoxville. Its big dam blocks the **Cheoah River**, turning it dry for 9 miles (except for 18 scheduled releases a year) as it sends its waters through a pipeline to a power station on Cheoah Lake, another old Tapoco project far below and far away. Santeetlah Lake has the best developed recreational opportunities of all the lakes in this area, with two private marinas and a Nantahala National Forest boat ramp at Cheoah Point. Santeetlah has a long and highly convoluted shoreline, most of it owned by the Nantahala National Forest; there are many **shoreline camping** spots within the national forest, and views are spectacular.

Hiwassee Lake. Water from the TVA's Hiwassee Dam backs up into the town of **Murphy**, 10 miles away. This long, skinny lake with many arms floods a long gorge of the Hiwassee River, with steep-sided hills rising out of the water, and the tall **Unicoi Mountains** visible to the north. Its main channel takes 20 miles to travel the 10 miles from the dam to Murphy, and its largest side channels extend another 10 miles—and nearly all of these 163 miles of shoreline are national forest lands, wild and open to the public. Recreational access is provided by the National Forest Service at **Hanging Dog Recreation Area**, and by TVA at the dam—a worthwhile site in itself.

* To See

CULTURAL SITES The Franklin Gem and Mineral Museum (828-369-7831; fgmm.org; franklingemsociety@fastmail.fm), 25 Phillips St., Franklin 28734. Open

May–Oct., weekdays noon–4, Sat. 11–3 and 6–9; Nov.–Apr., Sat., noon–4. Admission is free. The old Macon County Jail in downtown Franklin housed prisoners from 1850 until 1970. In 1976 it became the site of the Franklin Gem and Mineral Museum, run by the local rockhound club, the very active Franklin Gem and Mineral Society. The building remains very much an old jail, with gem and mineral exhibits in the cells. One such exhibit contains gems and minerals from North Carolina, including a most rare and valuable piece—an 18th-century Wedgewood porcelain made from clay taken from Franklin (then a Cherokee village). Another exhibit has minerals from every state in the Union. There are displays of wire-wrapped jewelry, of fluorescent minerals, of Native American artifacts, and of fossils.

Scottish Tartans Museum (828-524-7472; scottishtartans.org; tartans@scottish tartans.org), 86 E. Main St., Franklin 28734. Open Mon–Sat. 10–5. Adults $2, children $1. The official North American museum of the Scottish Tartan Society—the governing society for all tartans worldwide, located in Pitlochry, Scotland—occupies a storefront in downtown Franklin. Its museum displays Scottish tartans, and relates the tartans to Scottish history and culture. It has facilities for looking up family tartans, and a really great gift shop. The Scottish Tartans Museum sponsors the annual Taste of Scotland Festival (see *Special Events*).

John C. Campbell Folk School (800-365-5724; 828-837-2775; fax: 828-837-8637; folkschool.org), 1 Folk School Rd., Brasstown 28902. Open daylight hours. Founded in 1925 by New England social worker Olive Campbell and named after her late husband, the Campbell School occupies 380 acres in the rural community of Brasstown, 7 miles east of Murphy. The beautiful and well-kept campus looks like a large and prosperous farmstead, complete with barn and farmhouse; but these buildings hold studios and classrooms. The school sponsors an incredible list of six-day courses, with a large number going on at once and the courses changing every week. While all aspects of folk and fine art crafts are covered, the school is particularly strong in wood, textiles, and baskets. There are no restrictions on exploring the campus, and groups of four or fewer are welcome to peek into classes if there are no signs posted otherwise. They run a first-rate craft store and sponsor weekly concerts as well as bimonthly dances. From Murphy, go east on US 64 for 4.6 miles, to a right turn onto Settawig Road, and look for the signs.

Fields of the Wood (828-494-7855; fieldsofthewoodbiblepark.com), 10000 NC 294, Murphy 28906. Admission is free. This "biblical theme park," built in 1945 and run by the Church of God of Prophecy, commemorates its founding with monumental art deco sculptures in poured concrete. The enormous Ten Commandments are the most famous, covering a grassy hillside with 7-foot-tall concrete letters. However, the most impressive monument is the **Place of Prayer**, a 320-step landscaped path lined with gigantic concrete tablets engraved with biblical verses, leading to a prayer garden with wide views. Other monuments include a reconstruction of Golgotha and the tomb in which Jesus was buried, and a hilltop garden displaying the flags of all nations where the Church of God has congregations. There is also a large gift shop. Field of the Woods is 18 miles west of Murphy; take US 64/74 west for 10 miles, then go right on NC 294 for 8 miles.

HISTORIC SITES **Mountain Heritage Center** (828-227-7129; wcu.edu /2389.asp; collins@email.wcu.edu), Western Carolina University, 150 H. F.

Robinson Bldg., Cullowhee 28723. Open weekdays 8–5 all year, and Sun. 2–5, Apr.–Oct.; closed on university holidays. Admission is free. Run by Western Carolina University and located in its administrative building, this small museum tells the story of the pioneers who settled the deep coves and high hollows of the Smokies, and their descendants who followed the pioneer way of life. You'll also find changing displays on such diverse topics as blacksmithing, mountain trout, and handcrafting. In addition to running the small museum and maintaining its 10,000-item collection of mountain artifacts, the center publishes scholarly and educational material, puts on educational programs, and co-sponsors the highly popular **Mountain Heritage Day** in Cullowhee on the last Saturday in September.

Judaculla Rock is a large boulder completely covered by pictograms, sitting in on the edge of a lovely mountain meadow, 12.6 miles south of Sylva via NC 107 and Caney Fork Road (SSR 1737). The Cherokees credited the rock to their god of the hunt, Judaculla, a terrifying giant who lived in Judaculla Old Fields on the high Balsams crest. Examine the rock closely, and you can see the imprint of Judaculla's seven-fingered hand. Scholars cannot agree on the age or meaning of these carvings, or even if they were carved by the Cherokee. There is no office, visitors center, or even toilets on this county-owned site—just a few parking spaces in a field, and the strange stone.

The Stewart Cabin. This minor site is a fun side trip from the **Joyce Kilmer Memorial Forest** or the **Cherohala Skyway**. From the start of the Skyway, 2 miles south of Kilmer, FSR 81 drops down to the right to cross Santeetlah Creek in a mile, with good views over this handsome creek (and good access for fisher-

THE TUCKASEEGEE RIVER, NEAR SYLVA

men) from the bridge. Two miles farther, the Stewart Cabin sits in riverside meadows by the gravel road. It's a modest, handsome log cabin, framed by wildflowers and a split-rail fence. The Nantahala National Forest restored it, and preserves it as a historic site. Return the way you came.

Cheoah Dam. Located 15.6 miles north of Robbinsville on US 129, this is the most easily viewed of Alcoa's four **Tapoco dams**. Built in 1919, Cheoah was the tallest dam in the world at the time (at 225 feet) and had the largest turbines. The dam remains impressive nearly a century later, and gives you a good idea of the scale of Alcoa's early electrical project, very successful and still going full-tilt. It is now best known, however, as the site of Harrison Ford's famous dam jump in the movie *The Fugitive*—accomplished by tossing a dummy off the dam, combined with a matte to add the appropriate background above it. US 129 crosses the river just in front of the dam with wonderful views of it, and more views from the side of the road. Take a gander at the industrial Gothic turbine station in the gorge under the dam, a beautiful piece of architecture instantly recognizable in the movie. Incidentally, this section of highway is historic in itself—essentially unchanged since it was built in 1931, the first paved road into this remote corner of the mountains. The trailhead for the **Slickrock Wilderness Walk** is here as well, downstream on the left.

Hiwassee Dam. The TVA built this massive concrete structure in 1940 as part of efforts to bring economic development to the poorest areas of the South by providing them with cheap and plentiful electricity. Today paved SSR 1314 uses its top as a 0.25-mile-long bridge, with clear and somewhat disturbing views over the 300-foot vertical drop of the dam's downriver face. An excellent TVA picnic area sits on a grassy hill, shaded by large old trees, with sweeping views over Hiwassee Lake and Dam. From Murphy, take US 64/74 west 7.6 miles to a right onto NC 294; go north for 8.6 miles to a right onto SSR 1314, then north for 5.2 miles to the dam.

MOUNTAIN SCENERY The Nantahala Mountains dominate the middle of this chapter. Running almost due north from the Blue Ridge, the Nantahalas have always been a great green barrier, with more than a dozen peaks over 5,000 feet and only three gaps that barely dip below 4,000 feet. The Blue Ridge runs eastward, roughly along the SC–GA state line, from Lake Toxaway to merge with the southern end of the Nantahalas at **Standing Indian**. These are the major ridges, but there are others as well: Cowee Mountain, the Valley River Mountains, and the Unicoi Mountains along the Tennessee state line. All of these mountains are substantially federally owned, and all offer an incredible variety of things to see. Here are some of the best, from east to west.

Schoolhouse Falls. This **Panthertown Valley** waterfall forms where the headwaters of the **Tuckaseegee River** plunge over an overhanging 20-foot ledge into a large pool, not 0.5 mile from the crest of the Blue Ridge. Like many such waterfalls, it has formed a grotto that protects a variety of rare ferns and other plants, surrounding a large pool that serves as a popular swimming hole (complete with natural sand beach). Schoolhouse Falls is reached from the east gate of Panthertown Valley, from the trailhead at the end of Cold Mountain Road (SSR 1301). The round-trip walk is 2 miles, with a return climb of 250 feet.

Falls of the Horsepasture Wild and Scenic River. In 1986 the U.S. Congress acted to stop a California carpetbagger from destroying Cashier's little Horsepasture River in a hydroelectric scheme, by declaring it a Wild and Scenic River, the result of an extraordinary campaign by local residents. Waterfalls were the reason for this unusual congressional action—five of them. Three are easily accessible from NC 281 a mile south of Sapphire, then left into the **Gorges State Park** trailhead parking lot; an excellent, newly constructed path leads out of the park, into the adjacent Nantahala National Forest, and then down the river. First up is Drift Falls, a 30-foot slide rock with a large swimming hole at the bottom. Ten minutes farther down the path is Turtle Back Falls, which looks like water rolling over a turtle's back, with a 15-foot drop into the pool beneath. Some of the foolhardy (and one may doubt the *hardy* part) use this as a slide rock as well. Nobody uses the next waterfall as a slide rock. Rainbow Falls drops 150 feet straight down in a roar of water that puts up a perpetual mist in which rainbows form. Farther downstream the path becomes much steeper and quite difficult as it enters the state of North Carolina's Toxaway Game Lands, where the adventuresome will find Stairstep Falls and Windy Falls.

Whitewater Falls. One of several waterfalls claimed as the "tallest in the East," Whitewater Falls is an impressive sight. Located in the Nantahala National Forest, off NC 281 near the state line, it carries a huge flow of water 450 feet straight down in three great jumps. It has carved a great bowl for itself, and a projecting ledge (a short, flat walk from the parking lot) gives an unobstructed view of its entire length. The old pioneer-era road ran right by this waterfall, and its roadbed can be walked to its top. Downstream, Lower Whitewater Falls can be reached from Duke Power's **Bad Creek** facility, just south of the state line; drive right up and ask the guard at the gate.

WHITEWATER FALLS, BELIEVED TO BE THE TALLEST IN THE EAST, NEAR CASHIERS

Silver Run Falls. The only difficulty in exploring this isolated piece of the Nantahala National Forest is finding the parking area. It's on NC 107, 3.92 miles south of US 64, near Cashiers, a wide gravel area on the left; if it's summer, there are cars parked there. This is a justifiably popular swimming hole. The falls are lovely, one of those active little rivers that throws itself over a 15-foot ledge.

Whiteside Mountain. Reputed to be the highest continuous cliff in the East, Whiteside projects a mile out into the valley of the Chattooga River from the Blue Ridge Crest. Its gentle north slope, typical of the Blue Ridge, makes for a moderate walk to the clifftop.

The view must be seen to be believed—and the loop path follows this clifftop for a mile, opening up new vistas at every turn. Like most Blue Ridge cliffs, these start off as a gentle rock slope that gets gradually steeper; a foolhardy hiker can get quite a way down before noticing the extraordinary danger. A failed tourist attraction in the 1950s, the attraction's old tram bed makes for an easy but viewless walk to the top, where a loop trail follows the cliff line back to the parking lot. Whiteside is part of the Nantahala National Forest, which may charge a parking fee.

Norton Mill Creek Falls. One of the finest swimming holes in the mountains, this gem is little-known and little-visited—possibly because it's a bit of a walk. To reach it from US 64 in Cashiers, go south on NC 107 for 6.9 miles to Bull Pen Road, SSR 1603, then west 5.1 miles to the spectacular steel truss bridge with wonderful views of the Chattooga River far below; park where you can. From the steel bridge, the Chattooga River trail leads upstream 3 miles through a lovely riverine forest in a deep gorge, to this small, beautifully formed waterfall with a large, deep pool and sand beach. There's a steel footbridge over it, which the Forest Service helicoptered in.

Sunset Rock. Part of the town of Highland's Ravenel Park, Sunset Rock is a large bald overlooking Highlands. It sits on one side of the Blue Ridge Crest, here an unimpressive little ridgeline. From Sunset Rock this little mountaintop town looks particularly quaint and attractive, its downtown surrounded by forests and framed by mountain ridges. On the other side of the ridge, **Sunrise Rock** gives more limited views over the face of the Blue Ridge. You can walk up to Sunrise Rock from the **Highland's Nature Center**, or drive up a rough gravel road that goes right from Horse Cove Road (SSR 1603) to follow the Blue Ridge.

Glen Falls. Just west of Highlands, a violent little stream called the East Fork throws itself straight down the Blue Ridge escarpment, dropping 800 feet in 0.5 mile. On the way down it forms three impressive waterfalls, each bigger than the last. The national forest path, built by the CCC during the Depression, goes straight down as well, using interminable steps to drop through old-growth forest to views of the waterfalls.

Standing Indian—The Mountain. Well over a mile high, Standing Indian dominates the Southern Nantahala Wilderness. Known as "the grandstand of the Southern Appalachians," it has wide rocky balds with 180-degree views over the headwaters of the Nantahala River, framed by the 5,000-foot wall of the Nantahala Mountains. Reaching it is a bit of an adventure; paths up from Standing Indian Recreation Area are good, but climb a whopping 2,100 feet before reaching the top. However, there's an easier way up—a passable Forest Service road, FS 71, leads 6 miles to the **Appalachian Trail** at Deep Gap, reducing the hike to a short, steep 1,100-foot climb. You will find FS 71 on the left, 14.4 miles west of Franklin on US 64.

Pickens Nose. This easily reached high bald has wide and wonderful views over the much lower Georgia mountains to the south, and over the rich valley of the Little Tennessee River. A side ridge of the Nantahalas, it forms the eastern edge of the Southern Nantahala Wilderness. The path to it leaves the Standing Indian gravel road on the right, 8.7 miles from the campground, then follows a ridgeline for 0.7 mile, climbing 200 feet.

Wayah Bald. The 5,350-foot peak of Wayah Bald is crowned by a two-story stone tower that gives a full-circle panorama. There are more views from the nearby picnic area. This area's long-distance footpaths, the Appalachian Trail and the Bartram Trail, intersect just 500 feet north of the tower. The gravel Forest Service road to Wayah Bald (FS 69) climbs 1,100 feet in 4.5 miles, from its start in 4,200-foot Wayah Gap; on the way it passes **Wilson Lick**, one of the first National Forest Service ranger stations ever built, now preserved as a historic site.

✷ To Do

BICYCLE RENTALS **Smoky Mountain Bicycles** (828-369-2881; smokymtnbikes.com; sales@smokymtnbikes.com), 81 Bennett Rd., Franklin 28734. Located next to the Little Tennessee River Greenway, this bicycle shop rents bikes by the hour, day, or week, and sponsors road and mountain rides.

CANOES, KAYAKS, AND RAFTS **Rafting the Chattooga River**. The Chattooga River does not become floatable until it has put the high cliffs of the Blue Ridge well behind. The National Forest Service, which owns nearly all of the river, sets the upper limit of the floatable river at the SC 28 highway bridge—outside the area of this book. However, the two large regional float companies licensed by the Forest Service to run trips on the Chattooga are both in North Carolina and are listed elsewhere in this guide: the Nantahala Outdoor Center, and Wildwater Rafting.

✐ **Tuckaseegee Outfitters** (888-593-5050; 828-586-5050; tuckfloat.com), P.O. Box 1201, Dillsboro 28725. Open daily, May–Oct. Tuckaseegee Outfitters offers non-guided rentals of inflatables for downstream floats and paddles on the Tuckaseegee. You'll find them on the river, 5 miles west of Sylva on US 74/441.

VIEW FROM WAYAH BALD TOWER, NEAR FRANKLIN

Carolina Mountains Outdoor Center (888-785-2662; 828-586-5285; cmoc-rafting.com), 5303 US 74, Whittier 28789. Open daylight hours, May–Oct. Located on the Tuckaseegee River in Dillsboro, Carolina Mountains Outdoor Center offers immediate starts with a shuttle at the end of the 4.5-mile downstream float. They offer both guided and unguided trips on inflatables.

Great Smokey Mountain Fish Camp & Safaris (828-369-5295; fishcamp.biz), 81 Bennett Rd., Franklin 28734. Open daily, Apr.–Oct. This Little Tennessee River outfitter, just north of Franklin on NC 28 (near Cowee Valley), offers guided fishing trips, canoeing and kayaking, biking (including rentals), and a gourmet food store, in addition to its campground.

GUIDED WALKS AND HIKES **Slickrock Expeditions** (828-293-3999; slickrockexpeditions.com; slickrock@slickrockexpeditions.com), P.O. Box 1214, Cullowhee 28723. Burt Kornegay has been a professional guide since 1971, as well as being a freelance writer and past president of the NC Bartram Trail Society. His Slickrock Expeditions offers several unusual and interesting wilderness excursions in the western mountains of North Carolina.

HORSES AND LLAMAS **Arrowmont Stables and Cabins** (800-682-1092; 828-743-2762; arrowmont.com), 276 Arrowmont Trail, Cullowhee 28723. This stable offers fully guided trail rides, ranging from 45 minutes to two hours on the trail, on their 200-acre property deep in the mountains south of Cullowhee.

LAKE BOATING **Santeetlah Marina** (828-479-8180; santeetlahmarina.com; info@santeetlahmarina.com), 1 Marina Dr., Robbinsville 28771. Open daily, Apr.–Oct. This full-service marina is located on Lake Santeetlah, 5.2 miles north of Robbinsville just off US 129. They rent canoes, ski boats, and pontoon boats, as well as slips by the night and overnight vehicle and RV storage.

Deyton Camp Boat Rentals (828-479-7422; deytoncamp.com), NC 143, 1 mile north of Robbinsville. Open daily, spring–fall. Located on the south shore of Lake Santeetlah, Deyton Camp rents canoes, johnboats, ski boats, and pontoon boats.

Ron's Bait and Tackle (828-479-4467; fax: 828-479-4617; graham.main.nc.us/~rlofty; rlofty@graham.main.nc.us), US 129 N. Open daily. This small but well-equipped bait shop has house boats for rent on Lake Santeetlah, as well as pontoon boats and bass boats.

MINING AND PANNING **Cowee Valley**. This remote and pastoral valley is dotted with so many old farmhouses and barns that it has been declared a National Historic District. Its rolling farmlands are framed by the tall forested peaks of the Cowee Mountains, and easily visited from a network of country lanes. But that's not why its famous. No, it's the rubies. Cowee Valley has been a source of rubies since the 1870s. Not crummy, cloudy, gray-colored industrial corundum chunks, either, but big star rubies and sapphires, gem quality and weighing hundreds of carats. Gem-quality rubies are found in other mountain valleys as well. Be aware, however, that the large majority of the local "gem mines" salt their dirt with foreign corundum, the cheap industrial abrasive you get when the stones aren't gem quality. This guide lists only those mines that provide unsalted pay dirt from their own property.

Mason's Ruby and Sapphire Mine (828-369-9742; masonsrubyandsapphire mine.com), 6961 Upper Burningtown Rd., Franklin 28734. Open daily, all year. This ruby mine in the Nantahala Mountains west of Franklin allows miners to dig their own dirt, and does not practice salting. This mine is different from, and unconnected with, Mason Mountain Mine (which is near Cowee Valley and salts its dirt with foreign stones).

Sheffield Mine (828-369-8383; sheffieldmine.com; ruby@sheffieldmine.com), 385 Sheffield Farms Rd., Franklin 28734. Open Apr.–Oct., daily 10–5 (last admission at 3). This long-established Cowee Valley mine—open to the public since the 1940s but in existence before then—features unsalted dirt from its own property. It's one of the few places in the world where star rubies (purple red rubies that form a star when cabachoned) can be mined. They also sell salted dirt, clearly labeled as such; they do not salt rubies or sapphires. Their website has good information on ruby mining.

Cherokee Ruby and Sapphire Mine (828-349-2941; cherokeerubymine.com), 41 Cherokee Mine Rd., Franklin 28734. Open daily, Apr.–Oct. This mine, located in Cowee Valley, uses only unsalted dirt off their own property, and has produced some notable gem-quality stones since it opened in 1993.

✷ Lodging

HOTELS AND RESORTS **The Balsam Mountain Inn, Sylva-Dillsboro area** (800-224-9498; 828-456-9498; fax: 828-456-9298; balsaminn .com; relax@balsammountaininn.com), P.O. Box 40, Balsam 28707. $$$–$$$$. This beautifully restored Victorian railroad hotel is located well off the main road in Balsam Gap, 0.7 mile from the Blue Ridge Parkway's intersection with US 23/74. The 50 rooms all have original beadboard walls and ceilings. The comfortable furniture is rustic in style, covered in bright fabrics, with original prints on the walls, and either two double beds or a king bed; 16 of the rooms are expanded to include a large sitting area, and 8 are two-room suites. The breakfast (included in the tariff) is cooked to order and extremely good, while dinners (extra, by reservation) are of truly exceptional quality.

The Dillsboro Inn, Sylva-Dillsboro (866-586-3898; 828-586-3898; dillsboroinn.com; info@dillsboroinn .com), 146 N. River Rd., P.O. Box 270, Dillsboro 28725. Open all year. $$$–$$$$. This small B&B lodge overlooks a dam waterfall on the Tuckaseegee River, a short distance outside Dillsboro. It has 300 feet of landscaped riverfront, including a small fishing pier and a sitting area. Guests can enjoy wide views over the river and the falls from a large deck, or from a wood-burning hot tub. The rooms are very large and beautifully decorated, and WiFi is available.

The Greystone Inn, Lake Toxaway (800-824-5766; 828-966-4700; fax: 828-862-5689; greystoneinn.com; info@greystoneinn.com), Greystone Lane, Lake Toxaway 28747. $$$$$. This resort complex centers on a six-level Alpine-style 1915 mansion, built by local heroine Lucy Moltz (who lived there until her death in 1970); the 33 guest rooms and suites are split among the original Moltz Mansion and two new buildings. The resort strives to present gourmet meals to its guests, all included in the tariff—a full breakfast, an afternoon tea on the sunporch, wine and hors d'oeuvres before dinner, and a formal dinner with menu choices and dessert by the inn's pastry chef. An evening champagne cruise is offered free to guests, as are canoeing, kayaking, power boating, waterskiing, tennis, and lawn games. Golf privileges are available at nearby Lake Toxaway Country Club.

High Hampton Inn and Country Club, Cashiers (800-334-2551; 828-743-2411; highhamptoninn.com; Info@HighHamptonInn.com), P.O. Box 338, Cashiers 28717. $$$$. Located in Cashiers, this 1,400-acre resort has been run by the McKee family since 1922. However, it's older than that—Wade Hampton, a South Carolina planter, established the High Hampton estate as the family summer home in 1845, and the entire resort is a National Historic District. The large Hampton Lake, beside the main building, opens up vistas to the wide front of the Blue Ridge, which flanks the lake with great gray escarpments and granite crags. The 117 rooms are rustic, with board-and-batten paneling from wood logged on the estate and simple, country furniture. The tariff includes three meals a day, plus afternoon tea on the veranda; meals are hearty country fare, prepared fresh from scratch, and served buffet-style.

The Old Edwards Inn, Highlands (866-526-8008; 828-526-8008; fax: 828-526-8301; oldedwardsinn.com; info @oldedwardsinn.com), 445 Main St., P.O. Box 2130, Highlands 28741. $$$$–$$$$$. The oldest building in downtown Highlands, the 1878 Old Edwards Inn is a distinctive three-story brick building with a stone entrance (an early owner ran a rock quarry), plus a long wooden annex with a second-story veranda, almost as old as the main building. Rooms have 19th-century-style wall stenciling; most have balconies, and some have sitting areas.

The Main Street Inn, Highlands (800-213-9142; 828-526-2590; fax: 828-787-1142; mainstreet-inn.com; info@ mainstreet-inn.com), 270 Main St.,

DAWN VIEW OF THE VILLAGE OF WHITTIER, JUST SOUTH OF THE GREAT SMOKY MOUNTAINS

Highlands 28741. $$–$$$$. Built in 1885 and restored in 1998, this farmhouse sits in the middle of Highland's Main Street shopping district, surrounded by its own oak-shaded lawns. The 20 guest rooms vary greatly in size; some are small while others have individual sitting areas or balconies. A large country breakfast is served, as well as afternoon tea.

The Inn at Half Mile Farm, Highlands (800-946-6822; 828-526-8170; fax: 828-526-2625; halfmilefarm.com; stay@halfmilefarm.com), 214 Half-Mile Dr., P.O. Box 2769, Highlands 28741. $$$$–$$$$$. This 14-acre landscaped property has a large, traditional lodge overlooking a pond with 23 rooms and a restaurant, plus eight cabins. The tariff includes a full breakfast and evening hors d'oeuvres with wine.

Snowbird Mountain Lodge, Robbinsville area (800-941-9290; 828-479-3433; fax: 828-479-3473; snowbirdlodge.com; innkeeper@snowbirdlodge.com), 4633 Santeetlah Rd., Robbinsville 28771. $$$$–$$$$$. This 1941 rustic-style lodge sits on its own 100-acre tract high in the mountains above Lake Santeetlah, very near the Cherohala Parkway and Joyce Kilmer Forest. Built by a Chicago tour operator as a place to pamper guests, it features wide views from its native stone terrace. The lodge's rooms all have en suite private baths and are paneled in a variety of local hardwoods. The room tariff includes a full breakfast buffet, a picnic lunch, and a gourmet dinner.

✐ **The Blue Boar Inn, Robbinsville area** (866-479-8126; 828-479-8126; fax: 828-479-2415; blueboarinn.com; innkeeper@blueboarinn.com), 1283 Blue Boar Rd., Robbinsville 28771. $$$. Built in 1950 as a hunting lodge by Cincinnati's Bruckmann Brewery, the Blue Boar has been completely renovated into a elegant little bed & breakfast inn. The eight guest rooms all have outside private entrances with private porches. A full breakfast, included in the tariff, is served in dining room, as is lunch (open to the public), and dinner by reservation. The Blue Boar is located on Lake Santeetlah, just off NC 143.

BED & BREAKFASTS The Chalet Inn, Sylva-Dillsboro (800-789-8024; 828-586-0251; chaletinn.com; paradisefound@chaletinn.com), 285 Lone Oak Dr., Whittier 28789. $$–$$$$. This is a large, luxurious chalet, with an ample great room, seven guest rooms ranging in size from comfortable to huge, and a private balcony or porch for every room. The inn's 22-acre grounds are beautifully landscaped around a spring-fed mountain stream, and woven with graded footpaths. Rooms are simply but beautifully decorated, combining European flair with American amenities. Breakfast at the Chalet Inn is served in the style of a German *gasthaus*, a buffet including an exceptional variety of traditional German fare. Located in the Barkers Creek section of Jackson County down a tangle of paved country lanes, the Chalet Inn is only 2.4 miles from the four-lane US 23/74/441.

The Squire Watkins Inn, Sylva-Dillsboro (800-586-2429; 828-586-5244; squirewatkinsinn.com; info@SquireWatkinsInn.com), 657 Haywood Rd., P.O. Box 430, Dillsboro 28725. $$$. This large 1880 Queen Anne mansion just outside Dillsboro's center gives you the sensation of stepping back in time to visit your favorite wealthy Victorian aunt. When it was built, the Squire Watkins had a sweeping view over the brand-new railroad depot then being built, and the railroad's steam engine still passes by the inn's gardens, designed by the prominent mountain landscape architect

Doan Ogden in the early 1950s. Furnished completely in Victorian antiques, the four upstairs rooms are spacious and comfortable; all rooms are en suite and air-conditioned. The property also has three housekeeping units behind the main house, 1930s-style board-and-batten kitchenettes, very well kept and charmingly furnished in a country style. A full breakfast is included in the tariff.

The River Lodge, Sylva-Dillsboro area (877-384-4400; 828-293-5431; riverlodge-bb.com; rvrldg@dnet.net), 619 Roy Tritt Rd., Cullowhee 28723. $$$–$$$$. River Lodge sits on 6 landscaped acres, with views toward its 600 feet of Tuckaseegee River front, 10 miles south of Sylva and five minutes from the campus of Western Carolina University at Cullowhee. Its great room is particularly notable, with walls of century-old hand-hewn logs salvaged from derelict local cabins; old barn timbers support the massive roof span, while stairs made of half logs flow up to the second story. A huge stone hearth dominates one wall, and the antique Brunswick pool table occupies only a corner of this space. Furnishings combine Victorian oak, country vernacular, Mission-style designs, and Native American motifs. All rooms are en suite; most have either a claw-footed tub with a separate shower, or a double-sized shower. A full breakfast is included.

Buttonwood Inn, Franklin (888-368-8985; 828-369-8985; buttonwoodbb.com), 50 Admiral Dr., Franklin 28734. $$. This historic (1920s) board-and-batten lodge sits between the fifth and seventh greens of Franklin's golf course. It has a fire-engine-red exterior, and its four attractive, full-sized rooms are en suite. A full breakfast is included.

Angels Landing Inn, Murphy (828-835-8877; angelslandinginn.com), 94 Campbell St., Murphy 28906. $$. This beautifully decorated Victorian home with a wide rocking porch sits a block from Murphy's quaint downtown. The four rooms are large and with sitting areas, but only one is fully en suite; the rooms with partially or fully shared baths carry a lower tariff. Wireless Internet is available. The rate includes a full gourmet breakfast, afternoon snack, and evening sweet.

Huntingdon Hall Bed & Breakfast, Murphy (800-824-6189; 828-837-9567; fax: 828-837-2527; bed-breakfast-inn.com; info@bed-breakfast-inn.com), 272 Valley River Ave., Murphy 28906. $$. Huntingdon Hall is a 19th-century lawyer's house two blocks from downtown Murphy. Common rooms and guest rooms are furnished with period antiques, and business facilities (fax machines, phones, and a dataport) are available on request. The full breakfast is available on weekdays as early as 6 AM and as late as 9.

CABINS **The Cabins at Seven Foxes, Lake Toxaway** (828-877-6333; fax: 828-862-4132; sevenfoxes.com; cabins@sevenfoxes.com), P.O. Box 123; on Slick Fisher Rd., Lake Toxaway 28747. $$$–$$$$. Located 4 miles north of Lake Toxaway on the Blue Ridge, this group of five new cabins sits on 6 wooded acres. These one- and two-bedroom cabins, modestly styled on the outside, are comfortably furnished with antiques and reproductions, each with its own theme. All cabins have porches, gas fireplaces, fully equipped kitchens, and quilts.

Cabins in the Laurel, Cashiers (828-743-2621; cabinsinthelaurel.com; Info@NC-Cabins.com), P.O. Box 2475, Cashiers 28717. $$$–$$$$. These five modern-built rustic cabins are each the size of a small house, with either shingle or log exteriors, porches, fireplaces, and lots of interior wood. WiFi is available. The heavily wooded site is very close to the center of Cashiers.

🐾 **Cobb Creek Cabins, Murphy** (828-837-0270; fax: 828-837-9424; cobbcreekcabins.com; cobbcreekcabins@yahoo.com), 106 Cobb Circle, Murphy 28906. $$–$$$. The collection of six cabins occupies a quiet, rural site just off US 19, southwest of Murphy. Each cabin is an individual, but all share a high level of comfort. The site has a fishing pond, volleyball, and a horseshoe pitch, and includes an alpaca ranch.

✷ Where to Eat

DINING OUT The Balsam Mountain Inn, Sylva-Dillsboro area (800-224-9498; balsaminn.com; relax@balsammountaininn.com), P.O. Box 40, Balsam 28707. Open daily for breakfast and dinner; Sun. brunch. $$$$. This 1908 railroad hotel, 0.5 mile off US 74/23 near its intersection with the Blue Ridge Parkway, offers fine dining in a remote, rural setting. The hotel itself is worth a visit just to admire its authentically restored late-Victorian architecture, and its 100-foot-long porches on two floors. The menu typically combines several traditional items, such as fresh baked mountain trout or filet mignon, with two or three surprises. A sophisticated wine list (with a good selection under $30) completes the experience.

Lulu's Café, Sylva-Dillsboro (828-586-8989; luluscafe.com), 612 Main St., Sylva 28779. Open Mon.–Sat. for lunch and dinner. $$$$. This handsome restaurant, occupying three red-brick storefronts in downtown Sylva, has gained a wide reputation for its sophistication and intelligence. The lunch menu offers original salads and sandwiches, with specials such as black-bean-and-sweet-potato enchiladas and seafood gumbo. At dinner the sandwiches disappear, replaced by a selection of entrées and specials, typically nontraditional and frequently adventurous.

Madison's, Highlands (866-526-8008; 828-526-8008; fax: 828-526-8301; oldedwardsinn.com/dining; info@oldedwardsinn.com), 445 Main St., P.O. Box 2130, Highlands 28741. $$$–$$$$$. Located in the center of downtown Highlands, in the Old Edwards Inn, Madison's offers gourmet breakfasts, lunches, and dinners, as well as a Sunday brunch, all prepared by a professional culinary team. Recipes are unique and memorable, merging fresh flavors in imaginative ways. The low end of the price range is for breakfast.

On the Verandah, Highlands (828-526-2338; ontheverandah.com; otv1@ontheverandah.com), 1536 Franklin Rd., Highlands 28741. Open daily for dinner, and for Sun. brunch. $$$$$. Located west of Highlands on US 64, this family-owned restaurant occupies an old 1920s speakeasy overlooking Lake Sequoyah, with lovely views over the lake from its deck or enclosed veranda dining areas. Inside, the bright and attractive dining room is dominated by founding owner Alan Figel's collection of over 1,300 bottles of chili sauce (any one of which diners are welcome to try). The menu features a fusion of Caribbean, South American, and Asian approaches, always with fresh, local ingredients emphasized. There is a 200-bottle wine list, and a wine bar with an extensive choice of wines by the glass.

Ristorante Paoletti, Highlands (828-526-4906; paolettis.com), 440 Main St., Highlands 28741. Open for dinner, Mon.–Sat. $$$$$. This downtown Highlands storefront restaurant offers fine Italian dining with a rich choice of foods that go well beyond red sauce on pasta. The Paoletti has a long menu of gourmet pastas with a wide variety of treatments, any of which may be ordered as a main dish or as a side to one of their entrées—veal, lamb, fish, chicken, and filet mignon. Their wine list includes over 800 bottles.

Wolfgang's Restaurant and Wine Bistro, Highlands (828-526-3807; wolfgangs.net; wom1@gte.net), 474 Main St., Highlands 28741. Open daily for dinner. $$$–$$$$$. Located in a renovated house at the center of downtown, Wolfgang's combines German and American traditions in imaginative ways. They feature a pub menu in the bistro at reduced prices, more modest but just as original, as well as the full dinner menu in the restaurant.

THE CHEROHALA PARKWAY ON THE UNICOI CREST IN NORTH CAROLINA

EATING OUT Soul Infusion Teahouse and Bistro, Sylva-Dillsboro (828-586-1717; soulinfusion.com), 628 E. Main St. (NC 107), Sylva 28779. Open Tue.–Sat. for lunch and dinner. $. This lively local pub occupies a 1930s farmhouse on Sylva's Main Street. It features such fare as sandwiches and pizzas, but also has an ever-changing menu of specials. It has a good selection of microbrews on tap and in the bottle, wine, and of course 60 varieties of tea. There's live music most nights.

The Jarrett House, Sylva-Dillsboro (800-972-5623; 828-586-0265; fax: 828-586-6257; jarretthouse.com), P.O. Box 219, Dillsboro 28725. Open daily, Apr.–Dec., for lunch and dinner. $$. This historic inn in central Dillsboro, in continuous use since 1884, serves good, plain food and plenty of it. Lunch is served as a plate, while dinner is served family-style, out of big bowls. Desserts consist of vinegar pie, cobblers, and French silk pie. No beer or wine service.

Dillsboro Smokehouse, Sylva-Dillsboro (828-586-9556), 403 Haywood Rd., P.O. Box 269, Dillsboro 28725. Open Mon.–Sat. for lunch and dinner, and Sun. for lunch. $. This friendly spot in central Dillsboro is where the locals go. It features hearty, fresh food, including old-fashioned mountain barbeque.

Carolina Smokehouse, Cashiers (828-743-3200), US 64 W., Cashiers 28717. Open daily for lunch and dinner. $$. If you find yourself looking for a good, simple roadside eatery, this is your place. It occupies a plain little building with a covered deck, west of Cashiers on US 64. Inside it's just as plain, but clean and with a decor centering on old automobile tags. The barbeque is fresh and tasty, with a sweet tomato-based sauce, served up with the classic sides, and reasonably priced.

Pescado's Highland Burritos, Highlands (828-526-9313; pescados-highlands.us), 226 S. 4th St., Highlands 28741. Open for lunch Mon.–Sat., and for dinner Thu.–Fri. $$. Located half a block from Highland's town center in a handsome old stone building, this eatery features giant California-style burritos and tacos with shrimp and fish as well as the standard beef, pork, and chicken. Food is prepared from scratch, using fresh ingredients.

The Hidden Gem Café, Franklin (828-369-0575; fax: 828-369-1725; hiddengemcafe.com; info@chefandhiswife.com), 15 Courthouse Plaza, Franklin 28734. Open for lunch Mon.–Fri., and for dinner Tue.–Sat. $$–$$$. This popular eatery is on the Courthouse Square in the center of downtown Franklin. Lunch features hot dogs (good ones), fresh ½-pound burgers, and a variety of sandwiches (from roast beef on a kaiser to goat cheese and roasted red pepper on French bread). Dinners range from meat loaf and ribs, through a variety of steaks, to a good selection of fresh seafood.

ShoeBooties Café, Murphy (828-837-4589; fax: 835-8508; shoebootiescafe.com; info@shoebootiescafe.com), 25 Peachtree St., Murphy 28906. Open Tue.–Sat. for lunch and dinner. $–$$. This downtown Murphy storefront eatery has deli sandwiches and salads for lunch, and steak, seafood, chicken, pasta, and chef specialties for dinner. Wine is available.

✷ Entertainment

CLASSICAL **Highlands Chamber Music Festival** (828-526-9060), P.O. Box 1702, Highlands 28741. This summer series of chamber music performances is held at the Episcopal Church of the Incarnation, in July and August.

Highlands Playhouse (828-526-2695; fax: 828-526-0761; highlandsplayhouse.org; Highlandsplayhouse@msn.com), P.O. Box 896, Oak St., Highlands 28741. This respected summer theater performs plays and musicals in its shingle-clad playhouse behind downtown Highlands.

MOUNTAIN MUSIC **Friday Night Concerts at the Campbell Folk School** (800-365-5724; 828-837-2775; fax: 828-837-8637; folkschool.org). Most Friday nights the Campbell Folk School sponsors a showing of student work at 6:40, followed by a music concert at 7:30, featuring old-time mountain instruments and music. When weather permits concerts are held in the Festival Barn, so bring a lawn chair or be prepared to sit on a hay bale. They also hold a twice-monthly contra and square dance on Saturday evenings.

Pickin' on the Square (828-349-1212). There's free music and dancing every Saturday night at the gazebo on the square in downtown Franklin, in front of the County Courthouse. It starts with an open mike at 7, with the main band—either bluegrass or gospel—coming on at 8.

✷ Selective Shopping

Sylva and Dillsboro. These adjacent towns are a study in contrasts. Sylva has an old-style downtown that has changed remarkably little from the 1940s. Dillsboro, on the other hand, is a lively crafters town, whose 40-odd stores include quite a variety of studios and galleries. Both are fun for strolling, but if you have time for only one, Dillsboro is a must for any serious shopper.

Highlands's large concentration of million-dollar vacation cottages ensures that it has an equally large concentration of antiques shops and art galleries. In fact, Highlands has had a first-class collection of antiques shops for a number of decades, about half in its quaint downtown and the other half scattered about town. The chamber of commerce lists 16 antiques shops and art galleries, with five more craft galleries and shops, 14 gift shops, and two bookstores.

Franklin is an important market center for its surrounding region, and so takes on more of the look of a contemporary southern town than many of its peers in the mountains. Its three-block downtown is definitely worth a stroll, with gift, antiques, and gem shops as well as two museums and a nice town square.

John C. Campbell Folk School Craft Store (800-365-5724; 828-837-2775; fax: 828-837-8637; folkschool.org). Located on the beautiful campus of the Campbell Folk School east of Murphy, this craft shop has a juried selection of folk and fine arts by Campbell School students, faculty, and alumni.

✷ Special Events

Easter Sunday: **Dillsboro Easter Hat Parade**. Months before tourist season begins, Dillsboro residents celebrate the coming of the first flowers of spring by dressing up in creative hats and parading through the center of town, escorted by antique cars. Totally uncommercialized and completely local, this is great fun.

Mid-June: **Taste of Scotland Festival** (828-524-7472; tasteofscotlandfestival.org). Scottish food and Scottish music—what could be better? In this downtown Franklin festival people eat their haggis with a bagpipe accompaniment, and call it good. There's danc-

GRAHAM COUNTY RAMP FESTIVAL

(828-479-7971; terry.slaughter@ncmail.net), 49 S. Main St., Robbinsville 28771. Small communities throughout the North Carolina mountains traditionally support their volunteer fire departments and rescue squads with a ramp dinner. A ramp is a broadleaf wild leek with a strong onion-garlic flavor, one of the first plants to poke through the snow in the mountain forests. In the bad old days, people who were at the end of their winter food supplies would go into the forests and gather ramps as a healthy and hearty food until the crops came in. Ramps meant hope, and better things to come. And they taste good, too—both the greens and the bulbs are edible, and delicious. The Graham County Ramp Festival—held the last Sunday in April—is just such a traditional community get-together at the Rescue Squad building on Moose Branch Road in Robbinsville. They want everyone to come in and enjoy ramps cooked with mountain trout, chicken, baked beans, hushpuppies, corn bread, potato salad, and dessert.

ing, sheepdog demonstrations, and lots of Scottish stuff to buy at this annual event, sponsored by the Scottish Tartan Museum.

Fourth of July weekend: **Symphony Under the Stars** (828-743-2525; cashiersrotary.org/symphony.html). The Greenville Symphony Orchestra performs on the banks of cliff-ringed Fairfield Lake, east of Cashiers.

Last week in July: **Macon County Gemboree**. This annual rock show brings in gem and mineral dealers from all over, as well as custom jewelers. Sponsored by the Gem and Mineral Society of Franklin, it's been running every year since 1965.

Last Saturday in September: **Mountain Heritage Day** (828-526-9201), 5th and Main, Highlands 28741. The largest and most distinguished heritage festival in the North Carolina Smokies, Western Carolina University's Mountain Heritage Day features live performances, craft demonstrations, and a midway with over 200 mountain crafters and artists. Now in its third decade, this annual event draws tens of thousands of people to Western's beautiful rural campus, 5.8 miles south of Sylva.

First two weekends in December: **Dillsboro Lights and Luminaire**. Dillsboro merchants close out the season with a nighttime program of Christmas lights, candle-lined streets, and regional music, with homemade treats and hot beverages served in the shops.

INDEX

B

C

D

G

I

J

P

S

T

Y

Z